Taking Sides:
Clashing Views in
Lifespan Development, 5/e

Allison A. Buskirk-Cohen

http://create.mheducation.com

ISBN-10: 1259216187   ISBN-13: 9781259216183

Contents

Preface

Having used the *Taking Sides: Clashing Views in Lifespan Development* book in the courses that I teach, I was thrilled to accept the invitation to edit this edition. I have long considered myself both a teacher and student of lifespan development. As a college professor, I seek to balance theory and practice in the classroom. Though it is important to understand theories, concepts, and research findings, students also must know how to apply this knowledge in the real-world. And while I have gained expertise over the years, I am reminded (more often than I want to admit!) that there is always more to learn about development. New research findings emerge, along with new ways of looking at old data. Sometimes, a question about an issue in development seems to have an obvious answer. *Taking Sides* reminds readers that equally informed people can come to very different conclusions.

This book presents issues as controversies to stimulate critical thinking and reflection. Students often relate to the issues on a personal level, which can make it challenging to think critically and reflect on them appropriately. Students may be critical without offering any analysis. While an individual's personal experience is valuable as that person's lived experience, it is limited as such. Does one person's experience generalize to others? Can we really analyze our experience without bias? The selections in *Taking Sides* demonstrate how to support opinions with data and theory. They offer a guide for using information to establish credibility for an argument, and for engaging in an intellectual debate. Moreover, they represent the complexities inherent in lifespan development and the ongoing knowledge base of the field.

There have been some significant changes in this fifth edition compared with the previous one. Units, issues, and articles have changed in various respects. This newer edition has separated early and middle childhood into two different chapters to reflect the diversity of changes that occur during these stages of development. The unit previously titled "Youth and Emerging Adulthood" is now titled "Early Adulthood" to simplify the nomenclature. Six issues have been added and one issue was revised. The new issues address happiness, co-sleeping, preschool education, sexting, Facebook use, and grandparent visitation. The issue on religion and spirituality has been modified to look at how college students approach these topics, rather than whether they are interested in them. Finally, there are 19 new articles in this edition, representing current theory, research, and scholarly opinion. Of these articles, 12 support the new issues and 7 have replaced articles in issues that remain relevant.

I have used a chronological approach to organizing this book for a few reasons. First and foremost, I believe that it helps readers gain a better understanding of growth and change over time. Readers gain a sense of what are the pressing issues at each age and stage of development. Second, many developmental theories, such as those developed by Piaget and Erikson, for example, are organized by chronological age. Organizing this book chronologically provides an ease to matching articles with particular stages in the theories. However, some readers might prefer a topical approach, and *Taking Sides* can be used in this fashion as well. A Topic Guide lists the issue titles under corresponding subjects to aid instructors and students. The Correlation Guide provides a table identifying each issue and coordinating chapters in several lifespan textbooks—books that use a chronological approach and books that use a topical approach.

Additional support materials are available for both instructors and students. ***For instructors***, an *Instructor's Resource Guide* is available through the publisher for classroom use. This guide contains a brief synopsis of each issue along with suggestions for discussing each issue in class. Test questions are included as well, both multiple choice and essay, for each issue. Online materials for *Taking Sides* can be found at www.mhhe.com/createcentral.

Finally, as editor, I would like to acknowledge all those who have helped and supported me. I thank my students and colleagues at DelVal for their suggestions and feedback on material for this edition. In particular, I want to acknowledge the contributions of my graduate research assistants, Susan Sklaroff-Van Hook and Sarah Stout. To everyone in the RubinLab, thank you for teaching me how to think critically about lifespan development. Finally, I am so grateful to my family and friends for their support through all my endeavors. I especially want to thank my daughter, Sierra, who surprises and inspires me with her own development. I love you to the moon and back.

Allison A. Buskirk-Cohen
Delaware Valley University

Editor of This Volume

DR. ALLISON A. BUSKIRK-COHEN has been researching the social lives of children and adolescents for many years. She is interested in how peer and family relationships impact adjustment, particularly during significant transitions. Dr Buskirk-Cohen also studies teaching and learning in higher education. At Delaware Valley University, Dr Buskirk-Cohen authored the curriculum for the undergraduate counseling psychology major and coauthored the curriculum for the master's program in counseling psychology. Dr Buskirk-Cohen teaches courses at both the undergraduate and graduate levels in a variety of formats (face-to-face, hybrid and online modes). She uses a learner-centered approach in her teaching and emphasizes real-world applicability. At Delaware Valley University, Dr Buskirk-Cohen proudly serves on several committees, and is active in student organizations. Her work has been published in peer-reviewed journals and advanced textbooks, and presented at academic conferences around the world. Dr Buskirk-Cohen holds a doctorate in human development with a specialization in developmental sciences from the University of Maryland, and a master's degree in developmental psychology with a concentration in developmental psychopathology from Teachers College, Columbia University.

Academic Advisory Board Members

Members of the Academic Advisory Board are instrumental in the final selection of articles for *Taking Sides* books. Their review of the articles for content, level, and appropriateness provides critical direction to the editors and staff. We think that you will find their careful consideration reflected in this book.

Saundra Boyd
Houston Community College

Kimberly Brown
Ball State University

Mary Jane Labador-Farmer
Spartanburg Methodist College

Gina Langley
Eastern New Mexico University, Ruidoso

Dolores McCarthy
John Jay College

John Padgett
Capella Univeristy

Frank Provenzano
Greenville Technical College

Anne Marie Rakip
South Carolina State University

Norma Zunker
Texas A&M University—Corpus Christi

Introduction

I first discovered my interest and appreciation for lifespan development in college. I remember sitting in a psychology course, learning about various disorders. While I was fascinated by phobias, personality disorders, and the like, I could not help but wonder, "How did they develop? Where do these problems come from?" I did not believe that a person suddenly woke up one morning with clinical depression, for example. Instead, I thought there must be clues in a person's past that would predict or influence whether a person developed in a certain way. Similarly, when we discussed wellness and resiliency, I also wondered where people learned to develop these strengths. Thus, these questions marked the beginning of my commitment to a lifespan perspective. A lifespan perspective explores how individuals grow and change across their lifespan, and tries to identify specific factors that influence development. This fifth edition of *Taking Sides: Clashing Views in Lifespan Development* incorporates this perspective.

Theoretical Influences

Certain theorists have had monumental influence on how we approach lifespan development. Jean Piaget was one of the first psychologists to approach cognitive development with systematic observations. His work was published in the 1930s through the 1950s. Piaget created a cognitive stage theory that emphasized the role of both biology and the environment. He believed individuals inherit certain structures and ways of functioning, but that we adapt and respond to our environment in ways that allow our cognition to develop further. In order to advance, we must use assimilation and accommodation. Piaget's considered assimilation, the process by which we incorporate information into our cognitive structures, and accommodation, the manner by which cognitive structures change and adjust to new information. Piaget believed we try to establish equilibrium, a balance between these processes. They produce cognitive structures which combine with behavior to form schemes, Piaget's term for organized patterns of thought and action.

Our cognitive structures become more effective and sophisticated as a result of both age and experience. Piaget identified four stages of cognitive development. From birth through age two, Piaget believed individuals are in the sensorimotor stage. Sensory experiences with the environment develop cognitive structures for young infants. The next stage occurs in early childhood, with children roughly ages two through seven. In this preoperational stage, children come to understand the use of symbols, and language, in particular, as a way of communicating with the world. The concrete operational stage is Piaget's third stage of development and occurs in middle childhood. Children approximately ages seven through eleven can reason logically about concrete, physical objects and ideas. Their thinking becomes more flexible as they are able to consider different pieces of information simultaneously and to think about different perspectives. In the final formal operational stage, Piaget claimed that abstract thinking allows individuals to reason with more complex and sophisticated rationale. Consideration of Piaget's theory can be helpful in understanding the articles in issue on gender differences in learning, and the articles in issue on how young adults think about religion and spirituality.

While Piaget focused on these four stages of cognitive development, Erik Erikson identified eight separate stages of psychosocial development. Erikson's work, published in the 1950s and 1960s, emphasized the role of social interactions on lifespan development. Each of Erikson's stages is characterized by a crisis that must be resolved for positive development to occur. In this theory, the term *crisis* includes both risk and opportunity. The first four stages occur in the years prior to adolescence. From approximately birth through age two, Erikson believed infants face the crisis of basic trust versus mistrust. The main environmental influence is maternal, Erikson theorized. The importance of this stage can be understood in terms of the debate on co-sleeping addressed in Issue 6. During the next two years, Erikson thought young children must negotiate between autonomy and shame and doubt. Both parents or adult substitutes serve as the environmental influence for this stage. From approximately ages three through five, preschoolers face initiative versus guilt. Environmental influences include parents, family, and friends during this stage. Then, youth approximately ages five through twelve battle industry versus inferiority. School serves as the environmental influence in middle childhood.

The remaining four stages of Erikson's theory cover a much larger number of years. In what might be his most famous stage, adolescents face the crisis of identity versus identity confusion. At this time, peers serve as the main environmental influence on development. Young adults approximately ages 18 through 25 negotiate between intimacy and isolation. Partners, spouses, and friends all influence this developmental stage. Issue on marriage certainly speaks to this stage. Erikson identified middle age as encompassing all the years from 25 through 65. Individuals in this stage are influenced by family and society as they face generativity versus stagnation. Finally, in old age, individuals face the crisis of integrity versus despair, with all humans influencing this last stage. Erikson's theory emphasizes nurture (or experience) over nature (or biology), reflecting his own extensive study of people living in varied environments. While this theory continues to garner a lot of support, critics do wonder if the ages associated with each stage need to be adjusted to reflect modern aging. This idea is particularly relevant to issues regarding changes in late adulthood.

A more recent theory of development has been put forth by Urie Bronfenbrenner in the late 1970s. Bronfenbrenner's ecological theory suggests that reciprocal interactions between an individual and the environment shape that person's development. This perspective is often referred to as the bioecological model, since it incorporates reciprocal interactions among biopsychosocial characteristics. It contains four components: proximal processes, the person involved, the person's context, and time. Proximal processes consist of the reciprocal interactions between a person and the environment. In understanding the person involved, Bronfenbrenner emphasized the individual's temperament or disposition that triggers the proximal processes. The context includes the environmental features that either support or derail development. Last, Bronfenbrenner acknowledged that changes occur over time, the final component of this system. Interestingly, Bronfenbrenner was one of the founders of the Head Start program, which is further discussed in issue on preschool education.

He envisioned the environment as a set of nested systems that include the microsystem, mesosystem, exosystem, macrosystem, and chronosystem. The microsystem includes the most immediate and direct influences on an individual's development, such as a child's family, neighborhood, and school. The mesosystem represents the interconnections between the microsystems, such as the relationships between parents and teachers. The context that impacts a developing individual but does not directly impact him/her is included in the exosystem. For example, how a parent reacts to a child's behavior may be impacted by the stress encountered at work by the parent. The macrosystem is comprised of the cultural contexts of the individual. An individual living in a rural town in China would encounter drastically different influences than someone living in an urban city in England. The final level of Bronfenbrenner's system is the chronosystem, which includes how the systems interact over time, as well as sociohistorical circumstances. There are more educational opportunities available to girls and women today than there were 50 years ago, for example. The impact of the chronosystem is evident in the discussion on sexting in Issue 12, narcissism in Issue 13, and Facebook in Issue 15.

In addition to Bronfenbrenner, there are other non-stage theorists who have significantly impacted how we view development. Published in the 1930s through the 1950s, Skinner's theory of operant conditioning articulated the use of consequences like reinforcement and punishment to modify behavior. He defined reinforcement as anything that increases the likelihood of a response occurring in the future, and punishment as anything that decreases that likelihood. Issue 10, which addresses autism, includes information about applied behavior analysis, a highly regimented therapy designed around principles of operant conditioning. Bandura expanded Skinner's work to address social behavior. Introduced in the 1960s and 1970s, Bandura's social cognitive learning theory focused on how learning occurs through observation of others, even without reinforcement. From a developmental perspective, Bandura emphasized how children learn not always through direct instruction, but also by observation. In other words, what adults do is just as important (if not more!) than what they say. Bandura's theory has been most influential in terms of understanding the impact of violent television on children's behavior. Issue on violent video games presents new data that speaks to the role of observational learning.

One other non-stage theory has made a noteworthy impression on developmental psychology, Lev Vygotsky's sociocultural theory. This theory, developed in the late 1970s, emphasized the importance of social interactions in shaping children's cognitive development. He identified two paths of cognitive development that reflect both nature and nurture. Elementary processes are biological, while psychological processes are sociocultural; learning results from the interactions of these two processes. Problem solving, for Vygotsky, involves using speech to guide behavior combined with collaborative efforts with others. Vygotsky argued that cognitive development could be understood through social and cultural processes.

Social interaction encourages development through the guidance of others who are more skilled. Specially, Vygotsky's concept of the zone of proximal development (ZPD) embodies the influence of social and cultural factors on an individual. ZPD refers to a range of ability in a particular task, where the higher limit is achieved through interaction with others. The importance of culture on development can be seen in issues on Chinese parenting practices and on breastfeeding.

New Additions and Revisions

While these classic theories still remain influential, new discoveries and changes in how data is interpreted have transformed how we think about development. For example, the completion of the Human Genome Project in 2003 offered a new way of considering nature and nurture. Scientists were surprised to learn that a relatively small number of genes are responsible for all the diversity found in human beings. With these findings, a new field of epigenetics has emerged. Epigeneticists study cellular and physiological traits that play a role in inheritance but are not caused by changes in the DNA sequence. Thus, instead of simply identifying the presence (or absence) or certain genes, researchers now examine how genes interact with each other and the external environment. These findings also encourage researchers to revisit long-standing beliefs about development. Issue 1 further delves into this controversy, presenting more specific information about the role of genetics and also how culture can shape our biology.

Neuroscience has become an increasingly popular focus, with countries racing to learn more about the brain's structures and how they function. In the United States, the Obama administration announced The Brain Research through Advancing Innovative Neurotechnologies (BRAIN) Initiative in 2013. This initiative is based upon the Human Genome Project, and will seek to understand the subtleties of neuron activity in different animals, and try to achieve a comprehensive map of neural connections in the human brain. Similarly, the European Union is supporting the Human Brain Project. This 10-year project plans to simulate the complete human brain on supercomputers to better understand the brain's functions and to simulate drug treatments. This shift to emphasize neurological research can be explored further in Issue 11, which investigates the concept of a distinct adolescent brain. In the selected articles, scholars argue about how to interpret neurological data, and important task considering the BRAIN Initiative and Human Brain Project.

Relatedly, scholars are also reconsidering how we use our brains based on new research findings. Archaeologists examining fossilized seashells in 2007 discovered deliberate engravings of abstract patterns. The shells were dated to over 500,000 years ago, and were found at the same site where the first fossils of Homo erectus had been found in 1890. Archaeologists believe that these two discoveries suggest our hominin ancestor was more sophisticated than previously believed and capable of symbolic thought. Evolutionary developmental psychology incorporates such findings into our understanding of development. It assumes that our physiological and psychological systems resulted through evolution, and, particularly by natural selection. One question that stems from this perspective is whether certain disorders, such as autism, have some type of evolutionary benefit. Issue 10 considers the concept of neurodiversity in regards to autism, and the idea of accepting this condition rather than trying to cure it.

There are also questions about whether cognitive decline in old age is inevitable. Several years ago, Stanford scientists learned they could reverse cognitive decline in old mice by injecting them with blood from young mice. In 2014, several studies pointed to proteins as the mechanism for the rejuvenation. One study found that the GDF11 protein also rejuvenates the heart, skeletal muscle function, and exercise capability in mice. Another study found that a subset of macrophages, a class of blood cells, play a role in encouraging restoration through the protein Activin A. Human trials may soon focus on stopping the cognitive decline associated with Alzheimer's disease. This research speaks to Issue 19, which looks at the debate regarding finding a cure for old age. As with the autism debate, much of the discussion revolves around how much human beings should influence (or interfere) with natural development.

Another example of revisiting old beliefs about development can be found in the work of Sarah Blaffer Hrdy. Hrdy is an anthropologist and primatologist whose work has impacted evolutionary psychology. Rather than emphasizing survival through competition, she highlights the role of cooperation in our ancestral past. In her 2009 book, *Mother and Others: The Evolutionary Origins of Mutual Understanding*, Hrdy dispels historical myths about the nuclear family with the mother acting as primary caregiver for the children. Instead, she argues that alloparents, others who take part in a child's upbringing, have always been an integral part of development and are critical to the survival of the human species. Hrdy specifically points to the role of grandparents as alloparents. Issue 17 on grandparents' visitation rights certainly speaks to Hrdy's work. The articles selected for this issue debate the role grandparents play in their grandchildren's lives. Hrdy's work suggests that grandparents have always been important in helping to raise younger generations, while some scholars believe this marks a new cultural phenomenon.

Using theories to guide scientific thought and inquiry is much more complicated than one might think. New findings may cause us to refine, or even reject, old theories. Using data to guide our choices seems like a logical path; yet, defining an acceptable threshold is, again, a challenging decision. For example, should policy be created based on the results of one study? Four studies? How can we be certain research findings are not biased by cultural beliefs? Issue 4 debates whether pregnant women can safely consume alcohol. Certainly, the health risks are a fundamental part of this debate. However, there are facets relating to whether this decision is a private one or a matter of public concern. Similarly, Issue 3 deals with happiness, a topic once thought of as an individual pursuit. In past years, however, scholars have approached the study of happiness in a systematic and scientific way. The selected articles discuss whether happiness should be a goal for individuals and countries.

Like a detective searching for the missing piece of a puzzle, readers of *Taking Sides* may find themselves filled with anticipation as they hope to glean answers about lifespan development. For better or worse, this book is likely to provide more questions than answers. Just as we grow and change throughout our lifespan, so do the theories and data that guide us. The selected articles in this book highlight various factors that shape development, and demonstrate the complexities of these factors. While we can appreciate all the nuances that impact development, ultimately, choices must be made and "sides" chosen. It can be tempting to be persuaded by emotions, but in this book, readers will see how to use research to credibly support their arguments. By critically examining the 19 issues in this edition of *Taking Sides: Clashing Views in Lifespan Development*, readers can become more informed decision-makers.

Allison A. Buskirk-Cohen
Delaware Valley University

Unit 1

UNIT

General Issues in the Study of Lifespan Development

*A*lthough this book organizes development into a series of stages, several issues central to understanding the lifespan are not exclusive to one particular age. Traditionally, the study of lifespan development has included questions about continuity versus discontinuity, and the role of nature versus nurture. While these questions continue to be important, scholars have focused their attention on more specific aspects of these general themes. In this unit, the issues relate to a larger question about the nature of development: what forces and characteristics shape us into the people we become?

The issues in this section deal with this larger question and provide a foundation for thinking about specific developmental stages. The first issue directly addresses the role of genes and culture in shaping the thoughts, feelings, behaviors, and experiences that make us human. The second explores the role of parenting, examining whether there are culture differences in parenting practices. The final issue considers the role of positive psychology and whether studying happiness is a worthy goal for scholars. All of these issues emphasize the complex interactions that influence lifespan development.

Selected, Edited, and with Issue Framing Material by:
Allison A. Buskirk-Cohen, *Delaware Valley University*

ISSUE

Does the Cultural Environment Influence Lifespan Development More Than Our Genes?

YES: Rachael E. Jack et al., from "Facial Expressions of Emotion are Not Culturally Universal," *Proceedings of the National Academy of Sciences* (2012)

NO: Gary Marcus, from "Making the Mind: Why We've Misunderstood the Nature-Nurture Debate," *Boston Review* (2003/2004)

Learning Outcomes

After reading this issue, you will be able to:

- Understand that there are too few genes for any one gene to determine complex behavior by itself, but genes may shape behavior through cascades and combinations.
- Discuss how emotions are one example of how culture influences what was often thought of as a purely genetic expression.
- Understand that our brains are remarkably "plastic" in the sense of changing through development, but those changes are often constrained by genetic limits.
- Discuss the complexity of the nature-nurture debate issue, and how it's better understood as gene-environment interactions.

ISSUE SUMMARY

YES: Many believe that emotions are biologically hardwired; however, the research from Rachel Jack and colleagues questions that belief. The researchers compared facial expressions of emotions of individuals from Western and Eastern cultures, finding differences that highlight the influence of culture on how we represent emotions.

NO: Psychologist and researcher Gary Marcus asserts that research clearly demonstrates how a relatively small number of genes influence our environmental learning by "cascading" to determine the paths of our behavioral development.

Perhaps the most central question in the study of lifespan development is whether nature or nurture exerts more influence on our developing thoughts, feelings, and behavior. This debate takes many forms, and it underlies many of the important topics of study within lifespan development. Later issues described in this book revolve around this issue. For example, if intelligence is largely genetic, is preschool education necessary? Even in daily life, we regularly wonder about people—do they act that way because of things in their experience (nurture), or is it just the way they were born (nature)?

This debate finds its roots in philosophy and extends into psychology. Nativists such as Plato and Descartes believe that most behaviors and characteristics were inborn, and occurred regardless of environmental influences. Empiricists like John Locke believed that we develop as a result of our experiences. Chomsky's concept of a language acquisition device demonstrates a nativist theory within psychology. Chomsky believed that all children are born with an instinctive capacity for language use and production. Piaget's theory of development, on the other hand, stressed the importance of our experiences in shaping our schemes and how we interact with the world.

There are many complications to this issue, one of which is understanding exactly how genes operate. In the 1800s, Gregor Mendel offered a relatively simple theory of inheritance based on the idea of dominant and recessive genes. In the case of a child who inherits a dominant and recessive gene or a child who inherits two dominant genes, the dominant gene will be expressed. Recessive traits will be expressed only when an individual has inherited two recessive genes. Mendel's theory helps us determine certain physical characteristics such as eye color, dimples, and tongue-curling ability. However, this theory does not account for personality traits like shyness or aggression.

The Human Genome Project's original goal was to determine the sequence of genes making up human DNA and identifying all the genes within the human genome. Many experts hoped that the information gleaned from this project would lead to a better grasp of those more complicated characteristics. This project was declared complete in April 2003. Many individuals were surprised to learn that there are only about 19,000 genes in the human genome, which is not much different from the number of genes in a mouse. These findings led people to question exactly how genes operate. If we have such a small number of genes, why do we have such variation among all human beings?

Thus, researchers are trying to uncover the mechanisms to explain how complex and diverse human beings emerge from such a small number of genes. The study of genetics today focuses on how genes are edited and regulated. A new field has emerged—epigenetics—which examines how gene expression is varied by other DNA activities. In other words, epigenetics looks at traits that are not caused by changes in the DNA sequence. Instead, it is the study of stable, long-term alterations which may or may not be heritable. In psychology, epigenetics has been used to describe development as the result of an ongoing interaction between genes and the environment.

Another complication in the nature-nurture debate is how we define nurture. When some people think about the cultural environment of an individual, they may consider the role of parents, peers, teachers, and coaches. For others, culture may refer to an individual's nationality, race, social economic status, family, college or university, or religious affiliation. Without clear and agreed-upon definitions, it can be difficult to compare and contrast the results of various studies. Furthermore, research has shown that very few individuals experience the exact same environment in the exact same way. For example, twins and siblings who grow-up in the same household may have very different experiences.

One area in which the nature-nurture debate seemed to find common ground is emotions. In 1872, Charles Darwin published *The Expression of Emotions in Man and Animals*, putting forth the hypothesis that some basic facial expressions serve an adaptive and biological function. The universality hypothesis suggests that six basic emotions (i.e., happiness, surprise, fear, disgust, anger, and sadness) are expressed using the same facial expression across all cultures. Researchers believed that it was to our evolutionary advantage to express and perceive emotions in the same way. If I came across another human being who expressed disgust after eating an unusual plant, I would know to avoid eating that plant, for example. For many years, we have concluded that emotions must be biologically hardwired and that nurture plays a very small role in their expression.

In the YES selection, Rachael E. Jack and her colleagues from the University of Glasgow and the University of Fribourg challenge the universality hypothesis. Using a computer graphics platform, these researchers compared individuals from Western and Eastern cultures. They found two significant differences between these groups both in the facial movements used to represent emotions and in the eye activity representing emotional intensity. Thus, Jack and colleagues argue that our environment (in this case, cultural experiences) plays a larger role in the expression of emotions than do genetics.

In contrast, in the NO selection, New York University professor of psychology Gary Marcus takes a broader view of the nature-nurture debate. Although acknowledging that genes and the environment always interact, Marcus draws on extensive research with animals demonstrating that small genetic manipulations have dramatic influences on behavior. He also responds to the claim that there are not enough genes to control complex behaviors by insisting that relationships between genes and behavior do not have to be one to one. Genes often interact, or "cascade," in various patterns that account for a massive number of developmental outcomes.

Today, most experts agree that both nature and nurture, both genes and culture, shape development. The contemporary discussion is more about how they interact, and whether one leads the other. Historically, the pendulum of popular opinion has tended to swing back and forth. Thus, the current debate is mostly about the relative influence of each: does nature overwhelm nurture, or does nurture trump nature?

YES ↵

Rachael E. Jack et al.

Facial Expressions of Emotion Are Not Culturally Universal

As first noted by Darwin in *The Expression of the Emotions in Man and Animals* (1), some basic facial expressions originally served an adaptive, biological function such as regulating sensory exposure (2). By virtue of their biological origins (1–3), facial expressions have long been considered the universal language to signal internal emotional states, recognized across all cultures. Specifically, the *universality hypothesis* proposes that six basic internal human emotions (i.e., happy, surprise, fear, disgust, anger, and sad) are expressed using the same facial movements across all cultures (4–7), supporting universal recognition. However, consistent cross-cultural disagreement about the emotion (8–13) and intensity (8–10, 14–16) conveyed by gold standard universal facial expressions (17) now questions the universality hypothesis.

To test the universality hypothesis directly, we used a unique computer graphics platform (18) that combines the power of generative grammars (19, 20) with the subjectivity of visual perception to genuinely reconstruct the mental representations of basic facial expressions in individual observers (see also refs. 21, 22). Mental representations reflect the past visual experiences and the future expectations of the individual observer. A cross-cultural comparison of the mental representations of the six basic expressions therefore provides a direct test of their universality.

. . . Like a generative grammar (19, 20), we randomly generated all possible three-dimensional facial movements. Observers only categorized these random facial animations as expressive when the random facial movements correlated with their subjective mental representations— i.e., when they perceive an emotion. Thus, we can capture the subsets of facial movements that correlate with the subjective, culture-specific representations of the six basic emotions in individual observers and compare them.

Fifteen Western Caucasian (WC) and 15 East Asian (EA) observers (*Materials and Methods, Observers*) each categorized 4,800 such animations (evenly split between same and other-race face stimuli) by emotion (i.e., one of the six basic emotions or "don't know") and intensity (on a five-point scale ranging from "very low" to "very high").

To model the mental representation of each facial expression, we reverse correlated (23) the random facial movements with the emotion response (e.g., happy) that these random facial movements elicited (*Materials and Methods, Model Fitting*) (18). In total, we computed 180 models of facial expression representations per culture (15 observers × 6 emotions × 2 race of face). Each model comprised a 41-dimensional vector coding a composition of facial muscles—one dimension per muscle group, with six parameters coding its temporal dynamics and a set of intensity gradients coding how these dynamics change with perceived intensity (*Materials and Methods, Model Fitting*).

The universality hypothesis predicts that, in each culture, these mental models will form six distinct clusters—one per basic emotion, because each emotion is expressed using a specific combination of facial movements common to all humans. In addition, the mental models should also represent similar signaling of emotional intensity across cultures. Our data demonstrate cultural divergence on both counts.

Results

Six Basic Emotions Are Not Universal. We clustered the 41-dimensional models of expression representation in each culture independently. As predicted (24), WC models form six distinct and emotionally homogeneous clusters. However, EA models overlap considerably between emotion categories, demonstrating a different, culture-specific, and therefore not universal, representation of the basic emotions.

Representation of Emotional Intensity Varies Across Cultures. To identify *where* and *when* in the face each culture represents emotional intensity, we compared the

Jack et al., Facial expressions of emotion are not culturally universal, *Proceedings of the National Academy of Sciences*. May 8, 2012, vol. 109, no. 19, 7241–7244. Reprinted by permission.

models of expression representation according to how facial movements covaried with perceived emotional intensity across time. The temporal dynamics of the models revealed culture-specific representation of emotional intensity, as mirrored by popular culture EA emoticons: In EA, (^.^) is happy and (>.<) is angry. . . EA models represent emotion intensity primarily with early movements of the eyes in happy, fear, disgust, and anger, whereas WC models represent emotional intensity with other parts of the face.

Discussion

Using a FACS-based random facial expression generator and reverse correlation, we reconstructed 3D dynamic models of the six basic facial expressions of emotion in Western Caucasian and East Asian cultures. Analysis of the models revealed clear cultural specificity both in the groups of facial muscles and the temporal dynamics representing basic emotions. Specifically, cluster analysis showed that Western Caucasians represent the six basic emotions each with a distinct set of facial muscles. In contrast, the East Asian models showed less distinction, characterized by considerable overlap between emotion categories, particularly for surprise, fear, disgust, and anger. Cross-cultural analysis of the temporal dynamics of the models showed cultural specificity where (in the face) and when facial expressions convey emotional intensity. Together, our results show that facial expressions of emotion are culture specific, refuting the notion that human emotion is universally represented by the same set of six distinct facial expression signals.

To understand the implications of our results, it is important to first highlight the fundamental relationship between the perception and production of facial expressions. Specifically, the facial movements perceived by observers reflect those produced in their social environment because signals designed for communication (and therefore recognition) are those perceived by the observer. That is, one would question the logic and adaptive value of an expressive signal that the receiver could not or does not perceive. Thus, the models reconstructed here reflect the experiences of individual observers interacting with their social environment and provide predictive information to guide cognition and behavior. These dynamic mental representations, therefore, reflect both the past experiences and future expectations of basic facial expressions in each culture.

Cultural specificity in the facial expression models therefore likely reflects differences in the facial expression signals transmitted and encountered by observers in their social environment. For example, cultural differences in

the communication of emotional intensity could reflect the operation of culture-specific display rules (25) on the transmission (and subsequent experience) of facial expressions in each cultural context. For example, East Asian models of fear, disgust, and anger show characteristic early signs of emotional intensity with the eyes, which are under less voluntary control than the mouth (26), reflecting restrained facial behaviors as predicted by the literature (27). Similarly, culture-specific dialects (28) or accents (29) would diversify basic facial expression signals across cultures, giving rise to cultural hallmarks of facial behavior. "For example, consider the "happy models in Fig. 3—East Asian. . ."

Are the six basic emotions universal? We show that six clusters are optimal to characterize the Western Caucasian facial expression models, thus supporting the view that human emotion is composed of six basic categories (24, 31–33). However, our data show that this organization of emotions does not extend to East Asians, questioning the notion that these six basic emotion categories are universal. Rather, our data reflect that the six basic emotions (i.e., happy, surprise, fear, disgust, anger, and sad) are inadequate to accurately represent the conceptual space of emotions in East Asian culture and likely neglect fundamental emotions such as shame (34), pride (35), or guilt (36). Although beyond the scope of the current paper, such questions can now be addressed with our platform by constructing a more diverse range of facial expression models that accurately reflect social communication in different cultures beyond the six basic categories reported in the literature.

In sum, our data directly show that across cultures, emotions are expressed using culture-specific facial signals. Although some basic facial expressions such as fear and disgust (2) originally served as an adaptive function when humans "existed in a much lower and animal-like condition" (ref. 1, p. 19), facial expression signals have since evolved and diversified to serve the primary role of emotion communication during social interaction. As a result, these once biologically hardwired and universal signals have been molded by the diverse social ideologies and practices of the cultural groups who use them for social communication.

Materials and Methods

Observers. We screened and recruited 15 Western Caucasian (European, six males, mean age 21.3 y, SD 1.2 y) and 15 East Asian (Chinese, seven males, mean age 22.9 y, SD 1.3 y). All EA observers had newly arrived in a Western country (mean residence 5.2 mo, SD 0.94 mo) with

International English Language Testing System score ≥6,0 (competent user). All observers had minimal experience of other cultures (as assessed by questionnaire; *SI Observer Questionnaire*), normal or corrected-to-normal vision, gave written informed consent, and were paid £6/h in an ethically approved experiment.

Stimuli. On each experimental trial, a 4D photorealistic facial animation generator (18) randomly selected, from 41 core action units (AUs) (37), a subsample of AUs from a binomial distribution ($n = 5$, $P = 0.6$, median = 3). For each AU, the generator selected random values for each of the six temporal parameters (onset/peak/offset latency, peak amplitude, acceleration, and deceleration) from a uniform distribution. We generated time courses for each AU using a cubic Hermite spline interpolation (five control points, 30 time frames). To generate unique identities on each trial, we first obtained eight neutral expression identities per race (white WC: four female, mean age 23 y, SD 4.1 y; Chinese EA: four female, mean age 22.1 y, SD 0.99 y) under the same conditions of illumination (2,600 lx) and recoding distance (143 cm; Dimensional Imaging) (38). Before recording, posers removed any makeup, facial hair, visible jewelry, and/or glasses, and removed the visibility of head hair using a cap. We then created, for each race of face, two independent "identity spaces" for each sex using the correspondent subset of base identities and the shape and Red-Green-Blue (RGB) texture alignment procedures (18). We defined all points in the identity space by a [4 identities × 1] unit vector, where each entry corresponded to the weights assigned to each individual identity in a linear mixture. We then randomly selected each unit vector from a uniform distribution and constructed the neutral base shape and RGB texture accordingly. Finally, we retargeted the selected temporal dynamic parameters for each AU onto the identity created and rendered all facial animations using 3ds Max.

Procedure. Observers viewed stimuli on a black background displayed on a 19-inch flat panel Dell monitor with a refresh rate of 60 Hz and resolution of 1,024 × 1,280. Stimuli appeared in the central visual field and remained visible until the observer responded. A chin rest ensured a constant viewing distance of 68 cm, with images subtending 14.25° (vertical) and 10.08° (horizontal) of visual angle, reflecting the average size of a human face (39) during natural social interaction (40). We randomized trials within each block and counterbalanced (race of face) blocks across observers in each cultural group. Before the experiment, we established familiarity with the emotion categories by asking observers to provide correct synonyms and descriptions of each emotion category. We controlled stimulus presentation using Matlab 2009b.

Model Fitting. To construct the facial expression models for each observer, emotion, and intensity level, we followed established model fitting procedures (18). First, we performed a Pearson correlation between the binary activation parameter of each AU and the binary response variable for each of the observers' emotion responses, thus producing a 41-dimensional vector detailing the composition of facial muscles. To model the dynamic component of the models, we then performed a linear regression between each of the binary emotion response variables and the six temporal parameters for each AU. To calculate the intensity gradients, we fitted a linear regression model of each AU's temporal parameters to the observer's intensity ratings. Finally, to generate movies of the dynamic models, we combined the significantly correlated AUs with the temporal parameters derived from the regression coefficients.

Clustering Analysis and Mutual Information. To ascertain the optimal number of clusters required to map the distribution of the models in each culture, we applied k-means clustering analysis (41) ($k = 2$–40 inclusive) to the 180 WC and 180 EA models independently and calculated mutual information (41) (MI) for each value of k as follows. We randomly selected 90 models (15 per emotion) and applied k-means clustering analysis (Euclidian distance; 1,000 repetitions). Using the resulting k centroids, we then assigned the remaining 90 models to clusters on the basis of shortest Euclidean distance, and calculated MI, i.e., (model emotion label; cluster). We repeated the computation 100 times, averaged the 100 MI values, and normalized by an ideal MI (i.e., perfect association between cluster and emotion label).

References

1. Darwin C (1999) *The Expression of the Emotions in Man and Animals* (Fontana Press, London), 3rd Ed.

2. Susskind JM, et al. (2008) Expressing fear enhances sensory acquisition. *Nat Neurosci* 11:843–850.

3. Andrew RJ (1963) Evolution of facial expression. *Science* 142:1034–1041.

4. Ekman P, Sorenson ER, Friesen WV (1969) Pancultural elements in facial displays of emotion. *Science* 164:86–88.

5. Tomkins SS (1962) Affect, Imagery, and Consciousness (Springer, New York).

6. Tomkins SS (1963) Affect, Imagery, and Consciousness (Springer, New York).

7. Ekman P, Friesen W, Hagar JC, eds (1978) *Facial Action Coding System Investigators Guide* (Research Nexus, Salt Lake City, UT).

8. Biehl M, et al. (1997) Matsumoto and Ekman's Japanese and Caucasian facial expressions of emotion (JACFEE): Reliability data and cross-national differences. *J Nonverbal Behav* 21:3–21.

9. Ekman P, et al. (1987) Universals and cultural differences in the judgments of facial expressions of emotion. *J Pers Soc Psychol* 53:712–717.

10. Matsumoto D, et al. (2002) American-Japanese cultural differences in judgements of emotional expressions of different intensities. *Cogn Emotion* 16:721–747.

11. Matsumoto D (1989) Cultural influences on the perception of emotion. *J Cross Cult Psychol* 20:92–105.

12. Jack RE, Blais C, Scheepers C, Schyns PG, Caldara R (2009) Cultural confusions show that facial expressions are not universal. *Curr Biol* 19:1543–1548.

13. Moriguchi Y, et al. (2005) Specific brain activation in Japanese and Caucasian people to fearful faces. *Neuroreport* 16:133–136.

14. Yrizarry N, Matsumoto D, Wilson-Cohn C (1998) American-Japanese Differences in multiscalar intensity ratings of universal facial expressions of emotion. *Motiv Emot* 22:315–327.

15. Matsumoto D, Ekman P (1989) American-Japanese cultural differences in intensity ratings of facial expressions of emotion. *Motiv Emot* 13:143–157.

16. Matsumoto D (1990) Cultural similarities and differences in display rules. *Motiv Emot* 14:195–214.

17. Matsumoto D, Ekman P (1988), Japanese and Caucasian Facial Expressions of Emotion (JACFEE) and Neutral Faces (JACNeuF) Slides (San Francisco State University, San Francisco).

18. Yu H, Garrod OGB, Schyns PG (2012) Perception-driven facial expression synthesis. *Comput Graph* 36(3):152–162.

19. Chomsky N (1965) *Aspects of the Theory of Syntax* (MIT Press, Cambridge, MA).

20. Grenander U, Miller M (2007) *Pattern Theory: From Representation to Inference* (Oxford Univ Press, Oxford, UK).

21. Jack RE, Caldara R, Schyns PG (2011) Internal representations reveal cultural diversity in expectations of facial expressions of emotion. *J Exp Psychol Gen* 141:19–25.

22. Dotsch R, Wigboldus DH, Langner O, van Knippenberg A (2008) Ethnic out-group faces are biased in the prejudiced mind. *Psychol Sci* 19:978–980.

23. Ahumada A, Lovell J (1971) Stimulus features in signal detection. *J Acoust Soc Am* 49:1751–1756.

24. Levenson RW (2011) Basic emotion questions. *Emotion Review* 3:379–386.

25. Ekman P (1972) Universals and cultural differences in facial expressions of emotion, in *Nebraska Symposium on Motivation*, ed Cole J (Univ of Nebraska Press, Lincoln, NE).

26. Duchenne GB (1862–1990) The mechanisms of human facial expression or an electro-physiological analysis of the expression of the emotions, ed Cuthebertson R (Cambridge Univ Press, New York).

27. Matsumoto D, Takeuchi S, Andayani S, Kouznetsova N, Krupp D (1998) The contribution of individualism vs. collectivism to cross-national differences in display rules. *Asian J Soc Psychol* 1:147–165.

28. Elfenbein HA, Beaupré M, Lévesque M, Hess U (2007) Toward a dialect theory: Cultural differences in the expression and recognition of posed facial expressions. *Emotion* 7:131–146.

29. Marsh AA, Elfenbein HA, Ambady N (2003) Nonverbal "accents": Cultural differences in facial expressions of emotion. *Psychol Sci* 14:373–376.

30. Niedenthal PM, Mermillod M, Maringer M, Hess U (2010) The simulation of smiles (SIMS) model: Embodied simulation and the meaning of facial expression. *Behav Brain Sci* 33:417–433, discussion 433–480.

31. Ekman P (1992) An argument for basic emotions. *Cogn Emotion* 6:169–200.

32. Ekman P (1992) Are there basic emotions? *Psychol Rev* 99:550–553.

33. Ekman P, Cordaro D (2011) What is meant by calling emotions basic. *Emotion Review* 3:364–370.

34. Li J, Wang L, Fischer K (2004) The organisation of Chinese shame concepts? *Cogn Emotion* 18:767–797.

35. Tracy JL, Robins RW (2004) Show your pride: Evidence for a discrete emotion expression. *Psychol Sci* 15:194–197.

36. Bedford O, Hwang K-K (2003) Guilt and shame in Chinese culture: A cross-cultural framework from

the perspective of morality and identity. *J Theory Soc Behav* 33:127–144.

37. Ekman P, Friesen W (1978) *Facial Action Coding System: A Technique for the Measurement of Facial Movement* (Consulting Psychologists Press, Washington, DC).

38. Urquhart CW, Green DS, Borland ED (2006) 4D Capture using passive stereo photogrammetry. *Proceedings of the 3rd European Conference on Visual Media Production* (Institution of Electrical Engineers, Edison, NJ), p 196.

39. Ibrahimagić-Šeper L, Čelebić A, Petričević N, Selimović E (2006) Anthropometric differences between males and females in face dimensions and dimensions of central maxillary incisors. *Med Glas* 3:58–62.

40. Hall E (1966) *The Hidden Dimension* (Doubleday, Garden City, NY).

41. MacQueen J (1967) Some methods for classification and analysis of multivariate observations. Proceedings of the Fifth Berkeley Symposium on Mathematical Statistics and Probability (Univ of California Press, Berkeley, CA), 1:281–297.

42. Magri C, Whittingstall K, Singh V, Logothetis NK, Panzeri S (2009) A toolbox for the fast information analysis of multiple-site LFP, EEG and spike train recordings. *BMC Neurosci* 10:81.

RACHAEL E. JACK is a faculty member in the Institute of Neuroscience and Psychology at the University of Glasgow in Scotland. She investigates the psychological underpinnings of social interaction.

OLIVER G. B. GARROD is a research technologist in the Centre of Neuroscience at the University of Glasgow in Scotland. Currently, he is working on dynamic perception-based models of facial expression.

HUI YU is a faculty member with the Intelligent Systems and Robotics Group at the University of Portsmouth. His research interests include image/video processing and recognition; human behavior understanding and affective analysis (multidimensional); and geometric processing of human/facial performances.

ROBERTO CALDARA is a faculty member at the University of Fribourg in Switzerland. He currently serves as chair of cognitive neuroscience in the department of psychology. He investigates brain-behavior interactions on the study of human cognition.

PHILIPPE G. SCHYNS is the director of the Institute of Neuroscience and Psychology and a professor of psychology at the University of Glasgow in Scotland. He researches the information processing mechanisms of face, object, and scene categorization in the brain.

Gary Marcus  **NO**

Making the Mind: Why We've Misunderstood the Nature-Nurture Debate

What do our minds owe to our nature, and what to our nurture? The question has long been vexed, in no small part because until recently we knew relatively little about the nature of nature—how genes work and what they bring to the biological structures that underlie the mind. But now, 50 years after the discovery of the molecular structure of DNA, we are for the first time in a position to understand directly DNA's contribution to the mind. And the story is vastly different from—and vastly more interesting than—anything we had anticipated.

The emerging picture of nature's role in the formation of the mind is at odds with a conventional view, recently summarized by Louis Menand. According to Menand, "every aspect of life has a biological foundation in exactly the same sense, which is that unless it was biologically possible it wouldn't exist. After that, it's up for grabs." More particularly, some scholars have taken recent research on genes and on the brain as suggesting a profoundly limited role for nature in the formation of the mind.

Their position rests on two arguments, what Stanford anthropologist Paul Ehrlich dubbed a "gene shortage" and widespread, well-documented findings of "brain plasticity." According to the gene shortage argument, genes can't be very important to the birth of the mind because the genome contains only about 30,000 genes, simply too few to account even for the brain's complexity—with its billions of cells and tens of billions of connections between neurons—much less the mind's. "Given that ratio," Ehrlich suggested, "it would be quite a trick for genes typically to control more than the most general aspects of human behavior."

According to the brain plasticity argument, genes can't be terribly important because the developing brain is so flexible. For instance, whereas adults who lose their left hemisphere are likely to lose permanently much of their ability to talk, a child who loses a left hemisphere may very well recover the ability to speak, even in the absence of a left hemisphere. Such flexibility is pervasive, down to the level of individual cells. Rather than being fixed in their fates the instant they are born, newly formed brain cells—neurons—can sometimes shift their function, depending on their context. A cell that would ordinarily help to give us a sense of touch can (in the right circumstances) be recruited into the visual system and accept signals from the eye. With that high level of brain plasticity, some imagine that genes are left on the sidelines, as scarcely relevant onlookers.

All of this is, I think, a mistake. It is certainly true that the number of genes is tiny in comparison to the number of neurons, and that the developing brain is highly plastic. Nevertheless, nature—in the form of genes—has an enormous impact on the developing brain and mind. The general outlines of how genes build the brain are finally becoming clear, and we are also starting to see how, in forming the brain, genes make room for the environment's essential role. While vast amounts of work remain to be done, it is becoming equally clear that understanding the coordination of nature and nurture will require letting go of some long-held beliefs.

How to Build a Brain

In the nine-month dash from conception to birth—the flurry of dividing, specializing, and migrating cells that scientists call embryogenesis—organs such as the heart and kidney unfold in a series of ever more mature stages. In contrast to a 17th century theory known as preformationism, the organs of the body cannot be found preformed in miniature in a fertilized egg; at the moment of conception there is neither a tiny heart nor a tiny brain. Instead, the fertilized egg contains information: the three billion nucleotides of DNA that make up the human genome. That information, copied into the nucleus of every newly formed cell, guides the gradual but powerful process of successive approximation that shapes each of the body's organs. The heart, for example, begins as a simple sheet of cell that gradually folds over to form a tube; the tube sprouts bulges, the bulges sprout further bulges, and every day the growing heart looks a bit more like an adult heart.

Even before the dawn of the modern genetic era, biologists understood that something similar was happening in the development of the brain—that the organ of thought and language was formed in much the same way as the rest of the body. The brain, too, develops in the first instance from a simple sheet of cells that gradually curls up into a tube that sprouts bulges, which over time differentiate into ever more complex shapes. Yet 2,000 years of thinking of the mind as independent from the body kept people from appreciating the significance of this seemingly obvious point.

The notion that the brain is drastically different from other physical systems has a long tradition; it can be seen as a modernized version of the ancient belief that the mind and body are wholly separate—but it is untenable. The brain is a physical system. Although the brain's function is different from that of other organs, the brain's capabilities, like those of other organs, emerge from its physical properties. We now know that strokes and gunshot wounds can interfere with language by destroying parts of the brain, and that Prozac and Ritalin can influence mood by altering the flow of neurotransmitters. The fundamental components of the brain—the neurons and the synapses that connect them—can be understood as physical systems, with chemical and electrical properties that follow from their composition.

Yet even as late as the 1990s, latter-day dualists might have thought that the brain developed by different principles. There were, of course, many hints that genes must be important for the brain: identical twins resemble each other more than nonidentical twins in personality as well as in physique; mental disorders such as schizophrenia and depression run in families and are shared even by twins reared apart; and animal breeders know that shaping the bodies of animals often leads to correlated changes in behavior. All of these observations provided clues of genetic effects on the brain.

But such clues are achingly indirect, and it was easy enough to pay them little heed. Even in the mid-1990s, despite all the discoveries that had been made in molecular biology, hardly anything specific was known about how the brain formed. By the end of that decade, however, revolutions in the methodology of molecular biology—techniques for studying and manipulating genes—were beginning to enter the study of the brain. Now, just a few years later, it has become clear that to an enormous extent the brain really is sculpted by the same processes as the rest of the body, not just at the macroscopic level (i.e., as a product of successive approximation) but also at the microscopic level, in terms of the mechanics of how genes are switched on and off, and even in terms of which genes are involved; a huge number of the genes that participate in the development of the brain play important (and often closely related) roles in the rest of the body. . . .

The . . . power of genes holds even for the most unusual yet most characteristic parts of neurons: the long axons that carry signals away from the cell, the tree-like dendrites that allow neurons to receive signals from other nerve cells, and the trillions of synapses that serve as connections between them. What your brain does is largely a function of how those synaptic connections are set up—alter those connections, and you alter the mind—and how they are set up is no small part a function of the genome. In the laboratory, mutant flies and mice with aberrant brain wiring have trouble with everything from motor control (one mutant mouse is named "reeler" for its almost drunken gait) to vision. And in humans, faulty brain wiring contributes to disorders such as schizophrenia and autism.

Proper neural wiring depends on the behavior of individual axons and dendrites. And this behavior once again depends on the content of the genome. For example, much of what axons do is governed by special wiggly, almost hand-like protuberances at the end of each axon known as growth cones. Growth cones (and the axonal wiring they trail behind them) are like little animals that swerve back and forth, maneuvering around obstacles, extending and retracting feelers known as filopodia (the "fingers" of a growth cone) as the cone hunts around in search of its destination—say in the auditory cortex. Rather than simply being launched like projectiles that blindly and helplessly follow whatever route they first set out on, growth cones constantly compensate and adjust, taking in new information as they find their way to their targets.

Growth cones don't just head in a particular direction and hope for the best. They "know" what they are looking for and can make new plans even if experimentally induced obstacles get in their way. In their efforts to find their destinations, growth cones use every trick they can, from "short-range" cues emanating from the surface of nearby cells to long-distance cues that broadcast their signals from millimeters away—miles and miles in the geography of an axon. For example, some proteins appear to serve as "radio beacons" that can diffuse across great distances and serve as guides to distant growth cones—provided that they are tuned to the right station. Which stations a growth cone picks up—and whether it finds a particular signal attractive or repellent—depends on the protein receptors it has on its surface, in turn a function of which genes are expressed within.

Researchers are now in a position where they can begin to understand and even manipulate those genes. In 2000, a team of researchers at the Salk Institute in San Diego took a group of thoracic (chest) motor neurons that normally extend their axons into several different places, such as axial muscles (midline muscles that play a role in posture), intercostal muscles (the muscles between the ribs), and sympathetic neurons (which, among other things, participate in the fast energy mobilization for fight-or-flight responses), and by changing their genetic labels persuaded virtually the entire group of thoracic neurons to abandon their usual targets in favor of the axial muscles. (The few exceptions were a tiny number that apparently couldn't fit into the newly crowded axial destinations and had to find other targets.)

What this all boils down to, from the perspective of psychology, is an astonishingly powerful system for wiring the mind. Instead of vaguely telling axons and dendrites to send and accept signals from their neighbors, thereby leaving all of the burden of mind development to experience, nature in effect lays down the cable: it supplies the brain's wires—axons and dendrites—with elaborate tools for finding their way on their own. Rather than waiting for experience, brains can use the complex menagerie of genes and proteins to create a rich, intricate starting point for the brain and mind.

The sheer overlap between the cellular and molecular processes by which the brain is built and the processes by which the rest of the body is built has meant that new techniques designed for the study of the one can often be readily imported into the study of the other. New techniques in staining, for instance, by which biologists trace the movements and fates of individual cells, can often be brought to bear on the study of the brain as soon as they are developed; even more important, new techniques for altering the genomes of experimental animals can often be almost immediately applied to studies of brain development. Our collective understanding of biology is growing by leaps and bounds because sauce for the goose is so often sauce for the gander.

Nature and Nurture Redux

This seemingly simple idea—that what's good enough for the body is good enough for the brain—has important implications for how we understand the roles of nature and nurture in the development of the mind and brain.

Beyond the Blueprint

Since the early 1960s biologists have realized that genes are neither blueprints nor dictators; instead, as I will explain in a moment, genes are better seen as *providers of opportunity*. Yet because the brain has for so long been treated as separate from the body, the notion of genes as sources of options rather than purveyors of commands has yet to really enter into our understanding of the origins of human psychology.

Biologists have long understood that all genes have two functions. First, they serve as templates for building particular proteins. The insulin gene provides a template for insulin, the hemoglobin genes give templates for building hemoglobin, and so forth. Second, each gene contains what is called a regulatory sequence, a set of conditions that guide whether or not that gene's template gets converted into protein. Although every cell contains a complete copy of the genome, most of the genes in any given cell are silent. Your lung cells, for example, contain the recipe for insulin but they don't produce any, because in those cells the insulin gene is switched off (or "repressed"); each protein is produced only in the cells in which the relevant gene is switched on. So individual genes are like lines in a computer program. Each gene has an IF and a THEN, a precondition (IF) and an action (THEN). And here is one of the most important places where the environment can enter: the IFs of genes are responsive to the environment of the cells in which they are contained. Rather than being static entities that decide the fate of each cell in advance, genes—because of the regulatory sequence—are dynamic and can guide a cell in different ways at different times, depending on the balance of molecules in their environment.

This basic logic—which was worked out in the early 1960s by two French biologists, François Jacob and Jacques Monod, in a series of painstaking studies of the diet of a simple bacterium—applies as much to humans as to bacteria, and as much for the brain as for any other part of the body. Monod and Jacob aimed to understand how *E. coli* bacteria could switch almost instantaneously from a diet of glucose (its favorite) to a diet of lactose (an emergency backup food). What they found was that this abrupt change in diet was accomplished by a process that switched genes on and off. To metabolize lactose, the bacterium needed to build a certain set of protein-based enzymes that for simplicity I'll refer to collectively as lactase, the product of a cluster of lactase genes. Every *E. coli* had those lactase genes lying in wait, but they were only expressed—switched on—when a bit of lactose could bind (attach to) a certain spot of DNA that lay near them, and this in turn could happen only if there was no glucose around to get in the way. In essence, the simple bacterium had an IF-THEN—if lactose and not glucose, then build lactase—that is very much of a piece with the billions of IF-THENs that run the world's computer software.

The essential point is that genes are IFs rather than MUSTs. So even a single environmental cue can radically reshape the course of development. In the African butterfly *Bicyclus anynana*, for example, high temperature during development (associated with the rainy season in its native tropical climate) leads the butterfly to become brightly colored; low temperature (associated with a dry fall) leads the butterfly to become a dull brown. The growing butterfly doesn't learn (in the course of its development) how to blend in better—it will do the same thing in a lab where the temperature varies and the foliage is constant; instead it is genetically programmed to develop in two different ways in two different environments.

The lesson of the last five years of research in developmental neuroscience is that IF-THENs are as crucial and omnipresent in brain development as they are elsewhere. To take one recently worked out example: rats, mice, and other rodents devote a particular region of the cerebral cortex known as barrel fields to the problem of analyzing the stimulation of their whiskers. The exact placement of those barrel fields appears to be driven by a gene or set of genes whose IF region is responsive to the quantity of a particular molecule, Fibroblast Growth Factor 8 (FGF8). By altering the distribution of that molecule, researchers were able to alter barrel development: increasing the concentration of FGF8 led to mice with barrel fields that were unusually far forward, while decreasing the concentration led to mice with barrel fields that were unusually far back. In essence, the quantity of FGF8 serves as a beacon, guiding growing cells to their fate by driving the regulatory IFs of the many genes that are presumably involved in barrel-field formation.

Other IF-THENs contribute to the function of the brain throughout life, e.g., supervising the control of neurotransmitters and participating . . . in the process of laying down memory traces. Because each gene has an IF, every aspect of the brain's development is in principle linked to some aspect of the environment; chemicals such as alcohol that are ingested during pregnancy have such enormous effects because they fool the IFs that regulate genes that guide cells into dividing too much or too little, into moving too far or not far enough, and so forth. The brain is the product of the actions of its component cells, and those actions are the products of the genes they contain within, each cell guided by 30,000 IFs paired with

30,000 THENs—as many possibilities as there are genes. (More, really, because many genes have multiple IFs, and genes can and often do work in combination.)

From Genes to Behavior

Whether we speak of the brain or other parts of the body, changes in even a single gene—leading to either a new IF or a new THEN—can have great consequences. Just as a single alteration to the hemoglobin gene can lead to a predisposition for sickle-cell anemia, a single change to the genes involved in the brain can lead to a language impairment or mental retardation.

And at least in animals, small differences within genomes can lead to significant differences in behavior. A Toronto team, for example, recently used genetic techniques to investigate—and ultimately modify—the foraging habits of *C. elegans* worms. Some *elegans* prefer to forage in groups, others are loners, and the Toronto group was able to tie these behavioral differences to differences in a single amino acid in the protein template (THEN) region of a particular gene known as npr-1; worms with the amino acid valine in the critical spot are "social" whereas worms with phenylalanine are loners. Armed with that knowledge and modern genetic engineering techniques, the team was able to switch a strain of loner *C. elegans* worms into social worms by altering that one gene.

Another team of researchers, at Emory University, has shown that changing the regulatory IF region of a single gene can also have a significant effect on social behavior. Building on an observation that differences in sociability in different species of voles correlated with how many vasopressin receptors they had, they transferred the regulatory IF region of sociable prairie voles' vasopressin receptor genes into the genome of a less sociable species, the mouse—and in so doing created mutant mice, more social than normal, with more vasopressin receptors. With other small genetic modifications, researchers have created strains of anxious, fearful mice, mice that progressively increase alcohol consumption under stress, mice that lack the nurturing instinct, and even mice that groom themselves constantly, pulling and tugging on their own hair to the point of baldness. Each of those studies demonstrates how behavior can be significantly changed when even a single gene is altered.

Still, complex biological structures—whether we speak of hearts or kidneys or brains—are the product of the concerted actions and interactions of many genes, not just one. A mutation in a single gene known as FOXP2 can interfere with the ability of a child to learn language; an alteration in the vasopressin gene can alter a rodent's sociability—but this doesn't mean that FOXP2 is solely responsible for language or that vasopressin is the only gene a rat needs in order to be sociable. Although individual genes can have powerful effects, no trait is the consequence of any single gene. There can no more be a single gene for language, or for the propensity for talking about the weather, than there can be for the left ventricle of a human heart. Even a single brain cell—or a single heart cell—is the product of many genes working together.

The mapping between genes and behavior is made even more complex by the fact that few if any neural circuits operate entirely autonomously. Except perhaps in the case of reflexes, most behaviors are the product of multiple interacting systems. In a complex animal like a mammal or a bird, virtually every action depends on a coming together of systems for perception, attention, motivation, and so forth. Whether or not a pigeon pecks a lever to get a pellet depends on whether it is hungry, whether it is tired, whether there is anything else more interesting around, and so forth. Furthermore, even within a single system, genes rarely participate directly "on-line," in part because they are just too slow. Genes do seem to play an active, major role in "off-line" processing, such as consolidation of long-term memory—which can even happen during sleep—but when it comes to rapid on-line decision-making, genes, which work on a time scale of seconds or minutes, turn over the reins to neurons, which act on a scale of hundredths of a second. The chief contribution of genes comes in advance, in laying down and adjusting neural circuitry, not in the moment-by-moment running of the nervous system. Genes build neural structures—not behavior.

In the assembly of the brain, as in the assembly of other organs, one of the most important ideas is that of a cascade, one gene influencing another, which influences another, which influences another, and so on. Rather than acting in absolute isolation, most genes act as parts of elaborate networks in which the expression of one gene is a precondition for the expression of the next. The THEN of one gene can satisfy the IF of another and thus induce it to turn on. Regulatory proteins are proteins (themselves the product of genes) that control the expression of other genes and thus tie the whole genetic system together. A single regulatory gene at the top of a complex network can indirectly launch a cascade of hundreds or thousands of other genes leading to, for example, the development of an eye or a limb.

In the words of Swiss biologist Walter Gehring, such genes can serve as "master control genes" and exert

enormous power on a growing system. PAX6, for example, is a regulatory protein that plays a role in eye development, and Gehring has shown that artificially activating it in the right spot on a fruit fly's antenna can lead to an extra eye, right there on the antenna—thus, a simple regulatory gene leads directly and indirectly to the expression of approximately 2,500 other genes. What is true for the fly's eye is also true for its brain—and also for the human brain: by compounding and coordinating their effects, genes can exert enormous influence on biological structure.

From a Tiny Number of Genes to a Complex Brain

The cascades in turn help us to make sense of the alleged gene shortage, the idea that the discrepancy between the number of genes and the number of neurons might somehow minimize the importance of genes when it comes to constructing brain or behavior.

Reflection on the relation between brain and body immediately vitiates the gene shortage argument: if 30,000 genes weren't enough to have significant influence on the 20 billion cells in the brain, they surely wouldn't have much impact on the trillions that are found in the body as a whole. The confusion, once again, can be traced to the mistaken idea of genome as blueprint, to the misguided expectation of a one-to-one mapping from individual genes to individual neurons; in reality, genomes describe processes for building things rather than pictures of finished products: better to think of the genome as a compression scheme than a blueprint.

Computer scientists use compression schemes when they want to store and transmit information efficiently. All compression schemes rely in one way or another on ferreting out redundancy. For instance, programs that use the GIF format look for patterns of repeated pixels (the colored dots of which digital images are made). If a whole series of pixels are of exactly the same color, the software that creates GIF files will assign a code that represents the color of those pixels, followed by a number to indicate how many pixels in a row are of the same color. Instead of having to list every blue pixel individually, the GIF format saves space by storing only two numbers: the code for blue and the number of repeated blue pixels. When you "open" a GIF file, the computer converts those codes back into the appropriate strings of identical bits; in the meantime, the computer has saved a considerable amount of memory. Computer scientists have devised dozens of different compression schemes, from JPEGs for photographs to MP3s for music, each designed to exploit a different kind of redundancy. The general procedure is always the same: some end product is converted into a compact description of how to reconstruct that end product; a "decompressor" reconstructs the desired end product from that compact description.

Biology doesn't know in advance what the end product will be; there's no StuffIt Compressor to convert a human being into a genome. But the genome is very much akin to a compression scheme, a terrifically efficient description of how to build something of great complexity—perhaps more efficient than anything yet developed in the labs of computer scientists (never mind the complexities of the brain—there are trillions of cells in the rest of the body, and they are all supervised by the same 30,000-gene genome). And although nature has no counterpart to a program that stuffs a picture into a compressed encoding, it does offer a counterpart to the program that performs decompression: the cell. Genome in, organism out. Through the logic of gene expression, cells are self-regulating factories that translate genomes into biological structure.

Cascades are at the heart of this process of decompression, because the regulatory proteins that are at the top of genetic cascades serve as shorthand that can be used over and over again, like the subroutine of a software engineer. For example, the genome of a centipede probably doesn't specify separate sets of hundreds or thousands of genes for each of the centipede's legs; instead, it appears that the leg-building "subroutine"—a cascade of perhaps hundreds or thousands of genes—gets invoked many times, once for each new pair of legs. Something similar lies behind the construction of a vertebrate's ribs. And within the last few years it has become clear that the embryonic brain relies on the same sort of genetic recycling, using the same repeated motifs—such as sets of parallel connections known as topographic maps—over and over again, to supervise the development of thousands or even millions of neurons with each use of a given genetic subroutine. There's no gene shortage, because every cascade represents the shorthand for a different reuseable subroutine, a different way of creating more from less.

From Prewiring to Rewiring

In the final analysis, I think the most important question about the biological roots of the mind may not be the question that has preoccupied my colleagues and myself for a number of years—the extent to which genes prewire the brain—but a different question that until recently had never been seriously raised: the extent to which (and ways in which) genes make it possible for experience to *rewire* the brain. Efforts to address the nature-nurture question typically falter because of the false assumption that the two—prewiring and rewiring—are competing ideas. "Anti-nativists"—critics of the view that we might be born with significant mental structure prior to experience—often attempt to downplay the significance of genes by making what I earlier called "the argument from plasticity": they point to the brain's resilience to damage and its ability to modify itself in response to experience. Nativists sometimes seem to think that their position rests on downplaying (or demonstrating limits on) plasticity.

In reality, plasticity and innateness are almost logically separate. Innateness is about the extent to which the brain is prewired, plasticity about the extent to which it can be rewired. Some organisms may be good at one but not the other: chimpanzees, for example, may have intricate innate wiring yet, in comparison to humans, relatively few mechanisms for rewiring their brains. Other organisms may be lousy at both: *C. elegans* worms have limited initial structure, and relatively little in the way of techniques for rewiring their nervous system on the basis of experience. And some organisms, such as humans, are well-endowed in both respects, with enormously intricate initial architecture and fantastically powerful and flexible means for rewiring in the face of experience. . . .

GARY MARCUS is the director of the NYU Center for Language and Music, and a psychology professor at New York University. He has written numerous books looking at the integrated study of psychology, linguistics, and molecular biology.

EXPLORING THE ISSUE

Does the Cultural Environment Influence Lifespan Development More Than Our Genes?

Critical Thinking and Reflection

1. Do studies that show identical twins to be more alike than fraternal twins provide convincing evidence of genetic dominance? Why or why not?
2. How might twin studies also include environmental influences?
3. Evolutionary approaches to psychology have gained recent popularity; are these approaches correct? What might be other reasons for this popularity?
4. How might the complexity of gene-environment interactions make it difficult to analyze specific topics like emotions?

Is There Common Ground?

Although it has become common practice to talk about the "nature or nurture" debate, few experts today believe that our development is an either/or proposition. It is clear that genes are important, and it is clear that socialization through the cultural environment matters. The question here is really about the relative degree of influence of nature and nurture in different domains of development, and the processes through which genes and experiences interact. In fact, in their own ways, both of the above selections are emphasizing the importance of not oversimplifying human development.

Perhaps, then, the nature-nurture debate has been replaced by the study of interactions, with modern research findings that most traits reflect both genetic and environmental differences. Gene-environment correlations explain how nature and nurture may interact. Researchers have identified three types of causal gene-environment correlations: passive, evocative, and active. The degree of influence of genes (or the environment) is different for each of these correlations.

If we put too much stock in genes and evolutionary psychology, we risk implying that social roles are fixed by nature. But if we put too much stock in culture and socialization, we risk ignoring the natural constraints on our behavior and assuming that attitude is all that matters. So what is the right balance and how does that balance happen during the lived experience of lifespan development?

Create Central

www.mhhe.com/createcentral

Additional Resources

Ceci, S. J., & Williams, W. M. (Eds.). (1999). *The nature-nurture debate: The essential readings*. Blackwell Publishing.

Goldhaber, D. (2012). *The Nature-nurture debates: Bridging the gap*. Cambridge University Press.

Murata, A., Moser, J. S., & Kitayama, S. (2013). Culture shapes electrocortical responses during emotion suppression. *Social cognitive and affective neuroscience, 8*(5), 595–601.

Raval, V. V., & Martini, T. S. (2009). Maternal socialization of children's anger, sadness, and physical pain in two communities in Gujarat, India. *International Journal of Behavioral Development*.

Stiles, J., Braddick, O., Atkinson, J., & Innocenti, G. (2011). Brain development and the nature versus nurture debate. *Gene expression to neurobiology and behaviour: Human brain development and developmental disorders, 3*–22.

Internet References . . .

American Academy of Pediatrics

    http://www.aap.org

American Psychological Association

    http://www.apa.org

Nature Versus Nurture

    http://en.wikipedia.org/wiki/Nature_versus_nurture

Society for Research on Child Development

    http://www.srcd.org

Selected, Edited, and with Issue Framing Material by:
Allison A. Buskirk-Cohen, *Delaware Valley University*

ISSUE

Is Chinese Parenting Culturally Distinct?

YES: Amy Chua, from "Why Chinese Mothers Are Superior," *Wall Street Journal—The Saturday Essay* (2011)

NO: Markella B. Rutherford, from "The Social Value of Self-Esteem," *Society* (2011)

Learning Outcomes

After reading this issue, you will be able to:

- Discuss what is considered an optimal parenting style, and an optimal model of lifespan development, and how they vary significantly across both culture and social class.
- Understand how putting an emphasis on self-esteem as a key foundation of lifespan development is historically and culturally unusual, but underlies much of contemporary Western parenting.
- Explain how globalization and the global economy influence the way people think about the nature of successful development.

ISSUE SUMMARY

YES: Amy Chua, author of *The Battle Hymn of the Tiger Mother*, discusses strategies to achieve success in childrearing, highlighting the techniques of "Chinese" mothers. She argues that raising successful children is less about bolstering their self-esteem and more about instilling disciplined work habits and high standards, values that are important to academic and life success.

NO: Sociologist Markella B. Rutherford instead sees the "Tiger Mother" idea as just another example of the types of privileged parenting that ultimately prioritizes self-confidence, self-esteem, and perpetuates differences more dependent on class than on culture.

In an increasingly competitive and globalized world, what does it take for an individual to become a success? For many, the support of parents is the starting point, and most parents certainly want their children to succeed. But what does that mean in practice? For many modern Western parents, that often means emphasizing unconditional love and boosting self-esteem: We tend to believe that if we give our children enough attention and encouragement they will develop into successful adults. Although that belief may not seem terribly controversial, there are some interesting questions as to whether attention and encouragement is enough. Particularly with the growing global prominence of non-Western nations such as China, some are raising the question of whether

Western parents set their expectations too low. If parents raised their expectations, would children necessarily meet them, or is there more involved in successful parenting?

The optimal parenting style has long been a question of interest to scholars of lifespan development. One well-known scheme, developed by psychologist Diana Baumrind in the 1960s, identified three primary parenting styles that reflect differing combinations of demandingness and responsiveness. Authoritarian parents employ strict rules and unquestioned authority, while authoritative parents use a combination of some rules and some more democratic responsiveness. Permissive parent have few demands and many indulgences. Further research on parenting styles by Eleanor Maccoby and John Martin suggested a fourth style: uninvolved parenting which is characterized by low responsiveness and few demands. Most developmentalists have promoted authoritative parenting, though striking an effective balance between setting rules and being responsive is a persistent challenge. When does a parent know best, and when should the child be allowed to contribute to decision-making?

The question of optimal parenting style is further complicated by a growing recognition that cultural contexts can change the definition of "optimal." Some scholars have suggested, for example, that the American emphasis on self-esteem as the top priority for children is a curious cultural construction not considered essential in many cultural contexts. It reflects an American emphasis on individualism, rather than an appreciation for collectivism which other cultures value. Or, as another example, there is some research evidence suggesting that when raising children in crowded or dangerous communities, using an authoritarian parenting style can be more effective than an authoritative style. Economic status also plays a role in this debate. Certain activities simply cost more money than others. For example, taking private piano lessons is more expensive than playing outside in the backyard. Further complicating matters is the fact that culture itself is neither static nor clearly defined: The values, norms, and beliefs that shape what we consider optimal parenting and ideal development vary considerably both within and between communities.

Perhaps because defining optimal parenting is such a complicated task, people are often intrigued when experts claim to have figured it out. When such a claim also includes a provocative challenge to familiar cultural beliefs it can be all the more intriguing. This confluence was exactly what propelled Amy Chua's parenting memoir into national prominence in early 2011. Chua's essay claiming that "Chinese mothers are superior" in the pages of the *Wall Street Journal* drew broad attention, curiosity, and some outrage. Her claim that most "Western" parents are too easy on their children, and that the hard-driving style she identified as Chinese is better for ensuring children's success, led many to respond with a mix of defensiveness and recognition. The response implied that Western parents feel a close attachment to a developmental ideal based on affection and self-esteem, while simultaneously recognizing that success in modern society requires discipline, effort, and competitive excellence.

Much of the critical reaction to Chau's essay focused on the perceived harshness of her description

of Chinese parenting. Chua advocates emphasizing achievement in children—at all costs. As an example, one *Wall Street Journal* columnist proudly contrasted himself with the "Tiger Mother" by proclaiming himself a "Panda Dad" and extolling the virtues of allowing children the freedom to have fun and be creative. But Chua's daughters came to her defense, with one writing an essay of her own titled "Why I Love My Strict Chinese Mom." In this daughter's eyes, Chua's parenting style worked. The public outcry against the "Tiger Mother" emphasizes the confusion about what constitutes good parenting and how we define success. For Chua, parenting is about providing strict rules and discipline so that children achieve high grades in school and accolades in concert halls.

The scholarly reaction to the concept of the "Tiger Mother" has, however, been more considered. Many scholars have observed that Chua's perspective triggered broader global economic fears in the West that Chinese ways are the future, and consider the controversy to be as much about modern society as it is about individual parenting style. From that standpoint, Markella B. Rutherford's perspective as a sociologist interested in how child-rearing norms contribute to social inequalities brings together several lines of critique. In fact, Rutherford argues that at root the "Tiger Mother" style is less a cultural model of development and more another way privileged parents can give their children a head start in the global economy. As she notes in her essay, "The claims of cultural differences between so-called Chinese and American approaches are, in fact, red herrings; the 'tiger' and 'panda' approaches are different means for achieving the same goal—children with a strong sense of accomplishment and self-confidence."

Ultimately, then, this controversy invokes a variety of questions relevant to lifespan development. It starts as a consideration of the classic question of whether parents should be strict or lenient, proceeds to consider whether self-esteem matters and how it can be produced, and ends up raising issues about how social inequalities get reproduced. There also are questions about how much influence parents truly have. Does parenting really determine whether or not people develop into successful adults, however success is defined? Teachers, friends, siblings, movies, music, food—these are just a few examples of other influences on development. Whether it is culture, social class, or self-esteem, it all comes down to a question of what makes for successful lifespan development.

YES ↵

Amy Chua

Why Chinese Mothers Are Superior

A lot of people wonder how Chinese parents raise such stereotypically successful kids. They wonder what these parents do to produce so many math whizzes and music prodigies, what it's like inside the family, and whether they could do it too. Well, I can tell them, because I've done it. Here are some things my daughters, Sophia and Louisa, were never allowed to do:

- attend a sleepover
- have a playdate
- be in a school play
- complain about not being in a school play
- watch TV or play computer games
- choose their own extracurricular activities
- get any grade less than an A
- not be the No. 1 student in every subject except gym and drama
- play any instrument other than the piano or violin
- not play the piano or violin.

I'm using the term "Chinese mother" loosely. I know some Korean, Indian, Jamaican, Irish and Ghanaian parents who qualify too. Conversely, I know some mothers of Chinese heritage, almost always born in the West, who are not Chinese mothers, by choice or otherwise. I'm also using the term "Western parents" loosely. Western parents come in all varieties.

All the same, even when Western parents think they're being strict, they usually don't come close to being Chinese mothers. For example, my Western friends who consider themselves strict make their children practice their instruments 30 minutes every day. An hour at most. For a Chinese mother, the first hour is the easy part. It's hours two and three that get tough.

Despite our squeamishness about cultural stereotypes, there are tons of studies out there showing marked and quantifiable differences between Chinese and Westerners when it comes to parenting. In one study of 50 Western American mothers and 48 Chinese immigrant mothers, almost 70% of the Western mothers said either that "stressing academic success is not good for children" or that "parents need to foster the idea that learning is fun." By contrast, roughly 0% of the Chinese mothers felt the same way. Instead, the vast majority of the Chinese mothers said that they believe their children can be "the best" students, that "academic achievement reflects successful parenting," and that if children did not excel at school then there was "a problem" and parents "were not doing their job." Other studies indicate that compared to Western parents, Chinese parents spend approximately 10 times as long every day drilling academic activities with their children. By contrast, Western kids are more likely to participate in sports teams.

What Chinese parents understand is that nothing is fun until you're good at it. To get good at anything you have to work, and children on their own never want to work, which is why it is crucial to override their preferences. This often requires fortitude on the part of the parents because the child will resist; things are always hardest at the beginning, which is where Western parents tend to give up. But if done properly, the Chinese strategy produces a virtuous circle. Tenacious practice, practice, practice is crucial for excellence; rote repetition is underrated in America. Once a child starts to excel at something—whether it's math, piano, pitching or ballet—he or she gets praise, admiration and satisfaction. This builds confidence and makes the once not-fun activity fun. This in turn makes it easier for the parent to get the child to work even more.

Chinese parents can get away with things that Western parents can't. Once when I was young—maybe more than once—when I was extremely disrespectful to my mother, my father angrily called me "garbage" in our native Hokkien dialect. It worked really well. I felt terrible and deeply ashamed of what I had done. But it didn't damage my self-esteem or anything like that. I knew exactly how highly he thought of me. I didn't actually think I was worthless or feel like a piece of garbage.

As an adult, I once did the same thing to Sophia, calling her garbage in English when she acted extremely disrespectfully toward me. When I mentioned that I had done this at a dinner party, I was immediately ostracized. One guest named Marcy got so upset she broke down in tears and had to leave early. My friend Susan, the host, tried to rehabilitate me with the remaining guests.

The fact is that Chinese parents can do things that would seem unimaginable—even legally actionable—to Westerners. Chinese mothers can say to their daughters, "Hey fatty—lose some weight." By contrast, Western parents have to tiptoe around the issue, talking in terms of "health" and never ever mentioning the f-word, and their kids still end up in therapy for eating disorders and negative self-image. (I also once heard a Western father toast his adult daughter by calling her "beautiful and incredibly competent." She later told me that made her feel like garbage.)

Chinese parents can order their kids to get straight As. Western parents can only ask their kids to try their best. Chinese parents can say, "You're lazy. All your classmates are getting ahead of you." By contrast, Western parents have to struggle with their own conflicted feelings about achievement, and try to persuade themselves that they're not disappointed about how their kids turned out.

I've thought long and hard about how Chinese parents can get away with what they do. I think there are three big differences between the Chinese and Western parental mind-sets.

First, I've noticed that Western parents are extremely anxious about their children's self-esteem. They worry about how their children will feel if they fail at something, and they constantly try to reassure their children about how good they are notwithstanding a mediocre performance on a test or at a recital. In other words, Western parents are concerned about their children's psyches. Chinese parents aren't. They assume strength, not fragility, and as a result they behave very differently.

For example, if a child comes home with an A-minus on a test, a Western parent will most likely praise the child. The Chinese mother will gasp in horror and ask what went wrong. If the child comes home with a B on the test, some Western parents will still praise the child. Other Western parents will sit their child down and express disapproval, but they will be careful not to make their child feel inadequate or insecure, and they will not call their child "stupid," "worthless" or "a disgrace." Privately, the Western parents may worry that their child does not test well or have aptitude in the subject or that there is something wrong with the curriculum and possibly the whole school. If the child's grades do not improve, they may eventually schedule a meeting with the school principal to challenge the way the subject is being taught or to call into question the teacher's credentials.

If a Chinese child gets a B—which would never happen—there would first be a screaming, hair-tearing explosion. The devastated Chinese mother would then get dozens, maybe hundreds of practice tests and work through them with her child for as long as it takes to get the grade up to an A.

Chinese parents demand perfect grades because they believe that their child can get them. If their child doesn't get them, the Chinese parent assumes it's because the child didn't work hard enough. That's why the solution to substandard performance is always to excoriate, punish and shame the child. The Chinese parent believes that their child will be strong enough to take the shaming and to improve from it. (And when Chinese kids do excel, there is plenty of ego-inflating parental praise lavished in the privacy of the home.)

Second, Chinese parents believe that their kids owe them everything. The reason for this is a little unclear, but it's probably a combination of Confucian filial piety and the fact that the parents have sacrificed and done so much for their children. (And it's true that Chinese mothers get in the trenches, putting in long grueling hours personally tutoring, training, interrogating and spying on their kids.) Anyway, the understanding is that Chinese children must spend their lives repaying their parents by obeying them and making them proud.

By contrast, I don't think most Westerners have the same view of children being permanently indebted to their parents. My husband, Jed, actually has the opposite view. "Children don't choose their parents," he once said to me. "They don't even choose to be born. It's parents who foist life on their kids, so it's the parents' responsibility to provide for them. Kids don't owe their parents anything. Their duty will be to their own kids." This strikes me as a terrible deal for the Western parent.

Third, Chinese parents believe that they know what is best for their children and therefore override all of their children's own desires and preferences. That's why Chinese daughters can't have boyfriends in high school and why Chinese kids can't go to sleepaway camp. It's also why no Chinese kid would ever dare say to their mother, "I got a part in the school play! I'm Villager Number Six. I'll have to stay after school for rehearsal every day from 3:00 to 7:00, and I'll also need a ride on weekends." God help any Chinese kid who tried that one.

Don't get me wrong: It's not that Chinese parents don't care about their children. Just the opposite. They would give up anything for their children. It's just an entirely different parenting model.

Here's a story in favor of coercion, Chinese-style. Lulu was about 7, still playing two instruments, and working on a piano piece called "The Little White Donkey" by the French composer Jacques Ibert. The piece is really cute—

you can just imagine a little donkey ambling along a country road with its master—but it's also incredibly difficult for young players because the two hands have to keep schizophrenically different rhythms.

Lulu couldn't do it. We worked on it nonstop for a week, drilling each of her hands separately, over and over. But whenever we tried putting the hands together, one always morphed into the other, and everything fell apart. Finally, the day before her lesson, Lulu announced in exasperation that she was giving up and stomped off.

"Get back to the piano now," I ordered.

"You can't make me."

"Oh yes, I can."

Back at the piano, Lulu made me pay. She punched, thrashed and kicked. She grabbed the music score and tore it to shreds. I taped the score back together and encased it in a plastic shield so that it could never be destroyed again. Then I hauled Lulu's dollhouse to the car and told her I'd donate it to the Salvation Army piece by piece if she didn't have "The Little White Donkey" perfect by the next day. When Lulu said, "I thought you were going to the Salvation Army, why are you still here?" I threatened her with no lunch, no dinner, no Christmas or Hanukkah presents, no birthday parties for two, three, four years. When she still kept playing it wrong, I told her she was purposely working herself into a frenzy because she was secretly afraid she couldn't do it. I told her to stop being lazy, cowardly, self-indulgent and pathetic.

Jed took me aside. He told me to stop insulting Lulu—which I wasn't even doing, I was just motivating her—and that he didn't think threatening Lulu was helpful. Also, he said, maybe Lulu really just couldn't do the technique—perhaps she didn't have the coordination yet—had I considered that possibility?

"You just don't believe in her," I accused.

"That's ridiculous," Jed said scornfully. "Of course I do."

"Sophia could play the piece when she was this age."

"But Lulu and Sophia are different people," Jed pointed out.

"Oh no, not this," I said, rolling my eyes. "Everyone is special in their special own way," I mimicked sarcastically. "Even losers are special in their own special way. Well don't worry, you don't have to lift a finger. I'm willing to put in as long as it takes, and I'm happy to be the one hated. And you can be the one they adore because you make them pancakes and take them to Yankees games."

I rolled up my sleeves and went back to Lulu. I used every weapon and tactic I could think of. We worked right through dinner into the night, and I wouldn't let Lulu get up, not for water, not even to go to the bathroom. The house became a war zone, and I lost my voice yelling, but still there seemed to be only negative progress, and even I began to have doubts.

Then, out of the blue, Lulu did it. Her hands suddenly came together—her right and left hands each doing their own imperturbable thing—just like that.

Lulu realized it the same time I did. I held my breath. She tried it tentatively again. Then she played it more confidently and faster, and still the rhythm held. A moment later, she was beaming.

"Mommy, look—it's easy!" After that, she wanted to play the piece over and over and wouldn't leave the piano. That night, she came to sleep in my bed, and we snuggled and hugged, cracking each other up. When she performed "The Little White Donkey" at a recital a few weeks later, parents came up to me and said, "What a perfect piece for Lulu—it's so spunky and so *her*."

Even Jed gave me credit for that one. Western parents worry a lot about their children's self-esteem. But as a parent, one of the worst things you can do for your child's self-esteem is to let them give up. On the flip side, there's nothing better for building confidence than learning you can do something you thought you couldn't.

There are all these new books out there portraying Asian mothers as scheming, callous, overdriven people indifferent to their kids' true interests. For their part, many Chinese secretly believe that they care more about their children and are willing to sacrifice much more for them than Westerners, who seem perfectly content to let their children turn out badly. I think it's a misunderstanding on both sides. All decent parents want to do what's best for their children. The Chinese just have a totally different idea of how to do that.

Western parents try to respect their children's individuality, encouraging them to pursue their true passions, supporting their choices, and providing positive reinforcement and a nurturing environment. By contrast, the Chinese believe that the best way to protect their children is by preparing them for the future, letting them see what they're capable of, and arming them with skills, work habits and inner confidence that no one can ever take away.

Amy Chua is a professor at Yale Law School and author of *Day of Empire, World on Fire: How Exporting Free Market Democracy Breeds Ethnic Hatred and Global Instability,* and *Battle Hymn of the Tiger Mother.*

Markella B. Rutherford

The Social Value of Self-Esteem

A number of cultural skirmishes over the parenting practices of Americans have recently played out in the popular media and blogosphere. Often invoking inventive and colorfully descriptive labels, these rhetorical battles have pitted "Helicopter Parents" against "Free-Range Kids" and "Tiger Mothers" against "Panda Dads." Some parents insist that they should hover over their children, being immediately accessible and responsive at all times; others counter that we must encourage independent development and problem-solving by ensuring that children have opportunities to be on their own, unguarded. Some parents attempt to ensure children's future successes by providing a regimented round of enrichment activities; critics argue that children are over-scheduled and that we must protect children's down time for free play. A varied mixture of "confessionals" published by relatively privileged parents has intermingled with a wide array of diatribes against the contemporary parenting styles of affluent parents.

Of course, moral panics about proper parenting are not new. Before popular concerns about the "over-parenting" of the new professional elites, there were the "mommy wars" of the 1980s and 90s. Before that, there were misgivings about the seemingly relaxed morals of the 60s and 70s, which were themselves a kind of backlash against the conformist tendencies of the post-WWII era. Like critiques of previous generations' parenting practices, this latest round of debates still sometimes places mothers, specifically, in the cross-hairs of public disapproval; however, these contemporary debates are less about social control over adults' gender roles and more about a widespread sense of anxiety over whether parents can ensure their children's future success in an era that is increasingly characterized by risk and uncertainty.

The intense anxieties felt by Americans about parenting in the early-twenty-first century are grounded in the uncertainties of work in a post-industrial and global economy. They also point toward the individualized responsibility that has come to shape parenting in contemporary America, where cultural and community-level support for parenting are generally quite weak. This individualization of responsibility affects all parents, across the socioeconomic spectrum, but has led most intensely to a sense of isolation and status anxiety among the highly-educated and highly-credentialed professionals who make up the so-called "knowledge class" or "new elites." It is these parents, in particular, who are often the focus of discussion when contemporary parenting practices come under critique in the media. Unlike the uniform disapproval expressed whenever the parenting of less-affluent parents enters public discourse, there is a great deal of ambivalence about the practices of today's more elite professionals.

Although a relatively privileged group of parents are at the center of contemporary controversies about over-parenting, questions about how parents can ensure their children's success extend far beyond the relatively privileged bloggers and writers who provide easy targets for equally-privileged critics. Hot-button concerns about how much parenting is enough intersect with much more widespread public concerns about both the quality of public education and the limits of meritocracy. Are American kids "Waiting for Superman" and "Rac[ing] to Nowhere," as the titles of two recent documentary films assert? If the system of public education is failing our children, how should parents respond? Should they advocate for higher educational standards or for less homework? Should they insist on greater state investment in education (and the bureaucratic oversight that accompanies it) or should they focus their attention on local investments of targeted solutions and community volunteers? Uncertain about which investments will "pay off" for children in the future, contemporary parents are increasingly placing their trust in the talisman of children's self esteem; this central focus on self-esteem has led to many of the unique parenting practices of our time and is consistent with the divergent styles that engender such passionate debates in the media.

From *Society*, September 2011, pp. 407–412. Copyright © 2011 by Springer Science and Business Media. Reprinted by permission via Rightslink.

The "Magic" of Self-Esteem

Despite the exaggerated claims of difference in popular representations of the parenting wars, a common theme of building children's self-esteem is evident as a cornerstone of contemporary American parenting practices. Whether through a heavy-handed strategy or a more hands-off approach, the relatively privileged parents who write child-rearing confessionals profess a strikingly similar end: to build and enhance their children's self-concept, confidence, and emotional competence. Advocates of "free range kids" (see FreeRangeKids.wordpress.com) believe that allowing children ample independence and opportunities to make mistakes are key to developing self-confidence. Defenders of "helicopter parenting" believe that the best way to protect children's self-esteem is to be present and intervene liberally. Despite different strategies, both groups agree that their goal is to raise confident children.

Yale University Law Professor Amy Chua caused a media storm earlier this year with her book, *Battle Hymn of the Tiger Mother* (2011, Penguin Press), in which she asserted, among other things, that Western parents worry too much about their children's self-esteem. Nonetheless, her own measure of successful parenting takes self-confidence as its yardstick: "As a parent, one of the worst things you can do for your child's self-esteem is to let them give up. On the flip side, there's nothing better for building confidence than learning you can do something you thought you couldn't." One of Chua's critics was *Wall Street Journal* columnist Alan Paul, who called himself the "Panda Dad" in opposition. Paul advocates a "cuddlier" strategy of "controlled chaos," explaining his aversion to "Tiger" parenting specifically because he believes it conflicts with his parenting goals "to raise independent, competent, confident adults." According to Paul, his parenting strategy means that his kids are "constantly learning to take responsibility for their own homework, play time and everything else. Doing so allows them to take genuine pride in their accomplishments. They need to succeed for their own benefit . . ." The claims of cultural differences between so-called Chinese and American approaches are, in fact, red herrings; the "tiger" and "panda" approaches are different means for achieving the same goal—children with a strong sense of accomplishment and self-confidence.

Self-esteem has not always been the primary measure of good parenting. This new cultural development represents a particular context and set of conditions that are unique to a particular class position in a global, knowledge economy. Professional-class parents who are anxious about their own prospects for continued success in a risky economy turn toward emotional capital as a necessary supplement to educational end extra-curricular success to ensure generational reproduction of class advantages. Whether through a strictly-directed or laissez-faire approach, they explicitly seek to help their children discover and cultivate their passions and build their self-esteem through personalized successes.

In the myth of meritocracy, we believe that success depends upon talent and hard work. In reality, however, "achieved" statuses depend much more heavily upon received advantages than upon individual merit. Even if children's future successes do not depend wholly upon how good they are, the centrality of self-esteem in current parenting practices indicates that success may be influenced by how good children *believe* they are. Parents who make up the new professional knowledge class recognize that self-confidence and self-promotion are necessary, even if not sufficient, components of success. Thus, though it is certainly not the only form of cultural capital that matters in the reproduction of class advantages, self-esteem is an important kind of emotional capital that forms part of the *habitus* of today's elites.

Working- and lower-middle class parents also care about their children's self-esteem. In particular, those who are keen to foster upward mobility for their children seize upon the idea of self-esteem as a secret ingredient in the elusive recipe for success. Nonetheless, though these less-privileged parents care about their children's self-feelings, one rarely sees them engaging in debates over which strategy is best for cultivating self-esteem. Indeed, they may see positive self-esteem more as a feeling that develops in response to positive circumstances and that parents should support and encourage whenever possible. They do not engage in public philosophical debates about which elaborate strategies are best for the careful cultivation of self-confident children. Therefore, the kind of self-esteem targeted by more elite parents can be regarded a key form of contemporary cultural capital.

There is compelling sociological evidence that we should be paying more attention today to emotions as a form of cultural capital. In charting the emotional terrain of social class, self-esteem offers a particularly useful emotion to begin with. Self-esteem is a critical part of the sense of entitlement that Annette Lareau documents in *Unequal Childhoods* as emerging from the "concerted cultivation" childrearing approach of the middle class. (In contrast, Lareau argues that the result of the strategy of "accomplishment of natural growth," preferred by working-class parents, is an emerging sense of constraint.) In *Parenting Out of Control*, Margaret Nelson has recently documented, through her nuanced understanding of the interdependence of parenting practices and new technologies, that the sense of entitlement gained by privileged children begins from birth. Nelson documents that an elite parenting strategy of intensive responsiveness and availability is enacted through the use of baby monitors. This practical, technological choice is crucial to establishing, as one respondent told Nelson: "Part of the whole realm of invisible assumptions they have about life . . . if they cry someone will come, if they need help someone will help . . . knowing that someone will always respond." (Nelson 2010, 116) In my own work, I have documented that the approach to building self-esteem in current parenting advice literature hinges on teaching children emotional competency to recognize and express their feelings and the sense children develop that "my feelings matter."

Class Reproduction Among the New Elites

In order to see how a focus on emotional competency and self-esteem have become key components of the childrearing philosophies of today's elites, we must consider the ways that their parenting strategies grow out of the anxieties that upper-middle-class professionals feel about their ability to reproduce their class advantages. For quite some time, we sociologists have insisted that class-based childrearing practices reflect differences in working conditions. We accept that working class parents who are subject to considerable authority and hierarchy at work emphasize obedience in their childrearing, whereas middle-class parents who enjoy considerable autonomy at work emphasize independence and creativity. If we are to understand the foundations of the self-esteem-driven parenting style common today among the elite professional class, we must ask how this style both reflects the demands of professional working conditions and serves to reproduce that class position. If these parents are seeking to pass on their class advantages to their children, we should question: what, exactly is the nature of the advantage they are attempting to reproduce? How does this form of advantage require these strategies? Finally, what do parenting strategies reveal about the changing nature of social class and class reproduction in our time?

The new elites of today, composed of a class of professional, highly-credentialed knowledge workers, earn high incomes and enjoy a great deal of prestige. However, when compared with elites of previous eras, they have relatively low levels of wealth. This means that the reproduction of class advantage among these elites has to happen through a ricky set of mechanisms that is not as easily institutionalized as other historical forms of elite reproduction. In particular, the key source of these elites' status and earning potential—their degrees, credentials, and knowledge—are not (directly) heritable, making these advantages fundamentally different than strictly economic wealth. Because it depends so heavily upon educational credentials, the rise of these new elites signals an intensely individualized form of capital production and has been heralded as the rise of a "new meritocracy." Their class advantage stems not just from *private* property; indeed, it is a highly *personalized* property. The shift from physical and economic capital to the post-industrial capital of degrees and credentials requires new mechanisms for embodying cultural capital. Increasingly, emotional capital is an important element of class reproduction, with self-esteem playing a key role as one of its mechanisms.

Let us look closer at the working conditions of these privileged parents in order to understand why the habit of emphasizing self-esteem makes sense as a parenting strategy for reproducing their class advantages, as well as how the emphasis on self-esteem can unite the seemingly divergent styles through which it is enacted.

Professional Control

In her analysis of diverging class cultures of parenting and how parents make use of various surveillance technologies, Margaret Nelson draws on a Foucaultian framework to distinguish between parenting through discipline and parenting through control. Discipline, a la Foucault, means that hierarchical authority is exercised in such a way that it induces inmates to self-discipline. Children subject to discipline develop an inner compulsion to "do the right thing," thus becoming "docile bodies." In *Parenting Out of Control*, Nelson argues that while previous generations parented from discipline, today's upper-middle-class professionals parent from a strategy of control, which "relies less on enclosure and confinement than on constant communication, less on clear rules than on shifting possibilities, less on hierarchy than on intimacy, less on acknowledged surveillance than on the denial that it is necessary (because of trust), and less on the finished product that on the ongoing processes of shaping 'inmates.' Indeed in this model, there is no 'finished product' or launch into self-discipline" (Nelson 2010, 12). Nelson's analysis examines how these features influence parents' use of various technologies—baby monitors, cell phones, child locator devices, home drug testing—for surveillance and control.

Here, I wish to use these features of control to examine the conditions of contemporary capitalism as experienced in the occupational lives of professional, middle-class parents and to better understand why an emphasis on emotional capital and self-esteem are key aspects of these parents' attempts to reproduce class advantage.

Constant Communication and Shifting Possibilities

Nelson points out that elite parents today rely on constant communication and a set of shifting possibilities rather than either confinement or pre-established rules when dealing with their children. For example, parents stay in touch with kids by cell phone rather than establishing a curfew, making many decisions about what is allowable on a case-by-case basis as part of this steady stream of communication. In many ways these parenting strategies mirror the occupational lives of parents. Many elite professionals enjoy relatively flexible work hours and locations but remain in nearly-constant contact with their employers, colleagues, and clients through email and cell phones. Furthermore, a set of shifting possibilities rather than clear rules are necessary in professions that reward creative problem-solving abilities and encourage workers to find ways to recreate existing guidelines and overcome obstacles. Therefore, children growing up in families with fewer clearly-established boundaries and a considerable sense of latitude are being socialized into the kind of working conditions experienced by their professional parents.

Intimacy and Trust

The oft-criticized parenting philosophies of today's elite parents place great importance on intimacy and trust. These emotional elements of elite parenting undergird the concrete practices of latitude and constant communication described above. However, these are not free-floating parenting philosophies: intimacy and trust are also reflective of the emotional demands of a growing number of professional occupations. Increasingly, corporate capitalism has downplayed the appearance of strict hierarchy and come to favor instead a form of "soft power" that requires that managers and others placed in positions of relative power exhibit high levels of emotional competency and use strategies of therapeutic communication such as active listening (Illouz 2007). For corporate managers and for elite professionals, the ability to manage one's own emotions and respond subtly to the emotionality of others is increasingly a necessary skill for occupational

success. Recent trends of building kids' emotional intelligence through therapeutic communication and parent–child intimacy therefore serve to reproduce an emotional skill set that is needed for success in many upper-middle-class occupations under the contemporary conditions of capitalism.

Parents who emphasize emotional intimacy with their children are also likely to employ trust as a preferred disciplinary strategy. Nelson found that parents who eschewed certain technologies—such as automobile tracking devices, key stroke recorders, and home drug-testing kits—claimed it was because they value trust and that until trust was clearly broken they saw no need to use such blatant forms of surveillance. To these parents, this trust provided a foundation for the flexible discipline they offered through discussion, negotiation, and constant communication with their children.

Here, too, we can trace clear parallels to the working conditions of many contemporary professionals, who are subject to relatively low levels of short-term accountability at work. These are high prestige occupations in part because of the autonomy they offer. Most professionals are not subjected to the kinds of surveillance that other workers endure—time clocks, nanny cams, customer comment cards, tracking of computer use or online activities are the realm of a different class of workers. Such panoptic disciplinary measures are often unnecessary precisely because of the very high stakes for overall productivity in professional careers. Employer "trust" based on the metric of productivity is brittle and not easily restored once it is broken. Trust is therefore an effective strategy of control because elite workers know that if they do not produce desired results they will be fired, down-sized, or denied tenure. This precariousness of institutional trust creates some of the anxiety that contemporary professionals feel about both maintaining their own status and ensuring that they can pass on their status advantages to their children.

The intimacy and trust that are cornerstones of elites' parenting philosophies replicate their working conditions. These philosophies not only ensure that children will internalize parents' norms and values, they also socialize children into the emotional capital and self-concept that parents hope will help them be successful twenty-first-century professionals. Like the privileges and demands of professional autonomy, intimacy and trust offer children considerable disciplinary latitude while making heavy emotional demands. Children who grow up negotiating the emotional terrain of intimate communication with parents and trust-based, flexible discipline must test out for themselves the boundaries of their parents' latitude and of their own potential. Parents following this philosophy want their children to develop a particular kind of self-confidence that will serve as a basis for the creative risk-taking that is often required for professional success in contemporary capitalism. They presume that this philosophy will lead their children to develop the resilience that Richard Sennett claims is a necessary feature for workers in the unpredictable conditions of the "new capitalism."

An Ongoing Process With No Finished Product

Finally, strategies of control (as opposed to discipline) emphasize ongoing processes rather than finished products. The contemporary professional middle-class experiences anxiety for many reasons, not least of which are the current precarious economic conditions. However, anxiety is also built into the structure of elite jobs in contemporary capitalism. These highly accomplished new elites work under conditions in which the limits are not clearly spelled out and the bar always seems to be changing. Their jobs are structured to make them feel that they have never accomplished enough. Professional socialization into these high-status professions emphasizes that constant productivity matters more than the finished product. The "product," once it is produced, fades in importance, because ultimately what these elites are producing are their own careers, which are ongoing and never complete. Furthermore, because career paths are increasingly flexible and illegible, rather than linear and logical, the *real* product is the *self* that is being shaped and marketed in the package of a career.

Parents subject to this ongoing process of career control tend to favor parenting strategies that also revolve around the ongoing process of shaping children's selves. Because the child's self is an ongoing and unfinished project, self-esteem becomes a convenient gauge of how the project is going. Occasionally warning flags are raised about the intense anxieties of kids who are coping with a never-ending process of ever-increasing educational requirements: in primary and secondary schools, children learn that education is more targeted to standardized tests than the joy of discovery; kids are told that higher and higher levels of education are required as "tickets" to middle-class jobs; sports and extra-curricular activities are seen as resume-builders for college; college, too matters not just for its educational value, but as a prerequisite to a graduate or professional degree, or perhaps to an unpaid internship; and so on.

Despite the psychological toll that the extended gauntlet of adolescence and emerging adulthood exacts, parents and children are largely powerless to reshape the system both because this is how post-industrial capitalism operates and because the heavy emphasis on credentialing produces distinct economic and social benefits for elites. It is more complicated to pass on "achieved" class advantages than heritable wealth. These extended sifting mechanisms severely limit upward mobility and are therefore the price that the new elite pays to reproduce its class advantage. In the absence of systemic strategies to reshape the current game of post-industrial capitalism, then, parents rely upon the individualized task of building children's self-esteem in the hopes that it will see them through the ever-increasing years of education and credentialing, followed by career-building. Self-esteem becomes a critical form of cultural capital when this level of emotional endurance is called for.

The Future of Emotional Styles

Despite claims of difference about which strategies are most effective in producing self-confident children, today's parents agree that children's self-esteem is a vital measure of good parenting. The professional, upper-middle-class parents who have come under scrutiny in the past few years are not inventing a new pattern of childrearing so much as—just like parents in other social locations—they're adapting a pattern of occupational requirements and constraints to the task of childhood and adolescent socialization. Emotional competence and self-confidence are critical to success in contemporary professional spheres; therefore, these same characteristics have become the "gold standard" of good parenting. Though tactics may vary, the cultural goal of elite parenting styles is remarkably similar.

Based upon their experiences as upwardly mobile professionals and their understanding of what it takes to be successful as the new elite knowledge class, elite parents cultivate the same qualities through their childrearing strategies, whether these strategies are criticized as too strict or too lenient. Their distinctive parenting approaches are neither simply passing fads nor a mere generation gap. Instead, social and economic changes in the shift to a new capitalism have meant that the upwardly-mobile parents who make up the new elite have found themselves playing a game that operates by different rules than the ones their parents taught them. Control, much more than discipline, is a fundamental feature of the working conditions in the new elite professions. In their occupational lives, they are rewarded not for staying within clearly-defined limits, but for problem solving, overcoming obstacles, and "thinking outside the box." Because the institutions they work for have sought to flatten hierarchies, their work success requires emotional competence both in managing their own and others' feelings.

Because self-esteem forms a crucial part of the cultural capital that allows elite parents to reproduce their class advantages, it is no passing fad. By considering the structural experience of control in elite parents' occupational lives, we can see why professionals tend to prefer childrearing philosophies that hinge on communication, flexibility, intimacy, and trust. Furthermore, we can see in their working conditions the experiences that have caused them to focus in especially on the project of self in childrearing, making self-esteem both a desirable personal trait as well as cornerstone of class reproduction. In fact, the correspondence between professional control and parental control should cause us to question whether the popular ambivalence often expressed about the particular practices of contemporary parents might not mask a deeper anxiety about the conditions of elite status and its reproduction in contemporary capitalism. A new group of social elites requires new mechanisms for passing on status advantages to their offspring. The current group of professional elites is developing mechanisms of status reproduction that depend upon particular emotional styles. Further study should elucidate additional elements of these emotional styles in order to better understand the current workings of social inequality and the possibilities for social mobility.

Markella B. Rutherford is a faculty member in sociology at Wellesley College. She is the author of the book *Adult Supervision Required: Private Freedom and Public Constraints for Parents and Children.*

EXPLORING THE ISSUE

Is Chinese Parenting Culturally Distinct?

Critical Thinking and Reflection

1. How much does parenting, and by extension ideals about development, really vary by cultural context? What seem to be the points of potential difference and points of potential similarity?
2. There is a classic and persistent tension in parenting debates between being too strict and being too lenient. Why is that dimension in particular so difficult to negotiate?
3. Though Amy Chua's description of her parenting style can seem harsh, her own children seem to have appreciated her efforts with one personally defending Chua against popular criticism. Why? What about the "Tiger Mother" style might actually appeal to a child?
4. How does parenting differ by social class? Why does Markella B. Rutherford think privileged parents are able to subtly give advantages to their children despite the particular parenting style they adopt?
5. Does parenting really determine whether or not people develop into successful adults? What are the things that parents do and do not influence that relate to people's success in society?

Is There Common Ground?

Different models of parenting, whether across cultures or across social class lines, are crucial to understand beyond the issue of how individual parents influence individual children. It is important to note, however, that individuals do not parent in a bubble. The beliefs we hold about parenting and the behaviors we employ to reflect those beliefs are shaped by a plethora of influences. Our own experiences certainly shape our beliefs and behaviors, in ways we want to emulate or avoid our past experiences. Media, family environment, and culture are examples of other factors that can shape an individual's parenting style.

Models of parenting represent the very ideals we hold about lifespan development. When Amy Chua argues for the superiority of the "Chinese mother," she is implicitly advocating for the importance of discipline and achievement above fun and comfort. When Markella B. Rutherford highlights the way privileged parents confer subtle advantages to their children, she is pointing out the importance of how people are positioned to compete in the global economy. Both Chua and Rutherford thus see parenting as meaningful beyond the actual act of interacting with a child, and it

is worth thinking about how and why those meanings come into being.

Create Central

www.mhhe.com/createcentral

Additional Resources

Bornstein, M. H. (2013). Cross-cultural perspectives on parenting. *International perspectives on psychological science, 2,* 359–369.

Juang, L. P., Qin, D. B., & Park, I. J. (2013). Deconstructing the myth of the "tiger mother": An introduction to the special issue on tiger parenting, Asian-heritage families, and child/adolescent well-being. *Asian American Journal of Psychology, 4*(1), 1.

Kim, S. Y., Wang, Y., Orozco-Lapray, D., Shen, Y., & Murtuza, M. (2013). Does "tiger parenting" exist? Parenting profiles of Chinese Americans and adolescent developmental outcomes. *Asian American journal of psychology, 4*(1), 7.

Paul, A. M. (2011). Tiger moms: Is tough parenting really the answer? *Time Magazine.*

Internet References . . .

Amy Chua Website

www.amychua.com

Parenting Center

www.webmd.com/parenting

Positive Parenting

www.kidshealth.org/parent/positive

Selected, Edited, and with Issue Framing Material by:
Allison A. Buskirk-Cohen, *Delaware Valley University*

ISSUE

Should Happiness Be Our Goal?

YES: John Helliwell, Richard Layard, and Jeffrey Sachs (Eds.), from *World Happiness Report 2013* (UN Sustainable Development Solutions Network, 2013)

NO: Sharon Begley, from "Happiness: Enough Already," *Newsweek* (2008)

Learning Outcomes

After reading this issue, you will be able to:

- See how positive psychology emerged in an effort to shift our focus onto individuals' strengths rather than their weaknesses.
- Understand why it is important to consider how evolution has shaped our emotional experiences.
- Obtain a better understanding that what makes people happy means expanding definitions beyond materials success.

ISSUE SUMMARY

YES: In their introduction to the World Happiness Report, John Helliwell, Richard Layard, and Jeffrey Sachs argue for the need to assess happiness on a global level. They describe scientific approaches to the study of happiness from the perspectives of psychologists, economists, and others—and link it to sustainable development goals.

NO: Reporter Sharon Begley does not dispute the importance of happiness, but argues for a moderate approach to positive psychology. Moreover, she suggests that there is an evolutionary need to experience negative emotions.

For most of psychology's history, the focus has been on improving mental health by identifying ways to prevent and treat negative emotions. Anxiety and depression, certainly, are characterized by negative emotions. Even conduct disorder and ADHD might be thought of as disorders where people have difficulty controlling their negative emotions. Individuals with aggression or frustration problems have been targeted through prevention and intervention strategies. The DSM (Diagnostic and Statistical Manual), currently on its fifth edition, classifies and proposes treatment by describing such negative characteristics. By addressing those negative characteristics, mental health experts have believed we would improve our overall health and well-being.

However, in more recent years, the positive psychology movement has emerged, arguing that the absence of negative emotions does not equate well-being. Just because an individual does not meet the diagnostic criteria for depression, for example, it does not mean that person is living a satisfying, productive, or meaningful life. Martin Seligman and Mihaly Csikszentmihalyi are considered the founders of this movement, having written a paper detailing the focus of positive psychology in a paper published in 2000. These researchers believe we must scientifically study what actually contributes to happiness. Today, researchers of positive psychology study positive experiences, values, strengths, positive relationships, and social systems and institutions that promote positive well-being. Generally speaking, the focus is on individuals' strengths, not their weaknesses.

As with any movement, there are supporters and detractors. Those who advocate for positive psychology emphasize how it can help us better understand why and how some individuals thrive even in the most challenging of situations. One specific research area in positive psychology is the study of happiness. Researchers have examined how individuals (both within and across cultures) define happiness and what types of activities and situations make significant contributions to happiness. For example, many people think that a larger salary would make them happier. Interestingly, studies show that once an individual earns enough money for basic needs, additional income does not result in a huge increase in happiness. What does make people happy?

Popular media also has shifted attention to happiness, trying to answer this question through various mediums. In 2011, the documentary *Happy* was released. This film explored happiness from a variety of angles—interviews with researchers, world leaders, and everyday people provided a complex look at the topic. In 2014, Pharrell Williams wrote and performed the song "Happy," originally as part of the family film, *Despicable Me 2*. This song has sold over 10 million copies worldwide and has been nominated for numerous awards, signaling both public and critical acclaim. There are also a plethora of self-help books, like *Be Happy!, 10% Happier,* and *The Happiness Advantage*, dedicated to the search for happiness. With popular culture, scholars often question whether media leads society or whether media reflects society. Either way, there is a clearly a change afoot.

Should happiness be our goal? For some scholars, the research on happiness can and should be extended beyond the individual. They believe we have gleaned enough knowledge to begin enacting policy changes. In the YES selection, John Helliwell, Richard Layard, and Jeffrey Sachs of the Sustainable Development Solutions Network argue for the importance of studying happiness. They claim that well-being should be an important element of how countries assess their economic and social development. This selection includes the introduction to a long report that describes the state of world happiness, the causes of happiness and misery, policy implications, and case studies. Helliwell and colleagues describe research from psychologists, economists, sociologists, and others and point to how countries such as Bhutan have adapted the goal of Gross National Happiness rather than Gross National Product.

However, as with any movement, there are detractors. Critics question whether happiness can be studied scientifically. Is there a definition that fits all? They also wonder about the idea of happiness as a personality trait. Are happy people really just optimistic people? Perhaps more importantly, is dispositional optimism changeable and can pessimism be productive for some individuals? Lastly, there are questions about a moralism inherent to the positive psychology movement. Does it presume happiness itself is virtuous? Some scholars believe that positive psychology ignores the importance of life circumstances; not every context provides the same opportunities for psychological well-being. In other words, the search for happiness may be usurped by a search for food, shelter, and safety for some people.

Following this line of thought, in the NO selection, Sharon Begley emphasizes that the happiness movement has gone overboard. Her article discusses the development of positive psychology and the happiness movement, along with research on brain activity underlying well-being. In what might be a surprising twist, her conversations with mental health experts emphasize the potential dangers of extreme happiness and the benefits of experiencing negative emotions. Sadness, for example, may signal to others that we are in need of help. Begley describes how positive psychology and the happiness movement (ironically) have pathologized sadness. The experts Begley references suggest that we no longer allow negative reactions to events and circumstances. Instead of recognizing that someone has good reason to be sad, we diagnose that person with depression, for example. Begley's article argues for a broader view of human emotions that allows for authentic reactions to life experiences.

This issue tackles many big questions. What should be the main focus in psychology? Resources are limited, so where should researchers focus their attention, time, and money? If we shift to an emphasis on happiness, will disorders be left behind? Should individuals suffering from debilitating disorders be told to "focus on the positive" or do we need to prioritize disorders over happiness? Considering the knowledge we currently have, is it enough to shape countries' policies? Are governments responsible for their citizens' mental health and well-being? If researchers and governments concentrate on happiness, what happens to negative emotions? Are they a necessary part of the human experience or can we transcend them? The YES and NO selections in this issue do not answer all of these questions, but they do begin to frame the conversation and demonstrate how complicated happiness truly is.

YES

John Helliwell, Richard Layard, and Jeffrey Sachs

World Happiness Report 2013

We live in an age of stark contradictions. The world enjoys technologies of unimaginable sophistication; yet has at least one billion people without enough to eat each day. The world economy is propelled to soaring new heights of productivity through ongoing technological and organizational advance; yet is relentlessly destroying the natural environment in the process. Countries achieve great progress in economic development as conventionally measured; yet along the way succumb to new crises of obesity, smoking, diabetes, depression, and other ills of modern life.[1]

These contradictions would not come as a shock to the greatest sages of humanity, including Aristotle and the Buddha. The sages taught humanity, time and again, that material gain alone will not fulfi ll our deepest needs. Material life must be harnessed to meet these human needs, most importantly to promote the end of suffering, social justice, and the attainment of happiness. The challenge is real for all parts of the world.

As one key example, the world's economic superpower, the United States, has achieved striking economic and technological progress over the past half century without gains in the self-reported happiness of the citizenry. Instead, uncertainties and anxieties are high, social and economic inequalities have widened considerably, social trust is in decline, and confidence in government is at an all-time low. Perhaps for these reasons, life satisfaction has remained nearly constant during decades of rising Gross National Product (GNP) per capita.

The realities of poverty, anxiety, environmental degradation, and unhappiness in the midst of great plenty should not be regarded as mere curiosities. They require our urgent attention, and especially so at this juncture in human history. For we have entered a new phase of the world, termed the *Anthropocene* by the world's Earth system scientists. The Anthropocene is a newly invented term that combines two Greek roots: "anthropo," for human; and "cene," for new, as in a new geological epoch. The Anthropocene is the new epoch in which humanity, through its technological prowess and population of 7 billion, has become the major driver of changes of the Earth's physical systems, including the climate, the carbon cycle, the water cycle, the nitrogen cycle, and biodiversity.

The Anthropocene will necessarily reshape our societies. If we continue mindlessly along the current economic trajectory, we risk undermining the Earth's life support systems – food supplies, clean water, and stable climate – necessary for human health and even survival in some places. In years or decades, conditions of life may become dire in several fragile regions of the world. We are already experiencing that deterioration of life support systems in the drylands of the Horn of Africa and parts of Central Asia.

On the other hand, if we act wisely, we can protect the Earth while raising quality of life broadly around the world. We can do this by adopting lifestyles and technologies that improve happiness (or life satisfaction) while reducing human damage to the environment. "Sustainable Development" is the term given to the combination of human well-being, social inclusion, and environmental sustainability. We can say that the quest for happiness is intimately linked to the quest for sustainable development.

The Search for Happiness

In an impoverished society, the focused quest for material gain as conventionally measured typically makes a lot of sense. Higher household income (or higher Gross National Product per capita) generally signifies an improvement in the life conditions of the poor. The poor suffer from dire deprivations of various kinds: lack of adequate food supplies, remunerative jobs, access to health care, safe homes, safe water and sanitation, and educational opportunities. As incomes rise from very low levels, human well-being improves. Not surprisingly, the poor report a rising satisfaction with their lives as their meager incomes increase. Even small gains in a household's income can result in a child's survival, the end of hunger pangs, improved nutrition, better learning opportunities, safe childbirth, and prospects for ongoing improvements and opportunities in schooling, job training, and gainful employment.

Helliwell, John F., Richard Layard, and Jeffrey Sachs, eds. 2013. World Happiness Report 2013. New York: UN Sustainable Development Solutions Network. Reprinted by permission of United Nations Division for Sustainable Development.

Now consider the opposite end of the income spectrum. For most individuals in the high-income world, the basic deprivations have been vanquished. There is enough food, shelter, basic amenities (such as clean water and sanitation), and clothing to meet daily needs. In fact, there is a huge surfeit of amenities above basic needs. Poor people would swap with rich people in a heartbeat. Yet all is not well. The conditions of affluence have created their own set of traps.

Most importantly, the lifestyles of the rich imperil the survival of the poor. Human-induced climate change is already hitting the poorest regions and claiming lives and livelihoods. It is telling that in much of the rich world, affluent populations are so separated from those they are imperiling that there is little recognition, practical or moral, of the adverse spillovers (or "externalities") from their own behavior.

Yet the problems of affluence also strike close to home. Affluence has created its own set of afflictions and addictions. Obesity, adult-onset diabetes, tobacco-related illnesses, eating disorders such as anorexia and bulimia, psychosocial disorders, and addictions to shopping, TV, and gambling, are all examples of disorders of development. So too is the loss of community, the decline of social trust, and the rising anxiety levels associated with the vagaries of the modern globalized economy, including the threats of unemployment or episodes of illness not covered by health insurance in the United States.

Higher average incomes do not necessarily improve average well-being, the U.S. being a clear case in point, as noted famously by Professor Richard Easterlin, and U.S. GNP per capita has risen by a factor of three since 1960, while measures of average happiness have remained essentially unchanged over the half-century. The increased U.S. output has caused massive environmental damage, notably through green-house gas concentrations and human-induced climate change, without doing much at all to raise the well-being even of Americans. Thus, we don't have a "tradeoff" between short-run gains to well-being versus long-run costs to the environment; we have a pure loss to the environment without offsetting short-term gains.

The paradox that Easterlin noted in the U.S. was that at any particular time richer individuals are happier than poorer ones, but over time the society did not become happier as it became richer. One reason is that individuals compare themselves to others. They are happier when they are higher on the social (or income) ladder. Yet when everybody rises together, relative status remains unchanged. A second obvious reason is that the gains have not been evenly shared, but have gone disproportionately to those

at the top of the income and education distribution. A third is that other societal factors – insecurity, loss of social trust, a declining confidence in government – have counteracted any benefits felt from the higher incomes. A fourth reason is adaptation: individuals may experience an initial jump in happiness when their income rises but then at least partly return to earlier levels as they adapt to their new higher income.

These phenomena put a clear limit on the extent to which rich countries can become happier through the simple device of economic growth. In fact, there are still other general reasons to doubt the formula of everrising GNP per person as the route to happiness. While higher income may raise happiness to some extent, the *quest* for higher income may actually reduce one's happiness. In other words, it may be nice to have more money but not so nice to crave it. Psychologists have found repeatedly that individuals who put a high premium on higher incomes generally are less happy and more vulnerable to other psychological ills than individuals who do not crave higher incomes. Aristotle and the Buddha advised humanity to follow a middle path between asceticism on the one side and craving material goods on the other.

A further huge problem is the persistent creation of new material "wants" through the incessant advertising of products using powerful imagery and other means of persuasion. Since the imagery is ubiquitous on all of our digital devices, the stream of advertising is more relentless than ever before. Advertising is now a business of around $500 billion per year. Its goal is to overcome satiety by creating wants and longings where none previously existed. Advertisers and marketers do this in part by preying on psychological weaknesses and unconscious urges. Cigarettes, caffeine, sugar, and trans-fats all cause cravings if not outright addictions. Fashions are sold through increasingly explicit sexual imagery. Product lines are generally sold by associating the products with high social status rather than with real needs.

And finally, there is one further word of warning to those who expect to become happier by becoming richer. Even if gains in well-being can be eked out by further income gains, the evidence is quite overwhelming that after a certain point, the gains are very small. The key idea is known as the "diminishing marginal utility of income." Suppose that a poor household at $1,000 income requires an extra $100 to raise its life satisfaction (or happiness) by one notch. A rich household at $1,000,000 income (one thousand times as much as the poor household) would need one thousand times more money, or $100,000, to raise its well-being by the same one notch. Gains in income have to be of equal proportions to household income to have the same benefit in units of life satisfaction. This principle means that poor people benefit far more than rich people from an added dollar of income. This is a good reason why tax-and-transfer systems among high-income OECD countries on balance take in net revenues from high-income households and make net transfers to low-income households. Put another way, the inequality of household income is systematically lower net of taxes and transfers than before taxes and transfers.[2]

Rethinking the Keys to Happiness

The western economist's logic of ever higher GNP is built on a vision of humanity completely at variance with the wisdom of the sages, the research of psychologists, and the practices of advertisers. The economist assumes that individuals are rational decision-makers who know what they want and how to get it, or to get as close to it as possible given their budget. Individuals care largely about themselves and derive pleasure mainly through their consumption. The individual's preferences as consumers are a given or change in ways actually anticipated in advance by the individuals themselves. Some economists even say that drug addicts have acted "rationally," consciously trading off the early benefits of drug use with the later high toll of addiction. These economists may say this, but they don't dare examine such foolishness too closely!

We increasingly understand that we need a very different model of humanity, one in which we are a complicated interplay of emotions and rational thought, unconscious and conscious decision-making, "fast" and "slow" thinking. Many of our decisions are led by emotions and instincts, and only later rationalized by conscious thought. Our decisions are easily "primed" by associations, imagery, social context, and advertising. We are inconsistent or "irrational" in sequential choices, failing to meet basic standards of rational consistency. And we are largely unaware of our own mental apparatus, so we easily fall into traps and mistakes. Addicts do not anticipate their future pain; we spend now and suffer the consequences of bankruptcy later; we break our diets now because we aren't thinking clearly about the consequences.

We also understand (again!) that we are social animals through and through. We learn through imitation, and gain our happiness through meeting social norms and having a sense of belonging to the community. We feel the pain of others, and react viscerally when others are sad or injured. We even have a set of "mirror neurons" that enable us to feel things from the point of view of others. All of this gives us a remarkable capacity to cooperate even with strangers, and even when there is little chance of reward or reciprocity, and

to punish non-cooperators, even when imposing punishment on others is costly or puts us at risk ourselves. Of course there are limits to such cooperation and fellow feeling. We also cheat, bluff, deceive, break our word, and kill members of an out-group. We engage in identity politics, acting as cruel to outsiders as we are loving to our own group.

All these lessons of human nature matter more than ever, more even than when the Buddha taught humanity about the illusions of transient pleasures, and the Greeks warned us against the tempting Siren songs that could pull us off our life's course. For today we have more choices than ever before. In the ancient world, the choice facing most of humanity most of the time was little choice indeed: to work hard to secure enough to eat, and even then to face the risk of famine and death from bad weather or bad luck.

Now we face a set of real choices. Should the world pursue GNP to the point of environmental ruin, even when incremental gains in GNP are not increasing much (or at all) the happiness of affluent societies? Should we crave higher personal incomes at the cost of community and social trust? Should our governments spend even a tiny fraction of the $500 billion or so spent on advertising each year to help individuals and families to understand better their own motivations, wants, and needs as consumers?

Should we consider some parts of our society to be "off bounds" to the profit motive, so that we can foster the spirit of cooperation, trust, and community? A recent analyst of Finland's school system, for example, writes that Finland's excellence (ranking near the top of international comparisons in student performance) has been achieved by fostering a spirit of community and equality in the schools.[3] This is in sharp contrast to the education reform strategy at work in the U.S., where the emphasis is put on testing, measurement, and teacher pay according to student test performance.

There are reasons enough to believe that we need to rethink the economic sources of well-being, more so even in the rich countries than in the poor ones. High-income countries have largely ended the scourges of poverty, hunger, and disease. Poor countries rightly yearn to do so. But after the end of poverty, what comes next? What are the pathways to well-being when basic economic needs are no longer the main drivers of social change? What will guide humanity in the Anthropocene: advertising, sustainability, community, or something else? What is the path to happiness?

Taking Happiness Seriously

Most people agree that societies should foster the happiness of their citizens. The U.S. Founding Fathers recognized the inalienable right to the pursuit of happiness. British philosophers talked about the greatest good for the greatest number. Bhutan has famously adopted the goal of Gross National Happiness (GNH) rather than Gross National Product. China champions a harmonious society.

Yet most people probably believe that happiness is in the eye of the beholder, an individual's choice, something to be pursued individually rather than as a matter of national policy. Happiness seems far too subjective, too vague, to serve as a touchstone for a nation's goals, much less its policy content. That indeed has been the traditional view. Yet the evidence is changing this view rapidly.

A generation of studies by psychologists, economists, pollsters, sociologists, and others has shown that happiness, though indeed a subjective experience, can be objectively measured, assessed, correlated with observable brain functions, and related to the characteristics of an individual and the society. Asking people whether they are happy, or satisfied with their lives, offers important information about the society. It can signal underlying crises or hidden strengths. It can suggest the need for change.

Such is the idea of the emerging scientific study of happiness, whether of individuals and the choices they make, or of entire societies and the reports of the citizenry regarding life satisfaction. The chapters ahead summarize the fascinating and emerging story of these studies. They report on the two broad measurements of happiness: the ups and downs of daily emotions, and an individual's overall evaluation of life. The former is sometimes called "affective happiness," and the latter "evaluative happiness."

What is important to know is that both kinds of happiness have predictable causes that reflect various facets of our human nature and our social life. Affective happiness captures the day-to-day joys of friendship, time with family, and sex, or the downsides of long work commutes and sessions with one's boss. Evaluative happiness measures very different dimensions of life, those that lead to overall satisfaction or frustration with one's place in society. Higher income, better health of mind and body, and a high degree of trust in one's community ("social capital") all contribute to high life satisfaction; poverty, ill health, and deep divisions in the community all contribute to low life satisfaction.

What we learn in the chapters ahead is that happiness differs systematically across societies and over time, for reasons that are identifiable, and even alterable through the ways in which public policies are designed and delivered. It makes sense, in other words, to pursue policies to raise the public's happiness as much as it does to raise the public's national income. Bhutan is on to something path

breaking and deeply insightful. And the world is increasingly taking notice.

A household's income counts for life satisfaction, but only in a limited way. Other things matter more: community trust, mental and physical health, and the quality of governance and rule of law. Raising incomes can raise happiness, especially in poor societies, but fostering cooperation and community can do even more, especially in rich societies that have a low marginal utility of income. It is no accident that the happiest countries in the world tend to be high-income countries that also have a high degree of social equality, trust, and quality of governance. In recent years, Denmark has been topping the list. And it's no accident that the U.S. has experienced no rise of life satisfaction for half a century, a period in which inequality has soared, social trust has declined, and the public has lost faith in its government.

It is, of course, one thing to identify the correlates of happiness, and quite another to use public policies to bring about a society-wide rise in happiness (or life satisfaction). That is the goal of Bhutan's GNH, and the motivation of an increasing number of governments dedicated to measuring happiness and life satisfaction in a reliable and systematic way over time. The most basic goal is that by measuring happiness across a society and over time, countries can avoid "happiness traps" such as in the U.S. in recent decades, where GNP may rise relentlessly while life satisfaction stagnates or even declines.

The Bhutan case study tells the story of GNH in Bhutan, a story of exploration and progress since the King declared in 1972 the goal of happiness over the goal of wealth. Happiness became much more than a guidepost or inspiration; it became an organizing principle for governance and policy-making as well. The Gross National Happiness Index is the first of its kind in the world, a serious, thoughtful, and sustained attempt to measure happiness, and use those measurements to chart the course of public policy. I leave description of Bhutan's wonderful adventure, still unfolding while already inspiring others, to the case study.

Happiness and the Sustainable Development Goals

As the world enters the dangerous next decades of the Anthropocene, we must intensify our efforts to achieve a new course, one that ensures poor countries have the right to develop, and all countries have the right to happiness, while simultaneously curbing the human-induced destruction of the environment. It is too late to head off entirely climate change and loss of biodiversity. There is still time, though, to mitigate the damage and to build resilience to the changes ahead. The quest for happiness will be carried out in the context of growing environmental risks.

According to the recent recommendations of the UN Secretary-General's High-level Panel on Global Sustainability, the Millennium Development Goals, set to end in 2015, should be followed by a new set of Sustainable Development Goals. More succinctly, the MDGs should be followed by the SDGs. It is likely that the concept of the SDGs will be adopted by the UN member states at the Rio+20 Summit in Rio de Janeiro in June 2012.

The Sustainable Development Goals should have four pillars. The first should be to carry on the crucial work of the MDGs in order to **end extreme poverty** by 2030. The developing countries have successfully cut the overall poverty rate by half comparing 1990 and 2010, from around 44% to 22%. The biggest gains have come in China, while Africa has lagged behind, though Africa too is now on a path of poverty reduction. No later than 2030 the remaining extreme poverty and hunger should be eradicated. Happiness in the poorest countries would be strongly boosted by such an historic breakthrough.

The second pillar of the SDGs should be **environmental sustainability**. Without that, no gains against poverty, hunger, or disease can endure long. The environmental pillar of the SDGs may be guided by the concept of "planetary boundaries," the notion that humanity must avoid specific thresholds of environmental damage to avoid creating irreparable harms to the Earth and to future generations.

The third pillar should be **social inclusion**, the commitment of every society that the benefits of technology, economic progress, and good governance should be accessible to everybody, women as well as men, minority groups as well as the majority. Happiness must not be the preserve of a dominant group. The goal should be happiness for all.

The fourth pillar should be **good governance**, the ability of society to act collectively through truly participatory political institutions. Good governance is not only a means to an end, but also an end in itself, since good governance signifies the ability of people to help shape their own lives and to reap the happiness that comes with political participation and freedom.

Yet how shall we measure success, to know that our society is on track? Here is where new metrics of happiness can play a crucial role. To assess the four pillars of sustainable development, we need a new set of indicators that

extend well beyond the traditional GNP. The UN conferees have anticipated this need in the draft outcome document for Rio+20:

> Paragraph 111. We also recognize the limitations of GDP as a measure of well-being. We agree to further develop and strengthen indicators complementing GDP that integrate economic, social and environmental dimensions in a balanced manner. We request the Secretary-General to establish a process in consultation with the UN system and other relevant organizations.[4]

These are the kinds of indicators – economic, social, and environmental – now being collected by Bhutan's Gross National Happiness Commission in order to create Bhutan's GNH Index.

In addition to specific measures of economic, social, and environmental performance, governments should begin the systematic measurement of happiness itself, in both its affective and evaluative dimensions. The SDGs should include a specific commitment to measure happiness, so that the world as a whole, and each individual country, can monitor progress in sustainable development and can make comparisons with the achievements elsewhere. This massive effort of data collection has already begun. As this report discusses, survey data on happiness are now being collected in various means: the World Values Survey, covering up to 65 countries; the Gallup World Poll covering 155 countries; and several other national and international surveys mentioned in Chapters 2 and 3. The OECD is now developing important proposals for internationally standard measures explained in its case study. . . .

JOHN F. HELLIWELL is a Professor Emeritus of Economics at the University of British Columbia and an Arthur J. E. Child Foundation Fellow of the Canadian Institute for Advanced Research (CIFAR).

RICHARD LAYARD is the director of the Well-being Programme at the Centre for Economic Performance in the London School of Economics. He is also one of the first economists to work on happiness, and his main current interest is how better mental health could improve our social and economic life.

JEFFREY D. SACHS is the director of The Earth Institute, Quetelet Professor of Sustainable Development, and professor of Health Policy and Management at Columbia University. He has authored three *New York Times* bestsellers in the past seven years.

Notes

1 Editorial assistance provided by Claire Bulger.

2 On average across OECD countries, cash transfers and income taxes reduce inequality by one third. Poverty is around 60% lower than it would be without taxes and benefits. Even among the working-age population, government redistribution reduces poverty by about 50%. See OECD (2008).

3 Sahlberg, P (2007).

4 Rio+20 United Nations Conference on Sustainable Development. (2012).

Sharon Begley

 **NO**

Happiness: Enough Already

The push for ever-greater well-being is facing a backlash, fueled by research on the value of sadness

The plural of anecdote is not data, as scientists will tell you, but consider these snapshots of the emerging happiness debate anyway: Lately, Jerome Wakefield's students have been coming up to him after they break up with a boyfriend or girlfriend, and not because they want him to recommend a therapist. Wakefield, a professor at New York University, coauthored the 2007 book "The Loss of Sadness: How Psychiatry Transformed Normal Sorrow Into Depressive Disorder," which argues that feeling down after your heart is broken—even so down that you meet the criteria for clinical depression—is normal and even salutary. But students tell him that their parents are pressuring them to seek counseling and other medical intervention—"some Zoloft, dear?"—for their sadness, and the kids want no part of it. "Can you talk to them for me?" they ask Wakefield. Rather than "listening to Prozac," they want to listen to their hearts, not have them chemically silenced.

University of Illinois psychologist Ed Diener, who has studied happiness for a quarter century, was in Scotland recently, explaining to members of Parliament and business leaders the value of augmenting traditional measures of a country's wealth with a national index of happiness. Such an index would measure policies known to increase people's sense of well-being, such as democratic freedoms, access to health care and the rule of law. The Scots were all in favor of such things, but not because they make people happier. "They said too much happiness might not be such a good thing," says Diener. "They like being dour, and didn't appreciate being told they should be happier."

Eric Wilson tried to get with the program. Urged on by friends, he bought books on how to become happier. He made every effort to smooth out his habitual scowl and wear a sunny smile, since a happy expression can lead to genuinely happy feelings. Wilson, a professor of English at Wake Forest University, took up jogging, reputed to boost the brain's supply of joyful neurochemicals, watched uplifting Frank Capra and Doris Day flicks and began

sprinkling his conversations with "great!" and "wonderful!", the better to exercise his capacity for enthusiasm. When none of these made him happy, Wilson not only jumped off the happiness bandwagon—he also embraced his melancholy side and decided to blast a happiness movement that "leads to half-lives, to bland existences," as he argues in "Against Happiness," a book now reaching stores. Americans' fixation on happiness, he writes, fosters "a craven disregard for the value of sadness" and "its integral place in the great rhythm of the cosmos."

It's always tricky to identify a turning point, at least in real time. Only in retrospect can you accurately pinpoint when a financial market peaked or hit bottom, for instance, or the moment when the craze for pricey coffee drinks crested. But look carefully, and what you are seeing now may be the end of the drive for ever-greater heights of happiness. Fed by hundreds of self-help books, including the current "The How of Happiness: A Scientific Approach to Getting the Life You Want," magazine articles and an industry of life coaches and motivational speakers, the happiness movement took off in the 1990s with two legitimate developments: discoveries about the brain activity underlying well-being, and the emergence of "positive psychology," whose proponents urged fellow researchers to study happiness as seriously as they did pathological states such as depression. But when the science of happiness collided with pop culture and the marketplace, it morphed into something even its creators hardly recognized. There emerged "a crowd of people out there who want you to be happier," write Ed Diener and his son, Robert Biswas-Diener, in their book, "Rethinking Happiness," due for publication later this year. Somewhere out there a pharmaceutical company "is working on a new drug to make you happier," they warn. "There are even people who would like to give you special ozone enemas to make you happier." Although some 85 percent of Americans say they're pretty happy, the happiness industry sends the insistent message that moderate levels of well-being aren't enough: not only can we all be happier, but we practically have a duty to be so. What was once considered normal sadness is something to be smothered, even shunned.

The backlash against the happiness rat race comes just when scientists are releasing the most-extensive-ever study comparing moderate and extreme levels of happiness, and finding that being happier is not always better. In surveys of 118,519 people from 96 countries, scientists examined how various levels of subjective well-being matched up with income, education, political participation, volunteer activities and close relationships. They also analyzed how different levels of happiness, as reported by college students, correlated with various outcomes. Even allowing for imprecision in people's self-reported sense of well-being, the results were unambiguous. The highest levels of happiness go along with the most stable, longest and most contented relationships. That is, even a little discontent with your partner can nudge you to look around for someone better, until you are at best a serial monogamist and at worst never in a loving, stable relationship. "But if you have positive illusions about your partner, which goes along with the highest levels of happiness, you're more likely to commit to an intimate relationship," says Diener.

In contrast, "once a moderate level of happiness is achieved, further increases can sometimes be detrimental" to income, career success, education and political participation, Diener and colleagues write in the journal Perspectives on Psychological Science. On a scale from 1 to 10, where 10 is extremely happy, 8s were more successful than 9s and 10s, getting more education and earning more. That probably reflects the fact that people who are somewhat discontent, but not so depressed as to be paralyzed, are more motivated to improve both their own lot (thus driving themselves to acquire more education and seek ever-more-challenging jobs) and the lot of their community (causing them to participate more in civic and political life). In contrast, people at the top of the jolliness charts feel no such urgency. "If you're totally satisfied with your life and with how things are going in the world," says Diener, "you don't feel very motivated to work for change. Be wary when people tell you you should be happier."

The drawbacks of constant, extreme happiness should not be surprising, since negative emotions evolved for a reason. Fear tips us off to the presence of danger, for instance. Sadness, too, seems to be part of our biological inheritance: apes, dogs and elephants all display something that looks like sadness, perhaps because it signals to others a need for help. One hint that too much euphoria can be detrimental comes from studies finding that among people with late-stage illnesses, those with the greatest

sense of well-being were more likely to die in any given period of time than the mildly content were. Being "up" all the time can cause you to play down very real threats.

Eric Wilson needs no convincing that sadness has a purpose. In his "Against Happiness," he trots out criticisms of the mindless pursuit of contentment that philosophers and artists have raised throughout history—including that, as Flaubert said, to be chronically happy one must also be stupid. Less snarkily, Wilson argues that only by experiencing sadness can we experience the fullness of the human condition. While careful not to extol depression—which is marked not only by chronic sadness but also by apathy, lethargy and an increased risk of suicide—he praises melancholia for generating "a turbulence of heart that results in an active questioning of the status quo, a perpetual longing to create new ways of being and seeing." This is not romantic claptrap. Studies show that when you are in a negative mood, says Diener, "you become more analytical, more critical and more innovative. You need negative emotions, including sadness, to direct your thinking." Abraham Lincoln was not hobbled by his dark moods bordering on depression, and Beethoven composed his later works in a melancholic funk. Vincent van Gogh, Emily Dickinson and other artistic geniuses saw the world through a glass darkly. The creator of "Peanuts," Charles M. Schulz, was known for his gloom, while Woody Allen plumbs existential melancholia for his films, and Patti Smith and Fiona Apple do so for their music.

Wilson, who asserts that "the happy man is a hollow man," is hardly the first scholar to see melancholia as muse. A classical Greek text, possibly written by Aristotle, asks, "Why is it that all those who have become eminent in philosophy or politics or poetry or the arts are clearly melancholic?" Wilson's answer is that "the blues can be a catalyst for a special kind of genius, a genius for exploring dark boundaries between opposites." The ever-restless, the chronically discontent, are dissatisfied with the status quo, be it in art or literature or politics.

For all their familiarity, these arguments are nevertheless being crushed by the happiness movement. Last August, the novelist Mary Gordon lamented to The New York Times that "among writers … what is absolutely not allowable is sadness. People will do anything rather than to acknowledge that they are sad." And in a MY TURN column in NEWSWEEK last May, Jess Decourcy Hinds, an English teacher, recounted how, after her father died, friends pressed her to distract herself from her profound sadness and sense of loss. "Why don't people accept that after a parent's death, there will be years of grief?" she wrote. "Everyone wants mourners to 'snap out of it' because observing another's anguish isn't easy."

It's hard to say exactly when ordinary Americans, no less than psychiatrists, began insisting that sadness is pathological. But by the end of the millennium that attitude was well entrenched. In 1999, Arthur Miller's "Death of a Salesman" was revived on Broadway 50 years after its premiere. A reporter asked two psychiatrists to read the script. Their diagnosis: Willy Loman was suffering from clinical depression, a pathological condition that could and should be treated with drugs. Miller was appalled. "Loman is not a depressive," he told The New York Times. "He is weighed down by life. There are social reasons for why he is where he is." What society once viewed as an appropriate reaction to failed hopes and dashed dreams, it now regards as a psychiatric illness.

That may be the most damaging legacy of the happiness industry: the message that all sadness is a disease. As NYU's Wakefield and Allan Horwitz of Rutgers University point out in "The Loss of Sadness," this message has its roots in the bible of mental illness, the Diagnostic and Statistical Manual of Mental Disorders. Its definition of a "major depressive episode" is remarkably broad. You must experience five not-uncommon symptoms, such as insomnia, difficulty concentrating and feeling sad or empty, for two weeks; the symptoms must cause distress or impairment, and they cannot be due to the death of a loved one. Anyone meeting these criteria is supposed to be treated.

Yet by these criteria, any number of reactions to devastating events qualify as pathological. Such as? For three weeks a woman feels sad and empty, unable to generate any interest in her job or usual activities, after her lover of five years breaks off their relationship; she has little appetite, lies awake at night and cannot concentrate during the day. Or a man's only daughter is suffering from a potentially fatal blood disorder; for weeks he is consumed by despair, cannot sleep or concentrate, feels tired and uninterested in his usual activities.

Horwitz and Wakefield do not contend that the spurned lover or the tormented father should be left to suffer. Both deserve, and would likely benefit from, empathic counseling. But their symptoms "are neither abnormal nor inappropriate in light of their" situations, the authors write. The DSM definition of depression "mistakenly encompasses some normal emotional reactions," due to its failure to take into account the context or trigger for sadness.

That has consequences. When someone is appropriately sad, friends and colleagues offer support and sympathy. But by labeling appropriate sadness pathological, "we have attached a stigma to being sad," says Wakefield, "with the result that depression tends to elicit hostility and rejection" with an undercurrent of "'Get over it; take a pill.' The normal range of human emotion is not being tolerated." And insisting that sadness requires treatment may interfere with the natural healing process. "We don't know how drugs react with normal sadness and its functions, such as reconstituting your life out of the pain," says Wakefield.

Even the psychiatrist who oversaw the current DSM expresses doubts about the medicalizing of sadness. "To be human means to naturally react with feelings of sadness to negative events in one's life," writes Robert Spitzer of the New York State Psychiatric Institute in a foreword to "The Loss of Sadness." That would be unremarkable if it didn't run completely counter to the message of the happiness brigades. It would be foolish to underestimate the power and tenacity of the happiness cheerleaders. But maybe, just maybe, the single-minded pursuit of happiness as an end in itself, rather than as a consequence of a meaningful life, has finally run its course.

Sharon Begley is the senior health & science correspondent at Reuters. She was the science editor and the science columnist at *Newsweek* from 2007 to April 2011. She is the recipient of numerous awards for her writing on the topics of science writing, neuroplasticity, and science literacy.

EXPLORING THE ISSUE

Should Happiness Be Our Goal?

Critical Thinking and Reflection

1. What is the value in studying happiness? Would research funding be better utilized if focused on mental illness?
2. Is there an ideal level of happiness? Is there an ideal level of sadness?
3. How should researchers operationalize happiness? What might specific measures look like?
4. Does a society benefit from having individuals who vary on levels of happiness?

Is There Common Ground?

Certainly, the emotional experience of human beings is a complex topic. Does the human condition require the experience of all emotions? Must we experience sadness in order to experience happiness? These questions are pondered in the selected readings, though captured through different perspectives. Both selections focus on the study of well-being, which for much of psychology's history has been ignored, or relegated to the sidelines, at the very least.

This change marks an important shift, as researchers contemplate our higher needs and what they mean for us as individuals and as a group. Certainly, John Helliwell and his colleagues advocate for countries to consider the emotional and psychological well-being of their citizens. While Sharon Begley might not disagree with the importance of considering this perspective, her article cautions against any type of extremist movement—even one focused on happiness.

Additional Resources

Forgas, J. P. (2013). Don't worry, be sad! On the cognitive, motivational, and interpersonal benefits of negative mood. *Current Directions in Psychological Science*, *22*(3), 225–232.

Lazarus, R. S. (2003). Does the positive psychology movement have legs?. *Psychological Inquiry*, *14*(2), 93–109.

Lightsey Jr, O. R., Burke, M., Ervin, A., Henderson, D., & Yee, C. (2006). Generalized self-efficacy, self-esteem, and negative affect. *Canadian Journal of Behavioural Science/Revue canadienne des sciences du comportement*, *38*(1), 72.

Lyubomirsky, S., & Layous, K. (2013). How do simple positive activities increase well-being? *Current Directions in Psychological Science*, *22*(1), 57–62.

Create Central

www.mhhe.com/createcentral

Internet References . . .

Authentic Happiness

https://www.authentichappiness.sas.upenn.edu/

HAPPY Movie

www.thehappymovie.com/

Positive Psychology Center

www.positivepsychology.org

Unit 2

UNIT

Prenatal Development and Infancy

*O*ur most rapid and astonishing physical changes occur during approximately nine months prior to birth and during the first years of postnatal life. These are unique years in development because of our complete dependence on others. Being without language, a concept of self, and other complex capacities, it is easy to imagine these initial stages as a simple matter of accommodating needs and wants. There is, however, an increasing awareness that there is more to our earliest development than initially meets the eye.

This section considers three issues dealing with ways that our experiences during prenatal development and infancy provide a foundation for all the development that follows. The issues also involve questions about individual rights versus the role of the government. At what point should the government intervene or create policy mandating certain parenting practices? Or, should parents have the ultimate authority in how they raise their children—even if what they do contradicts current research? This unit provides information about the complexities inherent in decisions parents make for their children and emphasizes the implications of those decisions.

Selected, Edited, and with Issue Framing Material by:
Allison A. Buskirk-Cohen, *Delaware Valley University*

ISSUE

Is Drinking Alcohol While Pregnant an Unnecessary Risk to Prenatal Development?

YES: **Phyllida Brown**, from "Drinking for Two," *New Scientist* (2006)

NO: **Julia Moskin**, from "The Weighty Responsibility of Drinking for Two," *The New York Times* (2006)

Learning Outcomes

After reading this issue, you will be able to:

- Understand how many governments and researchers have become more stringent in recommending that pregnant women should not consume any alcohol, often making no distinction between heavy drinking and light drinking.
- Realize that the recognition of fetal alcohol syndrome (FAS) is relatively recent (only since the early 1970s), and while it causes a wide variety of problems with physical and mental health, it does not affect all children whose mothers drank during pregnancy.
- Discuss how magnetic resonance imaging (MRI) studies find some changes in brain structure of children whose mother drank during pregnancy, while animals studies suggest that exposure to alcohol during critical periods of brain development can cause neuronal cell death.
- Discuss how anxiety around maintaining perfect health behaviors may also have some negative effects during pregnancy, and some feel that society should be more trusting of women's ability to make intelligent choices.

ISSUE SUMMARY

YES: Science writer Phyllida Brown maintains that even a small amount of alcohol can damage a developing fetus and cites new research indicating that any alcohol consumed during pregnancy may be harmful.

NO: Journalist Julia Moskin argues that there are almost no studies on the effects of moderate drinking during pregnancy and that limited quantities of alcohol are unlikely to have much effect.

Drinking alcohol while pregnant carries a powerful negative stigma. Public health campaigns and government warnings have effectively conveyed the message that alcohol, along with other drugs, can harm prenatal development. Most people are now familiar with fetal alcohol syndrome (FAS), its symptoms, and its effects. Alcohol consumed during pregnancy can cross the placenta's barrier and stunt fetal growth and development. It can damage neurons and brain structures, resulting in intellectual disabilities, physical damage, and other psychological or behavioral problems. At any point during a pregnancy, alcohol exposure presents a risk of fetal brain damage. However, the first trimester tends to be the most critical point of development. Today, FAS is estimated to be between 0.2 and 2 in every 1,000 live births.

Given this information, however, it is interesting to note that FAS was only "discovered" in 1973. For generations women had consumed alcohol during pregnancy; doctors even prescribed alcohol as treatments. In the nineteenth century, champagne was used as a treatment for morning sickness and brandy served an appetite stimulant. Alcohol was used to sooth women's nerves and prepare them for labor well into the twentieth century. Some doctors even believed alcohol was an appropriate means to stop premature labor. In 1981, the Surgeon General of the United States began warning about the dangers of consuming alcohol when pregnant; drinking during pregnancy quickly became taboo. The combination of FAS's discovery and the Surgeon General's warning turned consuming alcohol from a moral and private behavior to a public health concern.

There has been a shift in how society views alcohol consumption since the 1980s and 1990s. Surveys find that in the United States today about a quarter of pregnant women report drinking alcohol at some point during their pregnancy. Of course, the rates differ when demographic variables, like age, educational level, and residence, are considered. Many women who consume alcohol draw inspiration (and justification) from European women. Drinking wine and eating raw-milk cheese are just a few of the "forbidden" activities that pregnant women in Europe enjoy. Of course, European women also have a list of prohibited foods, including salad in France. Many French obstetricians believe raw vegetables are risky for pregnant women to eat. There seem to be fewer judgments about pregnant women's choices today, with more women drinking publicly and speaking about the right to make their own decisions about their bodies.

Scientific research on this issue tends to devote less attention to stigma and more attention to the physical effects of prenatal exposure to alcohol and other teratogens. A teratogen is any external agent that causes malformation of organs and tissue during prenatal development. Researchers report that about four to five percent of birth defects are caused by teratogen exposure. Fetal exposure to external agents, most often through the mother, is not a process of direct transmission: there are widely varying degrees of detrimental influence on prenatal development. Timing also is important, with different teratogens having different impacts depending on what is developing in the fetus at that time. The central nervous system, for example, is sensitive to teratogens during the entire pregnancy. Thus, since alcohol affects the central nervous, at any time during pregnancy, alcohol might cause birth defects and health problems in the developing fetus.

Studies also may not reflect the typical experience of a pregnant woman drinking alcohol. There are both ethical and practical concerns in the existing literature. For ethical reasons, clinical trials are not performed on pregnant women. Instead, women are asked to self-report, which is subject to inaccuracies. Women may not remember how much they drink, or may feel a pressure to alter the truth. Thus, the majority of experimental research comes from animal studies. Determining the mouse equivalent of one human drink is challenging. Furthermore, the research on pregnancy and alcohol addresses only heavy drinking versus no drinking. Moderate drinking has not existed in the medical literature until very recently. It is reasonable to ask if research findings are really applicable and useful to the average individual person.

Further complicating matters, the relationship between teratogens and prenatal development does not necessarily correspond to popular perceptions of danger. In fact, according to ratings by the federal Food and Drug Administration, a drug such as aspirin has more established negative biological effects on a fetus than a drug such as cocaine. These biological effects, however, are often complicated by social context. Our society has a long history of extremist positions when it comes to alcohol consumption. The Prohibition era that started in the 1920s had the unintended consequences of fostering excessive drinking and intermingling private behavior with social/legal policy. Given the long list of teratogens pregnant women should avoid, there is bias inherent in deciding how to prioritize health education and policy decisions.

Understanding the relationship between exposure to alcohol and prenatal development is also complicated by the fact that many babies born to women who drank during pregnancy do not seem to suffer ill effects. Science writer Phyllida Brown, in arguing that it is safest to avoid all alcohol while pregnant, even acknowledges that "not all babies born to alcoholic women have FAS." So the relationship between a pregnant mother's alcohol consumption and prenatal development is imperfect and requires negotiating uncertain odds. The question then becomes about what sort of odds make drinking while pregnant worth the risk. From Brown's perspective, knowing that there is some chance alcohol can harm prenatal development means the only reasonable choice is complete abstinence. However, the question still remains as to whether that individual choice should be incorporated into policy.

Journalist Julia Moskin argues that a pregnant women can reasonably choose to drink lightly at certain points in a pregnancy. Moskin points out that while much research has been done comparing the effects of heavy drinking

Is Drinking Alcohol While Pregnant an Unnecessary Risk to Prenatal Development? by Buskirk-Cohen

during pregnancy with the effects of no drinking during pregnancy, significantly less research has considered the effects of light drinking. As such, when pressed, some doctors will acknowledge that light drinking at later points in pregnancy is not likely to have long-term effects on prenatal development. Moskin's underlying point is relevant to much of what we know about pregnancy: prenatal development is often too complicated a process to allow for simple certainties about what will or won't ensure the healthy children all parents desire.

YES ⤶

Phyllida Brown

Drinking for Two

AT FIRST, Susie's teachers thought she was a bright child. Her adoptive mother knew different. Give Susie a set of instructions and only a few seconds later she would have forgotten them. She was talkative, with a large vocabulary, but could not seem to form lasting friendships. Then, one day, Susie's adoptive mother heard a lecture that described fetal alcohol syndrome—a condition which affects some children born to heavy drinkers. "Bells went off in my head," she says. "The lecturer described eight traits, and my daughter had seven of them."

Children like Susie could well be just the tip of the iceberg. Fetal alcohol syndrome was once thought to affect only the children of heavy drinkers, such as Susie's biological mother, but a mounting body of research suggests that even a small amount of alcohol can damage a developing fetus—a single binge during pregnancy or a moderate seven small glasses of wine per week.

The new research has already prompted some governments to tighten up their advice on drinking during pregnancy. Others, however, say there is no convincing evidence that modest alcohol intake is dangerous for the fetus. With advice varying wildly from one country to another, the message for pregnant women has never been so confusing.

Last year the U.S. Surgeon General revised official advice warning pregnant women to limit their alcohol intake. Now they are told "simply not to drink" alcohol—not only in pregnancy, but as soon as they plan to try for a baby. France also advises abstinence, as does Canada. The UK's Department of Health says that pregnant women should avoid more than "one to two units, once or twice a week", but is finalising a review of the latest evidence, which it will publish within weeks. In Australia, women are advised to "consider" abstinence, but if choosing to drink should limit their intake to less than seven standard Australian drinks a week, with no more than two standard drinks on any one day.

Whichever guidelines women choose to follow, some level of drinking during pregnancy is common in many countries. The last time pregnant women in the UK were asked, in 2002, 61 percent admitted to drinking some alcohol. Even in the U.S., where abstinence is expected, and where pregnant women in some states have been arrested for drinking, 13 percent still admit to doing it.

Children with fetal alcohol syndrome (FAS) are generally smaller than average and have a range of developmental and behavioural problems such as an inability to relate to others and a tendency to be impulsive. They also have distinctive facial features such as a thin upper lip, an extra fold of skin in the inner corners of the eyes and a flattening of the groove between the nose and upper lip.

In recent years researchers investigating the effects of alcohol in pregnancy have begun to widen their definition of antenatal alcohol damage beyond the diagnosis of FAS. They now talk of fetal alcohol spectrum disorders, or FASD, an umbrella term that covers a range of physical, mental and behavioural effects which can occur without the facial features of FAS. Like children with FAS, those with FASD may have problems with arithmetic, paying attention, working memory and the planning of tasks. They may be impulsive, find it difficult to judge social situations correctly and relate badly to others, or be labelled as aggressive or defiant. In adulthood they may find it difficult to lead independent lives, be diagnosed with mental illnesses, or get into trouble with the law. Some have damage to the heart, ears or eyes.

While some children with FASD have been exposed to as much alcohol before birth as those with FAS, others may be damaged by lower levels, says Helen Barr, a statistician at the University of Washington, Seattle. Barr has spent 30 years tracking children exposed to alcohol before birth and comparing them with non-exposed children. The less alcohol, in general, says Barr, the milder the effects, such as more subtle attention problems or memory difficulties. Other factors that can affect the type of damage include the fetus's stage of development when exposed to alcohol and the mother's genetic make-up.

Although FASD is not yet an official medical diagnosis, some researchers estimate that it could be very common indeed. While FAS is thought to account for 1 in 500 live births, Ann Streissguth and her colleagues at the University of Washington believe that as many as 1 in every 100 babies born in the U.S. are affected by FASD. Others put the figure at about 1 in 300. Whichever figure is more accurate, it would still make the condition far more common than, say, Downs syndrome, which affects 1 in 800 babies born in the U.S.

Streissguth was among the first to study the long-term effects of moderate drinking in pregnancy. In 1993 she reported that a group of 7-year-olds whose mothers had drunk 7 to 14 standard drinks per week in pregnancy tended to have specific problems with arithmetic and attention. Compared with children of similar IQ whose mothers had abstained during pregnancy, they struggled to remember strings of digits or the details of stories read to them, and were unable to discriminate between two rhythmic sound patterns.

When Streissguth's team followed the alcohol-exposed children through adolescence and into their early twenties they found them significantly more likely than other individuals of similar IQ and social background to be labelled as aggressive by their teachers. According to their parents, these children were unable to consider the effects of their actions on others, and unable to take hints or understand social cues. As young adults, they were more likely to drink heavily and use drugs than their peers.

These findings were borne out by similar studies later in the 1990s by Sandra Jacobson and Joseph Jacobson, both psychologists at Wayne State University in Detroit, Michigan. To try and work out what dose of alcohol might be harmful, the Jacobsons ran a study of children born to 480 women in Detroit. In it, they compared the children born to women who, at their first antenatal appointment, said they drank seven or more standard U.S. drinks a week with the babies of women who drank less than seven, and with those whose mothers abstained altogether. The psychologists then tested the children's mental function in infancy and again at 7 years old. In the children whose mothers had seven drinks or more, the pair found significant deficits in their children's mental function in infancy, and again at age 7, mainly in arithmetic, working memory and attention (*Alcoholism: Clinical and Experimental Research,* vol 28, p. 1732). Where the mother drank less than that they found no effect.

Spread it Out

Seven drinks a week may be more than many pregnant women manage, but according to the Jacobsons, what's important is when you are drinking them, whether you have eaten, and how quickly your body metabolises alcohol. In their study, only one woman of the 480 drank daily; most of the others restricted their drinking to a couple of weekend evenings. If a woman is drinking seven standard drinks on average across the week, but having them all on two nights, she must be reaching four drinks on one night. That constitutes a binge. "Women don't realise that if they save up their alcohol 'allowance' to the end of the week, they are concentrating their drinking in a way that is potentially harmful," she says. This means that even women who have fewer than seven glasses per week could potentially be putting their babies at risk if they drink them all on one night.

There is also some evidence that fewer than seven drinks a week could have measurable effects on an unborn baby. Peter Hepper at Queen's University, Belfast, UK, examined the movements of fetuses scanned on ultrasound in response to a noise stimulus. Having asked women about their drinking habits, they compared the responses of fetuses exposed to low levels of alcohol—between 1 and 6 British units per week, each containing 10 millilitres of alcohol—and those exposed to none. When tested between 20 and 35 weeks, the fetuses exposed to alcohol tended to show a "startle response" usually found only in the earlier stages of pregnancy, when the nervous system is less developed. Five months after birth, the same babies showed different responses to visual stimuli from the babies whose mothers had abstained. Hepper interprets these findings as evidence that a low dose of alcohol has some as yet unexplained effect on the developing nervous system. Whether or not these differences will translate into behaviour problems in later life is as yet unknown.

When Ed Riley and colleagues at San Diego State University in California looked at children's brains using magnetic resonance imaging, they found obvious changes in the brain structure of children whose mothers drank very heavily, but also some changes in children born to moderate drinkers. For example, there were abnormalities in the corpus callosum, the tract of fibres connecting the right and left hemispheres of the brain. The greater the abnormality, the worse the children performed on a verbal learning task.

Despite these recent studies, the link between alcohol and fetal development is far from clear. Not all babies born to alcoholic women have FAS, yet other babies appear to be damaged by their mothers indulging in just a single binge. And if 61 percent of British women drink while pregnant, how come there are not hundreds of thousands of British children with FASD? Wouldn't we notice if 1 in 100 children being born were affected?

Hepper argues that few teachers would raise an eyebrow if they had two or three children in a class of 30 with marked behaviour difficulties, and several more with milder, manageable problems. He therefore thinks it is plausible to suggest that 1 in 100 children could have alcohol-related problems of some sort.

Hepper's research is widely quoted by anti-drinking campaigners such as FAS Aware, an international organisation which advertises in the women's bathrooms of bars to encourage pregnant women not to drink. The posters warn that "drinking in pregnancy could leave you with a hangover for life" and that "everything you drink goes to your baby's head."

Critics of these tactics point out that trying to scare women into abstinence is not helpful. There are reports in North America of women rushing off for an abortion because they had one drink before they knew they were pregnant or being racked with guilt about past drinking if they have a child with a mild disability.

Researchers like the Jacobsons acknowledge that it is hard to be certain about how alcohol affects a developing fetus on the basis of epidemiological studies, especially when they measure the notoriously messy subject of human behaviour. Any effect on the developing brain would vary depending on exactly when the fetus was exposed, and since some behavioural effects may not become apparent until several years after birth, it is difficult to pin down specific disabilities to specific antenatal exposure to alcohol.

To try and get around the epidemiological problem, John Olney, a neuroscientist at Washington University in St Louis, Missouri, has examined the impact of alcohol on developing rodent brains as a model for what happens in humans. Six years ago Olney and others showed that alcohol causes neurons in the developing rat brain to undergo programmed cell death, or apoptosis (*Science*, vol 287, p 1056).

Olney found that alcohol does the most serious damage if exposure happens during synaptogenesis, a critical time in development when neurons are rapidly forming connections. In rats, this happens just after birth, but in humans it begins in the second half of pregnancy and continues for two or more years. In the *Science* study, the team found that exposure to alcohol for baby

rats during this developmental stage, at levels equivalent to a binge lasting several hours, could trigger the suicide of millions of neurons, damaging the structure of the animals' forebrains. The alcohol seems to interfere with the action of receptors for two chemical signals or neurotransmitters, glutamate and GABA (gamma amino butyric acid), that must function normally for connections to form.

Lost Neurons

The changes to brain development in rodents, Olney believes, could explain some of the behavioural problems seen in children with FASD, including attention deficit, learning and memory problems. For example, in the rat study, large numbers of neurons were lost in the brain regions that comprise the extended hippocampal circuit, which is disrupted in other disorders of learning and memory (*Addiction Biology*, vol 9, p 137). Loss of cells in the thalamus, which is thought to play a role in "filtering" irrelevant stimuli, may partly explain why FASD children are easily distracted.

The timing of alcohol exposure during pregnancy dictates what type of damage will occur, Olney says: if it is early on, when facial structures are forming, the facial characteristics of FAS may be obvious. Later, when synapses are forming, mental function may be affected. This runs counter to the popular view that the fetus is only vulnerable in the first trimester; in fact, different stages may be vulnerable in different ways.

Olney has recently tried to find out exactly how much alcohol is enough to trigger apoptosis. This year he reported that, in infant mice whose brains are at the equivalent stage of development to a third-trimester fetus, some 20,000 neurons are deleted when they are exposed to only mildly raised blood alcohol levels, for periods as short as 45 minutes. In humans, he says, this is equivalent to deleting 20 million neurons with a 45-minute exposure to blood alcohol levels of just 50 milligrams per 100 millilitres of blood—which is well below the legal limit for driving, and easily achieved in "normal social" drinking (*Neurobiology of Disease*, DOI: 10.1016/j.nbd.2005.12.015). At blood alcohol levels below this, the team found no apoptosis.

Olney is quick to stress that, alarming as 20 million neurons sounds, it is "a very small amount of brain damage" in the context of the human brain, which is estimated to have trillions of neurons. He has no evidence that such small-scale damage would translate into any detectable effects on a child's cognitive abilities. "But if a mother is advised that one or two glasses of wine with dinner is OK, and if she then has two glasses with dinner three times a week, this is exposing the fetus to a little bit of damage three times a week," he says.

The bottom line is that, as yet, it's impossible to translate these findings into blanket advice for women about how many drinks they can or can't have when pregnant. A drink before food will raise blood alcohol concentrations faster than a drink with a meal; two drinks downed quickly will raise it more sharply than two drinks spread over 3 hours. Because of this uncertainty, some researchers—and some authorities—would rather take no chances. "The best possible advice I can give mothers is to totally abstain from alcohol the moment they know they are pregnant," Olney says.

PHYLLIDA BROWN is a writer based in the United Kingdom who has specialized in science journalism.

Julia Moskin  **NO**

The Weighty Responsibility of Drinking for Two

IT happens at coffee bars. It happens at cheese counters. But most of all, it happens at bars and restaurants. Pregnant women are slow-moving targets for strangers who judge what we eat—and, especially, drink.

"Nothing makes people more uncomfortable than a pregnant woman sitting at the bar," said Brianna Walker, a bartender in Los Angeles. "The other customers can't take their eyes off her."

Drinking during *pregnancy* quickly became taboo in the United States after 1981, when the Surgeon General began warning women about the dangers of alcohol. The warnings came after researchers at the *University of Washington* identified Fetal Alcohol Syndrome, a group of physical and mental birth defects caused by alcohol consumption, in 1973. In its recommendations, the government does not distinguish between heavy drinking and the occasional beer: all alcohol poses an unacceptable risk, it says.

So those of us who drink, even occasionally, during pregnancy face unanswerable questions, like why would anyone risk the health of a child for a passing pleasure like a beer?

"It comes down to this: I just don't buy it," said Holly Masur, a mother of two in Deerfield, Ill., who often had half a glass of wine with dinner during her pregnancies, based on advice from both her mother and her obstetrician. "How can a few sips of wine be dangerous when women used to drink martinis and smoke all through their pregnancies?"

Many American obstetricians, skeptical about the need for total abstinence, quietly tell their patients that an occasional beer or glass of wine—no hard liquor—is fine.

"If a patient tells me that she's drinking two or three glasses of wine a week, I am personally comfortable with that after the first trimester," said Dr. Austin Chen, an obstetrician in TriBeCa. "But technically I am sticking my neck out by saying so."

Americans' complicated relationship with food and drink—in which everything desirable is also potentially dangerous—only becomes magnified in pregnancy.

When I was pregnant with my first child in 2001 there was so much conflicting information that doubt became a reflexive response. Why was tea allowed but not coffee? How could all "soft cheeses" be forbidden if cream cheese was recommended? What were the real risks of having a glass of wine on my birthday?

Pregnant women are told that danger lurks everywhere: listeria in soft cheese, mercury in canned tuna, *salmonella* in fresh-squeezed orange juice. Our responsibility for minimizing risk through perfect behavior feels vast.

Eventually, instead of automatically following every rule, I began looking for proof.

Proof, it turns out, is hard to come by when it comes to "moderate" or "occasional" drinking during pregnancy. Standard definitions, clinical trials and long-range studies simply do not exist.

"Clinically speaking, there is no such thing as moderate drinking in pregnancy," said Dr. Ernest L. Abel, a professor at Wayne State University Medical School in Detroit, who has led many studies on pregnancy and alcohol. "The studies address only heavy drinking"—defined by the *National Institutes of Health* as five drinks or more per day—"or no drinking."

Most pregnant women in America say in surveys that they do not drink at all—although they may not be reporting with total accuracy. But others make a conscious choice not to rule out drinking altogether.

For me, the desire to drink turned out to be all tied up with the ritual of the table—sitting down in a restaurant, reading the menu, taking that first bite of bread and butter. That was the only time, I found, that sparkling water or nonalcoholic beer didn't quite do it. And so, after examining my conscience and the research available, I concluded that one drink with dinner was an acceptable risk.

My husband, frankly, is uncomfortable with it. But he recognizes that there is no way for him to put himself in my position, or to know what he would do under the same circumstances.

While occasional drinking is not a decision I take lightly, it is also a decision in which I am not (quite) alone. Lisa Felter McKenney, a teacher in Chicago whose first child is due in January, said she feels comfortable at her current level of three drinks a week, having been grudgingly cleared by her obstetrician. "Being able to look forward to a beer with my husband at the end of the day really helps me deal with the horrible parts of being pregnant," she said. "It makes me feel like myself: not the alcohol, but the ritual. Usually I just take a few sips and that's enough."

Ana Sortun, a chef in Cambridge, Mass., who gave birth last year, said that she (and the nurse practitioner who delivered her baby) both drank wine during their pregnancies. "I didn't do it every day, but I did it often," she said. "Ultimately I trusted my own instincts, and my doctor's, more than anything else. Plus, I really believe all that stuff about the European tradition."

Many women who choose to drink have pointed to the habits of European women who legendarily drink wine, eat raw-milk cheese and quaff Guinness to improve breast milk production, as justification for their own choices in pregnancy.

Of course, those countries have their own taboos. "Just try to buy unpasteurized cheese in England, or to eat salad in France when you're pregnant," wrote a friend living in York, England. (Many French obstetricians warn patients that raw vegetables are risky.) However, she said, a drink a day is taken for granted. In those cultures, wine and beer are considered akin to food, part of daily life; in ours, they are treated more like drugs.

But more European countries are adopting the American stance of abstinence. . . .

If pregnant Frenchwomen are giving up wine completely (although whether that will happen is debatable—the effects of warning labels are far from proven), where does that leave the rest of us?

"I never thought it would happen," said Jancis Robinson, a prominent wine critic in Britain, one of the few countries with government guidelines that still allow pregnant women any alcohol—one to two drinks per week. Ms. Robinson, who spent three days tasting wine for her Masters of Wine qualification in 1990 while pregnant with her second child, said that she studied the research then available and while she was inclined to be cautious, she didn't see proof that total abstinence was the only safe course.

One thing is certain: drinking is a confusing and controversial choice for pregnant women, and among the hardest areas in which to interpret the research.

Numerous long-term studies, including the original one at the University of Washington at Seattle, have established beyond doubt that heavy drinkers are taking tremendous risks with their children's health.

But for women who want to apply that research to the question of whether they must refuse a single glass of champagne on New Year's Eve or a serving of rum-soaked Christmas pudding, there is almost no information at all.

My own decision came down to a stubborn conviction that feels like common sense: a single drink—sipped slowly, with food to slow the absorption—is unlikely to have much effect.

Some clinicians agree with that instinct. Others claim that the threat at any level is real.

"Blood alcohol level is the key," said Dr. Abel, whose view, after 30 years of research, is that brain damage and other alcohol-related problems most likely result from the spikes in blood alcohol concentration that come from binge drinking—another difficult definition, since according to Dr. Abel a binge can be as few as two drinks, drunk in rapid succession, or as many as 14, depending on a woman's physiology.

Because of ethical considerations, virtually no clinical trials can be performed on pregnant women.

"Part of the research problem is that we have mostly animal studies to work with," Dr. Abel said. "And who knows what is two drinks, for a mouse?"

Little attention has been paid to pregnant women at the low end of the consumption spectrum because there isn't a clear threat to public health there, according to Janet Golden, a history professor at Rutgers who has written about Americans' changing attitudes toward drinking in pregnancy.

The research—and the public health concern—is focused on getting pregnant women who don't regulate their intake to stop completely.

And the public seems to seriously doubt whether pregnant women can be trusted to make responsible decisions on their own.

"Strangers, and courts, will intervene with a pregnant woman when they would never dream of touching anyone else," Ms. Golden said.

Ms. Walker, the bartender, agreed. "I've had customers ask me to tell them what the pregnant woman is drinking," she said. "But I don't tell them. Like with all customers, unless someone is drunk and difficult it's no one else's business—or mine."

Julia Moskin is a writer and journalist for *The New York Times* who writes primarily about food and dining.

EXPLORING THE ISSUE

Is Drinking Alcohol While Pregnant an Unnecessary Risk to Prenatal Development?

Critical Thinking and Reflection

1. If science was able to offer odds as to the likelihood of drinking during pregnancy causing developmental problems, what odds would be too great to risk? Is any risk at all too much, or does the potential comfort and familiarity of light drinking matter for mothers?
2. Why would government agencies be getting more conservative with their recommendations regarding drinking during pregnancy? Should mothers have the right to make informed decisions on their own, or is this really a public issue?
3. How likely does it seem that a good postnatal environment could make up for significant exposure to teratogens, such as alcohol, during prenatal development?
4. What would be the various advantages and disadvantages to labeling children exposed to alcohol during prenatal development as susceptible to fetal alcohol "disorders"? Is it possible such labels could themselves be a problem during development?
5. What are the particular challenges of researching prenatal development, and how might those challenges complicate efforts to understand the effects of alcohol on prenatal development?

Is There Common Ground?

Both Phyllida Brown and Julia Moskin would likely agree that the "discovery" of fetal alcohol syndrome in the early 1970s was beneficial to both individuals and society. Both would also likely agree that research into fetal alcohol syndrome has provided valuable information related to prenatal development. Understanding how different factors impact the fetus helps us ensure positive development.

Where they differ most is in what to do with that information. Because we have learned that alcohol can cause problems during prenatal development, even though we do not know the exact circumstances that produce those problems, is it fair to prohibit all drinking during pregnancy? When do we err on the side of caution, and when do we err on the side of trusting pregnant women to make good decisions? And if we do get more nuanced research findings of the sort that both Brown and Moskin would likely appreciate, when do we have enough to make definitive judgments about the risks of drinking during pregnancy?

An underlying theme is who makes decisions about the unborn child. Should women have ultimate control

over their bodies—and the child developing inside it? Or, should the government set laws to protect the fetus, even if those policies infringe on the rights of the pregnant woman? The idea of drinking alcohol while pregnant crosses multiple boundaries, and brings together issues of individual freedom, collective good, morality, and social policy.

Create Central

www.mhhe.com/createcentral

Additional Resources

Mattson, S. N., Roesch, S. C., Glass, L., Deweese, B. N., Coles, C. D., Kable, J. A., . . . & Riley, E. P. (2013). Further development of a neurobehavioral profile of fetal alcohol spectrum disorders. *Alcoholism: Clinical and Experimental Research, 37*(3), 517–528.

Meurk, C., Lucke, J., & Hall, W. (2014). A bio-social and ethical framework for understanding fetal alcohol spectrum disorders. *Neuroethics*, 1–8.

Muggli, E., Colleen, O., Forster, D., Anderson, P., Lewis, S., Nagle, C., . . . & Halliday, J. (2014). Study protocol: Asking questions about alcohol in pregnancy (AQUA): A longitudinal cohort study of fetal effects of low to moderate alcohol exposure. *BMC Pregnancy and Childbirth, 14*(1), 302.

Internet References . . .

Child Trends

www.childtrends.org

National Organization on Fetal Alcohol Syndrome (NOFAS)

www.nofas.org/

The American Pregnancy Association

www.americanpregnancy.org

The Mayo Clinic

www.americanpregnancy.org

Selected, Edited, and with Issue Framing Material by:
Allison A. Buskirk-Cohen, *Delaware Valley University*

ISSUE

Is Breastfeeding Inevitably Best for Healthy Development?

YES: **U.S. Department of Health and Human Services**, from *The Surgeon General's Call to Action to Support Breastfeeding* (Office of the Surgeon General, 2011)

NO: **Julie E. Artis**, from "Breastfeed at Your Own Risk," *Contexts* (2009)

Learning Outcomes

After reading this issue, you will be able to:

- Discuss how research suggests that the breastfeeding of infants can have positive health effects, psychosocial effects, economic effects, and environmental effects, but it is not a simple issue to research.

- Understand that the decision to breastfeed is not entirely the responsibility of individual mothers; the health care system, workplaces, family members, communities, and many other circumstances play both obvious and subtle roles in shaping breastfeeding rates.

- Recognize that the historical shifts and demographic differences in breastfeeding rates have depended upon cultural values that shape attitudes toward the "natural" and technology as part of healthy development.

- Realize breastfeeding may be an example of a broader ideology of "intensive mothering" where mothers feel obliged to sacrifice their own independence to take total responsibility for their children.

ISSUE SUMMARY

YES: As part of a broad mandate to advocate for public health, the U.S. Surgeon General cites numerous benefits of breastfeeding as part of "call to action" oriented toward increasing the practice among new mothers.

NO: Sociologist Julie E. Artis argues that the broad promotion of breastfeeding has the potential to unfairly stigmatize women who do not breastfeed while overstating the benefits.

"**B**reast is best." It is a catchy, alliterative, simple slogan that inundates parents trying to figure out how to ensure their children get off to the best possible developmental start. And most mothers do start their children on breast milk: according to the U.S. Surgeon General, 75 percent of American newborns are breastfed. The Surgeon General also notes, however, that those rates quickly decline: "only 13 percent of babies are exclusively breastfed at the end of six months." With the easy availability of formula as an alternative to breastfeeding, the challenges mothers face in needing to be constantly available to their infants, the physical limitations some mothers confront in producing breast milk, and numerous other barriers to exclusive breastfeeding, many parents use alternative means of feeding their babies despite hearing "breast is best." It turns out that for many parents breastfeeding may not be so simple after all.

There always have been alternatives to mothers' breastfeeding their children, since some mothers experience lactation problems or may die from childbirth. Infant feeding has experienced its own historical evolution including wet nursing, the invention of the bottle, and the use of formula. Using a wet nurse, another woman to breastfeed an infant, was common through the nineteenth and twentieth centuries, when the feeding bottle was introduced. Analysis of ancient artifacts indicates that animal's milk was used as a substitute for breastmilk as far back as 2000 B.C. The most common animal's milk used came from cows, though goats, sheep, donkeys, camels, pigs, and horses also could serve as substitutes. A human mother's milk still was considered ideal and in the eighteenth century, scientists tried to formulate nonhuman milk to resemble human milk using chemical analyses. In 1985, Justus von Liebig developed, patented, and marketed an infant formula that was considered "perfect" at the time. Since then, there have been numerous iterations of infant formula, some with greater success than others.

Today, few dispute the advantages of breastfeeding; yet, there are many mothers who still use formula as a substitute. Research has shown that breastfeeding benefits both mother and child, in terms of physical, cognitive, and emotional health. While there has been a recent increase in the number of mothers' breastfeeding, the rate is still lower than many health experts would like. There are also discrepancies by ethnicity, education, and income. Those families who might best benefit from breastfeeding may be least likely to do it. Also, many mothers do not breastfeed as long as the experts recommend. Despite all the campaigns dedicated to promoting knowledge about breastfeeding, why have there not been major changes in behavior?

One major complication related to breastfeeding is the mixed messages sent throughout our society. On the one hand, major public health campaigns such as that originating in the U.S. Surgeon General's office through the U.S. Department of Health and Human Services) heavily promote breastfeeding. Those campaigns are then complemented by the messaging of many health care providers and by advocacy groups such as the La Leche League. On the other hand, companies promoting baby food and formula produce extensive marketing suggesting their products can be similarly nutritious, while many workplaces and public spaces implicitly discourage breastfeeding through a lack of time or privacy. Those discouragements are then enhanced by confusing attitudes about public decency and the display of a breast.

The mixed messages around breastfeeding can become overwhelming to already anxious parents. In fact, sociologist Julie E. Artis argues that confusing messages about breastfeeding are one specific manifestation of a general anxiety that tends to characterize modern childrearing. Mothers in particular often feel as though they are responsible for every detail of infant development, and we are taught that infancy is a critical foundation for all later development. There are "right" ways to stimulate infants, to rest infants, to transport infants, to interact with infants, and perhaps nothing feels more important to get right than feeding. Artis is therefore concerned that women who are unable to breastfeed will end up feeling unnecessarily stressed and guilty.

Artis also offers an intriguing historical overview of generational changes in attitudes toward breastfeeding, noting that as recently as 1971 only 24 percent of American mothers breastfed newborns. She ties this to "technological advancements" that led many in the mid-to late-twentieth century to think "a scientifically developed substance [infant formula] was at least equivalent to, and possibly better than, breastmilk." This shift is part of an interesting general tension in lifespan development between relying on new technology and relying on "natural" tools and old ways that have worked for generations. It is worth remembering that infants have thrived for the whole of human history on a diet consisting primarily of breastmilk. But, it is similarly noteworthy that the 76 percent of American babies born in 1971 who were not breastfed have turned out fine.

Another challenge around both the importance of breastfeeding and the idealization of "natural" ways to facilitate infant development is to interpret the available science. The U.S. Surgeon General cites significant evidence suggesting that breastfed babies do better on measures ranging from physical health to IQ. But Artis points out that those findings may not be as definitive as they seem—research in this area often contrasts children of mothers who choose to breastfeed with children of mothers who choose not to breastfed, and there may be systematic differences between those groups. In support of that possibility, both the U.S. Surgeon General and Artis note that there are wide variations in breastfeeding rates between demographic groups differing by ethnicity, education, and so forth.

Most scholars and public health officials ultimately agree that breastfeeding seems to have general advantages for infant development. Mother's milk is remarkably well-suited to fulfill the needs of a newborn child, the process of breastfeeding can provide intensely valuable bonding experiences, and the whole endeavor offers an awe-inspiring example of the integral nature of lifespan development. But saying that breastfeeding has general advantages is not the same as assuming the breast is always best—campaigns to promote breastfeeding may do as much to promote a particular version of "intensive mothering" as to promote healthy infant development.

YES

U.S. Department of Health
and Human Services

The Surgeon General's Call to Action to Support Breastfeeding

Foreword from the Surgeon General, U.S. Department of Health and Human Services

For nearly all infants, breastfeeding is the best source of infant nutrition and immunologic protection, and it provides remarkable health benefits to mothers as well. Babies who are breastfed are less likely to become overweight and obese. Many mothers in the United States want to breastfeed, and most try. And yet within only three months after giving birth, more than two-thirds of breastfeeding mothers have already begun using formula. By six months postpartum, more than half of mothers have given up on breastfeeding, and mothers who breastfeed one-year-olds or toddlers are a rarity in our society.

October 2010 marked the 10th anniversary of the release of the *HHS Blueprint for Action on Breastfeeding*, in which former Surgeon General David Satcher, M.D., Ph.D., reiterated the commitment of previous Surgeons General to support breastfeeding as a public health goal. This was the first comprehensive framework for national action on breastfeeding. It was created through collaboration among representatives from medical, business, women's health, and advocacy groups as well as academic communities. The *Blueprint* provided specific action steps for the health care system, researchers, employers, and communities to better protect, promote, and support breastfeeding.

I have issued this *Call to Action* because the time has come to set forth the important roles and responsibilities of clinicians, employers, communities, researchers, and government leaders and to urge us all to take on a commitment to enable mothers to meet their personal goals for breastfeeding. Mothers are acutely aware of and devoted to their responsibilities when it comes to feeding their children, but the responsibilities of others must be identified so that all mothers can obtain the information, help, and support they deserve when they breastfeed their infants. Identifying the support systems that are needed to help mothers meet their personal breastfeeding goals will allow them to stop feeling guilty and alone when problems with breastfeeding arise. All too often, mothers who wish to breastfeed encounter daunting challenges in moving through the health care system. Furthermore, there is often an incompatibility between employment and breastfeeding, but with help this is not impossible to overcome. Even so, because the barriers can seem insurmountable at times, many mothers stop breastfeeding. In addition, families are often unable to find the support they need in their communities to make breastfeeding work for them. From a societal perspective, many research questions related to breastfeeding remain unanswered, and for too long, breastfeeding has received insufficient national attention as a public health issue.

This *Call to Action* describes in detail how different people and organizations can contribute to the health of mothers and their children. Rarely are we given the chance to make such a profound and lasting difference in the lives of so many. I am confident that this *Call to Action* will spark countless imaginative, effective, and mutually supportive endeavors that improve support for breastfeeding mothers and children in our nation.

Regina M. Benjamin, M.D., M.B.A.
Vice Admiral, U.S. Public Health Service
Surgeon General

The Importance of Breastfeeding

Health Effects

The health effects of breastfeeding are well recognized and apply to mothers and children in developed nations such as the United States as well as to those in developing countries. Breast milk is uniquely suited to the human infant's nutritional needs and is a live substance with unparalleled immunological and anti-inflammatory properties that protect against a host of illnesses and diseases for both mothers and children.

U.S. Department of Health and Human Services, 2011.

In 2007, the Agency for Healthcare Research and Quality (AHRQ) published a summary of systematic reviews and meta-analyses on breastfeeding and maternal and infant health outcomes in developed countries. The AHRQ report reaffirmed the health risks associated with formula feeding and early weaning from breastfeeding. With regard to short-term risks, formula feeding is associated with increases in common childhood infections, such as diarrhea and ear infections. The risk of acute ear infection, also called acute otitis media, is 100 percent higher among exclusively formula-fed infants than in those who are exclusively breastfed during the first six months (see Table 1).

The risk associated with some relatively rare but serious infections and diseases, such as severe lower respiratory infections and leukemia are also higher for formula-fed infants. The risk of hospitalization for lower respiratory tract disease in the first year of life is more than 250 percent higher among babies who are formula fed than in those who are exclusively breastfed at least four months. Furthermore, the risk of sudden infant death syndrome is 56 percent higher among infants who are never breastfed. For vulnerable premature infants, formula feeding is associated with higher rates of necrotizing enterocolitis (NEC). The AHRQ report also concludes that formula feeding is associated with higher risks for major chronic diseases and conditions, such as type 2 diabetes, asthma, and childhood obesity, all three of which have increased among U.S. children over time.

As shown in Table 1, compared with mothers who breastfeed, those who do not breastfeed also experience increased risks for certain poor health outcomes. For example, several studies have found the risk of breast cancer to be higher for women who have never breastfed. Similarly, the risk of ovarian cancer was found to be 27 percent higher for women who had never breastfed than for those who had breastfed for some period of time. In general, exclusive breastfeeding and longer durations of breastfeeding are associated with better maternal health outcomes.

The AHRQ report cautioned that, although a history of breastfeeding is associated with a reduced risk

Table 1

Excess Health Risks Associated with Not Breastfeeding

Outcome	Excess Risk* (%)
Among full-term infants	
Acute ear infection (otitis media)	100
Eczema (atopic dermatitis)	47
Diarrhea and vomiting (gastrointestinal infection)	178
Hospitalization for lower respiratory tract diseases in the first year	257
Asthma, with family history	67
Asthma, no family history	35
Childhood obesity	32
Type 2 diabetes mellitus	64
Acute lymphocytic leukemia	23
Acute myelogenous leukemia	18
Sudden infant death syndrome	56
Among preterm infants	
Necrotizing enterocolitis	138
Among mothers	
Breast cancer	4
Ovarian cancer	27

*The excess risk is approximated by using the odds ratios reported in the referenced studies.

of many diseases in infants and mothers, almost all the data in the AHRQ review were gathered from observational studies. Therefore, the associations described in the report do not necessarily represent causality. Another limitation of the systematic review was the wide variation in quality among the body of evidence across health outcomes.

As stated by the U.S. Preventive Services Task Force (USPSTF) evidence review, human milk is the natural source of nutrition for all infants. The value of breastfeeding and human milk for infant nutrition and growth has been long recognized, and the health outcomes of nutrition and growth were not covered by the AHRQ review.

Psychosocial Effects

Although the typical woman may cite the health advantages for herself and her child as major reasons that she breastfeeds, another important factor is the desire to experience a sense of bonding or closeness with her newborn. Indeed, some women indicate that the psychological benefit of breastfeeding, including bonding more closely with their babies, is the most important influence on their decision to breastfeed. Even women who exclusively formula feed have reported feeling that breastfeeding is more likely than formula feeding to create a close bond between mother and child.

In addition, although the literature is not conclusive on this matter, breastfeeding may help to lower the risk of postpartum depression, a serious condition that almost 13 percent of mothers experience. This disorder poses risks not only to the mother's health but also to the health of her child, particularly when she is unable to fully care for her infant. Research findings in this area are mixed, but some studies have found that women who have breastfed and women with longer durations of breastfeeding have a lower risk of postpartum depression. Whether postpartum depression affects breastfeeding or vice versa, however, is not well understood.

Economic Effects

In addition to the health advantages of breastfeeding for mothers and their children, there are economic benefits associated with breastfeeding that can be realized by families, employers, private and government insurers, and the nation as a whole. For example, a study conducted more than a decade ago estimated that families who followed optimal breastfeeding practices could save more than $1,200–$1,500 in expenditures for infant formula

in the first year alone. In addition, better infant health means fewer health insurance claims, less employee time off to care for sick children, and higher productivity, all of which concern employers.

Increasing rates of breastfeeding can help reduce the prevalence of various illnesses and health conditions, which in turn results in lower health care costs. A study conducted in 2001 on the economic impact of breastfeeding for three illnesses—otitis media, gastroenteritis, and NEG—found that increasing the proportion of children who were breastfed in 2000 to the targets established in *Healthy People 2010* would have saved an estimated $3.6 billion annually. These savings were based on direct costs (e.g., costs for formula as well as physician, hospital, clinic, laboratory, and procedural fees) and indirect costs (e.g., wages parents lose while caring for an ill child), as well as the estimated cost of premature death. A more recent study that used costs adjusted to 2007 dollars and evaluated costs associated with additional illnesses and diseases (sudden infant death syndrome, hospitalization for lower respiratory tract infection in infancy, atopic dermatitis, childhood leukemia, childhood obesity, childhood asthma, and type 1 diabetes mellitus) found that if 90 percent of U.S. families followed guidelines to breastfeed exclusively for six months, the United States would save $13 billion annually from reduced direct medical and indirect costs and the cost of premature death. If 80 percent of U.S. families complied, $10.5 billion per year would be saved.

Environmental Effects

Breastfeeding also confers global environmental benefits; human milk is a natural, renewable food that acts as a complete source of babies' nutrition for about the first six months of life. Furthermore, there are no packages involved, as opposed to infant formulas and other substitutes for human milk that require packaging that ultimately may be deposited in landfills. For every one million formula-fed babies, 150 million containers of formula are consumed; while some of those containers could be recycled, many end up in landfills. In addition, infant formulas must be transported from their place of manufacture to retail locations, such as grocery stores, so that they can be purchased by families. Although breastfeeding requires mothers to consume a small amount of additional calories, it generally requires no containers, no paper, no fuel to prepare, and no transportation to deliver, and it reduces the carbon footprint by saving precious global resources and energy.

Endorsement of Breastfeeding as the Best Nutrition for Infants

Because breastfeeding confers many important health and other benefits, including psychosocial, economic, and environmental benefits, it is not surprising that breastfeeding has been recommended by several prominent organizations of health professionals, among them the American Academy of Pediatrics (AAP), American Academy of Family Physicians, American College of Obstetricians and Gynecologists, American College of Nurse-Midwives, American Dietetic Association, and American Public Health Association, all of which recommend that most infants in the United States be breastfed for at least 12 months. These organizations also recommend that for about the first six months, infants be exclusively breastfed, meaning they should not be given any foods or liquids other than breast milk, not even water.

Regarding nutrient composition, the American Dietetic Association stated, "Human milk is uniquely tailored to meet the nutrition needs of human infants. It has the appropriate balance of nutrients provided in easily digestible and bioavailable forms." The AAP stated, "Human milk is species-specific, and all substitute feeding preparations differ markedly from it, making human milk uniquely superior for infant feeding. Exclusive breastfeeding is the reference or normative model against which all alternative feeding methods must be measured with regard to growth, health, development, and all other short- and long-term outcomes."

While breastfeeding is recommended for most infants, it is also recognized that a small number of women cannot or should not breastfeed. For example, AAP states that breastfeeding is contraindicated for mothers with HIV, human T-cell lymphotropic virus type 1 or type 2, active untreated tuberculosis, or herpes simplex lesions on the breast. Infants with galactosemia should not be breastfed. Additionally, the maternal use of certain drugs or treatments, including illicit drugs, antimetabolites, chemotherapeutic agents, and radioactive isotope therapies, is cause for not breastfeeding.

Federal Policy on Breastfeeding

Over the last 25 years, the Surgeons General of the United States have worked to protect, promote, and support breastfeeding. In 1984, Surgeon General C. Everett Koop convened the first Surgeon General's Workshop on Breastfeeding, which drew together professional and lay experts to outline key actions needed to improve breastfeeding rates. Participants developed recommendations in six distinct areas: 1) the world of work, 2) public education, 3) professional education, 4) health care system, 5) support services, and 6) research. Follow-up reports in 1985 and 1991 documented progress in implementing the original recommendations.

In 1990, the United States signed onto the *Innocenti Declaration on the Protection, Promotion and Support of Breastfeeding,* which was adopted by the World Health Organization (WHO) and the United Nations Children's Fund (UNICEF). This declaration called upon all governments to nationally coordinate breastfeeding activities, ensure optimal practices in support of breastfeeding through maternity services, take action on the *International Code of Marketing of Breast-milk Substitutes* (the Code), and enact legislation to protect breastfeeding among working women.

In 1999, Surgeon General David Satcher requested that a departmental policy on breastfeeding be developed, with particular emphasis on reducing racial and ethnic disparities in breastfeeding. The following year, the Secretary of the U.S. Department of Health and Human Services (HHS), under the leadership of the department's Office on Women's Health (OWH), released the *HHS Blueprint for Action on Breastfeeding.* This document, which has received widespread attention in the years since its release, declared breastfeeding to be a key public health issue in the United States.

Rates of Breastfeeding

Over the last few decades, rates of breastfeeding have improved, but in recent years, rates generally have climbed more slowly. Figure 1 presents data from 1970 through 2007 from two sources. Data before 1999 are from the Ross Mothers Survey. Data for 1999 through 2007 are from the Centers for Disease Control and Prevention's (CDC) annual National Immunization Survey (NIS), which includes a series of questions regarding breastfeeding practices.

National objectives for *Healthy People 2010,* in addition to calling for 75 percent of mothers to initiate breastfeeding, called for 50 percent to continue breastfeeding for six months and 25 percent to continue breastfeeding for one year. *Healthy People 2010* also included objectives for exclusive breastfeeding: targets were for 40 percent of women to breastfeed exclusively for three months and for 17 percent to do so for six months.

Figure 1

National Trends in Breastfeeding Rates

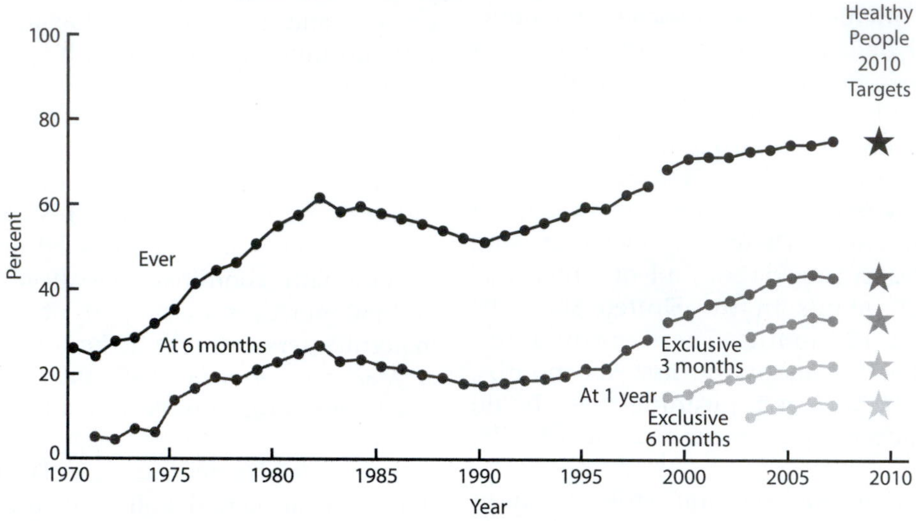

Note: Data from before 1999 are from a different source, as indicated by the line break.

Sources: 1970–1998, Ross Mothers Survey; 1999–2007, Centers for Disease Control and Prevention, National Immunization Survey.

The most recent NIS data shown in Figure 1 indicate that, while the rate of breastfeeding initiation has met the 2010 target, rates of duration and exclusivity still fall short of *Healthy People 2010* objectives. Among children born in 2007, 75 percent of mothers initiated breastfeeding, 43 percent were breastfeeding at six months, and 22 percent were breastfeeding at 12 months (see Figure 1). Although human milk is the only nutrition most babies need for about the first six months, many women discontinue breastfeeding or add other foods or liquids to their baby's diet well before the child reaches six months of age. Among breastfed infants born in 2007, an estimated 33 percent were exclusively breastfed through age three months, and only 13 percent were exclusively breastfed for six months.

Although much is known about rates of breastfeeding in the population, mothers' breastfeeding practices have not been well understood until recently. The Infant Feeding Practices Study II, conducted during 2005–2007 by the U.S. Food and Drug Administration (FDA) in collaboration with CDC, was designed to fill in some of the gaps. For this longitudinal study of women followed from late pregnancy through their infants' first year of life, participants were selected from across the United States. On average, members of the study group had higher levels

of education, were older, were more likely to be white, were more likely to have a middle-level income, and were more likely to be employed than the overall U.S. female population.

Some of the findings from this study were discouraging; for instance, almost half of breastfed newborns were supplemented with infant formula while they were still in the hospital after birth. Most healthy, full-term, breastfed newborns have no medical need to receive supplemental infant formula, and supplementing with infant formula can be detrimental to breastfeeding. In addition, more than 40 percent of infants in the Infant Feeding Practices Study II sample were consuming solid foods within the first four months after birth despite recommendations by the AAP that no infant, whether breastfed or formula fed, should be given any solid foods until at least the age of four months.

Disparities in Breastfeeding Practices

Despite overall improvements in breastfeeding rates, unacceptable disparities in breastfeeding have persisted by race/ethnicity, socioeconomic characteristics, and geography (see Table 2). For example, breastfeeding rates for black infants are about 50 percent lower than those for white

Table 2

Provisional Breastfeeding Rates Among Children Born in 2007*

Sociodemographic Factor	Ever Breastfed (%)	Breastfeeding at 6 Months (%)	Breastfeeding at 12 Months (%)
United States	75.0	43.0	22.4
Race/ethnicity			
American Indian or Alaska Native	73.8	42.4	20.7
Asian or Pacific Islander	83.0	56.4	32.8
Hispanic or Latino	80.6	46.0	24.7
Non-Hispanic Black or African American	58.1	27.5	12.5
Non-Hispanic White	76.2	44.7	23.3
Receiving WIC†			
Yes	67.5	33.7	17.5
No, but eligible	77.5	48.2	30.7
Ineligible	84.6	54.2	27.6
Maternal education			
Not a high school graduate	67.0	37.0	21.9
High school graduate	66.1	31.4	15.1
Some college	76.5	41.0	20.5
College graduate	88.3	59.9	31.1

*Survey limited to children aged 19–35 months at the time of data collection. The lag between birth and collection of data allows for tracking of breastfeeding initiation as well as calculating the duration of breastfeeding.

†WIC = Special Supplemental Nutrition Program for Women, Infants, and Children; U.S. Department of Agriculture.

Source: Centers for Disease Control and Prevention, National Immunization Survey.

infants at birth, age six months, and age 12 months, even when controlling for the family's income or educational level. On the other hand, the gap between white and black mothers in initiation of breastfeeding has diminished over time, from 35 percentage points in 1990 to 18 percentage points in 2007. Yet, the gap in rates of breastfeeding continuation at six months has remained around 15 percentage points throughout this period.

The reasons for the persistently lower rates of breastfeeding among African American women are not well understood, but employment may play a role. African American women tend to return to work earlier after childbirth than white women, and they are more likely to work in environments that do not support breastfeeding. Although research has shown that returning to work is associated with early discontinuation of breastfeeding,

a supportive work environment may make a difference in whether mothers are able to continue breastfeeding.

With regard to socioeconomic characteristics, many studies have found income to be positively associated with breastfeeding. For example, a study that included children participating in the U.S. Department of Agriculture's (USDA) Special Supplemental Nutrition Program for Women, Infants, and Children (WIC), which uses income to determine eligibility, found they were less likely to be breastfed than children in middle- and upper-income families. Educational status is also associated with breastfeeding; women with less than a high school education are far less likely to breastfeed than women who have earned a college degree. Geographic disparities are also evident; women living in the southeastern United States are less likely to initiate and continue breastfeeding than women in other areas of the country and women living in rural areas are less likely to breastfeed than women in urban areas. Understanding the reasons for these disparities is crucial for identifying, developing, and implementing strategies to overcome the barriers to breastfeeding that women and families experience throughout our country. Research suggests that 1) race and ethnicity are associated with breastfeeding regardless of income, and 2) income is associated with breastfeeding regardless of race or ethnicity. Other possible contributors to the disparities in breastfeeding include the media, which has often cited more difficulties with breastfeeding than positive stories, hospital policies and practices, the recommendations of WIC counselors, marketing of infant formula, policies on work and parental leave, legislation, social and cultural norms, and advice from family and friends.

Barriers to Breastfeeding in the United States

Even though a variety of evidence indicates that breastfeeding reduces many different health risks for mothers and children, numerous barriers to breastfeeding remain—and action is needed to overcome these barriers. . . .

THE U.S. DEPARTMENT OF HEALTH AND HUMAN SERVICES **(HHS)** is the U.S. government's principal agency for protecting the health of all Americans and providing essential human services, especially for those who are least able to help themselves.

Julie E. Artis

 **NO**

Breastfeed at Your Own Risk

For nearly two years, the U.S. Department of Health and Human Services spent $2 million on an ad campaign to promote breastfeeding by educating mothers about the risks of not doing so. Those risks were often communicated in provocative ways. One television ad, for example, showed a pregnant African American woman riding a mechanical bull, and then the message appears on the screen, "You wouldn't take risks before your baby is born. Why start after?"

This campaign was the culmination of three decades of increasing consensus among medical and public health professionals that, as the saying goes, "breast is best"— that there is no better nutrition for the first year of an infant's life than breastmilk. The endorsement of the medical establishment is echoed in advice books and parenting magazines that overwhelmingly recommend breastfeeding over formula. Communities have passed laws to support breastfeeding mothers in the workplace and to ensure public breastfeeding isn't legally categorized as indecency.

And rates of breastfeeding in the United States have increased dramatically—nearly 75 percent of mothers now breastfeed newborns, up from 24 percent in 1971. Rates of breastfeeding are even higher among middle-class, educated mothers. For these mothers, breastfeeding has become less of a choice and more of an imperative—a way to protect their infant's health and boost their IQ. Breastfeeding is a way to achieve so-called good mothering, the idealized notion of mothers as selfless and child-centered.

Taking a sociological look at the cultural imperative to breastfeed illustrates how mothering is shaped by discussions among scientists, doctors, and other experts, as well as policy recommendations that grow out of scientific findings. It also reveals that breastfeeding and infant feeding practices differ by culture, race, class, and ethnicity, and that the "breast is best" conventional wisdom doesn't take these differences into account. Thus, this campaign leaves many mothers feeling inadequate—and perhaps unnecessarily so because the scientific evidence about the benefits of breastfeeding are less clear-cut than mothers have been led to believe.

Historical Trends in Breastfeeding

Cultural ideas about motherhood and family in the United States have changed significantly over time, thanks in part to science and technology.

Religious authorities, midwives, and physicians encouraged mothers in the 17th and 18th centuries to breastfeed their infants. The practice through the mid-1800s, in a primarily farm-based society, was to nurse infants through their "second summer" to avoid unrefrigerated and possibly spoiled food and milk.

Wet nursing—breastfeeding a child who is not a woman's own—became necessary when a mother was severely ill or died during childbirth. Breastmilk was widely thought superior to "hand-feeding"—providing milk, tea, or "pap" (a mixture of flour, sugar, water, and milk)—in promoting infant health, but even so, according to historian Janet Golden in her study *A Social History of Wet Nursing,* families worried about having a wet nurse of "questionable" moral fitness, and these fears were exacerbated by race and class divisions. In the north, wet nurses were typically poor immigrant mothers; in the south, they tended to be African Americans, and it was common for female slaves to be wet nurses in the antebellum south. However, by the turn of the 20th century, the use of wet nurses had declined, in part because pasteurization made bottle-feeding a safe alternative to breastmilk. This was also the era in which children came to be seen as priceless, in need of protection, and worth extraordinary investment, sociologist Viviana Zelizer explained in *Pricing the Priceless Child.*

Technological advancements led to the development of mass-marketed infant formula in the 1950s. Doctors then began to recommend formula, saying a scientifically developed substance was at least equivalent to, and possibly better than, breastmilk. By the early 1970s, breastfeeding

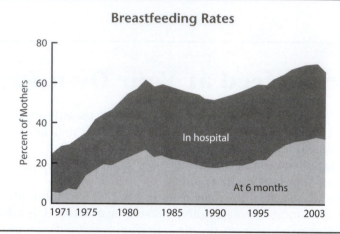

Breastfeeding Rates

Source: Mothers Survey, Ross Products Division of Abbott

rates in hospitals were at a low of approximately 24 percent, with only 5 percent of mothers nursing for several months following birth.

It was in this era that some feminist women's health groups and Christian women's groups such as La Leche League began challenging the medical model by promoting "natural" childbirth and breastfeeding. These groups promoted the benefits of breastfeeding and also raised public awareness about the activities of formula companies.

For example, some feminist health groups helped organize a boycott of Nestle in the late 1970s for promoting formula in developing countries. These groups claimed that Nestle's formula marketing tactics in Africa had led to 1 million infant deaths (from mixing powered formula with contaminated water, or feeding infants diluted formula because of the expense). The success of these small groups in challenging the corporate marketing of formula led to increasing consensus that breastfeeding was better than bottlefeeding. Soon, the medical establishment was embracing breastfeeding, based on scientific studies that confirmed the benefits La Leche League and other feminist health groups had been talking about for years. In 1978, the American Academy of Pediatricians (AAP) recommended breastfeeding over formula, marking the beginning of the shift in mainstream medical advice to mothers. Since then, scientific evidence and the medical establishment have continued to reaffirm the benefits of breastmilk.

Trends over the last 40 years gathered from a survey of mothers show how experts' recommendations and public discussions about breastfeeding have influenced breastfeeding rates. The graph above shows the sharp increase in

breastfeeding in the 1970s. In the 1980s, there is a slight decrease and plateau in breastfeeding initiation rates, and then, in the 1990s, the rate steadily rises to nearly 70 percent. The rates of breastfeeding until six months of age follow a very similar pattern, although overall the rates are quite lower than breastfeeding initiation; currently, only about one-third of mothers report breastfeeding at six months. This recent rise in breastfeeding rates can be explained, at least in part, by the ideology of intensive mothering.

Breastfeeding as Intensive Mothering

Childrearing advice books, pediatricians, parenting magazines, and even formula companies themselves now universally recommend breastmilk over formula. The consensus that "breast is best" is embedded in cultural ideals of motherhood.

In her book *The Cultural Contradictions of Motherhood*, sociologist Sharon Hays identifies an ideology of intensive mothering and describes how it's at work in the United States: Mothers—not fathers—serve as the primary caregivers of children; mothering practices are time-intensive, expensive, supported by expert advice, child-centered, and emotionally absorbing; and children are viewed as priceless, and the work that must be done to raise them can't be compared to paid work because it's infinitely more important.

The ideology of intensive mothering helps explain why we hear so much playground chatter and read so many magazine articles about getting children into the "best" school, the idea that natural childbirth is better than one assisted by medication or other medical interventions, and the recent discussion of "opt-out" mothers who leave high-powered jobs to stay home with their children. Hays contends the strength of the intensive mothering ideology is the result of an "ambivalence about a society based solely on the competitive pursuit of self-interest."

This may be one reason, for example, journalist Judith Warner, in her book *Perfect Madness: Motherhood in the Age of Anxiety*, felt such a difference when she was mothering in France compared to when she returned with her children to the United States. In France the state offers practical support to mothers, including subsidized childcare, universal healthcare, and excellent public education beginning at age 3. Furthermore, Warner explained that, as a new mother there, she found herself in the middle of an extensive and sympathetic support network that attended to her needs as a mother as much as they attended to the needs of her child. "It was a bad thing [for mothers] to go it alone," she wrote. In contrast, upon her return to the United States Warner felt isolated and anxious. She linked this directly to what she called the "American culture of rugged individualism." Mothers in the United States were under extraordinary pressure to be a "good mother"—otherwise, who else would protect their child from an individualistic, self-interested society?

The cultural imperative to breastfeed is part of the ideology of intensive mothering—it requires the mother be the central caregiver, because only she produces milk; breastfeeding is in line with expert advice and takes a great deal of time and commitment; and finally, the act of breastfeeding is a way to demonstrate that the child is priceless, and that whatever the cost, be it a loss of productivity at work or staying at home, children come first.

Since Hays links the intensive motherhood ideology to American individualistic sensibilities, it would seem to suggest that breastfeeding rates in the United States would be higher than other countries. To return to the example of France, only 50 percent of French mothers breastfeed their newborns, compared to 75 percent of American mothers. However, upon closer examination of statistics compiled by Le Leche League International, U.S. breastfeeding rates lag far behind many other countries, including European countries other than France (Germany, Italy, Spain, and the Scandinavian countries all have breastfeeding initiation rates around 90 percent). Most countries in Asia, Africa, and South America report breastfeeding initiation rates higher than the United States, as do New Zealand and Australia.

Clearly the cultural imperative to breastfeed in the United States has met some resistance. This resistance may be reflected in public debates about breastfeeding, which quickly dissolve into mud-slinging, judgmental arguments that pit mothers against mothers. Not "the mommy wars" in the traditional sense—working moms versus stay-at-home moms—but instead bottlefeeding versus breastfeeding moms.

Breastfeeding mothers, and a subset of those mothers who are deeply committed to breastfeeding promotion (sometimes referred to as "lactivists"), point to a continuing undercurrent of resistance to breastfeeding. Despite the fact that scientists and doctors recommend breastfeeding, and that these recommendations have been disseminated through a public health ad campaign and parenting magazines, breastfeeding remains controversial. While society wants mothers to breastfeed to protect and promote infant health, it wants them to do so behind closed doors. Indeed mothers are often asked to cover themselves while nursing in restaurants.

For example, in 2007 a nursing mother was asked by an Applebee's employee to cover herself while nursing or leave the restaurant. After repeated calls by enraged nursing mothers to the corporate headquarters, executives there insisted it was reasonable to ask the nursing mother to leave, despite a state law that extended mothers the right to nurse in public spaces. This incident resulted in "nurse-ins" at Applebee's locations all over the United States in protest. The social networking site Facebook found itself in a similar firestorm of controversy at the beginning of 2009 when it removed photos of breastfeeding mothers because they violated the site's decency standards. The resistance to nursing-in-public arises from the link between breasts and sexuality, including the idea that breasts are indecent.

Note that these public debates about breastfeeding and mothering in the United States emerge primarily from discussions by and about middle class mothers. The ideal of intensive mothering is much easier for these women to achieve. Even so, studies have explored the extensive labor middle class mothers must engage in just to meet current breastfeeding recommendations.

Sociologist Orit Avishai demonstrates through interviews of white, middle-class mothers that they treat breastfeeding not as a natural, pleasurable, connective act with their infant but instead as a disembodied project to be researched and managed. They take classes about breastfeeding, have home visits from lactation consultants postpartum, and view their bodies as feeding machines. When returning to work, they set up elaborate systems to pump breastmilk and store it. These middle-class women were accustomed to setting goals and achieving them—so when they decided to breastfeed for the one year the AAP recommends, they set out to do just that despite the physical and mental drawbacks. Although it's easier for middle-class mothers to meet the recommended breastfeeding standards than it is for less privileged mothers, they're at the same time controlled by a culture that equates good mothering with breastfeeding.

Variations in Class and Culture

In *At the Breast*, sociologist Linda Blum examined how mothers of different classes aspired to or rejected the intensive mothering ideology and mainstream cultural imperative to breastfeed. Through interviews with white middle-class mothers who were members of La Leche League, as well as with a sample of both white and black working-class mothers, Blum's study was the first (and is also the most extensive) to expose how the meaning of breastfeeding varies by class and race.

Her interviews with the La Leche mothers revealed the organization's emphasis on an intimate, relational bond between mother and child created through breastfeeding. They rejected medical, scheduled, and mechanized infant feeding and emphasized how important it is for mothers to read their babies' cues and be near them all the time. As such, a mother's care is seen as irreplaceable. One mother told Blum, "Only a mother can give what a child needs, nobody else can, not even a father. A father can give almost as close, but only a mother can give what they really need." Some of these mothers were also very critical of working mothers. "I'm pretty negative to people who just want to dump their kids off and go to work eight hours a day," one said. Ultimately, Blum contends La Leche League is a self-help group largely created by and for white, middle-class women.

In contrast, interviews with white working-class mothers revealed they understood the health benefits of breastfeeding and embraced the ideal of intensive mothering, but that they often didn't breastfeed because of constraints with jobs, lack of social support, inadequate nutrition, and limited access to medical advice. Working-class mothers were less likely to have jobs that allowed time and privacy to pump breastmilk and were less likely to have access to (paid or unpaid) maternity leave. Some felt it was embarrassing or restrictive. Yet, they still aspired to the middle class ideal of intensive mothering, so they were left feeling guilty and inadequate. Many reported feeling like their bodies had failed them. One mother, for example, said, "At first [breastfeeding] was great. I can't explain the feeling, but at first it was really great. [But then,] I felt . . . useless, if I couldn't nurse my baby, I was a flop as a mother."

Ethnic and racial differences were even more unique and revealing. Black working-class mothers in Blum's study were similar to white working-class mothers in understanding the health benefits of breastmilk. However, their discussions about not breastfeeding were, for the most part,

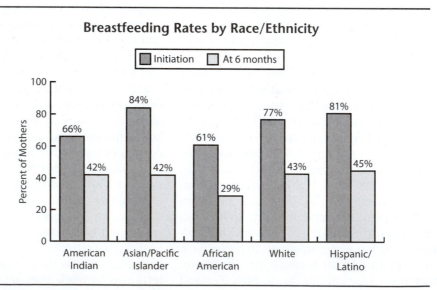

Breastfeeding Rates by Race/Ethnicity

Source: National Immunization Survey, CDC 2005

remarkably free of guilt. In short, black mothers rejected the dominant cultural ideal of intensive mothering, and had a more broadly construed definition of what it meant to be a good mother. Many African American women, for example, talked about the importance of involving older children and extended family in caring for the child, and insisted one way this could be accomplished was through bottlefeeding. Some black mothers reacted negatively to breastfeeding because they believed it reinforced long-standing racist stereotypes about the black female body as threatening or even animalistic. By rejecting medical advice about breastfeeding, black mothers asserted some control over their own bodies. "The doctors said that breastmilk was the best, but I told them I didn't want to. They tried to talk me into it, but they couldn't," one interviewee told Blum.

These cultural differences in the meaning of breast-feeding to white and African American mothers are reflected in breastfeeding initiation statistics. White, Asian, and Hispanic mothers have roughly similar rates of breastfeeding initiation, while African American and American Indian mothers have lower rates (above).

The importance of cultural differences and how they play out in breastfeeding practices has also been explored in studies of immigration. A study by public policy professor Christina Gibson-Davis and Jeanne Brooks-Gunn, co-director of the Columbia University Institute on Child and Family Policy, found that breastfeeding rates among Hispanics were related to the mother's country of birth. If the mother was born outside the United States and immigrated, she was more likely to breastfeed. Furthermore, for each additional year the mother had lived in the United States, her odds of breastfeeding decreased by 4 percent. These patterns suggest that the more acculturated the mother is in U.S. society, the less likely she is to breastfeed.

However, another study examining Vietnamese immigrant mothers in Quebec contradicts that model. Medical anthropologist Danielle Groleau and colleagues interviewed 19 Vietnamese mothers who immigrated to Quebec. They argue that geography and culture combine to create a context in which mothers decide not to breastfeed. In the Vietnamese traditional understanding of post-partum medicine and breastfeeding, women are said to suffer from excessive cold, which leads to fatigue, and the production of breastmilk that isn't fresh. In Vietnam, new mothers are cared for by extended family for several months post-partum in order to balance their health and allow them to produce "fresh" breastmilk. However, Vietnamese immigrants in Quebec had low rates of breastfeeding primarily because the lack of social support

and caregiving that would have been offered in Vietnam wasn't available in Canada. They saw bottlefeeding as optimal for their babies because their breastmilk wasn't fresh. These mothers weren't adopting the dominant Canadian cultural model and had retained their own cultural ideals about breastfeeding.

Problematic Science

The understanding that "breast is best" is based on scientific studies linking breastfeeding to a variety of health benefits. The breastfeeding recommendations issued by AAP, the World Health Organization, and other public health organizations state that breastfeeding increases IQ and lowers the likelihood of ear infections, diabetes, respiratory and gastrointestinal illnesses, and obesity. These benefits are transmitted to the public as unambiguous scientific findings. But upon closer examination, the science behind these claims is problematic.

Political scientist Joan Wolf, in the *Journal of Health Politics, Policy, and Law*, argues that the benefits of breast-feeding have been vastly overstated. Perhaps the largest problem is that it's impossible to conduct a controlled experiment—by asking some mothers to breastfeed and others to formula-feed—so all studies are observational. In other words, researchers have to tease out the characteristics of those who decide to breastfeed from the benefits of breastmilk itself. Mothers who choose to breastfeed may also promote a host of other health-protective and IQ-promoting behaviors in their children that go unmeasured in observational studies. The problem becomes even more pronounced when trying to examine the long-term health benefits of breastfeeding because there are even more potential unmeasured factors between infancy and adolescence that contribute to overall health.

Some researchers have attempted to control for potential unmeasured factors by studying the health of siblings who were fed differently as infants. Although these studies can't discern why the mother breastfed one child but not the other, they do control for parenting factors that go unmeasured in other studies. For example, a recent sibling study by economists Eirik Evenhouse and Siobhan Reilly, based on data from the National Longitudinal Study of Adolescent Health, suggests correlations between breast-feeding and a variety health benefits, including diabetes, asthma, allergies, and obesity, disappear when studying siblings within families. Only one outcome remains significant—that the breastfed sibling had a slightly higher IQ score (siblings who were ever breastfed scored 1.68 percentile points higher than siblings who were never breastfed).

Most of these studies can be critiqued for exaggerating the importance of small and weak associations; however, although these correlations are weak, they are consistently found. Furthermore, despite weak correlations, biomedical researchers have in some cases been able to identify the biological mechanisms that offer infants health protection. For example, one very consistent finding seems to be that breastmilk lowers the incidence, length, and severity of gastrointestinal illness because gut-protective antibodies, including IgA and lactoferrin, are passed from mother to child through breastmilk.

To be sure, not all biomedical research on breast milk identifies beneficial biological mechanisms. Medical researchers have found breastmilk to contain HIV, alcohol, drugs, and environmental toxins. How these findings are used by public health officials varies. To take the case of HIV, in parts of the world with high rates of infection, public health officials debate whether to recommend breastfeeding or not. Even if the mother is HIV positive, some argue the infant may gain other protective health benefits from breastmilk, especially in resource-poor countries plagued by inadequate water supply, limited refrigeration, and poor sanitary conditions. In the United States, however, mothers are now routinely advised to bottlefeed if they have HIV. Mothers in the United States are also advised to stop nursing if, for medical reasons, they have to take medication that passes through breastmilk and may be harmful to the baby. Nevertheless, the overwhelming public health message continues to be "breast is best."

Breastfeeding for Public Health

The "Babies Were Born to be Breastfed" public health ad campaign was designed to educate the public about the benefits of breastfeeding and the risks of not doing so. The campaign hoped to achieve goals established by the Department of Health and Human Services "Blueprint for Action on Breastfeeding"—75 percent of mothers initiating

breastfeeding and 50 percent breastfeeding their babies until five months by 2010.

But the campaign, along with doctors' advice and parenting publications, treat the decision to breastfeed as an individual choice without attending to the social and cultural situations in which this choice is made. The decision to breastfeed is shaped by a variety of social and cultural factors, including doctor-patient interaction, social support networks, labor force participation, child care arrangements, race and ethnicity, class, income, and education. Treating breastfeeding and other parenting practices as individual, decontextualized choices holds mothers solely responsible for their children's health.

In an analysis of discussions about mothering, bioethics professor Rebecca Kukla argues that we hold mothers accountable for all kinds of childhood health problems, including obesity, malnutrition, birth defects, and behavioral disorders. The fact that many of these health problems are disproportionately overrepresented among the lower class further demonizes poor, working-class mothers. Furthermore, by focusing on mothers' individual responsibility for child health and well-being, we aren't attending to other, more egregious societal issues that negatively affect children, such as pollution or lack of adequate health care.

Scientific research on infant health is incredibly important. However, as these findings are reported to the public, shaped into recommendations, and developed into public policy, it's important to view them with a critical eye. We need to consider the unintended consequences of breastfeeding promotion and other recommended parenting practices. These recommendations and policy based upon this science may inspire stress and guilt in mothers, especially poor and non-white mothers, when they don't measure up.

JULIE E. ARTIS is a faculty member in the sociology department at DePaul University. She studies motherhood, family, and law.

EXPLORING THE ISSUE

Is Breastfeeding Inevitably Best for Healthy Development?

Critical Thinking and Reflection

1. What research findings offer the most compelling support for the developmental importance of breastfeeding? What can researchers do to deal with the challenges of studying breastfeeding when those who choose to breastfeed often comprise distinct demographic groups?
2. Breastfeeding is one of several issues related to lifespan development that depends upon a contrast between doing what is "natural" and relying on "artificial" technology. What are the contexts in which "natural" ways of facilitating healthy infant development are best, and what are the ways that modern advances such as nutritious infant formula can have distinct advantages?
3. The U.S. Surgeon General notes that "a mother should not be made to feel guilty if she cannot or chooses not to breastfeed," but often that is easier said than felt. What are ways to promote breastfeeding when possible without implicitly criticizing those who do not or cannot breastfeed?
4. Artis critiques the ideology of "intensive mothering," but is it necessarily bad? What are the potential advantages and disadvantages of intensive mothering?

Is There Common Ground?

What would happen if we replaced the slogan "breast is best" with something like "breast is pretty good if there are no mitigating circumstances to prevent it"? Certainly not as catchy, but perhaps something the U.S. Surgeon General and Julie E. Artis could agree upon. In fact, both would likely agree that public messages about breastfeeding, whether from infant formula marketers or the La Leche League, help shape the decisions mothers make. That agreement also means infant development is shaped as much by the meanings we attach to breastfeeding as by the actual breastmilk consumed. In fact, no one here is arguing that the actual act of an infant consuming breastmilk is a bad thing; the difference comes in conveying its relative value in a fair way that does not negatively stigmatize mothers.

There may be ways to promote breastfeeding without implicitly criticizing those who do not or cannot breastfeed. Many health experts now incorporate motivational interviewing in their efforts to change health behaviors. Motivational interviewing refers to a counseling approach that works to facilitate and engage intrinsic motivation within the individual to change behavior. There are times, however, when negative and uncomfortable feelings can motivate change. When there is a mismatch between thoughts and behavior, individuals may experience cognitive dissonance, which can be highly motivating. In the case of breastfeeding, is stigma an inevitable consequence of an honest effort to promote healthy development? And, might that stigma, encourage change for some individuals?

Create Central

www.mhhe.com/createcentral

Additional Resources

Adamkin, D. H., & Radmacher, P. G. (2014). Donor human milk: No longer a place for formula in the neonatal intensive care unit?. *Current Pediatrics Reports*, 2(4), 276–283.

Kornides, M., & Kitsantas, P. (2013). Evaluation of breastfeeding promotion, support, and knowledge of benefits on breastfeeding outcomes. *Journal of Child Health Care*.

Li, R., Scanlon, K. S., May, A., Rose, C., & Birch, L. (2014). Bottle-feeding practices during early infancy and eating behaviors at 6 years of age. *Pediatrics*, 134(Supplement 1), S70–S77.

Llewellyn, K., Campus, R., & Chester, C. H. (2013). Breastfeeding benefits for mother and infant: A literature review. *New Scholar: The Journal for Undergraduates in Health and Social Care*, 16.

Wilson, C., & de Lange, C. (2014). Some breastfeeding benefits questioned by US study. *New Scientist*, 221(2959), 11.

Internet References . . .

Center on the Developing Child

http://developingchild.harvard.edu

La Leche League International

www.llli.org

The United Nations Children's Fund (UNICEF)

www.childinfo.org

Selected, Edited, and with Issue Framing Material by:
Allison A. Buskirk-Cohen, *Delaware Valley University*

ISSUE

Is Co-sleeping Safe for Baby?

YES: Wendy Middlemiss, from "Bringing the Parent Back into Decisions about Nighttime Care," *Clinical Lactation* (2013)

NO: Patricia G. Schnitzer, Theresa M. Covington, and Heather K. Dykstra, from "Sudden Unexpected Infant Deaths: Sleep Environment and Circumstances," *American Journal of Public Health* (2012)

Learning Outcomes

After reading this issue, you will be able to:

- Understand that parents face a barrage of decisions related to the safety and well-being of their infants.
- Realize that there are a number of factors that may influence how parents make decisions about infants' sleep.
- Know the typical locations for infant sleep include cribs, bassinettes, adult beds, sofas, and chairs.
- Recognize that sudden infant death syndrome (SIDS) continues to be a concern for parents and health care providers.
- Explain that while experts agree on the importance of SIDS prevention, they disagree on how to best communicate best sleep practices.

ISSUE SUMMARY

YES: Educational psychologist Wendy Middlemiss advocates that health care providers discuss options of nighttime care with parents, rather than providing specific advice that may conflict with parents' beliefs and preferences. Furthermore, she discusses ways for health care providers to address infant safety and health that best match the family unit.

NO: Patricia Schnitzer and colleagues analyzed data from sleep-related sudden unexpected infant deaths. They found that 70 percent of infants were not sleeping in a crib or on their back when found; many were sharing a sleep surface and/or sleeping with an adult. These findings stress the importance of infant sleep environment.

Sudden infant death syndrome (SIDS) is a condition in which an infant dies suddenly, usually during the night, without an identified cause. SIDS is the primary cause of death for infants under age one in industrialized nations. It is associated with early physical problems, including low birth weight, weak muscle tone, respiratory issues, and an irregular heartbeat. Some researchers believe that SIDS may be caused by problems with brain functioning that result in infants being unable to change their position if their breathing is hindered by clothing, bedding, or other materials. Parental factors like cigarette smoking and drug abuse also have been linked with SIDS. With all these associated risks in mind, caregivers have been encouraged to place infants on their backs to sleep, and to eliminate bedding and clothing that might interfere with infants' breathing.

Numerous professional organizations have come together in efforts to reduce SIDS. The National Institute of Child Health and Human Development partnered with the American Academy of Pediatrics, the Maternal and Child Health Bureau of the Health Resources and Services

Administration, the SIDS Alliance (now First Candle), and the Association of SIDS and Infant Mortality Programs in 1994 to launch the Back to Sleep campaign. The Back to Sleep campaign educated parents and caregivers about ways to reduce the risk of SIDS, focusing mostly on infants' sleep position. In the years that followed, the Back to Sleep campaign provided outreach efforts to different communities, with specific attention to culturally responsive training.

Around the same time that Back to Sleep was being developed, the Health Child Care America (HCCA) campaign began. The American Academy of Pediatrics along with over 100 other health and care child agencies launched the HCCA campaign in 1995. Now, the HCCA Child Care and Health Partnership marks a collaboration between health professionals and child care providers to improve the education, health, and safety of children in out-of-home child care. Their goals included increasing access to preventive health services, and improving safe physical environments. They also aimed to increase pediatrician participation and effectiveness in providing high-quality care.

In 2003, the American Academy of Pediatrics partnered with various organizations to bring together two related campaigns: The Back to Sleep Campaign and the Health Child Care America (HCCA) Campaign. The resulting Health Child Care America Back to Sleep campaign promotes safe sleep recommendations to child care providers. In 2012, the Back to Sleep campaign was expanded and renamed Safe to Sleep. Safe to Sleep continues to focus on safe sleep environments and back sleeping, but also incorporates research-based information on issues of safe infant sleep.

The Health Child Care American Back to Sleep campaign has four main objectives, all of which incorporate earlier goals set by the separate campaigns. First, it aims to promote the Back to Sleep message in child care programs. Second, it raises awareness and advocates to change practices in child care settings. Third, it disseminates information on national child care recommendations and standards related to SIDS risk reduction. Finally, it supports states to enhance existing and establish new child care regulations. Research has shown that countries with these types of public health campaigns have seen dramatic decreases in SIDS rates and an increase in infant back sleeping.

However, there are parents and other caregivers who do not follow these recommendations and guidelines for safe infant sleep. There are a multitude of reasons individuals do not adhere to these practices. Certainly, a lack of awareness may contribute. But what other factors might

play a role? For some infants, back sleeping may not be a comfortable position. Parents and other caregivers often find that infants who go to sleep on their stomachs have an easier time falling asleep and stay asleep for longer periods of time. Cultural beliefs and practices might impact sleep practices as well, with certain traditions being passed down from one generation to another.

In addition to making decisions about *how* infants sleep, caregivers also must consider *where* they sleep. Again, according to all of the aforementioned campaigns, infants should be placed in cribs or bassinets. However, many parents and caregivers choose to share a bed with the infant, which is referred to as "co-sleeping." Caregivers might choose to share a bed with their infant for emotional and practical reasons. Other movements in parenting, such as attachment parenting, emphasize the importance of having infants as close physical proximity to promote bonding. Breastfeeding advocates stress the importance of having the infant close for ease of feeding. Finally, some people do not believe the government should tell parents how to raise their children, especially when the research on preventing SIDS is still inconclusive.

With all of these conflicting messages and opinion, parents and caregivers often wonder if co-sleeping is safe. In the YES selection, Wendy Middlemiss argues that the best way to promote safe infant sleep is to discuss options with parents, rather than provide an authoritarian command of how and where infants should sleep. Middlemiss believes that one reason parents might ignore recommendations from the medical community is because the messages from these campaigns often conflicts with parents' beliefs and preferences. Instead, Middlemiss stresses the importance of honoring each family and responding in a culturally sensitive way. In this article, she discusses ways for health care providers to address infant safety and health that best match each family.

However, in the NO selection, Patricia Schnitzer and her colleagues claim that not all sleep environments should be accepted, regardless of individual preferences. In their study, Schnitzer and colleagues analyzed data from sleep-related sudden unexpected infant deaths. In the majority of these cases, infants were not sleeping in places recommended by the medical community, like bassinets or cribs. Their article stresses the strong association between sleep location and SIDS. While they acknowledge that there is no definitive cause for SIDS, these researchers believe prevention is more important than etiology. With the results of this study, Schnitzer and colleagues emphasize that efforts must be focused on changing parent and other caregiver behaviors to facilitate safe sleeping for all infants.

YES

Wendy Middlemiss

Bringing the Parent Back into Decisions about Nighttime Care

What Is the Allure of Reducing Nightwaking?

Healthcare providers often make specific recommendations about nighttime care that focus on reducing nightwakings, creating solitary sleep settings for infants, and limiting parents' contact with infants during their transitions to sleep. These recommendations for nighttime infant care reflect many common components of "best practice" recommendations (Morgenthaler et al., 2006) and American Academy of Pediatrics policy recommendations (American Academy of Pediatrics, 2000; 2011). However, recommendations can sometimes limit conversation about developmentally appropriate sleep routines, infant safety, and flexibility in parent choices.

Of importance then, in supporting parents in their early care decisions, is to find a balance between the essential aspects of best-practice and policy recommendations and parents' role in the decision making regarding care. With this, lactation consultants can help parents create sleep routines that are safe, incorporate best practice approaches, and fit the family's childrearing preferences. Finding this balance can be very important when discussing issues such as nighttime wakings and infants' ability to settle to sleep without parents' assistance or presence. In this article, support for different sleep approaches is examined—with an eye toward facilitating discussions between lactation consultants and parents.

Benefit or Risk?

Helping infants learn to sleep through the night without parents' help or attention is a compelling sleep goal. Controlled crying is one way that parents can achieve this end. Some healthcare providers like sleep-training approaches because they can be both simple to discuss, and *successful*, can result in fewer nightwakings requiring parent attention, and have outcomes that are easy to quantify.

Unfortunately, this successful approach does not take into account breastfeeding, parental responsiveness, normal fluctuations in infant sleep patterns at different ages, infant emotional regulation, maturity of infant autonomic functioning, infant settling and safety, or the parents' cultural preferences.

With this approach, infants can be "trained" to settle to sleep, and wake and resettle, without parental assistance through behavioral sleep interventions. Parents can be encouraged to focus on the goal of sleep consolidation. But is this an appropriate goal?

Certainly nightwakings, particularly in the context of helping infants settle to sleep, can be challenging for new parents. When infants wake, parents do too. This can influence parents' quality of sleep and their parenting efforts (McDaniel & Teti, 2013). Reducing nightwakings, then, benefits parents by increasing the duration of both their sleep and their infants' sleep. Advocates of sleep training believe that the benefits of their approach clearly outweigh any potential costs (Price et al., 2012).

As noted in this issue, however, the costs are far from negligible (see Miller & Commons, this issue). Infants *can* learn to settle themselves to sleep without parental assistance using behavioral-sleep interventions. However, even though infants stop crying for parents' attention, research has shown that infants continue to experience high levels of physiological distress (Middlemiss et al., 2012). What this means is that infants *appear* to be able to settle to sleep without distress—which is very relieving for parents if their infants had been crying at nighttime. But, infants are still experiencing distress even though they are no longer signaling that distress through crying. Considering that crying is an essential way for infants to communicate, the fact that they are no longer doing so is concerning.

This disconnect between infants' physiological experience of stress and their behavioral expression of this distress through crying is only one concern with behavioral approaches to nighttime care. There are other consequences when mothers are told to not respond to their babies' cries in order to eliminate nightwaking. Non-responsive parenting may encourage mothers to establish routines that interfere with breastfeeding, and that do not support infants' biological and physiological development. Taken together as a whole, the cry-it-out approach gives mothers an inflexible set of baby-care rules that do not accommodate the normal fluctuations in breastfeeding, nightwakings, and infant growth.

Parents Become Less Comfortable Providing Infant Care

Thus, it is important to create discussions with parents that neither begin nor end with considerations of night-wakings. Childrearing is complicated, and there are many factors that contribute to its complexity. Mothers differ in their childcare preferences and the ease with which they transition to the role of caregiver. In their recent study, Countermine and Teti (2010) examined a number of parenting factors, such as nighttime infant care, nightwakings, depression, and spousal agreement regarding infant care. They concluded that:

> The "best" sleep arrangements for infants may prove to be those that both parents are most comfortable with and that promote family harmony (p. 661).

Thus, rather than focusing on nightwakings—which is only one aspect of parenting—healthcare providers should help mothers find approaches that meet babies' needs and increase family well-being. Lactation consultants and other healthcare providers can help parents make informed, comfortable choices about caring for their infants.

Is Comfort with Care That Important?

Recent research on parental adaptation, defined as parental comfort with their abilities as parents, suggests that parents are more effective when they are confident about their parenting skills (Countermine & Teti, 2010). Researchers have found that parents' comfort with providing care is important in many different contexts. In looking specifically at infant nighttime care and adaptation, research indicates that when parents report high levels of stress, they have lower levels of parental self-efficacy (Jones & Prinz, 2005). When the parents are responsive to infants' needs, parental adaptation predicts higher

levels of functioning and adjustment in children over time (Countermine & Teti, 2010). In sum, parents who are well adapted, and have lower levels of parental stress, are more responsive during nighttime care, and report better quality of sleep (Ramos & Youngclarke, 2006). And when mothers are adapted, their babies sleep better too (Countermine & Teti, 2010).

Working with Parents to Develop a Strategy for Nighttime Care

Lactation consultants can help parents construct a system of care that meets their infants' needs, and is appropriate for their care-giving preferences. Parents feel respected when professionals listen to their concerns. When the practices healthcare providers recommend are consistent with parents' values and beliefs, parents are more likely to incorporate these practices into their parenting (Nobile & Drotar, 2003). Rather than simply focus on reducing nightwakings, you can work with parents to come up with strategies that address infants', mothers', and families' needs. You can incorporate their values into the nighttime-care plan, while encouraging parents to know their infants and trust their instincts for care. You can also help them be comfortable with different approaches to care and help them understand that their babies need them at night, and that parents also benefit when they are available to meet their infants' needs. Below are some strategies for parents to help them cope with nighttime care and adapt to parenthood.

Know Your Infant, Trust Your Instincts

One of the first steps is helping parents understand the nature of nighttime care and infants' developing and fluctuating sleep patterns. Sharing this information with parents helps focus on identifying realistic expectations and helping parents understand what is essential to their infants, their caregiving, and their child-rearing goals. With this refocusing of discussions about infant sleep, parents can ask questions about nighttime care choices and related benefits or risks.

For example, do parents want to sleep in the same bed and breastfeed their infant? If they do, then conversations can address the benefits of breastfeeding and infant safe-sleep environments, as well as likely sleep patterns. Do parents want infants to sleep through the night? If so, discussion can include how to help parents address this goal without compromising breastfeeding or infants' natural need for responsiveness and proximity. With this focus, responsiveness and breastfeeding are not considered within the framework of infant nightwakings. Nighttime wakings and crying become a natural and expected part of the sleep routine—one to be discussed, but not to be the central focus.

When parents are comfortable with their care choices, and feel efficacious and well adapted to their role as parents, everyone in the family benefits (Middlemiss, 2010). One benefit is lower likelihood of physiological distress at nighttime (Middlemiss, 2010). Infants receive care that builds their regulatory, social, and physiological systems and reflects their specific developmental needs. Mothers can feel confident that they are meeting their infants' needs, while still tending to their own mental health (Thome & Skulladottirr, 2005), and cooperating with their partners in parenting decisions (McDaniels & Teti, 2013).

Comfort with Adapting Care to Your Infants' Changing Patterns

By refocusing conversations on a diversity of acceptable nighttime-care practices (i.e., not only practices that may reduce nightwakings), parents can become comfortable with adapting their care to their infants' needs. When mothers accept that there are different care choices, they are more likely to be adapted to their care choice. This was demonstrated in a recent study of mothers. Mothers who chose to co-sleep still had higher stress levels when initiating the nighttime care than mothers whose babies slept alone. These findings were due, in part, to higher levels of stress associated with feelings of being criticized for their nighttime care choices (Middlemiss et al., 2009).

The co-sleeping mothers were asked why they were satisfied with their decision to co-sleep, yet still reported high levels of stress. These mothers indicated that they were uncomfortable because they knew that co-sleeping was generally not accepted. Their personal comfort with the routine was compromised by the sense that they were not taking care of their infant the way that they "should," i.e., in a manner that limited parental presence and focused on nightwakings. The mothers discussed, at length, their preferences for shared-sleep routines and the benefits they believed their infants derived from this type of care. Yet because they had heard that solitary sleep was the "best practice," they were uncomfortable with their care choice (Middlemiss et al., 2009).

Panchula (2012) discussed the importance of helping mothers be comfortable with their care routines. She noted that families' cultural framework is an important component of the type of care that the family will receive. In supporting families, it is essential to help them find solutions to problems that fit within the mothers' cultural preferences and their current situation. She emphasized that listening to parents is an important first step to any intervention. With this approach, parents feel comfortable expressing their preferences, and lactation consultants can provide guidance in a manner that resonates with parents' childrearing goals.

Helping parents feel comfortable with their childrearing choices is essential to successfully providing support and usable information (Ball et al., 2013; Cowan, 2012; Moon et al., 2008)—information that supports both continued breastfeeding and infant safety. Lactation consultants can assure parents that nightwaking is often a normal sleep pattern for infants andtoddlers. Infants' sleep varies by how they are fed; whether parents are present while they sleep; and individual variables, such as temperament, prematurity, or well-being. All of these variables influence the nature and quality of infant sleep. In their work, Thome and colleagues (2005) found that sharing information about normal infant sleep can have a positive impact on mothers' mental health.

Flexibility in Your Choices of Care

Mothers who wanted their infants to settle to sleep alone were less stressed when they were flexible with their care routines. In a study of infant sleep location, mothers who had firm beliefs about where babies should sleep were more stressed when they placed their infants in bed than mothers who were more flexible about sleep arrangements. Interestingly, this finding was true for both mothers who preferred that their infants sleep alone and mothers who believed they should be present while their infants slept (Yaure et al., 2011). Mothers in both groups with flexible care routines (i.e., remaining with infants until they had fallen asleep and then placing them down) had lower levels of stress. This was even true for mothers who preferred that their infants have solitary, self-settling routines. This flexibility in routine can be helpful for parents as infants' patterns of sleep fluctuate with developmental changes, illnesses, and other factors. With this flexibility, lactation consultants are better positioned to help parents incorporate continued breastfeeding into their nighttime care choices—a choice that is ultimately of great benefit for both infant and mother.

Maternal flexibility has long-term effects. One of our studies explored the association between mothers' comfort with the sleep routine their five-year-olds had as infants, and their ratings of their children's social competencies. Mothers' comfort with their care practices was related to their children's social competency at age five years. Parental presence vs. self-settling was not (Middlemiss et al., 2002).

Sorting Out the Quandary of Remaining Present with Infants and Nightwakings

When lactation consultants focus on how to best support breastfeeding and mother/infant sleep, they no longer need to focus solely on infant sleep location. This can help support parents in making choices that best fit their family and personal needs, as well as their infants' needs. For example, many parents prefer to be present during infants' nighttime routines, particularly as they transition to sleep (St. James-Roberts, 2007). This preference has been reported even for mothers focused on encouraging infant self-settling (Morgenthaler et al., 2006).

However, sometimes parents feel that they must choose between continued breastfeeding—often inclusive of nightwakings—or helping their infants learn self-settling routines. Self-soothing infants settle without parental assistance and sleep in locations *portrayed to be the most safe*. If healthcare providers do not discuss benefits and risks of various sleep locations, parents may feel that the only two options are bedsharing or letting their babies cry in another room. To facilitate mothers' adaptation to care and comfort with their care choices, healthcare providers must share information regarding different approaches to nighttime care and their benefits for families and infants. Below are some aspects of care that support choices across care routines.

Assurances of Infant Safety across Routines

Many parents prefer to remain with their infants during their transition to sleep, and many prefer to share sleep or bedshare. However, messages regarding the potential risk for infants in shared settings can lead parents to make choices that they do not feel comfortable with. In making their decisions about nighttime care, parents may inadvertently introduce unnecessary risk in the nighttime routines. For example, proximity at night, although associated with more parental awareness of nightwakings, has been linked to an increase in response to infant distress,

reducing infant stress reactivity, thus reducing this risk factor for future psychopathology (Tollenar et al., 2012).

Providing parents with information about safe infant sleep is critical. But such information needs to move beyond scare tactics and be more nuanced about what makes infant sleep healthy. It is important to assure parents that breastfeeding has been shown to reduce the risk of SIDS, particularly when bedsharing (AAP, 2011; McKenna, 2007). Breastfeeding while bedsharing places infants in a safe position from which they are least likely to roll over to an unsafe position. Finally, in a study examining the mother and infant sleep environments found mothers engaged in different methods of protecting infants across different sleep settings (Volpe, Ball, & McKenna, 2013). Thus, discussions of safe infant sleep need to address different sleep practices.

When information about infant safety is not provided increase. Information is not heard as applicable to parents based on their choices for care (Moon et al., 2012). The essentials of infant sleep are not discussed and parents often are left to ignore both the essential components of care protective of infants and the components of care that do not fit within their family system. Because infant safety can be assured across a diversity of sleep settings, sharing information about parents' preferred care routine is essential.

Understanding the Value of Responsiveness and Presence

Part of the quandary regarding nighttime care comes from the general sense that being present during nighttime care harms infants and keeps them from developing healthy sleep routines. Parents are particularly concerned that being present for their infants will lead to more nightwakings and poorer infant sleep. It is important, then, to assure parents that responsiveness is essential and help parents incorporate responsive within their preferred sleep routines. This may be the first step to helping parents establish and maintain breastfeeding across nighttime care.

Perceiving cries as needing attention has been found to be an important factor in mothers' response (Middlemiss et al., 2009). Mothers least likely to perceive infants' cries as needing attention were less likely to attend to infants. This lack of response, however, was associated with infants experiencing higher levels of physiological stress during their transition to sleep in comparison to infants whose mothers perceived their cries as indicating distress.

The value of responsiveness moves beyond that of its developmentally appropriate nature in supporting infants' development. Parents who respond to their infants' cries have higher levels of adaptation to parenting during nighttime care (Teti et al., 2010), and greater parental efficacy in comparison to parents who did not respond to their babies and practiced sleep training and other parental-sleep routines (Countermine & Teti, 2010). When parents ignored their babies' cries as a means of reducing nightwakings, it was problematic for parents and infants (France & Blampied, 2005; Morgenthaler et al., 2006). Not responding to infants' cries also led to higher levels of infant stress (Yaure et al., 2011). Telling parents about the benefits of responsive parenting can help them feel good about their parenting choices and/or help them be flexible in their nighttime parenting approaches.

Summary and Conclusions

Lactation consultants are one of the primary resources for new parents. What does this research on infant-sleep practices mean, then, for practice? Perhaps of greatest import is the message that mothers' comfort with and adaptation to the role of care provider is essential to helping families transition to parenting. By talking to parents about nighttime care practices in general, rather than focusing only on nightwakings, lactation consultants become guides who both share information with parents and gather information from them. In helping mothers establish early-care routines, you can actually support mothers, rather than "supporting" them by focusing on infants sleeping through the night, scheduled feedings, and other means of controlling a routine or schedule. These interventions, even when successful in the short term, may have high costs. You can support mothers by helping them understand the importance of knowing and having a relationship with their infants, and how to balance infant care with providing for their own needs. With a broader focus on normal infant sleep behavior, and realistic expectations for early care, parents can have a clearer understanding, and be more knowledgeable and accepting as they establish healthy and appropriate care routines.

Parents often anticipate that the "terrible twos"—whether terrible or not so bad—will be a time of toddlers proving that they are "able to do it by themselves." Adolescence can be a time of conflict between parents and teens. So it follows that infancy can be a time marked by nightwakings and that responsiveness is important to meeting these care needs. Thus, in working with new parents, it is important to help them understand that there are many times infants will wake, and that there are many options for care.

What may be most helpful is to let parents know that early nighttime care can be a challenging time, when parents are tired and sometimes frustrated or flustered. Discuss with parents what to expect, and how they can meet their babies' needs. This can provide parents with the assurance that they can find "their" best way to parent. The role of the lactation consultant is essential in providing parents with the tools to establish their routines, to meet the changes and challenges, and to be comfortable with how their care will provide a strong foundation for their child's developing emotional well-being, physical well-being, and brain.

References

American Academy of Pediatrics Task Force on Infant Sleep Position and Sudden Infant Death (2000). Changing concepts of sudden infant death syndrome: Implications for infant sleeping environment and sleep position. *Pediatrics, 105,* 650–656.

American Academy of Pediatrics, & Task Force on Sudden Infant Death Syndrome. (2011). Policy Statement: SIDSand other sleep-related deaths: Expansion of recommendations for a safe infant sleeping environment. *Pediatrics, 128*(5), 1030–1039.

Ball, H.L., & Volpe, L. (2013), Sudden Infant Death Syndrome (SIDS) risk reduction and infant sleep location—Moving the discussion forward. *Social Science & Medicine, 79,* 84–91.

Countermine, M.S. & Teti, D.M. (2010). Sleep arrangements and maternal adaptation in infancy. *Infant Mental Health Journal, 31*(6), 647–663. DOI: 10.1002/imhj.20276

Cowan, S. (2012). Creating change: How knowledge translates into action for protecting babies from Sudden Infant Death? *Current Pediatric Reviews, 6,* 86–94.

McDaniel, D. T., & Teti D. M. (2013). Coparenting quality during the first three months after birth: The role of infant sleep quality. *Journal of Family Psychology, 26,* 886–895.

McKenna, J. J., Mosko, S. S., & Richard, C. A. (1997) Bedsharing promotes breastfeeding. *Pediatrics, 100,* 214–219.

Meijer, A. M. (2011). Infant sleep consolidation: New perspectives. *Sleep Medicine Reviews, 15,* 209–210. doi:10.1016/j. smrv.2011.01.004

Middlemiss, W., Granger, D. A., Goldberg, W. A., & Nathans, L. (2012). Asynchrony of mother–infant hypothalamic–pituitary–adrenal axis activity following extinction of infant responses induced during the transition to sleep. *Early Human Development, 88,* 227–232. doi:10.1016/j.earlhumdev.2011.08.010

Middlemiss, W. (2010, August). *Working with families through a process orientation: Focusing on best practices through family strengths.* Invited paper presented at the International Scholar Series at Ewha Woman's University, Seoul, Korea.

Middlemiss, W. (2005). Prevention and intervention: Using resiliency-based multisetting approaches and a process-orientation. *Child and Adolescent Social Work Journal, 22,* 85–103.

Middlemiss, W. (2004a). Infant sleep: A review of normative and problematic sleep and interventions. *Early Child Development and Care, 174*(1), 99–122. doi:10.1080/0300443032000153516

Middlemiss, W. (2004b) Work in progress: Defining problematic infant sleep: Shifting the focus from deviance to difference. *Zero to Three, 24,* 46–51.

Moon, R. Y., Calabrese, T., & Aird, L. (2008). Reducing the risk of Sudden Infant Death Syndrome in child care and changing provider practices: Lessons learned from a demonstration project. *Pediatrics, 122,* 788–798.

Nobile, C., & Drotar, D. (2003). Research on the quality of parent-provider communication in pediatric care: Implications and recommendations. *Journal of Developmental & Behavioral Pediatrics, 24*(4), 279–290.

Panchula, J. (2012). Working with families of different cultures I. Lessons learned. *Clinical Lactation, 3-1,* 13–15.

Price, A. M. H, Wake, M., Ukoumunne, O. C., & Hiscock, H. (2012). Outcomes at six years of age for children with infant sleep problems: Longitudinal community-based study. *Sleep Medicine, 13,* 991–998. doi: 10.1016/j.sleep.2012.04.014

Sadeh, A., Tikotsky, L., Scher, A. (2010). Parenting and infant sleep. *Sleep Medicine Review, 14,* 89–96

St. James-Roberts, I. (2007). Infant crying and sleeping: Helping parents to prevent and manage problems. *Sleep Medicine Clinics, 2*(3), 363–375, DOI: 10.1016/j.jsmc.2007.05.015.

Teti, D. M., & Crosby, B. (2012). Maternal depressive symptoms, dysfunctional cognitions, and infant night waking: The role of maternal nighttime behavior. *Child Development, 83,* 939–953. DOI: 10.1111/j.1467–8624.2012.01760.x

Teti, D. M., Kim, B. -R., Mayer, G., & Countermine, M. (2010). Maternal emotional availability at bedtime predicts infant sleep quality. *Journal of Family Psychology, 24*(3), 307–315. doi: 10.1037/a0019306

Thome, M., & Skulladottir, A. (2005). Evaluating a family-centered intervention of infant sleep problems. *Journal of Advanced Nursing, 50,* 5–11.

Volpe, L. E., Ball, H. L., & McKenna, J. J. (2013). Nighttime parenting strategies and sleep-related risks to infants. *Social Science Medicine, 79,* 92–100.

Yaure, R., Middlemiss, W., & Huey, E. (2011, November). *Infant nighttime care: What should we consider?* Paper presented at the National Council on Family Relations Annual Conference Orlando, FL.

WENDY MIDDLEMISS is a faculty member of educational psychology at the University of North Texas, and is a certified family life educator. She researches the essentials of safe infant sleep.

**Patricia G. Schnitzer, Theresa M. Covington
and Heather K. Dykstra**

 **NO**

Sudden Unexpected Infant Deaths:
Sleep Environment and Circumstances

Each year in the United States, more than 4000 infants without prior known illness or injury die suddenly and unexpectedly.[1] Sudden unexpected infant deaths (SUIDs) may result from a variety of causes, some of which are discovered during autopsies or death investigations (e.g., previously undiagnosed metabolic disorders, homicides). One unifying factor is that, in many cases, the cause of death is not determined.

Consequently, more than half of SUIDs are ultimately classified as resulting from sudden infant death syndrome (SIDS).[2] SIDS is defined as the sudden death of an infant that remains unexplained after thorough investigation, including autopsy, death scene investigation, and a review of the infant's clinical history.[3] Approximately 14% of SUIDs are categorized as accidental suffocation, probably as a result of information obtained during death scene investigations. In the case of nearly 30% of SUIDs, the cause remains undetermined and is listed as such on the death certificate.[2] This may occur when the requirements for a SIDS classification are not met (e.g., no death scene investigation or autopsy is conducted).

Although SIDS remains a leading cause of infant mortality, SIDS mortality rates in the United States declined from 120.3 per 100 000 live births in 1992 to 54.6 per 100 000 in 2004[4]; much of this decline has been attributed to national campaigns introduced in 1992 that promoted supine sleep positions for infants.[5] During this same period, infant mortality rates resulting from suffocation and undetermined causes increased from 3.1 and 19.7 per 100 000 live births to 12.5 and 25.3 per 100 000, respectively.[2]

It has been noted that this decrease in SIDS and coinciding increase in mortality resulting from suffocation and undetermined causes, particularly since 1999, are the result of a "diagnostic shift" in classification of SUIDs.[2,6–8] The etiology of this diagnostic shift is not fully known; however, it is thought to be a consequence of an increase in death scene investigations and the role

Objectives. We sought to describe the characteristics and sleep circumstances of infants who die suddenly and unexpectedly and to examine similaritiesand differences in risk factors among infants whose deaths are classified as resulting from sudden infant death syndrome (SIDS), suffocation, orundetermined causes.

Methods. We used 2005 to 2008 data from 9 US states to assess 3136 sleep-related sudden unexpected infant deaths (SUIDs).

Results. Only 25% of infants were sleeping in a crib or on their back when found; 70% were on a surface not intended for infant sleep (e.g., adult bed).Importantly, 64% of infants were sharing a sleep surface, and almost half of these infants were sleeping with an adult. Infants whose deaths were classified as suffocation or undetermined cause were significantly more likely than were infants whose deaths were classified as SIDS to be found on a surface not intended for in fant sleep and to be sharing that sleep surface.

Conclusions. We identified modifiable sleep environment risk factors in a large proportion of the SUIDs assessed in this study. Our results make an important contribution to the mounting evidence that sleep environment hazards contribute to SUIDs. (Am J Public Health. 2012; 102:1204–1212. doi:10.2105/AJPH.2011. 300613)

of multidisciplinary child death review (CDR) programs in examining and consistently documenting the circumstances of child deaths, as well as more stringent adherence to the definition of SIDS.[2,6,7,9–11]

Recognition of the impact of hazards in the infant sleep environment on SUIDs has been increasing in the past several decades. Most of the etiological research on SUIDs has been conducted on deaths classified as SIDS. A recent review by Mitchell comprehensively summarized risk factors for SIDS, including modifiable risk factors

Source: Schnitzer, P. G., Covington, T. M., & Dykstra, H. K. (2012). Sudden unexpected infant deaths: Sleep environment and circumstances. *American Journal of Public Health*, 102(6), 1204–1212. Reprinted by permission of American Public Health Association.

related to the infant sleep environment such as prone sleep position, infants sharing a sleep surface with others, and the presence of blankets or other soft bedding.[12] Death certificate data have been used in conducting several large national studies of infant suffocation or deaths of undetermined causes.[2,13] Although use of death certificates allows calculation of rates, few data on sleep circumstances are available, even when written information from the cause of death section of the death certificate is analyzed.[2,4]

In a number of small studies, medical examiner records or CDR data from a single urban area or state have been used in assessing SUIDs.[9,14–17] Although these descriptive studies typically provide more detail on the circumstances of the sleep environment, they often involve small sample sizes that do not allow comparisons of characteristics across the 3 categories of SUIDs: SIDS, suffocation, and undetermined cause.

The Web-based National Child Death Review Case Reporting System (NCDR-CRS), developed to facilitate consistent collection and reporting of CDR program data, has been available to states since 2005 through the National Center for Child Death Review (NCCDR).[18] CDR typically involves a review of child deaths conducted by a local (e.g., county) or state-level multidisciplinary team. This reporting system includes important information, such as child and parent characteristics, presence of risk factors, and other pertinent circumstances (e.g., details on sleep circumstances), on all deaths related to the sleep environment.

The comprehensive compilation of relevant risk factors available in the NCDR-CRS presents a unique opportunity to examine the circumstances of SUIDs in the United States. We used these population-based multistate CDR program data to describe the characteristics and sleep circumstances of infants who die suddenly and unexpectedly and to assess similarities and differences in SUID risk factors among infants whose deaths are ultimately classified as resulting from SIDS, suffocation, or undetermined causes.

Methods

We obtained our data from the NCDR-CRS. The development, features, and limitations of this data system have been described in detail elsewhere.[18] Briefly, the NCDR-CRS serves as a Web-based system for the collection, analysis, and reporting of CDR program data. Individual case reports are entered into the system by a CDR team member who attended the death review. Although the system contains more than 1700 data

elements, many (e.g., risk factor details for mechanisms of common injury and natural-cause child deaths) are not pertinent to an analysis of SUIDs (a copy of the report form is available at http://www.childdeathreview.org/reports/CDRCaseReportForm2-1-11009. pdf). We selected covariates on the basis of their applicability to descriptive characteristics of the infant, caregiver, and sleep environment.

As of December 2010, 35 states were enrolled and entering data in the NCDR-CRS.[18] We asked 9 of these states (California, Delaware, Hawaii, Michigan, Nevada, Ohio, Pennsylvania, Tennessee, and Texas) for permission to use their de-identified data in aggregate for our analysis, and all agreed. Most of these states had been using the NCDR-CRS since it was launched in 2005 or began using it in early 2006; consequently, they had considerable experience with the system. As of June 2010, all 9 participating states confirmed that the data we used in our analyses were considered complete.

The study population included infants (defined as children younger than 1 year) who died between January 1, 2005, and December 31, 2008; whose death was identified as occurring while they were sleeping or in a sleeping environment; and whose cause of death, as recorded in the NCDR-CRS, was accidental asphyxia, SIDS, undetermined, or unknown. California, Texas, and Hawaii had not finalized their 2008 data in time for inclusion in this analysis, so only data from 2005 through 2007 were included from these 3 states. We excluded cases in which text narrative in the NCDR-CRS indicated the possibility of inflicted trauma.

A total of 3148 SUIDs met the study inclusion criteria; 12 deaths were excluded because of suspicion of inflicted injuries, resulting in 3136 deaths for analysis. We classified these 3136 SUIDs into 3 categories: SIDS (n = 960; 30.6%), suffocation (939; 29.9%), and undetermined cause (1237; 39.5%). The undetermined cause category included deaths recorded in the NCDR-CRS as cause undetermined and cause unknown.

We generated frequencies and proportions for the 3 SUID categories according to child, caregiver, and sleep environment characteristics. In the case of many NCDR-CRS variables, "unknown" is an option and is useful for distinguishing factors that may have been discussed during the death review but for which review team members did not have information. Missing items denote those for which no response option was marked. When applicable, frequencies and proportions of unknown and missing responses are presented.

We conducted χ^2 analyses to assess whether SUID classifications differed significantly ($\alpha = .05$) for each covariate. One-way analysis of variance was used to assess differences in the mean ages of infants and caregivers across SUID categories. We then conducted multivariate logistic regression analyses. Adjusted odds ratios and 95% confidence intervals were calculated to assess the independent associations of covariates with SUIDs while controlling for other important covariates.

We conducted 2 logistic regression analyses, each with a different dichotomous dependent variable. One analysis compared deaths classified as suffocation with those classified as SIDS, and the other compared deaths with an undetermined cause with those classified as SIDS. SIDS was selected as the reference group in these analyses because of the literature describing the shift in classification of SUIDs from SIDS to suffocation and undetermined cause over the past 15 years. We sought to assess differences in infant, caregiver, and sleep environment characteristics that might contribute to this diagnostic shift.

We selected covariates for inclusion in the final, adjusted multivariate regression models in the same way. Initially, variables with a statistically significant χ^2 value in the descriptive analysis were individually entered into a logistic regression model that included year of death and state as independent variables. Covariates with a significant effect estimate, as evidenced by a 95% confidence interval that excluded 1.0, were selected for inclusion in the final regression model.

Data available in the NCDR-CRS on the position of the infant (e.g., under, between) that was most relevant to the infant's death and the people or objects in the infant sleep environment relevant to this position were included in the descriptive analyses only. The "position relevant to death" variable, which did not have a not applicable option, was coded as unknown or missing for 50% of SUID deaths. The response options for the follow-up variable identifying the objects or persons relevant to the position allowed more than one response for each death. Because of these limitations in coding and response options, no statistical tests were conducted to assess differences across categories of these variables, nor were they assessed for inclusion in the logistic regression models because there was no obvious reference category.

Several of the covariates of interest contained missing values. Because records with missing values are excluded from regression analyses, imputation of missing values generally produces less biased results and is recommended.[19] In preparation for conducting the multivariate analyses, we used multiple imputation to impute missing values.[20] SPSS version 18 (SPSS Inc, Chicago, IL) was used in conducting all of the analyses.

Results

Of the 3136 SUIDs available for analysis, the majority occurred among male infants (57%) and infants younger than 4 months (71%). Forty-four percent of infants were identified as non-Hispanic White, whereas 32% were non-Hispanic Black and 19% were Hispanic. The majority of caregivers were female (83%) and were the infant's biological parent (93%); 41% were younger than 25 years, but information on age was missing for 28% of caregivers. Only 24% of infants were sleeping in a crib or bassinette at the time of death; 47% were in an adult bed, and another 13% were on a couch or chair. Twenty-five percent of infants were on their back, and 35% were on their stomach; position was unknown in 26% of deaths and missing in 5%.

Seventeen percent of infants were noted to have a partially or fully obstructed airway, but this information was missing for 41% of deaths. Sixty-four percent of all SUID victims were sleeping on the same surface as another person or animal when they died, and 49% were further identified as sleeping with an adult. More than 50% of the deaths were referred to a medical examiner, and an autopsy was performed on 94% of the infants included in our analysis. Table 1 presents the frequency distribution and proportion of deaths according to cause of death category and child, caregiver, and other selected characteristics.

When assessed individually, covariates associated with classifications of suffocation and undetermined cause were remarkably similar. Child age and race were associated with both undetermined cause and suffocation, whereas presence of disability or chronic disease was not associated with either classification. None of the caregiver characteristics were individually associated with either suffocation or undetermined cause, but most of the incident characteristics were, with the exception of place of death, referral to a medical examiner (vs a coroner), and whether an autopsy was performed. Unadjusted odds ratios are presented in Table 2.

Table 2 also presents the results of the adjusted multivariate logistic regression models comparing deaths classified as suffocation and undetermined cause with deaths classified as SIDS. The incident characteristics most strongly associated with classification of suffocation deaths were sleep surface and airway obstruction. Deaths of infants put to sleep on a surface not intended for infant sleep (e.g., adult bed, couch) were approximately twice as likely to be classified as resulting from suffocation than as resulting from SIDS. Sleeping with an adult remained significant even after control for sleep surface and position, although the more general classification of sleeping with a person or animal did not. The magnitude of the

Table 1

Child, Caregiver, and Incident Characteristics, by Cause of Death Category: Sudden Unexpected Infant Deaths, 9 US States, 2005–2008

	Sudden Unexpected Infant Death Category				
	Sudden Infant Death Syndrome, No. (%) or Mean	Suffocation, No. (%) or Mean	Undetermined, No. (%) or Mean	Total, No. (%) or Mean	*P*[a]
Total	960 (30.6)	939 (29.9)	1237 (39.5)	3136 (100)	
Child characteristic					
Age at death, mo					<.001
<2	264 (27.5)	331 (35.3)	420 (34.0)	1015 (32.4)	
2–3	409 (42.6)	331 (35.3)	468 (37.8)	1208 (38.5)	
4–5	191 (19.9)	147 (15.7)	216 (17.5)	554 (17.7)	
6–7	71 (7.4)	71 (7.6)	82 (6.6)	224 (7.1)	
≥ 8	25 (2.6)	59 (6.3)	51 (4.1)	135 (4.3)	
Mean age at death, mo	3.3	3.3	3.2	3.3	.51
Gender					.73
Male	555 (57.8)	531 (56.6)	712 (57.6)	1798 (57.3)	
Female	395 (41.1)	406 (43.2)	517 (41.8)	1318 (42.0)	
Missing	10 (1.0)	2 (0.2)	8 (0.6)	20 (0.6)	
Race/ethnicity					<.001
White, non-Hispanic	479 (49.9)	440 (46.9)	451 (36.5)	1370 (43.7)	
Black, non-Hispanic	249 (25.9)	327 (34.8)	414 (33.5)	990 (31.6)	
Hispanic	163 (17.0)	123 (13.1)	294 (23.8)	580 (18.5)	
Other	47 (4.9)	41 (4.4)	66 (5.3)	154 (4.9)	
Missing	22 (2.3)	8 (0.8)	12 (1.0)	42 (1.3)	
Gestational age, wk					.07
≥ 37	491 (51.2)	484 (51.5)	653 (52.8)	1628 (51.9)	
<37	172 (17.9)	145 (15.4)	227 (18.4)	544 (17.4)	
Missing	297 (30.9)	310 (33.0)	357 (28.9)	964 (30.7)	
Disability or chronic illness					<.001
No	624 (65.0)	689 (73.4)	866 (70.0)	2179 (69.5)	
Yes	34 (3.5)	38 (4.0)	78 (6.3)	150 (4.8)	
Missing	302 (31.5)	212 (22.6)	293 (23.7)	807 (25.7)	
Primary caregiver characteristic[b]					
Relationship to deceased					.55
Biological parent	894 (93.1)	872 (92.9)	1164 (94.1)	2930 (93.4)	
Other	31 (3.2)	30 (3.2)	40 (3.2)	101 (3.2)	
Missing	35 (3.7)	37 (3.9)	33 (2.7)	105 (3.4)	
Gender					<.001
Male	121 (12.6)	91 (9.7)	103 (8.3)	315 (10.0)	
Female	768 (80.0)	757 (80.6)	1064 (86.0)	2589 (82.6)	
Missing	71 (7.4)	91 (9.7)	70 (5.7)	232 (7.4)	
Age, y					.001
<20	106 (11.0)	115 (12.3)	204 (16.5)	425 (13.6)	
20–24	264 (27.5)	252 (26.8)	344 (27.8)	860 (27.4)	
25–29	161 (16.8)	166 (17.7)	198 (16.0)	525 (16.7)	
30–35	71 (7.4)	76 (8.1)	114 (9.2)	261 (8.3)	
35–39	43 (4.5)	27 (2.9)	53 (4.3)	123 (3.9)	
≥ 40	16 (1.7)	14 (1.5)	23 (1.9)	53 (1.7)	
Missing	299 (31.1)	289 (30.8)	301 (24.3)	889 (28.4)	
Mean age, y	25.0	24.7	24.6	24.7	.43

Continued

Table 1–Continued

Incident characteristic				
Place of death				<.001
Child's home	706 (73.5)	785 (83.6)	966 (78.1)	2457 (78.4)	
Friend's or relative's home	67 (7.0)	84 (9.0)	125 (10.1)	276 (8.8)	
Other	79 (8.2)	36 (3.8)	90 (7.3)	205 (6.5)	
Missing	108 (11.3)	34 (3.6)	56 (4.5)	198 (6.3)	
Infant sleep surface				<.001
Crib/bassinette	362 (37.7)	129 (13.7)	253 (20.5)	744 (23.7)	
Adult bed	322 (33.5)	486 (51.8)	658 (53.2)	1466 (46.8)	
Couch/chair	78 (8.1)	177 (18.8)	144 (11.6)	399 (12.7)	
Other	104 (10.8)	92 (9.8)	120 (9.7)	316 (10.1)	
Missing	94 (9.8)	55 (5.9)	62 (5.0)	211 (6.7)	
Position when found				<.001
On back	267 (27.8)	156 (16.6)	364 (29.4)	787 (25.1)	
On stomach	325 (33.9)	359 (38.2)	399 (32.3)	1083 (34.5)	
On side	73 (7.6)	85 (9.1)	153 (12.4)	311 (9.9)	
Unknown	258 (26.8)	267 (28.4)	281 (22.7)	806 (25.7)	
Missing	37 (3.9)	72 (7.7)	40 (3.2)	149 (4.8)	
Airway condition[c]				<.001
Unobstructed	314 (32.7)	95 (10.1)	328 (26.5)	737 (23.5)	
Partially obstructed	27 (2.8)	68 (7.2)	115 (9.3)	210 (6.7)	
Fully obstructed	21 (2.2)	204 (21.7)	86 (7.0)	311 (9.9)	
Unknown	181 (18.9)	162 (17.3)	253 (20.5)	596 (19.0)	
Missing	417 (43.4)	410 (43.7)	455 (36.8)	1282 (40.9)	
Infant sleeping with person/animal[d]				.001
No	29 (3.0)	13 (1.4)	29 (2.3)	71 (2.3)	
Yes	472 (49.2)	699 (74.4)	838 (67.7)	2009 (64.1)	
Missing	459 (47.8)	227 (24.2)	370 (29.9)	1056 (33.7)	
Infant sleeping with adult[e]				<.001
No/unknown/missing	662 (69.0)	365 (38.9)	559 (45.2)	1586 (50.6)	
Yes	298 (31.0)	574 (61.1)	678 (54.8)	1550 (49.4)	
Position relevant to death				
On top of[f]	100 (10.4)	67 (7.1)	152 (12.3)	319 (10.2)	
Under/between/tangled	75 (7.8)	277 (29.5)	191 (15.5)	543 (17.3)	
Wedged/pressed/rolled into	54 (5.6)	296 (31.5)	158 (12.8)	508 (16.2)	
Other	85 (8.9)	41 (4.4)	83 (6.7)	209 (6.7)	
Unknown	245 (25.5)	151 (16.1)	326 (26.4)	722 (23.0)	
Missing[g]	401 (41.8)	107 (11.4)	327 (26.4)	835 (26.6)	
Presence of people/objects in infant sleeping place[h]				
Adults	188 (19.6)	403 (42.9)	414 (33.5)	1005 (32.1)	
Children	31 (3.2)	85 (9.1)	104 (8.4)	220 (7.0)	
Soft bedding	225 (23.4)	307 (32.7)	414 (33.5)	946 (30.2)	
Mattress	107 (11.1)	148 (15.8)	129 (10.4)	384 (12.2)	
Couch/chair	43 (4.5)	97 (10.3)	64 (5.2)	204 (6.5)	
Crib rail/wall	7 (0.7)	44 (4.7)	11 (0.9)	62 (2.0)	
Other	59 (6.1)	107 (11.4)	79 (6.4)	245 (7.8)	
None listed	463 (48.2)	113 (12.0)	390 (31.5)	966 (30.8)	

Continued

Table 1–Continued

Authority to whom death was referred					<.001
Medical examiner	485 (50.5)	535 (57.0)	632 (51.1)	1652 (52.7)	
Coroner	335 (34.9)	333 (35.5)	539 (43.6)	1207 (38.5)	
Missing	140 (14.6)	71 (7.6)	66 (5.3)	277 (8.8)	
Autopsy performed					<.001
No	4 (0.4)	11 (1.2)	8 (0.6)	23 (0.7)	
Yes	850 (88.5)	901 (96.0)	1201 (97.1)	2952 (94.1)	
Missing	106 (11.0)	27 (2.9)	28 (2.3)	161 (5.1)	
Year of death					<.001
2005	286 (29.8)	213 (22.7)	301 (24.3)	800 (25.5)	
2006	262 (27.3)	238 (25.3)	317 (25.6)	817 (26.1)	
2007	299 (31.1)	301 (32.1)	432 (34.9)	1032 (32.9)	
2008	113 (11.8)	187 (19.9)	187 (15.1)	487 (15.5)	

Note. Percentages may not add to 100% because of rounding.

[a] P values were determined from a χ^2 test for all categorical variables and from a 1-way analysis of variance for continuous variables.

[b] The National Child Death Review Case Reporting System (NCDR-CRS) allows recording data on 2 primary caregivers. The data reported in this tables, summarize the information reported for primary caregiver 1. Nocaregiver 2 data were entered for 39% of the deaths analyzed. Among those with care giver 2 data, 91% of the caregivers were identified as biological parents, and 82% were male.

[c] Priorto January 1, 2008, documenting that the infant's face was "unobstructed" was the only option related to airway condition. Data entered with this option were placed in the"unobstructed by person or object" category when more specific airway questions were added on January 1, 2008.

[d] The response options for this question were changed with the release of version 2.1 of the data base in January 2010. Prior to that, only "yes" responses were recorded; there was not an option for "no" or "unknown." Some states may have used the later form in completing reviews of 2005–2008 deaths.

[e] This variable is completed only if there sponseto "infant sleeping with person/animal" is checked yes. It is not possible to distinguish "no" responses from missing data for this variable.

[f] This response option was added to the NCDR-CRS on January1, 2008.

[g] This may reflect circumstances for which the question on position was not applicable.

[h] Because more than one item could be recorded, totals are greater than 100%.

association between child race and suffocation death was reduced after controlling for all significant sleep environment characteristics.

Regression results for classification of undetermined cause deaths were similar but with generally lower effect estimates than suffocation deaths, except that child race remained significantly elevated for both Hispanic and non-Hispanic Black infants relative to White infants. After controlling for child age, race, and other sleep environment characteristics, infant sleep position and sleeping with a person or animal were not associated with classification of undetermined cause deaths. Similar to the results for suffocation deaths, sleeping with an adult remained significantly associated with classification of undetermined cause deaths relative to SIDS deaths.

Discussion

Our descriptive analysis of population-based multistate CDR program data showed that only one quarter of SUID victims were sleeping in a crib or on their back when found;

70% of infants were on a surface not intended for infant sleep, and 64% with documentation of their position when found were on their stomach or side. Importantly, 64% of SUID victims in our study were sharing a sleep surface, and 49% of these infants were sleeping with an adult. Infants whose deaths were classified as resulting from suffocation or undetermined causes were significantly more likely than were those whose deaths were classified as resulting from SIDS to be found in an adult bed, a couch or chair, or another surface not intended for infant sleep; they were also significantly more likely to be sharing that sleep surface with an adult.

Our findings are largely consistent with those of other studies that have described the sleep environment and other characteristics of SUIDs documented in CDR or medical examiner data from single (urban or state) jurisdictions.[9,14–17] Although these studies are not all directly comparable to ours because they report details on only suffocation deaths,[15] omit SIDS[16] or undetermined cause deaths,[17] or do not report findings by final classification of death,[14] the key findings are consistent and indicate that a large proportion of SUIDs involve hazards in the sleep environment such as non-supine sleep position, use of surfaces not intended for infant sleep, and the presence of people (bed sharing) or objects (bedding) in the sleep environment.

Our findings are also consistent with well-documented SIDS risk factors, although it is important to note that most studies identifying sleep risk factors for SIDS were conducted before the diagnostic shift in classifying SUIDs as suffocation and undetermined cause rather than SIDS.[12] In fact, it has been suggested that stricter adherence to the definition of SIDS might explain this diagnostic shift.[4] To be classified as SIDS, the sudden death of an infant must remain unexplained even after an autopsy, a thorough death scene investigation, and a review of the infant's clinical and medical history.[3]

In one example of strict adherence to the SIDS definition, the New York City Office of the Chief Medical Examiner classifies SUIDs according to a protocol that prohibits classifying a death as SIDS if any environmental events or sleep-related risk factors were present at the time of death.[16] Deaths are classified as suffocation when sufficient evidence of suffocation is present during the death scene investigation. Deaths in which there is insufficient evidence of suffocation but hazards in the environment are identified, such as an infant sleeping with others in an adult bed but no report or witness of overlay, would be classified as resulting from undetermined causes.

Medical examiners in other jurisdictions may be using similar criteria for classifying SUIDs, but such strict protocols are not universal. For example, in a study conducted in Kentucky, Shields et al. described a 3-month-old infant who "succumbed to sudden infant death syndrome" while sleeping with her mother,[21] a sleep-related circumstance defined as "consistent with SIDS" according to Kentucky's 2003 classification scheme for SUIDs.[22]

Our results are consistent with stricter adherence to the SIDS definition on the part of at least some of the death certifiers in the 9 states included in our analysis. That is, infants whose deaths were classified as suffocation were significantly more likely to be sleeping on a surface not intended for infant sleep, to be sharing that surface with an adult, and to have documentation of an obstructed airway when found.

In addition, the proportion of infant suffocation deaths for which there was documentation that the infant was found under, between, or tangled in or wedged, pressed, or rolled into people or objects such as soft bedding was 2-fold higher than the proportion of undetermined cause deaths and 4-fold higher than the proportion of SIDS deaths. These results indicate that

although sleep related risk factors were present for some of the deaths classified as SIDS, deaths with clearly documented hazards in the sleep environment were more likely to be classified as suffocation or, to a lesser extent, undetermined cause.

It is notable that the percentage of deaths in each SUID category differed from percentages reported previously in the literature. Shapiro-Mendoza et al. reported that, in 2004, 59% of SUIDs were classified as SIDS, 14% as suffocation, and 27% as unknown cause,[2] whereas in our 2005 to 2008 data 31 % were classified as SIDS, 29% as suffocation, and 39% as undetermined. This difference is likely caused, at least in part, by the different data sources used; Shapiro-Mendoza et al. reported cause-specific mortality data from death certificates, and we used data from CDR programs.

The National Center for Health Statistics (NCHS) assigns *International Classification of Diseases* (ICD) codes to death certificates based on the reported underlying cause of death. The SIDS code (R95) is assigned to death certificates with such designations as "infant death unknown cause" and "sudden unexpected infant death."[4] As a result, deaths identified as cause unknown in the NCDR-CRS might be coded as SIDS on the death certificate. This would result in a higher proportion of SUIDs being classified as SIDS in national mortality statistics than in CDR data. Another explanation for the inconsistency might be a continuation of the diagnostic shift from classification of SIDS to classification of suffocation or undetermined cause, given that nationally available mortality data typically lag several years and that we used CDR data from 2005 to 2008.

Limitations and Strengths

Our study is not without limitations. For example, although many state CDR programs attempt to review all child deaths, not all reviews are completed, and not all data are entered by the end of a calendar year (in fact, data on some deaths are not entered for more than a year after the death occurs). In addition, not all counties in one of the states included in our analysis participate in the NCDR-CRS. As a result of this lag time and incomplete coverage, we could not confidently determine an appropriate denominator for the deaths included in our study, precluding calculation of mortality rates. Furthermore, without access to a non-affected comparison group, risk cannot be determined. As a result, our analyses focused only on identifying the proportions of deaths in each of the 3 SUID categories across infant, caregiver, and sleep environment characteristics.

Table 2

Unadjusted and Adjusted Odds Ratios Comparing Suffocation and Undetermined Cause Deaths With SIDS Deaths, by Child and Incident Characteristics: 9 US States, 2005–2008

	Suffocation vs SIDS, OR (95% CI)	Suffocation vs SIDS,[a] AOR (95% CI)	Undetermined Cause vs SIDS, OR (95% CI)	Undetermined Cause vs SIDS,[b] AOR (95% CI)
Child characteristic				
Age at death, mo				
<2 (Ref)	1.0	1.0	1.0	1.0
2–3	0.6 (0.5, 0.8)	0.7 (0.6, 1.0)	0.7 (0.6, 0.8)	0.8 (0.6, 1.0)
4–5	0.6 (0.5, 0.8)	0.9 (0.6, 1.2)	0.7 (0.5, 0.9)	0.9 (0.7, 1.2)
6–7	0.8 (0.5, 1.2)	1.2 (0.8, 1.9)	0.7 (0.5, 1.0)	0.9 (0.6, 1.3)
≥ 8	1.7 (1.0, 2.9)	2.6 (1.5, 4.7)	1.1 (0.6, 1.8)	1.4 (0.8, 2.3)
Race/ethnicity				
White, non-Hispanic (Ref)	1.0	1.0	1.0	1.0
Black, non-Hispanic	1.3 (0.9, 1.7)	1.2 (0.8, 1.7)	1.9 (1.4, 2.4)	1.9 (1.4, 2.5)
Hispanic	1.6 (1.3, 2.0)	1.2 (0.9, 1.6)	2.0 (1.6, 2.5)	1.8 (1.4, 2.3)
Other	0.9 (0.5, 1.4)	0.7 (0.4, 1.3)	0.9 (0.6, 1.5)	1.0 (0.6, 1.6)
Incident characteristic				
Infant sleep surface				
Crib/bassinette (Ref)	1.0	1.0	1.0	1.0
Adult bed	4.3 (3.3, 5.7)	2.3 (1.6, 3.2)	2.8 (2.2, 3.4)	1.5 (1.2, 2.0)
Couch/chair	6.3 (4.2, 9.4)	2.8 (1.7, 4.8)	2.7 (1.9, 3.8)	1.6 (1.1, 2.4)
Other	2.3 (1.6, 3.4)	1.9 (1.2, 2.8)	1.6 (1.1, 2.2)	1.4 (1.0, 1.9)
Position when found				
On back (Ref)	1.0	1.0	1.0	1.0
On stomach	1.7 (1.3, 2.3)	1.8 (1.3, 2.6)	1.0 (0.8, 1.2)	1.1 (0.8, 1.4)
On side	1.9 (1.3, 3.0)	1.7 (1.0, 2.8)	1.4 (1.0, 1.9)	1.3 (0.9, 1.8)
Unknown	1.9 (1.4, 2.6)	1.3 (0.9, 1.9)	0.9 (0.7, 1.2)	0.8 (0.6, 1.1)
Airway condition				
Unobstructed (Ref)	1.0	1.0	1.0	1.0
Partially obstructed	3.3 (2.0, 5.4)	3.1 (1.8, 5.4)	2.1 (1.3, 3.3)	1.8 (1.1, 2.9)
Fully obstructed	6.9 (4.7, 10.0)	4.8 (3.3, 7.0)	1.8 (1.3, 3.3)	1.6 (1.1, 2.3)
Unknown	2.1 (1.6, 2.9)	1.7 (1.2, 2.3)	1.2 (0.9, 1.6)	1.2 (0.9, 1.6)
Infant sleeping with person/animal				
No (Ref)	1.0	1.0	1.0	1.0
Yes	3.7 (2.3, 5.9)	1.3 (0.7, 2.4)	2.1 (1.5, 3.1)	1.2 (0.8, 1.8)
Infant sleeping with adult				
No (Ref)	1.0	1.0	1.0	1.0
Yes	3.7 (3.0, 4.6)	2.7 (2.0, 3.5)	2.9 (2.4, 3.4)	2.2 (1.7, 2.8)

Note. AOR = adjusted odds ratio; CI = confidence interval; OR = odds ratio; SIDS = sudden infant death syndrome. Unadjusted ORs were obtained from individual logistic regression models that contained the variable listed as well as the covariates year of death and state; thus, year of death and state were controlled in each logistic regression model. AORs were obtained from logistic regression models that contained all of the variables listed as well as the covariates year of death and state.

[a] Area under the receiver operator curve for this multivariate model: 0.80 (95% CI = 0.78, 0.82).

[b] Area under the receiver operator curve for this multivariate model: 0.74 (95% CI = 0.72, 0.76).

The NCDR-CRS is a relatively new system and has grown rapidly in a short time. In her description of the system, Covington explained the potential limitations of the data in detail.[18] Of note, data quality can differ across states, particularly states new to the system. Although data from more than 3000 infant deaths were available for our analysis, inclusion of data from only 9 states may limit the generalizability of our results, especially given some of the documented differences in classification of SUIDs by jurisdiction.[16,22]

In addition, the database includes more than 1700 data elements, and large proportions of missing data are more likely when novice users are responsible for entering information into the system. The observation that the proportion of missing data submitted by a state decreases with time was a factor in selecting states that had participated in the database from early in its existence. Even so, several of the variables reported had large proportions of missing data, and we did not include other sleep environment data elements because they involved even larger proportions of missing data. Our imputation of missing data in our regression analyses allowed inclusion of all SUIDs and likely produced less biased results.[19] The reasons particular data elements involve large proportions of missing data are not known at this time; however, our findings can be used in future state training initiatives to improve data quality.

Finally, given the nature of the NCDR-CRS, only information on deceased infants was available for analysis. Although survey data are now available that describe usual infant sleep practices among living infants,[23,24] the etiological component of infant sleep environment characteristics with respect to risk of SUIDs cannot be determined without an analytic study in which the sleep environment and other characteristics of infants who die suddenly and unexpectedly are compared with the same characteristics in living infants. Such an investigation is beyond the scope of the NCDR-CRS data.

Despite their limitations, the NCDR-CRS data have a number of inherent strengths. For instance, these data are population based and consist of standard elements that allow aggregation of data across states. The NCCDR provides training and support for NCDR-CRS users, including a comprehensive data dictionary to facilitate consistency in completion of data elements across jurisdictions. The number of states participating in the NCDR-CRS continues to grow, and states are continually gaining experience in using the system; thus, although the NCDR-CRS data are relatively new, they have the potential to inform our understanding of the circumstances and risk factors associated with all causes of child death, particularly injury deaths. The use of these collective data for prevention is a goal of the NCCDR.

To our knowledge, this is the first population-based study in which CDR data from multiple states have been used to examine infant, care-giver, and sleep circumstances and to compare them across 3 SUID categories. Notably, we included sleep environment details for more than 3000 infant deaths, a sufficiently large number to allow calculation of stable proportions of specific infant, caregiver, and sleep environment characteristics stratified by SUID category and assessment of independent associations of key sleep environment risk factors.

This study makes an important contribution to the existing SIDS research and to the growing evidence from smaller SUID studies that identify hazards in the infant sleep environment as likely contributors to SUIDs. As such, our findings have important implications for preventing injuries and reducing SUID mortality. We identified modifiable sleep environment risk factors in a large proportion of SUIDs, regardless of the ultimate cause of death classification.

Conclusions

From a public health standpoint, it is not only important but at times more prudent to focus on prevention before etiology is definitively determined. Scientists have been attempting to determine the cause of SIDS for decades. Given the across-jurisdiction variability in application of SIDS definitions in the United States and the mounting evidence that sleep environment hazards probably contribute not only to SIDS but to all SUIDs, there is a critical need to develop effective interventions for ensuring a safe sleep environment for all infants.

The American Academy of Pediatrics recently published expanded recommendations on safe infant sleep practices that include placing infants supine on a firm crib mattress without soft bedding or other objects in the crib; bed sharing during sleep is discouraged.[25] Mitchell, going one step further, suggested that the most significant reductions in SUIDs would be achieved if the practice of infant bed sharing were eliminated.[12] Despite these expert recommendations, challenges to reducing hazards in the infant sleep environment remain, as evidenced by infant sleep surveys documenting a continual increase in infant bed sharing in the United States since 1993.[23,24] Future research should focus on development of novel interventions that facilitate behavior change and result in a safe infant sleep environment.

Acknowledgments

Funding for this study was received from the Maternal and Child Health Bureau, Health Resources and Services Administration, Department of Health and Human Services (grant R40 MC 17177).

We gratefully acknowledge the child death review coordinators in the participating states for their enthusiastic support of this project and efforts to finalize their data in time for inclusion in our analyses and Shaohui Zhai of the Michigan Public Health Institute for bio-statistical consultation.

Human Participant Protection

This study was approved by the institutional review board of the Michigan Public Health Institute.

References

1. Centers for Disease Control and Prevention. Sudden unexpected infant death (SUID). Available at: http://www.cdc.gov/sids/index.htm. Accessed February 15, 2012.

2. Shapiro-Mendoza CK, Kimball M, Tomashek KM, Anderson RN, Blanding S. US infant mortality trends attributable to accidental suffocation and strangulation in bed from 1984 through 2004: are rates increasing? *Pediatrics*. 2009;123(2):533–539.

3. Willinger M, James LS, Catz C. Defining the sudden infant death syndrome (SIDS): deliberations of an expert panel convened by the National Institute of Child Health and Human Development. *Pediatr Pathol*. 1991;11(5): 677–684.

4. Shapiro-Mendoza CK, Kim SY, Chu SY, Kahn E, Anderson RN. Using death certificates to characterize sudden infant death syndrome (SIDS): opportunities and limitations. *J Pediatr*. 2010;156(1):38–43.

5. Kinney HC, Thach BT. The sudden infant death syndrome. *N Engl J Med*. 2009;361(8):795–805.

6. Malloy MH, MacDorman M. Changes in the classification of sudden unexpected infant deaths: United States, 1992–2001. *Pediatrics*. 2005;115(5):1247–1253.

7. Mitchell E, Krous HF, Donald T, Byard RW. Changing trends in the diagnosis of sudden infant death. *Am J Forensic Med Pathol*. 2000;21(4):311–314.

8. Shapiro-Mendoza CK, Tomashek KM, Anderson RN, Wingo J. Recent national trends in sudden, unexpected infant deaths: more evidence supporting a change in classification or reporting. *Am J Epidemiol*. 2006; 163 (8):762–769.

9. Li L, Zhang Y, Zielke RH, Ping Y, Fowler DR. Observations on increased accidental asphyxia deaths in infancy while cosleeping in the state of Maryland. *Am J Forensic Med Pathol*. 2009;30(4):318–321.

10. Shapiro-Mendoza CK, Tomashek KM, Davis TW, Blanding SL. Importance of the infant death scene investigation for accurate and reliable reporting of SIDS. *Arch Dis Child*. 2006;91(4):373.

11. Tomashek KM, Shapiro-Mendoza C, Davis TW. Commentary on investigation of sudden unexpected deaths in infancy. *Forensic Sci Int*. 2005;155(2–3): 231–232.

12. Mitchell EA SIDS: past, present and future. *Acta Paediatr*. 2009;98(11):1712–1719.

13. Overpeck MD, Brenner RA, Cosgrove C, Trumble AC, Kochanek K, MacDorman M. National under-ascertainment of sudden unexpected infant deaths associated with deaths of unknown cause. *Pediatrics*. 2002;109(2):274–283.

14. Kemp JS, Unger B, Wilkins D, et al. Unsafe sleep practices and an analysis of bedsharing among infants dying suddenly and unexpectedly: results of a four-year, population-based, death-scene investigation study of sudden infant death syndrome and related deaths. *Pediatrics*. 2000;106(3):e41.

15. Takatsu A, Shigeta A, Sakai K, Abe S. Risk factors, diagnosis and prevention of sudden unexpected infant death. *Leg Med (Tokyo)*. 2007;9(2):76–82.

16. Senter L, Sackoff J, Landi K, Boyd L. Studying sudden and unexpected infant deaths in a time of changing death certification and investigation practices: evaluating sleep-related risk factors for infant death in New York City. *Matern Child Health J*. 2011;15(2):242–248.

17. Brixey SN, Kopp BC, Schlotthauer AE, Collier A, Corden TE. Use of child death review to inform sudden unexplained infant deaths occurring in a large urban setting. *Inj Prev*. 2011;17(suppl 1):i23–i27.

18. Covington TM. The US National Child Death Review Case Reporting System. *Inj Prev*. 2011;17(suppl 1): i34–i37.

19. Harrell FE Jr, Lee KL, Mark DB. Multivariable prognostic models: issues in developing models, evaluating assumptions and adequacy,

and measuring and reducing errors. *Stat Med* 1996;15(4):361–387.

20. Stuart EA, Azur M, Frangakis C, Leaf P. Multiple imputation with large data sets: a case study of the Children's Mental Health Initiative. *Am J Epidemiol.* 2009;169(9):1133–1139.

21. Shields LB, Hunsaker DM, Muldoon S, Corey TS, Spivack BS. Risk factors associated with sudden unexplained infant death: a prospective study of infant care practices in Kentucky. *Pediatrics.* 2005;116(1):e13–e20.

22. Walsh SL, Kryscio R, Holsinger JW, Krous HF. Statewide systematic evaluation of sudden, unexpected infant death classification: results from a national pilot project. *Matern Child Health J.* 2010;14(6):950–957.

23. Hauck FR, Signore C, Fein SB, Raju TN. Infant sleeping arrangements and practices during the first year of life. *Pediatrics.* 2008;122(suppl 2):S113–S120.

24. Willinger M, Ko CW, Hoffman HJ, Kessler RC, Corwin MJ. Trends in infant bed sharing in the United States, 1993–2000: The National Infant Sleep Position Study. *Arch Pediatr Adolesc Med.* 2003;157(1):43–49.

25. American Academy of Pediatrics Task Force on Sudden Infant Death Syndrome. SIDS and other sleep-related infant deaths: expansion of recommendations for a safe infant sleeping environment *Pediatrics.* 2011;128 (5):1030–1039.

Patricia G. Schnitzer is a registered nurse and faculty member with the Sinclair School of Nursing, University of Missouri, Columbia. Her areas of interest include injury epidemiology and prevention; child abuse and neglect; and methods for improving public health surveillance.

Theresa M. Covington is the director of the Center for Child Death Review at the Michigan Public Health Institute.

Heather K. Dykstra is with the Michigan Public Health Institute.

EXPLORING THE ISSUE

Is Co-sleeping Safe for Baby?

Critical Thinking and Reflection

1. What is the role of the government in everyday decisions such as where and how an infant sleeps?
2. How should parents be educated on best parenting practices?
3. Do we know enough about preventing SIDS to have "best practices" regarding infant sleep?
4. Who decides what the "best practices" are and how should these decisions be made?

Is There Common Ground?

Parents today face a barrage of information and opinions regarding every decision they make, from what type of food to provide to the best type of stroller. It is easy to feel overwhelmed simply by the sheer number of choices and the conflicting information about each choice. One of the most contentious areas of debate regards infant sleep, with both parents and health experts concerned about infant safety.

Both the YES and NO selections have the same goal of promoting healthy sleep for infants. Wendy Middlemiss recommends a discussion-based approach for parents and health care providers that respects the diverse needs and desires of each family. However, the research from Patricia Schnitzer and colleagues demonstrates that not all sleep choices are equal, with certain sleep environments being related to SIDS.

Perhaps then, the information in the NO selection represents *what* information should be communicated to parents and the information in the YES selection represents *how* that information should be communicated.

Create Central

www.mhhe.com/createcentral

Additional Resources

Ball, H. L. (2003). Breastfeeding, bed-sharing, and infant sleep. *Birth*, *30*(3), 181–188.

Carpenter, R., McGarvey, C., Mitchell, E. A., Tappin, D. M., Vennemann, M. M., Smuk, M., & Carpenter, J. R. (2013). Bed sharing when parents do not smoke: Is there a risk of SIDS? An individual level analysis of five major case-control studies. *BMJ Open*, *3*(5).

Colvin, J. D., Collie-Akers, V., Schunn, C., & Moon, R. Y. (2014). Sleep environment risks for younger and older infants. *Pediatrics*, *134*(2), e406–e412.

McKenna, J. J., & McDade, T. (2005). Why babies should never sleep alone: A review of the co-sleeping controversy in relation to SIDS, bed-sharing and breast feeding. *Paediatric Respiratory Reviews*, *6*(2), 134–152.

Internet References . . .

Cosleeping Organization

www.cosleeping.org

KidsHealth

www.kidshealth.org

Safe to Sleep Campaign

http://www.nichd.nih.gov/sts/Pages/default.aspx

Unit 3

UNIT

Early Childhood

*E**arly childhood** (sometimes referred to as toddlerhood) generally encompasses the years between two and six. These ages comprise a gradual transition into the social, psychological, and physical ways of being that orient any lifespan. Cognitive development, and language in particular, advances rapidly during early childhood. As such, scholars of development take particular interest in trying to ensure that these ways of being are healthy, hoping to give all children the chance to succeed in an increasingly sophisticated world.*

For many children, early childhood marks the start of "formal" schooling, and the opportunity to enhance development in a systematic way. The two issues in this section focus on how children should be educated to promote learning. The first issue questions how children learn, and whether these processes differ by gender. The second issue asks whether there is enough solid research to support universal preschool education. In essence, both issues encourage readers to consider how research should inform policy to make effective decisions.

Selected, Edited, and with Issue Framing Material by:
Allison A. Buskirk-Cohen, *Delaware Valley University*

ISSUE

Do Innate Gender Differences Influence How Children Learn?

YES: Kelley King, Michael Gurian, and Kathy Stevens, from "Gender-Friendly Schools," in *Educational Leadership* (November 2010)

NO: Lise Eliot, from "The Myth of Pink and Blue Brains," in *Educational Leadership* (November 2010)

Learning Outcomes

After reading this issue, you will be able to:

- Recognize that there are group-level differences between boys' and girls' performance in school, but many of those differences are relatively recent developments shifting a historical excess of opportunities for boys into an achievement gap favoring girls.

- Understand that average innate brain-based gender differences do exist, but they initially seem quite small and are difficult to interpret accurately because they always derive from an interaction between nature and nurture.

- Know that although some schools and school districts have had success explicitly attending to gender differences, there is research evidence suggesting efforts to emphasize gender equity can also be effective.

- Recognize that average group differences still allow for a great deal of individual variation, meaning that differences in learning related characteristics such as verbal ability and physical activity do not apply to all boys and girls.

ISSUE SUMMARY

YES: Kelley King, Michael Gurian, and Kathy Stevens, all affiliated with an institute that advocates for accommodating gender differences in learning, identify developmental differences between boys and girls that are deep enough to merit distinct educational practices.

NO: Lise Eliot explains how small gender differences in infancy become magnified through parental interactions with their children. She argues that teachers, as well, need to be aware of how they treat boys and girls so they do not exacerbate gender stereotypes.

Developmentalists emphasize the difference between sex and gender, describing sex as the biological and physiological characteristics of an individual and gender as socially constructed roles, behaviors, activities, and beliefs considered appropriate for individuals based on their sex. As the World Health Organization explains, "'male' and 'female' are sex categories, while 'masculine' and 'feminine' are gender categories." Sex characteristics tend to remain fairly consistent among cultures, while gender varies greatly. The gender binary, a relatively new term, refers to the social boundary that only allows for two categories of gender, rather than encouraging people to cross or mix gender roles together in a way that best fits each individual. Despite efforts to view gender on a continuum, many people continue to see it as a binary category. What being male or female means in any culture can have important developmental consequences.

Gender is one of the central organizing categories for lifespan development. From the very earliest prenatal screenings, when parents are asked if they want to know whether they will have a boy or a girl, to differences in infant clothing and toys, to voluntary segregation at school lunch tables and on teams at recess, to the negotiation of particular expectations around work and family in adulthood, gender matters. The very persistence of how greatly gender matters, despite much attention to the importance of gender equity, suggests to some people that gender differences must be hardwired in the brain. Seeing rambunctious boys ignoring calls to focus on their math problems, chatty girls telling artful tales during story hour, reinforces stereotypes in a way that makes it easy to assume those tendencies derive from natural predispositions. Perhaps, rather than fighting that nature, gender differences should be accommodated.

That line of thinking, however, quickly runs into the problem of history. In regard to learning and educational achievement, for example, it was not too many years back when boys were assumed to be more competent and girls less encouraged toward school achievement. There are numerous historical examples of segregating girls for biological reasons (e.g., menstruation). It has only been in recent decades, with a broad emphasis on creating opportunities for girls, that the gender pendulum has swung in schools. Increasingly, girls outperform boys on standardized tests in primary and secondary school, are more likely to attend and complete college, and more regularly pursue graduate degrees. For many schools and communities, in stark contrast to just a few decades prior, the concern is less that girls have fewer opportunities and more that boys are adrift. However, the glass ceiling remains intact with fewer women achieving top positions and earning incomes as high as their male counterparts.

Contemporary concerns about how gender differences might relate to learning and school achievement are evolving with technology allowing opportunities to better research the potential biological, genetic, and neurological dimensions of gender. Behavioral differences in classroom demeanor or math performance can now be correlated with brain scans analyzing cortical activation, for example. Some studies have found average, group-level differences in aspects of brain functioning between boys and girls. It is important to note that studies finding between group differences between girls and boys often also find within group differences, meaning that girls and boys show a range of abilities within their gender group. All of these differences are difficult to interpret. One of the wonders of the human brain is its plasticity, meaning that the brain simultaneously causes behavior and responds to experience. When basic gender differences show up in the brain, those differences can derive equally from innate predispositions and from lived experience.

The difficulty of interpreting new brain science has not, however, stopped people from trying to apply new research findings to practical settings such as schools. Kelley King, Michael Gurian, and Kathy Stevens have been at the forefront of many such applications through their work at the Gurian Institute, which is devoted to forwarding the lessons of Michael Gurian's many popular books on gender, including titles such as *Boys and Girls Learn Differently! A Guide for Teachers and Parents*. In the YES article, King, Gurian, and Stevens distill their perspectives on gender differences from their experiences working with these schools. They observe clear gender differences in tendencies such as physical activity and verbal acuity, noting that those differences seem to correspond with brain-based differences in characteristics such as frontal lobe development and neural rest states. From their perspective, such differences can be accommodated to ensure all children have the chance to thrive in school.

Lise Eliot, on the other hand, is focused less on educational practice and more on the ways neuroscience, her field of expertise, has been misinterpreted. Eliot, too, has written a popular book on gender differences, but her point in *Pink Brain, Blue Brain* is to emphasize that whatever small gender differences may be hardwired into the brain are insignificant when compared with constant social messages that accentuate and exaggerate the importance of gender. As a historical note, according to the Smithsonian, pink and blue were not promoted as gender signifiers until the start of World War I. At that time, pink was considered an appropriate color choice for boys and blue for girls; it was not until the 1940s that today's color designation appeared. In the NO article, Eliot draws on the concept of epigenetics to argue that most genetic influences on behavior and development only manifest through environmental activation. She suggests that concerns about gender differences are best addressed through emphasizing gender equity rather than treating boys and girls as if they were born to learn differently.

This controversy has other implications that go beyond classroom practice to the very design of our school system. In fact, Eliot was recently part of a team of distinguished scholars who published a paper in the prestigious journal *Science* titled "The Pseudoscience of Single-Sex Schooling" arguing against a trend to think of all-boy or all-girl schools as a salve for achievement gaps. Yet, at the level of group averages, those gaps do exist. Although there is a great deal of individual variation, boys and girls do tend to perform differently in school. Now the challenge is to figure out whether old history and new brain science can be reconciled to explain those differences.

YES

Kelley King, Michael Gurian, and Kathy Stevens

Gender-Friendly Schools

Diane Corner had been teaching "forever," so she was confident in her teaching abilities. In 2007, however, confronted with an extraordinarily wiggly group of 2nd grade boys in a chronically low-performing school, Diane told her principal, "I can't even get the boys to sit still for a short phonics lesson. I have to do something."

Desha Bierbaum, her principal, responded with a new possibility. "I've been learning about the differences in how boys and girls learn. Why don't you try letting the fidgety boys stand up and move around while you teach? That helps some boys' brains focus and learn better."

That conversation marked the beginning of the success story we became involved in at Wamsley Elementary School in Rifle, Colorado.

School Improvement Through Gender Equality

Fifty percent of Wamsley's students qualify for free or reduced-price lunch, 30 percent are English language learners, and the mobility rate is 43 percent. In fall 2007, Wamsley was on academic watch for not making adequate yearly progress (AYP).

Because boys underperformed girls by a significant margin at Wamsley, Principal Bierbaum decided to target her school's improvement efforts at achieving gender equality. The school staff acknowledged that it had a better understanding of how to teach girls than boys, but it resolved that any professional development approach the school implemented to give boys more opportunity must also be girl-friendly. Wamsley applied for and received a grant to provide whole-school online classes and strategies-oriented summer institute training for Wamsley's teachers, along with on-site professional development and coaching on the different learning needs of boys and girls. By the end of the first year of the initiative, student performance jumped markedly, and the school was taken off the AYP watch list. Wamsley became a national success story.

A year earlier, the Atlanta Public Schools in Georgia had embarked on a similar effort. In 2006, many Atlanta schools were not meeting AYP, and previous school reform initiatives had failed. When the district staff disaggregated data for gender, they noticed that gender gaps reflecting lower achievement for boys were present across all subgroups and were largest for boys of color and those living in poverty.

In fall 2007, the school district launched two single-sex middle school academies—the Business Engineering Science Technology Academy for Boys (the B.E.S.T. Academy), and the Coretta Scott King Young Women's Leadership Academy. We became involved at that point. Faculty and staff at the pilot schools received professional development (including coaching, online courses, on-site training, and summer institutes) on how boys and girls learn differently and how to strategically implement gender-friendly teaching strategies into all aspects of the school, from teaching to counseling services to athletics.

Like Wamsley, these schools are now success stories. Within two years, both made AYP. Grades and test scores improved, student attendance increased, discipline referrals decreased, and teachers felt more effective. The district is moving forward with plans to expand their two single-sex middle schools through grade 12.

Looking Through the Gender Lens

In the last two decades, we have supported efforts to close opportunity gaps in more than 2,000 schools across the United States. When educators look closely at test scores, grades, discipline referrals, homework completion rates, special education placements, and student motivation, they consistently realize how gender-related issues intersect and interfere with their ability to achieve school improvement goals. They notice the following areas of difficulty for girls:

- Lower learning and engagement in science and technology classes.
- Relational aggression in school and in cyberspace.
- Problems with self-esteem development in adolescence.

They notice a different set of core areas of difficulty for boys:

- Lower achievement scores in most classes—especially among low-income and racially/ethnically diverse students—with panicular problems in literacy.
- Lagging learning skills in such areas as note taking and listening.
- More struggles with homework.
- Lower grades in all classes, except some math and most science classes.
- Less motivation to learn and lower perception that the curriculum is relevant.

Both boys and girls tend to need help in specific areas. But data show that schools are now failing boys, as a group, in more areas than girls. More and more teachers are expressing the need for assistance in learning to teach boys effectively.

In March 2010, the Center on Education Policy echoed teachers' instincts when it released the report *Are There Gender Differences in Achievement Between Boys and Girls?* In preparing the report, the center examined state test data from all age groups in all 50 states, finding

> good news for girls but bad news for boys. In math, girls are doing roughly as well as boys, and the differences that do exist in some states are small and show no clear national pattern favoring boys or girls. But in reading, boys are lagging behind girls in all states with adequate data, and these gaps are greater than 10 percentage points in some states.

Dealing with this reality is an important challenge for all of us who care about education reform. If we do not recognize it and work to close the opportunity gaps boys are experiencing, millions of boys and men will lose out over the next decades.

The Elephant in the Room

Boys and girls, like men and women, are not stereotypes; they fall along a wide spectrum of learning preferences and styles. In fact, there is a great deal of overlap. Every day, teachers work with boys who are verbal, collaborative, and more emotive and with girls who are visual, competitive, and less emotive.

As a group, however, boys are much more likely than girls to be graphic thinkers and kinesthetic learners and to thrive under competitive learning structures. Some of the gender differences we observe in the classroom

(see a summary at www.ascd.org/ASCD/pdf/journals/ed_lead/el_201011_gurian_figure.pdf) are undoubtedly linked to societal influences, but some also stem from physical differences in the brain identified by neuroscientists.

Most of the teachers we work with realize that the preparation they received in graduate school and teacher certification programs to teach "all students" was in fact training for verbal and sedentary learning. This presents a large elephant in the room for teachers and schools. Given the structures, expectations, and teaching styles in today's classrooms, teachers generally have more difficulty teaching boys than girls. In a classroom of 25 students, we may notice that five to seven boys are having difficulties, whether these are overt issues or a tendency to check out of the learning process. They need a kind of instruction teachers have not been trained to provide, and the lack of such teaching profoundly affects the overall grades, test scores, and behavior of the class, as well as a teacher's sense of whether he or she is teaching effectively.

Strategies for Teaching Boys and Girls Effectively

Here are some examples of strategies that teachers we have worked with are using to close opportunity gaps between boys and girls.

Strategy 1: Add Movement

Chris Zust of Wellington School in Columbus, Ohio, gets her 1st grade boys and girls to stand up for reading group.

> I play a game when the children have finished reading. I let them spread out around the room, and I throw a beach ball to them that has eight prompts written on it. Each time a student catches the ball, he or she has to answer a prompt. My boys are far more engaged with this activity than they are when I have them sitting at the reading table.

Pairing learning with movement is especially important for many boys because it helps them stay out of the *neural rest* (boredom) state. But because it increases brain activity, movement can also help girls learn.

In addition to infusing movement into learning activities, teachers might also include regular brain breaks—frequent, brief opportunities to simply get up and move, such as doing jumping jacks, jogging in place, stretching, doing the wave from one side of the room to the other, or dancing in place with music.

Strategy 2: Build on the Visual

Fifth grade teacher Debbie Mathis and her teammates at Edith Wolford Elementary in Colorado Springs, Colorado, noticed that during traditional writing activities, boys were much slower getting started, wrote fewer words, used fewer sensory details, and got lower grades. After learning how graphically oriented boys' brains tend to be, Debbie and her teammates decided to use comic-strip pictures as prompts. "That really got the kids' imaginations flowing," Debbie shares. "The entire class was jazzed and wrote like crazy! Honestly, I was thrilled when even my most reluctant boys were eager to share."

HOW BOYS AND GIRLS LEARN DIFFERENTLY

- *Verbal/graphic differences.* Boys' brains tend to have more cortical areas, mainly in the right hemisphere, wired for spatial/mechanical processing than do girls' brains; girls' brains generally have greater cortical emphasis on verbal processing.
- *Frontal lobe development.* A girl's prefrontal cortex is generally more active than a boy's of the same age, and her frontal lobe generally develops earlier. These are the decision-making areas of the brain, as well as the reading/writing/word production areas.
- *Neural rest states.* Boys' brains tend to go into a more notable *rest state* than girls' brains do. Because the brain's first priority is survival, it scans its environment for information that would alert it to any threat, challenge, or information crucial to its survival. If the classroom is not providing any stimuli that the brain perceives as important, the male brain tends to more quickly slip into a rest state (which manifests itself as boredom, or "zoning out"). In the classroom, boys often try to avoid these natural male rest states by engaging in activities like tapping their pencils or poking at classmates.

Karen Combs, another teacher at Wolford, echoes this approach:

When I explained to my students that they were going to draw pictures as a way to plan their writing content, two of my boys looked at each other and said, "Sweet!" After about 30 minutes of writing, my most reluctant writer came toward me. I expected him to ask, "How much do I have to write?" Instead, he asked, "What if an hour isn't enough time to write everything that I've planned?"

Heather Peter, a language arts teacher at Broomfield High School in Broomfield, Colorado, notes that although boys are vocal about their enthusiasm for visual-spatial projects, girls also flourish when given the opportunity to create visual products to demonstrate their comprehension. Heather shares, "We recently finished a unit on *Hamlet* in which students had the choice to make a video, create a talk show, do a choral reading, or write a screenplay. Of the 38 female students, 35 chose a visual-spatial project."

Visual-spatial activities reach a broader spectrum of learners, harness learner strengths, help to stimulate and develop more neural pathways, and help close gaps for both boys and girls. They can be absolutely essential for some learners.

Strategy 3: Incorporate Student Interests and Choices

Tenth grader Will was like many of the boys struggling in Atlanta Public Schools. Will was not motivated in school, and it required superhuman effort to get him to do his schoolwork. But Will had a passion for sports. His teachers began to identify this passion in his classes and made sure to integrate it into his learning. English, social studies, and other teachers stocked classrooms with sports-relevant reading material, from graphic novels and technical magazines to sports magazines and biographies of football and basketball players.

His teachers reported consistent findings, which we've summarized here:

Since incorporating boys' interests into the curriculum, we have seen a measurable change in Will's body language. He comes in with his head up and is cheerful and making eye contact now. He has something he cares about to focus on in class and homework. Boys like him see school differently when their interests and passions are integrated into classes.

Broomfield's Heather Peter has also used strategies revolving around student interests to close opportunity gaps. She says,

I've had several students over the years tell me that they like literature more now because of all the projects that they were able to do. This is true not just for boys but also for girls. My student Alice told me, "I'll never forget *Hamlet* because I will always remember making my music video."

By bringing in novelty and topics of outside interest, these teachers are boosting all their students' motivation. For both boys and girls, motivation to learn can be the difference between success and failure.

A SNAPSHOT: BOYS IN SCHOOL

- On the most recent National Assessment of Educational Progress (NAEP) writing test, 26 percent of 12th grade males scored *below basic*, compared with 11 percent of females. Just 16 percent of males achieved at the *proficient/advanced* levels, compared with 31 percent of females.
- In reading, one-third of 12th grade males scored *below basic* on NAEP, compared with 22 percent of females; fewer than one-third of males (29 percent) were reading at the *proficient/advanced* levels, compared with 41 percent of females.
- Boys receive two-thirds of the *D*s and *F*s in schools, but fewer than one-half of the *A*s.
- Girls are more likely to attend and graduate from college. In 2003, there were 1.35 females for every male who graduated from a four-year college and 1.30 females for every male undergraduate.
- These and many other gender gaps for boys have been widening over the last decade.

Closing Gaps Now and in the Future

As districts, schools, and teachers close opportunity gaps, teach more effectively, and turn around low-performing schools, they explore and learn solutions they can apply right away—solutions inherent in the boys and girls they teach.

After 20 years of training teachers in both how to help boys and girls learn and strategies for teaching them effectively, we believe the next decade will open greater opportunities for teachers and schools to use the wisdom of the gender lens. This lens is an essential tool for education reform—one that not only enables schools to meet accountability goals in terms of higher test scores for all groups, but also reflects the deep humanity and love of all children that each of us brings to the schoolhouse.

KELLEY KING is a school administrator and staff member of the Gurian Institute, which identifies its mission as "helping boys and girls reach their full potential by providing professional development that increases student achievement, teacher effectiveness, and parent involvement."

MICHAEL GURIAN is an author of multiple books about gender and learning, and is the founder of the Gurian School. The Gurian Institute identifies its mission as "helping boys and girls reach their full potential by providing professional development that increases student achievement, teacher effectiveness, and parent involvement."

KATHY STEVENS is the executive director of the Gurian Institute, which identifies its mission as "helping boys and girls reach their full potential by providing professional development that increases student achievement, teacher effectiveness, and parent involvement."

Lise Eliot

 **NO**

The Myth of Pink and Blue Brains

Gender differences are a hot topic. But much of the recent discussion about boys' and girls' learning has generated more heat than light. As a neuroscientist who has studied children's cognitive and emotional abilities and, in particular, analyzed gender differences in children's brains, I hope to help set the record straight on this incendiary subject.

Boys and girls differ in many ways—in physical activity level; self-control; and performance levels in reading, writing, and math. Above all, they differ in interests. But most of these differences are nowhere near as large as popular ideas about a "Mars-Venus" gulf imply, nor are they as "hardwired" as current discourse portrays. The truth is that neuroscientists have identified very few reliable differences between boys' and girls' brains. Boys' brains are about 10 percent larger than those of girls, and boys' brains finish growing a year or two later during puberty (Lenroot et al., 2007). But these global differences reflect physical maturation more than mental development.

Few other clear-cut differences between boys' and girls' neural structures, brain activity, or neurochemistry have thus far emerged, even for something as obviously different as self-regulation. Boys and girls, on average, differ in self-regulatory *behavior*, with girls showing better ability to sit still, pay attention, delay gratification, and organize a take-home folder, for instance. We know that self-regulatory abilities depend on the prefrontal cortex of the brain, but neuroscientists have thus far been unable to show that this area develops earlier or is more active in girls (Barry et al., 2004).

The same is true of gender differences in the adult brain. In spite of what you may have read, women do not have a larger corpus callosum,[1] process language in a more symmetrical fashion, or have higher circulating levels of serotonin compared with men. The latest high-resolution MRI studies reveal small differences in brain lateralization or "sidedness" (Liu, Stufflebeam, Sepulcre, Hedden, & Buckner, 2009) and functional connectivity (Biswal et al., 2010), on the order of three-tenths of a standard deviation,

meaning there is more overlap between average males' and females' brains than differences between the average brain of each gender. These studies, based on thousands of subjects around the world, give us a better picture of the true size of neurologic sex differences than do the cherry-picked, single studies of a few dozen men and women that are often cited as proof of evolutionarily programmed gender differences.

Our actual ability differences are quite small. Although psychologists can measure statistically significant distinctions between large groups of men and women or boys and girls, there is much more overlap in the academic and even social-emotional abilities of the genders than there are differences (Hyde, 2005). To put it another way, the range of performance within each gender is wider than the difference between the average boy and girl.

Of course, teachers know this. Teachers recognize that girls *or* boys can be strong readers. On the playground, about one-third of girls are physically more active than the average boy. When it comes to academic achievement and even classroom behavior, gender is a very poor predictor of any individual student's performance.

So What's Behind Gender Gaps?

Society as a whole, however, cannot ignore the striking gender gaps in academic performance. Girls have outperformed boys in reading and boys have outscored girls in math (although by a smaller margin) on the National Assessment of Educational Progress (NAEP) in every year assessed since 1971 (U.S. Department of Education, 2005). Similar gender gaps exist on the Program for International Student Assessment (PISA) (Else-Quest, Hyde, & Linn, 2010).

At first glance, this stability suggests there is something inherently different about boys' and girls' academic abilities. But a closer look reveals that the gaps vary considerably by age, ethnicity, and nationality. For example, among the countries participating in PISA, the reading gap is more than twice as large in some countries

(Iceland, Norway, and Austria) as in others (Japan, Mexico, and Korea); for math, the gap ranges from a large male advantage in certain countries (Korea and Greece) to essentially no gap in other countries—or even reversed in girls' favor (Iceland and Thailand). What's more, a recent analysis of PISA data found that higher female performance in math correlates with higher levels of gender equity in individual nations.

This suggests that environmental factors are important in shaping gender gaps. The truth is that no mental ability—or ability difference—is "hardwired" into the brain. Abilities develop in a social-cultural context that includes each child's opportunities, relationships, sense of identity, and more. Biologists call such development *epigenetic*. Environmental factors—ranging from diet and chemical exposure to less tangible influences like parenting styles—are known to alter DNA structure, gene expression, and an organism's lifelong brain and behavioral function (Champagne & Curley, 2005). When it comes to gender gaps, boys and girls start out a little bit different, but these differences become rapidly magnified by a culture that sees them—and encourages them to see themselves—as fundamentally different creatures.

Three Little Differences—and How They Grow

Three small, early biases appear to be programmed by prenatal hormone exposure or sex-specific gene expression:

- Baby boys are modestly more physically active than girls (Campbell & Eaton, 1999).
- Toddler girls talk one month earlier, on average, than boys (Fenson et al., 1994).
- Boys appear more spatially aware (Quinn & Liben, 2008).

Such differences contribute to each gender's well-known toy preferences, which surface in the second year of life (Servin, Gohlin, & Berlin, 1999). Boys prefer more active playthings, like trucks and balls; girls choose more verbal-relational toys, especially dolls. In each of these cases, however, boy-girl differences are magnified through parental treatment. For example, parents encourage more physical risk-taking in sons than in daughters (Morrongiello & Dawber, 2000); mothers generally talk more to preschool-aged daughters than sons (Leaper, Anderson, & Sanders, 1998); and parents discourage "gender-inappropriate" play, especially in terms of boys showing too much interest in sister's Barbie collection (Lytton & Romney, 1991).

This is important, because children develop the skills they will bring into the classroom through such early play. Simply put, girls spend more time talking, drawing, and role-playing in relational ways, whereas boys spend more time moving, targeting, building, and role-playing as heroes. Each activity is beneficial, but because of the potency of early experience on children's brain wiring, the differences between typical "girl" and "boy" play have deep consequences for cognitive and emotional function.

For example, as boys and girls progress through childhood, clocking very different amounts of time throwing, catching, constructing, and playing high-speed driving and targeting games, their spatial skills grow increasingly disparate, with boys scoring higher in this area. The ability to visualize three-dimensional objects and their orientations, distances, and trajectories is important in higher math, science, and mechanical work—domains in which boys eventually pull ahead.

Alternatively, consider verbal skills. Thanks to their extra conversation with peers and parents, girls' small verbal advantage balloons by kindergarten into a significant gap in phonological awareness, the key stepping stone for learning to read. By 3rd grade, 20 percent more girls than boys score in the proficient range as readers, according to NAEP data—a gap that grows to 38 percent by 8th grade (Lee, Grigg, & Donahue, 2007) and a startling 47 percent by the end of high school (Grigg, Donahue, & Dion, 2007).

The numbers are stark, but they reveal that the reason boys don't read and write as well as girls has little to do with innate brain wiring and everything to do with the reality that girls engage more than boys with words: talking, reading, journal writing, or endless text-messaging. Only 25 percent of teenage boys around the world cite reading as one of their favorite hobbies, compared with 45 percent of teenage girls (Organisation for Economic Cooperation and Development, 2010).

So if we want to tackle academic gaps between boys and girls, we need to start early, nurturing skills and attitudes that will better prepare both genders for the modern classroom. We also need to make sure that the classroom remains a place where students' potential is broadened, rather than narrowed through misguided beliefs. As always, the best way to do this is to focus on each child's unique combination of cognitive and emotional talents.

Navigating Gender Differences

In spite of claims—and intentions—to the contrary, few parents or teachers are truly gender neutral. The good news is that attempts at gender equity do make a difference.

Students develop more stereotyped attitudes in classrooms that emphasize gender (such as by lining up boys and girls separately) and more egalitarian attitudes where it's deemphasized (Hilliard & Liben, in press).

So how should teachers pay attention to gender? Very carefully. As with all types of diversity, the challenge is to respect and honor differences without turning them into self-fulfilling prophecies. Just as we would never try to guess a student's math skill on the basis of skin or eye color, we must avoid prejudging any student's verbal, athletic, scientific, artistic, leadership, analytical, or social ability on the basis of chromosomes.

We must challenge gender stereotypes for *both sexes*. In mainstream U.S. culture, girls are rewarded for behaving like boys more than the other way around—which is great for girls' math and athletic skills, but not for boys' verbal and relational abilities. Boys hear that "girls can do anything" whereas the boys get boxed into smaller corners by their presumed limitations ("Boys are less verbal"); teachers' prohibitions ("No running"); and peers' narrow views of masculinity ("Art is gay"). Might this be why girls excel in many areas, while boys' success is shrinking to sports and a few select curricular zones?

Here are a few suggestions for reducing opportunity gaps between boys and girls:

Avoid stereotyping. I suspect most teachers try to do this, but I fear that the recent focus on boy-girl differences and claims of "hardwiring" have caused things to slip backwards. Some news reports about single-gender programs describe teachers guiding students into stereotyped activities, for instance, giving girls quiet spaces to "sit and discuss their feelings" while boys get extra opportunities for competition and physical play (Tyre, 2005). This approach is wrong: Both sexes need more physical exercise, and both need to be comfortable blending competition and cooperation.

Appreciate the range of intelligences. Beyond the three *R*s lie many zones of performance in which individual students may excel but which aren't typically recognized at school. Howard Gardner brought nontraditional kinds of intelligence and skill to teachers' attention years ago but with the new back-to-basics focus, some important domains—such as the arts and kinesthetic ability—have been forgotten. Broadening the range of abilities that we teach and affirm can help more students feel successful at school.

Strengthen spatial awareness. Spatial skills are arguably the most overlooked nontraditional abilities in the curriculum. Yet spatial cognition is important for understanding such areas as fractions, proportionality, calculus, geography, physics, and chemistry. Research supports the idea that practice in activities requiring spatial awareness improves such skills (Newcombe, Mathason, & Terlecki, 2002), but most training in this domain happens outside school. Beginning in preschool, teachers should formally teach spatial and mechanical skills using puzzles, map reading, targeting sports, and building projects that get students thinking in 3D.

Engage boys with the word. Parents and educators alike need to do a better job with this, starting early with the verbal and literary immersion that builds vocabulary, phonologic skill, and a love of books. The simple equation, "Language in = Language out" should remind teachers of the importance of engaging boys in one-on-one dialogue, word play, stories, songs, and every kind of text. Once they begin formal reading instruction, boys benefit from a wide variety of reading material that appeals to their sense of humor and frequent interest in action, adventure, and nonfiction.

Writing ability shows an even larger gender gap, but in a world that produced Shakespeare and Stephen King, it's absurd to suggest that boys are constitutionally incapable of writing as well as girls. The solution is time on task. Beginning in preschool, teachers should emphasize "mark-making" to promote writing using vivid markers, crayons, charcoal, or paint on large surfaces like appliance boxes—or fun ones like portable slates. The goal is not formal printing, but symbolic expression and fine-motor practice. Although penmanship is important, divorce it from composition by allowing students to dictate or type their thoughts.

Recruit boys into nonathletic extracurricular activities. When did the school newspaper, yearbook, and student council become all-female clubs? Unfortunately, many of these activities have reached a tipping point; when the number of boys falls below 25 percent, it becomes—perplexingly—"unmasculine" to join the chorus or run for class president. Just as we'd be appalled to host a science club without girls, we should not accept boys' absence from a wider variety of campus activities.

Bring more men into the classroom. The number of male teachers in elementary school has declined precipitously since the 1980s. We need to increase the ranks of young men who enter teaching, and bring more fathers and adult males into preschool and elementary classrooms as role models for intellectual engagement.

Treat teacher bias seriously. There still are teachers who believe "girls are good at reading and boys are good at math." There still are teachers who cannot tolerate physical exuberance or coloring outside the lines. Considering the potent effect of teacher expectations on student performance, we must train teachers about potential bias and evaluate them with respect to it. Just as girls have benefited from efforts to root out antifemale bias, boys deserve protection from teachers who may—consciously or unconsciously—regard them as "toxic."

In the past 15 years, claims about hardwired differences between boys and girls have propagated virally, with no genuine neuroscientific justification. In reality, culture, attitudes, and practices influence boy-girl academic gaps far more than prenatal testosterone does. The sooner teachers open their eyes to such influences, the sooner we can bring out the best in every child.

Note

1. The corpus callosum is a white matter tract that provides most of the connections between left and right cerebral hemispheres. Some studies have reported that it's larger in the female brain; others have found it larger in the male brain, but a meta-analysis of 49 studies found no significant difference in corpus callosum size between the genders (Bishop & Whalsten, 1997).

LISE ELIOT is a neuroscientist at the Chicago Medical School of Rosalind Franklin University and author of the book *Pink Brain, Blue Brain: How Small Differences Grow into Troublesome Gaps—And What We Can Do About It.*

EXPLORING THE ISSUE

Do Innate Gender Differences Influence How Children Learn?

Critical Thinking and Reflection

1. King, Gurian, and Stevens identify gender differences in learning and offer suggestions for teaching with those differences in mind. What are the potential advantages and disadvantages to gender-based teaching?

2. Eliot does not deny that gender differences exist; instead, she questions their significance and whether it is fair to consider them "hardwired." When do gender differences become significant enough to accommodate? If you were a teacher, what kind of evidence would you want to see to understand the development of gender differences?

3. What is the relationship between brain differences and genetic differences? Why is it the case that some brain-based differences may be unrelated to innate predispositions?

4. One of the challenges of confronting gender disparities in schools is that there is much individual variation: How can average differences between boys and girls be respected without condemning individual boys and girls who do not fit with the group norms?

Is There Common Ground?

Gender differences have long provoked contentious discussion, and it seems likely these discussions will continue. Although some radical thinkers have aspired to a gender-free society, most people on all sides of this issue acknowledge that gender differences are a real and unavoidable aspect of society. One of the most influential environments is children's development is the school system. Children spend much of their early lives in classroom, impacted by their teachers, peers, curricula, etc. All of the authors of the YES and NO selections recognize that schools are a key site for both demonstrating and shaping gender differences.

There are several important commonalities in these two selections. Both sides would likely agree that while girls have historically been marginalized in school, boys are now demonstrating struggles that deserve attention. Both would likely agree that schools should be constantly working to improve learning outcomes for all children. The core difference is whether that work requires accommodating or challenging gender norms. And that difference depends on how we understand the origin of those norms. Like all developmental domains, gender is a product of both nature and nurture—but what does our analysis of the relative importance of those forces mean for how our children learn?

Create Central

www.mhhe.com/createcentral

Additional Resources

Arroyo, I., Burleson, W., Tai, M., Muldner, K., & Woolf, B. P. (2013). Gender differences in the use and benefit of advanced learning technologies for Mathematics.

Fabes, R. A., Hayford, S., Pahlke, E., Santos, C., Zosuls, K., Martin, C. L., & Hanish, L. D. (2014). Peer influences on gender differences in educational aspiration and attainment. *Gender Differences in Aspirations and Attainment: A Life Course Perspective*, 29.

Guzzetti, B. J., Young, J. P., Gritsavage, M. M., Fyfe, L. M., & Hardenbrook, M. (2013). *Reading, writing, and talking gender in literacy learning*. Routledge.

Halpern, D. F. (2013). *Sex differences in cognitive abilities*. Psychology press.

Internet References . . .

Children's Defense Fund

www.childrendefense.org

National Association for the Education of Young Children

www.naeyc.org

Society for Research in Child Development

www.srcd.org

Selected, Edited, and with Issue Framing Material by:
Allison A. Buskirk-Cohen, *Delaware Valley University*

ISSUE

Is Preschool Education Worthwhile?

YES: **Hirokazu Yoshikawa, et al.**, from *Investing in Our Future: The Evidence Base on Preschool Education* (Society for Research in Child Development and Foundation for Child Development, 2013)

NO: **David J. Armor and Sonia Sousa**, from "The Dubious Promise of Universal Preschool," *National Affairs* (2014)

Learning Outcomes

After reading this issue, you will be able to:

- See that there is huge variation in the type of preschool education available to young children.
- Understand that high quality preschool education can result in gains in language, reading, and math skills.
- Discuss how the Head Start program has produced modest positive effects in the early years of children's lives.
- Understand that the long-term benefits of universal preschool are questioned by some experts, mainly due to questions of ensuring quality in such a program.

ISSUE SUMMARY

YES: Hirokazu Yoshikawa led a team of researchers from the Foundation for Child Development in an examination of the current research on early childhood education. They find that scientific research supports the academic, social, emotional, and economic benefits of preschool.

NO: Professors David Armor and Sonia Sousa, in contrast, point to disappointing results from the existing federal preschool program Head Start. They do not believe research overwhelmingly supports the benefits of preschool.

Young children today often experience care from other people than their parents. In the United States today, the majority of children under age five receive some kind of nonparental child care. The most recent reports estimate that there are at least eleven million children under age five in child care settings. Types of child care vary from a grandmother taking care of the family child to a stay-at-home mother caring for several neighborhood children to a privately owned business to a government-sponsored center. There are huge variations in the regulations for nonparental child care across states.

In some states, child care centers and family child care homes are not subject to state licensing regulations. Centers that are operated by a religious organization may apply for exemption from obtaining a license in some states. Family child care providers who care for five or fewer children may be exempt as well. Furthermore, in some of states, programs that are exempt from licensing but are legally operating, may not have to meet regulations regarding group size, child-staff ratios, staff education, educational activities, and materials. All of these decisions are reflected in costs.

Child care often differs dramatically in cost, with the average annual cost of full-time care for one child ranging from $5,000 to $15,000. The location of the child care setting impacts cost greatly, with costs being much higher in cities located in the northeastern section of the United States. The care of younger children is often higher than the cost of older children (partially because there is a higher care provider-child ratio.) There are typically additional fees if the child needs care beyond traditional hours (as defined by the provider). Optional enrichment activities, such as music or sports, often cost more as well.

How the day is structured in child care also differs, largely dependent upon the age of the child. Our expectations for how a six-month-old spends her day are quite different from expectations of a four-year-old. In recent years, our expectations for preschool-aged children have increased along with an expanding knowledge base of young children's development. Preschool also has been viewed as an opportune place for prevention and intervention. If we can improve young children's development, we might avoid later problems. In 1965, President Lyndon B. Johnson established the first publicly funded preschool program, Head Start. It was a half-day program for children of low-income families that provided education, nutrition, and health screenings for children, and support services for families.

The number of families interested in preschools has increased since the development of Head Start. In the 1960s, about 10 percent of preschool-aged children in the United States were enrolled in a preschool. There were many more families interested in preschools than were actual preschool programs available. By the 1980s, states began creating their own version of preschools for low-income children. By 2005, about 70 percent of young children are enrolled in some type of state preschool program. Many factors influence the increase in preschool programs. An increase of higher maternal employment rates, national antipoverty initiatives, and research on early development have been linked with national enrollment increase.

Despite these increases, there are individuals who still question the validity of preschool. In the YES selection, Hirokazu Yoshikawa and a team of researchers from the Foundation for Child Development review the research on preschool education. The data they examined includes programs like Head Start, the Perry Preschool, and Abecedarian program, as well as other lesser known programs. They find that scientific research supports the academic, social, emotional, and economic benefits of preschool. For example, they find that children gain about a third of a year of additional learning in language, reading, and math skills. In this selection, the researchers argue that large-scale public preschool programs can make a significant difference on children's development.

In this article, Yoshikawa and his colleagues do acknowledge some important discerning characteristics. They find that teacher-child interactions and effective use of curricula are the most important aspects of quality in preschool education. Furthermore, these authors discuss how interactions are most beneficial to children when they are supportive emotionally and educationally. Funding is required to train staff properly and continually; updating materials also requires funding. Given the financial strains already faced by families, and especially low-income families, that funding would have to come from another source, such as the government. Considering all of these limitations, the question about whether preschools are good or bad for children is not simple. However, even with these important challenges in mind, Yoshikawa and his colleagues do believe that preschool education is a good investment for the nation.

Professors David Armor and Sonia Sousa come to the opposite conclusion in the NO selection. Their article begins with a reference to President Barack Obama's 2013 State of the Union address, in which he called on Congress to expand access to high-quality preschool to every child in the country. His proposal called for a cost sharing partnership with the states to extend federal funds for low- and moderate-income children from families at or below 200 percent of poverty, approaching the concept of universal preschool (or "preschool for all."). In addition, the proposal described establishing standards, better training and pay for teachers, smaller class size, and continued funding for Head Start.

Armor and Sousa's article demonstrates how good intentions might be misplaced. Their article emphasizes the "disappointing results" from Head Start. The positive findings touted by proponents of Head Start have been modest and do not last more than one year. Armor and Sousa also review programs like the Perry Preschool program, and find similar results. They do not believe research overwhelmingly supports the benefits of preschool. As with the report from Yoshikawa and his colleagues, Armor and Sousa discuss the factors that qualify a preschool program as high quality. However, Armor and Sousa do not believe that there is a cost-effective way to create a high-quality universal preschool program. They argue that the existing programs would not likely create any kind of meaningful, long-term positive outcomes for children.

YES

Hirokazu Yoshikawa et al.

Investing in Our Future: The Evidence Base on Preschool Education

Early Skills Matter, and Preschool Can Help Children Build These Skills.

The foundations of brain architecture, and subsequent life-long developmental potential, are laid down in a child's early years through a process that is exquisitely sensitive to external influence. Early experiences in the home, in other care settings, and in communities interact with genes to shape the developing nature and quality of the brain's architecture. The growth and then environmentally based pruning of neuronal systems in the first years support a range of early skills, including cognitive (early language, literacy, math), social(theory of mind, empathy, prosocial), persistence, attention, and self-regulation and executive function skills (the voluntary control of attention and behavior). Later skills—in schooling and employment—build cumulatively upon these early skills. Therefore investment in early learning and development is more efficient and can generate more benefits than costs relative to investment later in the life cycle. The evidence reviewed below addresses the role of preschool in helping children build these skills.

Rigorous Evidence Suggests Positive Short-Term Impacts of Preschool Programs on Children's Academic School Readiness and Mixed Impacts on Children's Socio-Emotional Readiness.

Effects on Language, Literacy, and Mathematics. Robust evidence suggests that a year or two of center-based ECE for three- and four-year-olds, provided in a developmentally appropriate program, will improve children's early language, literacy, and mathematics skills when measured at the end of the program or soon after. These findings have been replicated across dozens of rigorous studies of early education programs, including small demonstration programs and evaluations of large public programs such as Head Start and some state Pre-K programs. Combining across cognitive (e.g., IQ), language (e.g., expressive and receptive vocabulary) and achievement (e.g., early reading and mathematics skills) outcomes, a recent meta-analysis including evaluations of 84 diverse early education programs for young children evaluated between 1965 and 2007 estimated the average post-program impact to be about .35 standard deviations. This represents about a third of a year of additional learning, above and beyond what would have occurred without access to preschool. These data include both the well-known small demonstration programs such as Perry Preschool, which produced quite large effects, as well as evaluations of large preschool programs like Head Start, which are characterized both by lower cost but also more modest effects. Two recent evaluations of at-scale urban prekindergarten programs, in Tulsa and Boston, showed large effects (between a half of a year to a full year of additional learning) on language, literacy and math.

Effects on Socio-Emotional Development. The effects of preschool on socio-emotional development are not as clear-cut as those on cognitive and achievement outcomes. Far fewer evaluation studies of general preschool (that is, preschool without a specific behavior-focused component) have included measures of these outcomes. And relative to measures of achievement, language and cognition, socio-emotional measures are also more varied in the content they cover and quality of measurement.

A few programs have demonstrated positive effects on children's socio-emotional development. Perry Preschool was found to have reduced children's externalizing

Hirokazu Yoshikawa et al., *Investing in Our Future: The Evidence Base on Preschool Education*, Foundation for Child Development, October 2013, behavior problems (such as acting out or aggression) in elementary school. More recently, the National Head Start Impact Study found no effects in the socio-emotional area for four-year-old children, although problem behavior, specifically hyperactivity, was reduced after one year of Head Start among three-year-olds. An evaluation of the Tulsa prekindergarten program found that prekindergarten attendees had lower levels of timidity and higher levels of attentiveness, suggesting greater engagement in the classroom, than was the case for other students who neither attended prekindergarten nor Head Start. However, there were no differences among prekindergarten and other children in their aggressive or hyperactive behavior. A recent explanation for the divergence of findings is suggested by meta-analytic work on aggression, which found that modest improvements in children's aggressive behavior occurred among programs that made improving children's behavior an explicit goal.

Effects on Health. The effects of preschool on children's health have been rigorously investigated only within the Head Start program; Head Start directly targets children's health outcomes, while many preschool programs do not. Head Start has been shown to increase child immunization rates. In addition, there is evidence that Head Start in its early years of implementation reduced child mortality, and in particular mortality from causes that could be attributed plausibly to aspects of Head Start's health services, particularly immunization and health screening (e.g. measles, diabetes, whooping cough, respiratory problems). More recently, the National Head Start Impact Study found somewhat mixed impacts on children's health outcomes between the end of the program and the end of first grade. Head Start had small positive impacts on some health indicators, such as receipt of dental care, whether the child had health insurance, and parents' reports of whether their child had good health, at some post-program time points but not at others. Head Start had no impact at the end of first grade on whether the child had received care for an injury within the last month or whether the child needed ongoing care. The positive impacts of Head Start on immunization, dental care and some other indicators may be due to features of its health component—the program includes preventive dental care, comprehensive screening of children, tracking of well-child visits and required immunizations, and assistance if needed with accessing a regular medical home. In contrast to the literature on Head Start and health outcomes, there are almost no studies of the effects of public prekindergarten on children's health.

A Second Year of Preschool Shows Additional Benefits.

Few studies have examined the relative impact of one vs. two years of preschool education, and none that randomly assigned this condition. All of the relevant studies focus on disadvantaged children. The existing evidence suggests that more years of preschool seem to be related to larger gains, but the added impact of an additional year is often smaller than the gains typically experienced by a four-year-old from one year of participation. Why the additional year generally results in smaller gains is unclear. It may be that children who attend multiple years experience the same curriculum across the two years rather than experiencing sequenced two-year curricula, as programs may mix three-year-old and four-year-olds in the same classroom.

Children Show Larger Gains in Higher-Quality Preschool Programs.

Higher-quality preschool programs have larger impacts on children's development while children are enrolled in the program and are more likely to create gains that are sustained after the child leaves preschool. Process quality features—children's immediate experience of positive and stimulating interactions—are the most important contributors to children's gains in language, literacy, mathematics and social skills. Structural features of quality (those features of quality that can be changed by structuring the setting differently or putting different requirements for staff in place, like group size, ratio, and teacher qualifications) help to create the conditions for positive process quality, but do not ensure that it will occur.

For example, smaller group sizes and better ratios of staff to children provide the right kind of setting for children to experience more positive interactions. But these conditions by themselves are not enough. Teacher qualifications such as higher educational attainment and background, certification in early childhood, or higher than average compensation for the field are features of many early education programs that have had strong effects. Yet here too, research indicates that qualifications alone do not ensure greater gains for children during the course of the preschool years. To promote stronger outcomes, preschool programs should be characterized by both structural features of quality and ongoing supports to teachers to assure that the immediate experiences of children, those provided through activities and interactions, are rich in content and stimulation, while also being emotionally supportive.

The aspects of process quality that appear to be most important to children's gains during the preschool years address two inter-related dimensions of teacher-child interaction. First, interactions explicitly aimed at supporting learning, that foster both higher-order thinking skills in general and learning of content in such specific areas as early math and language, are related to gains, as discussed further later in this brief. Second, learning across multiple domains is enhanced in the context of warm, responsive teacher-child relationships and interactions that are characterized by back and forth—serve and return—conversations to discuss and elaborate on a given topic. Both the warm and responsive interaction style and learning-focused interactions also predict the persistence of gains into the school years. Some evidence suggests that children who have more opportunities to engage in age-appropriate activities with a range of varied materials such as books, blocks, and sand show larger gains during the preschool years (and those gains are maintained into the school years).

Quality in Preschool Classrooms Is in Need of Improvement, with Instructional Support Levels Particularly Low.

Both longstanding and more recent research reveal that the average overall quality of preschool programs is squarely in the middle range of established measures. In large-scale studies of public prekindergarten, for example, only a minority of programs are observed to provide excellent quality; a comparable minority of programs are observed to provide poor quality. It is therefore not surprising that impacts of most of the rigorously evaluated public prekindergarten programs fall shy of those in Tulsa and Boston (showing gains in the small to moderate range for reading and math, that is, a few months of added learning, rather than the half-year to full-year of additional learning that was found in Tulsa and Boston). Head Start programs also show considerable variation in quality. While few programs are rated as having "poor" quality, research suggests that as in studies of many public prekindergarten programs, Head Start programs on average show instructional quality levels well below the midpoint of established measures. In sum, there is variation in quality in both Head Start and prekindergarten nationally, with no clear pattern of one being stronger in quality than

the other in the existing research. It is important to note here that funding streams are increasingly mixed on the ground, with prekindergarten programs using Head Start performance standards or programs having fully blended funds; thus, these two systems are no longer mutually exclusive in many locales.

High-quality programs implemented at scale are possible, according to recent research. Evaluation evidence on the Tulsa and Boston prekindergarten programs shows that high-quality public Pre-K programs can be implemented across entire diverse cities and produce substantial positive effects on multiple domains of children's development. Assuring high quality in these public programs implemented at scale has entailed a combination of program standards, attention to teacher qualifications and compensation, additional ongoing on-site quality supports such as the ones described previously, and quality monitoring.

A Promising Route to Quality: Developmentally Focused, Intensive Curricula with Integrated, In-Classroom Professional Development.

Curricula can play a crucial role in ensuring that children have the opportunity to acquire school readiness skills during the preschool years. Preschool curricula vary widely. Some, typically labeled "global" curricula, tend to have a wide scope, providing activities that are thought to promote socio-emotional, language, literacy, and mathematics skills and knowledge about science, arts, and social studies. Other curricula, which we label "developmentally focused," aim to provide intensive exposure to a given content area based on the assumption that skills can be better fostered with a more focused scope.

Few global curricula have been evaluated rigorously. However, existing evidence from independent evaluators suggests no or small gains associated with their use, when compared with other commercially available curricula, researcher-developed curricula or curricula developed by individual teachers. A revised version of a widely used global curriculum is currently being evaluated via a randomized trial.

As for developmentally focused curricula, several recent experimental evaluations have demonstrated moderate to large gains in the targeted domains of children's development, for math curricula, language and literacy curricula, and curricula directed at improving socio-emotional skills and self-regulation, compared with usual practice in preschool classrooms, which typically involve more global curricula. In these studies, for the group receiving the developmentally focused curriculum, it is generally added to a global curriculum that is already in place.

Most of the successful curricula in these recent evaluations are characterized by intensive professional development that often involves coaching at least twice a month, in which an expert teacher provides feedback and support for in-classroom practice, either in person or in some cases through observation of videos of classroom teaching. Some curricula also incorporate assessments of child progress that are used to inform and individualize instruction, carried out at multiple points during the preschool year. These assessments allow the teacher to monitor the progress of each child in the classroom and modify her content and approach accordingly.

This recent set of studies suggests that intensive, developmentally focused curricula with integrated professional development and monitoring of children's progress offer the strongest hope for improving classroom quality as well as child outcomes during the preschool years. However, more evidence is needed about the effectiveness of such curricula, particularly studies of curricula implemented without extensive support of the developer, or beyond initial demonstrations of efficacy. That is, the majority of rigorously conducted trials of developmentally focused curricula have included extensive involvement of the developer(s) and involve relatively small numbers of children. There have been only a few trials of curricula in "real world" conditions—meaning without extensive developer(s)' involvement and across a large program. Some notable recent results in "real world" conditions show promise that substantial effects can be achieved, but more such studies are needed given the widely noted difficulties in taking interventions to scale.

A recent development in early childhood curricula is the implementation of integrated curricula across child developmental domains (for example, socio-emotional and language; math and language), which retain the feature of defined scope for each area. In two recent successful instances, efforts were made to ensure feasible, integrated implementation; importantly, supporting coaches and mentor teachers were trained across the targeted domains and curricula.

In addition to in-classroom professional development supports, the pre-service training and education of teachers is of critical concern in the field of preschool education. However, here evaluation research is still scant. Recent innovations include increasing integration of practica and in-classroom experiences in higher education teacher preparation courses; hybrid web-based and in-person training approaches; and attention to overlooked areas of early childhood teacher preparation such as work with children with disabilities, work with children learning two languages, or teaching of early math skills. However, these innovations have yet to be fully evaluated for their impact on teacher capacities or preschool program quality.

Over the Course of Elementary School, Scores for Children Who Have and Have Not Attended Preschool Typically Converge. Despite This Convergence, There Is Some Evidence of Effects on Outcomes in Early Adulthood.

As children in preschool evaluation studies are followed into elementary school, the differences between those who received preschool and those who did not are typically reduced, based on the available primary-school outcomes of evaluations (chiefly test scores of reading and math achievement). This phenomenon of reduced effect sizes on test scores over time is often labeled "fadeout." We use the term convergence, as this term more accurately captures how outcomes like test scores of children who participated versus did not participate in preschool converge over time as the non-attenders catch-up. There is not yet a strong evidence base on reasons for the convergence of test scores in follow-up evaluations of children after early childhood. A number of factors may be involved—for example, low quality of primary schooling, particularly for students in disadvantaged areas,may fail to build on the gains created by early childhood education. Having students who attended and benefited from preschool may also permit elementary-school teachers to focus more on the non-attenders, and this extra attention may explain the convergence or catch-up pattern.

Persistence of Effects in Landmark, Small Demonstration Programs. A handful of small-scale demonstration programs show that while the language, literacy, and mathematics test scores of children participating versus not participating in preschool programs tend to converge as children progress through their K-12 schooling careers, the programs nonetheless appear to produce effects on a wide range of behavioral, health, and educational outcomes that persist into adulthood. The existing evidence pertains to low-income populations. The two most well-known randomized experimental tests of preschool interventions with long-term outcome data—Perry Preschool and Abecedarian—provided striking evidence of this. Both programs produced large initial impacts on achievement test scores. Though some effects remained, the size of these impacts fell in magnitude as children aged. Nonetheless, there were very large program effects on schooling attainment and earnings during adulthood. The programs also produced striking results for criminal behavior; fully 60–70% of the dollar-value of the benefits to society generated by Perry Preschool come from impacts in reducing criminal behavior. In Abecedarian, the treatment group's rate of felony convictions or incarceration by age 21 is fully one-third below that of the control group. Other effects included reductions in teen pregnancy in both studies for treatment group members and reductions in tobacco use for treatment group members in Abecedarian.

Persistence of Effects in Programs at Scale.   Patterns of converging test scores but emerging impacts in adulthood are present in some other noteworthy preschool programs as well. These also focus on disadvantaged populations. For example, in studies of Head Start, there appear to be long-term gains in educational, behavioral and health outcomes even after test score impacts decline to zero. Specifically, a number of quasi-experimental studies of Head Start children who participated in the program in the 1960's, 1970's and 1980's find test score effects that are no longer statistically significant within a few years after the children leave the program. But even though Head Start participants have test scores that look similar to other children by early to mid elementary school, these studies show that Head Start children wind up completing more years of schooling, earning more, being healthier, and (in at least some studies) may be less likely to engage in criminal behavior. Two studies have examined the medium-term persistence of gains of publicly funded state prekindergarten programs. One of these has followed children through third grade and found persistent mathematics gains, but not reading gains, through third grade for boys. The second study has followed children through first grade and has found convergence of participating and non-participating children's cognitive skills and mixed impacts on children's behavioral outcomes.

Future Directions in Sustaining Short-Term Gains from Preschool.   Despite several promising studies of long-term gains, we caution that the vast majority of preschool program evaluations have not assessed outcomes substantially beyond the end of the program. Strategies for sustaining short-term gains for children require more exploration and evaluation. One path to sustaining short-term gains may be to maximize the short-term impact by ensuring that quality of preschool is high, according to the approaches described previously. Another is to work towards greater continuity in learning goals and approaches across the preschool and early elementary years and ensuring instructional quality and support for health and socio-emotional learning in kindergarten and the early elementary grades. And finally, efforts to bolster three major influences that parents have on children's development—their psychological well-being; their parenting behaviors; and their economic security—have been a focus in Head Start but not in other preschool programs. Intensifying and further specifying these components may increase the impact of preschool. Recent advances in successful parenting interventions, which provide great specificity and intensive focus on the dimension of parenting behavior targeted (e.g., specific behavior management approaches or contingent responsiveness), have yet to be integrated with preschool systems. A recent meta-analytic study suggests that a parenting-focused component can be an important complement to preschool and produce added gains in children's cognitive skills. The key is that the component on parenting be delivered via modeling of positive interactions or opportunities for practice with feedback. Didactic workshops or classes in which parents merely receive information about parenting strategies or practices appeared to produce no additive benefits beyond those from the early education component of preschool alone. Efforts to integrate recent advances in adult education and workforce development programs(a new set of two- or dual-generation programs), similarly, are just now being evaluated.

Preschool's Effects for Different Subgroups.

Family Income.   **Recent evidence suggests that high-quality preschool positively contributes to the language, literacy, and mathematics skills growth of both low- and middle-income children, but has the greatest impact on children living in or near poverty.** Until recently, it has been difficult to compare the effectiveness of high-quality preschool across income groups, because almost all of the earlier studies focused on programs that targeted children from poor families. For example, the median percentage of families in poverty in rigorous early childhood education evaluations identified in a recent meta-analysis was 91%. One study from the 1980's of the positive impacts of preschool education on children from well-to-do families suggested substantial positive impacts on boys. More recently, the advent of universal prekindergarten in a small number of states and communities has permitted comparisons based on income. In two studies of public prekindergarten programs, positive and substantial impacts on language, literacy, and mathematics skills were found for both low- and middle-income children. In both of these studies, the impacts were larger for children living in or near poverty (as indicated by free- or reduced-lunch status), but still substantial for their less disadvantaged peers.

Race/Ethnicity. **Overall, the current research evidence suggests that children of different racial/ethnic groups benefit from preschool.** Many of the most prominent evaluations from the 1960's, 1970's and 1980's (e.g., Perry, Abecedarian, and the Chicago Child-Parent Centers) focused on African American students, with no comparisons of effects possible across different racial/ethnic groups. Several more recent studies have compared effects for students from different racial/ethnic backgrounds. The Head Start Impact Study reached somewhat different conclusions for three-year-olds and four-year-olds: for three-year-olds, positive post-program impacts were strongest for African Americans and Hispanics, relative to White, non-Hispanic children; for four-year-olds, positive impacts were smaller for Hispanics, again relative to White, non-Hispanic children. The Tulsa study found substantial improvements in school readiness for prekindergarten participants from all racial and ethnic groups. Effect sizes were moderate to large for all racial and ethnic groups studied (White, Black, Hispanic, Native American) but especially large for Hispanics. The Boston study found substantial benefits in language, literacy, mathematics, and executive functioning domains for children from all racial and ethnic groups. Effect sizes were especially large for Hispanics and for Asian Americans, though the sample size for Asian Americans was relatively small.

Dual Language Learners and Children of Immigrants. **Positive impacts of preschool can be as strong or stronger for dual language learners and children of immigrants, compared with their English-speaking or native-born counterparts.** Given the specific challenges and opportunities faced in school by dual language learner (DLL) students and the growing number of such students in the U.S., it is important to know how high-quality preschool programs impact them in particular, as well as the features of quality that are important to their development. National non-experimental evidence suggests that positive effects of preschool on early reading and math achievement are as strong for children of immigrants as for children of the native-born. In the Tulsa prekindergarten program, effects for Hispanic students who came from homes where Spanish was the primary spoken language (DLL students) were larger than effects for Hispanic students who came from homes where English was the primary spoken language. And the National Head Start Impact Study found significantly stronger positive impacts of Head Start on language and school performance at the end of kindergarten for DLL students, relative to their native speaking counterparts.

Generally, the same features of quality that are important to the academic outcomes of monolingual English speaking children appear to be important to the development of DLL children. However, a feature of early childhood settings that may be important specifically to the development of DLL children is language of instruction. There is emerging research that preschool programs that systematically integrate both the children's home language and English language development promote achievement in the home language as well as English language development. While there are no large meta-analytic studies of bilingual education in preschool, meta-analyses of bilingual education in elementary school and several experimental preschool studies have reached this conclusion. Home language development does not appear to come at the cost of developing English language skills, but rather strengthens them. Thus, programs that intentionally use both languages can promote emergent bilingualism, a characteristic that may be valuable in later development.

Children with Special Needs. **More research is needed replicating and extending initial findings of positive effects for children with special needs.** The Head Start Impact Study found that children with special needs randomly assigned to Head Start as 3-year-olds made significant gains in math and social-emotional development at the end of first grade compared with peers assigned to the control group. Research on the Tulsa prekindergarten program found that children with mild to moderate special needs who participated in prekindergarten experienced significant improvements—comparable to those for typically developing children—in their reading skills and writing skills, though not necessarily in math. There is a need to test these patterns in other studies.

The Benefits of Quality Preschool Outweigh the Costs.

High-quality preschool programs are one of many possible ways to support children's development, and it is important to ask whether the benefits from such programs can offset their considerable costs. Cost-benefit frameworks enable researchers to assess the value of social investments. Key to this technique is a systematic accounting of the costs and benefits of an intervention, based on a careful comparison of outcomes for those individuals who participated in the program and otherwise similar individuals who did not. Early childhood education costs refer to all expenditures necessary to provide the program, including staff time and capital investments. Benefits typically take one of two forms. First, benefits may come from cost savings, such as reduced spending for special education and grade retention, as well as lower involvement in the child protection, welfare, and criminal justice systems. Second, benefits may flow from greater economic productivity, especially higher earnings as adults. It is also important to note that benefits can accrue not only to the individuals who directly participated in preschool programs, but also to society (e.g., the value of not being a crime victim). When both costs and benefits are quantified, researchers can produce an estimate of a program's benefits relative to its costs.

Rigorous efforts to estimate benefit-cost ratios of preschool have yielded very positive results, suggesting that early childhood education can be a wise financial investment. Using data on the long-term life outcomes of program participants and non-participants, assessments of the Perry Preschool program and the Chicago Child-Parent Centers both yielded estimates of about 7 to 1 or higher. Estimates of the longer and thus more costly Abecedarian Project (program length of 5 years) have produced a lower estimate of approximately 2.5 to 1. Other scholars, lacking hard evidence on long-term impacts for program participants and non-participants who have not yet become adults, have made projections by blending evidence on short-term results from the program with evidence on the relationship between short-term results and adult outcomes from other sources. Such efforts have yielded estimates for universal prekindergarten programs (available to children from all income groups) that range from 3 to 1 to 5 to 1. The divergence of estimates across programs suggests that it may be hard to predict the exact rate of return for programs. However, the best current evidence suggests that the impact of quality preschool per dollar spent on cognitive and achievement outcomes is larger than the average impact of other well-known educational interventions per dollar spent, such as class-size reductions in elementary schools.

The consistent finding of benefits that substantially exceed preschool program costs indicates that high-quality early childhood education programs are among the most cost-effective educational interventions and are likely to be profitable investments for society as a whole.

Conclusion

The goal of this research brief has been to summarize the most recent rigorous research for inclusion in the important public discussion that is now occurring about preschool education. When taken together with earlier foundational studies, the growing body of research on preschool both confirms but also extends the previous evidence in important directions.

Recent meta-analyses drawing together the evidence across decades of evaluation research now permit us to say with confidence that preschool programs can have a substantial impact on early learning and development. Positive effects on children's development are found for language, literacy and early math skills; for social and emotional outcomes; and in children's health. Whereas earlier evidence was limited to small, tightly controlled demonstration projects, the more recent evidence supports this conclusion for rigorously evaluated high quality preschool programs implemented at scale. While earlier studies were limited to a focus on children from low-income families, some more recent studies of preschool implemented at scale encompass families from a wider socioeconomic range, and for the first time, make it possible to say that preschool education benefits children from middle-income as well as low-income families (although children from low-income children benefit more). The most recent research also makes clear that there are positive effects for dual language learner children as well as for those whose home language is English, and for children with special needs as well as for typically developing children.

While there is clear evidence that preschool education boosts early learning for children from a range of backgrounds, we also see a convergence of test scores during the elementary school grades so that there are diminishing differences over time on tests of academic achievement between children who did and did not attend preschool. Yet the most recent research is showing an accumulation of evidence that even when the difference in test scores declines to zero, children who have attended preschool go on to show positive effects on important adolescent and young adult outcomes, such as high school graduation, reduced teen pregnancy, years of education completed, earnings, and reduced crime. Why there are long term effects even with a convergence of test scores is an important focus of current research.

The evidence continues to grow that the foundation for positive effects on children are interactions with teachers that combine stimulation and support. Such interactions build children's higher-order thinking skills as well as knowledge of specific content (such as early math and language skills), and at the same time are warm, responsive and elicit reciprocal interactions. Features of quality that focus on structural elements, such as group size, ratio, and teacher qualifications are important in that they help to increase the likelihood of such interactions, but they do not ensure that simulating and supportive interactions will occur.

Multiple recent studies suggest a highly promising route to quality in preschool education: providing support for teachers to implement specific evidence-based curricula and instruction through coaching and mentoring. These studies have shown positive effects in strengthening both teacher-child interactions and children's learning in targeted domains. This evidence is particularly important given that large-scale studies of both state-funded preschool and Head Start show that there is a need to improve quality, and especially the quality of instruction.

Beyond coaching and mentoring in support of instruction and curricula, what other factors strengthen the boost provided to children from preschool education? There is evidence that a second year of preschool shows additional benefits to children. However, more work is needed to consider how a second year could intentionally build on children's growth in a first year of preschool. In addition, while comprehensive services can strengthen outcomes, the most recent research indicates that it is important to target such services so that they focus on evidence-based practices. For example, a recently conducted meta-analysis indicates that the positive effects of preschool education can be augmented when a parenting education component is added, but only when this component focuses on providing parents the opportunity to see modeling of positive interactions or to practice such interactions. Such effects do not occur when programs simply provide parents with information.

Finally, while it has been clear for some time that high-quality preschool education yields more in benefits to society than its initial costs, the most recent work indicates that there is a positive return on investment for a range of differing preschool programs, from those that are more intensive and costly to those that require less initial investment. In sum, quality preschool education is an investment in our future.

HIROKAZU YOSHIKAWA is the Courtney Sale Ross Professor of Globalization and Education at NYU Steinhardt and a University Professor at NYU. He is a community and developmental psychologist who studies the effects of public policies and programs related to immigration, early childhood, and poverty reduction on children's development.

CHRISTINA WEILAND is a faculty member in the School of Education at the University of Michigan. Her research focuses on the effects of early childhood interventions, developmental contexts, and public policies on children's development, particularly among children from low-income families, and on the mechanisms by which such effects occur.

JEANNE BROOKS-GUNN is a faculty member at Teachers College, Columbia University. Her research interests include child and family policy and programs; early childhood interventions and education; and adolescent transitions and development.

MARGARET R. BURCHINAL is a Senior Scientist at the Frank Porter Graham (FPG) Child Development Institute at the University of North Carolina, Chapel Hill. She directs FPG's Data Management and Statistics Unit. She is a faculty member in the department of psychology and the department of biostatistics there as well.

LINDA M. ESPINOSA is currently Co-PI for the Center for Early Care and Evaluation Research—Dual Language Learners (CECER-DLL) at Frank Porter Graham CDI at the University of North Carolina, Chapel Hill and Lead Consultant for the Best Practices for Young Dual Language Learners Project at the California State Department of Education, Child Development Division.

WILLIAM T. GORMLEY is a professor of public policy at Georgetown University and codirector for the Center for Research on Children in the United States (CROCUS). His interests include government reform and its consequences; functional and dysfunctional bureaucratic control mechanisms; developing and applying analytical frameworks to improve our understanding of public policy choices; and children and public policy.

JENS LUDWIG is the McCormick Foundation Professor of Social Service Administration, Law, and Public Policy in the School of Social Service Administration and Chicago

Harris, director of the University of Chicago Crime Lab, and codirector of the University of Chicago Urban Education Lab.

KATHERINE A. MAGNUSON is a faculty member in the School of Social Work at the University of Wisconsin-Madison. Her research interests include socioeconomic status and child development; early education and intervention; and welfare reform and family well-being.

DEBORAH PHILLIPS is a professor of psychology and associated faculty in the Public Policy Institute at Georgetown University. She was the first Executive Director of the Board on Children, Youth, and Families of the National Research Council and the Institute of Medicine and served as Study Director for the Board's report: From Neurons to Neighborhoods: The Science of Early Child Development.

MARTHA J. ZASLOW is the director of the Office for Policy and Communications of the Society for Research in Child Development (SRCD) and a Senior Scholar at Child Trends. She recently served on the Secretary's Advisory Committee for Head Start Research and Evaluation and on the Committee on Developmental Outcomes and Assessments of Young Children of the National Research Council.

David J. Armor and Sonia Sousa  **NO**

The Dubious Promise of Universal Preschool

In his 2013 state of the union address, President Obama proposed a "Preschool for All" initiative, pledging $75 billion in new federal funding over a period of ten years. In a partnership with the states, the federal government would provide the majority of funds needed for the implementation of "high-quality" preschool for all four-year-old children whose families make up to 200% of the poverty line. The federal government would also provide incentives for states to offer preschool to all remaining middle-class children, thus approaching "universal" preschool.

The idea of universal preschool is not new, and a handful of states already have such policies. Oklahoma, for instance, has the highest rate of four-year-old enrollment at about 70%. The president's endorsement and the offer of federal start-up money give a tremendous boost to this concept. Before we launch a universal preschool program and dedicate billions of dollars in federal funds, however, it is important that we take into account the outcomes of students participating in the existing federal preschool program: Head Start.

The Head Start program has been evaluated using the most sophisticated research designs available to social scientists, and the results have been disappointing. While Head Start appears to produce modest positive effects during the preschool years, these effects do not last even into kindergarten, much less through the early elementary years. These findings suggest that, if a new universal preschool program is to have greater success, something about the new program will have to be different.

Proponents of universal preschool stress that children need *high-quality* programs, implying that Head Start is not high quality and thereby explaining why the program has not produced the desired results. Evidence from comparative studies suggests, however, that Head Start programs are not significantly different from those commonly cited as being high quality, at least in attributes that produce better outcomes. The evidence suggests that we aren't exactly sure what kind of program would

succeed in leveling the playing field for low-income children. A review of the research on Head Start and other preschool programs, with a rigorous consideration of the benefits claimed by these programs and an informed cost-benefit analysis, must therefore be undertaken before the federal government spends billions of dollars on a new, untested program.

The State of Head Start

Head Start began in 1965 as a summer-school program intended to advance the ends of President Lyndon Johnson's War on Poverty. Policymakers quickly realized, however, that an eight-week intervention was not enough to overcome the disadvantages children suffered after four years of poverty, so Head Start was converted into a full-time program that served fewer students. In the early years of the summer-school program, about 700,000 students enrolled at the relatively low cost of $2 billion, for a per-capita cost of $2,000 to $3,000 (all in 2011 dollars). After the conversion to a full-time program, enrollment dropped to under 400,000 by the early 1970s. The figure on the next page tracks the growth of program enrollment and costs from 1967 to 2011.

From the early 1970s to about 1989, Head Start enrollment was relatively stable, increasing from just under 400,000 to about 450,000 children. Funding was also relatively stable, growing from $2 billion to $2.3 billion, and per-capita spending hovered around $5,000 per child in current dollars. In 1990, the program began a decade of rapid growth, starting in the first Bush administration and continuing through the Clinton years. Enrollment more than doubled to just over 900,000 children, and funding climbed even more steeply; by 2000, total appropriations had tripled to just under $7 billion per year, and per-capita expenditures increased to $8,000 per child. These funding increases, primarily meant to pay for curriculum changes and better-trained instructors, were partly in response to early evaluations of the Head Start program, which

Armor and Sousa, The Dubious Promise of Universal Preschool. *National Affairs*, 2014. p. 36–49. Reprinted by permission.

Trends in Head Start Enrollment and Appropriations

Source: U.S. Department of Health and Human Services, Fiscal Year 2011 Fact Sheet.

*Figures include $2.1 billion appropriated by the American Recovery and Reinvestment Act enacted in February 2009 and available over a two-year period.

showed gains that were very modest and tended to fade after children entered elementary school.

During the George W. Bush administration, enrollment remained stable around 900,000 children, but funding increased—jumping to $8.2 billion in 2002 and then slowly drifting downward to about $7.2 billion in 2008. In the first two years of the Obama administration, the American Recovery and Reinvestment Act added $2.1 billion to Head Start (divided between 2009 and 2010), and enrollment increased by 61,000. In 2011, program funding dropped back to $7.6 billion, serving approximately one million students.

The Head Start program was originally implemented to help children from low-income households catch up with middle-class children by the time they reached kindergarten. For decades, studies have shown that children who grow up in poverty are more likely to have social and behavioral problems, as well as cognitive challenges that can impede learning. Children who experience poverty in their preschool years, in particular, have a substantially higher risk of not graduating from high school and so of suffering all of the resulting economic consequences. Head Start was intended to mitigate some of those disadvantages through early intervention. The program is based on a "whole child" model, aimed at improving four main contributors to a child's readiness to enter regular school at age five: cognitive development; social-emotional development; medical, dental, and mental health; and parenting practices.

As part of a federal initiative under the Department of Health and Human Services, Head Start programs operate independently from local school districts and are most commonly administered through city or county social-services agencies. In general, classes are small or at least have low child-to-staff ratios of less than ten students per adult staff member. Individual Head Start programs develop their own curricula of academic and social activities with federal performance standards in mind. Though most Head Start teachers do not have a bachelor's degree and are not certified teachers, most of the teachers do have at least an associate's degree, and most have completed six or more courses in early-childhood education.

HHS demands that certain federal requirements be met in all Head Start programs, but because each program is run locally, there can be wide variations in the quality of the programs. In addition, Head Start does not require that teachers have the certification that regular public-school teachers are required to have.

As a result of these variations and trends, some champions of early-childhood intervention programs have argued that the Head Start program, in terms of staff and curriculum, is not a "high-quality" pre-school program. A high-quality program, according to these critics, must have a fully certified teacher and a standard curriculum approved by a state or local school board. Head Start officials dispute this assertion and argue that its instructors and curricula both meet high standards.

Does Head Start Kick-Start Kids?

After more than four decades of Head Start, there has been a considerable amount of research done on the program and its effects. The most comprehensive and rigorous evaluation to date is the Head Start Impact Study (HSIS), sponsored by the Administration for Children and Families in the Department of Health and Human Services. The study looked at 4,667 three- and four-year-old children applying for entry into Head Start in a nationally representative sample of programs across 23 states.

Children were randomly assigned to either a Head Start group (treatment group) or a non-Head Start group (control group), ensuring that the children in the two groups were similar in all measured and unmeasured characteristics at program entry, the only difference being their participation in Head Start. In order to verify this initial equivalence, and to estimate potential effects of attrition, pre-test assessments of all critical outcome measures were taken before the start of the preschool experience. Children in the non-Head Start control group could enroll in other non-Head Start child services chosen by their parents or remain at home in parent care. This allowed HSIS to assess how well the program performs compared to what children would experience in the absence of the program, rather than compared to an artificial condition where children were prevented from obtaining other child-care services. Nearly half of the control-group children did enroll in other preschool programs.

Outcome measures covered all four Head Start program goals: cognitive development, social-emotional development, health status and access to health care, and parenting practices. The table below summarizes only the positive effects on cognitive skills and social and behavioral outcomes (the health and parenting outcomes as well as some negative effects will be discussed separately).

Relative to children in the control group, Head Start participants showed positive effects in numerous cognitive skills during their Head Start years including letter-naming, vocabulary, letter-word identification, and applied math problems. However, these improvements did not carry into kindergarten or the later elementary grades. Only a few outcomes showed statistically significant improvements in the later grades, and they were not consistent across the three- and four-year-old cohorts (that is, they applied to different skills across cohorts and grades). This inconsistency makes it difficult to generalize about the success of the program in preparing students cognitively to keep up in later grades.

Participants showed fewer significant improvements in social and behavioral skills, even in the Head Start year, and results were inconsistent between the three- and four-year-old cohorts. The four-year-old cohort showed no significant improvements in the Head Start year or kindergarten, but in third grade they showed a significant reduction in total problem behavior according to their parents. The three-year-old cohort showed several significant improvements in social and behavioral skills, but only for outcomes assessed by parents. Not shown in the table, however, are several significant *negative* effects in relationships with teachers as rated by first-grade and third-grade teachers; in fact, there were no significant positive effects for this cohort as assessed by teachers for any of the elementary years. The three-year-old cohort showed several significant improvements in social and behavioral skills, but only as assessed by their parents.

Head Start also had some significant health-related effects, especially in increasing the number of children

Number of Significant and Positive Effects of Head Start on Cognitive and Behavioral Outcomes

Outcomes	Head Start Year	Kindergarten	First Grade	Third Grade
Cognitive Skills				
Head Start at age 4	7 out of 14	0 out of 19	1 out of 23	1 out of 11
Head Start at age 3	8 out of 14	1 out of 19	1 out of 23	0 out of 11
Social and Behavioral Skills				
Head Start at age 4	0 out of 9	0 out of 20	1 out of 20	2 out of 20
Head Start at age 3	2 out of 9	2 out of 20	2 out of 20	1 out of 20

Source: Authors' construction based on DHHS reports (2010, 2012). Significant means $p \leq .10$.

receiving dental care and having health-insurance coverage. These effects were not consistent, however. For example, participants did have increased health-insurance coverage, but not during their year in Head Start, and it did not extend into the third-grade year for either cohort, suggesting a possible short-term effect after leaving Head Start. There were also some significant effects on parenting practices, but they applied to the three-year-old cohort only. Most of these practices related to discipline, such as reduced spanking or use of time-outs. The reduced-spanking outcome occurred during the Head Start year and kindergarten, but it did not last into the first or third grades. During the Head Start year, there was also a significant effect on the amount of time parents spent reading to their children, but this effect did not last into kindergarten or first grade.

A secondary analysis of the HSIS evaluation was done by Peter Bernardy in his doctoral dissertation, entitled "Head Start: Assessing Common Explanations for the Apparent Disappearance of Initial Positive Effects." The study uses the HSIS data to test various hypotheses (including the quality argument) about *why* the initial effects of Head Start weaken and disappear during kindergarten and first grade. To begin, he examined whether other learning skills not examined in the HSIS might be affected more strongly than cognitive skills. These included child attention behavior, child persistence, and child confidence, as evaluated by teachers, parents, and independent assessors. Improvements in these skills could portend better longer-term outcomes in academic performance.

More important from a policy perspective, Bernardy also examined several programmatic and methodological issues frequently cited as explanations for why Head Start's positive effects fade after students enter regular grade school. He tested whether the quality of the Head Start curriculum and the quality of the elementary schools attended by Head Start students after preschool—two of the most common excuses for the failure of Head Start programs—affected the outcomes of students. Also addressed was the methodological problem arising from the fact that a significant portion of the control-group students attended some sort of other preschool program, meaning there was no true "no preschool" control group.

The table below summarizes the findings of Bernardy's study. The results are grouped under the four issues addressed: possible additional learning skills, Head Start program quality, elementary-school quality, and a no-preschool control group.

For additional learning skills, there was only one statistically significant positive effect out of the 43 possible comparisons, and there were none in the elementary grades. This single significant effect was the parent rating of attention at the end of the Head Start year for three-year-old children. This outcome was offset, however, by non-significant findings for attention as rated by independent assessors and teachers.

Children who participated in Head Start did exhibit several significant positive effects compared to children who had no preschool at all. All of these effects, however, were limited to the year they spent in the Head Start program; there were no significant positive effects in the kindergarten or first-grade years. In fact, there were two significant negative effects shown in cognitive skills for the three-year-old cohort, meaning the control group that did not participate in any preschool program had higher cognitive scores.

The failure of Head Start to produce long-term effects on its participants is often blamed on the quality of the Head Start curriculum. Using a common rating scale for assessing preschool curriculum quality, the Bernardy study showed no positive relationship between higher- quality Head Start programs and outcomes. Similarly, the evaluation of elementary-school quality yielded no significant positive effects after controlling for higher-quality schools.

This is why the Bernardy study is so valuable. It revealed no significant relationship between Head Start program quality and the major cognitive and social outcomes. And the long-term effects of participating in Head Start programs were not statistically different from not going to preschool at all.

The Quality Question

The evidence from the nationally representative HSIS evaluations, along with the Bernardy study, indicates that Head Start has small to moderate positive effects for several outcomes by the end of a child's preschool experience, but these initial positive effects do not endure even through kindergarten, let alone through the third grade. Proponents of publicly funded preschool contrast Head Start with other preschool programs that have, allegedly, better long-term outcomes, blaming the difference on the lower quality of Head Start. Some of the better-known "high-quality" programs created and evaluated within the last ten years include the Abbot program in New Jersey, the Boston preschool program, a preschool program in Tulsa, Oklahoma, and a Tennessee preschool program. Evaluators of the first three programs—none of which used the rigorous randomized designs used in the HSIS—claim very large cognitive effects, some nearly ten times those of the typical Head Start program. These stronger effects are attributed to the quality of the program offerings, namely,

Significant and Positive Effects of Head Start in the Bernardy Study*

	Head Start at Age 3				Head Start at Age 4		
	Age 3	Age 4	K	1st Grade	Age 4	K	1st Grade
Additional Learning Skills							
Attention: teacher rating	No	No	No	No	No	No	No
Attention: parent rating	Yes	No	No	No	No	No	No
Attention: independent rating	No	No	No	No	No	No	No
Attention: teacher/parent	–	–	No	No	–	No	No
Persistence: indep. rating	No	No	No	No	No	No	No
Confidence: indep. rating	No	No	No	No	No	No	No
Confidence: teacher/parent	–	–	No	No	–	No	No
Head Start Curriculum Quality							
Cognitive skills	No	No	No	No	No(–)	No	No
Social & behavioral skills	No	No	No	No	No	No	No
Attention: independent rating	No	No	No	No	No	No	No
Persistence: indep. rating	No	No	No	No	No	No	No
Confidence: indep. rating	No	No(–)	No	No	No	No	No
Elementary School Quality							
Cognitive skills	–	–	No	No	–	No	No
Social & behavioral skills	–	–	No	No	–	No	No
Attention: independent rating	–	–	No	No	–	No	No
Persistence: indep. rating	–	–	No	No	–	No	No
Confidence: indep. rating	–	–	No	No	–	No	No
Head Start vs. No Preschool							
Cognitive skills	Yes	No(–)	No(–)	No	Yes	No	No
Social & behavioral skills	No	No	No	No	No	No	No
Attention: independent rating	No	No	No	No	No	No	No
Persistence: indep. rating	Yes	No	No	No	Yes	No	No
Confidence: indep. rating	Yes	No	No	No	No	No	No

Source: Authors' construction based on Bernardy (2012). Significant means p≤.05.
*A minus sign denotes a significant negative effect.

a stronger curriculum and fully certified instructional staff with bachelor's degrees. But the Tennessee preschool evaluation, which had a randomized design, failed to find significant positive effects through first grade.

The argument that the large effects noted in New Jersey, Boston, and Tulsa are due to better curriculum and more qualified instructional staff—particularly more teachers with bachelor's degrees—is especially puzzling.

Research has shown that both curriculum quality and teacher education have very low correlations with cognitive and social-emotional outcomes in preschool programs. This was demonstrated both in Bernardy's study using the national sample of Head Start programs and in a 2007 study by a team led by Diane Early of the University of North Carolina, which used a diverse national sample of preschool programs including Head Start. The lack of correlation makes sense when one considers that the children in these preschool programs are only three or four years old. Teaching basic vocabulary or numeracy skills to this age group does not require years of formal study or a complex curriculum, otherwise untrained middle-class parents would not be such good teachers for their young children.

Furthermore, Head Start actually competes well on quality measures with preschools that have reputations for high quality. According to the ECERS-R index, a common measure of preschool classroom quality, the Head Start programs studied in the HSIS are actually of slightly higher quality than the "high-quality" Abbot program. The index ranges from 1 (poor) to 7 (excellent), and the Abbot preschool averaged 4.8 in a 2007 evaluation study led by Ellen Frede. For the national Head Start sample in the HSIS, the average ECERS-R index was 5.2 for the three-year-old Head Start cohort and 5.3 for the four-year-old cohort. (The Boston and Tulsa pre-K programs do not report ECERS scores.)

It is also important to note that there are potentially serious methodological problems in the New Jersey, Boston, and Tulsa evaluations. Because the preschool programs deal with very young children, often in challenging communities, it is difficult to achieve randomized designs. The Abbot, Boston, and Tulsa studies, therefore, used a quasi-experimental design called regression discontinuity design, or RDD.

There is no pre-test in RDD; the treatment group is assessed at the beginning of kindergarten, after children have completed the preschool program. The control group consists of students one year younger who are just starting pre-K. The treatment group can experience attrition, and children who drop out of a preschool program are quite likely to have lower test scores. In effect, the treatment group consists of only those students who complete a year of preschool, and we would expect their scores to be higher (adjusting for age) than a control group that includes everyone who starts the pre-K program. This could be a major reason why RDD studies of preschools show much higher program effects than the HSIS. The results of the Tennessee program, in contrast, look very similar to Head Start, with substantial effects in the Head Start year but no longer-term effects. The Tennessee program had the same quality characteristics as the other "high-quality" programs; the only difference is the use of a rigorous randomized design with a pre-test.

Having rigorous studies of these preschool-program outcomes is important to ensuring that children are receiving the quality of education they need. Quality-comparison studies are vital to making sure that the low-income children that Head Start was designed to help are actually getting the boost they need to keep up with their middle-class counterparts in kindergarten. From a policy perspective, such studies are also important for cost-benefit analysis, especially as a new universal-preschool program is being considered.

Costs and Benefits

Only a handful of cost-benefit studies have been carried out for pre-K programs. There is no need for a cost-benefit analysis of Head Start given the available evidence, because the program has only short-term effects and no quantifiable long-term benefits. The newer high-quality programs discussed earlier are too new for a meaningful cost-benefit study, and their treatment groups may be biased by program dropouts, meaning that a valid evaluation of long-term costs and benefits may not be possible using these newer studies.

Two older "high-quality" preschool programs mentioned frequently in the research literature are the HighScope Perry Preschool program from Ypsilanti, Michigan, and the Chicago Child-Parent Center (CPC) program. These programs include parent education and support and thus differ in significant ways from the type of preschool programs offered by Head Start, as well as the more recent "high-quality" programs. They are also much more expensive on a per-capita basis. Both the CPC and the HighScope Perry Preschool programs were started in the 1960s, and researchers have carried out long-term cost-benefit analyses for both programs. These analyses conclude that better long-term outcomes more than pay for their higher program costs, mainly in the form of higher career income and lower rates of criminal behavior.

For several reasons, however, these programs may not be reliable indicators of the long-term benefits of current pre-K proposals. First, while the Perry Preschool results are based on a randomized design, the CPC study, led by Arthur Reynolds and Judy Temple, used a quasi-experimental group without a pre-test for major outcome variables. In addition, the treatment group consisted of minority children who graduated from CPC preschool and kindergarten programs, while the control group is comprised of kindergarten students who participated in other pre-K and kindergarten programs. The treatment group could therefore be biased by program dropouts, just as in the newer programs' studies with the RDD designs. Further, without a pre-test, there is no way to test or adjust for these potential differences between the treatment and control groups.

Second, while the Perry Preschool study is a state-of-the-art cost-benefit analysis conducted by a highly professional team of economists led by James Heckman, it is not without flaws when it comes to comparing the small 58-student treatment group and the 65-student control group. The randomized design was also compromised by re-assigning two parents from the treatment to the control group because they were single mothers who were working and could not participate in the program. In addition, four children in the treatment group dropped out of the program. The authors argue that the re-assignments were taken into account by matching techniques, but no mention is made of the program dropouts. As in the RDD studies discussed above, program dropouts may be the most at-risk children with the worst prognoses for long-term outcomes. While the number of dropouts is small, their omission from the long-term follow-up study could overstate treatment-group success.

Finally, the family-intervention components of these programs make it impossible to compare them to the high-quality programs envisaged by the Obama proposal. It also makes these programs very costly compared to Head Start and other regular pre-K programs that have been implemented by several cities and states. For example, in 2006 the per-pupil cost for the Perry Preschool program was nearly $18,000 ($20,000 in current dollars). It is unlikely that many states would agree to invest those types of funds in a program that was tested 50 years ago on a very small group of children from a single small city.

Better Evaluations for More Cost-Effective Outcomes

It would be similarly unwise for the federal government to invest $75 billion in universal preschool when it is not at all clear that Head Start or other preschool programs have positive long-term effects on participants. The HSIS evaluation, the Bernardy study of the same data, and the Tennessee study remain the most rigorous studies conducted to date on the effectiveness of preschool programs. These studies do not find preschool to be effective in increasing long-term cognitive or social and emotional

outcomes. In cost-benefit terms, we cannot claim that the $8,000-per-child Head Start program is cost effective.

Despite the flaws in the evaluations of other "high-quality" programs, many education policy experts might nonetheless argue that some type of higher-quality pre-K program is needed for disadvantaged children. In response, we would urge President Obama to modify his proposal for universal pre-K. The president's plan as it has been proposed would be modeled after the curriculums of existing pre-K programs that are part of regular school systems, and the new program's teachers would be required to have certification. As we have seen, however, there is insufficient evidence to suggest that these changes will yield a program that will succeed where Head Start has failed.

Rather than implementing a full-blown program, the president should propose a national demonstration project for pre-K in a selected number of cities and states, accompanied by a rigorous randomized evaluation that would follow participants at least into the third grade. This demonstration project should also examine whether "preschool for all" closes achievement gaps between rich and poor, since it is possible that middle-class children will benefit more than disadvantaged children.

This randomized evaluation study should also assess what type of program characteristics are necessary for an effective yet affordable pre-K program. Such a randomized study should test the effect of each programmatic factor (staffing and curriculum characteristics, for instance) that other studies suggest is important in determining students' cognitive and social-emotional outcomes. The cost implications are quite substantial, because the cost of pre-K as a regular program in a K-12 system may be considerably higher than the cost of Head Start.

Given today's budget and deficit pressures, this national demonstration should be kept budget-neutral. Instead of new expenditures, a portion of current Head Start funds should be redirected to the national demonstration program and evaluation. Assuming a demonstration program for about 20,000 students spread across, say, 20 school districts, with average program costs of $10,000 per student, demonstration costs would be approximately $200 million per year; a rigorous evaluation should cost no more than one-tenth of that amount. With a current Head Start budget of about $8 billion, this demonstration project would consume only 2% to 3% of Head Start funds. It might be possible to locate the demonstration in communities that lose Head Start programs so that there would be no major reduction in services for children currently using Head Start.

Such a demonstration project would be vital to enabling a truly high-quality universal preschool program to work, especially in a cost-effective way. There is simply no evidence to date that indicates a program like the one President Obama has proposed would produce meaningful, long-term positive outcomes for participants. There is also no evidence that such a program would be cost-effective. If the federal government is going to create a new program to provide broad access to high-quality preschool education, it should ensure that the program can produce positive long-term results without wasting valuable funds. American taxpayers and their children deserve at least that much.

DAVID J. ARMOR is Professor Emeritus of Public Policy in the School of Policy, Government, and International Affairs at George Mason University, where he teaches graduate courses in multivariate statistics, culture and policy, social theory and policy, and program evaluation.

SONIA SOUSA is a researcher at the Big Innovation Centre where she leads the Big Data Action Group. Her research interests include the role of entrepreneurship and innovation in regional economic development; policy evaluation; statistical analysis; and macroeconomic analysis.

EXPLORING THE ISSUE

Is Preschool Education Worthwhile?

Critical Thinking and Reflection

1. How can we ensure that all preschools offer high-quality education?
2. What should learning outcomes for preschools look like?
3. Recognizing that there is a limit to funding, should society devote financial resources to preschool education? Why or why not?
4. What are the consequences of not providing government funding for preschool education?

Is There Common Ground?

Public education, funded by the local, state, and federal government, is available to all Americans. Included in public education is elementary, middle/junior high, and high school education. However, in recent years, there has been discussion about whether preschool education should be included as well. The researchers from the Foundation for Child Development describe the benefits of preschool in the YES selection, while David Armor and Sonia Sousa in the NO selection argue there is not enough evidence for that step.

Both articles emphasize the importance of educating young children. Research shows high-quality preschools support academic, social, and emotional growth. However, there is concern about maintaining high quality in all preschools. Some studies have found that preschools do not make a difference, and, in some cases, may actually be linked with problems for children, such as increases in aggression and conflict.

At what point do we have enough research to make policy decisions? How much agreement is needed among studies? There always will be exceptions, but when

should society be confident enough to make informed decisions?

Create Central

www.mhhe.com/createcentral

Additional Resources

Claessens, A., Engel, M., & Curran, F. C. (2013). Academic content, student learning, and the persistence of preschool effects. *American Educational Research Journal*.

Duncan, G. J., & Magnuson, K. (2013). Investing in preschool programs. *The Journal of Economic Perspectives, 27*(2), 109–132.

Graue, E. (2011). Are we paving paradise?. *Educational Leadership, 68*(7), 12–17.

Gronlund, G. (2001). Rigorous academics in preschool and kindergarten? Yes! Let me tell you how. *Young Children, 56*(2), 42–43.

Internet References . . .

National Association for the Education of Young Children

www.naeyc.org

National Education Association

www.nea.org

National Institute for Early Education

www.nieer.org

Unit 4

UNIT

Middle Childhood

*M*iddle childhood marks the growth of many areas of development, and typically encompasses children in the elementary-school years. Roughly, it includes children ages 5 through 12. The influences on the development of youth in middle childhood are numerous, and impact their physical, cognitive, social, and emotional growth. Their development tends to be more refined, and children apply their advances in their everyday lives through play, school, and other activities.

However, while there are certainly generalizations about development that hold true for most children, there are also many individuals who do not represent what is "typical." The first issue asks whether violent video games harm all children or just those predisposed to aggression. The second issue focuses on whether autism should be considered a disorder (to be treated and perhaps cured) or an example of neurodiversity. Both issues in this unit bring attention to individual differences in development.

Selected, Edited, and with Issue Framing Material by:
Allison A. Buskirk-Cohen, *Delaware Valley University*

ISSUE

Are Violent Video Games Necessarily Bad for Children?

YES: Craig A. Anderson, from "Violent Video Games and Other Media Violence (Parts 1 & 2)" in *Pediatrics for Parents* (January/February & March/April 2010)

NO: Cheryl K. Olsen, Lawrence Kutner, and Eugene Beresin, from "Children and Video Games: How Much Do We Know?" in *Psychiatric Times* (October 2007)

Learning Outcomes

After reading this issue, you will be able to:

- Discuss how research has established a consistent association between violent video game play and aggression, though it is difficult to ascertain if that association is long-term and causal.
- Understand that violent video games are not likely to cause significant problems for normal children doing well in other contexts, but may exacerbate existing problematic tendencies for children prone to aggression.
- Realize that children themselves, most particularly boys, often identify significant benefits to video game play, including having relatively safe outlets for aggression and opportunities for shared social experiences.

ISSUE SUMMARY

YES: Psychologist and researcher Craig A. Anderson finds that violent video game play consistently associates with aggression and problematic behavior, arguing that there is no good reason for making them available to children.

NO: Cheryl K. Olsen, Lawrence Kutner, and Eugene Beresin have all been affiliated with a Harvard Medical School center devoted to studying mental health and the media. In their work they recognize the potential risks of violent video games, but find that most children play video games in ways that pose little risk and offer some potential benefit.

Though debate about the value or harm of video games has existed since the first video games became widely distributed, the issue has rarely been as prominent as it was in 2011 when the U.S. Supreme Court decided a case called *Brown v. Entertainment Merchants Association.* The case derived from a proposed law in the state of California prohibiting the sale of violent video games to children. Ironically, the legislation was originally signed into law in 2005 by the then governor of California Arnold Schwarzenegger, who garnered fame largely through playing violent action heroes in Hollywood movies. During the process Schwarzenegger was reported as saying "We have a responsibility to our kids and our communities to protect against the effects of games that depict ultraviolent actions," taking for granted that those effects are negative. Although the Supreme Court ultimately sided with the video games makers and ruled the California prohibition on the sale of violent games unconstitutional, the decision was based largely on protecting free speech rather than protecting children. The case did, however, put a spotlight on much research relevant to lifespan development addressing the effects of video games on children.

New media of all types inundates the lives of today's children and youth, generating much debate among scholars about the developmental effects. How much television should children watch? Does time spent surfing the Internet erode social skills? Do social networking sites such as Facebook enhance or detract from personal relationships? Are video games more likely to be an engaging forum for fun and imagination or an addictive distraction that imparts questionable values? All of these questions are crucial issues for anyone concerned with healthy child and youth development, and accordingly they have received much scholarly attention. But they are also surprisingly challenging questions to research effectively.

Perhaps the single most challenging research issue is the classic social science question of causality. It is a question about selection versus socialization. For questions about the effects of video game violence, the issue is to isolate video game play as a causal agent—if aggressive children indulge themselves in violent video games, does the aggression or the video game play come first? The usual way researchers isolate causality is to do experimental studies where one randomly assigned group is exposed to violent media and another randomly assigned group is not; a classic example here is Alfred Bandura's famous "Bobo Doll" experiment where he found that children who watched an adult act aggressively toward a blow-up doll were more aggressive themselves than children who watched the adult act playfully with the doll. But although studies such as these have established that watching aggression can produce more aggression in the short-term, they are virtually impossible to undertake in the long term. It is both unethical and unfeasible to randomly assign children to long-term exposure to violent media. This means most research relies on short-term experiments or long-term observations comparing groups that may already differ in the predilection toward aggression and violence.

The challenges of researching media violence have not, however, stopped many scholars from specializing in studying the effects of media violence. Prominent among these is psychologist Craig A. Anderson, who summarizes his perspective on the research in the YES selection. Based on decades of his own research, Anderson finds that the evidence convincingly demonstrates an association between aggression and violent video games. He emphasizes that video games are teaching tools, so that aggressive video games teach aggression rather well. He acknowledges that some studies and researchers have found limited effects, but asserts that when quality studies are combined in meta-analyses, the results clearly show negative effects. Anderson also identifies potential mechanisms that are relevant to developmental processes, suggesting that extensive exposure to video game violence serves to make such violence familiar and acceptable.

In the NO selection, Cheryl K. Olsen, Lawrence Kutner, and Eugene Beresin offer a contrasting perspective, acknowledging that violent video games can exacerbate preexisting problems, but focusing on ways that violent video games do not necessarily harm children who are otherwise doing well. As they note, "The biggest fear of clinicians and the public alike—that violent video games turn ordinary children and adolescents into violent people in the real world—is not borne out by the data." They also draw on focus group research with video game players to identify potential benefits of video game play, including providing a reasonably safe outlet for aggressive feelings and providing opportunities for shared social experiences (particularly among boys). Their article also points out that while parents indicate concerns about video games, most youth report that their parents "rarely" or "never" play video games with them. Are video games really the problem, or is it parental uninvolvement?

Another important element of this debate is determining who decides which video games children play. Is it the role of the government or parents to regulate these decisions? Currently, the Entertainment Software Rating Board (ESRB) provides ratings regarding the content in video games so that parents and consumers can make informed choices. The ratings have three parts which suggest age appropriateness, indicate content that may be of concern, and inform about interactive aspects of the video game. The ESRB is relatively new, having been founded in 1994. Many parents and consumers may be unaware of intricacies of the rating system. Even with this information, many people believe that parents should be the responsible party in selecting and monitoring their children's video game activities. They do not believe that laws should restrict any kind of purchasing behavior. If parents want their children to have access to all types of video games, some believe they should be able to exercise that opinion.

Ultimately, while the U.S. Supreme Court addressed this issue as a constitutional question, the issue for children and families is developmental. Do video games have the potential to desensitize children to violence and socialize them to see aggression as a way to solve problems? Or, might violent video games offer a safe outlet for aggression? Considering another alternative, might video games also have the potential to increase prosocial behavior and adaptive problem-solving skills? Many of these same arguments were levied at children's television shows when they first emerged. Just as *Sesame Street* and *Blue's Clues* have become exemplars in positive programming, there may be opportunities for video games to positively influence children's development.

YES

Craig A. Anderson

Violent Video Games and Other Media Violence

Violent Video Games and Other Media Violence (Part I)

For my 2003 article on *The Influence of Media Violence on Youth,* a group of media scholars and I, selected by the National Institute of Mental Health, reviewed 50 years of research on media violence and aggression.

Early Research

Most of the early research focused on two questions:

1. Is there a significant association between exposure to media violence and aggressive behavior?, and
2. Is this association causal? (That is, can we say that violent television, video games, and other media are directly causing aggressive behavior in our kids?)

The results, overall, have been fairly consistent across types of studies (experimental, cross-sectional, and longitudinal) and across visual media type (television, films, video games). There is a significant relation between exposure to media violence and aggressive behavior.

Exposing children and adolescents (or "youth") to violent visual media increases the likelihood that they will engage in physical aggression against another person. By "physical aggression" we mean behavior that is intended to harm another person physically, such as hitting with a fist or some object.

A single, brief exposure to violent media can increase aggression in the immediate situation. Repeated exposure leads to general increases in aggressiveness over time. This relation between media violence and aggressive behavior is causal.

Early aggression researchers were interested in discovering how youth learn to be aggressive. Once they discovered observational learning takes place not only when youth see how people behave in the real world but also when they see characters in films and on television, many

began to focus on exactly how watching such violent stories increases later aggression. In other words, more recent research really focused on the underlying psychological mechanisms.

Current Research

In the last 10 years there has been a huge increase in research on violent video games. Based on five decades of research on television and film violence and one decade of research on video games, we now have a pretty clear picture of how exposure to media violence can increase aggression in both the immediate situation as well as in long-term contexts.

Immediately after consuming some media violence, there is an increase in aggressive behavior tendencies because of several factors:

1. Aggressive thoughts increase, which in turn increase the likelihood that a mild or ambiguous provocation will be interpreted in a hostile fashion
2. Aggressive (or hostile) emotion increases
3. General arousal (e.g., heart rate) increases, which tends to increase the dominant behavioral tendency
4. Youth learn new forms of aggressive behaviors by observing them, and will reenact them almost immediately afterwards if the situational context is sufficiently similar.

How Media Violence Increases Aggression

Repeated consumption of media violence over time increases aggression across a range to situations and across time because of several related factors. First, it creates more positive attitudes, beliefs, and expectations regarding aggressive solutions to interpersonal problems. In other words, youth come to believe that aggression is normal, appropriate, and likely to succeed.

From *Pediatrics for Parents,* January/February and March/April 2010. Copyright © 2010 by Craig A. Anderson. Reprinted by permission of the author.

It also leads to the development of aggressive scripts, which are basically ways of thinking about how the social world works. Heavy media violence consumers tend to view the world in a more hostile fashion. Additionally, it decreases the cognitive accessibility of nonviolent ways to handle conflict. That is, it becomes harder to even think about nonviolent solutions.

Media violence also produces an emotional desensitization to aggression and violence. Normally, people have a pretty negative emotional reaction to conflict, aggression, and violence, and this can be seen in their physiological reactions to observation of violence (real or fictional, as in entertainment media). For example, viewing physical violence normally leads to increases in heart rate and blood pressure, as well as to certain brain wave patterns. Such normal negative emotional reactions tend to inhibit aggressive behavior, and can inspire helping behavior. Repeated consumption of media violence reduces these normal negative emotional reactions.

Finally, repetition increases learning of any type of skill or way of thinking, to the point where that skill or way of thinking becomes fairly automatic. Repetition effects include learning how to aggress.

Effect of Violence in Passive Versus Active Media

Most of the research has focused on TV/film violence (so-called "passive" media), mainly because it has been around so much longer than video games. However, the existing research literature on violent video games has yielded the same general types of effects as the TV and cinema research.

At a theoretical level, there are reasons to believe that violent video games may have a larger harmful effect than violent TV and film effects. This is a very difficult research question, and there currently is no definite answer. But, recent studies that directly compare passive screen media to video games tend to find bigger effects of violent video games.

Violent Video Games and School Shootings

Mainstream media violence researchers do not believe that an otherwise normal, well-adjusted child who plays violent video games is going to become a school shooter. The best way to think about this issue is the risk factor approach. There are three important points to keep in mind.

First, there are many causal risk factors involved in the development of a person who frequently behaves in an aggressive or violent manner. There are biological factors, family factors, neighborhood factors, and so on. Media violence is only one of the top dozen or so risk factors.

Second, extreme aggression, such as aggravated assault and homicide, typically occurs only when there are a number of risk factors present. In other words, none of the causal risk factors are "necessary and sufficient" causes of extreme aggression. Of course, cigarette smoking is not a necessary and sufficient cause of lung cancer, even though it is a major cause of it. People with only one risk factor seldom (I'm tempted to say "never") commit murder.

Third, consumption of media violence is the most common of all of the major risk factors for aggression in most modern societies. It also is the least expensive and easiest risk factor for parents to change.

Playing a lot of violent games is unlikely to turn a normal youth with zero, one, or even two other risk factors into a killer. But regardless of how many other risk factors are present in a youth's life, playing a lot of violent games is likely to increase the frequency and the seriousness of his or her physical aggression, both in the short term and over time as the youth grows up.

Risk Groups for Aggression

There is some research that suggests that individuals who are already fairly aggressive may be more affected by consumption of violent video games, but it is not yet conclusive. Similarly, video game effects occasionally appear to be larger for males than females, but such findings are rare. Most studies find that males and females are equally affected, and that high and low aggressive individuals are equally affected.

One additional point is worth remembering: Scientists have not been able to find any group of people who consistently appear immune to the negative effects of television, film, or video game violence.

Realistic Versus Fantasy Violence

One of the great myths surrounding media violence is this notion that if the individual can distinguish between media violence and reality, then it can't have an adverse effect on that individual. Of course, the conclusion does not logically follow from the premise. And in fact, most of the studies that have demonstrated a causal link between exposure to media violence and subsequent aggressive behavior have been done with individuals who were fully aware that the observed media violence was not reality. For instance, many studies have used young adult participants who knew that the TV show, the movie clip, or the video game to which they were exposed was not "real." These studies still yielded the typical media violence effect on subsequent aggressive behavior.

Contradictory Studies

In any field of science, some studies will produce effects that differ from what most studies of that type find. If this weren't true, then one would need to perform only one study on a particular issue and we would have the "true" answer. Unfortunately, science is not that simple.

Why have different researchers found different results? Well, part of the problem is that many studies have used a sample size that is much too small to produce consistent results. But even with a larger sample sizes, we still would not get the exact same results in every study. Chance plays some role in the outcome of any experiment. So even if all the conditions of the test are exactly the same, the results will differ to some extent. Test conditions are complex. Each study differs somewhat from every other study, usually in several ways.

Given that scientific studies of the same question will yield somewhat different results, purely on the basis of chance, how should we go about summarizing the results of a set of studies? One way is to look at the average outcome across studies. This is essentially what a meta-analysis does. And when one does a comprehensive meta-analysis on the video game violence research literature, the clear conclusion is that the results are quite consistent. On average, there is a clear effect: exposure to violent video games increases subsequent aggression. This has been found for each of the three major research designs (experimental, cross-sectional, and longitudinal), for youth and for young adults, and for youth in North America, Japan, and Western Europe. Similar meta-analyses of the television and film violence research literatures produce the same, generally consistent effects.

In addition to the small sample size and chance factors, a third factor is that some of the few contradictory studies can be explained as being the result of poor methods. For example, one frequently cited study that failed to find a video game effect did not actually measure aggressive behavior; instead, it measured arguments with a friend or spouse. That same study also failed to show that participants in the "high video game violence" condition actually played more violent games than participants in the "low video game violence" condition.

When you separate studies into those that were well conducted versus those that had major flaws, you find that the well-conducted studies found bigger average effects of violent video games on aggression than did the poorly conducted studies. Some well-conducted, and some poorly conducted, studies suffer from a too-small sample size. But the main point is that even well-conducted studies with appropriate sample sizes will not yield identical results. For this reason, any general statements about a research domain must focus on the pooled results, not on individual studies.

Violent Video Games and Other Media Violence, (Part II)

Marketing Violence

Clearly, violence sells, at least in the video game market. But it is not clear whether the dominance of violent video games is due to an inherent desire for such games, or whether this is merely the result of the fact that most marketing dollars are spent on promoting violent games instead of nonviolent ones.

One great irony in all of this is that the industry belief that violence is necessary in their product in order to make a profit may be hurting their overall sales by failing to satisfy the market for nonviolent games. Another unfortunate consequence of the extreme marketing emphasis on violence is that the media industries have convinced many people in the U.S. that they like only violent media products. But nonviolent and low-violent products can be exciting, fun, and sell well.

Myst is a good example of an early nonviolent video game that sold extremely well for quite some time. More recent examples include The Sims, many sports and racing games, and many simulation games. In some of our studies, college students are required to play nonviolent video games. Interestingly, some of these students report that they have never played nonviolent games, and are surprised to learn that they like some of the nonviolent ones as much as their violent games.

Even more intriguing is recent research on the psychological motivations that underlie judgments about which games are the most fun and worthy of repeat business. Scholars at the University of Rochester conducted six studies on game players' ratings of game enjoyment, value, and desire for future play. They found that games that give the player a lot of autonomy (lots of choices within the game) and feelings of competence (for example, success in overcoming difficulties with practice) were rated much more positively than games without these characteristics, regardless of whether or not the games included violence. In other words, violent games are so popular mainly because such games tend to satisfy both autonomy needs and competence needs, not because they contain violence.

Media Violence "Experts"

The media industries seek out, promote, and support "experts" who make claims that there is no valid scientific evidence that links media violence to aggression. There are several such "experts" who have made their careers by bashing legitimate research. Examining their credentials is quite revealing.

Many do not have any research training in an appropriate discipline. Of those who do have advanced degrees in an appropriate discipline (for example, social psychology), almost none of them have ever conducted and published original media violence research in a top-quality peer-reviewed scientific journal; they have never designed, carried out, and published a study in which they gathered new data to test scientific hypotheses about potential media violence effects. In other words, they are not truly experts on media violence research. To get at the truth, one must distinguish between actual versus self-proclaimed (and often industry-backed) experts.

Interestingly, a number of professional organizations have asked their own experts to evaluate the media violence research literature. One of the most recent products of such an evaluation was a "Joint Statement on the Impact of Entertainment Violence on Children," issued by six medical and public health professional organizations at a Congressional Public Health Summit on July 26, 2000. This statement noted that ". . . entertainment violence can lead to increases in aggressive attitudes, values, and behavior, particularly in children." The statement also noted that the research points ". . . overwhelmingly to a causal connection between media violence and aggressive behavior in some children." The six signatory organizations were: American Academy of Pediatrics, American Academy of Child & Adolescent Psychiatry, American Medical Association, American Psychological Association, American Academy of Family Physicians, and the American Psychiatric Association.

Along the same line, several reports by the U.S. Surgeon General have concluded that exposure to media violence is a significant risk factor for later aggression and violence. Both the American Academy of Pediatrics and the American Psychological Association have specifically addressed the violent video game issue; both concluded that playing violent video games is a causal risk factor for later aggression against others, and called for a reduction in exposure of youth to this risk factor.

Public's Perception of Causal Effect

Some people claim the media violence/aggression issue today is very similar to the tobacco/lung cancer issue of 30 years ago. The tobacco industry was quite effective at keeping the public confused regarding the true causal effect of tobacco on lung cancer, and there are still sizable numbers of smokers who don't really believe this scientific fact. Among other tactics, the tobacco lobby promoted "experts" who claimed that the research was badly done, or was inconsistent, or was largely irrelevant to lung cancer in humans. The media industries have been doing much the same thing: seeking out, promoting, and supporting "experts" willing to bash legitimate media violence research.

The tobacco industry successfully defended itself against lawsuits for many years. There have been several lawsuits filed in the U.S. against various video game companies in recent years. As far as I know, none have been successful yet.

One big difference between the tobacco industry cases and the violent media cases is that the main sources of information to the public (e.g., TV news shows, newspapers, magazines) are now largely owned by conglomerates that have a vested interest in denying the validity of any research suggesting that there might be harmful effects of repeated exposure to media violence.

The tobacco industry certainly had some influence on the media because of their advertising revenues, but the violent media industries are essentially a part of the same companies that own and control the news media. Thus, it is likely to be much more difficult for the general public to get an accurate portrayal of the scientific state of knowledge about media violence effects than it was to get an accurate portrayal of the tobacco/lung cancer state of scientific knowledge.

Given that it took 30-some years for the public to learn and accept the tobacco/lung cancer findings, it seems unlikely that we'll see a major shift in the public's understanding of media violence effects in the near future. Indeed, a study that my colleague Brad Bushman and I published in 2001 suggests that the media violence/aggression link was firmly established scientifically by 1975, and that news reports on this research have become less accurate over time.

Another big difference between the tobacco case and the media violence case is in the proportion of people who were hooked on these risk factors as children. The vast majority of youth repeatedly consume violent media, well before they turn 18; this was never true of tobacco products. This is important in part because of the "third-person effect," a psychological phenomenon in which people tend to think that they personally are immune to risk factors that can affect others.

Current Video Game Research

Since 2000, a large number of new video game studies have been published. One of the most important developments is that now there have been several major longitudinal studies of violent video game effects on youth. In such studies, the research team gathers information about a child's video game habits and his typical level of aggressiveness at two separate points in time. The two time points may be separated by months or years.

Sophisticated statistical techniques are used to answer a simple question: Do those who played lots of violent video games at the first time measurement show larger increases in aggression over time than those who played few violent video games? Such longitudinal studies from North America, Europe, and Japan have all found the same answer: Yes.

In addition, my colleagues and I have done several meta-analyses of all of the video game studies. It is even clearer today than it was in 2000 that violent video games should be of concern to the general public. That is, even stronger statements can now be made on the basis of the scientific literature.

Advice

My colleagues and I are expert media violence researchers, not policy advocates. So, we tell the U.S. Senate (or anyone else who asks) what current scientific research literature shows as plainly and clearly as possible, and generally do not promote specific public policies.

Nonetheless, I believe that we need to reduce the exposure of youth to media violence. My preference for action is to somehow convince parents to do a better job of screening inappropriate materials from their children. It is not always an easy task for parents—in part because of poor ratings systems—and perhaps there are appropriate steps that legislative bodies, as well as the media industries, could take to make it easier for parents to control their children's media diet.

As long as the media industries persist in denying the scientific facts and persist in keeping the general public confused about those facts, many parents won't see a need to screen some violent materials from their children. Ironically, the industry's success in keeping parents confused and in making parental control difficult is precisely what makes many citizens and legislators willing to consider legislation designed to reign in what they perceive to be an industry totally lacking in ethical values. My colleagues and I recently published several pieces on the complexity of the public policy issues.

Conclusion

A well-designed video game is an excellent teaching tool. But what it teaches depends upon its content. Some games teach thinking skills. Some teach math. Some teach reading, or puzzle solving, or history. Some have been designed to teach kids how to manage specific illnesses, such as diabetes, asthma, and cancer.

But all games teach something, and that "something" depends on what they require the player to practice. If the player practices thinking in violent ways, deciding to solve conflicts with violent action, and then physically carrying out violent game actions, then those types of thinking, deciding, and behaving are what is learned and reinforced.

However, there are many nonviolent games that are fun, exciting, and challenging. Children, adolescents, and adults like them and can learn positive things from them. Some even get you to exercise muscles other than those in your hands. In moderation, such positive nonviolent games are good for youth. But parents and educators need to check the content of the games they are considering for the youth in their care. You can't simply use the game ratings, because many games rated by the industry as appropriate for children and for teens contain lots of violence. But with a bit of parental effort, and some household rules about game playing, the youth's gaming experience can be fun and positive.

Craig A. Anderson is a Distinguished Professor of Liberal Arts and Sciences in the Department of Psychology at Iowa State University and author of the book *Violent Video Game Effects on Children and Adolescents*.

Cheryl K. Olsen, Lawrence Kutner, and Eugene Beresin    **NO**

Children and Video Games: How Much Do We Know?

There is no shortage of hyperbole when politicians of all stripes describe the nature and effects of video games. Republican presidential candidate Mitt Romney proclaimed, "Pornography and violence poison our music and movies and TV and video games. The Virginia Tech shooter, like the Columbine shooters before him, had drunk from this cesspool." Democratic presidential candidate Hillary Clinton spoke of the game, *"Grand Theft Auto,* which has so many demeaning messages about women, and so encourages violent imagination and activities, and it scares parents."

Some researchers have echoed similar sentiments, noting that Columbine High School shooters Dylan Harris and Eric Klebold were avid computer gamers. Several television pundits quickly drew a link between the recent Virginia Tech shootings and video games, as well. (Ironically, Seung-Hui Cho's college roommates found it odd that he never joined them in playing video games.)

Do these assumptions about video-game violence leading to similarly violent behavior among child and adolescent players make sense? A review of the research gives us insights into which patterns of video game play may serve as potential markers of more serious problems among children and adolescents, and which are normal or even possibly beneficial.

Additional research and case studies may shed some light on parents' concerns, such as whether video games are addictive or dangerous. Finally, we will offer recommendations on what parents can do to reduce potential risks and to maximize potential benefits of video game play.

The biggest fear of clinicians and the public alike—that violent video games turn ordinary children and adolescents into violent people in the real world—is not borne out by the data. Analyses of school shooting incidents from the US Secret Service and the Federal Bureau of Investigation National Center for the Analysis of Violent Crime do not support a link between violent games and real-world attacks. But what does research show about more subtle behaviors, such as bullying or changes in game players' perceptions of violence?

Going from Lab to Street

An August 2007 search of the OVID database for titles incorporating some variation on "video game" yielded 30 articles; a similar search of PsycINFO (limited to peer-reviewed journals) found 418 articles. Most reports focused on studies of the effects of violent video games on aggressive cognitions, emotions, and behavior.

This body of research, however, is of limited use to clinicians for a range of reasons. The most-cited studies are laboratory experiments on college students, generally involving brief exposures to a single violent game. Correlational studies typically involve small, nonrepresentative samples, and assess playing time rather than game content. The terminology is vague, and some researchers use "aggression" and "violence" interchangeably, implying that one inevitably leads to the other. Studies done in the 1980s and 1990s are outdated because of rapidly evolving content and technologies. Recent studies that involve child or adolescent exposure to violent game content represent a tiny fraction of this literature.

In the sections below, we review some findings relevant to clinicians, including our own surveys and focus groups with young adolescents. Unless otherwise specified, "video games" refers to console and handheld games as well as games played on computers.

Normal Use

In a 2005 national sample, the Kaiser Family Foundation surveyed 2032 children in grades 3 to 12 about their media use, including computers and video games. On average, children aged 8 to 18 years spent 49 minutes per day on video games (console or handheld) and 19 minutes on computer games. Boys aged 8 to 10 years were the heaviest users of video games; 73% played on a typical day for an average of an hour and a half.

To learn more, we surveyed 7th- and 8th-grade students at two middle schools in Pennsylvania and South Carolina. Virtually all eligible children attending school on that day participated. For most, electronic game play was a routine activity. Of 1254 children surveyed, only 6% had not played any electronic games in the 6 months before the survey. (These nonplayers were excluded from most analyses.) Gender differences were striking. Boys typically said they played video games 6 or 7 days per week; girls typically played 1 day per week.

To assess exposure to various types of game content, we asked children to list the games they had played "a lot in the past months." We found that 68% of boys and 29% of girls aged 12 to 14 years included at least one M-rated (for those aged 17 years and older, often because of violent or sexual content) game on this list of frequently played games.

Why Kids Play

We presented children and adolescents with a list of 17 possible reasons for playing video games. More than half cited creative reasons for play, such as "I like to learn new things" and "I like to create my own world."

"To relax" was chosen as a reason to play by the majority of boys and close to half of girls. "To get my anger out" was selected by 45% of boys and 29% of girls; 25% of boys and 11% of girls said that they played to "cope with anger." Violent video games might provide a safe outlet for aggressive and angry feelings.

This use of video games to manage emotions came up repeatedly in focus groups we conducted with 42 young adolescent boys. A typical comment was, "If I had a bad day at school, I'll play a violent video game, and it just relieves all my stress."

Children also play violent electronic games for predictable developmental reasons, such as rebellion, curiosity about the forbidden, and testing the limits of acceptable behavior in a safe environment. "You get to see something that hopefully will never happen to you," said one boy in our focus groups. "So you want to experience it a little bit without actually being there."

In both surveys and focus groups, boys described video game play as a social activity. Although most boys played games alone at times, most also routinely played with one or more friends. Just 18% of boys and 12% of girls surveyed said they always played alone.

Markers of Problems

Our survey results, combined with other research, hint at some markers of abnormal (though not necessarily unhealthy) game play patterns. It is uncommon for girls to be frequent, heavy players of video games, especially violent games. One third of girls in our survey played electronic games for less than an hour per week on average. By contrast, it was unusual for boys to rarely or never play video games; just 8% of boys played for less than an hour per week. (Since game play is often a social activity for boys, nonparticipation could be a marker of social difficulties. These boys were also more likely than others to report problems such as getting into fights or trouble with teachers.) Finally, boys and girls who exclusively play games alone are atypical.

In our survey of young adolescents, we found significant correlations between routine play of M-rated games and greater self-reported involvement in physical fights, with a stronger association for girls. It is likely that aggressive or hostile youths may be drawn to violent games. There is limited but suggestive evidence that persons with trait anger or aggression may be affected differently by violent games. In one study, players tended to be less angry after playing a violent game, but this was not true for subjects who scored high on trait anger and aggression. Thus, another possible marker of unhealthy video game use may be increased anger after a round of play.

It must be emphasized that correlational studies, including ours, cannot show whether video games cause particular behaviors. Far too frequently, this important distinction between correlation and causation is overlooked.

Case Vignette: Games and Attention/Learning Disorders

Alex, a 13-year-old boy, spends 6 to 7 hours a day playing video games. He locks himself in his room, misses meals, and often stays up most of the night, which results in school tardiness. He learns "cheats" (tricks to find quick solutions to game-based problems) online, converses with players in chat rooms, and has accumulated a great deal of knowledge about the intricacies of the many, often violent, games he plays.

Although very bright, Alex has a nonverbal learning disability, social difficulties, poor athletic skills, and attention problems, and he was often made fun of at school. The primary source of his self-esteem, beyond academic achievement, is his video game prowess.

His parents have no understanding of the games, nor of the video games' central importance in his life. Other children in school often come to him for advice about games and strategies and ask to play with him. This has become his claim to fame in and out of school.

While his parents need to educate themselves about the games he is playing and to set limits on his game play, their initial response to curtail them has been modified over time, allowing for an important avenue in the socialization of their son.

Therapy for Alex and his parents involved their appreciation of the role and meaning of games in his life. His parents needed to understand that competence is a crucial component of positive self-esteem—something Alex needed tremendously in order to take on academic and social challenges. Video games provided a means for Alex to feel more confident in moving ahead in these areas. With a greater understanding of the role the games played in his life, his parents were much more tolerant of his game playing.

The therapist continues to work with Alex and his parents and teachers to find additional ways for him to build a stronger sense of himself, improve his self-worth, and learn new ways of connecting with peers. His increased sense of competence has translated into greater academic achievement and the development of friendships outside the realm of video games.

Little research has been done on how subgroups of children, including those with diagnosed mental illness or learning difficulties, may be differentially affected by video games—for better or worse. Our survey included Pediatric Symptom Checklist subscales on attention and internalizing symptoms. Boys whose responses put them over a threshold level for attention-deficit/ hyperactivity disorder (ADHD) symptoms were more likely than others to use games to cope with angry feelings.

Among girls with ADHD symptoms, twice as many (almost 1 in 4) played games to make new friends compared with girls who did not have ADHD. In moderation, these are probably healthy uses of video games. As in the case of Alex above, children with ADHD often are adept at playing video games and using computers. This can provide a highly valued source of self-esteem.

Might video games be helpful with other illnesses, such as depression? In our survey, children who endorsed internalizing symptoms, such as feeling sad, hopeless, and worthless were much more likely to select "to forget my problems" as a reason for playing video games. These children did not spend significantly more time with video games, but they were more likely to play alone. Unfortunately, we do not know enough to say whether using video games to manage emotions is healthy or unhealthy for depressed children in general, or any child in particular. It may be that temporary or intermittent immersion in a game is therapeutic, while playing games alone for hours most days after school makes matters worse. Talking with a child about where, when, why, and how he or she uses electronic games could provide some useful insights.

Parental Perceptions and Concerns

In our survey, more than three quarters of respondents said their parents "rarely" or "never" played video games with them. In focus groups, many parents expressed frustration about being too much in the dark about the games their children were playing. Many worried that their child spent too much time in game play to the detriment of homework, socializing, or sports.

For their part, boys liked the action, challenge, and excitement of their violent games. While *Grand Theft Auto* was the most popular game series among the boys we surveyed, the second most-cited series was *Madden NFL* football. For many, and perhaps most boys in middle school, violent and/or sports games are a key to initiating and structuring social interactions. As one boy in a focus group told us, "If I didn't play video games—it's like a topic of conversation—and so I don't know what I'd talk about, 'cause I talk about video games a lot."

Contrary to parental concerns, our focus groups—as well as a British study of college students—suggest that realistic sports games may actually encourage interest and participation in real-world sports.

CHERYL K. OLSEN is a cofounder of the Center for Mental Health and Media at Massachusetts General Hospital/ Harvard Medical School. She is also coauthor of the book *Grand Theft Childhood: The Surprising Truth About Violent Video Games and What Parents Can Do.*

LAWRENCE KUTNER is a cofounder of the Center for Mental Health and Media at Massachusetts General Hospital/ Harvard Medical School, and executive director of the Jack Kent Cooke Foundation. He is also coauthor of the book *Grand Theft Childhood: The Surprising Truth About Violent Video Games and What Parents Can Do.*

EUGENE BERESIN is a professor of psychiatry at Harvard Medical School, director of the Child and Adolescent Psychiatry Residency Training Program at Massachusetts General Hospital, and director of the Center for Mental Health and Media at Massachusetts General Hospital/ Harvard Medical School.

EXPLORING THE ISSUE

Are Violent Video Games Necessarily Bad for Children?

Critical Thinking and Reflection

1. One reason this issue has been an ongoing controversy is because it is challenging to research. Based on the readings, which types of research seem most convincing, and what more would you want to know about the relationship between video game play and child development?
2. The question of whether it should be illegal to sell violent video games to children was the target of a major case for the U.S. Supreme Court in 2011, which decided that the risks of the games did not trump free speech rights. From a developmental perspective, does this seem like the right decision? What would you say to the Supreme Court if they asked your opinion?
3. If it is problematic for children to play violent video games, is it also problematic for teens and adults? What are likely to be key effects of violent video game play that are particular to children in earlier developmental stages?

Is There Common Ground?

Playing violent video games is probably not anyone's idea of an ideal activity for children—except for some children themselves. The simple popularity of violent video games suggests that they may be serving some need, even if that need is antisocial. A key question thus becomes whether there are other ways to fill those needs. Craig A. Anderson thinks there are, suggesting that creative and educational video games can be an entertaining substitute rendering violent games pointless. Cheryl K. Olsen, Lawrence Kutner, and Eugene Beresin agree that other types of video games can be entertaining and worthwhile, but are not as concerned if some children still choose more violent games.

Both sides also agree that violent video games can be a bad idea for children who seem otherwise at risk. Returning to the idea of selection and socialization, for children with aggressive tendencies, violent video games may exacerbate their antisocial behavior. Ultimately, the difference in these sides comes down to a matter of who we can trust to ensure violent video games do not take development off track?

Additional Resources

Bavelier, D. (2014). Ever wondered what playing video games does to your brain? *Understanding Neuroscience*, *1*, 5.

DeLisi, M., Vaughn, M. G., Gentile, D. A., Anderson, C. A., & Shook, J. J. (2013). Violent video games, delinquency, and youth violence new evidence. *Youth Violence and Juvenile Justice*, *11*(2), 132–142.

Granic, I., Lobel, A., & Engels, R. C. (2013). The benefits of playing video games. Hasan, Y., Bègue, L., Scharkow, M., & Bushman, B. J. (2013). The more you play, the more aggressive you become: A long-term experimental study of cumulative violent video game effects on hostile expectations and aggressive behavior. *Journal of Experimental Social Psychology*, *49*(2), 224–227.

Maddison, R., Simons, M., Straker, L., Witherspoon, L., Palmeira, A., & Thin, A. (2013). Active video games—An opportunity for enhanced learning and positive health effects?

Create Central

www.mhhe.com/createcentral

Internet References . . .

**American Academy of Child
and Adolescent Psychiatry**

www.aacap.org

Entertainment Consumers Association (ECA)

www.theeca.com/video_games_government

Palo Alto Medical Association

www.pamf.org/...teens/.../videogames.html

**Reporters Committee for Freedom
of the Press**

www.rcfp.org

Selected, Edited, and with Issue Framing Material by:
Allison A. Buskirk-Cohen, *Delaware Valley University*

ISSUE

Should We Try to Cure Autism?

YES: Ruth Padawer, from "The Kids Who Beat Autism," *The New York Times* (2014)

NO: Aaron Rothstein, from "Mental Disorder or Neurodiversity?" *The New Atlantis: A Journal of Technology and Society* (2012)

Learning Outcomes

After reading this issue, you will be able to:

- Understand that while autism is considered a "lifelong developmental disorder," researchers have identified a small subset of children who experience the disappearance of the disorder as they mature.

- Explain how applied behavioral analysis (ABA) and other therapeutic approaches have seemed to contribute significantly toward the improvement of some individuals with autism.

- Discuss how advocates of neurodiversity point toward the intrinsic value of all individuals and view neurocognitive disorders such as autism, ADHD, dyslexia, and depression not simply as afflicting disorders, but rather integral parts of who these people are.

- Understand that balancing the application of scientific advances in improving the lives of individuals who are not neurotypical includes complicated ethical questions involving either the amelioration or improvement of presenting problems versus the elimination of diverse segments of society through the manipulation of genes and the elimination of the existence of certain groups of people considered by society to be "abnormal."

ISSUE SUMMARY

YES: Reporter Ruth Padawer describes how applied behavior analysis (A.B.A.) has seemingly "cured" some children of autism. She profiles these children, showcasing their individual responses to therapeutic programs.

NO: However, medical student Aaron Rothstein cautions that autism might be considered an example of neurodiversity, rather than a disorder. He describes how and why many autism advocates argue against the idea of a "cure." Instead, the focus of research should be on better understanding the complexity of human behavior.

The history of autism is as complex as the condition itself. In the early 1900s, Dr. Eugen Bleuler, a Swiss psychiatrist, used "autistic" to refer to a group of schizophrenia symptoms. In 1943, Dr. Leo Kanner published an article, entitled, "Autistic disturbance of affective contact" that described eleven socially isolated children with similar profiles. The children were all highly intelligent, preferred being alone, and disliked any changes in routines. Around the same time, a German scientist named Hans Asperger identified a similar condition, now called Asperger's

syndrome. For these reasons, autism and schizophrenia were associated with each other, with some psychiatrists viewing autism as a form of childhood schizophrenia.

In the 1960s and 1970s, researchers began to better understand autism as a distinct condition. However, their knowledge was still rather limited, with many believing that emotionally distant mothers (i.e., refrigerator mothers) caused autism in their children. The treatment, then, was to separate children from their mothers for long periods of time. This method proved ineffective. Once scientists discovered biological differences in brain development in children with autism, changes in treatment followed. Treatments focused on medications such as LSD, electric shock, and behavior modification programs relying on pain and punishment (for example, electric shock therapy). By the late 1970s, there was agreement that characteristics of autism included impaired social development, impaired language and communication skills, resistance to change, and onset in the first years of childhood. It is important to note, though, that autism was not included in the American Psychiatric Association's Diagnostic and Statistical Manual (DSM) until 1980.

Autism was recognized officially in the 1980 edition, DSM-III. With that inclusion, there was a monumental increase in the number of publications of peer-reviewed scientific papers. In the 1980s, Asperger's work was translated to English, which increased knowledge and awareness in the United States. Professionals started to believe that parenting did not have a role in the etiology of autism, but that neurological disturbances and other genetic factors were likely causal factors. In DSM-III-R, released in 1987, a developmental orientation was employed and both a single disorder and subthreshold category were described. The 1994 DSM-IV offered greater flexibility by adding Asperger syndrome to the autism spectrum. This version also aligned diagnostic criteria with another system, the World Health Organization's International Classification of Diseases (ICD-10), which resulted in another explosion of research papers since scientists could easily compare samples using the same list of characteristics. Behavior modification programs were the primary treatments for autism and related conditions during the 1980s and 1990s, but biochemical, neurosensory, and psychodynamic treatments were used as well.

In most respects, the most current version, the DSM-5, has a much broader definition of autism and the characteristics. Many people diagnosed with autism today probably would not have met the criteria in the 1980s. The DSM-5 uses a single autism spectrum term instead of the multiple disorders previously included. This change means that individuals are no longer diagnosed with autistic disorder, Asperger's disorder, childhood disintegrative disorder, or pervasive developmental disorder—not otherwise specified (PDD-NOS). The DSM-5 also eliminates subthreshold categories and relies heavily on diagnostic instruments. Treatments used today are varied and often have links to the past. A theory from the 1920s suggests that autism is caused by diet; today, research is still ongoing to investigate the impact of removing gluten and casein from a child's diet. Other researchers are investigated auditory integration training (AIT), which focuses on the auditory sensitivity first noted in the 1940s. Temple Grandin, a high functioning person with autism, developed a squeeze machine that provides total body pressure; researchers are evaluating this and other similar treatments as well.

One of the most widely used treatments today is applied behavior analysis (A.B.A.) therapy. Ivar Lovaas developed in in the 1960s, and continues to have dramatic success today. Successful A.B.A. programs are very intensive, often requiring up to 40 hours a week of therapy for several years. These types of programs include practice of skills in both structured and unstructured situation. In the YES selection, Reporter Ruth Padawer describes how A.B.A. has seemingly "cured" some children of autism. She describes A.B.A. programs in great detail and explains how individual children have responded to these therapeutic programs. However, Padawer also includes stories of children for whom A.B.A. has not been effective. Currently, there is no cure for autism. However, some children who have responded well to A.B.A. no longer meet the diagnostic criteria for autism spectrum.

Interestingly, while some individuals race toward this "cure," others are firmly against it. They do not view autism as something they have, but rather as part of who they are. This philosophical debate has its roots in the person-first language movement initiated in the late 1980s. Many advocates argued for describing "individuals with autism" rather than "autistic individuals" as a way of empowering people. Person-first language is meant to emphasize that there is more to a person than his or her autism. In a surprising twist, many advocates find person-centered language offensive. For them, autism is a part of them, not a separate disease. Identifying as an autistic individual, for some people, is no different than describing other traits (like tall, sweet, or funny.) In the NO selection, Aaron Rothstein provides a personal account explaining why many autism advocates argue against the idea of a "cure."

Instead, Rothstein and others want us to consider autism an example of neurodiversity. Neurodiversity suggests that normal variations in the human genome results in diverse neurological conditions. The term was coined by sociologist Judy Singer in the late 1990s; it stresses that neurological differences should be identified and valued as a social category, just like sexual orientation. Advocates of neurodiversity believe autism is a natural human variation, not a disorder, and it should be viewed as a valid form of human diversity. Advocates point to the historical evidence of autism; the stable prevalence in human beings suggests it is a normal and natural variation. Therapeutic support services should allow autistic individuals to live as they are, rather than trying to normalize their behavior to a clinical ideal. What do you think?

YES ↩

Ruth Padawer

The Kids Who Beat Autism

At first, everything about L.'s baby boy seemed normal. He met every developmental milestone and delighted in every discovery. But at around 12 months, B. seemed to regress, and by age 2, he had fully retreated into his own world. He no longer made eye contact, no longer seemed to hear, no longer seemed to understand the random words he sometimes spoke. His easygoing manner gave way to tantrums and head-banging. "He had been this happy, happy little guy," L. said. "All of a sudden, he was just fading away, falling apart. I can't even describe my sadness. It was unbearable." More than anything in the world, L. wanted her warm and exuberant boy back.

A few months later, B. received a diagnosis of autism. His parents were devastated. Soon after, L. attended a conference in Newport, R.I., filled with autism clinicians, researchers and a few desperate parents. At lunch, L. (who asked me to use initials to protect her son's privacy) sat across from a woman named Jackie, who recounted the disappearance of her own boy. She said the speech therapist had waved it off, blaming ear infections and predicting that Jackie's son, Matthew, would be fine. She was wrong. Within months, Matthew acknowledged no one, not even his parents. The last word he had was "Mama," and by the time Jackie met L., even that was gone.

In the months and years that followed, the two women spent hours on the phone and at each other's homes on the East Coast, sharing their fears and frustrations and swapping treatment ideas, comforted to be going through each step with someone who experienced the same terror and confusion. When I met with them in February, they told me about all the treatments they had tried in the 1990s: sensory integration, megadose vitamins, therapeutic horseback riding, a vile-tasting powder from a psychologist who claimed that supplements treated autism. None of it helped either boy.

Together the women considered applied behavior analysis, or A.B.A.—a therapy, much debated at the time, that broke down every quotidian action into tiny, learnable steps, acquired through memorization and endless repetition; they rejected it, afraid it would turn their sons into robots. But just before B. turned 3, L. and her husband read a new book by a mother claiming that she used A.B.A. on her two children and that they "recovered" from autism. The day after L. finished it, she tried the exercises in the book's appendix: Give an instruction, prompt the child to follow it, reward him when he does. "Clap your hands," she'd say to B. and then take his hands in hers and clap them. Then she would tickle him or give him an M&M and cheer, "Good boy!" Though she barely knew what she was doing, she said, "he still made amazing progress compared with anything he'd gotten before."

Impressed with B.'s improvement, both families hired A.B.A. specialists from the University of California, Los Angeles (where A.B.A. was developed), for three days of training. The cost was enormous, between $10,000 and $15,000, covering not only the specialists' fees but also their airfare and hotel stays. The specialists spent hours watching each boy, identifying his idiosyncrasies and creating a detailed set of responses for his parents to use. The trainers returned every couple of months to work on a new phase, seeking to teach the boys not just how to use language but also how to modulate their voices, how to engage in imaginative play, how to gesture and interpret the gestures of others. The families also recruited and trained people to provide A.B.A. to their sons, so each boy received 35 hours a week of one-on-one therapy.

The specialists taught the parents that if their child wanted something, they should hand it to him—but should not let go until he looked at them. Within a month, B. was looking at people when he asked them for something, having learned it was the only way to get what he wanted. Within four months, he was looking at people even when he wasn't soliciting help. Soon he learned to point to things he desired, a skill that required weeks of lessons. Once B. understood the power of pointing, he no longer pulled his mother to the refrigerator and howled till she happened upon the food he wanted; now he could point to grapes and get grapes. "Between the time he was age 1 and almost 3," L. said, "I remember only darkness, only fear. But as soon as I figured out how to teach him, the darkness lifted. It was thrilling. I couldn't wait to get up each morning and teach him something new. It wasn't work at all. It was a huge, huge relief." Soon B. began to use language to communicate, albeit inventively at first. One time when B. pointed to the grapes in the fridge, L. took them out, plucked them off the stem and handed them to him—at which point he started screaming. He threw himself on the ground, flailing in misery. L. was baffled. He had clearly pointed to the grapes. What had she misunderstood? Why were his tantrums so frustratingly arbitrary?

Suddenly, B. pleaded: "Tree! Tree!" It hit her: He wanted the grapes still attached to the stem. He wanted to pull them off himself! "It was like, Oh, my god, how many times have I thought his tantrums were random, when they weren't random at all? I felt so bad for him: What other things have you wanted that you couldn't tell me?"

After that, B.'s language blossomed quickly. By the time he finished kindergarten, he was chatty and amiable, though he remained socially awkward, hyperactive and unyieldingly obsessed with the animal kingdom—he knew every kind of dinosaur, every kind of fish. Whatever his preoccupation of the moment, he would talk about it incessantly to anyone who would, or wouldn't, listen. L. made three small laminated coupons, and each morning, she'd tuck them into B.'s front pocket and remind him that whenever he talked about his favorite animal or noticed kids walking away or changing the subject, he should move a coupon to his other pocket. Once he ran out of coupons, she told him, he had to find other things to talk about for the rest of the day. Whether because of the coupons or maturation or something else, B.'s monologues stopped by second grade. Around the same time, his fixations eased. B.'s doctor concluded that the last vestiges of his autism were gone; he no longer met the criteria, even in its mildest form.

L. was ecstatic, but she was also plagued by guilt. Though Jackie's son received the same treatments as B., he had made no such progress. Matthew still could not talk. He remained uninterested in other children and most toys. And despite efforts to teach him, Matthew's communication remained extremely limited: When he squealed loudly, he was happy. When he threw up—which for a year he did daily—his parents concluded that he was distressed, after a doctor assured them that there wasn't anything physically wrong with him.

"Jackie did everything for him," L. told me, her voice filled with angst. "Everything. She tried just as hard as I did. She hired the same people, did the same work. . . . "

Her voice trailed off. She was sure that the behavioral therapy had allowed her to reclaim her son, but she could not understand why it had not done the same for Matthew.

Autism is considered a lifelong developmental disorder, but its diagnosis is based on a constellation of behavioral symptoms—social difficulties, fixated interests, obsessive or repetitive actions and unusually intense or dulled reactions to sensory stimulation—because no reliable bio-markers exist. Though the symptoms of autism frequently become less severe by adulthood, the consensus has always been that its core symptoms remain. Most doctors have long dismissed as wishful thinking the idea that someone can recover from autism. Supposed cures have been promoted on the Internet—vitamin shots, nutritional supplements, detoxifiers, special diets, pressurized rooms filled with pure oxygen and even chelation, the potentially dangerous removal of heavy metals from the body. But no evidence indicates that any of them can alleviate any of the core symptoms of autism, let alone eradicate it.

The idea that autistic people could recover first took hold in 1987, after O. Ivar Lovaas, the pioneer of A.B.A., published a study in which he provided 19 autistic preschoolers with more than 40 hours a week of one-on-one A.B.A., using its highly structured regimen of prompts, rewards and punishments to reinforce certain behaviors and "extinguish" others. (An equal number of children, a control group, received 10 or fewer hours a week of A.B.A.) Lovaas claimed that nearly half the children receiving the more frequent treatment recovered; none in the control group did. His study was greeted with skepticism because of several methodological problems, including his low threshold for recovery—completing first grade in a "normal" classroom and displaying at least an average I.Q. The therapy itself was also criticized, because it relied, in part, on "aversives": sharp noises, slaps and even electric shocks. By the 1990s, after a public outcry, Lovaas and most of his followers abandoned aversives.

While subsequent studies did not reproduce Lovaas's findings, researchers did find that early, intensive behavioral therapy could improve language, cognition and social functioning at least somewhat in most autistic children, and a lot in some. A few studies claimed that occasionally children actually stopped being autistic, but these were waved off: Surely, either the child received a misdiagnosis to begin with or the recovery wasn't as complete as claimed.

In the last 18 months, however, two research groups have released rigorous, systematic studies, providing the best evidence yet that in fact a small but reliable subset of children really do overcome autism. The first, led by Deborah Fein, a clinical neuropsychologist who teaches at the University of Connecticut, looked at 34 young people, including B. She confirmed that all had early medical records solidly documenting autism and that they now no longer met autism's criteria, a trajectory she called "optimal outcome." She compared them with 44 young people who still had autism and were evaluated as "high functioning," as well as 34 typically developing peers.

In May, another set of researchers published a study that tracked 85 children from their autism diagnosis (at age 2) for nearly two decades and found that about 9 percent of them no longer met the criteria for the disorder. The research, led by Catherine Lord, a renowned leader in the diagnosis and evaluation of autism who directs a large autism center and teaches at Weill Cornell Medical College, referred to those who were no longer autistic as "very positive outcome."

Autism specialists hailed the reports. "Those of us who work closely with children with autism," says Geraldine Dawson, a psychologist and researcher at Duke University's department of psychiatry and the Institute for Brain Sciences, "have known clinically that there is this subgroup of kids who start out having autism and then, through the course of development, fully lose those symptoms—and yet people always questioned it. This work, in a very careful and systematic way, shows these kids exist." She told me that she and many of her colleagues estimated that 10 percent or more of their autistic patients no longer had symptoms.

The findings come at a time when the number of autism cases nationwide appears to be climbing rapidly. No nationally representative study of autism's prevalence exists, but the Centers for Disease Control and Prevention's most recent study of 11 communities in the United States found that one in 68 children has autism, up from one in 88 two years earlier. Experts attribute much of that increase to greater awareness of the disease and its symptoms, as well as to broader diagnostic criteria. Some researchers say additional factors—among them toxic substances and older parental age—may contribute to the rise as well. Scientists suspect that what is called autism may actually be an array of distinct conditions that have different genetic and environmental etiologies but happen to produce similar symptoms. If true, it could help explain why some children progress so much while others don't.

The research by Fein and Lord doesn't try to determine what causes autism or what exactly makes it go away—only that it sometimes disappears. There do, however, seem to be some clues, like the role of I.Q.: The children in Lord's study who had a nonverbal I.Q. of less than 70 at age 2 all remained autistic. But among those with a nonverbal I.Q. of at least 70, one-quarter eventually became nonautistic, even though their symptoms at diagnosis were as severe as those of children with a comparable I.Q. who remained autistic (Fein's study, by design, included only people with at least an average I.Q.) Other research has shown that autistic children with better motor skills, better receptive language skills and more willingness to imitate others also tend to progress more swiftly, even if they don't stop being autistic. So do children who make striking improvements early on, especially in the first year of treatment—perhaps a sign that something about their brains or their kind of autism enables them to learn more readily. Researchers also say that parental involvement—acting as a child's advocate, pushing for services, working with the child at home—seems to correlate with more improvements in symptoms. Financial resources, no doubt, help too.

For now, though, the findings are simply hints. "I've been studying autistic kids for 40 years," Fein says, "and I'm pretty good at what I do. But I can't predict who is going to get better and who's not based on what they look like when I first see them. In fact, I not only can't predict who is going to turn out with optimal outcome, but I can't even predict who will have high-functioning autism and who will be low-functioning. There's so much we still don't understand."

Mark Macluskie, an animated 16-year-old, is another of the children in Fein's study who no longer has autism. He spends his spare time playing video games, building robots, writing computer code and hanging out with friends at the local park near his home in a Phoenix suburb. He co-hosts a weekly Internet radio show called "Tech Team," which has 32,000 listeners. On the program, he and a buddy review apps, discuss tech news, tell (very) corny jokes and produce regular features like "Gadget on a Budget."

While he seems like a fairly typical geeky teenager now, it took years of hard work to get here. Just before he turned 3, he received a diagnosis of medium to severe autism. He showed no apparent interest in those around him and seemed to understand few words. He threw stunning tantrums. And even when he didn't seem angry, he would run headlong into walls and fall over, then get up and do it again, like a robot programmed to repeat the same pattern eternally, seemingly impervious to pain despite the bruises spreading across his forehead.

Mark's parents, Cynthia and Kevin, sent him to their district's preschool for developmentally delayed children, where he was placed in the highest-functioning class. But he only got worse, having more fits and losing even more language. Within a few months, he was moved to the lowest-functioning class. Cynthia said a neurologist told her to be prepared to someday institutionalize her only child.

In desperation, the Macluskies pulled Mark from school. They took out a $100,000 second mortgage so Cynthia could quit her job in human resources to work full time with Mark, even though she was the primary breadwinner. She scoured the Internet for guidance and vowed to try whatever might possibly work, as long as it didn't sound dangerous. She gave her son shots of vitamin B-12 and started him on a dairy-free, gluten-free and soy-free diet. She read books on various behavioral therapies, choosing what she liked and then training herself, because the family couldn't afford to hire professionals. In the end, Cynthia cobbled together a 40-hour-per-week behavioral program, on top of the five hours a week of speech and occupational therapy that the state provided.

They were difficult years. Early on, Mark would hurl eggs at the wall and pour milk on the floor, so the Macluskies padlocked the refrigerator with a heavy chain. They emptied their living room of furniture, replacing it with an inflatable trampoline encircled by rubber walls so that Mark could whap against them to get the sensory input he seemed to need without hurting himself. They made clear to Mark that if he wanted something to eat or drink, he would get it only if he conveyed his desires by using words or sign language or pointing to the relevant flashcard.

Cynthia decided to keep home-schooling Mark, having concluded that traditional school wouldn't sufficiently address his weaknesses or recognize his strengths. By the time he turned 8, his speech and behavior were on par with peers, but his social thinking remained classically autistic. "I sort of knew there were rules, but I just couldn't remember what those rules were," he told me recently by video chat. "It was hard to remember what you're supposed to do and what you're not supposed to do when you're interacting with people." He rarely noticed social cues, and he couldn't interpret them when he did. He was too rough, too tactile, too quick to intrude into other people's personal space.

Cynthia set out to address his social delays. She watched DVR recordings of "Leave It to Beaver" with Mark, stopping every few minutes to ask him to predict what might happen next, or what he thought Beaver was thinking, or why June reacted the way she did. When they had watched every episode, they moved on to "Little House on the Prairie" so Mark could practice reading facial expressions. "I remember it being hard to answer my mom's questions and being confused when I watched those shows. I knew she was doing all those things for a reason," he said appreciatively. "I just didn't know how it was going to help."

At parks and restaurants, they watched the faces of passers-by and played social detective, with Cynthia asking Mark to find clues to people's relationships or emotions. "He didn't seem to learn that stuff through osmosis like other kids do, so I'd have to walk him through it each time till he got it."

Around that time, his parents gave him a robot kit for Christmas, and he fell madly in love with it. Eager to find opportunities for Mark to practice socializing, Cynthia formed a robot club: Mark and four typically developing children, meeting in the Macluskies' living room two afternoons a week. At first they just built robots, but soon the five children began writing programming code and entering competitions. Two years ago, Mark made it to the robotics world competition. There he was partnered randomly with teenagers from Singapore and had to strategize with them on the fly. They won several rounds. By then, it had been three years since a specialist concluded that despite some lingering social deficits, Mark no longer met the criteria for autism. As Cynthia watched how well Mark worked with his teammates at that competition, she began sobbing so hard that she had to leave the auditorium.

Mark is also aware of how far he has come. "There's nothing wrong with being autistic, but my life is much easier not having it," he said. "For as long as I can remember, I've known I was autistic, but I never felt autistic. I just felt like me. That's all I knew how to feel."

Fein's study found that formerly autistic people often have residual symptoms, at least initially; these include social awkwardness, attention deficit hyperactivity disorder, repetitive movement, mild perseverative interests and subtle difficulties in explaining cause and effect. For Mark, the main remnant is his continued disgust at food that he considers slimy, like omelets, and his dislike for the texture of paper, which he avoids. His mother says that whenever she mentions that Mark once had autism, people look at her as if she's delusional. "Even doctors say, 'Well, he must have been misdiagnosed, because a person can't stop having autism,' " she said. "It's so frustrating. Mark worked so hard. To deny everything he did to get this far isn't fair."

No one has figured out what happens inside the brains of people who had autism but no longer do—whether, for example, their brains were different from those of other autistic children to begin with, or whether their brains were similar but then changed because of treatment. But recent research on autistic toddlers by Geraldine Dawson of Duke reveals just how malleable the autistic brain can be. Prior studies determined that autistic children show more brain engagement when they look at color photos of toys than at color photos of women's faces—even if the photo is of the child's mother. Typically developing children show the reverse, and the parts of their brain responsible for language and social interaction are more developed than those of autistic children.

Dawson wondered whether steering autistic children's attention to voices, gestures and facial expressions could alter their brain development. So in a randomized clinical trial published in 2012, she tracked two groups of autistic toddlers: one that received 25 hours a week of a behavioral therapy designed to increase social engagement, and a control group that received whatever treatments their community offered (some behavioral, some not). After two years, electroencephalograms showed that brain activity in the control group still strongly favored nonsocial stimuli, but the EEGs of the social-engagement group were now similar to those of typically developing children. It appeared that their brains had, in fact, changed. Though the children were still autistic, their I.Q.s had also increased and their language, social-engagement and daily-living skills had improved, while the children in the control group had progressed noticeably less.

How this relates to people who are no longer autistic is not entirely clear. Though many studies show that early intensive behavioral therapy significantly eases autism symptoms, most children who receive such therapy nevertheless remain autistic—and some who don't get it nevertheless stop being autistic. Only two of the eight no-longer-autistic children in Lord's study received intensive behavioral therapy, because at the time it wasn't commonly available where the research was conducted, in Illinois and North Carolina.

In Fein's study, children who lost the diagnosis were twice as likely to have received behavioral therapy as those who remained autistic; they also began therapy at a younger age and received more hours of it each week. But roughly one-quarter of Fein's formerly autistic participants did not get any behavioral therapy, including a boy named Matt Tremblay. Receiving an autism diagnosis at 2, Matt received speech, occupational and physical therapy until he was 7 or 8. But he wasn't given behavioral therapy because, his mother recalls, the pediatrician never suggested it and the schools in their town in upstate New York didn't provide it.

Matt's speech was the first thing to improve, but many of autism's telltale signs persisted. He remained obsessed with precision and order. He mentally kept track of the schedules and appointments for all five members of his family, knowing who had to be where at what time. "He'd even calculate exactly when each of us had to leave

the house, and he'd announce, 'We have three minutes before we must leave,' " his mother, Laurie, told me.

Cognitive and behavioral gains came next, but mastering social skills was a long, difficult process, as it is for most autistic children. Until well into middle school, Matt tended to blurt out whatever he was thinking, and it took him a while to put together the mechanics of conversation. "I remember when I was little that I had a hard time pronouncing things," Matt said, "and I remember it being frustrating. It was hard to make my mouth listen to my brain. And I remember that up until sixth grade, I didn't really know how to fit in, how to connect. I was afraid to talk to people. I put my head down when I was in the hall at school, walking to class or going home. I couldn't relate to other kids—or maybe I just didn't want to. I guess it was a bit of both."

After a while, Matt began to figure out social situations. "I think I was in seventh or eighth grade when I finally realized I was supposed to keep on topic," he said. "And I noticed that when I did that, I started to make more friends. I really don't know why it finally clicked for me then." By the time Matt finished eighth grade, his doctor said he no longer had autism.

These days, Matt is affable, conversational and funny, a rising senior in high school. During the school year, he plays trumpet in the band and tennis on the varsity team, works as a cashier, busboy and bakery stocker at Panera Bread for 15 to 20 hours a week and still manages to get good grades. He loves to hang out with family and friends. His bedroom, which he kept fanatically neat until adolescence, is now an utter mess—a shift that his mother jokes might be considered a sign of teenage normalcy, though not one she particularly welcomes.

Matt remembers a few things about being an autistic preschooler, like how he used to flap and rock. He remembers his fixation with the Little People School Bus and the calm, deep focus he felt when he drove the toy around and around the kitchen for hours, dropping Little People off all over the floor, then picking them up again. Mild echoes from his autistic days remain. He told me that he still can't stand wearing tight or stiff clothes, so he opts for sweatpants or loose khakis instead of jeans. And even though he's a jokester himself, by his own reckoning he still occasionally has difficulty figuring out when someone else is kidding. "I think he still sometimes interprets things more literally than other people do," said his mother, a pediatric nurse. "Maybe that's because he had to learn how to read people's emotions, facial expressions and mannerisms, where other kids just know, just learned it automatically."

When Matt is by himself watching an exciting game on TV, Laurie sometimes passes by and sees him flap his hands. "It just seems like a leftover from the autism, one he easily controls," she said. Later, I mentioned that to Matt and asked what he was feeling when he flapped. He was stunned to hear his mother's assessment. "Wow, I thought I stopped doing that at 13 or 14!" Matt insisted that his mother was misinterpreting his gestures. "That's just me being into sports, being like, 'Yeah!'—like anybody would if their team scored a goal."

Some people reject the idea that eliminating autism is the optimal outcome. "Autism isn't an illness in need of a cure," says Ari Ne'eman, the president of the Autistic Self Advocacy Network, a national group run by and for autistic adults. He says that it's important to remember that the particular qualities of autistic people, which may seem strange to the rest of the world, are actually valuable and part of their identity. Temple Grandin, for example, an author and animal scientist, credits her autism for her remarkable visual-spatial skills and her intense focus on detail, which allowed her to design her renowned humane-slaughter facilities for livestock.

Ne'eman and others strongly support treatments that improve communication and help people develop cognitive, social and independent-living skills. But they deeply resent the focus on erasing autism altogether. Why is no longer being autistic more of an optimal outcome than being an autistic person who lives independently, has friends and a job and is a contributing member of society? Why would someone's hand-flapping or lack of eye contact be more important in the algorithm of optimal than the fact that they can program a computer, solve vexing math questions or compose arresting music? What proof is there that those who lose the diagnosis are any more successful or happy than those who remain autistic?

"We don't think it is possible to fundamentally rewire our brains to change the way we think and interact with the world," Ne'eman says. "But even if such a thing were possible, we don't think it would be ethical." He and others argue that autism is akin to homosexuality or left-handedness: a difference but not a deficiency or something pathological. It's a view that was memorably articulated in 1993 when a man named Jim Sinclair wrote an open letter to parents of autistic children, igniting what would come to be known as the neurodiversity movement. Autism, Sinclair wrote, "colors every experience, every sensation, perception, thought, emotion and encounter, every aspect of existence. It is not possible to separate the autism from the person—and if it were possible, the person you'd have left would not be the same person you started with. . . . Therefore, when parents say, 'I wish my child did not have autism,' what they're really saying is, 'I wish the autistic child I have did not exist and I had a different (nonautistic) child instead.' . . . This is what we hear when you pray for a cure."

Ne'eman says society's effort to squelch autism parallels its historical effort to suppress homosexuality—and is equally detrimental. He points out that in the 1960s and '70s, Lovaas's team used A.B.A. on boys with "deviant sex-role behaviors," including a 4-year-old boy whom Lovaas called Kraig, with a "swishy" gait and an aversion to "masculine activities." Lovaas rewarded "masculine" behavior and punished "feminine" behavior. He considered the treatment a success when the boy looked "indistinguishable" from his peers. Years later, Kraig came out as gay, and at 38 he committed suicide; his family blamed the treatment.

Neurodiversity activists are troubled by the aspects of behavioral therapy that they think are designed less for the well-being of autistic people and more for the comfort of others. Autistic children are often rewarded for using "quiet hands" instead of flapping, in part so that they will not seem odd, a priority that activists find offensive. Ne'eman offered another example: "Eye contact is an anxiety-inducing experience for us, so suppressing our natural inclination not to look someone in the eye takes energy that might otherwise go toward thinking more critically about what that person may be trying to communicate. We have a saying that's pretty common among autistic young people: 'I can either look like I'm paying attention or I can actually pay attention.' Unfortunately, a lot of people tell us that looking like you're paying attention is more important than actually paying attention."

Indeed, Ne'eman argues that just as gay people "cured" of homosexuality are simply hiding their real self, people deemed no longer autistic have simply become quite good at passing, an illusion that comes at a psychic cost. Autism activists point out, for example, that one-fifth of the optimal-outcome participants in Fein's study showed signs of "inhibition, anxiety, depression, inattention and impulsivity, embarrassment or hostility."

Fein questions this interpretation. She acknowledges that people who stop being autistic are still vulnerable to the psychiatric difficulties that commonly coexist with autism. Nevertheless, optimal-outcome participants were much *less* likely than high-functioning autistic people to use antidepressants, anti-anxiety drugs or antipsychotics, Fein found in a subsequent study. Lord's study likewise found that formerly autistic subjects had far fewer psychiatric problems than autistic subjects of comparable I.Q.

Of course, none of this means that people who have autism should be pressed to become nonautistic, or change how they relate to the world simply because their interactions aren't typical. Still, now that it's clear some people really do shed autism, it's hard to imagine that parents won't be even more hopeful that their child's autism might one day disappear.

Carmine DiFlorio is another of the optimal-outcome teenagers in Fein's study. As a toddler, he seemed to hear nothing, even when his mother intentionally dropped heavy books next to him in the hopes of getting a reaction. Instead, he appeared immersed in an interior world, flapping his arms as if trying to take flight, jumping up and down and hollering "nehhh" over and over. He did not, however, seem unhappy.

After Carmine received an autism diagnosis at age 2, his hometown in central New Jersey provided him with three hours a week of therapy, and his parents, who run a construction business, paid for four more. In a video of a session, a therapist shows Carmine pictures of common objects and tries to teach him vocabulary. She shows him a picture of a glass of milk. His gaze wanders. To get his attention, she taps his knee, calls his name and wiggles the photo in front of him. He looks past her. "Mmmilkkkk," she enunciates slowly. She sticks the photo right up to his face and turns his chin toward her with her finger. When that doesn't work, she coaxes: "Pay attention! Milk!" She clutches his head and swivels it to face her. "Ook," he offers, and she responds: "Good try! Milk!" Later, she tries to get him to practice following simple directions. "Do this," she says as she pats her thighs. He does nothing for a moment, but then raises his hands and drops them in his lap. It's close enough: "Yay!" the therapist exclaims. "What a good boy!" She tickles him, and he squeals in glee.

In sessions with another therapist, Carmine rocks when he doesn't want to do the exercises. Or he pumps his body up and down. Sometimes when he flaps his hands—which he does frequently in those sessions, whenever he's excited, frustrated, confused or engaged— the therapist holds them down. It's uncomfortable to watch. The prevailing view at the time was that repetitive movements should be extinguished, for fear that they would preoccupy the child and repel peers. (It's still a common view, though instead of restraining children, many clinicians redirect them. Some ignore flapping if it doesn't impede the child's engagement with other things.)

Carmine learned much more quickly once he started attending a full-time, year-round preschool for children with developmental delays, where he received intensive behavioral therapy throughout the day. When Carmine was a month shy of 5, his teachers sent home a detailed performance report based on a multitude of tests. It revealed that his communication, behavior, sensory, social, daily-living and fine motor skills were on par with those of a typically developing child. Only his gross motor skills were delayed. The other concern the school noted was his flapping and jumping when he was excited; for that, teachers directed him to a "more appropriate way of expressing excitement, such as clapping his hands or giving high-fives." By the summer before he started kindergarten, the neurologist who gave Carmine his diagnosis was shocked, and declared his autistic characteristics essentially gone.

Carmine doesn't recall all those efforts to get him to quit flapping. "And I don't remember why excitement translated into flapping my arms," he added. "But I definitely do remember the excitement." He also recalls his kid sister teasing him about flapping when he was 6 or 7, and he remembers deciding then to try to control the impulse. It took years. "When I wanted to flap, I'd put my hands in my pockets. I think I came up with that on my own. It was frustrating for those two years. It was like smiling and then someone telling you that you shouldn't smile, that smiling was wrong. Remembering to put my hands in my pockets made me less excited because I had to think about it so much. But as time goes on, you get in the habit. So by the time I was 10 or 11, I wasn't even feeling the urge to flap."

It's hard to square the Carmine I saw on those early videos with the 19-year-old I met a few months ago. Today, Carmine is sunny and gregarious; there's nothing idiosyncratic about his eye contact, gestures or ways of interacting. In the fall, he'll be a sophomore at the Berklee College of Music in Boston. He says he loves the friends he's made, the classes he's taken and the freedom of living independently.

I asked him if there was anything he missed about being autistic. "I miss the excitement," he said. "When I was little, pretty often I was the happiest a person could be. It was the ultimate joy, this rush in your entire body, and you can't contain it. That went away when my sister started teasing me and I realized flapping wasn't really acceptable. Listening to really good music is the main time I feel that joy now. I still feel it in my whole body, but I don't outwardly react to it like I used to."

Carmine's mother, Carol Migliaccio, told me that watching him improve during those early years was thrilling, but she became painfully aware of how unusual his experience was. At first, when Carmine made swift progress at his preschool, his parents gushed publicly. "We were like: 'Oh, my god! He shared the cake! He's talking! He's doing better!'" Carol said. But they quickly realized that most of his schoolmates were progressing far more slowly. "I had that guilt," Carol said. "He was just climbing mountains, and the others weren't. Having all seven kids in a room with the same teachers, you could see who was still spinning in their own world, who was still not talking. You just feel bad. The other mothers ask you, 'What are you doing that I haven't done?' And you have nothing to tell them."

For many parents, it is surely tempting to scrutinize the new studies for hidden clues or a formula for how to undo autism. But many mysteries still remain about autism's trajectory, and researchers urge parents to keep the results in perspective. "I see a lot of parents of 2-year-olds," Catherine Lord says, "who have heard stories about kids growing out of autism, and they tell us, 'I want my kid to be one of those kids.'" She reminds them that only a minority of children lose their symptoms, and she counsels parents to focus instead on helping their child reach his or her potential, whatever it is, instead of feeling that nothing short of recovery is acceptable. "When you get too focused on 'getting to perfect,' you can really hurt your child. A typical kid fights back against that kind of pressure, but a kid with autism might not. It's fine to hope—it's good to hope—but don't concentrate so much on that hope that you don't see the child in front of you."

Negotiating how best to raise a child with autism—or one who no longer has it—is clearly complicated. For L. and her husband, that involved deciding to move once B. had made significant progress. The summer after kindergarten, the family settled into a new school district. "We moved so no one would know, so people would approach him with an open mind," L. said. "We didn't even tell his teachers at the new school." In fact, L. and her husband didn't even tell B. about his autism until he was 12 or 13. When they did, he was shocked—dead quiet and shaken. L. said he asked, "Why didn't you ever tell me this?" L. said, "I didn't think you were ready to hear it." He responded, "I don't think I'm ready to hear it now."

B. is in his early 20s and recently graduated from a select university. L. told me that although he battled A.D.H.D. and occasional social anxiety, he got good grades, studied abroad, had good friends and a girlfriend.

He majored in psychology, focusing on its potential to change people's lives.

B.'s past is a secret that he and his family still keep, even from close friends. L. is afraid people will be disturbed by the idea that B. was once autistic or will think the family is exaggerating his past. L. says she and her husband don't bring up autism with B., because they fear it might upset him—which is why L. refused to ask B. if he'd talk with me and insisted that I not ask him myself. But sometimes B. brings up autism with his parents. Usually he asks what he was like when he was autistic, but recently he asked his mother a different question: Was it horrible for you? L. told me she paused, trying to figure out how to be honest without upsetting him. "I told him that it was really, really scary. But the hard times were short-lived, because he responded so quickly and so well once we figured out what to do. We've told him many times that so few people have that outcome and that he's one of the lucky ones."

Jackie's son, Matthew, now 24, has not had that conversation with his parents. In fact, he barely has conversations at all. At the group home where he now lives, near a horse farm in the Berkshires, the staff can generally interpret the sounds he makes. Sometimes he types clues on the iPod Touch his parents gave him, because he long ago learned to spell the things that matter to him. But mostly he seems absorbed by his interior life. He is calmed by the routines there, including his assigned chore of brushing the horses, even though he does that for only a few seconds before he wanders away. Every day, the caregivers take him to swim in an indoor pool, where he squeals in a piercingly high pitch of delight. In the evenings, he is happiest watching Disney videos and crooning along in a sort of indistinct warbling. The words he does pronounce clearly are "Mama" and "Daddy."

His parents see him most weekends. During those visits, Matthew sometimes gets wiggly, which can be a signal that he wants something he doesn't have. Jackie will say, "Show me," and hand him her smartphone, and Matthew will type a text. She showed me some of his recent messages: "Eat lunch. Chicken nuggets. Fries. Ketchup. Brownie. Ice cream. Cookies." And "Peter Pan. Watch a tape." To communicate with her, he doesn't ask for her phone, or point to it, or reach toward it, or mime texting. He doesn't seem to understand that those are ways to express his wishes, despite 20 years of effort to teach him so.

The idea that Matthew won't recover no longer pains Jackie. "At some point," she told me, "I realized he was never going to be normal. He's his own normal. And I realized Matthew's autism wasn't the enemy; it's what he is. I had to make peace with that. If Matthew was still unhappy, I'd still be fighting. But he's happy. Frankly, he's happier than a lot of typically developing kids his age. And we get a lot of joy from him. He's very cuddly. He gives us endless kisses. I consider all that a victory."

RUTH PADAWER is a contributing writer at *The New York Times Magazine*, focusing primarily on gender and social issues. She has freelanced for the radio show "This American Life," as well as *USA Today* and *MSNBC* online. Her work has also appeared in *The Guardian*, *The Week*, *Marie Claire* France, *Haaretz* Magazine, *Internazionale* and *GEO*. She earned an MS from Columbia's journalism school, where she has taught since 1992, and a BA in history from the University of Wisconsin-Madison.

Aaron Rothstein    **NO**

Mental Disorder or Neurodiversity?

One of the most famous stories of H. G. Wells, "The Country of the Blind" (1904), depicts a society, enclosed in an isolated valley amid forbidding mountains, in which a strange and persistent epidemic has rendered its members blind from birth. Their whole culture is reshaped around this difference: their notion of beauty depends on the feel rather than the look of a face; no windows adorn their houses; they work at night, when it is cool, and sleep during the day, when it is hot. A mountain climber named Nunez stumbles upon this community and hopes that he will rule over it: "In the Country of the Blind the One-Eyed Man is King," he repeats to himself. Yet he comes to find that his ability to see is not an asset but a burden. The houses are pitch-black inside, and he loses fights to local warriors who possess extraordinary senses of touch and hearing. The blind live with no knowledge of the sense of sight, and no need for it. They consider Nunez's eyes to be diseased, and mock his love for a beautiful woman whose face feels unattractive to them. When he finally fails to defeat them, exhausted and beaten, he gives himself up. They ask him if he still thinks he can see: "No," he replies, "That was folly. The word means nothing—less than nothing!" They enslave him because of his apparently subhuman disability. But when they propose to remove his eyes to make him "normal," he realizes the beauty of the mountains, the snow, the trees, the lines in the rocks, and the crispness of the sky—and he climbs a mountain, attempting to escape.

Wells's eerie and unsettling story addresses how we understand differences that run deep into the mind and the brain. What one man thinks of as his heightened ability, another thinks of as a disability. This insight about the differences between ways of viewing the world runs back to the ancients: in Plato's *Phaedrus*, Socrates discusses how insane people experience life, telling Phaedrus that madness is not "simply an evil." Instead, "there is also a madness which is a divine gift, and the source of the chiefest blessings granted to men." The insane, Socrates suggests, are granted a unique experience of the world, or perhaps even special access to its truths—seeing it in a prophetic or artistic way.

Today, some psychologists, journalists, and advocates explore and celebrate mental differences under the rubric of *neurodiversity*. The term encompasses those with Attention Deficit/Hyperactivity Disorder (ADHD), autism, schizophrenia, depression, dyslexia, and other disorders affecting the mind and brain. People living with these conditions have written books, founded websites, and started groups to explain and praise the personal worlds of those with different neurological "wiring." The proponents of neurodiversity argue that there are positive aspects to having brains that function differently; many, therefore, prefer that we see these differences simply as differences rather than disorders. Why, they ask, should what makes them *them* need to be classified as a disability?

But other public figures, including many parents of affected children, focus on the difficulties and suffering brought on by these conditions. They warn of the dangers of normalizing mental disorders, potentially creating reluctance among parents to provide treatments to children—treatments that researchers are always seeking to improve. The National Institute of Mental Health, for example, has been doing extensive research on the physical and genetic causes of various mental conditions, with the aim of controlling or eliminating them.

Disagreements, then, abound. What does it mean to see and experience the world in a different way? What does it mean to be a "normal" human being? What does it mean to be abnormal, disordered, or sick? And what exactly would a cure for these disorders look like? The answers to these questions may be as difficult to know as the minds of others. Learning how properly to treat or accommodate neurological differences means seeking answers to questions such as these—challenging our ideas about "normal" human biology, the purpose of medical innovation, and the uniqueness of each human being.

Not coincidentally, the neurodiversity movement accompanies an apparent boom in the number of people with mental disorders, especially children. In locations

Rothstein, A. (2012). Mental disorder or neurodiversity. *The New Atlantis: A Journal of Technology and Society*, 36, 99–115. Reprinted by permission of The New Atlantis.

monitored by the Centers for Disease Control and Prevention (CDC), the number of children with diagnosed autism spectrum disorders nearly doubled between 2002 and 2008, from one in 156 to one in 88. Autism was not even included in the American Psychiatric Association's *Diagnostic and Statistical Manual of Mental Disorders* (DSM) until its third edition was published in 1980. Similar stories are true of other disorders. In the 1970s, ADHD was known as "Hyperkinetic Reaction of Childhood Disorder," and was not well known. Following revisions to the DSM, diagnosis has become increasingly common, especially in children. Psychiatrists' improved ability to identify and treat such conditions has much to do with their increased profile, though there is some question whether environmental factors may be responsible as well.

A diagnosis of autism, ADHD, dyslexia, or depression does not necessarily mean that a patient has some definite set of observable traits. Each disorder exists on a spectrum, such that some cases are more evident than others—which complicates diagnosis as well as judgment of the patient's wellbeing. But as psychologist Thomas Armstrong writes in *Neurodiversity* (2010; title changed in paperback to *The Power of Neurodiversity*), there are generally at least a few characteristics of each disorder that hold across the spectrum and cause difficulty for those affected.

Autistics, writes Armstrong, tend to be much better at understanding systems than understanding people. Perhaps the most famous person with autism is Temple Grandin, an animal scientist at Colorado State University, who wrote an autobiography on growing up with autism called *Thinking in Pictures* (1995). To demonstrate the systematic thought process of autistics, Grandin describes an experiment conducted by Uta Firth, a British researcher on cognition:

> Joe, Dick, and a person with autism are sitting at a table. Joe places a candy bar in a box and shuts the lid. The telephone rings, and Dick leaves the room to answer the phone. While Dick is gone, Joe eats the candy bar and puts a pen in the box.

When the experimenter asks the autistic person what Dick thinks is in the box, the autistic person will say, "a pen." Autistics do not know how to predict what others think.

Consequently, autistics have great difficulty socializing. In his book *An Anthropologist on Mars* (1995), neurologist Oliver Sacks describes this difficulty as a state of mental aloneness. Autistics cannot read emotions and do not know how to interact with other people, so they often make others uncomfortable. Grandin recounts that it has taken her years of practice and observation to learn how

to introduce herself and converse, and that she still feels deeply uncomfortable doing it; the title of Sacks's book comes from Grandin's description of what it feels like to be around "normal" people.

For these reasons, autistics tend to enjoy working with computers and machines. The logic behind machines is simple; outcomes are consistent rather than dependent on the unpredictability of human emotions and the incompleteness of human knowledge. Furthermore, autistics often think about the world in terms of images rather than words. Grandin writes, "my imagination works like the computer graphics programs that created the lifelike dinosaurs in *Jurassic Park*. When I do an equipment simulation in my imagination or work on an engineering problem, it is like seeing it on a videotape in my mind." Grandin also describes the "video library in my imagination" that includes "video memories of every item I've ever worked with," which she can retrieve and recombine with great precision.

The processing of visual imagery and verbal thought, as Grandin notes, occur in different areas of the brain. In autistics, the visual area may become more active as compensation for a verbal deficit. People with autism also largely rely on visualization to understand concepts that are not inherently visual. In his 2007 memoir *Born on a Blue Day*, Daniel Tammet, who is an autistic savant—someone with autism who possesses prodigious skills or capacities—describes the unusual way he experiences ideas:

> I see numbers as shapes, colors, textures and motions. The number 1, for example, is a brilliant and bright white, like someone shining a flashlight into my eyes. Five is a clap of thunder or the sound of waves crashing against rocks. Thirty-seven is lumpy like porridge, while 89 reminds me of falling snow.

Tammet, who has a remarkable talent for learning languages, also sees words as images: "when I read a word or phrase or sentence written down, I close my eyes, see it in my head and can remember it perfectly." But his ability to remember chunks of words is very poor when he hears rather than sees them. This trait, common in autistics, often is a barrier to learning language, which most children acquire through listening. Their literal-mindedness also makes it difficult for autistics to understand idiomatic language: for instance, when Tammet first heard the phrase "under the weather," he thought, "Isn't everyone under the weather?"

One of the most common neurological diagnoses is Attention Deficit/Hyperactivity Disorder. As described by

Thomas Armstrong, psychiatrists and psychologists classify the three major symptoms of ADHD as hyperactivity, generally defined as an inability to sit still; impulsivity, or an inability to control one's actions; and inattention, or an inability to concentrate and a tendency to be easily distracted. As with autism, ADHD exists on a spectrum of severity and type. One type of ADHD manifests primarily as inattention; another primarily as impulsivity and hyperactivity; and the third main type manifests as all three kinds of behavior.

Biologically, Armstrong explains, ADHD patients have disruptions within the neurological circuitry that connects the "restraint and planning areas of the brain (the prefrontal lobes) and the emotional and motor areas of the brain (the basal ganglia and the cerebellum)." The result is that people with ADHD suffer from impulsivity. Often, the parts of the brain that are disrupted in children with ADHD eventually develop normally, but lag behind the growth of children without ADHD by about three years.

Counterintuitively, people with ADHD also suffer from *under*-stimulation of the neurological system. They have a natural shortage of dopamine, a neurotransmitter that helps to control motor activity. It is this shortage of dopamine that creates a constant need for external stimulation; as Armstrong writes, "what stimulates the average person is not enough for them. They need a higher dose of thrills and chills." This is why ADHD patients are often treated using psychostimulants, which increase dopamine in the brain and help stimulate the nervous system.

Dyslexia, which literally means "difficulty with words," like ADHD is also fairly common. It affects between 5 and 20 percent of schoolchildren (depending on the diagnostic criteria) and seems to be caused by problems in the brain—specifically, in the left hemisphere, which is associated with logic, language, and arithmetic. According to Armstrong, the posterior left hemisphere is underactive in dyslexics, so that they tend to rely more on the anterior left hemisphere, which is associated with spoken language, and the right hemisphere, which is generally associated with visual-spatial skills, including facial and pattern recognition.

Dyslexics have basic difficulties with reading and writing even short letters or compositions. This impairment exacts a painful toll on the psyche: in a culture where reading and writing are integral to the education of children, dyslexics face enormous challenges in coping with the basic requirements of school. Thomas G. West, a writer who himself had learning difficulties in childhood that he did not recognize until later in life, describes the lives of dyslexics and creative visual thinkers in his book *In the Mind's Eye* (1991; not to be confused with Oliver Sacks's

2010 book *The Mind's Eye*). West notes that patients commonly hide their dyslexia—sometimes even from themselves. One woman, "on learning in college of the basis of the problems that had tortured her during her early educational experience, wept for weeks."

Perhaps the most well-known mental disorder, but the one that is least often viewed in terms of cognitive impairment or difference, is depression. Though also strongly associated with problems in the brain, the characteristics of depression are markedly different from those of autism, ADHD, and dyslexia. Neurological theories of depression hold that it is caused by deficiencies or imbalances in neurotransmitters, such as serotonin, which is thought to stabilize moods. The most common class of antidepressant medications is that of the selective serotonin reuptake inhibitors, such as Prozac, Zoloft, and Paxil, which increase serotonin levels between neurons by keeping the cells from reabsorbing it. This helps to maintain the level of activity and firing between the neurons.

The symptoms of depression are all too familiar. Ludwig van Beethoven described the experience in an 1802 letter:

> With joy I hasten towards death—if it comes before I shall have had an opportunity to show all my artistic capacities it will still come too early for me despite my hard fate and I shall probably wish it had come later—but even then I am satisfied, will it not free me from my state of endless suffering? Come when thou will I shall meet thee bravely.

Beethoven would live another twenty-five years, but wrote this while suffering from deep depression, and while losing his hearing. Armstrong notes that, over the course of their lifetimes, nearly 13 percent of Americans experience major depressive disorders—classified as episodes of "low mood, negativity, insomnia, and other indicators" lasting for at least two weeks. Depression may last far longer than this, however, and often recurs for years or across a lifetime. Without psychotherapy or medication, people suffering from depression are at a high risk for harming themselves.

The disadvantages of autism, ADHD, dyslexia, and depression are very real, and are what lead them to be considered disorders. But what those clamoring for cures often neglect, and what the term "neurodiversity" seeks to recognize, is that these disorders often also bring unusual abilities. For example, people with Asperger's syndrome (AS), a high-functioning type of autism, have an uncanny capacity to see details. They score higher than non-autistics on block-design tests, in which children are asked to use colored blocks to match a pattern given to them.

They have better abilities to identify shapes, and are more likely to have prodigious talents, such as perfect pitch and highly accurate memories.

Temple Grandin, the accomplished animal scientist with AS, has heightened visual-spatial abilities that grant her both a knack for envisaging the workings of machinery and a keen insight into the way that animals perceive the world. As a consultant for McDonald's, she has combined these talents to revolutionize the way that slaughterhouses are run, designing them to minimize the pain and fear that animals feel during processing. (Her work in this area was the focus of HBO's 2010 biographical movie *Temple Grandin*.)

Daniel Tammet, who also has AS, memorized over twenty thousand digits of pi and recited them in five hours. In his book, Tammet shows a diagram he used to memorize all of these digits. To most people, it would appear to just be a line graph with peaks and troughs, but Tammet associated these peaks and troughs with thousands of numbers. Many employers highly value such visual-spatial skills and orientation to detail. Thomas Armstrong describes Thorkil Sonne, the executive of a Danish software company, who searches for people with AS to serve as his software testers; Sonne's company benefits from their fastidiousness, amazing memory, and ability to concentrate.

ADHD has potential benefits similar to those of autism. Although the notion is now perhaps too well-worn that our biological evolution lags behind our cultural development and our traits are best suited for an environment in which we no longer live, the idea is rather more plausible when it comes to ADHD. As Armstrong argues, people with what is now called ADHD would, in a hunter-gatherer setting, have been "always moving, always vigilant," making them more wary of potential threats. They may have been more likely to be explorers or to discover new sources of food.

The advantages ADHD might have had for our hunter-gatherer ancestors may seem ill-suited to an era that requires focus more than restlessness and vigilance. But in addition to the roving style of attention that often makes people with ADHD seem inattentive and restless, they also often possess an ability to focus for hours on specific activities or tasks that greatly stimulate or interest them. This "homing attention," as Armstrong calls it, is evident in "rock climbers negotiating steep mountain cliffs" and "surgeons engaged in twelve-hour sessions in the operating room." Certain professions actually demand characteristics that are much more prevalent in people with ADHD.

People with dyslexia also have certain impressive skills generally lacking in non-dyslexics. They can easily recognize patterns and anomalies in patterns. They sometimes also possess greater visual-spatial abilities, including ease with visualizing objects and systems in three dimensions. Similar to the abilities of autistics like Temple Grandin, they can sometimes visualize machines in their mind, and can tinker with these images—changing, adding to, and subtracting from them. Dyslexics also tend to be especially creative, for, as Thomas G. West notes, "one might see visual thinking, spatial ability, pattern recognition, problem solving, and related forms of creativity as linked together in a continuum."

The creativity of dyslexics can enable them to make groundbreaking discoveries and, sometimes, to compensate professionally for their disability. West tells of Susan Hampshire, a dyslexic and an actress, who could not read scripts for the stage. Instead, she "devised a personal system of pictures, symbols and other cues to help her." Baruj Benacerraf, a dyslexic who is a former president of the Dana-Farber Cancer Institute and a Nobel laureate for his work in immunology, claims that his ability to visualize objects in three dimensions has greatly aided him in his research.

While depression may seem simply dysfunctional, even this condition has some advantages for those who suffer from it—although it is difficult to establish a biological connection between the symptoms of depression and the special abilities of those who suffer from it. These abilities seem to be tied to the closely related disorder of manic depression. Kay Redfield Jamison, a psychiatrist who has written extensively on this topic, claims that manic depression is correlated with artistic temperament. In *Touched with Fire* (1993), she recounts various studies showing that artists have far higher rates of manic depression than the general population. Jamison herself studied forty-seven British writers and visual artists who were highly accomplished in their respective fields, and found that 38 percent of them had been treated for a mood disorder, with most of those requiring medication or hospitalization. In the 1970s, another researcher at the University of Iowa examined thirty creative writers and found that 80 percent had had at least one episode of major depression. Jamison also cites Harvard psychologist Ruth Richards, who found that manic depressives, as well as their relatives, showed higher creativity than those without such family histories. The state of mania apparently heightens performance on certain creative tests, like the ability to produce original responses on word-association tasks. People in manic states also have increased abilities to produce rhymes, puns, and sound associations.

Moreover, although many people assume that high creative production leads to elevated mood and low creative production leads to depression, studies seem to suggest that the order works in reverse: In what sounds like a clinical reformulation of the old notion of visitation from the Muses, Jamison found that "writers and artists . . . reported pronounced elevations in mood just prior to their periods of intense creative activity." Describing in *Scientific American* the biological uniqueness of the manic-depressive mind, Jamison writes that it is "an alert, sensitive system that reacts strongly and swiftly. It responds to the world with a wide range of emotional, perceptual, intellectual, behavioral, and energy changes."

There is a risk, however, in romanticizing the advantages of neurological disorder, and forgetting how painful and difficult these disorders can be. Romanticizing the connection between depression and artistic creativity, for instance, is not only dubious but also dangerous. Those heightened creative capacities are mostly associated with mania—which occurs only in some depressives, and even for them only intermittently. Not all depressives can write poetry or music, and the suffering of the artists themselves is at least as great as the works that it inspires. Even if there are special advantages conferred to the depressive mind, it seems problematic, even cruel, to apply the term *neurodiversity* to those who need intensive therapy and medication simply to live and appreciate living.

Similar cautions apply to our understanding of other neurological disorders. For instance, while there are obvious advantages to the heightened visual-spatial cognition of autistics, they have other traits that are much less clearly beneficial. Their nervous systems are hypersensitive, so that a simple knock on the door, tolerable to a normal child, can send shock waves through autistic children, much as a high-pitched fire alarm brings most people to plug their ears and recoil in pain. Temple Grandin tells of how, as a child, she was "scared to death" of balloons popping because the sound caused so much pain in her ears. Some autistic people, she says, can even sense the flicker of household fluorescent lights turning on and off sixty times every second.

This sensitivity also extends to touch. Grandin "wanted to experience the good feeling of being hugged, but it was just too overwhelming. It was like a great all-engulfing tidal wave of stimulation, and I reacted like a wild animal. Being touched triggered flight; it flipped my circuit breaker." But autistics still need physical contact and pressure in order to relax. Ultimately, Grandin built a contraption that provides this to her on a regular basis: called a "squeeze machine," it puts pressure on her body and calms her nervous system. Oliver Sacks writes of Grandin that this device opens a door "into an otherwise closed emotional world and allows her, almost teaches her, to feel empathy for others."

The difficulties of cognitive disorders are much more pronounced for individuals at the lower-functioning ends of the spectrums of these conditions. They are also harder to see—for these are just the individuals who tend to be much less vocal and visible in public discussions. The kinds of autism, for example, that the public most often hears about and sees depicted in media are usually the high-functioning ones, such as AS. Spokesmen like Temple Grandin or Daniel Tammet are able to write books about their condition; they adjust to society, find jobs, and learn to deal with people. The darker side of autism has few voices. Low-functioning autistics typically don't have blogs, books, or jobs.

Many times, autistics grow up mute, rocking back and forth, flinging their hands up and down, unable to interact with others. Additionally, parents may shoulder great responsibilities when they have children with autism. Grandin writes that "young children with autism need at least twenty hours a week of intensive one to one teaching by an adult." Parents must also pay for and participate in these sessions and deal with inexplicable temper tantrums, a child's inability to speak, and a child's social and emotional isolation, including difficulty in even hugging a parent. For many autistics, it seems condescending to label their conditions as cases to be appreciated under the rubric of neurodiversity rather than genuine disorder.

ADHD also causes great frustration, as Blake E. S. Taylor recounts in his memoir *ADHD and Me*, which he wrote during high school and published while a student at Berkeley. Taylor describes how, while taking a test on the *Odyssey*, he found his mind wandering: "I think about slalom racing down the packed powder, cold dry air on my face. . . . The distractions, like Circe, entice you and beckon you to daydream and enjoy yourself." Even during a test, which forces most young people to concentrate— and when concentration is most crucial—those with ADHD have little ability to control their thoughts and focus. Nor are these the kinds of distractions which most people would face for a fleeting moment when thinking about epic poetry; under many circumstances, they can be all-consuming.

Another scene in Taylor's book vividly illustrates how far the impulsivity of a patient with ADHD goes beyond that of a normal child. One evening, Taylor watched as his sister played with a lighter. Though he had been taught safety procedures and understood the consequences and hazards of fire, he could "only think of lighting something—anything—on fire to see what will happen." Taylor took a bottle of eyeglass cleaner and poured it on the flame—creating a blaze that nearly burned down his house. This is a classic story of ADHD: a child doesn't specifically want to cause mischief, but craves stimulation and lacks self-control.

ADHD is perhaps the neurological disorder most closely associated with childhood: according to the CDC, 7 percent of Americans between ages six and eleven have been diagnosed with it. But it is not just children who confront these difficulties. In the *Wall Street Journal*, adult ADHD patient Ali Bauman writes, "I had a messy bedroom and a string of minor accidents that I could never explain. I couldn't keep the house clean, pay bills, get things done on time. It wasn't that I didn't want to do it, I just wasn't capable of doing it." Over 4 percent of U.S. adults have also been diagnosed with ADHD. Like children with the disorder, these adults often require medications like Ritalin to allow the focus required to keep their lives in order.

Dyslexics may face even greater difficulties because of the relative lack of understanding the general public has about their condition. People with dyslexia often hide their disability because of the stigma and misunderstanding surrounding it; many people consider dyslexia and its symptoms to be a sign of stupidity, even though dyslexics have the same range of intelligence as the average population. As Thomas G. West writes, "there are no rewards for revelation, and the penalties can take the most humiliating forms."

Though dyslexics sometimes find their niche in society because of their visual-spatial and creative abilities, their disorder makes it difficult for them to perform the linguistic tasks necessary for passing through even elementary school. West recounts the stories of children who are laughed at by their peers for being unable to stand up and read fluently in class. Worse yet, teachers can fail to understand why certain students cannot read, and often end up putting dyslexics in special-education classes intended for children with below-average intelligence. All of these factors may take a heavy emotional toll, and can combine to keep dyslexic students from aspiring to greater goals—perhaps handicapping them for life.

The question of whether autism, ADHD, depression, and dyslexia should be considered disorders or appreciated as a matter of neurodiversity is not, as it might appear, simply a matter of terminology or political correctness. For at stake is not only how people with these conditions should be regarded—pitied or perhaps ennobled—but whether and how they should be included, treated, or cured.

For one group of advocates, the move to normalize neurological disorders is a form of gross medical irresponsibility—an ignorant act of cruelty rather than of

toleration toward people who are suffering. Lenny Schafer, who has an adopted son with severe autism, in a recent issue of the online Schafer Autism Report notes research finding that boys with autism are more likely to be bullied, and that obesity, hypertension, and diabetes are linked to the risk of autism. Schafer told *New York* magazine that "it's like stealing money from the tin cup of a blind man when you say that it's not an illness."

The difficulty, however, does not simply lie in whether to treat or not to treat. Even within the realm of treatment, the question remains whether to work *with* or *against* the unique traits of the individual. Thomas Armstrong, who has had years of teaching experience, including at the primary-school level, argues that this is a problem with special education under the current system. Special ed, he says, bases its approach "on deficit, damage, and dysfunction" rather than "strengths, talents, and aptitudes." In other words, the purpose of special ed is to cater to the slower learners. But many of these "slow" learners actually have talents that should be nurtured by teachers. A primary goal for ameliorating the plight of children with neurological conditions, then, would be to change the perception of special ed as a place for people who are not smart. This means also changing the approach: the question should be less whether, say, autistics as a group are gifted or defective, and more how to recognize and work well with each individual's weaknesses and strengths—as an effective educational program should for any child.

The questions of treatment, intended to benefit or change the lives of those already affected, are complicated by and easily confused with the more stark ethical questions of prevention and cures. Scientists have already identified many genes that contribute to neurological conditions, and are working to find more. For example, some variations of the dopamine receptor D4 gene may be one of the factors that contribute to ADHD; and there is strong evidence that other disorders are heritable. Studies on the heritability of autism show that it almost certainly has a genetic component—although researchers estimate that as many as a hundred genes may be involved. Thomas G. West claims that families share dyslexic traits. And genetic predisposition is believed to play a significant role in depression, too.

The ultimate goal of this research, of course, is not simply to learn the causes of these disorders but to help eliminate them. Mark Daly, an associate professor of medicine at Massachusetts General Hospital, argues that the "pieces are in place" to head in the direction of identifying gene variants and using that information to eventually develop more effective treatments—perhaps even by manipulating the genes in living patients. But pronouncements about such theoretical possibilities are prone to mislead about the immense pragmatic and ethical difficulties inherent in such an undertaking. And Armstrong, despite his sincere call for better understanding and appreciation of children with neurological disorders, scarcely explores in his book the practical difficulties and moral problems associated with manipulating human genetics.

In the first place, we do not necessarily know how a cure would work for each individual person. The human body is not like a machine: tinkering with one part will not always have predictable consequences for the other parts. Because we are biologically distinct, subtle biological variations mean that every person's body will respond differently to the same treatment. This is especially true for psychiatric conditions, which involve not only our bodies but our personalities as well; a drug that is considered successful in a psychiatric context may only work for some modest fraction of patients, and provide only modest improvements. Complicating factors and side effects are often not well understood, and treatments are often based not on definite diagnoses, as in more traditional disease models, but on an unsystematic trial-and-error approach. This is why there are many different kinds of medications for any given neurological disorder. For ADHD, for instance, doctors can prescribe Ritalin, Adderall, Dexedrine, Cylert, or various other stimulants or combinations of stimulants.

Treatment becomes even more complicated when it involves the manipulation of genes. Such treatment is still only hypothetical in human beings, and if it were to become possible would likely be extremely difficult and unpredictable. The role of individual genes in the development of traits and the functioning of an organism tends to be enormously complicated; one can only imagine how unpredictable the effects of manipulating the nearly hundred genes associated with autism would be. We need to understand not only how this would affect the autistic traits of a patient, but the other traits as well, which are far from neatly independent from each other in the first place.

The likelihood that disordered traits are too enmeshed in the biological makeup of individuals to be targeted separately underscores the broader point made by many advocates that their disorders are integrated into who they are. Many of those who are born with these differences and are able to advocate for themselves are wary of research into eliminating their conditions, on the basis that it would eliminate much of what makes them *them*. To search for a "cure" denies their distinctiveness as human beings.

Disability rights advocate Ari Ne'eman, who has AS and was appointed by President Obama to the National Council on Disability, argues in a 2010 interview with Wired.com that the traditional focus of the autism community has been on "narrow questions of causation and cure." And the focus of the national dialogue on matters like the vaccine controversy has led to the exclusion of "the voices of the people who should be at the center: those who are on the [autism] spectrum ourselves." Rather than focusing on how to make a world where autistic people "have the rights and support they deserve," more traditional activism has aimed to "create a world where there aren't any autistic people."

When asked whether he would take a pill to cure his autism, Ne'eman replies that "that's an intensely silly question . . . predicated on the strange idea that there was or is a normal person somewhere inside me, hidden by autism, and struggling to get out." This response gets to the heart of the beliefs underlying the neurodiversity movement: these conditions are not simply disorders afflicting otherwise healthy individuals, but are integral parts of who these individuals are. These advocates hold that the way to address the problems they face is to change the world to make it more inclusive of them and their particular needs, not to change them to fit what the world sees as normal or appropriate.

This point becomes disturbingly concrete when one considers that the more likely application for knowledge of genetic causes of these disorders will not be to find cures through genetic manipulation for existing patients, but rather to test and screen fetuses and embryos so as to eliminate before birth those that have a mental disorder. There is a telling precedent in the case of Down syndrome, which is already widely tested for in the womb, resulting in abortion for over 90 percent of fetuses with positive diagnoses. As Ne'eman has written in these pages, "To disability-rights advocates, this indicates a fundamental prejudice against the disabled" (see "Disability Politics," Spring 2009).

Might the same thing happen with fetuses with autism? Despite the activities of the neurodiversity movement, the inclination to consider neurological differences to be disorders or defects still predominates. So it seems quite plausible that the trend we see against fetuses with Down syndrome could expand to include fetuses with other sorts of brain differences, if similar tests for them were to become available. How might we decide at what point a case of neurological disorder becomes too severe to be acceptable and who will get to make such decisions? The precedent would leave these choices in the hands of parents—but, as Ne'eman notes is already the case with parents who receive a prenatal diagnosis of Down syndrome, "many . . . are given patently false information about the characteristics of the people they are being encouraged to prevent."

There is, of course, an immediate practical difficulty for such decision-making in the fact that, unlike the test for Down syndrome, new tests for other disorders are likely to provide far less certain results. The difficulty of predicting complex traits such as autism or depression based on genes or other biological factors easily detectable during pregnancy means that at best, such tests would likely only express a probability of certain neurological disorders, and would be even worse at predicting severity. Individual decisions of whether to abort would be muddled from the start, unable to rely on solid information that a child will or will not have a certain set of defects. Parents who abort a potentially defective fetus would likely have to face the possibility that their child would have suffered only mild abnormalities or none at all, while parents who choose only to carry to term fetuses that test sufficiently normal might still end up having to raise a child suffering from disabilities due to inadequate test results—a child they would have aborted had they correctly known his or her condition—with disturbing ramifications for how the parents might feel about and care for that child.

Considered at the societal level, the question is: If we were able, would we move to eliminate large segments of the population and the different ways of experiencing the world that characterize them? Doing so would arise from a judgment that the lives of people with neurological differences are less worthy than the rest of ours—as is already clearly the judgment so many parents are making with respect to Down syndrome pregnancies.

The cases of people with autism, dyslexia, ADHD, and depression who are able to lead successful, productive and well-adapted lives speak powerfully. Advocates with autism and other neurological differences say that they would never eliminate their singular traits—that those are much of what gives them their identity. Temple Grandin, Blake E. S. Taylor, Beethoven, and innumerable others show the kind of contributions such individuals are able to make to society. They show us how wrong we would have been were we to have tried to change them to be other than they are, or worse, never given these individuals a chance at life.

The heart of the matter of neurodiversity is not the hypothetical question of how we might use genetic testing in the future, but the very immediate question of how we are to regard and treat those who are already here. And important though the high-functioning individuals are as

examples, the worth of a life should not have to be justified by extraordinary achievements. One of the lessons of H. G. Wells's story is that the narrowness of our vision easily obscures the value of the lives of others, especially when they seem to us impaired.

Every life has joy and triumph, pain and hardship, aspiration and frustration—all parceled out unequally, and this only in part because of the different biological hands we are dealt. In labeling certain individuals "defective" or "disordered," we act in part to wall off some people as the unfortunate, tacitly claiming that the rest of us are whole, avoiding the truth that we are all flawed, struggling with deficiencies, working with and against aspects of ourselves we would like to overcome. In labeling others as "disabled," we must ask whether we are motivated by sympathy and compassion, or by fear and the difficulty of knowing the minds of others.

But even as we should not pass judgment on the value of the lives of others, neither should we presume to know their pain and difficulties. In a way, the neurodiversity movement shares a premise with the movement to eliminate individuals with neurological differences: namely, it says that individuals are to some extent identical with and defined by their nameable neurological traits. But in both cases, there is a danger of focusing on abstractions instead of the uniqueness of each individual.

We should celebrate the many treatments available for people who are suffering: anti-anxiety medications to help autistics, antidepressants for the depressed, Ritalin for people with ADHD, along with a wide variety of cognitive and behavioral therapies. The scientific community will and should continue to develop and improve these medications and therapies, especially for those who suffer on the extreme ends of the spectrums of neurological disorders.

The struggle remains one of understanding not only the causes of neurological disorders, but also to what extent prevention and treatment means valuing or devaluing the lives of affected individuals. Perhaps progress in these areas will necessarily remain idiosyncratic—and we would do well to be wary of solutions presented as absolute "cures." The line between difference, advantage, and suffering may not always be clear, and will be different for each individual, as will what counts as desirable treatment versus troubling manipulation.

In considering the question of how to deal with the diversity of neurological conditions, we would do well to remember H. G. Wells's story, where "normal" is a fluid term. Nunez thinks of the blind as abnormal, but so do they of him. That each human being is biologically unique is, in fact, the norm. These biological differences are, in turn, inextricably intertwined with the different ways we have of seeing and being in the world. Eliminating this rich biological and psychological diversity in the ostensible interests of ameliorating or preventing suffering would in the end diminish our humanity. It would make us less visibly like the country of the blind, but more like them in their prejudice. Rather than working to create another set of public labels, the real value of the neurodiversity movement may be in helping us to recognize that we each face challenges and opportunities—and that a decent society is one in which we are each able to strive to make the best of what we are given.

Aaron Rothstein is a third year student at the Wake Forest School of Medicine. He graduated from Yale University with a BA in history and has written for *The New Atlantis*, the *Wall Street Journal*, the *Weekly Standard*, and *Commentary*.

EXPLORING THE ISSUE

Should We Try to Cure Autism?

Critical Thinking and Reflection

1. How do these inequities in the cost of services relate to inequality in our society?
2. How might the implications of neurodiversity regarding disability rights and advocacy impact people with other types of disabilities? How does this conversation apply to the deaf community in particular?
3. When considering how to fund research related to autism, should we as a society be focused on curative measures, investigating the etiology of autism, or on accommodations for people living with autism? How do these decisions affect governmental policy?
4. How will a person's identity be affected by the realization that they had autism in the past and are no longer diagnosed with the disorder?
5. Since autism is understood as a spectrum disorder, is there some point at which particular behaviors become less acceptable than others?

Is There Common Ground?

Autism has become more common in recent years, partially due to broadening diagnostic criteria and the increasing awareness of this condition. In the YES selection, Ruth Padawer reports on children who, after receiving intensive applied behavior analysis (A.B.A.), no longer meet the criteria for autism. Aaron Rothstein, in the NO selection, advocates for a different view of autism. He argues that individuals with autism should not be cured; instead, we should try to better understand them as examples of neurodiversity.

Both selections emphasize the importance of recognizing the individual. Today, mental health experts view all disorders on a continuum so that no two people experience any disorder in an identical manner. Padawer's article, in fact, recognizes that some children with autism do not respond to A.B.A. treatment, and that we still do not understand why. Continued research into the intricacies of autism and other conditions, with attention to individual differences, will help us better understand neurodiversity among all human beings.

Create Central

www.mhhe.com/createcentral

Additional Resources

Ameis, S. H., Corbettdick, P., Cole, L., & Correll, C. U. (2013). Decision making and antipsychotic medication treatment for youth with autism spectrum disorders: Applying guidelines in the real world. *The Journal of clinical psychiatry, 74*(10), 1022–1024.

Evans, B. (2013). *Chloe Silverman, Understanding autism: Parents, doctors and the history of a disorder.* Princeton, NJ: Princeton University Press, 2012; 340; reviewed by Bonnie Evans. *Psychoanalysis and History, 15*(1), 116–119.

Eyal, G. (2013). For a sociology of expertise: The social origins of the autism epidemic. *American Journal of Sociology, 118*(4), 863–907.

Itkonen, T., & Ream, R. (2013). Autism advocacy: A network striving for equity. *Peabody Journal of Education, 88*(1), 48–59.

McGuire, A. E. (2013). Buying time: The S/pace of advocacy and the cultural production of autism. *Canadian Journal of Disability Studies, 2*(3), 98–125.

Internet References . . .

**American Institute for Learning
and Human Development**

> http://www.institute4learning.com/bio.php

Autism Self Advocacy Network

> http://autisticadvocacy.org/

Autism Society

> http://www.autism-society.org/about-the
> -autism-society/

Unit 5

UNIT

Adolescence

*D*eveloping adolescents cope with dramatic physical changes that often seem to combine a mature body with an immature mind. Further, because adolescence is associated with increasing independence and responsibility, adolescents seem both powerful and vulnerable. Society is compelled to provide adolescents care and opportunity, while simultaneously fearing that they will rebel. The issues in this section deal with the nature of success and failure in adolescence by asking two questions about the range of adolescent experiences.

On the surface, it appears that the first issue is about biology and the second about the environment. However, the selections selected for the first issue demonstrate that understanding the adolescent brain is more than simply addressing biological changes. In this issue, the chosen selections show that making sense out of environmental patterns is also quite complex. The second issue in this unit involves the newer trend of sexting. Authors of both selections agree it is occurring, but disagree over whether it has reached epidemic proportions. Both issues emphasize the challenges scholars face when interpreting data.

Selected, Edited, and with Issue Framing Material by:
Allison A. Buskirk-Cohen, *Delaware Valley University*

ISSUE

Does the Adolescent Brain Make Risk Taking Inevitable?

YES: Laurence Steinberg, from "Risk Taking in Adolescence: New Perspectives from Brain and Behavioral Science," *Current Directions in Psychological Science* (2007)

NO: Robert Epstein, from "The Myth of the Teen Brain," *Scientific American Mind* (2007)

Learning Outcomes

After reading this issue, you will be able to:

- Advances in brain science have added a new dimension to our understanding of adolescent risk taking.
- Brain science does carry with it a risk of "biodeterminism," oversimplifying the complicated reality of why people at any age take risks.
- Understanding adolescent risk taking involves neurological information combined with data about alcohol and substance abuse, dangerous driving, and other life-threatening behaviors.
- There are multiple explanations for why variables are related; we cannot assume that one causes the other.

ISSUE SUMMARY

YES: Although adolescent risk taking has proved difficult to study and explain, psychology professor Laurence Steinberg claims brain science is now demonstrating that basic biological changes explain much about the issue.

NO: Robert Epstein claims that difficulties in adolescence are better explained by cultural factors than by a "teenage brain." He provides examples of how genes and the environment shape the brain over time. Epstein cautions that images of brain activity do not identify causes, just correlations.

One of the most common stereotypes of adolescents is that they are prone to take risks without adequately accounting for consequences. Much attention has been directed toward influencing adolescents to be more careful and safe. But, despite all the attention, this stereotype persists, which raises the interesting developmental question of whether the stereotype is true. For many years, researchers believed adolescents view of their own immortality led to this risky behavior. Theorists also referred to adolescents' tendency to create personal fables, where they think of themselves in heroic or mythical terms. In these personal fables, adolescents tend to exaggerate their own abilities and their invincibility. However, in more recent years, people have looked to biological reasons to explain adolescents' tendency to take risks.

The idea of adolescence as a tumultuous period that inevitably results in "storm and strain" has long been a controversial issue for developmental research. Some researchers point to societal factors that emphasize the chaos of adolescence. Teenage rebellion is viewed as adolescents' way of asserting their independence and autonomy. It also has been popular to attribute whatever tumult research finds to biological changes—most often to "raging hormones." In fact, adolescence is the rare stage in the lifespan with a clear biological marker: puberty.

And, because puberty does produce dramatic physical changes, it is not hard to imagine that psychological changes would follow.

Even puberty, though, is hard to define using biological markers. For females, menarache, a girl's first menstruation might mark her entrance into adolescence. For males, however, there is not such a defining biological event. Some researchers suggest using semenarche, a boy's first ejaculation, a similar marker. Others might prefer using hair growth in the pubic region, armpit, and legs. Adolescent boys typically see increased width in their shoulders; adolescent girls experience growth in their hips. All of these biological changes typically occur at different ages, though, and may be difficult for outsiders to observe.

There are important changes occurring in the brain as well during this time period. The cortex, where thought and memory processes are based, experiences significant growth and development. The volume of gray matter, which forms the cortex, increases during early adolescence. In early adolescence, the prefrontal cortex also develops rapidly. The prefrontal cortex is the center of planning, decision making, and the intersection of cognitive and social behavior. Throughout adolescence, myelination and synaptic pruning occur, which results in less gray matter and more efficient and effective neural connections. There is some evidence that these changes are linked with experience, with the brains of some adolescents maturing faster than others.

The abilities to process information and think critically also change drastically throughout adolescence. Compared with children, teenagers have improved executive functioning skills. Executive function includes making complex decisions, in which information must be organized, weighing advantages and disadvantages of choices, monitoring performance, and shifting thought, emotion, and behavior. It occurs mainly in the prefrontal cortex, and while it develops during adolescence, current research suggests it does not peak until the mid-twenties. Relatedly, critical-thinking skills also improve in adolescence. Adolescents learn how to use both convergent and divergent thinking. Convergent thinking refers to following a series of steps to arrive at one correct answer to a problem. On the other hand, divergent thinking is used when a problem can be solved in a multitude of ways. These specific types of critical-thinking skills have not received as much attention by developmental researchers.

Advances in technology and brain science seem to have only perpetuated debates about the nature of adolescent behavior. Most of these debates continue to focus on the development of executive functioning in adolescence. As described above, there are ways in which the adolescent brain seems, on average, to function differently than the brain at other ages. Unfortunately, while those differences are often interpreted as indicating biological inevitabilities, patterns of brain activity alone tell us very little about the causes of behavior: social experiences activate the brain just as do genetic programs. Brain activity is both a cause and an effect of behavior. Just as participation in challenging coursework in schools might lead to changes in gray matter, for example, the changes in gray matter might allow an individual to accomplish challenging coursework. Therefore, one of the great challenges that comes with technological advancement is the art and science of interpretation.

Laurence Steinberg, in the YES selection, explains that the brain's ability to reason and logically think through problems matures more consistently than its ability to manage social and emotional stimulation. Steinberg thinks this difference helps explain a paradox of adolescent risk taking: despite effective educational efforts to help teens logically understand the consequences of risk taking, they often act as if they do not care. He rejects the idea that adolescents are irrational, ignorant, or hold delusions of invincibility. This selection discusses research on the brain's cognitive-control system, and why the maturation of function in the teen brain makes risk taking nearly inevitable.

However, according to Robert Epstein in the NO selection, we cannot draw causal conclusions from images of brain activity. Scientists long have warned that correlation does not equal causation. In this selection, Epstein argues that cultural factors are responsible for adolescent turmoil, not biological factors. Anthropological and cross-cultural research is reviewed, showing that the experiences of today's American adolescents are quite different from those in the past and those in other cultures. Furthermore, Epstein believes that adolescents are capable of achieving much more than we expect, and that our culture damages their potential. He puts forth the possibility that it is risk-taking behaviors that cause neurological differences.

However we interpret the findings of modern brain research, it is clear that new technologies raise as many questions as they answer. The intersection of biology and social behavior is not new; however, we now have the ability to assess it in very exciting ways. Our challenge is to ensure that our interpretations are correct so that we are not merely confirming our own biases.

Laurence Steinberg

Risk Taking in Adolescence: New Perspectives from Brain and Behavioral Science

...Adolescents and college-age individuals take more risks than children or adults do, as indicated by statistics on automobile crashes, binge drinking, contraceptive use, and crime; but trying to understand why risk taking is more common during adolescence than during other periods of development has challenged psychologists for decades.... Numerous theories to account for adolescents' greater involvement in risky behavior have been advanced, but few have withstood empirical scrutiny....

False Leads in Risk-Taking Research

Systematic research does not support the stereotype of adolescents as irrational individuals who believe they are invulnerable and who are unaware, inattentive to, or unconcerned about the potential harms of risky behavior. In fact, the logical-reasoning abilities of 15-year-olds are comparable to those of adults, adolescents are no worse than adults at perceiving risk or estimating their vulnerability to it . . . , and increasing the salience of the risks associated with making a potentially dangerous decision has comparable effects on adolescents and adults. . . . Most studies find few age differences in individuals' evaluations of the risks inherent in a wide range of dangerous behaviors, in judgments about the seriousness of the consequences that might result from risky behavior, or in the ways that the relative costs and benefits of risky activities are evaluated. . . .

Because adolescents and adults reason about risk in similar ways, many researchers have posited that age differences in actual risk taking are due to differences in the information that adolescents and adults use when making decisions. Attempts to reduce adolescent risk taking through interventions designed to alter knowledge, attitudes, or beliefs have proven remarkably disappointing, however. . . . Efforts to provide adolescents with information about the risks of substance use, reckless driving, and unprotected sex typically result in improvements

in young people's thinking about these phenomena but seldom change their actual behavior. Generally speaking, reductions in adolescents' health-compromising behavior are more strongly linked to changes in the contexts in which those risks are taken (e.g., increases in the price of cigarettes, enforcement of graduated licensing programs, more vigorously implemented policies to interdict drugs, or condom distribution programs) than to changes in what adolescents know or believe.

The failure to account for age differences in risk taking through studies of reasoning and knowledge stymied researchers for some time. Health educators, however, have been undaunted, and they have continued to design and offer interventions of unproven effectiveness, such as Drug Abuse Resistance Education (DARE), driver's education, or abstinence-only sex education.

A New Perspective on Risk Taking

In recent years, owing to advances in the developmental neuroscience of adolescence and the recognition that the conventional decision-making framework may not be the best way to think about adolescent risk taking, a new perspective on the subject has emerged. . . . This new view begins from the premise that risk taking in the real world is the product of both logical reasoning and psychosocial factors. However, unlike logical-reasoning abilities, which appear to be more or less fully developed by age 15, psychosocial capacities that improve decision making and moderate risk taking—such as impulse control, emotion regulation, delay of gratification, and resistance to peer influence—continue to mature well into young adulthood. . . . Accordingly, psychosocial immaturity in these respects during adolescence may undermine what otherwise might be competent decision making. The conclusion drawn by many researchers, that adolescents are as competent decision makers as adults are, may hold true only under conditions where the influence of psychosocial factors is minimized.

Evidence from Developmental Neuroscience

Advances in developmental neuroscience provide support for this new way of thinking about adolescent decision making. It appears that heightened risk taking in adolescence is the product of the interaction between two brain networks. The first is a socioemotional network that is especially sensitive to social and emotional stimuli, that is particularly important for reward processing, and that is remodeled in early adolescence by the hormonal changes of puberty. It is localized in limbic and paralimbic areas of the brain, an interior region that includes the amygdala, ventral striatum, orbitofrontal cortex, medial pre-frontal cortex, and superior temporal sulcus. The second network is a cognitive-control network that subserves executive functions such as planning, thinking ahead, and self-regulation, and that matures gradually over the course of adolescence and young adulthood largely independently of puberty. . . . The cognitive-control network mainly consists of outer regions of the brain, including the lateral prefrontal and parietal cortices and those parts of the anterior cingulate cortex to which they are connected.

In many respects, risk taking is the product of a competition between the socioemotional and cognitive-control networks . . . , and adolescence is a period in which the former abruptly becomes more assertive (i.e., at puberty) while the latter gains strength only gradually, over a longer period of time. The socioemotional network is not in a state of constantly high activation during adolescence, though. Indeed, when the socioemotional network is not highly activated (for example, when individuals are not emotionally excited or are alone), the cognitive-control network is strong enough to impose regulatory control over impulsive and risky behavior, even in early adolescence. In the presence of peers or under conditions of emotional arousal, however, the socioemotional network becomes sufficiently activated to diminish the regulatory effectiveness of the cognitive-control network. Over the course of adolescence, the cognitive-control network matures, so that by adulthood, even under conditions of heightened arousal in the socioemotional network, inclinations toward risk taking can be modulated.

It is important to note that mechanisms underlying the processing of emotional information, social information, and reward are closely interconnected. Among adolescents, the regions that are activated during exposure to social and emotional stimuli overlap considerably with regions also shown to be sensitive to variations in reward magnitude. . . . This finding may be relevant to understanding why so much adolescent risk taking—like drinking, reckless driving, or delinquency—occurs in groups. . . . Risk taking may be heightened in adolescence because teenagers spend so much time with their peers, and the mere presence of peers makes the rewarding aspects of risky situations more salient by activating the same circuitry that is activated by exposure to nonsocial rewards when individuals are alone.

The competitive interaction between the socioemotional and cognitive-control networks has been implicated in a wide range of decision-making contexts, including drug use, social-decision processing, moral judgments, and the valuation of alternative rewards/costs. . . . In all of these contexts, risk taking is associated with relatively greater activation of the socioemotional network. For example, individuals' preference for smaller immediate rewards over larger delayed rewards is associated with relatively increased activation of the ventral striatum, orbitofrontal cortex, and medial prefrontal cortex—all regions linked to the socioemotional network—presumably because immediate rewards are especially emotionally arousing (consider the difference between how you might feel if a crisp $100 bill were held in front of you versus being told that you will receive $150 in 2 months). In contrast, regions implicated in cognitive control are engaged equivalently across decision conditions. . . . Similarly, studies show that increased activity in regions of the socioemotional network is associated with the selection of comparatively risky (but potentially highly rewarding) choices over more conservative ones. . . .

Evidence from Behavioral Science

Three lines of behavioral evidence are consistent with this account. First, studies of susceptibility to antisocial peer influence show that vulnerability to peer pressure increases between preadolescence and mid-adolescence, peaks in mid-adolescence—presumably when the imbalance between the sensitivity to socioemotional arousal (which has increased at puberty) and capacity for cognitive control (which is still immature) is greatest—and gradually declines thereafter. . . . Second, as noted earlier, studies of decision making generally show no age differences in risk processing between older adolescents and adults when decision making is assessed under conditions likely associated with relatively lower activation of brain systems responsible for emotion, reward, and social processing (e.g., the presentation of hypothetical decision-making dilemmas to individuals tested alone under conditions of low emotional arousal. . . . Third, the presence of peers increases risk taking substantially among teenagers, moderately among college-age individuals, and not at all among adults, consistent with the notion that the development of the cognitive-control network is gradual and extends beyond the teen years. In one of our lab's studies, for instance, the presence of peers more than doubled the number of risks teenagers took in a video driving game and increased risk taking by 50% among college undergraduates but had no effect at all among adults. . . . In adolescence, then, not only is more merrier—it is also riskier.

What Changes During Adolescence?

Studies of rodents indicate an especially significant increase in reward salience (i.e., how much attention individuals pay to the magnitude of potential rewards) around the time of puberty . . . , consistent with human studies showing that increases in sensation seeking occur relatively early in adolescence and are correlated with pubertal maturation but not chronological age. . . . Given behavioral findings indicating relatively greater reward salience among adolescents than adults in decision-making tasks, there is reason to speculate that, when presented with risky situations that have both potential rewards and potential costs, adolescents may be more sensitive than adults to variation in rewards but comparably sensitive (or perhaps even less sensitive) to variation in costs. . . .

It thus appears that the brain system that regulates the processing of rewards, social information, and emotions is becoming more sensitive and more easily aroused around the time of puberty. What about its sibling, the cognitive-control system? Regions making up the cognitive-control network, especially prefrontal regions, continue to exhibit gradual changes in structure and function during adolescence and early adulthood. . . . Much publicity has been given to the finding that synaptic pruning (the selective elimination of seldom-used synapses) and myelination (the development of the fatty sheaths that "insulate" neuronal circuitry)—both of which increase the efficiency of information processing—continue to occur in the prefrontal cortex well into the early 20s. But frontal regions also become more integrated with other brain regions during adolescence and early adulthood, leading to gradual improvements in many aspects of cognitive control such as response inhibition; this integration may be an even more important change than changes within the frontal region itself. Imaging studies using tasks in which individuals are asked to inhibit a "prepotent" response—like trying to look away from, rather than toward, a point of light—have shown that adolescents tend to recruit the cognitive-control network less broadly than do adults, perhaps overtaxing the capacity of the more limited number of regions they activate. . . .

In essence, one of the reasons the cognitive-control system of adults is more effective than that of adolescents is that adults' brains distribute its regulatory responsibilities across a wider network of linked components. This lack of cross-talk across brain regions in adolescence results not only in individuals acting on gut feelings without fully thinking (the stereotypic portrayal of teenagers) but also in thinking too much when gut feelings ought to be attended to (which teenagers also do from time to time). In one recent study, when asked whether some obviously dangerous activities (e.g., setting one's hair on fire) were "good ideas," adolescents took significantly longer than adults to respond to the questions and activated a less narrowly distributed set of cognitive-control regions. . . . This was not the case when the queried activities were not dangerous ones, however (e.g., eating salad).

The fact that maturation of the socioemotional network appears to be driven by puberty, whereas the maturation of the cognitive-control network does not, raises interesting questions about the impact—at the individual and at the societal levels—of early pubertal maturation on risk taking. We know that there is wide variability among individuals in the timing of puberty, due to both genetic and environmental factors. We also know that there has been a significant drop in the age of pubertal maturation over the past 200 years. To the extent that the temporal disjunction between the maturation of the socioemotional system and that of the cognitive-control system contributes to adolescent risk taking, we would expect to see higher rates of risk taking among early maturers and a drop over time in the age of initial experimentation with risky behaviors such as sexual intercourse or drug use. There is evidence for both of these patterns. . . .

Implications for Prevention

What does this mean for the prevention of unhealthy risk taking in adolescence? Given extant research suggesting that it is not the way adolescents think or what they don't know or understand that is the problem, a more profitable strategy than attempting to change how adolescents view risky activities might be to focus on limiting opportunities for immature judgment to have harmful consequences. More than 90% of all American high-school students have had sex, drug, and driver education in their schools, yet large proportions of them still have unsafe sex, binge drink, smoke cigarettes, and drive recklessly (often more than one of these at the same time . . .). Strategies such as raising the price of cigarettes, more vigilantly enforcing laws governing the sale of alcohol, expanding adolescents' access to mental-health and contraceptive services, and raising the driving age would likely be more effective in limiting adolescent smoking, substance abuse, pregnancy, and automobile fatalities than strategies aimed at making adolescents wiser, less impulsive, or less shortsighted. Some things just take time to develop, and, like it or not, mature judgment is probably one of them.

The research reviewed here suggests that heightened risk taking during adolescence is likely to be normative, biologically driven, and, to some extent, inevitable. There is probably very little that can or ought to be done to either attenuate or delay the shift in reward sensitivity that takes place at puberty. It may be possible to accelerate the maturation of self-regulatory competence, but no research has examined whether this is possible. In light of studies showing familial influences on psychosocial maturity in adolescence,

understanding how contextual factors influence the development of self-regulation and knowing the neural underpinnings of these processes should be a high priority for those interested in the well-being of young people.

Laurence Steinberg is the Distinguished University Professor and Laura H. Carnell Professor of Psychology at Temple University. An internationally recognized expert on psychological development during adolescence, Dr. Steinberg's research has focused on a range of topics in the study of contemporary adolescence, including adolescent brain development, risk-taking and decision-making, parent-adolescent relationships, school-year employment, high school reform, and juvenile justice.

Robert Epstein  **NO**

The Myth of the Teen Brain

We blame teen turmoil on immature brains. But did the brains cause the turmoil, or did the turmoil shape the brain?

It's not only in newspaper headlines—it's even on magazine covers. *TIME, U.S. News & World Report* and even *Scientific American Mind* have all run cover stories proclaiming that an incompletely developed brain accounts for the emotional problems and irresponsible behavior of teenagers. The assertion is driven by various studies of brain activity and anatomy in teens. Imaging studies sometimes show, for example, that teens and adults use their brains somewhat differently when performing certain tasks.

As a longtime researcher in psychology and a sometime teacher of courses on research methods and statistics, I have become increasingly concerned about how such studies are being interpreted. Although imaging technology has shed interesting new light on brain activity, it is dangerous to presume that snapshots of activity in certain regions of the brain necessarily provide useful information about the causes of thought, feeling and behavior.

This fact is true in part because we know that an individual's genes and environmental history—and even his or her own behavior—mold the brain over time. There is clear evidence that any unique features that may exist in the brains of teens—to the limited extent that such features exist—are the *result* of social influences rather than the *cause* of teen turmoil. As you will see, a careful look at relevant data shows that the teen brain we read about in the headlines—the immature brain that supposedly causes teen problems—is nothing less than a myth.

Cultural Considerations

The teen brain fits conveniently into a larger myth, namely, that teens are inherently incompetent and irresponsible. Psychologist G. Stanley Hall launched this myth in 1904 with the publication of his landmark two-volume book *Adolescence*. Hall was misled both by the turmoil of his times and by a popular theory from biology that later proved faulty. He witnessed an exploding industrial revolution and massive immigration that put hundreds of thousands of young people onto the streets of America's burgeoning cities. Hall never looked beyond those streets in formulating his theories about teens, in part because he believed in "recapitulation"—a theory from biology that asserted that individual development (ontogeny) mimicked evolutionary development (phylogeny). To Hall, adolescence was the necessary and inevitable reenactment of a "savage, pigmoid" stage of human evolution. By the 1930s the recapitulation theory was completely discredited in biology, but psychologists and the general public

---

FAST FACTS
Troubled Teens

1 Various imaging studies of brain activity and anatomy find that teens and adults use their brains somewhat differently when performing certain tasks. These studies are said to support the idea that an immature "teen brain" accounts for teen mood and behavior problems.

2 But, the author argues, snapshots of brain activity do not necessarily identify the *causes* of such problems. Culture, nutrition and even the teen's own behavior all affect brain development. A variety of research in several fields suggest that teen turmoil is caused by cultural factors, not by a faulty brain.

3 Anthropological research reveals that teens in many cultures experience no turmoil whatsoever and that teen problems begin to appear only after Western schooling, movies and television are introduced.

4 Teens have the potential to perform in exemplary ways, the author says, but we hold them back by infantilizing them and trapping them in the frivolous world of teen culture.

Epstein, R. (2007). The myth of the teen brain. Scientific American, 17(2), 68–75. Reprinted by permission of Scientific American, Inc.

never got the message. Many still believe, consistent with Hall's assertion, that teen turmoil is an *inevitable* part of human development.

Today teens in the U.S. and some other Westernized nations do display some signs of distress. The peak age for arrest in the U.S. for most crimes has long been 18; for some crimes, such as arson, the peak comes much earlier. On average, American parents and teens tend to be in conflict with one another 20 times a month—an extremely high figure indicative of great pain on both sides. An extensive study conducted in 2004 suggests that 18 is the peak age for depression among people 18 and older in this country. Drug use by teens, both legal and illegal, is clearly a problem here, and suicide is the third leading cause of death among U.S. teens. Prompted by a rash of deadly school shootings over the past decade, many American high schools now resemble prisons, with guards, metal detectors and video monitoring systems, and the high school dropout rate is nearly 50 percent among minorities in large U.S. cities.

But are such problems truly inevitable? If the turmoil-generating "teen brain" were a universal developmental phenomenon, we would presumably find turmoil of this kind around the world. Do we?

In 1991 anthropologist Alice Schlegel of the University of Arizona and psychologist Herbert Barry III, of the University of Pittsburgh reviewed research on teens in 186 preindustrial societies. Among the important conclusions they drew about these societies: about 60 percent had no word for "adolescence," teens spent almost all their time with adults, teens showed almost no signs of psychopathology, and antisocial behavior in young males was completely absent in more than half these cultures and extremely mild in cultures in which it did occur.

Even more significant, a series of long-term studies set in motion in the 1980s by anthropologists Beatrice Whiting and John Whiting of Harvard University suggests that teen trouble begins to appear in other cultures soon after the introduction of certain Western influences, especially Western-style schooling, television programs and movies. Delinquency was not an issue among the Inuit people of Victoria Island, Canada, for example, until TV arrived in 1980. By 1988 the Inuit had created their first permanent police station to try to cope with the new problem.

Consistent with these modern observations, many historians note that through most of recorded human history the teen years were a relatively peaceful time of transition to adulthood. Teens were not trying to break away from adults; rather they were learning to *become* adults. Some historians, such as Hugh Cunningham of

the University of Kent in England and Marc Kleijwegt of the University of Wisconsin–Madison, author of *Ancient Youth: The Ambiguity of Youth and the Absence of Adolescence in Greco-Roman Society* (J. C. Gieben, 1991), suggest that the tumultuous period we call adolescence is a very recent phenomenon—not much more than a century old.

My own recent research, viewed in combination with many other studies from anthropology, psychology, sociology, history and other disciplines, suggests the turmoil we see among teens in the U.S. is the result of what I call "artificial extension of childhood" past puberty. Over the past century, we have increasingly infantilized our young, treating older and older people as children while also isolating them from adults. Laws have restricted their behavior. Surveys I have conducted show that teens in the U.S. are subjected to more than 10 times as many restrictions as are mainstream adults, twice as many restrictions as active-duty U.S. Marines, and even twice as many restrictions as incarcerated felons. And research I conducted with Diane Dumas as part of her dissertation research at the California School of Professional Psychology shows a positive correlation between the extent to which teens are infantilized and the extent to which they display signs of psychopathology.

The headlines notwithstanding, there is no question that teen turbulence is *not* inevitable. It is a creation of modern culture, pure and simple—and so, it would appear, is the brain of the troubled teen.

Dissecting Brain Studies

A variety of recent research—most of it conducted using magnetic resonance imaging (MRI) technology—is said to show the existence of a teen brain. Studies by Beatriz Luna of the department of psychiatry at the University of Pittsburgh, for example, are said to show that teens use prefrontal cortical resources differently than adults do. Susan F. Tapert of the University of California, San Diego, found that for certain memory tasks, teens use smaller areas of the cortex than adults do. An electroencephalogram (EEG) study by Irwin Feinberg and his colleagues at the University of California, Davis, shows that delta-wave activity during sleep declines in the early teen years. Jay Giedd of the National Institute of Mental Health and other researchers suggest that the decline in delta-wave activity might be related to synaptic pruning—a reduction in the number of interconnections among neurons—that occurs during the teen years.

This work seems to support the idea of the teen brain we see in the headlines until we realize two things. First, most of the brain changes that are observed during the teen years lie on a continuum of changes that take place over much of our lives. For example, a 1993 study by Jésus Pujol and his colleagues at the Autonomous University of Barcelona looked at changes in the corpus callosum—a massive structure that connects the two sides of the brain—over a two-year period with individuals between 11 and 61 years old. They found that although the rate of growth declined as people aged, this structure still grew by about 4 percent each year in people in their 40s (compared with a growth rate of 29 percent in their youngest subjects). Other studies, conducted by researchers such as Elizabeth Sowell of the University of California, Los Angeles, show that gray matter in the brain continues to disappear from childhood well into adulthood.

Second, I have not been able to find even a single study that establishes a *causal* relation between the properties of the brain being examined and the problems we see in teens. By their very nature, imaging studies are correlational, showing simply that activity in the brain is associated with certain behaviors or emotions. As we learn in elementary statistics courses, correlation does not even imply causation. In that sense, no imaging study could possibly identify the brain as a causal agent, no matter what areas of the brain were being observed.

Is it ever legitimate to say that human behavior is caused by brain anatomy or activity? [See "Brain Scans Go Legal," by Scott T. Grafton, Walter P. Sinnott-Armstrong, Suzanne I. Gazzaniga and Michael S. Gazzaniga; SCIENTIFIC AMERICAN MIND, December 2006/January 2007.] In his 1998 book *Blaming the Brain*, neuroscientist Elliot Valenstein deftly points out that we make a serious error of logic when we blame almost any behavior on the brain—especially when drawing conclusions from brain-scanning studies. Without doubt, all behavior and emotion must somehow be reflected (or "encoded") in brain structure and activity; if someone is impulsive or lethargic or depressed, for example, his or her brain must be wired to reflect those behaviors. But that wiring (speaking loosely) is not necessarily the cause of the behavior or emotion that we see.

Considerable research shows that a person's emotions and behaviors continuously change brain anatomy and physiology. Stress creates hypersensitivity in dopamine-producing neurons that persists even after they are removed from the brain. Enriched environments produce more neuronal connections. For that matter, meditation, diet, exercise, studying and virtually all other activities alter the brain, and a new study shows that smoking produces brain changes similar to those produced in animals given heroin, cocaine or other addictive drugs. So if teens are in turmoil, we will necessarily find some corresponding chemical, electrical or anatomical properties in the brain. But did the brain

cause the turmoil, or did the turmoil alter the brain? Or did some other factors—such as the way our culture treats its teens—cause both the turmoil and the corresponding brain properties?

Unfortunately, news reports—and even the researchers themselves—often get carried away when interpreting brain studies. For instance, a 2004 study conducted by James Bjork and his colleagues at the National Institute on Alcohol Abuse and Alcoholism, at Stanford University and at the Catholic University of America was said in various media reports to have identified the biological roots of teen laziness. In the actual study, 12 young people (ages 12 to 17) and 12 somewhat older people (ages 22 to 28) were monitored with an MRI device while performing a simple task that could earn them money. They were told to press a button after a short anticipation period (about two seconds) following the brief display of a symbol on a small mirror in front of their eyes. Some symbols indicated that pressing the button would earn money, whereas others indicated that failing to respond would cost money. After the anticipation period, subjects had 0.25 second to react, after which time information was displayed to let them know whether they had won or lost.

Areas of the brain that are believed to be involved in motivation were scanned during this session. Teens and adults were found to perform equally well on the task, and brain activity differed somewhat in the two groups—at least during the anticipation period and when $5 (the maximum amount that could be earned) was on the line. Specifically, on those high-payment trials the average activity of neurons in the right nucleus accumbens—but not in other areas that were being monitored—was higher for adults than for teens. Because brain activity in the two groups did not differ in other brain areas or under other payment conditions, the researchers drew a very modest conclusion in their article: "These data indicate qualitative similarities overall in the brain regions recruited by incentive processing in healthy adolescents and adults."

But according to the Long Island, N.Y., newspaper *Newsday*, this study identified a "biological reason for teen laziness." Even more disturbing, lead author James Bjork said that his study "tells us that teenagers love stuff, but aren't as willing to get off the couch to get it as adults are."

In fact, the study supports neither statement. If you truly wanted to know something about the brains of lazy teens, at the very least you would have to have some lazy teens in your study. None were identified as such in the Bjork study. Then you would have to compare the brains of those teens with the brains of industrious teens, as well as with the brains of both lazy and industrious adults. Most likely, you would then end up finding out how, on average, the brains in these four groups differed from one another. But even this type of analysis would not allow you to conclude that some teens are lazy "because" they have faulty brains. To find out why certain teens or certain adults are lazy (and, perforce, why they have brains that reflect their lazy tendencies), you would still have to look at genetic and environmental factors. A brain-scanning study can shed no light.

Valenstein blames the pharmaceutical industry for setting the stage for overinterpreting the results of brain studies such as Bjork's. The drug companies have a strong incentive to convince public policymakers, researchers, media professionals and the general public that faulty brains underlie all our problems—and, of course, that pharmaceuticals can fix those problems. Researchers, in turn, have a strong incentive to convince the public and various funding agencies that their research helps to "explain" important social phenomena.

The Truth about Teens

If teen chaos is not inevitable, and if such difficulty cannot legitimately be blamed on a faulty brain, just what is the truth about teens? The truth is that they are extraordinarily competent, even if they do not normally express that competence. Research I conducted with Dumas shows, for example, that teens are as competent or virtually as competent as adults across a wide range of adult abilities. And long-standing studies of intelligence, perceptual abilities and memory function show that teens are in many instances far superior to adults.

Visual acuity, for example, peaks around the time of puberty. "Incidental memory"—the kind of memory that occurs automatically, without any mnemonic effort, peaks at about age 12 and declines through life. By the time we are in our 60s, we remember relatively little "incidentally," which is one reason many older people have trouble mastering new technologies. In the 1940s pioneering intelligence researchers J. C. Raven and David Wechsler, relying on radically different kinds of intelligence tests, each showed that raw scores on intelligence tests peak between ages 13 and 15 and decline after

that throughout life. Although verbal expertise and some forms of judgment can remain strong throughout life, the extraordinary cognitive abilities of teens, and especially their ability to learn new things rapidly, is beyond question. And whereas brain size is not necessarily a good indication of processing ability, it is notable that recent scanning data collected by Eric Courchesne and his colleagues at the University of California, San Diego, show that brain volume peaks at about age 14. By the time we are 70 years old, our brain has shrunk to the size it had been when we were about three.

Findings of this kind make ample sense when you think about teenagers from an evolutionary perspective. Mammals bear their young shortly after puberty, and until very recently so have members of our species, *Homo sapiens*. No matter how they appear or perform, teens *must* be incredibly capable, or it is doubtful the human race could even exist.

Today, with teens trapped in the frivolous world of peer culture, they learn virtually everything they know from one another rather than from the people they are about to become. Isolated from adults and wrongly treated like children, it is no wonder that some teens behave, by adult standards, recklessly or irresponsibly. Almost without exception, the reckless and irresponsible behavior we see is the teen's way of declaring his or her adulthood or, through pregnancy or the commission of serious crime, of instantly *becoming* an adult under the law. Fortunately, we also know from extensive research both in the U.S. and elsewhere that when we treat teens like adults, they almost immediately rise to the challenge.

We need to replace the myth of the immature teen brain with a frank look at capable and savvy teens in history, at teens in other cultures and at the truly extraordinary potential of our own young people today.

ROBERT EPSTEIN is a contributing author for *Scientific American Mind* and the former editor of *Psychology Today*. Currently, he serves as a senior research psychologist at the American Institute for Behavioral Research and Technology.

EXPLORING THE ISSUE

Does the Adolescent Brain Make Risk Taking Inevitable?

Critical Thinking and Reflection

1. What qualifies as "risk taking" in adolescence? What might be some other ways to operationalize or define this term?
2. How might researchers with expertise in different areas work together to better understand adolescent risk taking?
3. What experiences might aid in adolescents' development?
4. How might we look to other cultures for a better understanding of neurological development in adolescents?
5. What are the important public policies that might change depending on how we understand adolescent risk taking and brain development?

Is There Common Ground?

Brain-based research is extremely popular in most areas of contemporary developmental science, and neurological research had advanced quickly amidst technological improvements. Both authors in the YES and NO selections recognize that interpreting this brain science is a key skill for those interested in adolescent development. For Laurence Steinberg, however, those interpretations offer practical suggestions about mitigating risk. For Robert Epstein, on the other hand, we need to consider an alternative explanation that culture impacts brain development.

In some ways, then, this issue becomes a matter of analysis. At the microlevel of neuronal activity in the brain, risk taking looks very different from the macro level of societal inequities. Those these two authors clearly disagree, the prominence of brain-based research makes it important to think about ways those different levels of analysis might become complementary rather than contentious.

Additional Resources

Albert, D., Chein, J., & Steinberg, L. (2013). The teenage brain peer influences on adolescent decision making. *Current Directions in Psychological Science, 22*(2), 114–120.

Bessant, J. (2008). Hard wired for risk: Neurological science, "the adolescent brain" and developmental theory. *Journal of Youth Studies, 11*(3), 347–360.

Bessant, J., & Watts, R. (2012). The mismeasurement of youth: why adolescent brain science is bad science. *Contemporary Social Science, 7*(2), 181–196.

Choudhury, S. (2009). Culturing the adolescent brain: What can neuroscience learn from anthropology? *Social Cognitive and Affective Neuroscience.*

Peper, J. S., & Dahl, R. E. (2013). The teenage brain surging hormones—Brain-behavior interactions during puberty. *Current Directions in Psychological Science, 22*(2), 134–139.

Create Central

www.mhhe.com/createcentral

Internet References . . .

The National Institute of Mental Health (NIMH)

www.nimh.nih.gov

Society for Neuroscience

http://www.sfn.org/

Society for Research on Adolescence

http://www.s-r-a.org/

Selected, Edited, and with Issue Framing Material by:
Allison A. Buskirk-Cohen, *Delaware Valley College*

ISSUE

Is There a Sexting Epidemic?

YES: The National Campaign to Prevent Teen and Unplanned Pregnancy and Cosmogirl.com, from "Sex and Tech: Results from a Survey of Teens and Young Adults," *The National Campaign to Prevent Teen and Unplanned Pregnancy and Cosmogirl.com* (2008)

NO: Joyce Kerstens and Wouter Stol, from "Receiving Online Sexual Requests and Producing Online Sexual Images: The Multifaceted and Dialogic Nature of Adolescents' Online Sexual Interactions." *Cyberpsychology: Journal of Psychosocial Research on Cyberspace* (2014)

Learning Outcomes

After reading this issue, you will understand that:

- Researchers and the public have become increasingly concerned with the intersection of adolescent behavior in cyberspace and adolescent attitudes and behaviors toward sex.
- Some research indicates that there is a wide prevalence of "sexting" among adolescents; other research disagrees.
- Translating research findings into information for the public can be a challenging task.
- It is difficult to make comparisons across research studies since they often differ in how they define "sexting."

ISSUE SUMMARY

YES: The National Campaign to Prevent Teen and Unplanned Pregnancy and CosmoGirl.com commissioned a survey to examine sexting. Over 1,000 adolescents and young adults responded to an online survey. The results from this survey suggest that a significant number of adolescents have engaged in sexting.

NO: Researchers at the Cybersafety Research Group analyzed data from a national survey among 4,453 Dutch adolescents. They compared the prevalence of receiving online sexual requests with the prevalence of producing online sexual images, finding that receiving sexual requests is common while producing sexual images is relatively rare.

Sexting refers to sending sexually explicit messages, images, or videos using mobile phones, emails, and social media websites. It is a relatively new term to describe a trend that incorporates electronic media, sex, and messaging. The first time this term appeared in publication was a 2005 article in the *Sunday Telegraph* magazine. Sexting was included in the Merriam-Webster's Collegiate Dictionary for the first time in 2012. As a phenomenon, sexting began primary through the extensive use of text messaging common among young adults. While this fact may be surprising to some individuals, research shows that many couples use sexting to enhance their relationship and sexual satisfaction within that relationship. Today, sexting seems to be prevalent among many age groups.

The Anthony Weiner scandals highlighted the sexting trend. The first scandal involved Weiner's use of the social networking site Twitter to send a sexually suggestive image link to a young woman. Weiner admitted to sexting with this woman and others both before and during his marriage. He officially resigned in June of 2011. Weiner attempted to return to politics two years later when he ran for New York

City mayor. That summer, a website released more sexting images and messages allegedly sent by Weiner. Again, Weiner admitted to sexting with at least three women. While he did not drop out of the mayoral race, he did not win the vote.

Clearly, there are some important risks associated with sexting. One risk is that the messages, images, and videos can be easily disseminated without the sender's permission. In fact, with sexting, the material can be sent to thousands of others within seconds. Individuals who sext may be at risk for cyberbulling, social problems, mental health difficulties, and legal issues. As Anthony Weiner learned, there may be employment repressions as well. Many individuals do not consider the consequences when sending or receiving sexts. Sexting may be associated with problematic attachment styles and contribute to problems in relationships. Studies have suggested that those who have sexts stolen may be at risk for anxiety and depression. The risks become that much more severe when adolescents are involved.

The legal and legislative communities are unsure of how to handle sexting among minors. Many state legislatures are introducing anti-sexting statutes into their criminal laws. In many states, sexting may relate to sexual harassment and stalking laws. When one person pressures another person to engage in sexting, that coercion may constitute sexual harassment. Sexting also might be subject to child pornography laws if a minor is involved. All fifty states have laws that protect minors from exploitation through the distribution of sexually implicit images, which would include sexting. However, what happens when minors both consent and engage in that distribution? In 2012, 13 states had introduced bills or resolutions involving sexting among minors. Hawaii, New York, Pennsylvania, and South Dakota had enacted legislation that same year.

Some adolescents who have sexted images have been charged with distribution of child pornography. If a state does not have specific laws about sexting between minors, a minor may be charged under the child pornography laws. There are up to three potential felony charges, including possession, distribution, and promotion. There are cases of prosecutors who have tried using child pornography laws to make sexting a criminal act. There are also states that have separated these issues. In 2009, Vermont lawmakers have introduced a bill to legalize the consensual exchange of sexting for individuals ages 13 through 18. Legislative bills lessening the penalty for consenting minors who sext was introduced in both Connecticut and Ohio. Instead of being charged with a felony, these minor would instead face a misdemeanor for sexting.

Part of the push for legal and legislative action has been media attention declaring an epidemic of texting among adolescents. In the YES selection, results from a survey commissioned by the National Campaign to Prevent Teen and Unplanned Pregnancy and CosmoGirl.com are discussed. Their survey included over 1,000 adolescents and young adults (ages 13 through 26) who responded to an online poll. About 20 percent of respondents indicated that they had participated in sexting, with some response rates to specific questions being higher. This report also lists cautionary information for adolescents and young adults before they engage in sexting. It also provides suggestions for how parents should talk to their children about sex and technology. The results of this report have been used to support the idea of a sexting epidemic.

In the NO selection, published by researchers at the Cybersafety Research Group in The Netherlands, the argument is made that a more complex view on adolescents' sexting behavior is warranted. This study analyzed data from a 2011 national survey of 4,453 Dutch adolescents. The researchers found that while receiving sexual requests is common among adolescents, producing sexual images is rare. Most adolescents self-reported that such incidences were non-problematic. However, negative experiences were more likely to occur when adolescents interacted with strangers online. Researchers also identified a link between problematic experiences and cyberbullying. Lastly, they were able to identify characteristics of adolescents vulnerable to engaging in both types of sexual communications.

There are two main questions to consider when reading the selections in this issue. First, how should sexting be defined for research purposes? Do all messages and images with sexual content qualify, or should researchers focus only on those that might be subject to some kind of legal consequence? Agreeing on a definition allows researchers to compare results across studies so that we can have a general understanding of behavior. A more inclusive definition allows us to explore related behaviors, but it may also lead to findings that do not capture the information we want. On the other hand, a more restricted definition helps prioritize the research agenda, but may leave out details and important pieces of information.

The other main question concerns how we define an epidemic. Traditionally, epidemics were used to describe a disease that affected many individuals at the same time and spread rapidly. In other words, epidemics referred to diseases that were highly contagious and extremely prevalent. Is it appropriate to apply the word "epidemic" to a behavioral trend like sexting? How quickly must the rates have increased for it to be considered highly contagious? How common must sexting be within a certain population, in this case, adolescents, for it to be considered extremely common? No one doubts that sexting may have serious ramifications, especially for adolescents, but have we truly reached a sexting epidemic?

YES

The National Campaign to Prevent Teen and Unplanned Pregnancy and Cosmogirl.com

Sex and Tech: Results from a Survey of Teens and Young Adults

In an effort to better understand the intersection between sex and cyberspace with respect to attitudes and behavior, The National Campaign to Prevent Teen and Unplanned Pregnancy and *CosmoGirl.com* commissioned a survey of teens and young adults to explore electronic activity. This is the first public study of its kind to quantify the proportion of teens and young adults that are sending or posting sexually suggestive text and images.

The survey of those ages 13–26 was conducted by TRU, a global leader in research on teens and 20-somethings. The survey was fielded online to a total of 1,280 respondents—653 teens (ages 13–19) and 627 young adults (ages 20–26)—between September 25, 2008 and October 3, 2008.

Please visit *www.TheNationalCampaign.org/sextech* for additional data from the survey, relevant tips for teens and parents, and other related materials. Visit *CosmoGirl.com* for teen perspectives on sending and receiving sexually suggestive content. (For more information on the survey, please see page 5.)

Key Findings

Note: Unless otherwise stated, *teen* means ages 13–19 and *young adult* means ages 20–26.

A significant number of teens have electronically sent, or posted online, nude or semi-nude pictures or video of themselves.

How many teens say they have sent/posted nude or seminude pictures or video of themselves?

- 20% of teens overall
- 22% of teen girls
- 18% of teen boys
- 11% of young teen girls (ages 13–16)

Sending and posting nude or semi-nude photos or videos starts at a young age and becomes even more frequent as teens become young adults.

How many young adults are sending or posting nude or seminude images of themselves?

- 33% of young adults overall
- 36% of young adult women
- 31% of young adult men

Sexually suggestive messages (text, email, IM) are even more prevalent than sexually suggestive images.

How many teens are sending or posting sexually suggestive messages?

- 39% of all teens
- 37% of teen girls
- 40% of teen boys
- 48% of teens say they have received such messages

How many young adults are sending or posting sexually suggestive messages?

- 59% of all young adults
- 56% of young adult women
- 62% of young adult men
- 64% of young adults say they have received such messages

Although most teens and young adults who send sexually suggestive content are sending it to boyfriends/girlfriends, others say they are sending such material to those they want to hook up with or to someone they only know online.

Who are these sexually suggestive messages and images being sent to?

- 71% of teen girls and 67% of teen guys who have sent or posted sexually suggestive content say they have sent/posted this content to a boyfriend/girlfriend.
- 21% of teen girls and 39% of teen boys say they have sent such content to someone they wanted to date or hook up with.

Sex and Tech: Results from a Survey of Teens and Young Adults, 2008, pp. 2–6. Reprinted with permission from The National Campaign to Prevent Teen and Unplanned Pregnancy.

- 15% of teens who have sent or posted nude/sem-inude images of themselves say they have done so to someone they only knew online.
- 83% of young adult women and 75% of young adult men who have sent sexually suggestive content say they have sent/posted such material to a boyfriend/girlfriend.
- 21% of young adult women and 30% of young adult men who have sent/posted sexually suggestive content have done so to someone they wanted to date or hook up with.
- 15% of young adult women and 23% of young adult men who have sent sexually suggestive material say they have done so to someone they only knew online.

Teens and young adults are conflicted about sending/posting sexually suggestive content—they know it's potentially dangerous, yet many do it anyway.

How do teens and young adults feel about sending/posting sexually suggestive content?

- 75% of teens and 71% of young adults say sending sexually suggestive content "can have serious negative consequences."
- Yet, 39% of teens and 59% of young adults have sent or posted sexually suggestive emails or text messages—and 20% of teens and 33% of young adults have sent/posted nude or semi-nude images of themselves.

Teens and young adults are sending sexually explicit messages and images, even though they know such content often gets shared with those other than the intended recipient.

How common is it to share sexy messages and images with those other than the intended recipient?

- 44% of both teen girls and teen boys say it is common for sexually suggestive text messages to get shared with people other than the intended recipient.
- 36% of teen girls and 39% of teen boys say it is common for nude or semi-nude photos to get shared with people other than the intended recipient.
- 44% of young adult women and 50% of young adult men say it is common for sexually suggestive text messages to get shared with people other than the intended recipient.
- 48% of young adult women and 46% of young adult men say it is common for nude or semi-nude photos to get shared with people other than the intended recipient.

Five Things to Think about Before Pressing "Send"

Don't assume anything you send or post is going to remain private.
Your messages and images will get passed around, even if you think they won't: 40% of teens and young adults say they have had a sexually suggestive message (originally meant to be private) shown to them and 20% say they have shared such a message with someone other than the person for whom is was originally meant.

There is no changing your mind in cyberspace—anything you send or post will never truly go away.
Something that seems fun and flirty and is done on a whim will never really die. Potential employers, college recruiters, teachers, coaches, parents, friends, enemies, strangers and others may all be able to find your past posts, even after you delete them. And it is nearly impossible to control what other people are posting about you. Think about it: Even if you have second thoughts and delete a racy photo, there is no telling who has already copied that photo and posted it elsewhere.

Don't give in to the pressure to do something that makes you uncomfortable, even in cyberspace.
More than 40% of teens and young adults (42% total, 47% of teens, 38% of young adults) say "pressure from guys" is a reason girls and women send and post sexually suggestive messages and images. More than 20% of teens and young adults (22% total, 24% teens, 20% young adults) say "pressure from friends" is a reason guys send and post sexually suggestive messages and images.

Consider the recipient's reaction.
Just because a message is meant to be fun doesn't mean the person who gets it will see it that way. Four in ten teen girls who have sent sexually suggestive content did so "as a joke" but many teen boys (29%) agree that girls who send such content are "expected to date or hook up in real life." It's easier to be more provocative or outgoing online, but whatever you write, post or send does contribute to the reallife impression you're making.

Nothing is truly anonymous.
Nearly one in five young people who send sexually suggestive messages and images, do so to people they only know online (18% total, 15% teens, 19% young adults). It is important to remember that even if someone only knows you by screen name, online profile, phone number or email address, that they can probably find you if they try hard enough.

Young people who receive nude/semi-nude images and sexually suggestive texts and emails are sharing them with other people for whom they were never intended.

How many teens and young adults say they have been shown nude/semi-nude content originally meant for someone else?

- 38% of teen girls and 39% of teen boys say they have had sexually suggestive text messages or emails—originally meant for someone else— shared with them.
- 25% of teen girls and 33% of teen boys say they have had nude or semi-nude images—originally meant for someone else—shared with them.
- 37% of young adult women and 47% of young adult men have had sexually suggestive text messages or emails—intended for someone else— shared with them.
- 24% of young adult women and 40% of young adult men say they have had nude or semi-nude images—originally meant for someone else— shared with them.

Teens and young adults admit that sending/posting sexually suggestive content has an impact on their behavior.

Does sending sexually suggestive text and images affect what happens in real life?

- 22% of teens and 28% of young adults say they are personally more forward and aggressive using sexually suggestive words and images than they are in "real life."
- 38% of teens and 40% of young adults say exchanging sexually suggestive content makes dating or hooking up with others more likely.
- 29% of teens and 24% of young adults believe those exchanging sexually suggestive content are "expected" to date or hook up.

5 Tips to Help Parents Talk to Their Kids about Sex and Technology

Talk to your kids about what they are doing in cyberspace.
Just as you need to talk openly and honestly with your kids about real life sex and relationships, you also want to discuss online and cell phone activity. Make sure your kids fully understand that messages or pictures they send over the Internet or their cell phones are not truly private or anonymous. Also make sure they know that others might forward their pictures or messages to people they do not know or want to see them, and that school administrators and employers often look at online profiles to make judgments about potential students/employees. It's essential that your kids grasp the potential short-term and long-term consequences of their actions.

Know who your kids are communicating with.
Of course it's a given that you want to know who your children are spending time with when they leave the house. Also do your best to learn who your kids are spending time with online and on the phone. Supervising and monitoring your kids' where-abouts in real life and in cyberspace doesn't make you a nag; it's just part of your job as a parent. Many young people consider someone a "friend" even if they've only met online. What about your kids?

Consider limitations on electronic communication.
The days of having to talk on the phone in the kitchen in front of the whole family are long gone, but you can still limit the time your kids spend online and on the phone. Consider, for example, telling your teen to leave the phone on the kitchen counter when they're at home and to take the laptop out of their bedroom before they go to bed, so they won't be tempted to log on or talk to friends at 2 a.m.

Be aware of what your teens are posting publicly.
Check out your teen's MySpace, Facebook and other public online profiles from time to time. This isn't snooping—this is information your kids are making public. If everyone else can look at it, why can't you? Talk with them specifically about their own notions of what is public and what is private. Your views may differ but you won't know until you ask, listen, and discuss.

Set expectations.
Make sure you are clear with your teen about what you consider appropriate "electronic" behavior. Just as certain clothing is probably off-limits or certain language unacceptable in your house, make sure you let your kids know what is and is not allowed online either. And give reminders of those expectations from time to time. It doesn't mean you don't trust your kids, it just reinforces that you care about them enough to be paying attention.

Teens and young adults give many reasons for sending/posting sexually suggestive content. Most say it is a "fun and flirtatious" activity.

Why do teens and young adults send or post sexually suggestive content?

- 51% of teen girls say pressure from a guy is a reason girls send sexy messages or images; only 18% of teen boys cited pressure from female counterparts as a reason.
- 23% of teen girls and 24% of teen boys say they were pressured by friends to send or post sexual content.

Among teens who have sent sexually suggestive content:

- 66% of teen girls and 60% of teen boys say they did so to be "fun or flirtatious"—their most common reason for sending sexy content.
- 52% of teen girls did so as a "sexy present" for their boyfriend.
- 44% of both teen girls and teen boys say they sent sexually suggestive messages or images in response to such content they received.
- 40% of teen girls said they sent sexually suggestive messages or images as "a joke."
- 34% of teen girls say they sent/posted sexually suggestive content to "feel sexy."
- 12% of teen girls felt "pressured" to send sexually suggestive messages or images.

Among young adults who have sent sexually suggestive content:

- 72% of young adult women and 70% of young adult men say they did so to be "fun or flirtatious."
- 59% of young adult women sent/posted sexually suggestive content as a "sexy present" for their boyfriend.

- 41% of young adult women and 51% of young adult men say they sent sexy messages or images in response to such content they received.

Definition of Terms

To ensure accurate interpretation, respondents were shown (and reminded of) the following definitions/explanations during the survey:

- *Sexually suggestive pictures/video:* semi-nude or nude personal pictures/video taken of oneself and not found on the Internet, or received from a stranger (like spam), etc.
- *Sexually suggestive messages:* sexually suggestive written personal texts, emails IMs, etc.—and not those you might receive from a stranger (like spam), etc.
- *Messages* only refers to those written electronically (in emails, texts, IMs, etc.)—and *pictures/video* only refers to those captured electronically (on a cellphone or digital camera/camcorder), etc.

About the Survey

This survey was fielded online to a total of 1,280 respondents—653 teens (ages 13–19) and 627 young adults (ages 20–26) between September 25, 2008 and October 3, 2008. It was conducted by **TRU**, a global leader in research on teens and 20-somethings.

At present, it is estimated that about 90% of teens and young adults are online. Respondents for this survey were selected from among those who have volunteered to participate in TRU's online surveys. Respondents were stratified according to the U.S. Census and the data have been weighted to reflect the demographic composition of teens and young adults. Respondents do not constitute a probability sample.

This document contains the precise language used in the survey and separate results for teens and young adults, as well as the total combined. For additional data, please visit *www.TheNationalCampaign.org/sextech* or contact The National Campaign at 202.478.8500. . . .

The National Campaign to Prevent Teen and Unplanned Pregnancy is a U.S. nonprofit organization that provides statistics on adolescent pregnancy, poll results, and analyses of factors affecting teenage sexual behavior and sex education.

Joyce Kerstens and Wouter Stol

Receiving Online Sexual Requests and Producing Online Sexual Images: The Multifaceted and Dialogic Nature of Adolescents' Online Sexual Interactions

Introduction

The Internet is playing an increasingly central role in the exploration and expression of adolescents' sexuality. Adolescents engage in various online sexual activities: they search for information about sex (Suzuki & Calzo, 2004), they engage in implicit and explicit sexual conversations and make obscene and flirtatious comments (Subrahmanyam & Šmahel, 2011) and, they produce and send sexual self-images (Lenhart, 2009). Research suggests that the Internet provides adolescents with opportunities to explore and express their sexuality (Valkenburg & Peter, 2011). However, adolescents' online sexual activities may also entail adverse consequences which might be detrimental to their sexual development. Adolescents may feel bothered by receiving online sexual requests from other online individuals. Feeling bothered can be an indication for having experienced harm online. Looking back, adolescents may also negatively evaluate their own online sexual behaviour. A negative evaluation can be an indication that adolescents' online sexual behaviour has led to unintended consequences. In the understanding of the adverse consequences of adolescents' online sexual interactions, many factors come into play. This study examines the incident characteristics and the characteristics of adolescents who received online sexual requests and who produced online sexual images, thereby focusing on requests perceived as bothersome and sexual behaviour evaluated as negative. Identifying which incident characteristics and characteristics of adolescents are related to adverse consequences of online sexual interactions, is a prerequisite to design personalized tools for adolescents that will enable them to recognize and counter online sexual interactions that might entail adverse consequences.

Prevalence of Receiving Online Sexual Requests and Producing Online Sexual Images

Receiving online sexual requests refers to receiving requests to talk about sex, questions about private parts and, requests for sexual intercourse or to undress in front of a webcam. Prior research predominantly investigated the prevalence of unwanted online sexual requests, i.e., online sexual solicitations (e.g., Ybarra, Espelage, & Mitchell, 2007). The three *Youth Internet Safety Surveys* conducted in the United States show a decline in receiving unwanted sexual solicitations: from 19% to 9% between 2000 and 2010. These studies also investigated the impact of the solicitations. The percentage of adolescents who reported feeling distressed declined from 5% in 2000 to 3% in 2010 (Jones, Mitchell, & Finkelhor, 2012). These studies did not encompass questions about wanted sexual solicitations, i.e., developmentally normal and/or consensual sexual requests as a part of adolescents' sexual exploration (e.g., Subrahmanyam & Šmahel, 2011). The *EU Kids Online* survey, a representative sample of children aged 9–16 years in 25 European countries, investigated the prevalence of receiving and seeing online sexual messages and found that 15% of the surveyed children had received or seen sexual messages on the Internet and that 4% of the surveyed children reported being bothered by these messages (Livingstone, Haddon, Görzig, & Ólafsson, 2011). However, the questions about sexual messaging included items about seeing posts from others and seeing other people perform sexual acts, i.e., the survey did not limit sexual messaging exclusively to online interactions, but included passively seeing sexual content from others.

Cyberpsychology: Journal of Psychosocial Research on Cyberspace, 8(1), article 8. doi: 10.5817/CP2014-1-8.

To our knowledge, no study has investigated the prevalence of receiving online sexual requests and how many adolescents perceived this as bothersome.

Producing online sexual images refers to making and sending sexual images of someone else and sexual self-exposure in front of a webcam. Prior research primarily investigated the prevalence of producing and distributing online sexual self-images and sexual images of peers through the Internet or by mobile phone. In research, this behaviour is labelled as 'sexting' (Lounsbury, Mitchell, & Finkelhor, 2011; Ringrose, Gill, Livingstone, & Harvey, 2012). Since sexting is a relatively new practice, studies on sexting are still scarce. The prevalence rates found in the—predominantly North-American—studies differ considerably, ranging from 2% to 20% (Livingstone et al., 2011; Mitchell, Finkelhor, Jones, & Wolak, 2012). Lounsbury et al. (2011) state that methodological inadequacies—for example, lack of consensus on definitions—account for the large differences in the studies they reviewed. No prior research has investigated how adolescents evaluated having produced online sexual material. Therefore, we asked:

RQ1: What is the prevalence of (a) receiving online sexual requests and (b) producing online sexual images?

RQ2: How many adolescents (a) perceive receiving online sexual requests as bothersome and how many adolescents (b) evaluate producing online sexual images as negative?

Incident Characteristics

Insight in the context of adolescents' online sexual interactions is important to understand why these interactions may entail adverse consequences. The concerns about adolescents' online sexual interactions primarily address two issues: (1) male perpetrators sending online sexual requests to minors for the purpose of sexual abuse and exploitation and (2) adolescents inability to realistically estimate the risks of their own online sexual behaviour. Sender characteristics (age, gender, familiarity) are important to gain insight in the context of online sexual interactions. However, adolescents who receive online sexual requests may also engage in sending these requests. This can indicate that sending and receiving sexual requests is reciprocal, for example to initiate a romantic relationship, or that sending sexual requests is related to adolescents' developing sexuality.

Little is known about the incident characteristics of receiving online sexual requests and producing online

sexual images. The aforementioned *Youth Internet Safety Surveys* found that more males than females were identified as senders of online sexual requests and most youth whose contact with senders was limited to the Internet were not certain of the sender's age. Furthermore, the proportion of senders of sexual requests personally known increased between 2000 and 2010 and most senders were identified as same-aged peers (Jones et al., 2012; Wolak, Mitchell, & Finkelhor, 2006). This tendency to communicate within the context of existing relationships is consistent with findings from the *EU Kids Online* survey (Livingstone et al., 2011). A survey conducted in the United States found that sexting occurs most often in the following contexts: solely between two romantic partners, first between partners and then shared with others and, between adolescents hoping to enter a romantic relationship (Lenhart, 2009). Findings from a qualitative study indicate that sexual images are being used as "a form of 'relationship currency' with boys asking for them and with 'pressures' upon girls to produce/share such images" (Ringrose et al., 2012, p. 13). To date, no study has investigated the relation between sexual requests perceived as bothersome, evaluating producing online sexual material as negative and incident characteristics. To our knowledge, no study has investigated adolescents' own role—either as sender or receiver—in online sexual interactions or investigated the motives for engaging in online sexual behaviour. To understand why online sexual requests and producing online sexual images may and may not entail adverse consequences, we asked:

RQ3: What are incident characteristics of sexual requests perceived as bothersome and behaviour evaluated as negative, in terms of (a) the characteristics of the communication partner, (b) the own role of adolescents in communication and, (c) motives for exposing?

Investigating incident characteristics provides insight into the way receiving online sexual requests and producing online sexual materials are embedded within a broader communicative context and existing offline and online relations.

Characteristics of Adolescents

Prior research primarily investigated the socio-demographic characteristics of adolescents who receive online sexual requests and who produce online sexual images (e.g., Jones et al., 2012; Lenhart, 2009; Livingstone et al., 2011). An overall picture of adolescents who receive requests and produce images is missing (e.g., Ringrose et al., 2012). Prior research revealed that adolescents' online victimization can be associated with the frequency of Internet use, online disinhibition, a lower level of psychological wellbeing, a lower level of self-control and, being cyberbullied (e.g., Barak, 2005; Bossler & Holt, 2010; Ybarra et al., 2007). Producing online sexual images is categorized as risk-taking behaviour. Prior research revealed that risk-taking behaviour can be associated with the afore-mentioned characteristics (e.g., Grasmick, Tittle, Bursik, & Arneklev, 1993; Livingstone & Helsper, 2007). Parental mediation generally refers to parental management of children's media use. Parental mediation of adolescents' Internet use might reduce the likelihood of online risks and might decrease online risk-taking behaviour (Pardoen & Pijpers, 2006; van den Eijnden & Vermulst, 2006). To develop an integrative perspective that helps us to understand why online sexual interactions may and may not entail adverse consequences for adolescents, we asked:

RQ4: What are the characteristics of (a) adolescents who reported bothersome online sexual requests and (b) adolescents who evaluated their behaviour negatively?

We compared the characteristics of these adolescents with the characteristics of adolescents who were not bothered and who did not evaluate their behaviour as negative. Knowing who is vulnerable online and why and; conversely who is not, is a prerequisite for the protection and ultimately the empowerment of vulnerable adolescents.

Method

Sample and Procedure

For this cross-sectional study a sample was taken from *Youth & Cybersafety*, a 4-year Dutch research project on online risks for children (2009–2013) commissioned by the Dutch Ministry for Education, Culture and Science[1]. The questionnaire on online sexual risks and online sexual risk-taking behaviour was developed in co-operation with *Rutgers WPF*, a Dutch knowledge centre on sexual and reproductive health and rights. The questionnaire was developed on the basis of feedback from 25 adolescents and tested in a pilot study for validity and reliability and, to refine question wording, sequence and questionnaire length. 442 adolescents participated in the pilot study. In total, 4538 adolescents filled in the online questionnaire. Validity checks for nonsensical answers resulted in the removal of 85 respondents of our dataset. The data-analysis was based on 4453 completed questionnaires

filled in by respondents attending secondary schools (51.2 % male). The age range of the adolescent sample was 11 to 18 years ($M = 13.9$, $SD = 1.48$). Younger adolescents (11 to 14 years) were over-represented. Data were collected between January 2011 and April 2011. Parental consent and adolescents' assent were obtained before participation.

Adolescents were not directly recruited; we randomly sampled secondary schools. Schools exclusively providing special or practical education were excluded from the sample, since pupils attending these schools require a different research approach. Schools were sent a letter asking them to participate in the *Youth & Cybersafety* research project. Seventeen secondary schools from three different levels—pre-vocational education (vmbo), higher general secondary education (havo) and pre-university education (vwo) participated. Each participating school received a report in which the findings from the school were compared with the overall findings. A detailed account of the recruitment and sampling procedures can be found elsewhere (Kerstens & Stol, 2012).

Data were collected using an online survey. The questionnaire was filled in at school during class in the presence of researchers and supervisors. We redesigned classrooms in order to create privacy for each respondent. Each respondent was provided with a unique number code making it impossible to link answers to identifying information of the participant. At the start of the questionnaire, participants were notified that: (1) the questionnaire would be about the internet and online sexual risks; (2) that the investigators had no chance to identify who had given the answers; (3) that they could stop at any point in time if they wished.

Measures

Prevalence and Adolescents' Perception

Receiving sexual requests. Participants were asked if they had received online sexual requests: questions about sex, requests for sexual intercourse, questions about private parts, requests to undress in front of a webcam. Response categories were 1 (*never*), 2 (*once*) and 3 (*several times*). Participants who reported receiving online sexual requests were asked how they perceived the incidences. Response categories were 1 (*pleasant*), 2 (*common*) and 3 (*bothersome*).

Producing sexual images. Since not all adolescents are familiar with the term 'sexting', the term 'sexting' was not used in the questionnaire (e.g., Ringrose et al., 2012). Two types of producing and distributing sexual images were investigated. Participants were asked (1) if they had made sexual images of someone else within the past 12 months: photo or video of intimate body parts, masturbation and sexual intercourse. Response categories were 1 (*never*), 2 (*once*) and 3 (*several times*). Participants were asked (2) if they had exposed their breasts and/or private parts in front of a webcam within the past 12 months. Response categories were 1 (*never*), 2 (*once*) and 3 (*several times*). Participants who reported having exposed their breasts and/or private parts in front of a webcam were asked how they evaluated their exposure in retrospect. Response categories were 1 (*pleasant*), 2 (*common*), 3 (*bad*).

Incident Characteristics

Gender of sender and webcam partner. To measure the gender of the sender of sexual requests and webcam partner, we asked participants to indicate whether they knew the gender of the sender. Measures of knowing the gender of the sender of sexual requests and the webcam partner were: 1 (*male*), 2 (*female*) and 3 (*don't know*).

Estimated age of sender and webcam partner. Measures of knowing the age of the sender of sexual requests and the webcam partner were: 1 (*more than 5 years younger*), 2 (*more than 2 years younger*), 3 (*approximately the same age*), 4 (*more than 2 years older*), 5 (*more than 5 years older*) and 6 (*don't know*).

Familiarity with sender and webcam partner. To measure the familiarity with sender and webcam partner, we asked if participants if they knew senders and webcam partners in real life. Response categories were: 1 (*I know the other person well in real life (for example, from school)*), 2 (*I have met the other person in real life, but I don't know him/her very well*) and 3 (*I know the other person only via the Internet*).

Receiver's role in online communication. Participants who reported having received online sexual requests were asked if they had sent online sexual requests themselves.

Characteristics of Adolescents

Frequency of Internet use. Participants were asked to indicate how many hours per day on average they were active on the Internet, for example engaging in activities such as gaming, sending emails or chatting.

Online disinhibition. Online disinhibition—a lower level of behavioural inhibitions in the online environment—may be particular significant when considered in the context of sexual risks and sexual risk-taking behaviour on the Internet (Whittle, Hamilton-Giachritsis, Beech, & Collings, 2013). Online disinhibition was measured using a 7-item scale based on studies on the online disinhibition effect (Suler, 2004) and a study by Schouten, Valkenburg, and Peter (2007). The items were rated on a 5-point Likert scale from 1 (*agree entirely*) to 5 (*disagree entirely*). The Cronbach's alpha was 0.86.

Parental mediation. We measured adolescents' perspective on parental mediation by asking questions about the four basic strategies of parental mediation: supervision (parent is present while using the Internet), restrictive mediation (parent sets rules), monitoring (parent checks records afterwards) and active mediation (parent communicates on Internet use and safety). The items were rated on a 3-point Likert scale: 1 (*(almost) always*), 2 (*sometimes*) and 3 (*never*).

Psychological well-being. Psychological well-being can be defined as "people's positive evaluations of their lives" (Diener & Seligman, 2004, p. 1). Psycho-social well-being was measured using a 12-item scale based on the study by Vandebosch, Van Cleemput, Mortelmans, and Walrave (2006) in which items from the *Self-Description Questionnaire* by Ellis, March, and Richards and the *SHIELDS Questionnaire* by Gerson were implemented. The items were rated on a 5-point Likert scale from 1 (*agree entirely*) to 5 (*disagree entirely*). The Cronbach's alpha was 0.85.

Self-control. Low self-control is an individual trait associated with risk-taking behaviour. Grasmick, Tittle, Bursik, and Arneklev (1993) developed a 24-item scale to measure self-control. We abbreviated the original scale to 13 items. The six sub-components of the original scale—impulsivity, simple tasks, risk-taking, physical activities, self-centredness, and temper—were represented. The 13 items were rated on a 3-point Likert scale from 1 (*(almost) never*) to 3 (*often*). The Cronbach's alpha was 0.74.

Cyberbulling. We asked respondents if they had been the target of one or more negative actions conducted by others via Internet or mobile phones within the past three months: spreading malicious rumors, posting threats or embarrassing information, deliberately exclusion and/or posting embarrassing photos or videos on the Internet. If respondents answered affirmative at one or more of the questions and evaluated these actions as offensive, we labeled them as cyberbully victims: a dichotomous variable (0–1).

Results

Prevalence and Adolescents' Perception

How prevalent are incidences of receiving online sexual requests and producing online sexual images (*RQ1*) and how did adolescents perceive and evaluate the incidences (*RQ2*)? Of the overall sample, 25.4% of the adolescents reported having received one or more online sexual requests. Table 1 depicts the percentages of participants who received specific sexual requests. Percentages are presented according to gender, age and educational level. Among all sexual requests, asking general questions about sex had the highest prevalence, whereas requests to undress before the webcam had the lowest prevalence. Female participants did not differ from male participants, although female participants more often received requests to do something sexual. Levels of receiving online sexual requests differed according to age and educational level. As adolescents get older, they are more likely to receive online sexual requests. Adolescents attending pre-university education received fewer requests.

Table 2 depicts the perception of receiving online sexual requests. Percentages are presented according to gender, age and educational level. The majority of the adolescents who received online sexual requests perceived the incidences as pleasant or common (71.2%). Less than one-third of the adolescents (28.8%) perceived the incidences as bothersome. Of the overall sample, 7.0% of the participants reported bothersome incidences (*n* = 312).

Percentages of reported bothersome incidences differed according to gender, age and educational level. Female participants and adolescents attending pre-vocational education reported more bothersome incidences and, younger adolescents reported more bothersome incidences than older adolescents.

Table 3 depicts the percentages of participants who indicated having produced online sexual images: exposing breasts and/or private parts in front of a webcam and, making photos or videos of intimate body parts, masturbation and/or sexual intercourse. Percentages are presented according to gender, age and educational level. A minority of the participants reported having produced online sexual images (3.0%).

Percentages of producing online sexual images differed according to gender and age: male adolescents produced more online sexual images than female adolescents

Table 1

	Questions about sex	Requests for sexual intercourse	Questions about breasts and/or genitals	Requests to undress on webcam	One or more of the mentioned requests
Percentages of Incidences of Online Sexual Requests (N = 4453).					
Gender	*	NS	**	**	NS
Boys	23.3%	15.9%	10.3%	7.5%	25.4%
Girls	20.6%	16.1%	14.1%	10.7%	25.3%
Age	**	**	**	**	**
≤ 12 year	9.9%	6.7%	6.0%	5.6%	12.7%
13–14 year	18.6%	13.3%	11.5%	8.2%	22.7%
15–16 year	35.1%	26.8%	17.2%	13.1%	37.7%
≥ 17 year	38.2%	26.8%	17.1%	11.8%	40.5%
Educational level	**	**	**	**	**
Lower pre-vocational education	23.8%	19.2%	13.7%	10.7%	28.5%
Higher general secondary education	23.5%	17.2%	12.9%	9.5%	26.6%
Pre-university education	18.8%	11.6%	9.8%	6.9%	20.9%
Total	**22.0%**	**16.0%**	**12.1%**	**9.1%**	**25.4%**

**P<0.01, Chi-Square, *P<0.05, Chi-Square, NS difference is not significant.

Table 2

Perception of Having Received Online Sexual Requests (*n* = 1108).

	Pleasant	Common	Bothersome
*Gender ******			
Boys	28.3%	59.6%	12.1%
Girls	9.9%	44.8%	45.3%
*Age ******			
≤ 12 year	11.3%	46.4%	42.3%
13–14 year	16.4%	51.2%	32.4%
15–16 year	21.7%	55.2%	23.0%
≥ 17 year	33.3%	53.9%	12.7%
*Educational level ******			
Lower pre-vocational education	14.7%	49.1%	36.2%
Higher general secondary education	23.2%	54.7%	22.1%
Pre-university education	23.7%	55.8%	20.6%
Total	**19.4%**	**52.4%**	**28.2%**

**$P<0.01$, Chi-Square.

Table 3

Percentages of Incidences of Producing Online Sexual Images (*N* = 4453).

	Exposing breasts and/or genitals on webcam	Making photos or videos of intimate body parts, masturbation and/or sexual intercourse	One or more of the mentioned activities
Gender	NS	**	**
Boys	1.7%	2.6%	3.7%
Girls	1.4%	1.2%	2.3%
Age	**	*	**
≤ 12 year	0.7%	1.0%	1.7%
13–14 year	1.3%	1.7%	2.7%
15–16 year	2.4%	2.5%	4.1%
≥ 17 year	2.8%	4.0%	5.6%
Educational level	NS	**	**
Lower pre-vocational education	1.3%	1.6%	2.4%
Higher general secondary education	2.3%	3.0%	4.7%
Pre-university education	1.3%	1.5%	2.6%
Total	**1.5%**	**1.9%**	**3.0%**

**$P<0.01$, Chi-Square, *$P<0.05$, Chi-Square, NS difference is not significant.

Table 1

Evaluation in Retrospect About Exposing Breasts and/or Private Parts in Front of a Webcam (*n* = 68).	Pleasant	Common	Bad
Gender			
Boys	44.7%	28.9%	26.3%
Girls	23.3%	36,7%	40,0%
Age			
≤ 12 year	16.7%	33.3%	50.0%
13–14 year	36.7%	36.7%	26.7%
15–16 year	32.0%	28.0%	40.0%
≥ 17 year	57.1%	28.6%	14.3%
Educational level			
Lower pre-vocational education	43.5%	17.4%	39.1%
Higher general secondary education	20.8%	50.0%	29.2%
Pre-university education	42.9%	28.6%	28.6%
Total	**35.3%**	**32.4%**	**32.4%**

and older adolescents produced more online sexual images than the younger ones.

Table 4 depicts how adolescents evaluated having exposed breasts and/or private parts in front of a webcam in retrospect. Percentages are presented according to gender, age and educational level. 32.4% of the participants felt bad about their behaviour. Of the overall sample, 0.5% of the participants felt badly about their sexual exposure (*n* = 22).

Some cells had an expected count less than 5; therefore, statistic tests to find out whether differences are significant were not possible. However, more females than males, more young adolescents than older adolescents and, more adolescents attending lower pre-vocational education felt bad about their online sexual behaviour. The most frequently reported negative consequences were sexual harassment, bullying and, negative comments—offline as well as online—and general regret.

Incident Characteristics

Research question 3 asked what specific incident characteristics are related to receiving online sexual requests and exposing breasts and/or private parts in front of a webcam, in terms of (1) the characteristics of the communication partner, (2) the role of the adolescent him/herself in online communication and, (3) motives for exposing. Table 5 depicts the percentages of incident characteristics of receiving online sexual requests between participants who perceived these requests as bothersome and those who did not. Percentages are presented according to gender and age of sender, familiarity with sender and, the receiver's role in online sexual communication.

If we compare online sexual requests that are perceived as pleasant or common with sexual requests that are perceived as bothersome, it appears that sexual requests perceived as bothersome more often originated from males or from senders whose sex is unknown, from senders more than 5 years older than the recipient and, from senders solely known from the Internet. The role of the receivers of online sexual requests was also significant: being passive in online sexual communication, i.e., not sending online sexual requests to others is related to perceiving online sexual requests as bothersome. The results indicate that anonymity in online sexual communication makes it more likely that online sexual requests are perceived as bothersome.

Table 6 depicts the percentages of incident characteristics of exposing breasts and/or private parts in front of a webcam between participants who felt bad about their behaviour in retrospect and those who did not. A negative

Table 5

Prevalence of Incident Characteristics of Receiving Online Sexual Requests for Adolescents Who Perceived this as Pleasant or Common ($n = 796$) and, for Those Who Perceived this as Bothersome ($n = 312$).

	Perceived as pleasant or common	Perceived as bothersome
Gender of sender **		
Male	38.2%	64.7%
Female	50.1%	9.9%
Gender unknown	11.7%	25.3%
Total	100.0%	100.0%
Age of sender **		
Peer (about the same age)	81.3%	53.8%
>5 years older	4.5%	12.2%
Age unknown	14.2%	34.0%
Total	100.0%	100.0%
Familiarity with sender **		
Well acquainted, also offline	69.8%	27.9%
Little acquainted	17.3%	23.4%
Acquainted only online	12.8%	48.7%
Total	100.0%	100.0%
Receiver's role in online sexual communication **		
Active: sent sexual requests to others	54.0%	18.3%
Passive: did not sent sexual requests to others	46.0%	81.7%
Total	100.0%	100.0%

** $P < 0.01$, Chi-Square.

evaluation of sexual behaviour is related to reported negative consequences. Percentages are presented according to gender and age of sender, familiarity with sender and, motives of participants.

Some cells had an expected count less than 5; therefore, statistic tests to find out whether differences are significant were not possible. However, participants more often felt bad about their behaviour when the webcam partner was male and when the webcam partner was known only from the Internet. A positive evaluation of sexual behaviour more often occurred when the webcam partner was a peer. It is not surprising that a negative evaluation is related to negative motives for engaging in sexual behaviour in front of a webcam.

Characteristics of Vulnerable and Risk-Taking Adolescents

Research question 4 asked (1) what are the characteristics of adolescents who received online sexual requests and perceived this as bothersome and, (2) what are the characteristics of adolescents who produced online sexual images and felt bad about it in retrospect. Table 7 depicts the characteristics of participants who received online sexual requests and perceived this as bothersome and participants who did not. The analysis includes 6 characteristics: sociodemographic characteristics, Internet use, parental mediation, individual characteristics, negative online experiences and, initiative in online sexual communication.

Table 6

Prevalence of Incident Characteristics of Exposing Breasts and/or Private Parts in Front of a Webcam for Adolescents Who Felt Bad About Their Behaviour in Retrospect (*n* = 22) and Those Who Did Not (*n* = 46).

	No bad feelings in retrospect *n* = 46	Bad feelings in retrospect *n* = 22
Gender of the webcam partner		
Male	39.1%	50.0%
Female	54.3%	27.3%
Gender unknown	6.5%	22.7%
total	100.0%	100.0%
Age of the webcam partner		
Peer (about the same age)	89.1%	54.4%
>5 years older	2.2%	0.0%
Age unknown	8.7%	45.5%
total	100.0%	100.0%
Familiarity with the webcam partner		
Well acquainted, also offline	58.7%	22.7%
Little acquainted	15.2%	13.6%
Acquainted only online	26.1%	63.6%
total	100.0%	100.0%
Motives for exposure		
Positive motives (excitement, enjoyment)	93.5%	59.13%
Negative motives (social pressure, coercion)	6.5%	40.9%
Total	100.0%	100.0%

Table 7 reveals that receiving online sexual requests and perceiving this as bothersome (*n* = 312) is associated with being female and being younger, a higher level of online disinhibited behaviour, a lower level of psychological well-being and, being cyberbullied. Conversely, a greater likelihood of receiving online sexual requests and perceiving this as pleasant or common (*n* = 796) is associated with being male, a lower level of parental mediation and, a high frequency of Internet usage. Age is strongly associated with a positive perception: as adolescents get older, the likelihood of perceiving online sexual requests as bothersome decreases. A lower level of self-control is associated with receiving online sexual requests, regardless of a positive or negative perception. Adolescents who take initiative in online sexual interaction are less likely to perceive receiving online sexual requests as bothersome.

Table 8 depicts the characteristics of participants who produced online sexual images. The columns of Table 8 show the results for (1) exposing breasts and/or private parts in front of a webcam and a negative evaluation; (2) exposing breasts and/or private parts in front of a webcam and no negative evaluation and, (3) making photos or videos of intimate body parts, masturbation or sexual intercourse. We included the following characteristics: socio-demographic characteristics, Internet use, parental mediation, individual characteristics and negative online experiences. Exposing breasts and/or private parts in front of a webcam and feeling bad about this (*n* = 22) is associated with a higher level of online disinhibited behaviour and being cyberbullied. Conversely, a greater likelihood of reporting no negative feelings after exposing breasts and/or private parts (*n* = 46) is associated with a high frequency of Internet usage and a lower level of self-control.

Table 7

Logistic Regression Analysis for Variables Predicting Receiving Online Sexual Requests for Adolescents Who Perceived this as Bothersome (*n* = 796) and Adolescents Who Perceived this as Pleasant or Common (*n* = 312).

Predictor	Perceived the requests as bothersome		Perceived the requests as pleasant or common	
	OR	95% CI	OR	95% CI
Socio-demographic characteristics				
Girl	4.04 *	2.96–5.51	0.75	0.59–0.94
Age	1.04	0.95–1.13	1.31 *	1.22–1.40
Internet use				
Frequency	1.09	1.00–1.20	1.14 *	1.06–1.23
Online disinhibition	1.28 *	1.09–1.50	1.10	0.96–1.26
Parental mediation				
Parental supervision while using the Internet	1.03	0.78–1.35	0.91	0.72–1.16
Rules about internet use and activities	0.95	0.72–1.25	0.79	0.63–0.99
Monitoring internet use (afterwards)	1.03	0.89–1.19	0.91	0.81–1.03
Communication on internet use and safety	0.98	0.87–1.11	0.89	0.80-0.98
Individual characteristiscs				
Psychological well-being	0.72 *	0.59–0.88	1.12	0.94–1.34
Self-control	0.42 *	0.28–0.62	0.24 *	0.17–0.33
Negative online experiences online				
Was bullied online	2.70 *	1.97–3.69	1.32	0.92–1.88
Initiative in online sexual communication				
Produced sexual images (photo,video,cam)	1.48	0.83–2.64	2.03 *	1.23–3.37
Sent sexual requests	1.33	0.92–1.92	17.84 *	13.88–22.94
$\div^2$	254.65		1335.08	
Nagelkerke R^2	0.15		0.46	

Note: N = 4453. Results of girls were compared with boys (reference group). *p<.05,*p<.01**.

Age is strongly associated with a positive evaluation: as adolescents get older, the likelihood of feeling bad about sexual exposure in front of a webcam decreases.

Making photos and videos of intimate body parts, masturbation and/or sexual intercourse (*n* = 83) is associated with being male and being older, a high frequency of Internet use, a higher level of online disinhibited behaviour and, a lower level of self-control.

Discussion

This article investigated adolescents receiving online sexual requests and adolescents engaging in producing online sexual images. Our purpose was to enhance our understandings of the complex nature of these online sexual interactions in terms of (1) their perception and

evaluation, (2) incident characteristics and, (3) the characteristics of adolescents involved. The findings suggest that a more nuanced view on adolescents' online sexual interactions is required. Prior studies on online sexual risks primarily framed adolescents either as victims—passively being at risk and vulnerable—or as perpetrators—actively engaging in risky and deviant behaviour. This strict distinction conceals the multifaceted, dialogic and developmentally normal nature of adolescents' online sexual interactions.

Our findings indicate that receiving online sexual requests is quite common among adolescents. Requests for information about sex had the highest prevalence. This is in line with previous research (Ward, 2004). The levels of receiving requests did not differ considerably for male and female adolescents, although female adolescents

Table 8

Logistic Regression Analysis for Variables Predicting Exposing in Front of Webcam for Adolescents Who Felt Bad About this (*n* = 22) and Adolescents Who Did Not (*n* = 46) and, for Variables Predicting Making Sexual Photos or Videos (*n* = 83).

Predictor	Sexual exposure feeling bad		Sexual exposure no bad feelings		Making sexual photos or videos	
	OR	95% CI	OR	95% CI	OR	95% CI
Socio-demographic characteristics						
Girl	1.32	0.50–3.45	0.79	0.41–1.54	0.53 **	0.32–0.88
Age	1.19	0.99–1.43	1.34 *	1.03–1.73	1.18 **	1.02–1.36
Internet use						
Frequency	1.37	0.99–1.88	1.43 **	1.14–1.78	1.35 **	1.15–1.58
Online disinhibition	2.74 **	1.74–4.32	1.37	0.98–1.91	1.43 **	1.12–1.83
Parental mediation						
Parental supervision	.63	0.20–2.06	0.42	0.13–1.33	1.45	0.90–2.34
Rules about internet use	1.10	0.43–2.84	0.85	0.43–1.72	0.9	0.54–1.50
Monitoring internet use (afterwards)	1.22	0.76–1.96	0.96	0.67–1.39	0.89	
Communication on internet use	.64	0.41–1.00	1.00	0.75–1.33	0.95	0.77–1.18
Individual characteristiscs						
Psychological well-being	.93	0.48–1.81	1.06	0.64–1.74	1.01	0.70–1.45
Self-control	1.32	0.39–4.51	0.14 **	0.06–0.34	0.16 **	0.09–0.31
Negative online experiences						
Was bullied online	4.61 **	1.65–12.93	0.81	0.24–2.72	1.47	0.70–3.07
$\div^2$	47.34		70.06		105.88	
Nagelkerke R²	0.18		0.15		0.14	

Note: N = 4453. Results of girls were compared with boys (reference group). *p<.05,*p<.01**.

more often receive requests to do something sexual. The likelihood of receiving sexual requests increases when adolescents get older. An increased interest in sexuality and sexual relationships is developmentally normal for adolescents (Subrahmanyam & Šmahel, 2011). Producing online sexual images is relatively rare. Older adolescents are more likely to produce sexual materials than younger adolescents. This finding is in line with other studies (Lenhart, 2009; Livingstone et al., 2011). Male adolescents send more sexts than female adolescents. Findings in other studies, however, are inconclusive.

One-fourth of the adolescents who received an online sexual request perceived this as bothersome. Looking back, one-third of the adolescents who exposed breasts and/or private parts in front of a webcam felt bad about their behaviour. Adolescents reported negative consequences such as sexual harassment, bullying and negative comments—offline as well as online. The finding that

female and younger adolescents more often perceive sexual request as bothersome is in line with previous research (Jones et al., 2012; Livingstone et al., 2011). The degree of sexual interest and subsequent sexual activity increases with adolescents' age (Cubbin, Santalli, Brindis, & Braveman, 2005). Therefore, receiving sexual requests might be developmentally-inappropriate for younger adolescents. Female adolescents use the Internet for communication purposes more often, which increases the likelihood of experiencing the downsides of communicating online (Mitchell, Finkelhor, & Wolak, 2003).

Online sexual requests originating from senders who are male and whose age and sex are unknown were more often perceived as bothersome. Requests originating from peers and senders adolescents were well acquainted with were more often perceived as pleasant or common. Although anonymity might be beneficial for adolescents who send sexual requests (Valkenburg & Peter, 2011), our findings suggest that this is not the case for adolescents who receive these requests. The same picture emerges for adolescents who exposed themselves in front of a webcam. Not surprisingly, a negative assessment of this behaviour is related to negative motives such as social pressure and coercion. Previous research has shown that sexting is often coercive (Ringrose et al. 2012). Interestingly, being passive in online communication is associated with a negative perception. Receivers of requests who send sexual requests themselves are less likely to perceive these as bothersome. Trust, reciprocity and equivalence are essential for adolescents in exploring their sexuality and engaging in romantic relationships (Subrahmanyam & Šmahel, 2011). Therefore, negative experiences are more likely to occur when adolescents interact with people relatively unknown and when an intrinsic motivation for engaging in sexual interaction is missing. Our findings suggest that incident characteristics play an important role in explaining why sexual communication is perceived as bothersome or not.

There are striking similarities in the profiles of vulnerable adolescents; i.e. adolescents who perceived receiving sexual requests as bothersome and adolescents who evaluated their online sexual activities as negative. Likewise, the profiles of adolescents who have did not perceive these requests as bothersome and who did not evaluate their activities as negative show significant similarities. Therefore, it is possible to give an overview of risk factors and protective factors. Firstly, bothersome and negative experiences do not stand alone. There is a strong relation with other negative online experiences, such as being cyber bullied. Secondly, there is a strong relation between adolescents' Internet usage and receiving sexual requests or engaging in sexting. An above average score on online disinhibition increases the likeliness of being involved in bothersome and negative incidences. Conversely, very frequent internet use increases the likeliness of being involved in non-problematic incidences. Therefore, it seems that being frequently online is a protective factor. Possibly, learning-by-doing helps adolescents to early recognize and counter negative online situations. Thirdly, adolescents with low self-control are more likely to engage in both sexual communications as well as in producing online sexual material, whether this leads to bothersome incidences or not. However, adolescents who also score low on psychological well-being are more likely to perceive incidences as bothersome, although the direction of this relation is unclear. Lastly, age and taking initiative in online interactions are both very important factors in protecting adolescents from harm.

The older adolescents get, the more they developmentally are interested in sex and, the more they voluntarily become involved in online sexual communications and activities. Conversely, younger adolescents who are passively confronted with sexual requests from others feel intimidated or bothered. Therefore, this group needs special attention.

Our study has several limitations that need to be addressed in future research. First, our data is cross-sectional which allowed us to identify relations between variables, but it did not allow us to investigate temporal sequence or causality. Second, we did not investigate long-term effects, neither of receiving online sexual requests nor of producing online sexual images. Third, the sample size of the models explaining sexting (Table 8) is quite small. Therefore, caution need to be used in the interpretation of the findings and the inferences to the population. Although the represented models describe the variables that significantly correlated with sexting, a more elaborated rationale for studying psychological variables in relation to sexting is needed to understand psychological processes which shape youth's motivations and experience with this type of online activity.

Conclusion

The binary conceptions 'being at risk-risk-taking', 'victim-perpetrator', 'online-offline' do not grasp the reality of adolescents' multifaceted and dialogic online sexual interactions and the ways in which these interactions are integrated within and shaped by adolescents' offline lives. However, the online environment differs from its offline counterpart in terms of the extent to which people are disembodied or anonymous and, the extent to which people may interact with a known or unknown other. Furthermore, adolescents are no homogeneous group, neither online nor offline. In addition, adolescents are constantly developing themselves, gaining experience, acquiring skills and building resilience. A personalized rather than general approach in which the adolescent is central, and that fosters the empowerment of adolescents is more likely to entail an outcome in the interest of adolescents.

Note

1. This research project was undertaken in accordance with the Code of Research established by the HBO-council (Andriessen, Onstenk, Delnooz, Smeijsters, & Peij, 2010).

References

Andriessen, D., Onstenk, J., Delnooz, P., Smeijsters, H., & Peij, S. (2010). *Gedragscode praktijkgericht onderzoek voor het hbo; Gedragscode voor het voorbereiden en uitvoeren van praktijkgericht onderzoek binnen het Hoger Beroepsonderwijs in Nederland* [Dutch Code of conduct for research in applied sciences]. Delft: Elan Strategie & Creatie.

Barak, A. (2005). Sexual harassment on the Internet. *Social Science Computer Review, 23*, 77–92. http://dx.doi.org/10.1177/0894439304271540

Bossler, A. M., & Holt, T. J. (2010). The effect of self-control on victimization in the cyberworld. *Journal of Criminal Justice, 38*, 227–236. http://dx.doi.org/10.1016/j.jcrimjus.2010.03.001

Cubbin, C., Santelli, J., Brindis, C. D., & Braveman, P. (2005). Neighborhood context and sexual behaviors among adolescents: Findings from the National Longitudinal Study of Adolescent Health. *Perspectives on Sexual and Reproductive Health, 37*, 125–134. http://dx.doi.org/10.1363/3712505

Diener, E., & Seligman, M. E. P. (2004). Beyond money: Toward an economy of well-being. *Psychological Science in the Public Interest, 5*, 1–31. http://dx.doi.org/10.1111/j.0963-7214.2004.00501001.x

Eijnden, R.J.J.M. van den, & Vermulst, A. (2006). *Online communicatie, compuslief internetgebruik en het psychosociale welbevinden van jongeren* [Online communication, compulsive Internet use and psychosocial well-being among youth]. In Jaarboek IVCT en samenleving 2006. De digitale generatie (pp. 25–44). Amsterdam: Boom.

Grasmick, H. G., Tittle, C. R., Bursik Jr. R. J., & Arneklev, B. J. (1993). Testing the core empirical implications of Gottfredson and Hirschi's general theory of crime. *Journal of Research in Crime and Delinquency, 30*, 5–29. http://dx.doi.org/10.1177/0022427893030001002

Jones, L. M., Mitchell, K. J., & Finkelhor, D. (2012). Trends in youth internet victimization: Findings from three youth internet safety surveys 2000-2010. *Journal of Adolescent Health, 50*, 179–186. http://dx.doi.org/10.1016/j.jadohealth.2011.09.015

Kerstens, J., & Stol, W. P. (2012). *Jeugd en Cybersafety: Online slachtoffer- en daderschap onder Nederlandse jongeren* [Youth & Cybersafety: Online victimization and perpetration among Dutch youth]. Den Haag: Boom Lemma uitgevers.

Lenhart, A. (2009). *Teens and sexting: how and why minor teens are sending sexually suggestive or nearly nude images via text messaging.* Washington, D.C.: Pew Internet & American Life Project.

Livingstone, S., Haddon, L., Görzig, A., & Ólafsson, K. (2011). *Risks and safety on the Internet: The perspective of European children. Full Findings.* LSE, London: EU Kids Online.

Livingstone, S., & Helsper, E. (2007). Taking risks when communicating on the Internet: The role of offline social-psychological factors in young people's vulnerability to online risks. *Information, communication and society, 10*, 619–643. http://dx.doi.org/10.1080/13691180701657998

Lounsbury, K., Mitchell, K. J. & Finkelhor, D. (2011). *The true prevalence of sexting.* Crimes Against Children Research Centre, University of New Hampshire, Durham, New Hampshire.

Mitchell, K. J., Finkelhor, D., Jones, L. M., & Wolak, J. (2012). Prevalence and characteristics of youth sexting: a national study. *Pediatrics,129*, 13–20. http://dx.doi.org/10.1542/peds.2011-1730

Mitchell, K. J., Finkelhor, D., & Wolak, J. (2003). The exposure of youth to unwanted sexual material on the internet: A national survey of risk, impact, and prevention. *Youth & Society, 34*, 330–358. http://dx.doi.org/10.1177/0044118X02250123

Pardoen, J., & Pijpers, R. (2006). *Mijn kind online: Hoe begeleid je als ouder je kind op internet?* [My child online: guidelines for parents to mediate their children's Internet use]. Amsterdam: SWP.

Ringrose, J., Gill, R., Livingstone, S., & Harvey, L. (2012). *A Qualitative Study of Children, Young People and 'Sexting'.* London: NSPCC.

Schouten, A. P., Valkenburg, P. M., & Peter, J. (2007). Precursors and underlying Processes of adolescents' online self-disclosure: Developing and testing an "Internet-attribute-perception" model. *Media Psychology, 10*, 292–314. http://dx.doi.org/10.1080/15213260701375686

Subrahmanyam, K, & Šmahel, D. (2011). *Digital Youth: The Role of Media in Development.* New York: Springer.

Suler, J. R. (2004). The online disinhibition effect. *CyberPsychology & Behavior, 7*, 321–326. http://dx.doi.org/10.1089/1094931041291295

Suzuki, L. K., & Calzo, J. P. (2004). The search for peer advice in cyberspace: An examination of online teen bulletin boards about health and sexuality. *Journal of Applied Developmental Psychology, 25*, 685–698. http://dx.doi.org/10.1016/j.appdev.2004.09.002

Valkenburg, P. M., & Peter, J. (2011). Online communication among adolescents: An integrated model of its attraction, opportunities, and risks. *Journal of Adolescent Health, 48*, 121–127. http://dx.doi.org/10.1016/j.jadohealth.2010.08.020

Vandebosch, H., van Cleemput, K., Mortelmans, D., & Walrave, M. (2006). *Cyberpesten bij jongeren in Vlaanderen* [Cyberbullying among youth in Flanders]. Brussel: viWTA.

Ward, L. M. (2004). Wading through the stereotypes: Positive and negative associations between media use and black adolescents' conceptions of self. *Developmental Psychology, 40,* 284–294. http://dx.doi.org/10.1037/0012-1649.40.2.284

Whittle, H., Hamilton-Giachritsis, C., Beech, A., & Collings, G. (2013). A review of online grooming: Characteristics and concerns. *Aggression and Violent Behavior, 18,* 62–70. http://dx.doi.org/10.1016/j.avb.2012.09.003

Wolak, J., Mitchell, K., & Finkelhor, D. (2006). *Online Victimization of Youth: Five years later.* Alexandria, VA: National Center for Missing & Exploited Children Bulletin - #07-06-025.

Ybarra, M. L., Espelage, D. L., & Mitchell, K. J. (2007). The co-occurrence of Internet harassment and unwanted sexual solicitation victimization and perpetration: Associations with psychosocial indicators. *Journal of Adolescent Health, 41,* S31–S41. http://dx.doi.org/10.1016/j.jadohealth.2007.09.010

JOYCE KERSTENS is a senior researcher at the Cybersafety research Group (NHL University). Her research activities have mainly focused on policy and evaluation research in the field of safety and security.

WOUTER STOL is chairholder in Cybersafety at NHL University of Applied Sciences and the Police Academy, and professor in Police Studies at the Open University. He served as the chief of police in Amsterdam until 1992. He has written about 100 publications; the main theme of his research is safety and information and communications technology.

EXPLORING THE ISSUE

Is There a Sexting Epidemic?

Critical Thinking and Reflection

1. At what point does a behavior qualify as an "epidemic"? How do we measure it?
2. What are the consequences of sexting for an adolescent? Are adolescents capable of considering these consequences before engaging in this behavior?
3. How might researchers better communicate their findings to the media and the public?
4. What responsibility does the media have in communicating with the public? What is the public's responsibility?

Is There Common Ground?

The topic of sex and adolescents has long been a controversial subject. The intersection of media, sex, and adolescents is a relatively new area for researchers to investigate. Both selections in this issue find that adolescents are sexting—using the Internet to send messages or images that are sexual in nature. However, the extent of this behavior is up for debate. According to the YES selection, the rates of adolescent sexting are high enough to constitute an epidemic. However, in the NO selection, the authors present a more nuanced description of online sexual interactions.

Both selections find that adolescents are increasingly using media to explore aspects of their sexuality. Sexual identity, in terms of attitudes and behaviors, is not something that develops overnight. Rather, it is a lengthy process and the role media plays in that process is not something that can be ignored.

Additional Resources

Hack, L. (2014). Sexting suggests more than just words and pictures.

Houck, C. (2013). Youth sexting: Balancing media representations and emerging data. *The Brown University Child and Adolescent Behavior Letter, 29*, 1–8.

Lounsbury, K., Mitchell, K., & Finkelhor, D. (2011). The true prevalence of "sexting." *Durham, NH, Crimes Against Children Research Center, University of New Hampshire.*

Podlas, K. (2011). Legal Epidemiology of the Teen Sexting Epidemic: How the Media Influenced Legislative Outbreak, *The Pittsburgh Journal of Technology Law & Policy, 12*, 1.

Ringrose, J., Harvey, L., Gill, R., & Livingstone, S. (2013). Teen girls, sexual double standards and "sexting": Gendered value in digital image exchange. *Feminist Theory, 14*(3), 305–323.

Create Central

www.mhhe.com/createcentral

Internet References . . .

Cyberbullying Research Center

www.cyberbullying.us

Do Something

https://www.dosomething.org/facts/11-facts
-about-sexting

The National Campaign

www.thenationalcampaign.org/resource
/sex-and-tech

Unit 6

Early Adulthood

*S*electing a name for this stage of development is controversial in and of itself. Some people use the term youth, while others prefer emerging adults. Generally, this period of early adulthood is when a person is developing the characteristics of adulthood but does not yet have adult responsibilities (such as a career and marriage) or the full psychological sense of responsibility. In many contemporary societies, this period of life seems longer and more intense because of increasing educational expectations, later average ages for starting a family, and more time allocated to self-exploration.

Youth and emerging adulthood are primarily times where people gradually make the transition to fully adult roles. That transition involves both psychological and practical challenges, several of which are dealt with in the issues covered in this section. The three issues all focus on the experiences of early adults in the college environment, asking how this generation differs from previous generations. The selections question the presence of certain personality traits, the role of religion, and how technology influences development. The selections for the three issues are as multifaceted as the stage itself.

Selected, Edited, and with Issue Framing Material by:
Allison A. Buskirk-Cohen, *Delaware Valley University*

ISSUE

Is There a "Narcissism Epidemic" among Contemporary Young Adults?

YES: Jean M. Twenge, from "The Age of Anxiety? Birth Cohort Change in Anxiety and Neuroticism, 1952–1993," *Journal of Personality and Social Psychology* (2000)

NO: Pew Research Center, from "Millennials: Confident. Connected. Open to Change," Pew Internet and American Life Project (2010)

Learning Outcomes

After reading this issue, you will be able to:

- Know that there is some evidence that college student scores on the Narcissistic Personality Inventory have risen significantly in recent decades, though the magnitude of those changes depends upon the data being interpreted.
- Understand that other research suggests that college students do report high confidence, but also report a variety of other positive characteristics.
- Recognize that the study of generational differences is complex with values often reflecting life cycle effects, period effects, and cohort effects.

ISSUE SUMMARY

YES: Jean Twenge's article presents the results from two meta-analyses examining self-reports of anxiety and neuroticism. Her findings demonstrate that both college students and schoolchildren report increases in these characteristics. She suggests low social connectedness and environmental threat are responsible for these changes.

NO: In the overview of this report, the Pew Research Center describes findings on the study of roughly 50 million Millennials. They describe this generation as confident, self-expressive, liberal, positive, and open to change—quite different from the negative characteristics often assigned.

In the hit 2004 Disney movie *The Incredibles*, Dash, the boy child in a family movie of superheroes, finds himself frustrated by his mother's insistence that he not use his super-speed to beat other children in running races—despite his father telling him his powers make him "special." His mother explains to Dash that beating the other children would make them feel bad, and that "everyone's special." "Which," according to Dash, "is another way of saying that nobody is." Though the movie was imaginary, it touches on a very real issue for contemporary children and youth: emphasizing the idea that "everyone is special"

may create a culture where young people believe they are extraordinary regardless of their actual accomplishments or aptitudes.

Many scholars attribute the contemporary emphasis on ways that "everyone is special" to the prominence of the self-esteem movement and to the importance of individualism in Western cultures. Although the value of individual rights has long been emphasized, there is a sense that the priority on individualism in contemporary society is new and extreme. Back in 1943, Abraham Maslow identified esteem needs as one of the higher needs existing in all human beings. He differentiated between a lower version of esteem which is focused on respect from others, while a higher version is focused on respect from the self. Might the extreme emphasis on self-reflection and self-awareness today be an example of this lower version Maslow described? Returning to the quote from the family movie *The Incredibles*, does Dash only feel special when judging his speed in relation to the running abilities of others?

Twenge thinks our contemporary emphasis on self-esteem and individualism has created an entire group characterized by self-absorption: a phenomenon leading her, along with psychologists W. Keith Campbell, to title their 2009 book *The Narcissism Epidemic*. Narcissism, according to the book website, "is a positive, inflated and grandiose sense of self … Along with this inflated sense of self is a lack of warm, emotionally intimate or caring relationships with others. This does not mean a lack of social relationships—often the opposite is the case—but a lack of emotionally deep relationships." Psychologists also have a technical classification for "Narcissistic Personality Disorder" that highlights the traits associated with narcissism as problematic for normal functioning. Characteristics for this disorder include an inflated sense of self importance, a deep need for admiration from others, and a lack of empathy for others. Clinical narcissists often appear confident, but actually have a very delicate sense of self that is extremely sensitive to any type of criticism.

In the YES selection, Twenge presents some of her earliest work finding increases in negative personality traits among the younger generation. This selection includes two studies that provide an in-depth look at neuroticism and anxiety in contemporary college students and schoolchildren. In both cases, Twenge finds significant increases of anxiety and neuroticism over time. She suggests that the increases in these two negative traits are caused by low social connectedness and high environmental threat. This research has been implicated in later studies, adding to her argument that American culture has become more self-focused. Twenge believes that the rises in anxiety, neuroticism, environmental threat combined with low social connectedness contribute to today's narcissism epidemic.

However, in addition to the main question concerning the concept of a narcissism epidemic, there are two other important questions to consider about their findings. First, have all Americans increased in narcissism? Twenge and her colleagues have not conducted cross-sectional analysis, measuring narcissism in other cohorts. It is possible that other age groups also would report increases in narcissism. Second, where is the clinical cut-off for

narcissism? The questionnaire used by Twenge and colleagues is for research purposes; it does not diagnose individuals with Narcissistic Personality Disorder. Thus, while scores have increased, it may be possible these high scores still remain within a healthy boundary. Confidence is associated with many positive mental health outcomes, while narcissism is not. However, differentiating between confidence and narcissism can be difficult.

In fact, in the NO selection, scholars from the Pew Research Center use the term confident, not narcissistic, in describing the current generation. They prefer calling them Millennials, and report that this generation is self-expressive, liberal, optimistic, and open to change. These characteristics are especially interesting when considered in terms of the environmental changes this generation has experienced. For example, despite the rising costs of college tuition and the country's economic recession, according to the Pew Research Center's report, the Millennials are on their way to becoming the most educated generation yet. While this generation has seen its share of political scandals, they are civic-minded and tend to trust the government. In many ways, this report highlights the contradictory behaviors and beliefs of this generation.

Assigning a label to an entire generation is always a difficult task. While Twenge and colleagues prefer the label Generation Me, the Pew Research Center uses Millennials. Still, others have used the label Trophy Kids, Generation 9/11, and the Homeland Generation. Today's generation is not the first to receive multiple labels. Which name sticks is anyone's guess. Naming a generation is as much an art as it a science. Sometimes generations are named to describe collective values and behaviors, but not every individual identifies with the label selected for their generation. The labels are useful to scholars, media outlets, and advertising executives—but not necessarily to the people they are describing. At their worst, generational labels can lead to stereotypes and discrimination.

The broader issue here relates to other controversial questions in the study of lifespan development. The fact that there may be significant differences in narcissism between ethnic groups, for example, raises questions about the influence of cultural differences in child rearing. In addition, the question of whether the term Generation Me is accurate relates to questions about how to characterize age groups at any point in the lifespan. And, finally, the broad question of self-esteem has been the subject of much debate. Scholars have realized that while emphasizing self-esteem for children is popular, that emphasis produced mixed results.

YES ⬅

Jean M. Twenge

The Age of Anxiety? Birth Cohort Change in Anxiety and Neuroticism, 1952–1993

Over the last few decades, people seem to have become more anxious, worrying about safety, social acceptance, and job security more than in the past (e.g., Rosen, 1998; Sloan, 1996). The perceived trend is so strong that some authors have labeled the twentieth century "the age of anxiety" (e.g., Spielberger & Rickman, 1990, p. 69). These descriptions imply that modern life produces higher levels of anxiety. But does it? Have people actually grown more anxious, or does hindsight bias lead us to believe that people were less anxious in the past? If anxiety has increased, what are the causes? Why is modern life anxiety-producing?

These questions hint at a deeper one: Are there environmental influences on personality outside the individual family? If levels of anxiety have changed over a 30-year time span, the most likely cause is changes in the larger sociocultural environment. Recent research and theory in psychology has recognized that environments vary between countries and regions, producing differences in personality, emotion, perception, and behavior (e.g., Choi, Nisbett, & Norenzayan, 1999; Heine & Lehman, 1997; Markus & Kitayama, 1991; Markus, Kitayama, & Heiman, 1996; Markus, Kitayama, & Vanden Bos, 1996; Nisbett & Cohen, 1996; Suh, Diener, Oishi, & Triandis, 1998). Environments vary over time and generations in a similar way (e.g., the U.S. in the 1950s was a very different environment than the U.S. in the 1990s). Yet very little research has explored the effect of changing times on personality. Such research might help answer the challenge posed by Matthews and Deary (1998): "... with so much good evidence for broad heritability effects," they wrote, "the onus is on environmentalists to make clear hypotheses about the effects of specific environmental factors on personality and test them" (p. 120).

Most previous work on environmental effects (especially within countries) has focused on family environment. Although some of this research has been successful (e.g., Reiss, 1997), much of it has failed to find that growing up in the same house and with the same parents has much measurable effect on personality (e.g., Bergeman, Plomin, McClearn, Pedersen, & Friberg, 1988; Langinvaionio, Kaprio, Koskenvuo, & Lonngvist, 1984; Loehlin, 1992; Rowe, 1990; Shields, 1962). These studies do not include environmental effects outside the family; in fact, most seem to assume that there are no environmental influences outside the family (e.g.,Bergeman et al., 1988; Bouchard, 1994; Loehlin, 1989, 1992; Pedersen, Plomin, McClearn, & Friedberg, 1988; Shields, 1962).For example, in their study of identical twins reared apart, Bergeman et al. (1988) stated that "in the absence of selective placement, any similarity" between the twins "is due to genetic influences" (p. 400). Loehlin (1989) made a similar statement (p. 1285). Thus, it is not surprising that at least one review of personality research discusses only two types of environmental influences: "those shared by family members and those unique to the individual"(Matthews & Deary, 1998; p. 106).

Such statements are true only if we consider genetics and family or individual environment to be the only two variables influencing personality. However, the larger sociocultural environment can also affect personality. Each generation effectively grows up in a different society; these societies vary in their attitudes, environmental threats, family structures, sexual norms, and in many other ways. A large number of theorists have suggested that birth cohort—as a proxy for the larger sociocultural environment—can have substantial effects on personality (e.g., Caspi, 1987; Elder,1974, 1981; Gergen, 1973; Kertzer, 1983; Lambert, 1972; Nesselroade & Baltes, 1974; Ryder, 1965; Schaie, 1965; Sloan, 1996; Stewart & Healy, 1989; Woodruff & Birren, 1972). In addition, previous empirical studies have found strong cohort effects on a number of psychopathology, attitude, and life outcome variables (Duncan & Agronick, 1995; Dyer, 1987; Klerman & Weissman, 1989; Lewinsohn, Rohde,

Twenge, J. M. (2000). The age of anxiety? The birth cohort change in anxiety and neuroticism, 1952–1993. *Journal of Personality and Social Psychology*, 79(6), 1007. Reprinted by permission of American Psychological Association.

Seeley, & Fischer, 1993; Twenge, 1997a, 1997b, in press; Twenge & Campbell, 2000; Woodruff & Birren, 1972).

Thus, birth cohort, as a proxy for the larger sociocultural environment, may be a significant source of previously unexplored environmental effects on personality. Given the weak effects for environment found in much previous research, it seems prudent to test such theories. Even if genetics explain about 40% of the variance in anxiety/neuroticism, and family environment about 10%, that still leaves 50% of the variance unexplained. It is difficult (as well as distressing) to believe that half of the variance in personality is error variance. Birth cohort should not be ignored as a possible contributor to that 50%.

Acknowledging birth cohort differences would also resolve a striking paradox in personality research: Longitudinal studies have often found remarkable consistency in personality traits as people age (e.g., Conley, 1984; Costa & McCrae, 1988; Costa, McCrae, & Arenberg, 1980; Finn, 1986; Kelly, 1955), whereas cross-sectional studies purporting to measure age differences have often found large effects (e.g., Bendig, 1960; Costa et al., 1986; H. J. Eysenck & S. B. G. Eysenck, 1975; S. B. G. Eysenck & H. J. Eysenck, 1969; Gutman, 1966). Birth cohort can explain this: In a cross-sectional study, the individuals of different ages also belong to different birth cohorts (Baltes & Nesselroade, 1972; Buss, 1974; Nesselroade & Baltes, 1974; Schaie, 1965; Woodruff & Birren, 1972). Thus, at least some of the conflict between the results of longitudinal and cross-sectional studies may be explained by birth cohort differences in personality traits. This also suggests that cohort differences may be widespread.

Examining changes in anxiety might be particularly important. More people visit doctors for anxiety than for colds, and anxiety is now more common than depression (Barlow, 1988). Anxiety is a predisposing factor to major depression (Bagby, Joffe, Parker, Kalemba, & Harkeness, 1995; Surtees & Wainwright, 1996) and to suicide attempts (Coryell, Noyes, & Clancy, 1982; Coryell, Noyes, & House, 1986). Researchers have also linked self-reports of anxiety to a wide variety of physical ailments, including asthma, coronary heart disease, irritable bowel syndrome, ulcers, and inflammatory bowel disease (for a review, see Edelmann, 1992). Psychological consequences are also important. Out of the Big Five traits, neuroticism (closely related to anxiety) was the strongest predictor of life satisfaction, happiness, and negative affect in a recent meta-analysis (DeNeve & Cooper, 1998). High levels of trait anxiety impair cognitive performance (Seipp, 1991) [including in everyday tasks (Matthews, Coyle, & Craig, 1990)], predispose people to marital problems (O'Leary & Smith, 1991), and sometimes lead

to alcohol and drug abuse (Chambless, Cherney, Caputo, & Rheinstein, 1987; Mullaney & Trippett, 1979; Smail, Stockwell, Canter, & Hodgeson, 1984). Thus, if anxiety level shave increased, it would have implications for mental and physical health.

Before beginning a discussion of relevant theories of anxiety, a definition is necessary. In this article, *anxiety* should be read to mean *trait anxiety*, often described as "relatively stable individual differences in anxiety-proneness" (Spielberger & Rickman, 1990, p. 76). This definition is in contrast to state anxiety, usually understood as a transient emotion experienced in a particular situation. In addition, anxiety and neuroticism are treated as synonymous; the two concepts have a great deal in common (e.g., Barlow, 1988; H. J. Eysenck & S. B. G. Eysenck, 1991), and measures of anxiety and neuroticism often correlate .80 or more (Twenge, 2000).

Theories of Anxiety

If there are birth cohort differences in anxiety, why did they occur? That is, what specific changes in the larger sociocultural environment may lead to higher levels of anxiety? Three theories on the origin of anxiety, usually used to explain individual differences, are also informative in the discussion of change over time. The three models are *overall threat* (anxiety increases as environmental threat increases), *economic conditions* (anxiety increases as economic conditions deteriorate), and *social connectedness* (anxiety increases as social bonds weaken). Using social statistics from corresponding years (e.g., crime rates, unemployment rates, divorce rates), I tested each of these models for their effects on anxiety scores, both individually and in regression equations including all three models. These tests should demonstrate not only if anxiety has changed but which influences were the most important (and which were not). In addition, these statistics can be lagged to show if changes in the environment occurred before changes in anxiety or vice versa. If the former, this would suggest that the environment is shaping personality; if environmental changes occur after changes in anxiety, it would suggest instead that shifts in personality traits affected the environment.

Overall Threat

Overview

At one time, anxiety was conceptualized as an organism's fear reaction, or the emotional response evoked when the organism is physically threatened (e.g., Darwin, 1872). More recent theorists acknowledge that threats leading to anxiety can be physical or psychological (Barlow, 1988; May, 1979; Spielberger & Rickman, 1990). Evolutionary theory holds that emotions are adaptive—that they serve specific purposes for the survival of the individual. Anxiety and fear primarily serve to warn of potential danger and trigger defensive physiological and psychological reactions (Darwin, 1872). Simply the anticipation of physical threat can cause anxiety; whereas both anxiety and depression appear after a loss, only anxiety appears when a loss is threatened (Rholes, Riskind, & Neville, 1985).

An additional component of this model involves the act of appraising environmental threat. Beck and his colleagues (Beck, 1985; Beck & Emery, 1985) have argued that anxiety stems from a disordered perception of reality as dangerous. These cognitions, a result of faulty information processing, elicit the emotional response of anxiety. Under this viewpoint, the individual's cognitive appraisal of the situation is the most important step (e.g., Lazarus, 1966; Lazarus & Folkman, 1984; Spielberger, 1972).

Change Over Time

Under this model, we would expect anxiety to increase over time if physical and psychological threats have increased. By all accounts, most threats increased between 1952 and 1993 (e.g., Bronfenbrenner, McClelland, Wethington, Moen, & Ceci, 1996; Fukuyama, 1999). These include violent crime (U.S. Bureau of the Census, 1998), worries about nuclear war (Diamond & Bachman, 1986; Kramer, Kalick, & Milburn, 1983), fear of diseases such as AIDS (Henker, Whalen, & O'Neil, 1995; Wilkins & Lewis, 1993), and the entrance of women into higher education and the workforce (possibly a threat to men and a source of stress to women; e.g., Rosen, 1998). Composite measures, such as the Index of Social Health, suggest increases in threat even since the 1970s (Miringoff & Miringoff, 1999). Media coverage has also led to a greater perception of environmental threat (Cohl, 1997; Glassner, 1999).

Economic Conditions

Overview

Some authors have suggested that economic hardship is the modern equivalent of physical (and sometimes emotional) threat (Barlow, 1988). In the modern world, economic difficulties are detrimental to optimal survival and reproduction and thus might also be seen as a threat, producing anxiety. Economic difficulties can increase anxiety for children as well as adults; unemployment, for example, increases anxiety in children by straining relationships with parents (McLoyd, Jayaratne, Ceballo, &

Borquez, 1994). If this model is correct, poor economic times should lead to increased anxiety as people feel their livelihoods threatened.

Change Over Time

Changes in economic conditions have been less linear than changes in other threats. Nevertheless, a general pattern of economic downturn emerges for this particular period. While the economy was booming from the 1950s to the late 1960s, it faltered in the 1970s and did not fully recover until the mid-1980s. Even then the upswing was not continuous (e.g., the stock market crash of 1987 and the recession of the early 1990s). Only after 1993 (when this study ends) did the economy experience continuous, sustained growth. Thus, the later part of the time period studied here experienced more economic hardship. Child poverty also increased even during some of the better economic times (Holtz, 1995; Howe & Strauss, 1993; Miringhoff & Miringhoff, 1999).

Social Connectedness

Overview

The social connectedness model focuses on social exclusion as particularly important to anxiety (Baumeister & Tice, 1990). Baumeister and colleagues (Baumeister & Leary, 1995; Baumeister & Tice, 1990) have proposed that anxiety is an adaptive response to being excluded from social groups and/or relationships. An influential review (Cohen & Wills, 1985) concluded that social support is correlated with lower self-reports of anxiety and depression.

Other authors have noted that the effect of social exclusion is not limited to individuals; lack of connection in a society may produce alienation and feelings of loneliness and despair. Fukuyama (1999) argued that Western societies have experienced a noticeable decrease in "social capital" (broadly defined as social connectedness and a sense of community) since the 1960s (see also Bronfenbrenner et al, 1996; Putnam, 2000).

Change Over Time

Many social statistics point to a breakdown in social connectedness. The divorce rate has increased, the birth rate has dropped, people marry later in life, and many more people now live alone (11% in 1950, compared with 25% in 1997). In addition, Putnam (2000) found that Americans are now less likely to join community organizations and visit friends than they once were. Connectedness can also be measured by levels of trust (Fukuyama, 1999), and these levels have also declined (only 18.3% of high school seniors in 1992 agreed that you can usually trust people, compared with 34.5% in 1975; Smith, 1997).

Empirical Evidence for Change

Although no known studies have examined change in anxiety over the time period studied, some evidence on related variables suggests that anxiety should increase over time. First, large panel studies have consistently found that younger cohorts show more, and longer, episodes of depression (Klerman & Weissman, 1989; Lewinsohn et al., 1993). Some psychologists have gone so far as to label this effect a modern *epidemic of depression* (Seligman, 1988, 1995) or *age of melancholy* (Hagnell, Lanke, Rorsman, & Ojesjo, 1982). Anxiety and depression are highly correlated (e.g., Tanaka-Matsumi & Kameoka, 1986), indicating that anxiety should also have increased. However, some authors have argued that anxiety and depression are distinct (e.g., Barlow, 1988; Tellegen, 1985; Torgersen, 1993).

Another limitation is more important: The depression studies are based on retrospective accounts, with participants self-reporting past episodes of depression. As the authors of these studies acknowledge (e.g., Klerman & Weissman, 1989; Lewinsohn et al., 1993), this method has obvious drawbacks. Respondents may not remember incidents, or their memory may exaggerate episodes. Also, the definition of a depressive episode might differ between age and cohort groups.

More direct evidence comes from authors who have examined self-reports of anxiety. These authors have found that more recent cohorts score higher on anxiety measures (Schonberg, 1974; Sutton-Smith, Rosenberg, & Morgan, 1961; Veroff, Douvan, & Kulka, 1981; cited in Veroff, Kulka, & Douvan, 1981, p. 36). These studies also have substantial limitations, however. They provide no data later than 1976, compare only a few samples against each other, and use nonstandard or outdated measures (none use the popular anxiety/neuroticism measures examined in this study).

Overview and Methods

This article aims to explore change over time in anxiety and the reasons behind these changes. Study 1 examines 170 samples of American college students collected from the literature, computing the correlation between mean scores on anxiety measures and year of data collection. I also report correlations between anxiety scores and social statistics to determine the causes behind changes in anxiety

and the likely direction of causation. Study 2 analyzed 99 samples of children who completed an anxiety measure. Examining child samples accomplished two goals: (a) it ensured that changing college populations and/or the unique composition of college samples was not responsible for the results of Study 1, and (b) it determined if the cohort differences in anxiety originated early in life. Both of these studies gather data from the literature, using a modified meta-analysis technique called *cross-temporal meta-analysis* that has been used in four previous studies (Twenge, 1997a, 1997b, in press; Twenge & Campbell, 2000).

Study 1

This study uses meta-analytic techniques to gather and analyze data from samples of American college students between the years 1952 and 1993. These samples completed self-report measures of anxiety and neuroticism under normal conditions. Because college students are roughly the same age, data collected at different times provides a test of birth cohort differences. Assuming an average age of 20, the participants in the collected studies were born between 1932 and 1973. As discussed more extensively in the *Methods* section, college populations have necessarily changed over time; however, these changes have not been large, and the average income of students' parents did not change between the mid-1960s and the early 1990s (Dey, Astin, & Korn, 1992). In addition, trends in the percentage of high school students enrolling in college have been curvilinear rather than linear since the late 1960s.

Method

Locating Studies   I conducted a preliminary search using PsycInfo to determine the most popular measures of anxiety and neuroticism for college students. Researchers were most likely to use and list means for the Taylor Manifest Anxiety scale (TMAS; Taylor, 1953), the Eysenck Personality Inventory (EPI; H. J. Eysenck, 1968), the Eysenck Personality Questionnaire (EPQ; H. J. Eysenck & S. B. G. Eysenck, 1975), and the State-Trait Anxiety Inventory (STAI; Spielberger, Gorsuch, & Lushene, 1970; Spielberger, Gorsuch, Lushene, Vagg, & Jacobs, 1983; only the trait form was collected here). Year of data collection was coded as 2 years prior to publication unless another date was mentioned in the article (this technique was also used by Oliver & Hyde, 1993).

Published articles. The main source of studies was the Social Science Citation Index (SSCI), which was searched for studies that cited the above test sources. The SSCI begins its listings in 1956, three years after the publication of the TMAS scale. To find datapoints on the TMAS for these years (1953–1955), a manual search was conducted of the following journals: *Journal of Abnormal and Social Psychology, Journal of Social Psychology, Journal of Personality* (formerly *Character and Personality*), *Journal of Applied Psychology, Journal of Psychology, American Journal of Psychology, Journal of Consulting Psychology, Educational and Psychological Measurement, Psychological Reports, and Perceptual and Motor Skills*. In addition, the 1956 edition of the Buros Mental Measurement handbook was searched for references to the TMAS.

Dissertation Abstracts. Dissertations and masters' theses are major sources of unpublished data. Dissertation Abstracts catalogs master's theses and dissertations from 1861 to the present. I searched this database using the names of the scales as keywords.

Inclusion Rules   Possible studies for the analysis were included or excluded on the basis of specific rules. To be included in the analysis, a study had to meet the following criteria: (a) participants were undergraduates at conventional 4-year institutions; (b) participants were attending college in the United States (thus samples from all other countries were eliminated; it is expected that the differing cultural and political climates in these countries would confound the results because samples from other countries tend to score differently on the measures used here, e.g., Jamison, 1984); (c) the study included at least 10 male or 10 female participants; (d) participants were not clients at a counseling center or any other group singled out for being maladjusted; (e) means were reported for unselected groups of students, not groups that were extremely high or extremely low on a measure; and (f) means were broken down by sex. A number of studies did not provide means for the personality measures they used; most studies excluded from the analysis were eliminated for not including means rather than for violating any other criterion. The breakdown of means by sex is important given the sex differences in the variables under examination and the changing numbers of women in college psychology samples. In addition, the direction and magnitude of any personality change may differ for men and women. Thus, simply controlling for the number of women in the sample might not illustrate the true nature of the change.

These data collection and inclusion strategies yielded 170 studies, including 148 samples of men and 134 samples of women. In total, these studies included 40,192 college students (21,173 women and 19,019 men). A reference list of the studies included in the analyses is available on request.

Analyses   Two types of analyses can be performed on anxiety/neuroticism mean scores: (a) correlations between means and year within measure and (b) analyses summarizing across measures. Because these analyses examine means of specific measures, traditional meta-analytic techniques cannot be used to summarize across measures. Two methods were applied here: (a) a weighted average using conversions to z scores and (b) z scoring within measure and then combining the results across all measures to examine the correlation with year (see Table 1). This second method assumes homoscedasticity for all measures across the time period. Three of the four measures (EPI, EPQ, STAI) cover about the same time period (late 1960s/early 1970s to the early 1990s) and demonstrate homoscedasticity for this time period. However, the TMAS, first published in 1953, has considerably more datapoints from the 1950s and 1960s. Thus, any z score will place the mean for the TMAS much earlier than for the other measures, skewing the results. To correct for this, I examined the z scores for the EPI and STAI for the period 1968–1975, when the TMAS z score was near 0. The EPI and STAI samples showed z scores of $-.73$ for men and $-.53$ for women during this time (based on 16 samples of men and 18 samples of women). Thus, the z scores for the TMAS were adjusted downward by these amounts in the analyses including all four measures. Because this method is an approximation, I also report results separately by time period (the TMAS from 1952–1967, and z score results for the EPI, EPQ, and STAI only for the period 1968–1993). However, this bootstrap method may be the only way to summarize results across the entire time period.

Sources for Social Statistics   As noted previously, direct correlations can be computed between anxiety scores and social statistics. Most of these statistics were obtained from the Statistical Abstract of the United States (these were divorce rate, percentage of people living alone, women's age at first marriage, birth rate, unemployment, violent crime rate, AIDS cases, the suicide rate for people aged 15–24, women's labor force participation rate, and the percentage of bachelor's degrees awarded to women). Two statistics were obtained from the Monitoring the Future survey of American high school seniors (Bachman, Johnston, & O'Malley, 1998): the percentage of *often* responses to "How often do you worry about the chance of nuclear war?" and the percentage of *trust* responses to "Generally speaking, would you say that most people can be trusted or that you can't be too careful in dealing with people?" Most of these statistics were available for the entire time period. Others were only available for the last 20–25 years:

Table 1

Weighted Correlations Between Year of Scale Administration and College Students' Anxiety/Neuroticism Scores, 1952–1993

Measure or composite	Time span	Men		Women	
		Bivariate	w/controls	Bivariate	w/controls
Entire time period					
TMAS	1952–1993	.62*** (41)	.61*** (41)	.48*** (32)	.50*** (32)
EPI-N	1969–1991	.26* (25)	.31** (25)	.43*** (25)	.48*** (25)
EPQ-N	1973–1993	.65*** (22)	.76*** (22)	.65*** (23)	.89*** (23)
STAI	1968–1993	.65*** (60)	.49*** (60)	.45*** (54)	.37** (54)
Overall weighted average	1952–1993	.56*** (148)	.54*** (148)	.49*** (134)	.58*** (134)
Within-scale Z scores (All measures; TMAS adjusted)	1952–1993	.52*** (148)	.64*** (148)	.39*** (134)	.53*** (134)
Within time periods					
TMAS	1952–1967	.48** (29)	.48** (29)	.64*** (24)	.37** (24)
Overall weighted average (EPI, EPQ, & STAI)	1968–1993	.54*** (107)	.52*** (107)	.49*** (102)	.58*** (102)
Within-scale Z scores (EPI, EPQ, & STAI)	1968–1993	.53*** (107)	.43*** (107)	.48*** (102)	.44*** (102)

Note: TMAS = Taylor Manifest Anxiety Scale; EPI-N = Eysenck Personality Inventory Neuroticism; EPQ-N = Eysenck Personality Questionnaire Neuroticism; STAI = State-Trait Anxiety Inventory. *N* of groups is shown in parentheses. Correlations are weighted for sample size of study.
*$p < .05$. **$p < .01$. ***$p < .001$.

The two questions from Monitoring the Future begin in 1975, and AIDS cases were reported beginning in 1981.

These particular statistics were chosen using two main criteria. First, the social indicators had to be readily available and easily quantified as meaningful continuous variables. Some interesting statistics are not readily available (e.g., average geographical mobility). Others are difficult to quantify as continuous variables (e.g., improvements in birth control technology). Second, the statistics were chosen to be representative of general trends. For example, statistics on the percentage of law, medical, and doctorate degrees awarded to women are available; however, they follow almost exactly the same pattern as the more broadly representative statistics on the percentage of undergraduate degrees awarded to women. Thus, the latter statistic was used. Economic statistics are another example of representativeness. Unemployment, which was included, is arguably the best economic indicator. Others, such as gross national product, tend to increase steadily even when adjusted for inflation and are thus not meaningful indicators of the nation's economic health.

Control Variables and Limitations It is possible that samples may differ in region and type of college in a way that confounds with birth cohort. These two variables were recorded for each datapoint; region was coded as East, Midwest, South, or West according to the U.S. Census designations, and type of college was coded as public or private according to a list of U.S. colleges and universities. These two variables were used as controls in the analyses (with region coded using dummy variables). Most studies did not report information on the racial or socioeconomic status composition of the samples; thus, it was not possible to use these variables as controls. Specific measure (e.g., TMAS, STAI) was entered to control for variance between methods/scales.

Another possible limitation is changes in the college population over the time period. One measure of this might be the median income of college students' parents, an indicator of socioeconomic status. Dey et al.'s (1992) summary of a national, yearly sample found that the median income of college students' families did not change from 1966 to 1991 when adjusted for inflation (although variations from 1952 to 1965 are unknown). As for the racial composition of college samples, this changed only slightly (Black students were 6% of the college population in 1960 and are now about 10%; Asians increased from 2% to 5%; and Hispanics increased from 4% to 7%).

One statistic that has changed more is the number of people going to college. Reliable data on the percentage of high school graduates enrolling in college was available beginning in 1960 (U.S. Bureau of the Census, 1998). In 1960, 45% of high school graduates enrolled in college; in 1967 (the year before data are available for the more recent measures of anxiety/neuroticism), this figure was 52%. This 7% rise was fairly linear, increasing about 1% per year. For the time period covered by the more recent measures, the percentage rose from 55% (in 1968) to 62% (in 1993). However, even this small change was not linear; college enrollment actually declined during the 1970s, not reaching the 1968 figure of 55% again until 1984. Thus, the available statistics suggest that change in the college population is likely to most strongly affect the pre-1968 era, when this statistic changed fairly quickly (about 1% a year) and in a linear fashion; here, this mainly affects the results for the TMAS.

Results

Correlations Between Mean Scores and Year Have college students' self-reported levels of anxiety and neuroticism increased from 1952 to 1993? The results show unequivocally that they have. In regressions weighted by sample size, every measure produced a significant positive correlation with year (see Table 1), with most correlations over .40 and many over .60.

In the weighted regressions, the larger samples—as better estimates of the population mean—were proportionally weighted in computing the average distance from the regression line. These regressions differ from simple bivariate correlations only in their weighting by n. Correlations unweighted for sample size produced very similar, though sometimes stronger, results (e.g., the correlation between women's STAI scores and year rose to .40, $p < .001$, in the unweighted analyses). Correlations were also similar when controls for type of college (public vs. private), region, and specific measure were included in a multiple regression to test for the unique effect of year (betas for year are reported in Table 1).

When did the increase in anxiety begin? An analysis of the TMAS, the most popular measure of anxiety between 1952 and 1967, showed that anxiety increased during this time period. Thus, the increase began during the 1950s (see Table 1). The increase continued throughout the 1970s and 1980s; z-scored scale combinations of the EPI, EPQ, and STAI also demonstrated a significant increase in anxiety/neuroticism scores from 1968 to 1993.

z scores (with the correction applied to the TMAS) over the entire time period (1952–1993) also showed a clear, linear rise in scores, as did the correlations mathematically averaged over the measures (using Fisher's r to z transform; see Table 1). Although the betas for men appear to be larger than those for women in many cases, the differences between the betas were not significant when compared (using Fisher's r to z and the formula for comparing two correlations in Wolf, 1986, p. 36).

Sex differences in anxiety, calculated using the formula to compute d and weighted by w (e.g., Wolf, 1986) were $d = .24$ across 118 samples of college students, meaning that women scored about a quarter of a standard deviation higher than men. The effect size did not show a significant correlation with year when entered into a regression equation with all samples included. However, there was a significant correlation with year for the TMAS samples collected 1952–1967, $r = .33$ ($k = 15$), $p < .05$. This result indicates that sex differences were increasing during the postwar period, with women reporting more anxiety compared with men over time. There was no significant correlation between the d for sex differences and year for samples collected 1968–1993. Thus, for the most recent era, men's and women's anxiety changed at about the same rate.

Magnitude of Change The above results show that anxiety has increased in a linear manner. But how much has anxiety increased? After all, it is possible to have change that is linear yet small in magnitude. Analyses using the regression equations demonstrate that this is not the case here: Anxiety scores have risen about a standard deviation from the 1950s to the 1990s, explaining about 20% of the variance.

I used the regression equations to compute the average score at the beginning and end of the regression lines. These computations were performed both with and without the controls; with the controls, the mean score was computed using the 0 values of the dummy variables (here, a public university in the East). The controls produced no major changes (greater than .05 standard deviations) for most groups; the only differences occurred for women on the TMAS. Thus, means without controls are reported for most groups, with both estimates reported for women's TMAS scores. The meta-analytic d (difference in terms of standard deviations) allows for standardization across measures; thus, the change is reported in terms of d.

In this study, the TMAS is the sole measure of anxiety from 1952 to 1967. Men's TMAS scores began at 12.88 and rose to 15.84; with an average SD of 7.24 in these samples, this was an increase of $d = .41$. Without controls applied, women's scores rose from 13.15 to 19.76 ($SD = 7.48$), $d = .88$. However, these samples were confounded with type of college; with the controls applied, women's scores rise from 14.30 to 18.17, $d = .52$.

Three measures were available from 1968–1993 (the EPI, EPQ, and STAI); for each, means were calculated representing 1968 and 1993. On the EPI, men's scores rose from 8.75 to 10.05, a change of $d = .27$ ($SD = 4.85$). Women's scores increased from 9.78 to 11.91 ($SD = 4.79$), $d = .45$. Changes on the EPQ were larger; for men, scores advanced from 9.06 to 12.29 ($SD = 5.19$), $d = .62$. Women's scores rose from 11.48 to 14.06 ($SD = 4.94$), $d = .65$. As for the STAI, men's scores increased from 36.37 to 40.73 ($SD = 7.75$), $d = .56$; women's scores rose from 37.94 to 41.92 ($SD = 8.01$), $d = .50$. Weighting by n, this averaged to a change of .47 SDs for men and .52 SDs for women over the period 1968–1993. Cohen (1977) would classify these as medium effect sizes ($d = .50$).

Adding these results with those for the TMAS (1952–1967), women's anxiety scores rose 1.40 standard deviations (without controls) or $d = 1.04$ SDs (with controls) from 1952 to 1993; men's scores rose $d = .88$. Weighting by n, this averages to a change of .97 standard deviations for both sexes combined. By Cohen's (1977) definition, these are large effect sizes (greater than. 80). These effect sizes convert to $r = .40$ for men and $r = .46$ for women (with the controls applied); thus, birth cohort (as a proxy for the larger sociocultural environment) explains between 16% and 21% of the variance in personality, considerably more than family environment explains in most studies.

The regression equations can also be used to estimate mean anxiety scores for the past and future. If the regression equation for the TMAS is used to compute a predicted score for 1945, scores have risen 1.28 to 1.82 standard deviations for women between the end of World War II and 1993, and $d = 1.07$ for men. If this pattern continued from 1993 to 2000 (a debatable point), scores have risen $d = 1.42$ to 1.96 for women and 1.21 for men between 1945 and 2000 (1.18 to 1.54 for women and 1.02 for men between 1952 and 2000).

Correlations Between Mean Scores and Social Statistics Thus, it seems clear that anxiety has increased considerably over time. Why has this occurred? Correlating anxiety scores directly with social statistics provides a view of possible causes and outcomes of the rise in college students' anxiety scores. The social statistics are facets of the sociocultural environment; what is important is not a higher crime rate itself, for example, but that more people are the victims of crime, and more people feel unsafe. Overall, the results suggest that low social connectedness

and high overall threat predict higher anxiety scores; economic conditions are not related to anxiety when controlled for the other two influences.

These statistics were matched with the anxiety data in five ways: ten years before the data were collected, 5 years before, the year of data collection, 5 years after, and 10 years after. These analyses report correlations between these social statistics and the z-scored scale combinations of TMAS, EPI, EPQ, and STAI scores, with the TMAS adjusted as described previously. They are computed both for individual statistics (betas with only one predictor in the equation) and, at the bottom of the table, in a regression equation including both composites controlled for each other (economic conditions, and social connectedness plus other threats).

Social connectedness predicted anxiety scores well (see Tables 2 and 3). The divorce rate and birth rate preceded anxiety levels; correlations were highest for the childhood (10 years prior) and adolescent (5 years prior) time periods (for the divorce rate, the correlations for the 10 years prior and actual year, 5, and 10 years after were significantly different at $p < .05$; there were no significant differences for birth rate). People living alone and women's average age at first marriage both showed fairly consistent correlations over the time periods. Trust was significantly correlated for the adolescent and college years (a result that might be expected, given that the item was from a survey of high school seniors). For the most part, the correlations are stronger when lagged into the past or matched with the present, suggesting that environmental change is preceding personality change (and thus that the environment is causing personality change). The few significant correlations during the future years could have occurred for two reasons. They may be an artifact of the steady linear increase of some variables (e.g., women's age at first marriage). Alternatively, they could represent the influence of personality (here, anxiety) on society-wide behavior; for example, perhaps women who are anxious marry later.

Overall threat also predicted anxiety scores. Crime rates demonstrated significant correlations for all periods except 10 years after data collection. Correlations for AIDS cases were somewhat higher for the adolescent, college, and young adult (5 years after) time periods, which might be expected for a variable more relevant for the sexually active, single person (10 years prior was significantly different from 5 years after at $p < .05$). Worry about nuclear war showed a significant positive correlation for the adolescent years; however, the correlation was negative for 5 years after college (significantly different at $p < .01$, most likely because worry about nuclear

Table 2

Correlations Between Social Indicators and *Z*-Scored Scale Combinations of Men's Anxiety/Neuroticism Scores, Weighted for Sample Size, 1952–1993

Social indicator	10 years prior	5 years prior	Actual year	5 years after	10 years after
Overall threat					
Crime rate	.34***	.43***	.36***	.40***	.21
AIDS cases	.29**	.37***	.49***	.54***	.30**
Worry about nuclear war	−.04	.47***	−.26	−.61***	−.19
Suicide rate, ages 15–24	.51***	.26**	.25*	.14	.14
Women's LFPR	.54***	.55***	.50***	.45***	.39***
College degrees awarded to women	.23*	.52***	.47***	.44***	.27**
Index of social health (reverse)	−.45**	−.66***	−.23*	−.20	.00
Economic conditions					
Unemployment rate	.43***	.29***	.07	.05	.08
Percentage of children in poverty	−.06	.19	−.02	.01	.00
Low social connectedness					
Divorce rate	.48***	.32***	.25**	.27**	.24
Percentage of people living alone	.46***	.48***	.44***	.41***	.30**
Women's age at first marriage	.44***	.58***	.56***	.42***	.48***
Birth rate (reverse)	−.40***	−.30***	−.35***	−.29**	−.25
Trust (reverse)	−.12	−.44***	−.59***	−.09	.14
Regression with total scales					
Economic conditions	−.23	.27	−.39**	−.25	.07
Social connectedness 1 other threats	.76***	.44**	.59***	.24	.21

Note. n varies from 56 to 148 because of missing indicators for some years. LFPR = Labor force participation rate.
$*p < .05.$ $**p < .01.$ $***p < .001.$

war has been declining since the late 1980s). Statistics measuring women's status (LFPR, college degrees) displayed fairly consistent correlations with anxiety for both men and women.

Economic conditions showed more mixed results. Unemployment rates correlated with anxiety scores when lagged 10 and 5 years into the past, particularly for men. These correlations were significantly different from those 5 and 10 years after college at $p < .05$, suggesting that parental unemployment precedes later anxiety. However, the percentage of children in poverty did not correlate significantly with anxiety scores, even when lagged into the respondents' childhood and adolescent years.

These analyses suggest that several aspects of the larger environment may have influenced levels of anxiety. But which are the strongest influences, when controlled for the others? Unfortunately, the influences of social connectedness and overall threat cannot be separated; when the statistics in each category are z scored and added into an index, social connectedness and overall threat correlate over .95. This is a simple historical fact: For example, the divorce rate and crime rate increased at about the same rate during the late 1960s and 1970s. (The decrease in social connectedness and the increase in crime are probably related: see, e.g., Sampson & Laub, 1990; Twenge, Baumeister, Tice, Faber, & Stucke, 2000). Thus,

Table 3

Correlations Between Social Indicators and *Z*-Scored Scale Combinations of Women's Anxiety/Neuroticism Scores, Weighted for Sample Size, 1952–1993

Social indicator	10 years prior	5 years prior	Actual year	5 years after	10 years after
Overall threat					
Crime rate	.32**	.33***	.22*	.29**	.06
AIDS cases	.19	.27**	.39***	.47***	.24*
Worry about nuclear war	.04	.36***	−.16	−.49***	−.25*
Suicide rate, ages 15–24	.42***	.19	.21*	.04	.07
Women's LFPR	.42***	.41***	.38***	.32***	.31**
College degrees awarded to women	.19	.39***	.33***	.34***	.13
Index of social health (reverse)	−.34**	−.53***	−.26*	−.17	.07
Economic conditions					
Unemployment rate	.29**	.22*	.05	−.03	−.09
Percentage of children in poverty	2.04	.22*	.10	.09	−.07
Low social connectedness					
Divorce rate	.39***	.23*	.11	.11	.19
Percentage of people living alone	.35***	.36***	.32***	.28*	.17
Women's age at first marriage	.34***	.44***	.44***	.34***	.37***
Birth rate (reverse)	−.31***	−.15	−.19	−.14	−.29*
Trust (reverse)	−.18	−.33*	−.46***	−.15	.10
Regression with total scales					
Economic conditions	−.23	.31*	−.20	−.08	−.27
Social connectedness 1 other threats	.65***	.39**	.44***	.26	.15

Note. *n* varies from 54 to 134 because of missing indicators for some years. LFPR = Labor force participation rate.
*$p < .05$. **$p < .01$ ***$p < .001$.

the two composites display too much multicollinearity to be entered separately into a regression equation. However, economic conditions have fluctuated more and correlate only .65 with an index combining social connectedness and overall threat.

Thus, the index of economic conditions (unemployment and child poverty) and the social connectedness/threat index were entered into a regression equation together (and thus the results at the bottom of Tables 2 and 3 show the two composites controlled for each other). The results are clear: When controlled for social connect-

edness/threat, economic conditions do not correlate significantly with anxiety levels. Thus, the environmental attributes of low social connectedness and high threat explain high levels of anxiety, but poor economic conditions do not necessarily lead to high anxiety (at least during this 40-year period).

Study 2

Anxiety clearly increases among college students from the 1950s to the 1990s. Does this result replicate for samples of children, who are both younger and less susceptible to biased sampling? College student samples have a possible limitation: The number and types of people who go to college changes from year to year, and these samples are often not representative of their age group at large. As discussed previously, this is more a problem in the samples collected during the 1950s and early 1960s. However, it cannot be fully ruled out as an explanation for any of the time periods. In addition, college students come from the middle and higher classes; perhaps economic conditions do not explain changes in college students' anxiety scores because they did not experience the brunt of hard economic times.

In addition, college students are typically 18 years of age or older, an age usually described as late adolescence or early adulthood. These individuals have already passed through the developmental stages of childhood and most of adolescence. Thus, it is impossible to know when the rise in anxiety and neuroticism scores began for these birth cohorts. It could be that the later birth cohorts became more anxious than their predecessors only after they entered college; on the other hand, they could have been more anxious since childhood. Many theories maintain that anxiety tendencies begin in childhood (Barlow, 1988), and this study provides a partial test of those theories. The correlations with social statistics in Study 1 suggested that the childhood environment is particularly important, but a direct examination seemed warranted.

Study 2 attempts to address these questions by examining samples of schoolchildren of approximately the same birth cohorts as the college students studied above. Using children (especially those under the age of 16) virtually eliminates the selection bias inherent in the college samples (both its possible changes in composition and its general SES bias). For the time period in question (1950s–early 1990s), almost all normal children were enrolled in school, and this did not change much from year to year. In addition, studies using children usually report information on the racial and socioeconomic composition of the samples, allowing these variables to be used as controls.

The samples of college students examined above completed the measures of anxiety and neuroticism between the years 1952 and 1993. Subtracting 10 years estimates when these participants were 10 years old (a typical age for completing a children's anxiety measure; see following). Thus, these birth cohorts were common in child samples between about 1942 and 1983. No widely used measures of children's anxiety were available before the 1950s. In 1956, a group of authors published the Children's Manifest Anxiety scale (CMAS; Castaneda, McCandless, & Palermo, 1956), which soon became the most popular measure of children's anxiety and remained so until the late 1970s–early 1980s. This scale was normed on 4th- to 6th-grade

children (thus about 9 to 11 years old) and was most often used for this age group. Thus, Study 2 used the same cross-temporal meta-analysis method used in Study 1 to examine samples of children who completed the CMAS from the mid-1950s to the 1980s.

Method

Locating Studies   Similar to the method used in Study 1, published studies were located using PsycInfo and the SSCI. PsycInfo was used as a preliminary search technique using the keywords "Children's Manifest Anxiety" and "children and manifest anxiety." Serendipitously, the SSCI begins its coverage in 1956, the year the CMAS was published. Studies that cited the CMAS source (Castaneda et al., 1956) were located. Dissertation Abstracts was used to locate unpublished datapoints with the same keywords used in the PsycInfo search.

Inclusion Rules   Studies were included in the analyses if (a) participants were children between the ages of 9 and 17 (grades 4–12) (the scale was normed on 4th–6th graders, and children in the 3rd grade or younger often score considerably higher on the measure; e.g., Holloway, 1961; Rie, 1963); (b) samples were collected in the United States; (c) participants were not clients at a counseling center or any other group singled out for being maladjusted; (d) means were reported for unselected groups of students, not groups that were extremely high or extremely low on the measure; and (e) means were reported, either broken down by sex or for an entire sample. In Study 1, only means broken down by sex were included; analyses for mixed-sex samples are included here for comparison because many fewer samples from the 1970s–1980s reported means broken down by sex. In addition, the sex composition of the child samples is very stable, in contrast to the studies of college students where the percentage of women in the samples is highly confounded with year.

Year of data collection was coded as 2 years prior to publication unless another date was mentioned in the article (Oliver & Hyde, 1993). Birth cohort was computed by subtracting the sample's mean age from the year of data collection (range = 1940–1978). If only a grade level was provided, 5 years were added to estimate age. Studies reporting separate means for different age/grade groups were entered as separate samples. Studies were also coded for region, race composition, urban/rural location, and socioeconomic status.

This method yielded 99 samples reporting means on the CMAS, including 6,600 boys and 5,456 girls (total n = 12,056). The samples were primarily collected between 1954 and 1981 (only one sample was collected after 1981, in 1988). This roughly corresponds to the middle and later birth cohorts of college students included in Study 1: Assuming that the college student samples were 10 years older than the child samples, this is equivalent to the years 1964–1991 for the college samples.

Results

Correlations Between Mean Scores and Year The results for the child samples exactly parallel those for college students: Self-reported anxiety increases in a linear fashion. Correlations weighted by sample size appear in Table 4. All correlations between CMAS means and year are .58 or above, with the mixed-sex samples showing a correlation of .77 (most likely because of a greater number of datapoints post-1970, when CMAS scores continued to rise). The correlations are similar (or even higher) when controls are added to the regression for region, urban versus rural location, socioeconomic status, and race.

Because these samples ranged in age from 9 to 17 years old, age differences in anxiety may be confounded with year (e.g., if more of the younger samples were collected later). In addition, the effect for year of data collection could be either a time period or a birth cohort effect. Thus, the correlation between birth year and CMAS scores was also computed. As shown in Table 4, these correlations are very similar to those with year, suggesting that the data are not confounded by age and that much of the change can be attributed to birth cohort. Because the majority of the datapoints were children 13 years and younger (most 9–11 years), I analyzed the data using only this age group; the results were almost identical to the results when all the age groups were included.

Magnitude of Change The increases in anxiety for children were large as well as linear. I again quantified the changes by using the regression equations and the average standard deviation of the samples. These computations were performed both with and without the controls and were virtually identical; computations without the controls are reported. Samples of boys increased from 14.94 on the CMAS in 1954 to 19.91 in 1981, a change of .67 standard deviations. Samples of girls increased from 16.32 to 22.46, a shift of .79 standard deviations. Mixed-sex samples, which include more samples after 1970, demonstrate even larger changes, increasing from 15.08 to 22.42 from 1954 to 1981, an increase of .99 standard deviations. The latest mixed-sex datapoint was actually collected in 1988, when the regression line computes an average score of 24.33, reflecting a change of 1.25 standard deviations between 1954 and 1988. By Cohen's (1977) criteria, almost all of these changes qualify as large (.80 or over). Thus, children's anxiety scores increase about a standard deviation over the time period, again explaining about 20% of the variance in scores.

It is also interesting to compare the scores of more recent samples with a 1957 sample of child clinic patients admitted with psychiatric problems (Levitt, 1959). The mean score of the 1957 psychiatric sample was 20.82, about the same as the mean score of the normal child samples collected between 1970 and 1988 (20.59). By 1980–1988, the average score for normal children was 23.26. Thus, by the 1980s normal children were scoring higher than 1950s child psychiatric patients on self-reported anxiety. This difference demonstrates the change in interpretation produced by an increase of one standard deviation.

Table 4

Weighted Correlations Between Year, Birth Cohort, and Responses to the Children's Manifest Anxiety Scale

Analysis	Time span	Boys	Girls	Mixed-sex
Bivariate				
Year of data collection	1954–1981	.58*** (67)	.62*** (59)	.77*** (89)
Birth year	1940–1970	.63*** (67)	.61*** (59)	.76*** (89)
With controls				
Year of data collection	1954–1981	.60*** (67)	.72*** (59)	.78*** (89)
Birth year	1940–1970	.62*** (67)	.70*** (59)	.77*** (89)

Note. N on which correlations are based is shown in parentheses.
*$p < .05$. **$p < .01$. ***$p < .001$.

To directly compare the results for children with those for college students, I projected the mean scores for 1952 and 1993 (using the regression equation) to calculate the effect size over the same time period. For boys, the effect size was 1.01, for girls 1.20, and for mixed-sex samples, 1.50 standard deviations. These effect sizes are very similar to (though a little higher than) the changes for the college students, which were .88 for men and 1.04 for women.

Across the 50 studies including both boys and girls, the weighted d for sex differences was .22. The effect size differs between age groups; it is smaller among the 37 samples of elementary school children (ages 9–11) where $d = .20$ and larger among the 13 samples of adolescents (ages 12–17), where $d = .31 (p < .05$ by a chi-square for moderator variables). Thus, in both age groups, girls score higher on anxiety measures than boys do; this difference increases during adolescence. The effect size does not show a significant correlation with year.

Correlations Between Mean Scores and Social Statistics   Child samples increased in anxiety just as college students did, but were the antecedents of these changes the same? Table 5 shows correlations between mixed-sex samples (where the most data were available) and the lagged social statistics. The average age of the children in these samples is 11, so these statistics correspond(respectively) to infancy, 6 years old, 11 years old, 16 years old, and 21 years old. Three statistics included in the analyses in Study 1 were not included because they were only available beginning in the mid-1970s or later (trust, fear of nuclear war, and AIDS cases) and there were not enough data from this time period.

Table 5

Correlations Between Social Indicators and Children's Manifest Anxiety Scores, Weighted for Sample Size, 1954–1988

Social indicators	10 years prior	5 years prior	Actual year	5 years after	10 years after
Overall threat					
Crime rate	.70***	.79***	.75***	.73***	.76***
Suicide rate, ages 15–24	.52***	.70***	.72***	.69***	.70***
Women's LFPR	.67***	.74***	.74***	.76***	.76***
College degrees awarded to women	−.38**	.77***	.72***	.76***	.74***
Economic conditions					
Unemployment rate	.32**	.42***	.41***	.34**	.24*
Percentage of children in poverty	−.48***	−.55***	−.22*	−.43**	.16
Low social connectedness					
Divorce rate	−.22	.58***	.71***	.69***	.66***
Percentage of people living alone	.70***	.68***	.77***	.75***	.74***
Women's age at first marriage	.34**	.60***	.70***	.72***	.74***
Birth rate (reverse)	−.47***	−.69***	−.71***	−.68***	−.46**
Regression with total scales					
Economic conditions	.03	.13	.04	2.08	.00
Social connectedness 1 other threats	.67***	.81***	.76***	.77***	.74***

Note. n varies from 61 to 99 because of missing indicators for some years. LFPR = Labor force participation rate.
*$p < .05$. **$p < .01$. ***$P < .001$.

Strong, significant correlations appear between social connectedness and anxiety, as well as between overall threat and anxiety. Changes in the divorce rate, the birth rate, and the crime rate are all highly correlated with children's anxiety. In general, it appears that lower social connectedness and higher threat led to higher anxiety.

These samples were drawn from a more diverse range of socioeconomic status than the college samples, and thus we might expect more of an influence from economic conditions. However, this was not the case: Economic conditions were not correlated with anxiety, similar to the college samples. Unemployment rates are positively correlated with children's anxiety, particularly for the study year and 5 years prior. In contrast, the percentage of children in poverty is actually negatively correlated with anxiety. One might think that when more children were living in poverty, the overall average anxiety score would go up. However, the percentage of children in poverty decreased during the 1960s, exactly when anxiety scores began to zoom upward. When the index for economic conditions was entered into a regression equation with a social connectedness/threat index, its influence was negligible (see Table 5). Thus, even in a sample diverse in socioeconomic status, economic conditions do not explain the rise in anxiety.

The correlations between mean scores and social connectedness/threat were strong and relatively consistent across the measurement years. However, the correlations were generally strongest for the year of data collection and 5 years afterward, corresponding to the years of middle childhood and adolescence (the difference between the correlations were significant at $p < .05$ or greater for the divorce rate, women's age at first marriage, and college degrees awarded to women). This result parallels the results found for college students, where many correlations were stronger for those years; in the college-student analyses, this corresponded to 5 and 10 years prior to data collection.

General Discussion

Two meta-analyses find that self-reports of anxiety/neuroticism have increased substantially from the 1950s to the early 1990s. Thus, the larger sociocultural environment—an influence on personality beyond genetics and individual family environment—has a considerable effect on a major personality trait. Samples of college students between 1952 and 1993 show increases on four different measures of anxiety and neuroticism. Study 2 replicates this increase for samples of schoolchildren, showing that sampling bias was not responsible for the college-student results. Both meta-analyses find that self-reports of anxiety increase about one standard deviation over 30–40 years, explaining about 20% of the variance (considerably more than family environment explains in most studies). The birth cohort change in anxiety is so large that by the 1980s normal child samples were scoring higher than child psychiatric patients from the 1950s (Levitt, 1959). In both studies, anxiety levels are correlated with low social connectedness and high environmental threat; economic conditions do not explain the rise in anxiety, even among the socioeconomically diverse samples in Study 2.

Theoretical Implications

A Third Influence on Personality

What do these studies tell us about personality and its development? First, they demonstrate the impact of the larger sociocultural environment. Clearly, the larger environment should be considered a third influence on individual differences in personality, taking a place next to the more recognized effects of genetics and family/individual environment. Researchers have often found that family environment has little effect on personality, making the recognition of sociocultural environment and birth cohort all the more important.

The Importance of Childhood Environment

Correlations between anxiety and social indicators are somewhat higher in the childhood and adolescent years than in adulthood, no matter what the age of the sample. In addition, children's anxiety scores showed a strong birth cohort effect. These results suggest that personality is most susceptible to the larger environment during the childhood years. Because the environmental changes precede the personality changes, it is likely that environment is causing personality rather than vice versa. This is also consistent with the research finding stability in personality traits after late adolescence (e.g., Conley, 1984; Costa & McCrae, 1988; Costa et al., 1980; Finn, 1986; Kelly, 1955). The significant correlations between anxiety and future social conditions may be an artifact of steady linear change; on the other hand, they could reflect the influence of the person on the situation. Perhaps people who are anxious marry later, commit more crimes, and are more likely to live alone. However, this is speculative; further research should investigate the effect of personality on societal change.

One might well have assumed that children would mainly be affected by family influences whereas adults would be affected by broader social trends. The present data do not support that analysis, however; they suggest that childhood is the time of the greatest societal influence (of course, some of these effects could be mediated through the immediate family). Contrary to views that children have nothing to worry about except bullies and Oedipal dynamics, these findings indicate that children's anxiety strongly reflects what is happening in the society at large. Theories of personality development may benefit by incorporating some understanding that children live in the society as a whole rather than in a narrow, circumscribed world.

The Effects of Low Social Connectedness and High Threat

What social forces have led to the increase in anxiety? The two most important are low social connectedness and high environmental threat. These results demonstrate the singular importance of social bonds and attachment to other human beings (e.g., Baumeister & Leary, 1995; Bowlby, 1969; Fukuyama, 1999; Putnam, 2000; Twenge et al., 2000). Societies with low levels of social integration produce adults prone to anxiety. Societies with high levels of environmental threat have much the same effect. This may be a society-wide demonstration of human beings' natural tendency to become anxious when threatened (e.g., Barlow, 1988; Darwin, 1872). These threats can be physical (such as violent crime) or more psychological (worry about nuclear war or women's roles; May, 1979). Many of these changes (both in social connectedness and in threat) stem from the increasing individualism and freedom of American society. As Schwartz (2000) has noted, too much freedom can lead to poor outcomes, in which we are paralyzed by our choices and then blame ourselves when things do not go well. Our greater autonomy may lead to increased challenges and excitement, but it also leads to greater isolation from others, more threats to our bodies and minds, and thus higher levels of free-floating anxiety.

Perhaps surprisingly, economic indices had very little independent effect on anxiety. Apparently, children are less concerned with whether their family has enough money than whether it is threatened by violence or dissolution. Why might this be? First, economic conditions might be relative: If the economy is doing badly and you are poor, many other people are probably poor as well. This theory is consistent with the concept of relative deprivation (e.g., Collins, 1996; Wood, 1989); one feels less deprived when everyone else is deprived too. As several authors have suggested, it may be the perception rather than the reality that is most important for producing anxiety (e.g., Beck & Emery, 1985; Lazarus & Folkman, 1984; Spielberger, 1972). Similarly, the material benefits of good economic times might be more than out weighed by the stress they produce. When everyone is doing well, there is more pressure to succeed, leading to anxiety. This argument also explains why women's anxiety would rise even as they obtained greater opportunities; greater opportunities lead to greater expectations and more stress. Last, it might be that economic conditions are just not that important to anxiety levels, especially in the samples studied here (who are too young to support themselves and thus are not worrying as much about economic conditions—either their own or the country's overall). This finding is similar to research on happiness: Beyond a certain level of survival, having more money does not lead to greater happiness (Myers & Diener, 1995).

Strengths and Practical Implications

The replication of the results over samples and measures increases confidence in the conclusions. Increases in anxiety appear in all of the measures of anxiety and neuroticism included, and the results for college students replicate in child samples. This result is especially important because college samples may differ over time in basic characteristics, whereas child samples remain more similar.

The increase in anxiety is not merely consistent across measures and samples; it is also large. Cohen (1977) classified any effect size over .80 as large; averaging across all samples, the effect size for cohort effects on anxiety in this study was .98, almost a standard deviation (and this calculation is conservative, relying on analyses with controls and only changes for years where data exist for a particular measure). In a normal distribution, a shift of one standard deviation moves the median score from the 50th percentile to the 84th percentile. In other words, the average respondent from 1993 would score at the 84th percentile on a distribution of self-reports of anxiety collected in the 1950s. As another means of comparison, the birth cohort difference reported here is larger than almost all psychological sex differences (e.g., sex differences in aggression are $d = .29$ in adults, $d = .50$ in children). They are even larger than many physical sex differences (e.g., grip strength, long jump, throw accuracy, and the 50-yard dash; Ashmore, 1990).

Another strength of this study is that it is based on current self-reports rather than retrospective recollections. All of the studies of birth cohort differences in depression rely on the retrospective reports of participants, a method with obvious drawbacks (e.g., Klerman & Weissman, 1989). In contrast, the two meta-analyses reported here are based on self-reports of anxiety actually completed at different points in time. It thus collects the true responses of participants many years into the past, rather than asking people to remember their traits or experiences.

These findings have specific implications relevant to clinical and applied concerns. First, the results suggest that cases of depression will continue to increase in the coming decades, as anxiety tends to predispose people to depression (Bagby et al.,1995; Surtees & Wainwright, 1996). Anxiety is also highly correlated with alcohol abuse and other substance abuse (Mullaney & Trippett, 1979; Smail et al., 1984); usually anxiety precedes the onset of drinking or substance abuse (Chambless et al., 1987; Mullaney & Trippett, 1979; Smail et al., 1984). This suggests that the United States will continue to grapple with the problem of substance abuse. There are also implications for physical health. Research has found that anxious people have a higher mortality rate, most likely because anxiety has been linked to higher occurrences of asthma, irritable bowel syndrome, ulcers, inflammatory bowel disease, and coronary heart disease (Edelmann, 1992). Although some of these health problems are decreasing because of changes in health habits and better care (e.g., coronary heart disease), others (e.g., asthma, irritable bowel syndrome) are on the increase. If anxiety accounts for some of this trend, the increases are likely to continue.

A Limitation

The results presented here all involve self-reports of anxiety and neuroticism. Thus, change over time on the scales could reflect either true shifts in personality traits or the respondents' willingness to describe themselves in different terms, perhaps because of changes in social desirability (e.g., Edwards, 1957). This limitation cannot be completely overcome; it is difficult to study trait (as opposed to state) anxiety without relying on self-report (especially in a meta-analysis, which must gather the available data). Thus, self-report measures are the best data available for studying change over time in anxiety. This concern can also be addressed in several ways. First, previous empirical evidence suggests that anxiety should increase over time (e.g., the studies of birth cohort differences in lifetime depression). In addition, it is unlikely that any large discrepancy between self-reported and actual anxiety would remain that way for long; the experienced self will likely change to meet the expressed self (Tice, 1994).

Conclusion: If There is an Epidemic of Anxiety, What is the Cure?

Self-reports of anxiety have risen about a standard deviation between the 1950s and 1990s, a result consistent across samples of college students and children and across different measures. Anxiety is so high now that normal samples of children from the 1980s outscore psychiatric populations from the 1950s (Levitt, 1959). If this is true, how can we reduce feelings of anxiety on a societal level? Seemingly, anxiety will decrease when threat decreases and social connectedness increases. Economic conditions will not have much of an effect, at least for child, adolescent, and young adult samples. Many environmental threats have declined somewhat in the years since the end of this study (1994–2000): Crime rates are down, for example, and worries about nuclear war have decreased. These are good signs for stopping or even reversing increases in anxiety. However, social connectedness has not improved very much. Although divorce rates have decreased somewhat, the percentage of people living alone continues to increase, and levels of trust are still declining. Improvements in these statistics—and a general feeling of belongingness and closeness in our communities—would likely decrease feelings of anxiety. Until people feel both safe and connected to others, anxiety is likely to remain high.

References

Ashmore, R. D. (1990). Sex, gender, and the individual. In L. A. Pervin (Ed.), *Handbook of personality theory and research* (pp. 486–526). New York: Guilford Press.

Bachman, J., Johnston, L., & O'Malley, P. (1998). *Monitoring the future: Questionnaire responses from the nation's high school seniors, 1998*. Ann Arbor, MI: University of Michigan, Institute for Social Research.

Bagby, R. M., Joffe, R. T., Parker, J. D. A., Kalemba, V., & Harkeness, K. L. (1995). Major depression and the five-factor model of personality. *Journal of Personality Disorders, 9*, 224–234.

Baltes, P. B., & Nesselroade, J. R. (1972). Cultural change and adolescent personality development. *Developmental Psychology, 7*, 244–256.

Barlow, D. H. (1988). *Anxiety and its disorders*. New York: Guilford.

Baumeister, R. F., & Leary, M. R. (1995). The need to belong: Desire for interpersonal attachments as a fundamental human motivation. *Psychological Bulletin, 117*, 497–529.

Baumeister, R. F., & Tice, D. M. (1990). Anxiety and social exclusion. *Journal of Social and Clinical Psychology, 9*, 165–195.

Beck, A. T. (1985). Theoretical perspectives on clinical anxiety. In A. H.Tuma & D. Maser (Eds.), *Anxiety and the anxiety disorders* (pp. 153–196). Hillsdale, NJ: Erlbaum.

Beck, A. T., & Emery, G. (1985). *Anxiety disorders and phobias: A cognitive perspective*. New York: Basic Books.

Bendig, A. W. (1960). Age differences in the inter scale factor structure of the Guilford-Zimmerman Temperament Survey. *Journal of Consulting Psychology, 24*, 134–138.

Bergeman, C. S., Plomin, R., McClearn, G. E., Pedersen, N. L., & Friberg, L. T. (1988). Genotype-environment interaction in personality development: Identical twins reared apart. *Psychology and Aging, 3*, 399–406.

Bouchard, T. J. (1994). Genes, environment, and personality. *Science, 264*, 1700–1701.

Bowlby, J. (1969). *Attachment and loss: Vol. 1. Attachment*. New York: Basic Books.

Bronfenbrenner, U., McClelland, P., Wethington, E., Moen, P., & Ceci, S.(1996). *The state of Americans: This generation and the next*. New York: Free Press.

Buss, A. R. (1974). Generational analysis: Description, explanation, and theory. *Journal of Social Issues, 30*, 55–71.

Caspi, A. (1987). Personality in the life course. *Journal of Personality and Social Psychology, 53*, 1203–1213.

Castaneda, A., McCandless, B. R., & Palermo, D. S. (1956). The children's form of the manifest anxiety scale. *Child Development, 27*, 317–326.

Chambless, D. L., Cherney, J., Caputo, G. C, & Rheinstein, B. J. (1987). Anxiety disorders and alcoholism: A study with inpatient alcoholics. *Journal of Anxiety Disorders, 1*, 29–40.

Choi, I., Nisbett, R. E., & Norenzayan, A. (1999). Causal attribution across cultures: Variation and universality. *Psychological Bulletin, 125*, 47–63.

Cohen, J. (1977). *Statistical power analysis for the behavioral sciences*. New York: Academic Press.

Cohen, S., & Wills, T. A. (1985). Stress, social support, and the buffering hypothesis. *Psychological Bulletin, 98*, 310–357.

Cohl, H. A. (1997). *Are we scaring ourselves to death?* New York: St. Martin's Press.

Collins, R. L. (1996). For better or worse: The impact of upward social comparison on self-evaluation. *Psychological Bulletin, 119*, 51–69.

Conley, J. J. (1984). The hierarchy of consistency: A review and model of longitudinal findings in adult individual differences in intelligence, personality

and self-opinion. *Personality and Individual Differences, 5*, 11–26.

Coryell, W. H., Noyes, R., & Clancy, J. (1982). Excess mortality in panic disorder: A comparison with primary unipolar depression. *Archives of General Psychiatry, 39*, 701–703.

Coryell, W. H., Noyes, R., & House, D. (1986). Mortality among outpatients with anxiety disorders. *American Journal of Psychiatry, 143*, 508–510.

Costa, P. T., & McCrae, R. R. (1988). Personality in adulthood: A six-year longitudinal study of self-reports and spouse ratings on the NEO Personality Inventory. *Journal of Personality and Social Psychology, 54*, 853–863.

Costa, P. T., McCrae, R. R., & Arenberg, P. (1980). Enduring dispositions in adult males. *Journal of Personality and Social Psychology, 38*, 793–800.

Costa, P. T., McCrae, R. R., Zonderman, A. B., Barbano, H. E., Lebowitz, B., & Larson, D. M. (1986). Cross-sectional studies of personality in a national sample: 2. Stability in neuroticism, extraversion, and openness. *Psychology and Aging, 1*, 144–149.

Darwin, C. R. (1872). *The expression of emotion in man and animals*. London: John Murray.

DeNeve, K. M., & Cooper, H. (1998). The happy personality: A meta-analysis of 137 personality traits and subjective well-being. *Psychological Bulletin, 124*, 197–229.

Dey, E. L., Astin, A. W., & Korn, W. S. (1992). *The American freshman: Twenty-five year trends, 1966–1990*. Los Angeles: Higher Education Research Institute.

Diamond, G., & Bachman, J. (1986). High-school seniors and the nuclear threat, 1975–1984: Political and mental health implications of concern and despair. *International Journal of Mental Health, 15*, 210–241.

Duncan, L. E., & Agronick, G. S. (1995). The intersection of life stage and social events: Personality and life outcomes. *Journal of Personality and Social Psychology, 69*, 558–568.

Dyer, E. D. (1987). Ten-year differences in level of entering students' profile on the California Psychological Inventory. *Psychological Reports, 60*, 822.

Edelmann, R. J. (1992). *Anxiety theory, research and intervention in clinical and health psychology*. New York: Wiley.

Edwards, A. L. (1957). *The social desirability variable in personality assessment and research*. New York: Dryden Press.

Elder, G. H. (1974). *Children of the Great Depression: Social change and life experience*. Chicago: University of Chicago Press.

Elder, G. H. (1981). History and the life course. In D. Bertaux (Ed.), *Biography and society: The life history approach in the social sciences*. Beverly Hills, CA: Sage.

Eysenck, H. J. (1968). *Manual of the Eysenck Personality Inventory*. San Diego, CA: EDITS.

Eysenck, H. J., & Eysenck, S. B. G. (1975). *Manual of the Eysenck Personality Questionnaire*. San Diego, CA: EDITS.

Eysenck, H. J., & Eysenck, S. B. G. (1991). *The Eysenck Personality Questionnaire-Revised*. Sevanoaks, Kent, UK: Hodder & Staughton.

Eysenck, S. B. G., & Eysenck, H. J. (1969). Scores on three personality variables as a function of age, sex, and social class. *British Journal of Social and Clinical Psychology, 8*, 69–76.

Finn, S. E. (1986). Stability of personality self-ratings over 30 years: Evidence for an age/cohort interaction. *Journal of Personality and Social Psychology, 50*, 813–818.

Fukuyama, F. (1999). *The great disruption: Human nature and the reconstitution of social order*. New York: Free Press.

Gergen, K. J. (1973). Social psychology as history. *Journal of Personality and Social Psychology, 26*, 309–320.

Glassner, B. (1999). *The culture of fear: Why Americans are afraid of the wrong things*. New York: Basic Books.

Gutman, G. M. (1966). A note on the MPI: Age and sex differences in extraversion and neuroticism in a Canadian sample. *British Journal of Social and Clinical Psychology, 5*, 128–129.

Hagnell, O., Lanke, J., Rorsman, B., & Ojesjo, L. (1982). Are we entering an age of melancholy? Depressive illnesses in a prospective epidemio-logical study over 25 years: The Lundby Study, Sweden. *Psychological Medicine, 12*, 279–289.

Heine, S. J., & Lehman, D. R. (1997). Culture, dissonance, and self-affirmation. *Personality and Social Psychology Bulletin, 23*, 389–400.

Henker, B., Whalen, C. K., & O'Neil, R. (1995). Worldly and workaday worries: Contemporary concerns of children and young adolescents. *Journal of Abnormal Child Psychology, 23*, 685–702.

Holloway, H. D. (1961). Normative data on the Children's Manifest Anxiety Scale at the rural third-grade level. *Child Development, 32*, 129–134.

Holtz, G. T. (1995). *Welcome to the Jungle: The why behind Generation X*. New York: St. Martin's Press.

Howe, N., & Strauss, W. (1993). *13th Gen: Abort, retry, ignore, fail?* New York: Vintage Books.

Jamison, R. N. (1984). Differences in personality between American and English children. *Personality and Individual Differences, 5*, 241–244.

Kelly, E. L. (1955). Consistency of the adult personality. *American Psychologist, 10*, 659–681.

Kertzer, D. J. (1983). Generation as a sociological problem. *Annual Review of Sociology, 9*, 125–149.

Klerman, G. L., & Weissman, M. M. (1989). Increasing rates of depression. *Journal of the American Medical Association, 261*, 2229–2235.

Kramer, B. M, Kalick, S. M., & Milburn, M. A. (1983). Attitudes toward nuclear weapons and nuclear war: 1945–1982. *Journal of Social Issues, 39*, 7–24.

Lambert, T. A. (1972). Generations and change: Toward a theory of generations as a force in historical process. *Youth and Society, 4*, 21–46.

Langinvaionio, H., Kaprio, J., Koskenvuo, M., & Lonngvist, J. (1984). Finnish twins reared apart: 3. Personality factors. *Acta Geneticae Medicae of Gemellogiae, 33*, 259–264.

Lazarus, R. S. (1966). *Psychological stress and the coping process*. New York: McGraw-Hill.

Lazarus, R. S., & Folkman, S. (1984). *Stress appraisal and coping*. New York: Springer.

Levitt, E. E. (1959). A comparison of parental and self-evaluations of psychopathology in children. *Journal of Clinical Psychology, 15*, 402–404.

Lewinsohn, P., Rohde, P., Seeley, J., & Fischer, S. (1993). Age-cohort changes in the lifetime occurrence of depression and other mental disorders. *Journal of Abnormal Psychology, 102*, 110–120.

Loehlin, J. C. (1989). Partitioning environmental and genetic contributions to behavioral development. *American Psychologist, 44*, 1285–1292.

Loehlin, J. C. (1992). *Genes and environment in personality development*. Newbury Park, CA: Sage.

Markus, H. R., & Kitayama, S. (1991). Culture and the self: Implications for cognition, emotion, and motivation. *Psychological Review, 98*, 224–253.

Markus, H. R., Kitayama, S., & Heiman, R. J. (1996). Culture and "basic" psychological principles. In E. T. Higgins & A. W. Kruglanski (Eds.), *Social psychology: Handbook of basic principles* (pp. 857–913). New York: The Guilford Press.

Markus, H. R., Kitayama, S., & VandenBos, G. R. (1996). The mutual interactions of culture and emotion. *Psychiatric Services, 47*, 225–226.

Matthews, G., Coyle, K., & Craig, A. (1990). Multiple factors of cognitive failure and their relationships with stress vulnerability. *Journal of Psychopathology and Behavioral Assessment, 12*, 49–64.

Matthews, G., & Deary, I. (1998). *Personality traits.* Cambridge, UK: Cambridge University Press.

May, R. (1979). *The meaning of anxiety.* New York: Washington Square Press.

McLoyd, V. C, Jayaratne, T. E., Ceballo, R., & Borquez, V. (1994). Unemployment and work interruption among African-American single mothers: Effects on parenting and adolescent socioemotional functioning. *Child Development, 65*, 562–589.

Miringoff, M., & Miringoff, M. L. (1999). *The social health of the nation: How America is really doing.* New York: Oxford University Press.

Mullaney, J. A., & Trippett, C. J. (1979). Alcohol dependence and phobias: Clinical description and relevance. *British Journal of Psychiatry, 135*, 565–573.

Myers, D. G., & Diener, E. (1995). Who is happy? *Psychological Science, 6*, 10–19.

Nesselroade, J. R., & Baltes, P. B. (1974). Adolescent personality development and historical change, 1970–1972. *Monographs of the Society for Research in Child Development, 39* (1, Serial No. 154).

Nisbett, R. E., & Cohen, D. (1996). *Culture of honor: The psychology of violence in the South.* Boulder, CO: Westview Press.

O'Leary, K. D., & Smith, D. A. (1991). Marital interactions. *Annual Review of Psychology, 42*, 191–212.

Oliver, M. B., & Hyde, J. S. (1993). Gender differences in sexuality: A meta-analysis. *Psychological Bulletin, 114*, 29–51.

Pedersen, N. L., Plomin, R., McClearn, G. E., & Friedberg, L. (1988). Neuroticism, extraversion, and related traits in adult twins reared apart and reared together. *Journal of Personality and Social Psychology, 55*, 950–957.

Putnam, R. D. (2000). *Bowling alone: The collapse and revival of American community.* New York: Simon & Schuster.

Reiss, D. (1997). Mechanisms linking genetic and social influences in adolescent development: Beginning a collaborative search. *Current Directions in Psychological Science, 6*, 100–105.

Rholes, W. S., Riskind, J. H., & Neville, B. (1985). The relationship of cognitions and hopelessness to depression and anxiety. *Social Cognition, 3*, 36–50.

Rie, H. E. (1963). An exploratory study of the Children's Manifest Anxiety Scale lie scale. *Child Development, 34*, 1003–1017.

Rosen, B. C. (1998). *Winners and losers of the information revolution: Psychosocial change and its discontents.* Westport, CT: Praeger.

Rowe, D. C. (1990). As the twig is bent? The myth of child-rearing influences on personality development. *Journal of Counseling and Development, 68*, 606–611.

Ryder, N. B. (1965). The cohort as a concept in the study of social change. *American Sociological Review, 30*, 843–861.

Sampson, R. J., & Laub, J. H. (1990). Crime and deviance over the lifecourse: The salience of adult social bonds. *American Sociological Review, 55*, 609–627.

Schaie, K. W. (1965). A general model for the study of developmental problems. *Psychological Bulletin, 64*, 92–107.

Schonberg, W. B. (1974). Modification of attitudes of college students overtime: 1923–1970. *Journal of Genetic Psychology, 125*, 107–117.

Schwartz, B. (2000). Self-determination: The tyranny of freedom. *American Psychologist, 55*, 79–88.

Seipp, B. (1991). Anxiety and academic performance: A meta-analysis of findings. *Anxiety Research, 4*, 27–41.

Seligman, M. E. P. (1988). Boomer blues. *Psychology Today, 22*, 50–53.

Seligman, M. E. P. (1995). *The optimistic child.* New York: Harper.

Shields, J. (1962). *Monozygotic twins brought up apart and together.* London: Oxford University Press.

Sloan, T. (1996). *Damaged life: The crisis of the modern psyche.* New York: Routledge.

Smail, P., Stockwell, T., Canter, S., & Hodgson, R. (1984). Alcohol dependence and phobic anxiety states: I. A prevalence study. *British Journal of Psychiatry, 144,* 53–57.

Smith, T. W. (1997). Factors relating to misanthropy in contemporary American society. *Social Science Research, 26,* 170–196.

Spielberger, C. D. (1972). *Anxiety: Current trends in theory and research* (Vol. 1). New York: Academic Press.

Spielberger, C. D., Gorsuch, R. L., & Lushene, R. E. (1970). *Manual for the State-Trait Anxiety Inventory*. Palo Alto, CA: Consulting Psychologists Press.

Spielberger, C. D., Gorsuch, R. L., Lushene, R., Vagg, P. R., & Jacobs,G. A. (1983). *Manual for the State-Trait Anxiety Inventory (Form Y)*. Palo Alto, CA: Consulting Psychologists Press.

Spielberger, C. D., & Rickman, R. L. (1990). Assessment of state and trait anxiety. In N. Sartorius, V. Andreoli, G. Cassano, L. Eisenberg, P.Kielkolt, P. Pancheri, & G. Racagni (Eds.), *Anxiety: Psychobiological and clinical perspectives* (pp. 69–83). New York: Hemisphere Publishing.

Stewart, A. J., & Healy, J. M. (1989). Linking individual development and social changes. *American Psychologist, 44,* 30–42.

Suh, E., Diener, E., Oishi, S., & Triandis, H. C. (1998). The shifting basis of life satisfaction judgments across cultures: Emotions versus norms. *Journal of Personality and Social Psychology, 74,* 482–493.

Surtees, P. G., & Wainwright, N. W. J. (1996). Fragile states of mind: Neuroticism, vulnerability, and the long-term outcome of depression. *British Journal of Psychiatry, 169,* 338–347.

Sutton-Smith, B., Rosenberg, B. G., & Morgan, E. F. (1961). Historical changes in the freedom with which children express themselves on personality inventories. *Journal of Genetic Psychology, 99,* 309–315.

Tanaka-Matsumi, J., & Kameoka, V. A. (1986). Reliabilities and concurrent validities of popular self-report measures of depression, anxiety, and social desirability. *Journal of Consulting and Clinical Psychology, 54,* 328–333.

Taylor, J. A. (1953). A personality scale of manifest anxiety. *Journal of Abnormal and Social Psychology, 48,* 285–290.

Tellegen, A. (1985). Structures of mood and personality and their relevance to assessing anxiety, with an emphasis on self-report. In A. H. Tuma & J. D. Maser (Eds.), *Anxiety and the anxiety disorders* (pp. 681–706). Hillsdale, NJ: Erlbaum.

Tice, D. M. (1994). Pathways to internalization: When does overt behavior change the self-concept? In T. M. Brinthaust & R. P. Lipka (Eds.), *Changing the self: Philosophies, techniques, and experience* (pp. 229–250). Albany, NY: State University of New York Press.

Torgersen, S. (1993). Relationship between adult and childhood anxiety disorders: Genetic hypothesis. In C. Last (Ed.), *Anxiety across the life span: A developmental perspective* (pp. 26–48). New York: Springer.

Twenge, J. M. (1997a). Changes in masculine and feminine traits overtime: A meta-analysis. *Sex Roles, 36,* 305–325.

Twenge, J. M. (1997b). Attitudes toward women, 1970–1995: A meta-analysis. *Psychology of Women Quarterly, 21,* 35–51.

Twenge, J. M. (2000). *Similarities and differences in past and present personality measures*. Unpublished manuscript, University of Michigan.

Twenge, J. M. (in press). Birth cohort changes in extraversion: A cross-temporal meta-analysis, 1966–1993. *Personality and Individual Differences*.

Twenge, J. M., Baumeister, B. F., Tice, D. M., Faber, J. E., & Stucke, T. S. (2000). *If you can't join them, beat them: The effects of social exclusion on antisocial vs. prosocial behavior*. Unpublished manuscript.

Twenge, J. M., & Campbell, W. K. (2000). *Age and birth cohort differences in self-esteem: A cross-temporal meta-analysis*. Unpublished manuscript.

U.S. Bureau of the Census. *Statistical Abstract of the United States*. Various years, 1925–1998. Washington, DC: U.S. Government Printing Office.

Veroff, J., Douvan, E., & Kulka, R. (1981). *The inner American*. New York: Basic Books.

Veroff, J., Kulka, R. A., & Douvan, E. (1981). *Mental health in America: Patterns of help-seeking from 1957 to 1976*. New York: Basic Books.

Wilkins, R., & Lewis, C. (1993). Sex and drugs and nuclear war: Secular,developmental and Type A influences upon adolescents' fears of then uclear threat, AIDS and drug addiction. *Journal of Adolescence, 16,* 23–41.

Wolf, F. M. (1986). Meta-analysis: Quantitative methods for research synthesis. In *Sage University Paper Series on Quantitative Applications in the Social Sciences* (pp. 7–59). Newbury Park, CA: Sage.

Wood, J. V. (1989). Theory and research concerning social comparisons of personal attributes. *Psychological Bulletin, 106*, 231–248.

Woodruff, D. S., & Birren, J. E. (1972). Age changes and cohort differences in personality. *Developmental Psychology, 6*, 252–259.

JEAN M. TWENGE is a professor in the department of psychology at San Diego State University.

Pew Research Center

Millennials: Confident. Connected.
Open to Change

Overview

Generations, like people, have personalities, and Millennials—the American teens and twenty-somethings who are making the passage into adulthood at the start of a new millennium—have begun to forge theirs: confident, self-expressive, liberal, upbeat and open to change.

They are more ethnically and racially diverse than older adults. They're less religious, less likely to have served in the military, and are on track to become the most educated generation in American history.

Their entry into careers and first jobs has been badly set back by the Great Recession, but they are more upbeat than their elders about their own economic futures as well as about the overall state of the nation.

They are history's first "always connected" generation. Steeped in digital technology and social media, they treat their multi-tasking hand-held gadgets almost like a body part—for better and worse. More than eight-in-ten say they sleep with a cell phone glowing by the bed, poised to disgorge texts, phone calls, emails, songs, news, videos, games and wake-up jingles. But sometimes convenience yields to temptation. Nearly two-thirds admit to texting while driving.

They embrace multiple modes of self-expression. Threequarters have created a profile on a social networking site. One-in-five have posted a video of themselves online. Nearly four-in-ten have a tattoo (and for most who do, one is not enough: about half of those with tattoos have two to five and 18% have six or more). Nearly one-in-four have a piercing in some place other than an earlobe—about six times the share of older adults who've done this. But their look-at-me tendencies are not without limits. Most Millennials have placed privacy boundaries on their social media profiles. And 70% say their tattoos are hidden beneath clothing.

Despite struggling (and often failing) to find jobs in the teeth of a recession, about nine-in-ten either say that they currently have enough money or that they will eventually meet their long-term financial goals. But at the moment, fully 37% of 18- to 29-year olds are unemployed or out of the workforce, the highest share among this age group in more than three decades. Research shows that young people who graduate from college in a bad economy typically suffer long-term consequences—with effects on their careers and earnings that linger as long as 15 years.[1]

Whether as a by-product of protective parents, the age of terrorism or a media culture that focuses on dangers, they cast a wary eye on human nature. Two-thirds say "you can't be too careful" when dealing with people. Yet they are less skeptical than their elders of government. More so than other generations, they believe government should do more to solve problems.

They are the least overtly religious American generation in modern times. One-in-four are unaffiliated with any religion, far more than the share of older adults when they were ages 18 to 29. Yet not belonging does not necessarily mean not believing. Millennials pray about as often as their elders did in their own youth.

Only about six-in-ten were raised by both parents—a smaller share than was the case with older generations. In weighing their own life priorities, Millennials (like older adults) place parenthood and marriage far above career and financial success. But they aren't rushing to the altar. Just one-in-five Millennials (21%) are married now, half the share of their parents' generation at the same stage of life. About a third (34%) are parents, according to the Pew Research survey. We estimate that, in 2006, more than a third of 18 to 29 year old women who gave birth were unmarried. This is a far higher share than was the case in earlier generations.[2]

Millennials are on course to become the most educated generation in American history, a trend driven largely by the demands of a modern knowledge-based economy, but most likely accelerated in recent years by the millions of 20-somethings enrolling in graduate schools, colleges or community colleges in part because they can't find a job. Among 18 to 24 year olds a record share–39.6%—was enrolled in college as of 2008, according to census data.

They get along well with their parents. Looking back at their teenage years, Millennials report having had fewer spats with mom or dad than older adults say they had with their own parents when they were growing up. And now, hard times have kept a significant share of adult Millennials and their parents under the same roof. About one-in-eight older Millennials (ages 22 and older) say they've "boomeranged" back to a parent's home because of the recession.

They respect their elders. A majority say that the older generation is superior to the younger generation when it comes to moral values and work ethic. Also, more than six-in-ten say that families have a responsibility to have an elderly parent come live with them if that parent wants to. By contrast, fewer than four-in-ten adults ages 60 and older agree that this is a family responsibility.

Despite coming of age at a time when the United States has been waging two wars, relatively few Millennials—just 2% of males—are military veterans. At a comparable stage of their life cycle, 6% of Gen Xer men, 13% of Baby Boomer men and 24% of Silent men were veterans.

Politically, Millennials were among Barack Obama's strongest supporters in 2008, backing him for president by more than a two-to-one ratio (66% to 32%) while older adults were giving just 50% of their votes to the Democratic nominee. This was the largest disparity between younger and older voters recorded in four decades of modern election day exit polling. Moreover, after decades of low voter participation by the young, the turnout gap in 2008 between voters under and over the age of 30 was the smallest it had been since 18- to 20-year-olds were given the right to vote in 1972.

But the political enthusiasms of Millennials have since cooled—for Obama and his message of change, for the Democratic Party and, quite possibly, for politics itself. About half of Millennials say the president has failed to change the way Washington works, which had been the central promise of his candidacy. Of those who say this, three-in-ten blame Obama himself, while more than half blame his political opponents and special interests.

To be sure, Millennials remain the most likely of any generation to self-identify as liberals; they are less supportive than their elders of an assertive national security policy and more supportive of a progressive domestic social agenda. They are still more likely than any other age group to identify as Democrats. Yet by early 2010, their support for Obama and the Democrats had receded, as evidenced both by survey data and by their low level of participation in recent off-year and special elections.

Our Research Methods

This Pew Research Center report profiles the roughly 50 million Millennials who currently span the ages of 18 to 29. It's likely that when future analysts are in a position to take a fuller measure of this new generation, they will conclude that millions of additional younger teens (and perhaps even pre-teens) should be grouped together with their older brothers and sisters. But for the purposes of this report, unless we indicate otherwise, we focus on Millennials who are at least 18 years old.

What's in a Name?

Generational names are the handiwork of popular culture. Some are drawn from a historic event; others from rapid social or demographic change; others from a big turn in the calendar.

The Millennial generation falls into the third category. The label refers those born after 1980—the first generation to come of age in the new millennium.

Generation X covers people born from 1965 through 1980. The label long ago overtook the first name affixed to this generation: the Baby Bust. Xers are often depicted as savvy, entrepreneurial loners.

The Baby Boomer label is drawn from the great spike in fertility that began in 1946, right after the end of World War II, and ended almost as abruptly in 1964, around the time the birth control pill went on the market. It's a classic example of a demography-driven name.

The Silent generation describes adults born from 1928 through 1945. Children of the Great Depression and World War II, their "Silent" label refers to their conformist and civic instincts. It also makes for a nice contrast with the noisy ways of the anti-establishment Boomers.

The Greatest Generation (those born before 1928) "saved the world" when it was young, in the memorable phrase of Ronald Reagan. It's the generation that fought and won World War II.

Generational names are works in progress. The zeitgeist changes, and labels that once seemed spot-on fall out of fashion. It's not clear if the Millennial tag will endure, although a calendar change that comes along only once in a thousand years seems like a pretty secure anchor.

We examine their demographics; their political and social values; their lifestyles and life priorities; their digital technology and social media habits; and their economic and educational aspirations. We also compare and contrast Millennials with the nation's three other living generations—Gen Xers (ages 30 to 45), Baby Boomers (ages 46 to 64) and Silents (ages 65 and older). Whenever the trend data permit, we compare the four generations as they all are now—and also as older generations were at the ages that adult Millennials are now.[3]

Most of the findings in this report are based on a new survey of a national cross-section of 2,020 adults (including an oversample of Millennials), conducted by landline and cellular telephone from Jan. 14 to 27, 2010; this survey has a margin of error of plus or minus 3.0 percentage points for the full sample and larger percentages for various subgroups. The report also draws on more than two decades of Pew Research Center surveys, supplemented by our analysis of Census Bureau data and other relevant studies.

Some Caveats

A few notes of caution are in order. Generational analysis has a long and distinguished place in social science, and we cast our lot with those scholars who believe it is not only possible, but often highly illuminating, to search for the unique and distinctive characteristics of any given age group of Americans. But we also know this is not an exact science.

We acknowledge, for example, that there is an element of false precision in setting hard chronological boundaries between the generations. Can we say with certainty that a typical 30-year-old adult is a Gen Xer while a typical 29-year-old adult is a Millennial? Of course not. Nevertheless, we must draw lines in order to carry out

the statistical analyses that form the core of our research methodology. And our boundaries—while admittedly too crisp—are not arbitrary. They are based on our own research findings and those of other scholars.

We are mindful that there are as many differences in attitudes, values, behaviors and lifestyles within a generation as there are between generations. But we believe this reality does not diminish the value of generational analysis; it merely adds to its richness and complexity. Throughout this report, we will not only explore how Millennials differ from other generations, we will also look at how they differ among themselves.

The Millennial Identity

Most Millennials (61%) in our January, 2010 survey say their generation has a unique and distinctive identity. That doesn't make them unusual, however. Roughly two-thirds of Silents, nearly six-in-ten Boomers and about half of Xers feel the same way about their generation.

But Millennials have a distinctive reason for feeling distinctive. In response to an open-ended follow-up question, 24% say it's because of their use of technology. Gen Xers also cite technology as their generation's biggest source of distinctiveness, but far fewer—just 12%—say this. Boomers' feelings of distinctiveness coalesce mainly around work ethic, which 17% cite as their most prominent identity badge. For Silents, it's the shared experience of the Depression and World War II, which 14% cite as the biggest reason their generation stands apart.

Millennials' technological exceptionalism is chronicled throughout the survey. It's not just their gadgets—it's the way they've fused their social lives into them. For example, three-quarters of Millennials have created a profile on a social networking site, compared with half of

What Makes Your Generation Unique?

	Millennial	Gen X	Boomer	Silent
1.	Technology use (24%)	Technology use (12%)	Work ethic (17%)	WW II, Depression (14%)
2.	Music/Pop culture (11%)	Work ethic (11%)	Respectful (14%)	Smarter (13%)
3.	Liberal/tolerant (7%)	Conservative/Trad'l (7%)	Values/Morals (8%)	Honest (12%)
4.	Smarter (6%)	Smarter (6%)	"Baby Boomers" (6%)	Work ethic (10%)
5.	Clothes (5%)	Respectful (5%)	Smarter (5%)	Values/Morals (10%)

Note: Based on respondents who said their generation was unique/distinct. Items represent individual, open ended responses. Top five responses are shown for each age group. Sample sizes for sub-groups are as follows: Millennials, n = 527; Gen X, n = 173; Boomers, n = 283; Silent, n = 205.

Xers, 30% of Boomers and 6% of Silents. There are big generation gaps, as well, in using wireless technology, playing video games and posting selfcreated videos online. Millennials are also more likely than older adults to say technology makes life easier and brings family and friends closer together (though the generation gaps on these questions are relatively narrow).

Work Ethic, Moral Values, Race Relations

Of the four generations, Millennials are the only one that doesn't cite "work ethic" as one of their principal claims to distinctiveness. A nationwide Pew Research Center survey taken in 2009 may help explain why. This one focused on differences between young and old rather than between specific age groups. Nonetheless, its findings are instructive.

Nearly six-in-ten respondents cited work ethic as one of the big sources of differences between young and old. Asked who has the better work ethic, about three-fourths of respondents said that older people do. By similar margins, survey respondents also found older adults have the upper hand when it comes to moral values and their respect for others.

It might be tempting to dismiss these findings as a typical older adult gripe about "kids today." But when it comes to each of these traits—work ethic, moral values, respect for others—young adults *agree* that older adults have the better of it. In short, Millennials may be a self-confident generation, but they display little appetite for claims of moral superiority.

That 2009 survey also found that the public—young and old alike—thinks the younger generation is more racially tolerant than their elders. More than two decades of Pew Research surveys confirm that assessment. In their views about interracial dating, for example, Millennials are the most open to change of any generation, followed closely by Gen Xers, then Boomers, then Silents.

Likewise, Millennials are more receptive to immigrants than are their elders. Nearly six-in-ten (58%) say immigrants strengthen the country, according to a 2009 Pew Research survey; just 43% of adults ages 30 and older agree.

The same pattern holds on a range of attitudes about nontraditional family arrangements, from mothers of young children working outside the home, to adults living together without being married, to more people of different races marrying each other. Millennials are more accepting than older generations of these more modern family arrangements, followed closely by Gen Xers. To be sure, acceptance does not in all cases translate into outright approval. But it does mean Millennials disapprove less.

A Gentler Generation Gap

A 1969 Gallup survey, taken near the height of the social and political upheavals of that turbulent decade, found that 74% of the public believed there was a "generation gap" in American society. Surprisingly, when that same question was asked in a Pew Research Center survey last year—in an era marked by hard economic times but little if any overt age-based social tension—the share of the public saying there was a generation gap had risen slightly to 79%.

But as the 2009 results also make clear, this modern generation gap is a much more benign affair than the one that cast a shadow over the 1960s. The public says this one is mostly about the different ways that old and young use technology—and relatively few people see that gap as a source of conflict. Indeed, only about a quarter of the respondents in the 2009 survey said they see big conflicts between young and old in America. Many more

Weighing Trends in Marriage and Parenthood, by Generation
% saying this is a bad thing for society

	Millennial	Gen X	Boomer	Silent
More single women deciding to have children	59	54	65	72
More gay couples raising children	32	36	48	55
More mothers of young children working outside the home	23	29	39	38
More people living together w/o getting married	22	31	44	58
More people of different races marrying each other	5	10	14	26

Note: "Good thing", "Doesn't make much difference", and "Don't know" responses not shown.

see conflicts between immigrants and the native born, between rich and poor, and between black and whites.

There is one generation gap that *has* widened notably in recent years. It has to do with satisfaction over the state of the nation. In recent decades the young have always tended to be a bit more upbeat than their elders on this key measure, but the gap is wider now than it has been in at least twenty years. Some 41% of Millennials say they are satisfied with the way things are going in the country, compared with just 26% of those ages 30 and older. Whatever toll a recession, a housing crisis, a financial meltdown and a pair of wars may have taken on the national psyche in the past few years, it appears to have hit the old harder than the young.

But this speaks to a difference in outlook and attitude; it's not a source of conflict or tension. As they make their way into adulthood, Millennials have already distinguished themselves as a generation that gets along well with others, especially their elders. For a nation whose population is rapidly going gray, that could prove to be a most welcome character trait.

Notes

1. Lisa B. Kahn. "The Long-Term Labor Market Consequences of Graduating from College in a Bad Economy," Yale School of Management, Aug. 13, 2009 (forthcoming in *Labour Economics*).

2. This Pew Research estimate is drawn from our analysis of government data for women ages 18 to 29 who gave birth in 2006, the most recent year for which such data is available. Martin, Joyce A., Brady E. Hamilton, Paul D. Sutton, Stephanie J. Ventura, Fay Menacker, Sharon Kirmeyer, and TJ Mathews. Births: Final Data for 2006. National Vital Statistics Reports; vol 57 no 7. Hyattsville, Maryland: National Center for Health Statistics. 2009.

3. We do not have enough respondents ages 83 and older in our 2010 survey to permit an analysis of the Greatest Generation, which is usually defined as encompassing adults born before 1928. Throughout much of this report, we have grouped these older respondents in with the Silent generation. However, Chapter 8 on politics and Chapter 9 on religion each draw on long-term trend data from other sources, permitting us in some instances in those chapters to present findings about the Greatest Generation.

THE PEW RESEARCH CENTER is a nonpartisan fact tank that informs the public about the issues, attitudes, and trends shaping America and the world. It conducts public opinion polling, demographic research, media content analysis, and other empirical social science research.

EXPLORING THE ISSUE

Is There a "Narcissism Epidemic" Among Contemporary Young Adults?

Critical Thinking and Reflection

1. What qualifies as a "generation" of young adults? What types of social forces might have influenced the increasing emphasis on self-esteem?
2. Do you believe that the shift in narcissism is specific to young adults or has our entire society become more self-involved?
3. Why might different researchers find such contrasting findings regarding traits and values of contemporary young adults?
4. What are the implications of viewing young adults through a negative lens? What are the implications of viewing them through a positive lens?
5. What are some of the strengths and challenges of interpreting generational data?

Is There Common Ground?

The inexact science of labeling a generation means that concepts such as "Generation Me," as coined by Jean M. Twenge, are bound to generate debate. Both sides of this debate would likely agree that college students today have come of age amidst social trends that are meaningfully different from those of past decades. The issue here is whether data supports the suggestion that narcissism particularly characterizes this generation. Or are there other possibilities?

In contrast to Jean Twenge's article, the Pew Research Center's report describes the same generation as confident, self-expressive, liberal, positive, and open to change. Perhaps the answer lies in the difference between narcissism and confidence. It is important to consider the individuals responding to surveys presented in both selections. Might there be certain factors that elicit narcissism from some individuals and confidence from others?

Create Central

www.mhhe.com/createcentral

Additional Resources

Arnett, J. J. (2007). Suffering, selfish, slackers? Myths and reality about emerging adults. *Journal of youth and adolescence*, *36*(1), 23–29.

Gentile, B., Twenge, J. M., & Campbell, W. K. (2010). Birth cohort differences in self-esteem, 1988–2008: A cross-temporal meta-analysis. *Review of General Psychology*, *14*(3), 261.

Lester, S. W., Standifer, R. L., Schultz, N. J., & Windsor, J. M. (2012). Actual versus perceived generational differences at work: An empirical examination. *Journal of Leadership & Organizational Studies*, *19*(3), 341–354.

Internet References . . .

The B.I.T. Group

www.thebitgroup.com

The Narcissism Epidemic

http://www.narcissismepidemic.com/

TRU

www.tru-insight.com

Selected, Edited, and with Issue Framing Material by:
Allison A. Buskirk-Cohen, *Delaware Valley University*

ISSUE

Do Religion and Spirituality Mean the Same Thing to Today's College Students?

YES: **Diane Winston**, from "iFaith in the Amen Corner: How Gen Y Is Rethinking Religion on Campus," in the Social Science Research Council Essay Forum on the Religious Engagements of American Undergraduates (2007)

NO: **Chelsi A. Creech et al.**, from "Changing Trends in Ritual Attendance and Spirituality Throughout the College Years," *Psychology* (2013)

Learning Outcomes

After reading this issue, you will be able to:

- Discuss how in past decades, college has been associated with a decline in religious involvement, but contemporary college students may be countering that trend through new forms of religious engagement.
- Understand that college students are increasingly aware of religious traditions different from their own, though that awareness has not necessarily led to the widespread adoption of new practices or beliefs.
- Understand that while religiosity and spirituality may intersect, they are different constructs and must be considered uniquely.
- Explain how a multidimensional view of religiousness may be more helpful in understanding college students today.

ISSUE SUMMARY

YES: Religion scholar Diane Winston describes interacting with students at her university and finding that the students have vibrant religious engagements despite eschewing traditional types of religiosity.

NO: The study from Chelsi Creech and colleagues indicates that religion is better understood from a multi-dimensional perspective. They found first-year and upper-class students differed in terms of their religious attendance and reported daily spiritual experiences.

Interestingly, many developmental textbooks do not include information about religion or spirituality until their chapters on death and dying. However, we know that many individuals live religious and/or spiritual lives that do not begin at the end of life. Polls and surveys show that an overwhelming majority of Americans believe in the existence of God or a supreme being, and indicate that religion plays a significant role in their daily lives. Many Americans grow up in households that identify with a specific religious denomination, and children often have little choice about religious service attendance. In middle

and later adulthood, when most have settled into routines and communities, religious involvement offers an anchor. But in-between, with the relative independence that often accompanies leaving home and finding one's own path, religious involvement has been considered easy to set aside. That ease does not, however, make the relationship between young adults and religion an easy one.

One way of thinking about this topic is to consider an individual's religious identity development. Theoretically, it is considered one aspect of identity formation. Religious identity might refer to specific religious group membership regardless of one's activity of participation in organized events. Religious identify has many implications on identity development and one's sense of self; however, the crux of research using Erik Erikson's model of identity development has not focused on religious identity development. Instead, much work has been devoted to the study of ethnic, gender, and vocational identity formation. Researchers have examined and identified factors that impact the strength of religious identity over time, and found that gender, ethnicity, and generational status are important predictors.

An increasing number of studies have started to focus on religious identity, but there are some significant challenges in this work. Many researchers use religious identity, religiosity, and spirituality interchangeably. Does it necessary require involvement in religious congregations and attending services regularly? Or can religious engagement encompass more general spiritual explorations that involve searching for meaning in ways that may or may not include God? Until the 1960s, scholars did not consider religiousness and spirituality as separate constructs or belief systems. It was not until the past 15 to 20 years that researchers began making a distinction between the two terms.

In the 1950s and 1960s, not only did researchers begin defining these terms, they also shifted their focus to examine religion and spirituality in college students. Many studies noted a "religious revival" occurring on college campuses. In the 1970s, researchers started using multidimensional measures of religiousness and spirituality, understanding that these terms encompassed a variety of beliefs and behaviors. Through the 1970s and 1980s, researchers also looked at consequences for college students who endorsed high levels of religiosity and spirituality, finding that they tended to wield a positive influence on well-being. Interestingly, a split then occurred in which scientists and scholars viewed religion and spirituality as an additional (not necessary) part of an individual's life and development. Though research did not stop, it did slow down compare with that of earlier decades.

When researchers did return their attention to religious identify, they tended to study adolescents, not college students. Perhaps this trend reflects Erikson's original emphasis on adolescence as a time of identity exploration. However, the increased independence and diverse experiences of college life makes this an opportune time to study religious and spiritual development. Many colleges feature a diverse array of club and activities associated with different religions. Coursework may involve issues of religion and spirituality, either through religious studies department or other relating academic areas.

Today, scholars (and young adults) often distinguish between "religiosity" and "spirituality," with the former referring more to traditional religious practices and the latter referring more to personal attention to values, meanings, and one's "inner life." Religiosity or religiousness often refers to an individual's involvement with a specific religious institution and traditions. Some researchers find the terms are used relatively interchangeably despite attempts to specify the differences between them. It is almost a cliché among young adults to define themselves as "spiritual but not religious," and social scientists have usually observed the same pattern: contemporary young adulthood is often characterized less by traditional religious involvement than by exploring spiritual interests.

In the YES selection, Diane Winston, a professor of media and religion at the University of Southern California, offers the perspective of a teacher interacting with students around issues of religion and spirituality. She finds her students engaged in religion in innovative ways, committed to their own religious orientation while also intrigued to learn about other traditions. At one point, Winston notes, she had thought students would start merging religious traditions into a personal faith, but she finds that "cafeteria-style" religion less common than she expected. Drawing on both surveys and personal experience, Winston finds many college students committed to their faith while simultaneously curious about others.

In the NO selection, Chelsi Creech and colleagues investigated undergraduate college students' responses to measures of religiousness and spirituality. This selection highlights ways of measuring both constructs that cover a variety of beliefs and behaviors that may apply to college students today. The measure of religiousness used by Creech and colleagues was multidimensional, assessing ritual attendance, non-ritual attendance, and religious beliefs and practices. Three separate measures of spirituality were collected as well. The results of this study highlight the specificity needed when studying religiousness and spirituality. Differences were found on a variety of variables, including ritual attendance, non-ritual attendance, student year (first-year versus upper-class), and spirituality. The researchers emphasize the difficulty inherent in measuring these constructs, and call for continued student.

Returning to our lifespan perspective, the concept of an identity lockbox seems directly against the characteristics most scholars associate with emerging adulthood. Transitioning from the protections of childhood, but not yet committed to one's own family life, college can be a time of healthy exploration. Returning to Erikson's theory (and the work elaborating it by James Marcia), exploration and commitment are necessary for positive identity development. Certainly, many college students want to include religion in their explorations. But does that interest constitute genuine engagement?

YES ↵

Diane Winston

iFaith in the Amen Corner: How Gen Y Is Rethinking Religion on Campus

I had to ask.

If you saw one student, then another and another wearing an "I am a Whore" tee shirt around campus, wouldn't you want to ask?

My chance came when a young woman wore the eye-popping black shirt to class. But a big red patch now hid the bold letters of sexual provocation. The new message? "FORGIVEN."

Was it an upcoming film? A fabulous new scent? A velvet-roped all-night bar?

No, the reference was to the Biblical story of Hosea, the Hebrew prophet whom God commanded to marry a faithless prostitute. The account, understood as an allegory of God's unwavering love for Israel, is shocking on many levels—which is why 250 students chose it for their religious witness that spring.

The students, members of Campus Crusade for Christ, wanted to be asked what the shirts meant. That opening would allow them to share the good news that God loves and forgives us, whether or not we deserve it.

I work at the University of Southern California (USC) where 77 religious groups, representing everyone from Asian evangelicals to Wiccans vie for student support. That support is both greater and more tenuous than in years past. According to recent surveys, members of Generation Y—which includes today's college students—exhibit a deep and thoughtful commitment to religion and spirituality. But since they also are, in the words of one study, "redefining faith in the iPod era," they're not in the market for package deals. Instead they want to create their own playlists. So even if youthful fervor is growing, don't count on a new crop of listeners for the Old Time Gospel Hour.

The combination of religious commitment and intellectual independence initially confounded me. As a journalist and historian, I have tracked American religion for more than two decades. I thought I knew what an evangelical was. Sarah Glass, who'd worn the black tee to the class I teach on American religious history, obviously was one.

She'd averred the need to reach people—however, wherever—with the gospel message. But then she said she wanted to be a minister—an unlikely career choice for a female true believer.

"You can't limit God to whom he's going to call," Sarah told me, explaining why she did not agree with the evangelical prohibition against ordaining women. "The Bible is full of contradictions. In I Timothy, women are told to submit to men, but in Acts women teach men. God changes his mind all the time."

That's not the standard view at Campus Crusade, a 56-year old mission "to turn lost students into Christ-centered laborers." One of the largest Christian ministries in the world, the US arm of the international organization works on 1,300 campuses with over 55,000 students. Still, despite its immersion in the edgy richness of campus life, the group is not known for pushing the envelope on either social or theological issues.

But Sarah's mix of religious commitment and social progressivism squares with the findings of "OMG! How Generation Y is Redefining Faith in the iPod Era," as well as data collected by UCLA's Higher Education Research Institute on collegiate religion and spirituality. Both studies found a high level of religious tolerance and acceptance among college students. The UCLA survey focused more on beliefs, while Greenberg examined social and political attitudes, too. Her bottom line? "Respect for difference and diversity" is a core value. Members of Generation Y—even the most "Godly"—tend to be more liberal on social issues than their elders. Recent HERI data supports similar findings.

This coincides with what I've heard in classes. These new religious conservatives are eloquent in defense of gay rights and women's ordination. They are happy, even eager, to discuss their own faith, but go to great lengths to understand others: a staunch Catholic gingerly explained Mormonism's three-tiered heaven, an evangelical explored why some Muslim women choose to veil, and a young Jew grappled with the Religious Right. I teach in three different departments—Religion, Journalism, and

Communications—and students in each one invariably are curious about what others believe and why.

While other contributors to the SSRC Forum on Religion and Higher Education have analyzed the sociological, historical, theological and pedagogical issues surrounding religion on campus; the relationship between faith and reason, and the moral development of today's young people, my focus is the classroom. I am interested in how my colleagues' analyses look on the ground. And having compared my own observations with those from a range of colleges and universities nationwide, my experiences do not appear out of the ordinary.

Here at USC, some 10,000 out of 33,000 undergraduate and graduate students are on the campus' religious organization listserv, and 4,200 of these are actively involved in faith groups. Forty-seven percent of students consider themselves "above average" in seeking to integrate spirituality into their lives, and 67 percent say they understand other religions better since coming to USC.

Seventeen percent list their religious choice as different from either of their parents.

In 2006, freshmen completed an online assignment as part of orientation and were invited to state their religious interests. Of the 3,637 new students, 1,087 used the website to state a religious interest and 149 chose instead to fill in a low-tech postcard. Of the 1,236 responses, the largest number (1,072) identified as Christian: 235 Roman Catholics, 126 non-denominational and 99 Presbyterian (followed by 23 other denominations). The next largest number of freshman were Jewish (198), Buddhist (99) and atheist/agnostic (77)—followed by 14 other designations including Falun Gong, Pagan, Unitarian and Zoroastrian.

My own classes do not reflect such diversity. Although I teach in three different areas, the subject matter of my classes (writing about religion, religion in American history, religion and the entertainment media) leads to self-selection among students. The majority has some religious inclination (ranging from deeply committed to marginally identified) and a minority want to know why religion is such a big deal. This year's class in American religious history—the same one Sarah Glass attended two years ago—had 21 students who identified as Protestant (8), Jewish (5), Catholic (4), Muslim (1) and None (3).

This spring I also taught "Religion, Media and Hollywood," a Communications class that explored religion, spirituality and ethics in post 9/11 television drama. At the end of the semester I asked the 33 students to answer a short questionnaire I had written. Of the 20 who participated, 13 identified as Christian, 5 as nothing, one as Muslim and one as Jewish. Asked to select how religious and spiritual they were on a scale of 1 to 5 (one being the lowest and five highest),

they arrayed themselves evenly over the religious spectrum, but clustered at the high end of the one measuring spirituality. Twelve said this was their first college religion course while two were Religion majors or minors.

When I gave the Religion class the same questionnaire, 16 responded. Eight were taking a religion course for the first time while six were Religion majors or minors. This group skewed less religious and less spiritual than the Comm. students. Members of both classes listed prayer as a central religious practice, and several said they followed their own spiritual practices. A handful expressed a preference for the term religion over spirituality, noting the two were intertwined. Those who listed a religious affiliation were quite clear: They were Catholic, Methodist, Lutheran, Jewish or Muslim. Evangelicals called themselves Christian. But no one identified with more than one faith tradition. Overall, my modest data collection tracked with UCLA's findings from 112,232 students.

That was far from the experience I had when interviewing college students about religion and spirituality in the late 1990s. Working on a research project for Robert Wuthnow, I found many young people (and older ones too) who had constructed a spiritual regime based on religious sampling. One young woman—the epitome of this trend—was a Methodist, Taoist, Native American, Quaker, Russian Orthodox, Jew. But she was faithful in her fashion. She worked for world peace, practiced yoga and meditation, attended church, sat in sweat lodges, and participated in additional spiritual activities with her housemates.

At the time, I speculated that the growth of religious diversity in our society was paralleled by an increased diversity in individual religious practice. Inveighing against language that demeaned such eclecticism—specifically the whimsical yet market-driven description of "cafeteria-style" religion, I suggested the term "transreligiousity," a concept used by African scholars to describe conjoined spiritual beliefs and ritual practices.

Sadly, my bid to expand our descriptive vocabulary was no more prescient than my prediction of a new religious phenomenon. There has been no groundswell of students identifying in religious multiples. They are interested in learning about others' practices but not in adopting them. When I send out my class to explore local religious sites—visiting hitherto unfamiliar traditions from Sikhism and Hinduism to Wiccan and Self-Realization, they come back enthused by new discoveries but disinclined to integrate them into their lives.

Rather, students will try out variations within a familiar theme—Christians will go to InterVarsity, Campus Crusade and a Bible student fellowship—and stick with the one that feels right for them. If there aren't a lot of options, students make do with what exists: Jewish students attend Hillel, and Muslims gather at on-campus Islamic groups or nearby mosques. Religious students don't mix and match, they practice and participate. Even those from interfaith marriages fall on one side of the fence or the other.

At least most do, and those who don't are often seeking.

"My dad comes from a Jewish family in New York and my mom is a German Methodist," said one senior, who grew up in Santa Monica. Although his parents celebrated holidays from both traditions, he identified as a Christian—partly to distinguish himself in his heavily Jewish neighborhood. "Now I don't associate with a church but I'm graduating in two weeks so I've been thinking a lot about spirituality. I want something to hold onto before my life falls apart so I'm on a quest."

The USC students seem similar to their peers nationwide. The UCLA/HERI results—on the heels of 9/11, the Iraqi war and the upsurge of "values voters"—inspired a spate of stories on campus religion. Most reported an upswing in student interest and activity. At Stanford University, the Office of Religious Life reported half of the student body claim religious affiliation. The Rev. Scotty McLennan, Dean of Religious Life and a Unitarian Universalist minister told Stanford magazine that student interest in religion had doubled over the past 20 years, "The immigration laws of the '60s brought a lot of people from other religious traditions and our student body mirrors that. And another part is the failure of science and rationality to answer and solve all our problems."

At Oberlin College, Catholic chaplain Father Edward Kordas saw a similar rise in religious interest. "Some of them are flipping back to the spiritual forms of their grandparents," he told the college alumni magazine. Erica Seager, a senior when interviewed, agreed, "There has always been spirituality here. Ties to nature, service to others, people doing yoga. But definitely, in the last several years, there has been more interest in traditional religion and, along with that, an increasing desire of religions to work together."

It's the same story further east at Rensselaer Polytechnic Institute. According to the university magazine, "the Institute's religious population is larger, more active and more diverse than it was a decade ago." Rick Hartt, director of the Rensselaer Union and a member of RPI's class of 1970, reported significant differences between religion on campus then and now, "It used to be that your religious beliefs were private—except for Mass on Sunday morning. Now we try to create an environment where [students] can feel comfortable exploring their faith. I've really seen interest grow in the last five years. These students see the big picture."

The big picture, as the UCLA/HERI survey suggests, is that today's students "show a high degree of spiritual interest and involvement." To understand why, I tried an in-class experiment. After lecturing on the large sweep of 20th century American religion—highlighting post-war events including the Second Vatican Council, changed immigration laws, the Age of Aquarius, the integration of Jews and Catholics into the religious mainstream and the rise of evangelicalism—I asked students how their own family histories fit in.

Nick Street, my teaching assistant, and I began by discussing how our religious odysseys crossed paths with the Vietnam anti-war movement, psychedelicism, feminism, gay liberation, new religious movements, Southern Baptists, yoga, Buddhism and Reconstructionist Judaism.

I'd never before asked students to speak personally about their families or their religious identities, but the stories that Nick and I told established a level of trust and intimacy that enabled class members to speak freely. We subsequently discovered that five were children of first generation immigrants (who tended to have strong religious backgrounds) while another five had parents who had been "60s hippies" and wanted nothing to do with organized religion. Three were from intermarried families (one was raised Jewish and the other two Christian) and another five, who came from conservative Christian homes, remained so. Students raised in non-religious homes had little interest in becoming religious; several who had some religious education were still "searching."

"I'm open to everything," said a student who had attended Catholic, Lutheran and Baptist primary and secondary schools. "I've done lots of reading in Christian apologetics but I still have no idea what I believe."

Afterwards, students questioned each other. A non-believer asked an evangelical, "Can you accept me?" A Jew asked a Christian how she reconciled religious truths that were different from her own. A born-again asked an atheist why she got out of bed in the morning; in other words, what gave her life meaning. Great questions all, they underscored the challenges that religion poses in a secular, pluralist environment as well as the reasons why its study and practice has experienced a renaissance on many American campuses.

Two years ago, Stanley Fish, Dean Emeritus at the University of Illinois at Chicago, opined that religion "is now where the action is." While some may agree, others—steeped in the culture of secular fundamentalism—remain unconverted. Last fall, when a Harvard task force on curriculum reform proposed a "faith and reason" requirement, many faculty responded as if Al Queda had breached the ivy-covered walls.

Given longstanding intellectual paradigms, emotional prejudices and a pervasive system of financial rewards that work against the academic study of religion, can the field move from side show to center stage in secular research universities? When I posed the question at an American Academy of Religion meeting in 2003, I spoke from my position as a program officer at the Pew Charitable Trusts. Pew invested more than $30 million in ten centers of excellence to mainstream the study of religion at ten, top-tier research universities. As part of my portfolio I helped select and oversee the centers that the foundation hoped would end the ghettoization of religious studies.

On my own campus, the Pew-supported Center for Religion and Civic Culture (CRCC) has reinvigorated the academic discussion of religion through high-profile programming, funding for interdisciplinary research and leveraging Pew support to garner additional funding. Is religion center stage at USC? That is for others to decide, but CRCC's research and academic programs combined with extracurricular activities through the Office of Religious Life and faculty and student interest provide a high profile.

That's not to say that religion holds the same hallowed spot that engineering, business, and the sciences do. These areas attract the most funding, some of the best students and a significant slice of cultural capital. Yet religion has made inroads in each of these fields through programming, research and interdisciplinary projects that remind faculty (as well as students) that some of our most pressing questions—*why do you get up in the morning*—are religious in nature.

For me, these questions exemplify why religion has a central role to play in the academy. All our studies must be leavened by inquiries into the ethical and existential meaning of the knowledge we seek and the responsibilities it bears. But even though I believe these questions are fundamentally religious in nature, I am cautious about framing the discussions that follow lest I—or anyone else—appear to have ultimate answers. I balk when others try to impress their truth claims on me, as when evangelical colleagues claim that all truth is mediated through the Christian revelation. I am glad that many of our great universities are no longer religious institutions and I pray they remain so. I want my students to be free to choose which tee shirts to wear around campus.

"If Jesus came back he would be just as liberal for today as he was for his time," Sarah told me. "He'd go to the people whom nobody loves just like he went to the prostitutes and those who were unclean and unworthy. That's his example."

To drive home her point, Sarah wore another black tee shirt to a Campus Crusade meeting. This one read, "Gay? Fine By Me."

The leadership immediately pulled her aside.

"They wanted to talk about it and look at the Bible," she recalled. "I never saw anything in the Bible that said being a homosexual is evil. It says two guys having sex is bad, but not that you're going to hell if you're born gay."

After much discussion, Sarah and the leadership agreed to disagree.

"They gave me the postmodern view that everyone has to come to the truth their own way," she observed. "But I'm socially liberal and most of them aren't."

Me, I'm still coming to terms with a generation that doesn't automatically tie Biblical truth to social conservatism. If my students are indicative, these young believers may have more in common with nineteenth century evangelicals, crusaders for abolition, suffrage and labor reform—than with the today's Christian right. Now can somebody say Amen?

DIANE WINSTON holds the Knight Chair in Media and Religion at the Annenberg School for Communication & Journalism at the University of Southern California. A national authority on religion and the media as both a journalist and a scholar, her expertise includes religion, politics, and the news media as well as religion and the entertainment media.

Chelsi A. Creech et al.

Changing Trends in Ritual Attendance and Spirituality throughout the College Years

Introduction

Until the 1960s, religiousness and spirituality were not considered as separate belief systems (Hood Jr., Hill, & Spilka, 2009). For this reason, religion and spirituality were not researched as separate constructs until more recently (Zinnbauer et al., 1997). In the last fifteen years, a body of research has developed regarding the differences between the two constructs, but the constructs are operationalized in almost as many different ways as there are studies (Zinnbauer et al., 1997). In a 1993 study, Gorsuch suggested the following definitions: spirituality encompasses a person's beliefs, values, and behavior, whereas religiousness is a personal involvement in a specific religious institution and traditions (Hood Jr. et al., 2009). Some researchers, however, suggest that there is no such thing as spirituality outside of institutional religion (Hood Jr. et al., 2009). Other studies, such as Zinnbauer et al. (1997), show a frequent interchanging of the two terms, despite attempting to highlight differences between them.

In their textbook on the subject, Hood Jr. et al. (2009) high-lighted five key characteristics they say to separate the two constructs. Spirituality is personal and subjective, without an institutional or organized structure, and with high importance placed on commitments to personal values. It may not include a deity. Religiousness, by this definition, is a type of spirituality. It always involves spirituality and is objective, institutional and creedal, but spirituality need not always include religiousness. This confusion about the definitions has made concrete distinctions difficult to come by, but what has been clear is the growing trend in American culture to identify as spiritual and not religious, when participants are asked to self-identify. Most recently, in 2010 the Pew Research on Religion and Public Life Project (PEW), it is found that around 30% of the American public would self-identify as "spiritual but not religious". The 2012 PEW poll found that 20% of Americans do not claim any religious affiliation. Based on these numbers, it seems clear that people in general feel there is a difference between the two terms, despite difficulties in researching such differences.

Supporting the notion that religiousness may be a subset of spirituality, Kneipp, Kelly and Cyphers (2009) found that high scores on the Spiritual Well Being scale accounted for 16% of the differences between students on the Student Adaptation to College Questionnaire. Religiousness, measured by the Religiousness Measure/Demographic Questionnaire, only accounted for another 6% of the variance between the students. Along with suggesting that there is some overlap between the two constructs, this study also showed the importance of spirituality and religiousness in college adjustment. Those with higher scores on the spirituality and religiousness scales also generally had higher scores on the measure of college adjustment. However, this study looked only at the levels of spirituality and religiousness in the first year of college and did not track the changes that may occur throughout the college years.

Evidence suggests that levels of religiousness decrease throughout the college years (Uecker, Regnerus, & Vaaler, 2007; Astin, Astin, & Lindholm, 2011; Scheitle, 2011). However, Lee (2002) reported a decrease in ritual attendance during college, and also reported an increase in religious conviction across the college years. This finding is of importance because it focuses on what aspect of religion is measured in studies concerned with an increase or decrease in religion during the college years. Apparently, the issue of measurement originated in the early studies of religion which equated a decrease in ritual attendance with a decrease in religious belief (Feldman, 1968). More recently, Uecker et al. (2007) found that college students' religious convictions decreased less than their non-college attending peers. Based on this result, they posited that it was not a decrease in belief that changed, but rather only religious attendance.

Contradictory results were reported by Astin et al. (2011) who analyzed data from the Higher Education Research Institute's Spirituality in Higher Education project. Their results showed that students who self-identified as Christian as first year students and attended Evangelical-affiliated schools showed an increase in overall religiousness throughout college, but Christian students at schools of other affiliations or secular institutions decreased in religiousness, as measured by the Religious Tradition measure (RELTRAD). Students who self-identified as members of a minority religion (e.g., Buddhism, Islam, Judaism) and attended an Evangelical affiliated school decreased in religiousness. Catholic and secular institutions showed equal rates of decline in religiousness among all students. At the Catholic institutions, this was equally true of the Catholic students as well as those not affiliated with the Catholic religion.

The literature is unclear about the relationship between religion and the college years. The literature shows a decrease in religion, but it is unclear what is really decreasing—is it religious belief, conviction, or religious attendance? These discrepancies seem to be a problem of measurement, namely what is being measured; is it ritual attendance, or religious attendance, or religious beliefs or religious convictions. Additionally, it is notable that there is little research investigating the spirituality during the college years.

The present study investigated the relationship between religion and the college years by using a multidimensional measure of religiousness, which assessed ritual attendance, non-ritual attendance, and religious beliefs and practices. Additionally, this study investigated the relationship between spirituality and the college years by using three measures of spirituality, the Daily Spiritual Experiences Scale (DSES), the Spiritual Transcendence Scale (STS), and the Spiritual Involvement and Beliefs Scale (SIBS).

Method

Participants

Participants were 280 undergraduate students from a private Midwestern university. The study included students between the ages of 18 and 24 ($M = 19.91$, $SD = 3.47$). Of the 280, 190 were female (66%) and 196 were Caucasian (69%). There were 147 Catholics (52%), 56 other Christians (20%), 29 were atheist or agnostic (9%), 15 were Hindus (5%), 6 were Muslims (2%), and 25 were some other religion (9%). Two participants chose not to report their religious affiliation. Freshmen or first year students numbered 169 (60%) of the sample. Sophomore participants numbered 52 (19%). Juniors numbered 42 (15%), and seniors numbered 15 (5%). Because of the small N of juniors and seniors, they were combined for analysis, for an N of 57 (20%).

Measures

Spirituality Measures

The 2004 Daily Spiritual Experiences Scale (DSES) is measured by a 16-item index. Participants were asked to indicate how often they have certain spiritual experiences.

The responses range from never (coded 1), to many a day (coded 6). Items were coded in the direction that higher scores reflected a greater level of daily spiritual experiences ($a = .96$). Scores were summed for each respondent and then averaged across the 16 items. One of these items ("In general, how close do you feel to God?") is reverse scored in a 4-point metric (not at all, somewhat close, very close, as close as possible) instead of a 6-point likert scale. To be consistent with the directionality (Underwood, 2002), the raw score of this item is reversed coded and the 4-point scale is adjusted to fit the 6-point spectrum. The adjusted score is averaged for this subscale into the total for the resulting mean score. Further, the scale was divided into two subscales: a "theistic" subscale, with an alpha reliability of .95 and a "non-theistic (self-transcendent)" subscale, with an alpha reliability of .90 (Ellison & Fan, 2007).

The Spiritual Transcendence Scale (STS) is a 24-item scale, developed by Piedmont (2009), which consists of three subscales: universality, prayer fulfillment, and connectedness. Universality is the belief in the unity and purpose of life, prayer fulfillment is a feeling of joy and contentment that results from prayer or meditation, and connectedness is a sense of personal responsibility and connection to others. The scale items were answered on a 1 (strongly agree) to 5 (strongly disagree) likert-type scale. Piedmont (2009) showed these scales to have acceptable reliabilities for the subscales: .83 for universality, .87 for prayer fulfillment, and .64 for connectedness (Akyalcin, Greenway, & Milne, 2008).

The Spiritual Involvement and Beliefs Scale (SIBS) (Hatch et al., 1998) was designed to measure participants' spiritual status. It consists of four sub-scales. The first is the external/ ritual scale, which is a 13-item scale that reflects belief in a greater power. Second is the internal/fluid scale, with 11 items that reflect internal beliefs and growth. The third is the existential/meditative subscale, seven items which reflect existential issues. Finally is the humility/personal application subscale with four items that reflect humility and application of spiritual principles. Internal reliability statistics for three of the subscales are satisfactory: external/ritual, $\alpha = .98$; internal/fluid, $\alpha = .74$; existential/meditative, $\alpha = .70$) but perhaps, as Hatch et al. (1998) suggest, not for humility/personal application sub-scale ($\alpha = .51$). The internal consistency of the SIBS was reportedly high (Cronbach's alpha $= .92$) and presented a test-retest reliability of $r = .92$. This scale strengthens measures of spirituality by evading the usage of cultural-religious bias, and assessment of beliefs and actions (Maltby & Day, 2001).

Religiousness Measures

The PRI (Lipsmeyer, 1984) is a 45-item, nine scale, multidimensional measure of religiosity. The scales measure personal prayer (PRP); ritual attendance (RA); non-ritual, church-related activity (NRA); belief in God (BLFGOD); belief in an afterlife (AFTLIFE); perceived congruence of a person's religious beliefs with their attitudes on social and moral issues (RSM); the extent to which an individual's ideas about religion guide their philosophy or way of life (IDEO); the subjective experience of feeling close to God (CLOSEGOD) ; and integration or the extent to which persons perceive that their relationship with God influences their cognition, affect, and behavior (INT). Most of the items use a 6-point Likert response format; however, others use a multiple-choice or yes/no format.

According to Lipsmeyer, test-retest reliability coefficients over a one-week period were between .83 and .97 for the nine scales in an adult population. Additionally, Lipsmeyer found that the PRI had high concurrent validity; religious professionals (e.g., priests, ministers, nuns) scored significantly higher on all scales than the general public. Also, Lipsmeyer reported that atheists, agnostics, and those with no religious preference scored significantly lower than other major religious groups. Lipsmeyer reported that each subscale of the PRI correlated highest with integration (INT), and that it had the highest stability coefficient and was the best single measure of religion (Ross, Handal, Clark, & Vander Wal, 2009).

The Duke University Religion Index (DUREL) is a five-item measure of religious involvement that is incorporated in epidemiological surveys inspecting the affiliation between religion and health outcomes (Koenig & Bussing, 2010). This brief measure of religiosity was established for use in both cross-sectional and longitudinal studies. It evaluates three main dimensions of religiosity: organizational religious activity, non-organizational religious activity, and intrinsic/subjective religiosity. The scale assesses each of these components by a separate "subscale", and correspondences between health outcomes should be examined by subscale in different models. The scale as a whole displayed high test-retest reliability (intra-class correlation = .91), high internal consistence (Cronbach's alpha's = .78 − .91) and has high convergent validity with other religiosity measures (r's = .71 − .86).

Demographic Measure

The participants also completed a 22-item demographic questionnaire. These items asked about a participant's age, ethnicity, sex, religious affiliation, college living arrangement, volunteer and work positions, and finally whether a participant identified as spiritual, religious or both.

Procedure

Participants were recruited from undergraduate psychology classes. Some classes (approximately 66%) offered class credit for participation, while the other classes were not offered incentives for participation. Participants accessed the study via SONA, a university-approved research recruitment program, or through a link provided to them by professors who helped with recruitment. After accessing the study, they were directed to a link to the Qualtrics site that was hosting the survey. Participants first answered the demographic questionnaire. Next, the participants progressed through the Duke University Religious Index, the Personal Religious Inventory, the Daily Spiritual Experience Scale, the Spiritual Transcendence Scale, and the Spiritual Involvement and Beliefs Scale. Participants were encouraged to complete all sections in order, but were able to progress through the questionnaires at will. Participants were able to end the survey at any time, and were able to skip any questions they chose.

Results

In order to determine whether significant differences existed on the measures on religion and spirituality, a series of analyses of variance were computed and for significant F-values, follow up Tukey's HSD were computed to determine differences be-tween groups. Results of these analyses revealed that significant differences existed on measures of ritual attendance ($F(2, 286) = 5.09$, $p < .007$), non-ritual attendance ($F(2, 286) = 3.63$, $p < .027$), and the Daily Spiritual Experiences Scale ($F(2, 286) = 4.88$, $p < .008$). No significant differences were found on the other religion and spirituality measures.

Results for Ritual attendance revealed that first year students reported significantly higher levels of Ritual attendance (RA) ($M = 13.04$, $SD = 5.13$) than upper-class students ($M = 11.28$, $SD = 5.55$, $p < .01$). There were no significant differences be-tween the sophomore participants and either the first-year or the upper-class participants, with regard to ritual attendance.

Results for Non-Ritual attendance (NRA) revealed that, first year participants reported significantly higher levels of NRA ($M = 10.65$, $SD = 4.59$) than upper-class participants ($M = 9.27$, $SD = 4.56$, $p < .01$). There were no significant differences between the sophomore participants and either the first year or the upper-class participants, with regard to religious attendance.

Finally, first year participants reported significantly higher scores on the Daily Spiritual Experiences Scale

(M = 57.73, SD = 16.54) than upper-class participants (M = 51.56, SD = 18.56, $p < .009$). There were no significant differences between the sophomore participants and either the first year or the upper-class participants, with regard to religious attendance.

Discussion

The results of this study, namely that ritual attendance and non-ritual attendance decreases during college, support the findings reported by Lee (2002) and extend them in terms of our finding that non-ritual attendance also decreases during college. This later finding is not surprising since it may be expected that attendance at non-ritual church events would decrease because college students appear to be decreasing their attendance at ritual events.

It is notable that no significant differences were reported for the DUREL measure, which is a measure of religion. It is likely that differences were found with the PRI and not with the DUREL because the PRI is a multidimensional measure, with separate scales for each of nine dimensions, whereas the DUREL, although it has one item that asks about church attendance, consists of a total score, which precludes a sensitivity to the specific area of ritual and non-ritual attendance.

Additional results revealed that spirituality, as measured by the DSES, decreased during the college years. However, this finding did not occur on the other measures of spirituality, namely the STS and the SIBS. It is possible that these results are due to the fact that the DSES purports to measure how often certain spiritual experiences occur, while the other two scales purport to measure beliefs in unity, contentment, a greater power and other internal beliefs. It may be that the DSES is more experiential and the other measures are more cognitive. These results are intriguing and certainly require additional research.

This study reflects the existence of an ongoing difficulty in research in the area of religion and spirituality, namely the difficulty that exists in measuring the constructs of religion and spirituality. Contradictory findings may be explained by the difference in the measures employed in a particular study as operation definitions of the constructs of religion and spirituality.

Our results were found with a relatively small sample, which would lend itself to a Type II error. It would be important that additional research occur with a larger sample across each year level to replicate our findings and to determine whether a Type II error occurred on the other measures of spirituality.

References

Akyalcin, E., Greenway, P., & Milne, L. (2008). Measuring transcendence: Extracting core constructs. *The Journal of Transpersonal Psychology, 40*, 41–59.

Astin, A. W., Astin, H. A., & Lindholm, J. A. (2011). Assessing students' spiritual and religious qualities. *Journal of College Student Development, 52*, 39–61. http://dx.doi.org/10.1353/csd.2011.0009

Ellison, C. G., & Fan, D. (2008). Daily spiritual experiences and psychological well-being among US adults. *Social Indicators Research, 88*, 247–271. http://dx.doi.org/10.1007/s11205-007-9187-2

Feldman, K. (1968). Change and stability of religious orientations during college: Part I. freshman-senior comparisons. *Review of Religious Research, 11*, 40–60. http://dx.doi.org/10.2307/3510552

Hatch, R. L., Burg, M. A., Naberhaus, D. S., & Hellmich, L. K. (1998). The Spiritual Involvement and Beliefs Scale: Development and testing of a new instrument. *The Journal of Family Practice, 46*, 476–486.

Hood Jr., R., Hill, P., & Spilka, B. (2009). *The psychology of religion.* (4th ed.). New York: The Guilford Press.

Koenig, H. G., & Bussing, A. (2010). The Duke University Religion Index (DUREL): A five-item measure for use in epidemiological studies. *Religions, 1*, 78–85. http://dx.doi.org/10.3390/rel1010078

Kneipp, L. B., Kelly, K. E., & Cyphers, B. (2009). Feeling at peace with college: Religiosity, spiritual well-being, and college adjustment. *Individual Differences Research, 7*, 188–196.

Lee, J. J. (2002). Religion and college attendance: Change among students. *The Review of Higher Education, 25*, 369–384. http://dx.doi.org/10.1353/rhe.2002.0020

Lipsmeyer, M. E. (1984). *The measurement of religiosity and its relationship to mental health/impairment.* Unpublished Doctoral Dissertation, St. Louis, MO: Saint Louis University.

Maltby, J., & Day, L. (2001). Spiritual involvement and belief: The relationship between spirituality and Eysenck's personality dimensions. *Personality and Individual Differences, 30*, 187–192. http://dx.doi.org/10.1016/S0191-8869(00)00024-6

PEWResearch (2012). Religion and the unaffiliated. http://www.pewforum.org/2012/10/09/nones- on-the-rise-religion/

Piedmont, R. L., Ciarrochi, J. W., Dy-Liacco, G. S., & Williams, J. G. (2009). The empirical and conceptual value of the spiritual transcendence and religious involvement scales for personality research. *Psychology of Religion and Spirituality*, 1, 162–179. http://dx.doi.org/10.1037/a0015883

Ross, K., Handal, P., Clark, E., & Vander Wal, J. (2009). The relationship between religion and religious coping: Religious coping as a moderator between religion and adjustment. *Journal of Religion and Health*, 48, 454–467. http://dx.doi.org/10.1007/s10943-008-9199-5

Scheitle, C. P. (2011). Religious and spiritual change in college: Assessing the effect of a science education. *Sociology of Education*, 84, 122–136. http://dx.doi.org/10.1177/0038040711401811

Uecker, J. E., Regnerus, M. D., & Vaaler, M. L. (2007). Losing my religion: The social sources of religious decline in early adulthood. *Social Forces, 85*, 1667–1687. http://dx.doi.org/10.1353/sof.2007.0083

Underwood, L. G., & Teresi, J. T. (2002). The Daily Spiritual Experience Scale: Development, theoretical description, reliability, exploratory factor analysis, and preliminary construct validity using health-related data. *Annals of Behavioral Medicine, 24*, 22–31. http://dx.doi.org/10.1207/S15324796ABM2401_04

Zinnbauer, B. J., Pargament, K. I., Cole, B., Rye, M. S., Butter, E. M., Belavich, T. G., Hipp, K. M., & Scott, A. B. (1997). Religion and spirituality: Unfuzzying the fuzzy. *Journal for the Scientific Study of Religion, 36*, 549–564. http://dx.doi.org/10.2307/1387689

CHELSI A. CREECH is a student at Saint Louis University studying psychology and theology.

PAUL J. HANDAL is a faculty member at Saint Louis University. His research interests include relation of marital status, family climate and conflict on child, adolescent and adult adjustment; relation of religion, spirituality, and religious coping to adjustment; relation of death anxiety to adjustment; relation of physical/sexual abuse and witnessing violence on adjustment; primary prevention, community psychology and community mental health.

SEAN A. WORLEY is associated with Saint Louis University.

TRAVIS J. PASHAK is a clinical psychology graduate student at Saint Louis University.

EUNICE J. PEREZ is a clinical psychology graduate student at Saint Louis University.

LEA CAVER is a psychology student at Saint Louis University.

EXPLORING THE ISSUE

Do Religion and Spirituality Mean the Same Thing to Today's College Students?

Critical Thinking and Reflection

1. Why might college students be more or less religiously involved? What factors might influence their attitudes and behaviors?
2. How do religiosity and spirituality overlap? How are they distinct?
3. Do you believe religiosity or spirituality is more important for development?
4. What examples of nontraditional religious engagement among college students have you observed?

Is There Common Ground?

Given threats of terrorism, environmental disasters, and an uncertain economic climate, it is not surprising that college students look for a great meaning to their existence. Religion and spirituality offer the opportunity to question personal philosophy and practices. Both selections view attitudes toward religion and spirituality as an interesting dimension of college life.

Scholars debate the reasons for religious engagement and disengagement, but they often share an appreciation for college as a time when young adults could potentially explore their religious and spiritual life—something integral to development across the lifespan. Erik Erikson's original model of identity development stressed the importance of exploration before commitment. Questioning the role of religion and spirituality may be one way contemporary college students explore this particular aspect of their identity.

Create Central

www.mhhe.com/createcentral

Additional Resources

Johnson, C. V., & Hayes, J. A. (2003). Troubled spirits: Prevalence and predictors of religious and spiritual concerns among university students and counseling center clients. *Journal of Counseling Psychology, 50*(4), 409.

Kuhre, B. E. (1971). The religious involvement of the college student from a multi-dimensional perspective. *Sociology of Religion*, 32(1), 61–69.

Mayhew, M. J., & Bryant, A. N. (2013). Achievement or arrest? The influence of the collegiate religious and spiritual climate on students' worldview commitment. *Research in Higher Education, 54*(1), 63–84.

Internet References . . .

Institute for American Values

http://americanvalues.org/

Social Science Research Council

http://religion.ssrc.org/reforum

Society for the Psychology of Religion and Spirituality

www.division36.org

Selected, Edited, and with Issue Framing Material by:
Allison A. Buskirk-Cohen, *Delaware Valley University*

ISSUE

Is Facebook Bad for College Students' Health?

YES: Brian A. Feinstein, et al., from "Negative Social Comparison on Facebook and Depressive Symptoms: Rumination as a Mechanism," *Psychology of Popular Media Culture* (2013)

NO: Amy L. Gonzales and Jeffrey T. Hancock, from "Mirror, Mirror on My Facebook Wall: Effects of Exposure to Facebook on Self-esteem," *Cyberpsychology, Behavior, and Social Networking* (2011)

Learning Outcomes

After reading this issue, you will be able to:

- Discuss how social networking experiences may put individuals at risk for depression and other mental health concerns.
- Understand that some research shows that social networking sites, such as Facebook, may increase likelihood of negative social comparisons which are associated with rumination, one pathway leading to depressive symptoms.
- Understand that other research indicates that Facebook enhances self-esteem through selective self-presentation which leads to intensified relationship formation.
- Recognize the nuances in how individuals use social networking sites may help explain differences in research findings.

ISSUE SUMMARY

YES: Researchers Brian Feinstein and colleagues explore the link between use of social networking sites and depressive symptoms. Their study examined undergraduate students' use of Facebook. They argue that negatively comparing oneself with others is linked with rumination, which is linked with depression.

NO: The research from Amy Gonzales and Jeffrey Hancock presents a different view of the impact of social networking sites on mental health. Their research demonstrates how viewing one's Facebook profile actually enhances self-esteem through selective self-presentation.

Social networking sites (SNS) are platforms that allow individuals to build social networks with others who share something in common—typically interests, activities, backgrounds, or other connections. SNS are web-based services that allow individuals to create a public profile, create a list of users to share connections with, and link with other users within the system. Most SNS allow users to interact using some type of messaging system. They offer social, informational and communication tools, such as the sharing of videos, photos, and links to other sources. SNS emerged in the 1990s, with many of the early communities, like Geocities and Tripod, using chat rooms to bring users together. In the late 1990s, user profiles became a popular feature that allows users to create lists of "friends" and search for others who share their interests. By the end of the decade, new developments provided more advanced features to find and manage "friend" lists. Friendster and MySpace became extremely popular, and SNS had become a part of mainstream society.

One of the most popular SNS today is Facebook. It launched in 2004 and had become the largest SNS in the world by 2009. Founded by college roommates Mark Zuckerberg and Eduardo Saverin, Facebook was originally limited to Harvard students as a way to connect with each other. It then expanded its membership options to other Ivy League colleges. Facebook grew in popularity, and was incorporated in the summer of 2004. By September 2006, everyone age thirteen and older was invited to join Facebook using a valid email address. By late 2007, Facebook had 100,000 business pages that allowed companies to attract users and communicate with them. By early 2011, Facebook had become the largest online photo host. By spring of 2014, Facebook had over one billion monthly active users. (Active users are defined as those individuals who have logged in to Facebook during the past thirty days. This statistic means that Facebook actually has a greater number of total users than the number reported.)

SNS differ in terms of who their users are and how they behave online. According to the Pew Research Center, Facebook continues to dominate the SNS scene in terms of numbers of users. In the United States, women are more likely than men to use Facebook. It remains the top SNS for American adolescents; Facebook has more daily adolescent users than any other SNS. It is still considered a top site for college students. About one quarter of all Facebook users are college-aged individuals (ages 18 through 24). There are also differences in how users behave on Facebook compared with other SNS. The majority of Facebook users visit the site at least once a day, if not more.

Researchers have asked about potential consequences of Facebook use. Initially, people assumed that SNS would be beneficial, since there is a plethora of research showing the benefits of social contact. However, a study by University of Michigan psychologist Ethan Kross and his colleagues garnered the media's attention, with headlines warning readers about "Facebook depression." In the actual study, Kross and colleagues found that the more people used Facebook, the more their overall satisfaction declined. Past research has claimed that the Internet can be alienating, and tends to have negative socialization effects. The more people use the web, and Facebook in particular, the more lonely, depressed, and jealous they feel. However, some experts believe the opposite is true. Sebastián Valenzuela and his colleagues at the Pontificia Universidad Catolica de Chile found that using Facebook makes us happier. They also found that it increases social trust and engagement, and encourages political participation. The Pew Research Center's study of demographics also found that Facebook users are more politically engaged than other users.

In the YES selection of this issue, researchers Brian Feinstein and colleagues present findings from a study that help explain why Facebook use is linked with negative mental health outcomes. These researchers investigated two mechanisms that might explain this link by evaluating self-report measures from a large group of undergraduate college students. The first mechanism explored was negative social comparisons. They believed that Facebook use might increase likelihood of negative social comparisons, since users can see frequent updates of their "friends" accomplishments. Negative social comparisons can maintain or exacerbate negative self-appraisals, which lead to poorer well-being. The other mechanism they considered was rumination. Rumination occurs when an individual repetitively focuses on his or her own distress, obsessing over potential causes and consequences. It has been linked with negative mental health, including depression. In fact, Feinstein and colleagues did find that individuals engaging in negative social comparisons while using Facebook placed themselves as risk for rumination, and, consequently, depressive symptoms.

However, might Facebook use involve behaviors other than negative social comparisons? Indeed, in the NO selection, Amy Gonzales and Jeffrey Hancock's study focuses on the consequences of viewing one's own Facebook profile. These researchers suggest that the ability to socialize may have important positive benefits. For example, having multiple "friends" comment positively about a post might increase the user's happiness, at least temporarily. Specifically, Gonzales and Hancock investigated whether Facebook would increase self-esteem among users. The mechanism they explored was selective self-presentation through the hyperpersonal model. Joseph Walther developed the hyperpersonal model in 1996; it suggests that computer mediated communication has a greater ability to develop and edit self-presentation than face-to-face communication, so it creates a selective and optimized presentation of one's self to others. In terms of Facebook, individuals can carefully select the aspects of themselves that they would like to present to other users in terms of both text and images. When Gonzales and Hancock surveyed undergraduate college students, they found that viewing one's Facebook profile did enhance self-esteem through selective self-presentation.

Thus, the question of whether Facebook and other SNS are bad for college students' health is quite complex. Upon reading the YES and NO selections, you might reflect on your own SNS usage. It appears that Facebook use on its own may not be detrimental, but how one spends that time could be advantageous or problematic. Do you believe the results from either study are significant enough to warrant education of college students on SNS? Colleges might offer courses teaching how to use Facebook and other SNS to increase emotional well-being and avoid negative mental health outcomes. What's your opinion?

YES ⤶

Brian A. Feinstein et al.

Negative Social Comparison on Facebook and Depressive Symptoms: Rumination as a Mechanism

As social networking sites such as Facebook have become more popular, researchers have become increasingly interested in understanding the potential consequences of their use. Initially, it was suggested that Internet use was associated with negative mental health outcomes such as depressive symptoms. However, as data accumulated, the results became increasingly mixed; some studies supported the associations between Internet use and mental health problems (Kraut et al., 1998; Selfhout, Branje, Delsing, ter Bogt, & Meeus, 2009; van den Eijnden, Meerkerk, Vermulst, Spijkerman, & Engels, 2008), whereas others demonstrated positive effects of Internet use (Bessière, Kiesler, Kraut, & Boneva, 2008; Morgan & Cotten, 2003; Valkenburg & Peter, 2007). To reconcile discrepant findings, Davila et al. (2012) examined the amount of time spent engaging in social networking activities as well as the quality of interactions people had while using social networking mediums. Consistent with the larger literature on mood and anxiety disorders and interpersonal functioning, the authors hypothesized that poorer quality interactions, rather than use alone, would be associated with negative mental health outcomes. As predicted, in cross-sectional and 3-week prospective analyses, more negative and less positive self-reported social networking interactions were associated with depressive symptoms, whereas time spent engaging in social networking was not (Davila et al., 2012).

As Facebook use becomes virtually ubiquitous, it is important to continue to identify the specific behaviors and processes that may be "risky." Previous research on Facebook use has garnered a great deal of media attention, particularly a clinical report claiming that researchers had documented a phenomenon called "Facebook depression," or depression that results from spending too much time on Facebook (O'Keeffe & Clarke-Pearson, 2011). In fact, no research supports this claim, and, although scholars have attempted to clarify this (Davila, 2011; Magid, 2011), such false claims emphasize the importance of testing hypothesis-driven research questions that shed light on specific mechanisms that may lead to poorer well-being in the context of social networking. As noted, Davila et al. (2012) suggest that it is the quality rather than the frequency of social networking experiences that predicts negative mental health outcomes, but it remains unclear what specifically takes place on social networking sites beyond poor quality interactions that may be pathogenic.

Social networking sites provide venues for people to engage in a variety of behaviors, such as actively interacting with others (e.g., instant messaging), passively interacting with others (e.g., posting a message on someone's profile), and obtaining information about others (e.g., looking at someone's profiles). Similar to traditional social activities, these online activities provide individuals with ample opportunity to compare themselves with others on numerous characteristics such as appearance, popularity, and success. When people are presented with information about others, they tend to relate that information to themselves (Mussweiler, Ruter, & Epstude, 2006), and this social comparison provides them with self-evaluative information that can be used to make positive or negative self-judgments (Festinger, 1954). For instance, if a person sees that many of his or her friends are getting jobs and he or she is unemployed and having a difficult time getting a job, then he or she might feel inadequate in that domain. In contrast, if a person sees that many of his or her friends are unemployed and he or she has just gotten a job, then he or she might feel especially adequate in that domain. Importantly, social comparison is a pervasive and automatic feature of relating to others on an individual and group level (Pratto, Sidanius, Stallworth, & Malle, 1994; Sidanius, Pratto, & Bobo, 1994; Wood, 1989), making it nearly impossible to circumvent.

Feinstein, B. A., Hershenberg, R., Bhatia, V., Latack, J. A., Meuwly, N., & Davila, J. (2013). Negative social comparison on Facebook and depressive symptoms: Rumination as a mechanism. *Psychology of Popular Media Culture*, 2(3), 161–170. Reprinted by permission of American Psychological Association.

Social comparison is not in itself problematic, and indeed, even negative[1] social comparisons (i.e., comparisons with others who are perceived as superior) can have positive effects (e.g., self-improvement and self-enhancement; Wood, 1989). Still, negative social comparison can also maintain or exacerbate negative self-appraisals (for reviews, see Ahrens & Alloy, 1997; Suls & Wheeler, 2000; Swallow & Kuiper, 1988; Wood & Lockwood, 1999). Notably, individuals report increases in negative affect subsequent to negative social comparisons (Ahrens & Alloy, 1997; Antony, Rowa, Liss, Swallow, & Swinson, 2005; Giordano, Wood, & Michela, 2000; Wheeler & Miyake, 1992). Despite evidence that negative social comparison may lead to poorer well-being in general, little research exists on this process in the context of social networking. As an exception, a qualitative study found that users of MySpace, another social networking site, reported engaging in social comparison on the site and reported negative self-views subsequent to such comparison (Manago, Graham, Greenfield, & Salimkhan, 2008). Chou and Edge (2012) also found that individuals who spent more time on Facebook were more likely to agree that others were "happier" and "had better lives." Finally, Haferkamp and Krämer (2011) found that individuals who looked at profile pictures of attractive members of the same-sex reported less positive affect than those who looked at nonattractive members of the same-sex. This emerging body of research provides preliminary support for a social networking site such as Facebook to provide a context for engaging in negative social comparison, which may be associated with negative consequences.

In addition to examining the relationship between specific processes taking place in the context of social networking and mental health outcomes, it is important to understand the mechanisms that may account for these associations. One possible factor that may account for the association between negative social comparison on Facebook and depressive symptoms is the tendency to engage in maladaptive emotion regulation strategies, such as rumination. Rumination refers to repetitively focusing on one's distress, including its potential causes and consequences (Nolen-Hoeksema, Wisco, & Lyubomirsky, 2008), and has been consistently linked to negative mental health outcomes, including depression (for a meta-analytic review, see Aldao, Nolen-Hoeksema, & Schweizer, 2010). Although there has been little research on social comparison and emotion regulation, one study found that social comparison was positively associated with rumination (Cheung, Gilbert, & Irons, 2004). Building on these cross-sectional findings, the present study tests the hypothesis that negative social comparison on Facebook will lead to increases in the use of rumination as an emotion regulation

strategy. Given that negative social comparison may be associated with rumination, and that rumination has consistently been linked to depressive symptoms, it is likely that rumination may act as a mechanism through which negative social comparison increases depressive symptoms. Notably, Locatelli, Kluwe, and Bryant (2012) found that rumination mediated the association between negative status updates on Facebook and depressive symptoms. Although their study provides preliminary support for our meditation hypothesis, the current study extends this to social comparison and uses a prospective design to test changes over time.

In sum, to refine our understanding of the processes that render individuals at risk when using social networking sites, the current study used a 3-week prospective design to examine a mediation model, wherein it was hypothesized that negative social comparison on Facebook would be associated with increases in depressive symptoms 3 weeks later *through* its association with increases in rumination. We controlled for general social comparison tendencies (i.e., social comparison not specific to Facebook) to examine the *specific* effects of Facebook social comparison. Additionally, given that there are some data to suggest bidirectional associations between rumination and depressive symptoms (Nolen-Hoeksema, Larson, & Grayson, 1999; Nolen-Hoeksema, Stice, Wade, & Bohon, 2007; for an exception, see McLaughlin, Hatzenbuehler, Mennin, & Nolen-Hoeksema, 2011), we examined an alternate mediation model with depressive symptoms as the mediator and rumination as the outcome. By examining both models, we hoped to gain a better sense of the direction of the proposed mediation effect. The current study extended previous research in several ways, including examining a specific process that may put individuals at risk for depressive symptoms in the context of social networking, using path analysis to test mediation models to better understand mechanisms of action, and controlling for general social comparison tendencies to provide a more stringent test.

Method

Participants

Eligible participants were at least 18 years old and enrolled in a psychology course for which they earned research credits for study participation. The present study was posted on the online system used by the psychology department to advertise research projects and track student credit. Participants included 105 male and 181 female students from Stony Brook University. Nine participants did not complete the follow-up assessment (retention rate = 96%), and nine additional participants did not complete one or more of the measures.

These 18 participants were excluded from analyses; they did not significantly differ from the rest of the sample on gender, race/ethnicity, age, Facebook social comparison, general social comparison, rumination, or depressive symptoms (*ps* range from .07 to .68). The final sample included 268 individuals (62% female), with an average age of 19.66 years (*SD* = 2.29) and a racial/ethnic distribution including Caucasian (40%), Asian (42%), Latino/a (5%), African American (4%), Middle-Eastern (3%), and other (6%).

Procedure

Participants completed an online survey (Time 1; T1) consisting of questionnaires assessing social comparison (in general and specific to Facebook), rumination, and depressive symptoms. To assess change over time, a follow-up online survey was conducted 3 weeks later (Time 2; T2). Given that the surveys were administered online, respondents were able to participate from any location that had Internet access. Participants received course credit for their participation. This research was approved by the Stony Brook University Committee on Research Involving Human Subjects.

Measures

Social comparison on Facebook. The tendency to engage in social comparison when using Facebook was assessed with the Social Comparison Rating Scale (SCR; Allan & Gilbert, 1995), an 11-item self-report measure that presents respondents with an incomplete sentence followed by a series of bipolar constructs. We modified the instructions so that participants endorsed items based on social comparison while using Facebook. Specifically, whereas the original scale began using the stem, "In relationship to others I generally feel. . ." we used the stem, "When I compare myself to others on Facebook, I feel. . ." Participants selected a number from 1 to 10 that best described their perceived position between two poles (e.g., inferior/superior, incompetent/more competent, unlikeable/more likable, undesirable/ more desirable). We reverse coded and summed all responses to compute a total score in which higher values indicated more negative selfperceptions compared with others. Possible total scores could range from 11 to 110, and in our sample, ranged from 13 to 110 at T1. Allan and Gilbert (1995) reported internal consistency (alpha) of .88 and significant correlations with measures of psychopathology, including depression. In the current sample, the alpha was .94 at T1.

General social comparison. The general tendency to engage in social comparison was assessed with the Iowa-Netherlands Comparison Orientation Measure (INCOM; Gibbons & Buunk, 1999), which is an 11-item self-report measure. Participants were instructed to rate their degree of agreement with each statement, ranging from 1 (I disagree strongly) to 5 (I agree strongly). Sample items include, "I often compare how my loved ones are doing with how others are doing," "If I want to learn more about something, I try to find out what others think about it," and "If I want to find out how well I have done something, I compare what I have done with how others have done." Responses to all items were summed to create a total score, where higher scores reflected a greater tendency to compare oneself with others. Possible total scores could range from 11 to 55, and our sample had a large distribution (15–54 at T1). Gibbons and Buunk (1999) demonstrated internal consistencies (alphas) ranging from .78 to .84, 3 to 4 week test–retest reliability of .71, and significant convergent and divergent validity across numerous samples. The alpha was .85 at T1 in the current sample.

Rumination. Rumination was assessed with the Ruminative Responses Scale (RRS; Nolen-Hoeksema & Morrow, 1991). The RRS is a 22-item self-report measure that assesses how frequently individuals experience or engage in various thoughts, feelings, and actions during a depressed mood. Sample items include "Think about how sad I feel" and "Analyze recent events to try to understand why I am depressed." Each item is rated on a 1 (almost never) to 4 (almost always) scale, and responses are summed to compute a total score, which could range from 22 to 88, with higher scores representing higher levels of rumination. At both time points in our sample, we had a full range of scores. Excellent internal consistency and a significant correlation with depressive symptom severity have been reported (Nolen-Hoeksema & Morrow, 1991). In this sample, the alpha was .94 at T1 and .96 at T2.

Depressive symptoms. Depressive symptoms were assessed with the Center for Epidemiological Studies-Depression Scale (CES-D; Radloff, 1977). The CES-D was specifically designed for use with community samples and included 20 items assessing past week experience of depressive symptoms. Responses ranged from 0 (*rarely or none of the time*) to 3 (*most or all of the time*), with greater scores indicating greater depressive symptoms. Sample items included, "I was happy" (reverse scored), "I felt that I could not shake off the blues even with help from my family and friends," and "I felt hopeful about the future" (reverse scored). Construct validity, internal reliability, and other psychometric strengths of the CES-D have been widely supported (Radloff, 1977). Possible total scores could range from 0–60. In this sample, scores ranged from 1 to 44 at T1 and 0 to 51 at T2. The alpha was .88 at T1 and .89 at T2.

Results

Table 1 presents the means, standard deviations, and zero-order correlations for all of the variables. As hypothesized, Facebook social comparison was significantly and positively associated with general social comparison, and both were significantly and positively associated with rumination and depressive symptoms at both time points. Rumination was also significantly and positively associated with depressive symptoms at both time points. Notably, the correlation between Facebook social comparison and general social comparison was modest ($r = .18$), suggesting that they are distinct constructs.

Path analysis with measured variables was conducted using IBM SPSS Amos Version 20 to examine the primary hypothesized mediation model (see Figure 1). Path analysis has the advantage of being able to simultaneously test the associations among multiple predictor and outcome variables. The hypothesized model proposed that Facebook social comparison at T1 would lead to increases in depressive symptoms at T2 through increases in rumination at T2. Given the prospective design, we controlled for rumination and depressive symptoms at T1. Additionally, general social comparison was controlled for to test the specific effect of Facebook social comparison. To test the significance of the hypothesized indirect effect of Facebook social comparison on depressive symptoms mediated through rumination, we conducted bootstrapping analyses to estimate bias-corrected confidence intervals (cf. Mackinnon, Lockwood, & Williams, 2004). Less than 1% of the data from the final sample was missing, and it was handled by imputing a participant's mean score on a measure in place of a missing value on one of the measure's items. All paths included in the model were estimated freely, and two paths were not included, thus they were set to 0 (the path from T1 rumination to T2 depressive symptoms and the path from T1 depressive symptoms

to T2 rumination). Model fit was assessed by the comparative fit index (CFI), the Tucker–Lewis index (TLI), and the root-mean-square error of approximation (RMSEA), with acceptable model fit indicated by a CFI and TLI > .90 and an RMSEA < .06 (Hu & Bentler, 1999; Kline, 2005).

Results indicated that the hypothesized model fit the data very well, $\chi^2(2, N = 268) = 1.78$, $p = .41$, CFI = 1.00, TLI = 1.00, and RMSEA = .00 (90% CI = [.00–.12]). The model demonstrated that Facebook social comparison was significantly associated with increases in rumination, which, in turn, were significantly associated with depressive symptoms[2] (see Table 2). Bootstrapping analyses supported the significance of the indirect effect of Facebook social comparison on increases in depressive symptoms through increases in rumination, $\beta = .05$, bias-corrected 90% CI = [.02–.09], $SE = .02$. The direct effect of Facebook social comparison on increases in depressive symptoms was not significant in the model, but it was significant when the mediator (rumination) was not included in the model (standardized path coefficient = .11, $p = .03$). Together, these findings provide support for the hypothesized mediation effect. Further, the significance of the indirect effect of *general* social comparison on depressive symptoms through rumination was *not* significant, $\beta = .004$, bias-corrected 90% CI = [.02 to .03], $SE = .01$, suggesting that this effect may be specific to negative social comparison on Facebook.

Given that the mediator (rumination) and the outcome (depressive symptoms) were both measured at the T2 assessment, we also examined an alternate model with depressive symptoms as the mediator and rumination as the outcome. Results indicated that the alternate model did *not* fit the data well, $\chi^2(2, N = 268) = 9.36$, $p = .01$, CFI = .99, TLI = .90, and RMSEA = .12 (90% CI = [.05–.20]). Although bootstrapping analyses indicated that the indirect effect of Facebook social comparison on increases in rumination through increases in depressive symptoms

Table 1

Means, Standard Deviations, and Zero-Order Correlations

Variable	1	2	3	4	5	6	Mean (*SD*)
1. T1 Facebook social comparison	—	—	—	—	—	—	57.38 (16.95)
2. T1 General social comparison	.18*	—	—	—	—	—	35.68 (7.21)
3. T1 Rumination	.42**	.37**	—	—	—	—	49.63 (14.82)
4. T1 Depressive symptoms	.38**	.19*	.57**	—	—	—	12.89 (8.50)
5. T2 Rumination	.42**	.26**	.66**	.43**	—	—	48.07 (15.23)
6. T2 Depressive symptoms	.35**	.16*	.49**	.69**	.54**	—	13.07 (8.60)

*$p < .01$. **$p < .001$.

Figure 1

Path model depicting the significant indirect effect of Facebook social comparison on increases in depressive symptoms *through* increases in rumination.

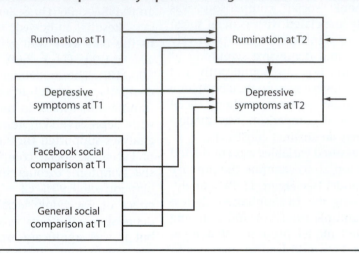

Note. Correlations among all T1 variables are included in the model, but not depicted for parsimony; paths representing the mediation component of the model are emphasized in bold.

was significant, β = .03, bias-corrected 90% CI = [.01–.06], SE = .02, this should be interpreted with caution because of the poor model fit. In sum, results provide stronger support for our primary model than our alternate model, suggesting that rumination mediates the association between negative social comparison on Facebook and depressive symptoms.

Discussion

As the use of Facebook becomes increasingly commonplace, it is important to identify the behaviors and processes that may place users at risk for negative consequences. Given the inherently social nature of Facebook, we tested the hypothesis that negatively comparing oneself with others

Table 2

Standardized Path Coefficients, Unstandardized Path Coefficients, and Standard Errors

Path	Standardized path coefficient	Unstandardized path coefficient	Standard error
T1 Facebook social comparison → T2 Rumination	.17*	.15*	.05
T1 Facebook social comparison → T2 Depressive symptoms	.03	.01	.02
T2 Rumination → T2 Depressive symptoms	.29*	.16*	.03
T1 General social comparison → T2 Rumination	.01	.03	.10
T1 General social comparison → T2 Depressive symptoms	−.02	−.03	.05
T1 Rumination → T2 Rumination	.58*	.60*	.05
T1 Depressive symptoms → T2 Depressive symptoms	.56*	.57*	.05
T2 Depressive symptoms error term	—	33.40*	2.89
T2 Rumination error term	—	125.97*	10.90

Note. → = predicting.

*$p < .001$.

on Facebook leads to increases in depressive symptoms. Further, to better understand the mechanism underlying this association, we tested the hypothesis that negative social comparison would lead to increases in rumination, and this passive and repetitive focus on distress would in turn be associated with depressive symptoms. We review key findings below.

First, Facebook social comparison, rumination, and depressive symptoms were all positively and significantly associated with one another. As noted, the correlation between general social comparison and Facebook social comparison was modest at T1 and nonsignificant at T2, suggesting that these are distinct constructs. When we included all of the variables in the proposed path model, we found a strong fit to the data. Specifically, controlling for the general tendency to engage in social comparison, negatively comparing oneself with others while using Facebook predicted increases in rumination, which in turn was associated with increases in depressive symptoms. The significant indirect effect of Facebook social comparison on depressive symptoms through rumination coupled with the nonsignificant direct effect with the mediator in the model provides preliminary support for the possibility that rumination does indeed mediate the association in question. Further, the nonsignificant indirect effect of general social comparison on depressive symptoms through rumination suggests that this effect may be specific to engaging in negative social comparison on Facebook rather than the general tendency to compare oneself with others. Notably, when we tested an alternate model with depressive symptoms as the mediator and rumination as the outcome, the model fit was poor. This provides additional support for the proposed direction of the mediation effect in our primary model, and it is consistent with previous research that failed to find a significant association between depressive symptoms and increases in emotion dysregulation over time (McLaughlin et al., 2011). However, other studies *have* demonstrated that depressive symptoms are associated with increases in rumination over time (Nolen-Hoeksema et al., 1999, 2007). Thus, although findings suggest that rumination may be a mechanism underlying the association between negative social comparison on Facebook and depressive symptoms, it will be important for future research to collect at least three time points and include the *prospective* association between the mediator and outcome.

Findings are consistent with and expand previous research in several meaningful ways. Consistent with findings that link negative social comparison with increases in negative affect (Ahrens & Alloy, 1997; Antony et al., 2005; Giordano et al., 2000; Wheeler & Miyake, 1992), we found

support for a significant association between Facebook social comparison and depressive symptoms in the zero-order correlations. This suggests that social networking sites can provide novel opportunities for individuals to compare themselves with others, and these comparisons can have negative influences on well-being. Further, this provides insight into what specifically may be happening on social networking sites that has the potential to be pathogenic—namely, comparing oneself with others who are perceived as superior. We also found that negative social comparison on Facebook predicted increases in rumination at a 3-week follow-up, which extends previous cross-sectional findings (Cheung et al., 2004). Why might this be the case? Some evidence suggests that individuals tend to self-disclose more positive information about themselves on Facebook compared with "real life" (Qiu, Lin, Leung, & Tov, 2012), and individuals who spend more time on Facebook are more likely to agree that others are "happier" and have "better lives" (Chou & Edge, 2012). As such, given that rumination involves passive and repetitive focus on one's distress, social comparison may provide ample opportunity to mull over causes and consequences of perceived inferiority.

Finally, consistent with the larger literature on risk factors for depression, we found that rumination was associated with depressive symptoms. If an individual ruminates on his or her perceived inferiority subsequent to negatively comparing oneself with others on Facebook, he or she is engaging in an emotion regulation strategy known to maintain and exacerbate distress. Nolen-Hoeksema et al. (2008) speculated that rumination may prolong and increase depression, in part, because it is associated with reduced interpersonal problem solving, less willingness to engage in pleasant activities to lift mood when given the chance, and more pessimistic views about positive events in the future. Thus, rather than problem solving (i.e., changing the situation that led to the negative social comparison) or switching the focus of attention to more positive or rewarding aspects of their environment, these individuals may continue to passively focus on distress (perhaps via increased time spent on the site) and/or seek out others in potentially problematic ways (e.g., corumination, excessive reassurance seeking). The significant indirect effect of Facebook social comparison on depressive symptoms through rumination is also consistent with a recent study that found that rumination mediated the association between negative status updates on Facebook and depressive symptoms (Locatelli et al., 2012). Together, these findings lend confidence to the notion that rumination may play a mechanistic role in the associations between negative social networking experiences and depressive symptoms, as two studies have now demonstrated similar meditational effects despite different predictor variables and methodological features.

It is useful to note that research on Facebook use and mental health has important public health implications. First, given the bidirectional and transactional nature of depression and problematic interpersonal functioning (see Joiner & Timmons, 2009), in order to continue to understand the bounds of their association it is incumbent upon researchers to examine interpersonal processes in the contexts in which they currently occur, which includes social networking sites. Next, the media has taken a particular interest in research on social networking, and has oft made large-scale claims about the "dangers" of Facebook use (e.g., "Facebook depression"). As scientists developing a programmatic line of research to test a priori hypotheses regarding Facebook use and mental health, we hope to shed light on the processes that may render individuals more vulnerable to negative effects of Facebook use.

The current study has several strengths, including a large and racially/ethnically diverse sample, a prospective design, and the use of path analysis to test the proposed mediation model. Nevertheless, it is important to keep in mind the following limitations that underscore the importance of replicating and extending these findings. We relied on a one-time selfreport assessment of social comparison tendencies, and findings would be strengthened by a laboratory manipulation of this process. Additionally, our sample was composed of nonclinical emerging adults and may not generalize to older or younger adults or a more clinically depressed sample. That said, that this effect was so robust in a nonclinical sample that commonly uses social networking sites is quite notable and suggests that this process may be especially relevant for those with elevated symptomatology. Consistent with current interventions designed to enhance adaptive emotion regulation (see Kring & Sloan, 2010), findings suggest that targeting rumination in a clinical context may minimize the negative consequences of engaging in negative social comparison. It will be useful for future research to test more complex models that account for the various types of maladaptive emotion regulation strategies that individuals may engage in to regulate their mood subsequent to negative social comparison on Facebook, as well as additional types of mental health outcomes that may be affected by these processes. Future research could also benefit from assessing specific behaviors related to rumination that may take place in the context of social networking (e.g., rereading posts on Facebook that contribute to one's dysphoria). Finally, our study focused on only one set of variables that may contribute to associations between Facebook use and depressive symptoms. Ongoing development of theory about the function of social networking, the contexts in which it occurs, and the ways in which it is related to self-concept and identity may provide new avenues of research that will allow for further understanding of its effect on people of all ages.

Notes

1. Several different terms have been used throughout the literature to describe the process wherein an individual compares himself or herself with others who are perceived as superior. Although most studies refer to this process as upward social comparison, others have referred to it as downward social comparison or negative social comparison. We chose to use the term negative social comparison throughout this article, as it seems to be the least ambiguous.

2. Given that rumination and depressive symptoms were both measured at the T2 assessment, it is worth noting that, in a separate regression analysis, rumination at T1 was associated with depressive symptoms at T2, controlling for depressive symptoms at T1 ($\beta = .14$, $p = .01$). Thus, even though the model included a path from rumination at T2 to depressive symptoms at T2, it is likely that rumination does, in fact, predict increases in depressive symptoms over time (as demonstrated by our data and previous research).

References

Ahrens, A. H., & Alloy, L. B. (1997). Social comparison processes in depression. In B. P. Buunk & F. X. Gibbons (Eds.), *Health, coping, and wellbeing: Perspectives from social comparison theory* (pp. 389–410). Mahwah, NJ: Erlbaum Publishers.

Aldao, A., Nolen-Hoeksema, S., & Schweizer, S. (2010). Emotion-regulation strategies across psychopathology: A meta-analytic review. *Clinical Psychology Review, 30*, 217–237. doi:10.1016/j.cpr.2009.11.004

Allan, S., & Gilbert, P. (1995). A social comparison scale: Psychometric properties and relationship to psychopathology. *Personality and Individual Differences, 19*, 293–299. doi:10.1016/0191-8869(95)00086-L

Antony, M. M., Rowa, K., Liss, A., Swallow, S. R., & Swinson, R. P. (2005). Social comparison processes in social phobia. *Behavior Therapy, 36*, 65–75. doi:10.1016/S0005-7894(05)80055-3

Bessière, K., Kiesler, S., Kraut, R., & Boneva, B. S. (2008). Effects of Internet use and social resources on changes in depression. *Information, Communication, & Society, 11*, 47–70. doi:10.1080/13691180701858851

Cheung, M. S., Gilbert, P., & Irons, C. (2004). An exploration of shame, rank, and rumination in relation to depression. *Personality and Individual Differences, 36*, 1143–1153. doi:10.1016/S0191-8869(03)00206-X

Chou, H., & Edge, N. (2012). 'They are happier and having better lives than I am': The impact of using Facebook on perceptions of others' lives. *Cyberpsychology, Behavior, and Social Networking, 15*, 117–121. doi:10.1089/cyber.2011.0324

Davila, J. (2011). *The "Facebook Depression" controversy.* Retrieved from http://www.psychology.sunysb.edu/jdavila-/webpage/facebook%20depression%20controversy.htm

Davila, J., Hershenberg, R., Feinstein, B. A., Gorman, K., Bhatia, V., & Starr, L. (2012). Frequency and quality of social networking experiences: Associations with depressive symptoms, rumination, and co-rumination. *Psychology of Popular Media Culture, 1*, 72–86. doi:10.1037/a0027512

Festinger, L. (1954). A theory of social comparison processes. *Human Relations, 7*, 117–140. doi:10.1177/001872675400700202

Gibbons, F. X., & Buunk, B. P. (1999). Individual differences in social comparison: Development of a scale of social comparison orientation. *Journal of Personality and Social Psychology, 76*, 129–142. doi:10.1037/0022-3514.76.1.129

Giordano, C., Wood, J. V., & Michela, J. L. (2000). Depressive personality styles, dysphoria, and social comparisons in everyday life. *Journal of Personality and Social Psychology, 79*, 438–451. doi:10.1037/0022-3514.79.3.438

Haferkamp, N., & Krämer, N. C. (2011). Social comparison 2.0: Examining the effects of online profiles on social-networking sites. *Cyberpsychology, Behavior, and Social Networking, 14*, 309–314. doi:10.1089/cyber.2010.0120

Hu, L., & Bentler, P. M. (1999). Cutoff criteria for fit indexes in covariance structure analysis: Conventional criteria versus new alternatives. *Structural Equation Modeling, 6*, 1–55. doi:10.1080/10705519909540118

Joiner, T. E., & Timmons, K. A. (2009). Depression in its interpersonal context. In I. H. Gotlib & C. L. Hammen (Eds.), *Handbook of depression* (2nd ed., pp. 322–339). New York, NY: Guilford Press.

Kline, R. B. (2005). *Principles and practice of structural equation modeling* (2nd ed.). New York, NY: Guilford Press.

Kraut, R., Patterson, M., Lundmark, V., Kiesler, S., Mukopadhyay, T., & Scherlis, W. (1998). Internet paradox: A social technology that reduces social involvement and psychological well-being? *American Psychologist, 53*, 1017–1031. doi:10.1037/0003-066X.53.9.1017

Kring, A. M., & Sloan, D. M. (2010). *Emotion regulation and psychopathology: A transdiagnostic approach to etiology and treatment.* New York, NY: Guilford Press.

Locatelli, S. M., Kluwe, K., & Bryant, F. B. (2012). Facebook use and the tendency to ruminate among college students: Testing meditational hypotheses. *Journal of Educational Computing Research, 46*, 377–394. doi:10.2190/EC.46.4.d

Mackinnon, D. P., Lockwood, C. M., & Williams, J. (2004). Confidence limits for the indirect effect: Distribution of the product and resampling methods. *Multivariate Behavioral Research, 39*, 99–128. doi:10.1207/s15327906mbr3901_4

Magid, L. (2011). "Facebook Depression": A nonexistent condition. *The Huffington Post.* Retrieved from http://www.huffingtonpost.com/larry-magid/facebook-depression-nonexistent_b_842733.html

Manago, A. M., Graham, M. B., Greenfield, P. M., & Salimkhan, G. (2008). Self-presentation and gender on MySpace. *Journal of Applied Developmental Psychology, 29*, 446–458. doi:10.1016/j.appdev.2008.07.001

McLaughlin, K. A., Hatzenbuehler, M. L., Mennin, D. S., & Nolen-Hoeksema, S. (2011). Emotion dysregulation and adolescent psychopathology: A prospective study. *Behaviour Research and Therapy, 49*, 544–554. doi:10.1016/j.brat.2011.06.003

Morgan, C., & Cotten, S. R. (2003). The relationship between Internet activities and depressive symptoms in a sample of college freshmen. *CyberPsychology & Behavior, 6*, 133–142. doi:10.1089/109493103321640329

Mussweiler, T., Ruter, K., & Epstude, K. (2006). The why, who and how of social comparison: A socialcognition perspective. In S. Guimond (Ed.), *Social comparison processes and social psychology* (pp. 33–54). Cambridge, England: Cambridge University Press.

Nolen-Hoeksema, S., Larson, J., & Grayson, C. (1999). Explaining the gender difference in depressive symptoms. *Journal of Personality and Social Psychology, 77*, 1061–1072. doi:10.1037/0022-3514.77.5.1061

Nolen-Hoeksema, S., & Morrow, J. (1991). A prospective study of depression and distress following a natural disaster: The 1989 Loma Prieta earthquake. *Journal of Personality and Social Psychology, 61*, 115–121. doi:10.1037/0022-3514.61.1 .115

Nolen-Hoeksema, S., Stice, E., Wade, E., & Bohon, C. (2007). Reciprocal relations between rumination and bulimic, substance abuse, and depressive symptoms in female adolescents. *Journal of Abnormal Psychology, 116*, 198–207. doi:10.1037/0021-843X.116.1.198

Nolen-Hoeksema, S., Wisco, B. E., & Lyubomirsky, S. (2008). Rethinking rumination. *Perspectives on Psychological Science*, 3, 400–424.

O'Keeffe, G. S., & Clarke-Pearson, K. (2011). The impact of social media on children, adolescents, and families. *Pediatrics, 127*, 800–804.

Pratto, F., Sidanius, J., Stallworth, L. M., & Malle, B. (1994). Social dominance orientation: A personality variable predicting social and political attitudes. *Journal of Personality and Social Psychology, 67*, 741–763. doi:10.1037/0022-3514.67.4 .741

Qiu, L., Lin, H., Leung, A. K.-y., & Tov, W. (2012). Putting their best foot forward: emotional disclosure on facebook. *Cyberpsychology, Behavior, and Social Networking, 15*, 569–572. doi:10.1089/cyber.2012.0200

Radloff, L. S. (1977). The CES-D scale: A self-report depression scale for research in the general population. *Applied Psychological Measures, 1*, 385–401. doi:10.1177/014662167700100306

Selfhout, M. H., Branje, S. J., Delsing, M., ter Bogt, T. F., & Meeus, W. H. (2009). Different types of Internet use, depression, and social anxiety: The role of perceived friendship quality. *Journal of Adolescence, 32*, 819–833. doi:10.1016/j.adolescence.2008.10.011

Sidanius, J., Pratto, F., & Bobo, L. (1994). Social dominance orientation and the political psychology of gender: A case of invariance? *Journal of Personality and Social Psychology, 67*, 998–1011. doi:10.1037/0022-3514.67.6.998

Suls, J., & Wheeler, L. (2000). *A selective history of classic and neo-social comparison theory.* Handbook of Social Comparison. New York: Kluwer Academic/Plenum Press Publishers. doi:10.1007/978-1-4615-4237-7

Swallow, S. R., & Kuiper, N. A. (1988). Social comparison and negative self-evaluations: An application to depression. *Clinical Psychology Review, 8*, 55–76. doi:10.1016/0272-7358(88)90049-9

Valkenburg, P. M., & Peter, J. (2007). Preadolescents' and adolescents' online communication and their closeness to friends. *Developmental Psychology, 43*, 267–277. doi:10.1037/0012-1649.43.2.267

van den Eijnden, R. M., Meerkerk, G., Vermulst, A. A., Spijkerman, R., & Engels, R. E. (2008). Online communication, compulsive Internet use, and psychosocial well-being among adolescents: A longitudinal study. *Developmental Psychology, 44*, 655–665. doi:10.1037/0012-1649.44.3.655

Wheeler, L., & Miyake, K. (1992). Social comparisons in everyday life. *Journal of Personality and Social Psychology, 62*, 760–773. doi:10.1037/0022-3514.62.5.760

Wood, J. V. (1989). Theory and research concerning social comparisons of personal attributes. *Psychological Bulletin, 106*, 231–248. doi:10.1037/0033-2909.106.2.231

Wood, J. V., & Lockwood, P. (1999). Social comparisons in dysphoric and low self-esteem people. In R. Kowalski & M. Leary (Eds.), *The social psychology of emotional and behavioral problems: Interfaces of social and clinical psychology* (pp. 97–135), Washington, DC: American Psychological Association. doi:10.1037/10320–004.

BRIAN A. FEINSTEIN is a doctoral candidate at SUNY Stony Brook. His research interests include ways in which psychopathology and interpersonal relationships affect one another, with an emphasis on the unique ways in which sexual orientation and other minority statuses (e.g., race, gender) influence these domains.

RACHEL HERSHENBERG is postdoctoral research fellow at the Philadelphia VA and University of Pennsylvania School of Medicine. Her research interests include depression, positive emotions, interpersonal behavior, behavioral activation, and evidence-based practice and clinical training.

VICKIE BHATIA is a doctoral candidate at SUNY Stony Brook. Her research focuses on examining the mechanisms involved in the bidirectional relationship between depression and romantic relationship dysfunction.

JESSICA A. LATACK is a doctoral candidate at SUNY Stony Brook. Her research focuses on the ways in which childhood sexual abuse and later sexual trauma may affect individuals' behavior in adult romantic relationships.

NATHALIE MEUWLY is a research fellow of the University of Fribourg, Switzerland. She is interested in what role intimate relationships play for our well-being and health, particularly within adolescent relationships.

JOANNE DAVILA is a psychology faculty member at SUNY Stony Brook. Her research focuses on the development and course of interpersonal functioning and psychopathology among adolescents and adults, with a particular emphasis on the interpersonal causes and consequences of depression and anxiety disorders, risk factors for the early development of romantic relationship dysfunction in adolescents, the role of attachment representations in interpersonal functioning, and well-being among LGBT individuals.

**Amy L. Gonzales and
Jeffrey T. Hancock**

 **NO**

Mirror, Mirror on My Facebook Wall: Effects of Exposure to Facebook on Self-Esteem

Introduction

Over a decade ago, INTERNET USE WAS THOUGHT to promote negative psychosocial well-being, including depression and loneliness.[1] Having attracted attention in and out of the research community, these findings prompted researchers to take a more nuanced look at the relationship between Internet use and psychosocial health,[2,3] at times finding evidence that Internet use could be beneficial.[3,4] The present study extends this research by examining the effects of the social-networking site Facebook (http://facebook.com), which represents a popular new form of Internet communication, on self-esteem.

Previous work has addressed the role of Facebook and the ability to socialize, and the role that socializing online plays in supporting self-esteem and various forms of social capital.[5,6] For example, one recent study found that Facebook can enhance "social self-esteem," measured as perceptions of one's physical appearance, close relationships, and romantic appeal, especially when users received positive feedback from Facebook friends.[5] Also, individuals with low self-esteem may see particularly positive benefits from the social opportunities provided by Facebook.[6]

The effect of Facebook exposure on general self-esteem has not been explored. Yet Facebook, and other social-network sites, have the potential to affect temporary states of self-esteem. Social-network sites are designed to share information about the self with others, including likes/dislikes, hobbies, and personal musings via "wall posts," and "status updates." This information could make people aware of their own limitations and shortcomings, which would lower self-esteem,[7] or it could be that this information represents selective and therefore positively biased aspects of the self, which might raise self-esteem.[8] Does Facebook operate on self-esteem in the same way non-digital information does, by decreasing self-esteem? Or does the opportunity to present more positive information about the self

while filtering negative information mean that reviewing one's own Facebook site enhances self-esteem? The following piece examines these questions, by exploring the theoretical predictions of Objective Self-Awareness (OSA) theory[9] and the Hyperpersonal Model.[8]

Objective Self-Awareness

One theoretical approach relevant to the effects of social-networking sites on self-esteem is OSA theory, one of the first experimentally tested psychological theories of the self. The theory assumes that humans experience the self as both subject and object.[9] For example, the self as subject is found in daily experiences of life (e.g., waiting for the bus, eating lunch, watching TV[10]). In those experiences the self is an active participant in life and is not self-conscious. However, people become the "object of [their] own consciousness" when they focus attention on the self,[9 (p2)] which can have both positive and negative effects.

In a state of objective self-awareness, Duval and Wicklund[9] claim that people are prone to self-evaluations based on broader social standards and norms. This usually results in a greater sense of humility, or downgraded ratings of self, and increased pro-social behavior. For example, people report feeling greater responsibility for social injustice,[11] or are less likely to take an extra helping of candy without being observed.[12] On the other hand, because most people often fall short of social standards when self-awareness is heightened, positive affect and self-esteem typically decrease when people are exposed to objective self-awareness stimuli.[13]

The stimuli used to evoke objective self-awareness is most commonly a mirror,[13] although other stimuli include images of the self,[14] audio feedback,[15] having a video camera pointed at participants,[16] or having participants write autobiographical information.[11] These stimuli cause people to view themselves as they believe others do, even if they are not immediately under observation. Exposure

Gonzales, A. L., & Hancock, J. T. (2011). Mirror, mirror on my Facebook wall: Effects of exposure to Facebook on self-esteem. *Cyberpsychology, Behavior, and Social Networking*, 14(1–2), 79–83. Reprinted by permission of Mary Ann Liebert, Inc.

to these stimuli is what leads to pro-social behavior and decreases in self-esteem.

Given that social-networking profiles include information about the self similar to the type of information that is used to prompt objective self-awareness (e.g., photos, autobiographical information), viewing one's profile should prompt a downgrading of self-esteem according to OSA theory. That is, viewing one's Facebook profile should negatively affect one's self-esteem. Furthermore, research in computer-mediated communication has found that information online is often over-interpreted relative to the same information provided offline,[17] leading to exaggerated or stereotyped impressions.[18] Is it possible that this same process could occur for impressions of the self? If Facebook acts on self-esteem in the same way as previous OSA stimuli, only to a more extreme degree, one prediction is:

H1: Exposure to one's Facebook site will have a more negative effect on self-esteem than traditional objective self-awareness stimuli (e.g., mirror).

Selective Self-Presentation

A second relevant theoretical approach to understanding effects of Facebook use is the Hyperpersonal Model.[8] Walther posits that affordances of the Internet allow users to *selectively self-present* themselves in asynchronous media. People can take their time when posting information about themselves, carefully selecting what aspects they would like to emphasize. Evidence of selective self-presentation is found in a variety of Internet spaces, including e-mails,[19] discussion boards,[20] and online dating Web sites.[21,22]

In addition to evidence that online self-presentations are especially positive presentations, recent research in computer-mediated communication (CMC) suggests that online self-presentations can become integrated into how we view ourselves, especially when the presentations take place in a public, digital space.[23] This phenomenon, known as *identity shift*, demonstrates that self-presentations enacted in online space can impact users' self-concepts.

Self-presentations online can be optimized through selective self-presentation, and online self-presentation affects attitudes about the self. Facebook profiles may provide sufficiently positively biased stimuli to counter the traditional effects of objective self-awareness, and instead prompt a positive change in self-esteem. From this perspective, the hyperpersonal prediction of exposure to Facebook is:

H2: Exposure to one's Facebook site will have a more positive effect on self-esteem than a control condition or traditional self-awareness stimuli (e.g., mirror).

Furthermore, if exposure to one's own Facebook profile increases self-esteem due to selective self-presentation, then behaviors associated with selective self-presentation should correlate with changes in self-esteem. For example, because self-stimuli are most likely to be on one's own profile page, we would expect that participants who only view their own profile page would report higher self-esteem than participants who view other profiles within Facebook. Thus:

H3: Participants who exclusively examine only their own profile will report higher self-esteem than participants who view other profiles in addition to their own profiles.

Finally, selective self-presentation should be reflected primarily in editing of one's online self-presentation, according to Walther.[8] That is, the ability to edit one's self-presentation after the fact is a unique attribute of asynchronous, textbased communication. Thus, according to the Hyperpersonal Model, we predict that:

H4: Participants who make changes to their profile during the experiment will report higher self-esteem than participants who do not.

Each of these predictions is tested in the following study, comparing the effect of viewing one's Facebook site, viewing one's own image in a mirror, and being in a control condition on self-reported self-esteem.

Methods

Participants

A total of 63 students (16 males, 47 females) from a large, Northeastern university participated in this study for extra credit. The study consisted of three conditions: exposure to a mirror, exposure to one's own Facebook site, and a control condition in which participants used the same room without any treatment. Participants were randomly assigned to one of the three conditions, with a total of 21 participants taking part in each of the three conditions.

Procedure

Each participant was told that the study was designed to examine "people's attitudes about themselves after exploring different Internet sites." People in both offline conditions were told that they were in a control condition, and thus would not be online. In the online condition, participants were asked to examine their own Facebook site.

In the Facebook stimulus condition, after logging on to Facebook, participants were instructed to click on the "Profile" tab after the experimenter left the room. The profile page contains the primary source of information on an individual user. Participants were told to look through any of the tabs on that page (Wall posts, Photos, Info, Boxes). Participants were given no specific instructions about making changes to their profile during the study. In addition to the main profile photo, the profile page has information on recent activity on Facebook sent to and from the site owner, personal demographic information, photos, and quizzes completed by the site owner. After being on Facebook for 3 minutes, the experimenter returned with a survey. Participants were instructed to keep the profile page open while completing the questionnaire.

Participants in the offline conditions were taken to the same small computer cubicle used in the online condition. In the objective self-awareness stimulus condition, a mirror was placed against the computer screen. To reduce suspicion of the mirror, they were also told that the cubicle was being used for another experiment and that they should not move anything. Other items were laid about the room in all conditions (e.g., intercoms, a television) in order to enhance the perception that the room was being used for another experiment. Participants were given a survey of questions, which were answered while being exposed to their own reflection in the mirror.

In the offline control condition, participants sat in the same room as participants in the previously mentioned two conditions, but without the mirror present and without the computer screen turned on. Participants were left with the survey and given instructions to buzz the experimenter when they had finished completing the survey. In all conditions, experimenters returned to collect the survey, and participants were then debriefed and probed for suspicion or failure to comply with instruction.

Measures

Self-esteem. Self-esteem was measured using the Rosenburg Self-Esteem scale,[24] in which 10 items were used to assess self-esteem ($\alpha = 0.82$). Half of the items were reverse coded. Responses were scored on a 4-point scale, ranging from "strongly agree" to "strongly disagree." Although this scale is generally used to measure trait self-esteem, as mentioned above, previous studies of objective self-awareness have used this measure to capture temporary changes in self-esteem due to awareness-enhancing stimuli.[7]

Selective self-presentation. In order to examine behaviors predicted by the Hyperpersonal Model, we asked participants in the Facebook condition about their behavior while they were on Facebook. Questions included, "Did you leave your profile at any time during the study?" ($1 = $ "yes," $2 = $ "no"), and "Did you change your profile while you were on the Web site?" ($1 = $ "yes," $2 = $ "no").

Results

To establish that the objective self-awareness stimuli had an effect on self-esteem, an analysis of variance (ANOVA) was first performed. Gender was also included in the model as a covariate, given previous research suggesting that gender may predict differences in self-esteem.[25] The following analyses all reflect significant differences using two-tailed tests of significance, unless otherwise noted. Indeed, the stimuli did have an effect on self-esteem, $F(1, 59) = 4.47$, $p = 0.02$, $n^2 = 0.13$. However, gender was not a significant predictor of self-esteem, $F(1, 60) = 0.94$, $p = 0.34$. This finding reveals that self-reported self-esteem did vary by condition.

To test the hypothesis that Facebook had a more negative effect on self-esteem than traditional objective self-awareness stimulus (H1), a linear contrast analysis was performed with a weight 0 assigned to the traditional objective self-awareness stimulus condition (i.e., mirror, $M = 2.97$, $SD = 0.51$), a weight of -1 assigned to the Facebook condition ($M = 3.35$, $SD = 0.37$), and a weight of 1 assigned to the control condition ($M = 3.23$, $SD = 0.40$). The results of this test were not significant, $F(1, 60) = 0.95$, $p = 0.33$.

To test the opposing hypothesis that Facebook has a positive impact on self-esteem (H2), a different linear contrast analysis was performed. A contrast weight of -1 was assigned to the traditional objective self-awareness stimuli condition, 0 was assigned to the control condition, and $+1$ was assigned to the Facebook condition. This contrast analysis was significant, $F(1, 59) = 8.60$, $p < 0.01$, $n^2 = 0.13$, demonstrating support for H2 and suggesting that Facebook has a positive effect on self-esteem relative to a traditional objective self-awareness stimulus.

Given that viewing Facebook enhanced self-esteem, is there additional evidence that the process of selective self presentation was responsible for influencing self-esteem? Our first method of testing this question included examining whether participants who exclusively viewed their own profile reported having higher self-esteem than participants who also viewed the profiles of others. An ordinary least squares (OLS) regression of self-esteem on viewing behavior (self-only profile vs. self and other profiles) and gender revealed a significant effect on viewing behavior, $b = 0.40$, $p = 0.03$ (one-tailed, $1 = $ "yes," $2 = $ "no"), indicating that participants who left their profile during the study reported lower self-esteem than those participants who exclusively viewed their own profile site, supporting H3. The relationship between gender and self-esteem was not significant, $b = 0.33$, $p = 0.12$ (1 = female, 2 = male).

Finally, we expected that changes to any part of the profile (i.e., status, photo, etc.) during the study would increase participant self-esteem (H4), as editing is a primary means of optimizing self-presentation, according to the Hyperpersonal Model.[8] We tested this hypothesis using OLS regression, and once again included gender in the analysis. In support of this hypothesis, participants who changed their profile during the study reported higher self-esteem than those who did not change their profile, $b = \_0.53$, $p = 0.01$, (1 = "yes," 2 = "no"). These data suggest that, because asynchronous social-network profiles allow for added time and energy to construct positive self-presentations, profiles contain information that prompts positive, rather than negative, effects on self-esteem. Men reported having greater self-esteem than women after controlling for the likelihood that participants changed their profile, $b = 0.45$, $p = 0.03$. However, this result cannot be fairly interpreted due to the very small number of men (17 women, 4 men).

Discussion

This study was designed to test the effects of exposure to Facebook on self-esteem relative to traditional self-awareness enhancing stimuli, such as a mirror or photo of oneself. The study suggests that selective self-presentation, afforded by digitally mediated environments can have a positive influence on self-esteem.

These findings are in contrast to predictions from OSA theory, which posits that stimuli that prompt self-awareness (e.g., mirror, photo, autobiographical information) activate discrepancies between oneself and social standards,[9] and consequently lower self-esteem.[13,15] Instead, the results demonstrate that exposure to information presented on one's Facebook profile enhances self-esteem, especially when a person edits information about the self, or *selectively self-presents*. These findings are consistent with Walther's Hyperpersonal Model[8] and suggest that the process of *selective self-presentation*, which takes place in mediated spaces due to increased time for creating a self-presentation, makes Facebook a unique awareness-enhancing stimuli.

This study is a preliminary step toward understanding how selective self-presentation processes, which have been previously discussed in the context of interpersonal impression formation,[19,20,22] may also influence impressions of the self. Whereas a non-edited view of the self

(i.e., mirror) is likely to decrease self-esteem, these findings suggest that the extra care involved in digital self-presentations may actually improve self-esteem. By allowing people to present preferred or positive information about the self, Facebook is a unique source of self-awareness stimuli in that it enhances awareness of the optimal self. This finding is consistent with previous work that has found that digital self-presentations can shape self-assessments.[23] In this case, however, the findings are striking because they contradict previous work on the negative effect of self-awareness enhancing information on self-assessments.

Previous work examining self-esteem suggests that consistency between the actual and the ideal self is an important factor in understanding how information can affect self-esteem.[26] Although participant perceptions between the actual and ideal self were not measured, it is possible that Facebook activates the ideal self. Future research on implications of self evaluations on self-esteem is needed to test this possibility.

Facebook may also be unique in that the public nature of the site may contribute to objective self-awareness. In previous work, autobiographical information or photos have prompted objective self-awareness.[11,14,15] We tested OSA in Facebook because these features are present there. However, Facebook is a public site, which should also remind users of self-evaluation. In this case, the same information that is prompting OSA is *actually* viewed and evaluated by others as well. Further work is necessary to determine whether public Internet audiences alone may stimulate OSA. In this case, we can only speculate that the high visibility of one's Facebook profile further adds to a sense of objective self-awareness. The difference is that that while Facebook may prime awareness of an audience and self-evaluation, it is a more optimal self that is being evaluated. Thus the effect of self-esteem is positive rather than negative.

Limitations

An important limitation of this study was our failure to account for the effect of the number of Facebook friends on self-esteem. As previous research has demonstrated, the social opportunities in Facebook contribute to an enhanced feeling of social competence.[5,6] We cannot rule out the possibility that reminders of one's social connections are partially responsible for the increase in self-esteem. On the other hand, social connection does not seem to be completely responsible for this effect. Changes to one's profile and attention to one's profile (vs. others' profiles) have a positive effect on self-esteem, which suggests that selective self-presentation is a factor in shaping the resultant self-reports of self-esteem.

Another limitation is that we cannot know the long term implications of using Facebook on self-esteem from a single study. The measure of self-esteem used in this study is generally used as a measure of stable self-esteem, but has been used on other occasions to measure temporary shifts in self-esteem.[7,13,15] Though difficult to perform in an experimental setting, research that examines long-term effects of social network sites, such as Facebook, would be valuable. Also, incorporating pre- and post-test measures of self-esteem and other relevant psychological measures would be useful in future work.

The focus in the present study is on Facebook, although we make arguments about social-network sites in general regarding their effect on self-esteem. While future research will be required to extend these findings beyond Facebook, the Facebook interface has several advantages over other sites, such as MySpace (http://myspace.com), including a more uniform layout and the sheer popularity of the site. Given that every person must view their own site, the increased uniformity and popularity of Facebook made it a useful starting point for examining digital self-awareness stimuli and self-esteem.

Finally, participants in the offline conditions did not have the same 3-minute lapse between coming into the room and completing the questionnaire as participants in the Facebook condition. We were concerned, however, that including a filler task would potentially introduce an additional and unintended manipulation into the study. It seems unlikely that the time lapse alone was part of the reason for the different ratings of self-esteem, but to be sure, future research will need to account for this effect by providing an appropriate filler task for participants in the non-digital environments.

Conclusion

The Internet has not created new motivation for self presentation, but provides new tools to implement such motives. The negative effects of objective self-awareness on self-esteem originated from work in the early 1970s.[9,13-15] Social-networking sites, a product of the 21st century, provide new access to the self as an object. By providing multiple opportunities for selective self-presentation—through photos, personal details, and witty comments—social-networking sites exemplify how modern technology sometimes forces us to reconsider previously understood psychological processes. Theoretical development can benefit from expanding on previous "offline" theories by incorporating an understanding of how media may alter social processes.

References

1. Kraut R, Patterson M, Lundmark V, et al. Internet paradox: A social technology that reduces social involvement and psychological well-being? American Psychologist 1998; 53:1017–31.

2. Bessière K, Kiesler S, Kraut R, et al. Effects of Internet use and social resources on changes in depression. Information, Communication & Society 2008; 11:47–70.

3. McKenna KYA, Bargh JA. Plan 9 from cyberspace: The implications of the Internet for personality and social psychology. Personality & Social Psychology Review 2000; 4:57–75.

4. Shaw LH, Gant LM. In defense of the Internet: The relationship between Internet communication and depression, loneliness, self-esteem, and perceived social support. CyberPsychology & Behavior 2002; 5:157–71.

5. Valkenburg PM, Peter J, Schouten AP. Friend networking sites and their relationship to adolescents' well-being and social self-esteem. CyberPsychology & Behavior 2006; 9:484–590.

6. Ellison NB, Steinfield C, Lampe C. The benefits of Facebook "friends": Social capital and college students' use of online social network sites. Journal of Computer-Mediated Communication 2007; 12: 1. jcmc.indiana.edu/vol12/issue4/ ellison.html (Accessed Jan. 27, 2009).

7. Heine SJ, Takemoto T, Moskalenko S, et al. Mirrors in the head: Cultural variation in objective self-awareness. Personality & Social Psychology Bulletin 2008; 34:879–87.

8. Walther JB. Computer-mediated communication: Impersonal, interpersonal, and hyperpersonal interaction. Communication Research 1996; 23:3–43.

9. Duval S, Wicklund RA. (1972) *A theory of objective self awareness*. New York: Academic Press.

10. Moskalenko S, Heine SJ. Watching your troubles away: Television viewing as a stimulus for a subjective self-awareness. Personality & Social Psychology Bulletin 2003; 29:76–85.

11. Duval S, Duval VH, Neely, R. Self-focus, felt responsibility, and helping behavior. Journal of Personality & Social Psychology 1979; 37:1769–78.

12. Beaman AL, Klentz B, Diener E, et al. Self-awareness and transgression in children: Two field studies.

Journal of Personality & Social Psychology 1979; 37:1835–46.

13. Fejfar MC, Hoyle RH. Effect of private self-awareness on negative affect and self-referent attribution: A quantitative review. Personality & Social Psychology Review 2000; 4:132–42.

14. Storms MD. Videotape and the attribution process: Reversing actors' and observers' points of view. Journal of Personality & Social Psychology 1973; 27:165–75.

15. Ickes WJ, Wicklund RA, Ferris CB. Objective self-awareness and self-esteem. Journal of Experimental Social Psychology 1973; 9:202–19.

16. Duval T, Duval V, Mulilis J. Effects of self-focus, discrepancy between self and standard, and outcome expectancy favorability on the tendency to match self to standard and withdraw. Journal of Personality & Social Psychology 1992; 62:340–8.

17. Hancock JT, Dunham PJ. Impression formation in computermediated communication. Communication Research 2001; 28:325–47.

18. Epley N, Kruger J. When what you type isn't what they read: The perseverance of stereotypes and expectancies over e-mail. Journal of Experimental Social Psychology 2005; 41:414–22.

19. Duthler KW. The politeness of requests made via email and voicemail: Support for the hyperpersonal model. Journal of Computer-Mediated Communication 2006; 11. jcmc.indiana .edu/vol11/issue2/duthler.html (accessed Jan. 13, 2009).

20. Walther JB. Selective self-presentation in computer-mediated communication: Hyperpersonal dimensions of technology, language, and cognition. Computers in Human Behavior 2007; 23:2538–57.

21. Ellison N, Heino R, Gibbs J. Managing impressions online: Self-presentation processes in the online dating environment. Journal of Computer-Mediated Communication 2006; 11.//jcmc.indiana.edu/vol11/issue2/ellison.html (Accessed Sept. 12, 2007).

22. Toma CL, Hancock JT, Ellison NB. Separating fact from fiction: An examination of deceptive self-presentation in online dating profiles. Personality & Social Psychology Bulletin 2008; 4:1023–36.

23. Gonzales AL, Hancock JT. Identity shift in computermediated environments. Media Psychology 2008; 11:167–85.

24. Rosenberg M. (1965) *Society and the adolescent self-image*. Princeton, NJ: Princeton University Press.

25. Josephs RA, Markus HR, Tafarodi RW. Gender and self-esteem. Journal of Personality & Social Psychology 1992; 63:391–402.

AMY L. GONZALES is a faculty member in the department of telecommunications at Indiana University Bloomington. Her research examines the effects that communication technologies have on individual identity, social support, and well-being.

JEFFREY T. HANCOCK is a professor in the Communications and Information Science departments at Cornell University and is the Chair of the Information Science department. He is interested in social interactions mediated by information and communication technology, with an emphasis on how people produce and understand language in these contexts.

EXPLORING THE ISSUE

Is Facebook Bad for College Students' Health?

Critical Thinking and Reflection

1. Do different social networking sites offer different benefits and drawbacks?
2. Is there an ideal number of "friends" or connections individuals have on Facebook that can improve their mental health?
3. What factors might influence whether Facebook has negative influences, like links with depression, versus positive influences, such as boosts in self-esteem?
4. Do social networking sites have any responsibility in promoting mental health in their users? If so, how might they go about doing so?

Is There Common Ground?

The number of young adults using social networking sites has increased dramatically in the past few years, along with the amount of time these individuals dedicate to these sites. Does such use have positive or negative consequences? Both selections focused on college undergraduate students' Facebook usage, one specific social networking site. While Brian Feinstein and colleagues in the YES selection find that it increases depressive symptoms, Amy Gonzales and Jeffrey Hancock in the NO selection find that Facebook usage enhances self-esteem.

How could two studies have such contrasting results? It is important to note the mechanisms by which each outcome was reached. Feinstein and colleagues found that negative comparison of oneself with others was linked with rumination, which was then linked with depression. Gonzales and Hancock, on the other hand, found that viewing one's own profile was a form of selective self-presentation, which was then linked with increases in self-esteem. Thus, it appears that *how* individuals use Facebook may be more significant than simply whether or not individuals use the site. These selections emphasize the importance of sophisticated analysis and looking beyond the surface of an issue.

Create Central

www.mhhe.com/createcentral

Additional Resources

Davila, J., Hershenberg, R., Feinstein, B. A., Gorman, K., Bhatia, V., & Starr, L. R. (2012). Frequency and quality of social networking among young adults: Associations with depressive symptoms, rumination, and corumination. *Psychology of Popular Media Culture, 1*(2), 72.

Ellison, N. B., Steinfield, C., & Lampe, C. (2007). The benefits of Facebook "friends": Social capital and college students' use of online social network sites. *Journal of Computer-Mediated Communication, 12*(4), 1143–1168.

Lee, S. J. (2009). Online communication and adolescent social ties: Who benefits more from Internet use? *Journal of Computer-Mediated Communication, 14*(3), 509–531.

Internet References . . .

American Psychiatric Association

www.psychiatry.org

The Jed Foundation

https://www.jedfoundation.org

National Alliance on Mental Illness

www.nami.org

Society for Research on Adult Development

http://www.adultdevelopment.org

Unit 7

UNIT

Middle Adulthood

Middle adulthood is generally conceptualized as the years between the mid-30s and the mid-60s. It encompasses a time when individuals have asserted their independence and autonomy, and have found ways to engage with society. In conventional terms, middle adulthood is often the most productive portion of the lifespan. During middle adulthood, most people deeply engage with families, the workforce, and communities. As such, some versions of the lifespan present middle adulthood as the peak of development.

However, middle adulthood also produces significant challenges and new expectations. The first issue in this unit discusses the role in marriage in intimate relationships. It begs the question of whether delays in marriage signify the end of marriage as an institution. The second issue in this unit focuses on the increased role grandparents play in their grandchildren's lives. When marriages (or other romantic relationships) do break up, should grandparents continue to be involved? These selections emphasize how as society has changed, so have the roles and expectations for middle adults.

Selected, Edited, and with Issue Framing Material by:
Allison A. Buskirk-Cohen, *Delaware Valley University*

ISSUE

Do Adults Need to Place More Value on Marriage?

YES: W. Bradford Wilcox, from *Why Marriage Matters: Thirty Conclusions from the Social Sciences—3rd ed.* (Institute for American Values, 2011)

NO: Brenda McKerson, from "Raising the Next Generation: What's Gender Got to Do with It?" *Plaza: Dialogues in Language and Literature* (2014)

Learning Outcomes

After reading this issue, you will be able to:

- Asses the dramatic increases in divorce rates during the second half of the twentieth century have leveled off, such that some social scientists consider cohabitation a more significant threat to traditional marriage.

- Understand that although adults increasingly see cohabitation as a viable option for long-term relationships, there is evidence to suggest that cohabitation does not associate with as positive of outcomes as marriage.

- See how long-term relationship norms vary significantly across historical periods and cultural settings, suggesting that it may be worth devoting attention to providing social support for relationships other than traditional marriage.

- Understand that it is important to consider significant relationships that are not heterosexual; there is huge variation in outcomes of heterosexual, gay and lesbian couples.

- Explain how interpretations of long-term relationships may reflect cultural biases rather than statistical differences.

ISSUE SUMMARY

YES: Sociologist W. Bradford Wilcox led a team of prominent family scholars to draw conclusions about the contemporary state of marriage as an institution, and the consequences of being married. They conclude that although marriage patterns are changing, traditional marriages still benefit adults and society.

NO: Brenda McKerson draws parallels between racial discrimination in the 1960's and discrimination faced by same-sex couples today. She argues that research on "nontraditional" couples often reflects heterosexist norms. Furthermore, McKerson believes that as generations become more accepting of different family structures, research findings will change to reflect this acceptance.

Marriage is one significant markers of the adult lifespan. Both historically and cross-culturally, adulthood is often defined by getting married and starting a family. In contemporary society, this norm is gradually changing—for both heterosexual and homosexual couples. Although there has always been a diversity of family types, expectations regarding marriage have changed. It is much more likely for people to wait until later adulthood to get married, or to not get married at all. The average age of first marriage has been rising, with individuals hoping to be more mature and financially stable before committing to a marital partnership. This trend has generated tremendous controversy among those interested in considering the relationship between marriage and lifespan development.

Definitions of marriage have differed dramatically throughout different time periods. Historically, marriage was viewed as a way of forming strategic alliances between and within families. Individuals had little say in terms of who they would marry and when. While many people regard monogamy as central to a healthy marital relationship today, that belief was not always the case. Through the sixth century in Western societies, polygamy was often preferred, perhaps as a way of maintaining gender hierarchies and assuring reproductive success. Even when monogamous marriages were confirmed, society in many ways favored extramarital affairs among men. The state was not regularly involved in marriages until the nineteenth century when marriage licenses became common in the United States. Along with civil rights and feminist movements, women gained more power in their marital relationships, both in the eyes of society and the law.

Have all of these changes benefited the institution of marriage? Some of the controversy about marriage derives from high divorce rates today. From 1960 to 1980, divorce rates almost tripled, and then have flattened and decreased in recent years. It is common to hear that half of all marriages in the United States end in divorce—though that figure is generally used more as a high-end estimate than the probability of any particular marriage working out. Although statistics can be manipulated to serve varying agendas, it is true that divorce is a common outcome of contemporary marriage. The history of divorce is just as complex as the history of marriage. There is some evidence claiming the ancient Athenians held very liberal attitudes toward divorce, while divorce was very rare in Ancient Rome. Divorce was uncommon throughout Medieval Europe related to the influence of the Church. Throughout the 1600s and 1700s, divorce became more acceptable as the independence and autonomy of the individual was recognized.

In addition to controversy around divorce, a current trend toward adults choosing cohabitation over marriage is new and raises interesting questions. Cohabitation refers to sharing a residence and personal assets without being married. There has been a large increase in the number of couples' cohabitating since the 1960s. A recent study by the Population Studies Center at the University of Michigan-Ann Arbor finds that cohabitation is the new norm. In their multi-year study, the researchers found that cohabitation rates had jumped among all

women, almost regardless of race or ethnicity, or advanced education level. Cohabitation has been a norm in other countries for quite a while, and in such accepting environments, cohabitation tends be associated with more positive outcomes.

The reasons individuals cohabit are quite diverse. For some individuals, cohabitation is in lieu of marriage; for others, it is a preparatory step. A recent Pew Research Center poll showed that among Americans who cohabitated, about two-thirds reported they thought about it as a step toward marriage. Societal views toward homosexual relationships and marriage have changed as well. In 2014, 35 states have legalized same-sex marriage. In an additional 10 states, judges have ruled in favor of same-sex marriages. It is important to note that many cohabitation studies only include men and women living together. The experience of living together is different for different people. Are traditionalists concerned about marriage in general, or just among heterosexual individuals?

In the YES selection, W. Bradford Wilcox and a team of family scholars note that the prevalence of cohabitation has risen dramatically. They see this rise as the major current threat to marriage, having overtaken divorce. Data does suggest that cohabitation on average associates with more negative outcomes than marriage. Even when comparing divorce rates among couples who had initially cohabitated and those who had not, for example, many have been surprised to learn that prior cohabitation associates with less successful marriages.

However, there may be other social forces at play. It may well be the case, for example, that cohabitating couples have had less success than married couples precisely because such relationships have been marginalized. Because marriage has long been a marker of adulthood, many social support systems focus on marriage: accessing health care, financial planning, parental duties, and more may all be easier for those in traditional marriages. Considering the changes in society noted in paragraphs above, is the argument posed by Wilcox and colleagues still valid?

According Brenda McKerson in the NO selection, we need to examine the lens through which we view marriage and cohabitation. Her article emphasizes the cultural forces that impact family structures and outcomes. McKerson describes the discrimination faced by same-sex couples today as similar to that of the racial discrimination experiences in the 1960's. Her article specifically critiques the New Family Structures Study, arguing that it reflects heterosexist norms in how data is interpreted. McKerson believes that as society becomes more accepting of various family structures, research on child outcomes will look quite different.

Just as the research on cohabitation emphasized the importance of social support, research on gay and lesbian couples also find social support integral to the success of their marital relationships. Studies on family structure and child outcomes may have very different results if and when same-sex marriage has become the norm. It is important to recognize how our own biases may influence the ways in which we interpret data. The ultimate question remains: is marriage itself beneficial? Or, is the support gleaned from being in a relationship recognized and supported by society?

YES

W. Bradford Wilcox

Why Marriage Matters: Thirty Conclusions from the Social Sciences

Executive Summary

In the latter half of the twentieth century, divorce posed the biggest threat to marriage in the United States. Clinical, academic, and popular accounts addressing recent family change—from Judith Wallerstein's landmark book, *The Unexpected Legacy of Divorce,* to Sara McLanahan and Gary Sandefur's award-winning book, *Growing Up with a Single Parent,* to Barbara Dafoe Whitehead's attention-getting *Atlantic* article, "Dan Quayle Was Right"—focused largely on the impact that divorce had upon children, and rightly so. In the wake of the divorce revolution of the 1970s, divorce was the event most likely to undercut the quality and stability of children's family lives in the second half of the twentieth century.

No more. In fact, as divorce rates have come down since peaking in the early 1980s, children who are now born to married couples are actually more likely to grow up with both of their parents than were children born at the height of the divorce revolution (see figure 1). In fact, the divorce rate for married couples with children has fallen almost to pre-divorce revolution levels, with 23 percent of couples who married in the early 1960s divorcing before their first child turned ten, compared to slightly more than 23 percent for couples who married in the mid 1990s.

Today, the rise of cohabiting households with children is the largest unrecognized threat to the quality and stability of children's family lives. In fact, because of the growing prevalence of cohabitation, which has risen fourteen-fold since 1970, today's children are much more likely to spend time in a cohabiting household than they are to see their parents divorce (see figure 2).

Now, approximately 24 percent of the nation's children are born to cohabiting couples, which means that more children are currently born to cohabiting couples

Figure 1

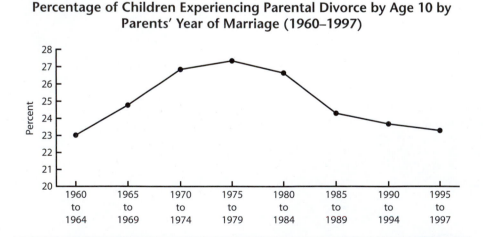

Percentage of Children Experiencing Parental Divorce by Age 10 by Parents' Year of Marriage (1960–1997)

Source: SIPP Data, 2001, 2004, and 2008. Women with premarital births excluded.

Figure 2

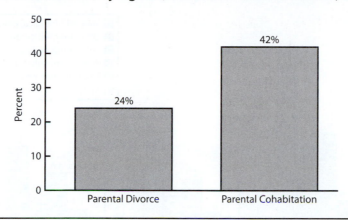

Percentage of Children Experiencing Parental Divorce/Separation and Parental Cohabitation, by Age 12; Period Life Table Estimates, 2002–07

Source: Kennedy and Bumpass, 2011. Data from National Survey of Family Growth. Note: The divorce/separation rate only applies to children born to married parents.

than to single mothers. Another 20 percent or so of children spend time in a cohabiting household with an unrelated adult at some point later in their childhood, often after their parents' marriage breaks down. This means that more than four in ten children are exposed to a cohabiting relationship. Thus, one reason that the institution of marriage has less of a hold over Americans than it has had for most [of] our history is that cohabitation has emerged as a powerful alternative to and competitor with marriage.

For this reason, the third edition of *Why Marriage Matters* focuses new attention on recent scholarship assessing the impact that contemporary cohabitation is having on marriage, family life, and the welfare of children. This edition also picks up on topics that surfaced in the first two editions of the report, summarizing a large body of research on the impact of divorce, stepfamilies, and single parenthood on children, adults, and the larger commonwealth. The report seeks to summarize existing family-related research into a succinct form useful to policy makers, scholars, civic, business, and religious leaders, professionals, and others interested in understanding marriage in today's society.

Five New Themes

1. ***Children are less likely to thrive in cohabiting households, compared to intact, married families.*** On many social, educational, and psychological outcomes, children in cohabiting households do significantly worse than children in intact, married families, and about as poorly as children living in single-parent families. And when it comes to abuse, recent federal data indicate that children in cohabiting households are markedly more likely to be physically, sexually, and emotionally abused than children in both intact, married families and single-parent families (see figure 3). Only in the economic domain do children in cohabiting households fare consistently better than children in single-parent families.

2. ***Family instability is generally bad for children.*** In recent years, family scholars have turned their attention to the impact that transitions into and out of marriage, cohabitation, and single parenthood have upon children. This report shows that such transitions, especially multiple transitions, are linked to higher reports of school failure, behavioral problems, drug use, and loneliness, among other outcomes. So, it is not just family structure and family process that matter for children; family stability matters as well. And the research indicates that children who are born to married parents are the least likely to be exposed to family instability, and to the risks instability poses to the emotional, social, and educational welfare of children.

3. ***American family life is becoming increasingly unstable for children*** (see figure 4). Sociologist Andrew Cherlin has observed that Americans are stepping "on and off the carousel of intimate

Figure 3

Incidence Per 1,000 Children of Harm Standard Abuse by Family Structure and Living Arrangement, 2005–2006

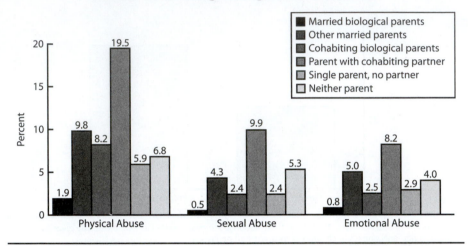

Source: Figure 5-2 in Fourth National Incidence Study of Child Abuse and Neglect (NIS-4): Report to Congress.

Figure 4

Percent of 16-Year-Olds Living with Mother and Father, 1978–1984 and 1998–2004

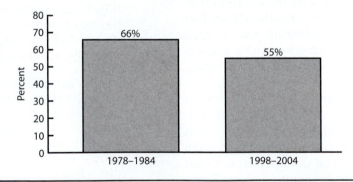

Source: General Social Survey, 1980–2010.

relationships" with increasing rapidity. This relational carousel spins particularly quickly for couples who are cohabiting, even cohabiting couples with children. For instance, cohabiting couples who have a child together are more than twice as likely to break up before their child turns twelve, compared to couples who are married to one another (see figure 5). Thus, one of the major reasons that children's lives are increasingly

turbulent is that more and more children are being born into or raised in cohabiting households that are much more fragile than married families.

4. ***The growing instability of American family life also means that contemporary adults and children are more likely to live in what scholars call "complex households,"*** where children and adults are living with people who are half-siblings, stepsiblings, stepparents, stepchildren,

Figure 5

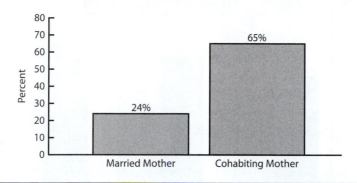

Percent of Children Experiencing Parental Separation by Age 12 by Mother's Relationship Status at Birth; Period of Life Table Estimates, 2002–07

Source: Kennedy and Bumpass, 2011. Data from National Survey of Family Growth.

or unrelated to them by birth or marriage. Research on these complex households is still embryonic, but the initial findings are not encouraging. For instance, one indicator of this growing complexity is multiple-partner fertility, where parents have children with more than one romantic partner. Children who come from these relationships are more likely to report poor relationships with their parents, to have behavioral and health problems, and to fail in school, even after controlling for factors such as education, income, and race. Thus, for both adults and children, life typically becomes not only more complex, but also more difficult, when parents fail to get or stay married.

5. ***The nation's retreat from marriage has hit poor and working-class communities with particular force.*** Recent increases in cohabitation, nonmarital childbearing, family instability, and family complexity have not been equally distributed in the United States; these trends, which first rose in poor communities in the 1970s and 1980s, are now moving rapidly into working-class and lower-middle-class communities. But marriage appears to be strengthening in more educated and affluent communities. As a consequence, since the early 1980s, children from college-educated homes have seen their family lives stabilize, whereas children from less-educated homes have seen their family lives become increasingly unstable (see figure 6). More generally, the stratified character of family trends means that the United States is "devolving into a separate-and-unequal family regime,

where the highly educated and the affluent enjoy strong and stable [families] and everyone else is consigned to increasingly unstable, unhappy, and unworkable ones."

We acknowledge that social science is better equipped to document whether certain facts *are* true than to say *why* they are true. We can assert more definitively that marriage is associated with powerful social goods than that marriage is the sole or main cause of these goods.

A Word About Selection Effects

Good research seeks to tease out "selection effects," or the preexisting differences between individuals who marry, cohabit, or divorce. Does divorce cause poverty, for example, or is it simply that poor people are more likely to divorce? Scholars attempt to distinguish between causal relationships and mere correlations in a variety of ways. The studies cited here are for the most part based on large, nationally representative samples that control for race, education, income, and other confounding factors. In many, but not all cases, social scientists used longitudinal data to track individuals as they marry, divorce, or stay single, increasing our confidence that marriage itself matters. Where the evidence appears overwhelming that marriage *causes* increases in well-being, we say so. Where marriage probably does so but the causal pathways are not as well understood, we are more cautious.

We recognize that, absent random assignment to marriage, divorce, or single parenting, social scientists

Figure 6

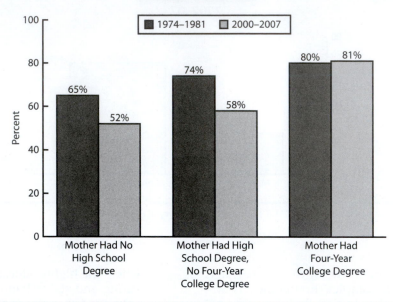

Percent of 14-Year-Old Girls Living with Mother and Father, by Mother's Education and Year

Source: National Survey of Family Growth, 1982 and 2006–08.

must always acknowledge the possibility that other factors are influencing outcomes. Reasonable scholars may and do disagree on the existence and extent of such selection effects and the extent to which marriage is causally related to the better social outcomes reported here.

Yet, scholarship is getting better in addressing selection effects. For instance, in this report we summarize three divorce studies that follow identical and nonidentical adult twins in Australia and Virginia to see how much of the effects of divorce on children are genetic and how much seem to be a consequence of divorce itself. Methodological innovations like these, as well as analyses using econometric models, afford us greater confidence that family structure exercises a causal influence for some outcomes.

Departures from the norm of intact marriage do not necessarily harm most of those who are exposed to them. While cohabitation is associated with increased risks of psychological and social problems for children, this does not mean that every child who is exposed to cohabitation is damaged. For example, one nationally representative study of six- to eleven-year-olds found that only 16 percent of children in cohabiting families experienced serious emotional problems. Still, this rate was much higher than the rate for children in families headed by married biological or adoptive parents, which was 4 percent.

While marriage is a social good, not all marriages are equal. Research does not generally support the idea that remarriage is better for children than living with a single mother. Marriages that are unhappy do not have the same benefits as the average marriage. Divorce or separation provides an important escape hatch for children and adults in violent or high-conflict marriages. Families, communities, and policy makers interested in distributing the benefits of marriage more equally must do more than merely discourage legal divorce.

But we believe good social science, despite its limitations, is a better guide to social policy than uninformed opinion or prejudice. This report represents our best judgment of what current social science evidence reveals about marriage in our social system.

Our Fundamental Conclusions

1. ***The intact, biological, married family remains the gold standard for family life in the United States,*** insofar as children are most likely to thrive—economically, socially, and psychologically—in this family form.

2. ***Marriage is an important public good,*** associated with a range of economic, health, educational, and safety benefits that help local, state, and federal governments serve the common good.

3. ***The benefits of marriage extend to poor, working-class, and minority communities,*** despite the fact that marriage has weakened in these communities in the last four decades.

Family structure and processes are only one factor contributing to child and social well-being. Our discussion here is not meant to minimize the importance of other factors, such as poverty, child support, unemployment, teenage childbearing, neighborhood safety, or the quality of education for both parents and children. Marriage is not a panacea for all social ills. For instance, when it comes to child well-being, research suggests that family structure is a better predictor of children's psychological and social welfare, whereas poverty is a better predictor of educational attainment.

But whether we succeed or fail in building a healthy marriage culture is clearly a matter of legitimate public concern and an issue of paramount importance if we wish to reverse the marginalization of the most vulnerable members of our society: the working class, the poor, minorities, and children.

W. BRADFORD WILCOX is director of the National Marriage Project at the University of Virginia, associate professor of sociology at the University of Virginia, and senior fellow at the Institute for Family Studies. He has published articles on marriage, cohabitation, parenting, and fatherhood.

Brenda McKerson

Raising the Next Generation: What's Gender Got to Do with It?

One year after passage of the landmark Civil Rights Act of 1964, the United States government declared itself on the precipice of what it regarded as a new crisis in race relations—how to ensure its Black citizens' equality in the wake of their newly found liberty. For this cause, then Assistant Secretary of Labor and sociologist, and later U.S. Senator Daniel Patrick Moynihan was tasked with defining the root cause of Black poverty in America. What resulted was the report titled "The Negro Family: The Case for National Action." The report, more familiarly known as "The Moynihan Report," while acknowledging the effect of limited educational and employment opportunities resulting from racial discrimination and injustice, focused on the matriarchal structure of the poor Black family, calling it the country's most "dangerous social problem." Moynihan argued that this unconventional family structure was unstable to the point of being "pathological" because of its lack of a strong father figure, and that, if it were allowed to persist it would result in the cycle of poverty and disadvantage repeating itself among these families' children who would continue to blight society at large.

Fast forward a half century to today when the focus is no longer Black families but rather same-sex families. In his article "Children of Homosexuals Fare Worse on Most Outcomes," Peter Sprigg, Senior Fellow for Policy Studies at the Family Research Council, lauds the research of University of Texas sociologist Mark Regnerus, calling it "the most careful, rigorous, and methodologically sound study ever conducted"—the "gold standard" in its field. Sprigg is referring to Regnerus' New Family Structures Studies and related report, titled "How Different are the Adult Children of Parents who Have Same-Sex Relationships?" According to Sprigg, Regnerus' "virtually irrefutable" research shows that statistically significant outcomes exist in the differences between children of married heterosexual parents (which Regnerus terms "intact biological families") and the children of homosexual parents. According to Sprigg, Regnerus' research shows that the latter "are much more

likely to have received welfare . . . to have lower educational attainment . . . to suffer from depression . . . to have been arrested more often . . . and, if female, to have had more sexual partners—both male and female." Further, Sprigg writes that Regnerus' research supports findings that children of lesbian mothers additionally "are more likely to be currently cohabiting . . . are more likely to have 'attachment' problems . . . use marijuana more frequently . . . are more likely to be sexually abused." When Moynihan assesses the "social pathology afflicting the Negro community" in 1965, he finds its center to be a nontraditional family structure which he criticizes as detrimental to its children and "out of line with the rest of American society." Similarly, when Regnerus analyzes results from the 2012 New Family Structures Study, he finds that the same-sex family structure, by the very nature of its being different, is subject to "forces uniquely problematic for child development" (766). Each of these researchers is looking at an alternative family style within a minority population and finding it out of step with the mainstream. Could it be that Regnerus' "Findings from the New Family Structures Study" is the new "Moynihan Report," and "gay" is the new "Black?"

The subject of same-sex parenting, barely a blip on the radar a decade ago, now accounts for a paradigm shift in family research. Social scientists, psychologists, proponents and detractors of same-sex parenting alike are weighing in on the possible outcomes for children with same-sex parents. They are seeking to determine whether this family form provides an environment for children that is equivalent to the traditional, marriage-based, nuclear family (having a male father and a female mother), or whether "having gay parents or the stigma of gay parents is detrimental to a child's development" (Rimalower and Caty 18). This paper examines some of the issues raised and opinions voiced as a result of studies performed on behalf of notable authorities and stake holders in the debate on same-sex parenting (e.g. the American Psychological Association, National Council on Family

Relations, Family Research Council, etc.). This paper concludes that the findings of these studies do not form the basis for consensus and that parenting is not a monolith to be evaluated on a single factor.

In her 1989 review of literature concerning children of lesbian and gay parents, Julie Schwartz Gottman looks at the issue from the perspective of clinical implications and judicial decisions related to child custody. Gottman's research comes at a time when an increasing number of lesbian and gay parents are no longer hiding their gender identities and are attempting to maintain guardianship of their children during court custody disputes, despite social stereotypes that confront their abilities to parent.

Gottman first reviews the literature and finds that problems surrounding same-sex parents raising their children resulted more from societal forces than from the parenting itself:

> In general, none of the ... studies on children of lesbian mothers and gay fathers reported negative effects on children relative to their parent's sexual orientation. Children did not appear deviant in gender identity, sexual orientation or social adjustment. Issues that emerged during their upbringing related more to society's rejection of homosexuality than to poor parent-child relationships. (186)

Then, citing the limitations of the above studies due to their lack of control groups, their small sample sizes, and their predominate focus on younger children, Gottman conducts her own study in an attempt to address some of these weaknesses—particularly in light of her contention that "it is difficult to predict sexual orientation, gender identity, and social adjustment in children of homosexual parents without looking at later adult development" (187).

From the standpoint of their legal implications, Gottman's own findings support those of the earlier research in their assessment of the apparent normalcy of the children of lesbian mothers and gay fathers with regard to gender identity, sexual orientation, and social adjustment. In addition, Gottman concludes that "Parental homosexuality does not appear to directly or indirectly harm the child. Children may have issues to contend with concerning how society perceives them when a parent's homosexuality is revealed. However, it appears that children develop strategies to protect themselves when necessary" (191).

From the standpoint of their clinical implications, Gottman's findings support the conclusions that although "children do not demonstrate pathology related to their parents' homosexual orientation ... there appear to be issues that the clinician should be sensitive to in children of gay and lesbian parents":

> [P]arental homosexuality does not in itself signal pathology in the family or in the child ... The time and manner in which parents disclose their homosexuality to children appears to be important ... Adolescents seem the hardest hit by disclosure ... The children would probably do best if the parent was secure in both his or her sexual identity and parental role ... given the implications of homosexuality in a homophobic culture. (191–192)

In their 1995 assessment of the prevailing mainstream family literature regarding how sexual orientation impacts family experience, particularly the psychological and social development of children from same-sex families, Katherine Allen and David Demo find that the body of research is limited, primarily because "Sexist and heterosexist assumptions continue to underlie most of the research on families by focusing on heterosexual partnerships and parenthood" (112). Elucidating their theory as to the absence of what may be an uncomfortable subject from researchers' studies of family phenomena, Allen and Demo define heterosexism as a bias that cannot conceptualize human experience in other than strictly heterosexual terms and that, consequently, ignores and invalidates other relationships and lifestyles:

> Heterosexism operates in personal belief systems and in institutional practices. Like racism, sexism, and classism, heterosexism is a form of institutional oppression designed to ridicule, limit, or silence alternative discourses about identity and behavior. Societal institutions reinforce heterosexism by shaping and controlling knowledge. (122)

Allen and Demo further assert that this heterosexual bias reflects society's belief that "gayness and family are mutually exclusive concepts, a belief that prevails because the same-sex family, more than any other form, challenges fundamental patriarchal notions of family and gender relations" (112). Despite finding a void in same-sex family research, Allen and Demo's investigation cites a 1993 Downey and Powell study analyzing 35 social, psychological, and educational outcomes of children in different living arrangements in order to evaluate what they refer to as the "same-sex parent argument" which insists that "the presence of and identification with the same-sex parent is necessary for the child's healthy emotional adjustment and appropriate gender role development" (118). It would follow, then, from this argument that a heterosexual female daughter could not identify appropriately with a lesbian mother, and a heterosexual male son could not achieve appropriate emotional adjustment and gender role development when raised by a gay father. No evidence was found by the Downey and Powell study to support this argument, which Allen and Demo find is used to challenge the competency and adequacy of lesbian and gay parents.

Another implication cited by the Allen and Demo research, and one worth noting here because of its effect on children, is the need to further explore the liminal aspect of the same-sex family. Allen and Demo's position, based on a 1989 Brown study, is that lesbian mothers and gay fathers exhibit "Biculturalism—the contradiction of being between two cultures" in the sense that they interact as parents of their children within the mainstream heterosexual culture while relating as peers with the gay community in which they share a same-sex identity (122). Further, Allen and Demo, citing the Brown study and a 1993 Laird study, find that this biculturality offers a collateral advantage of "resilience and creative adaptation" in an environment of minority group oppression—similar to the "dual socialization that many Black parents provide for their children, preparing them for institutionalized racism they will confront and at the same time helping them to become self-sufficient, competent adults" (123).

A decade after Allen and Demo survey the landscape for studies pertaining to same-sex parenting and find it lacking, Lucy Rimalower and Caren Caty find that a slowly emerging body of research exists from which to conclude that "children raised by same-sex parents are not disadvantaged compared with their peers raised in households headed by heterosexual parents" (17). With their focus on the effects of gay parents on a child's development, Rimalower and Caty review literature and studies of this "highly contended issue" from the perspectives of the involvement of same-sex parents in their children's school system; the role of heterosexism, gender identity, and sexual orientation in the lives of same-sex families; and the emotional and developmental issues facing children of same-sex parents in contrast with children having heterosexual parents.

Noting that children with same-sex parents—regardless of their parents' legal or biological status—are entering school systems, creating issues for both the families and the faculties, Rimalower and Caty cite 2004 Wainright, Russell, and Patterson research finding that children with same-sex parents are more connected to their school communities than their peers with heterosexual parents. This suggests, they observe, the importance of same-sex parents' efforts toward making school a welcoming and safe place for their children. Because

having same-sex parents is not necessarily an obvious trait, same-sex parents and their children are confronted with the issue of if, when, and how to disclose their non-traditional family structure to school personnel and other families. And while these children may have no problem understanding and describing their families to others and may start school feeling proud of their families, Rimalower and Caty site research which finds that negative reactions and disapproval from these children's teachers and/or peers, or the children's being discriminated against or excluded from the family norm at school can negatively impact these children's well-being and "denies these children a sense of legitimacy and inhibits their sense of future potential" (22).

Maintaining that homophobia and heterocentrism continue to be socially relevant and politically charged issues for same-sex families, Rimalower and Caty cite the 2004 Clarke, Kitzinger, and Potter study indicating that these factors may cause school-aged children, particularly adolescents, of these families to be bullied, harassed, ostracized, stigmatized, taunted and rejected by their peers and schoolmates, and even assumed to have the same sexual orientation as their parents (25). These same studies, finding a negative correlation between experiencing stigma and self-esteem and a positive correlation between positive coping and self-esteem, speak to the importance of children and families having support groups as well as engaging in conversations about sexual orientation in the same ways and degrees that heterosexual parents might educate their children about relationships and sexuality.

Addressing another issue surrounding same-sex parenting research—gender identity and sexual orientation—Rimalower and Caty cite research that dispels stereotypes which assume, for example, that gay mothers are less maternal than heterosexual mothers, or that effeminacy in gay fathers precludes children's ability to achieve their own healthy gender development (26). In addition Rimalower and Caty refute the notion that gay fathers and gay mothers necessarily raise gay children by citing the American Psychological Association's positions that, first, homosexuality is not a psychological disorder and, second, that "there is no evidence ... that children raised by homosexual parents are more likely to have sexual or romantic attraction to the same sex than children raised by heterosexual parents" (27).

Finally, Rimalower and Caty look at research that questions whether, all else being equal, there are significant differences important to the well-being of the children in households with same-sex parents versus those with heterosexual parents. Rimalower and Caty point to research that shows "there are no significant differences across a spectrum of dimensions including emotional functioning, gender identification, sexual orientation, and social relationships" and "no significant differences in psychiatric disorders and psychological problems." Further, despite the unique challenges facing same-sex parents, Rimalower and Caty cite research reporting that "there are more similarities than differences in parenting styles between heterosexual and homosexual parents" (27).

From the studies included in their review, Rimalower and Caty conclude most notably that no significant differences exist that would impair the development of children raised by same-sex parents compared to children raised within traditional family structures. Further, they find that the research overwhelmingly demonstrates that "it is the quality of parent-child relationships, more than biological or legal status, which has an impact on children's development" (Rimalower and Caty 29).

While echoing many of the same sentiments and findings as the Rimalower-Caty report on the subject of same-sex families, a 2011 *Journal of Nursing Law* article examines the issue from a different standpoint: the impact of recognizing the legal relationship of same-sex parenting couples on family health and well-being. To illustrate the extent to which this impact could be felt, the article cites figures from the 2000 U.S. Census; approximately 960,000 children younger than the age of 18 being raised by 740,000 lesbian or gay parents, including more than 200,000 female-female or male-male couples. The article asserts that, as a social construction, parenting and family life are central to participation in society and to the experience of full citizenship (Weber 39). Further, it cites 2004 R. J. Green research suggesting that these citizenship relations inherently provide the advantages of "links to economic progress, legal protections for partner relationships, and increased parental rights that ... strengthen legal rights of children" (Weber 43). Conversely, as indicated by G. M. Herek's 2004 research, lacking access to these legal frameworks causes sexual minorities (and by implication, their children) to experience more difficulty and a kind of social inadequacy (Weber 42). So important is family, the article contends, that most people trace their well being and social status to traditional features of family life and partnered relationship recognition. Therefore, the article maintains, "the well-being of children raised by lesbian and gay couples is undermined when laws and social customs do not recognize their families," causing the stability and cohesiveness of these families to be weakened (Weber 43). Accordingly, the article cites G. M. Herek's 2006 research suggesting that government recognition of same-sex partnership is likely to affect children positively because it can afford them "a stable legal bond

with the parent that gives the child much needed security and continuity and minimizes the likelihood of conflicting or competing claims by nonparents for the child's custody" (Weber 46).

So, where are we in the academic debate over same-sex parenting? Among others, including some research cited here, findings from the American Academy of Pediatrics, the American Psychological Association, the National Council on Family Relations, and the National Longitudinal Lesbian Family Study are that sexual orientation of parents is not a major determinant in children's emotional development and that what really matters is the quality of parenting and the family's economic health. Still, others argue that many of these studies lack the quality and amount of demographic data that would make them definitive. And the earlier research of Julie Gottman seems to dispel the assumption that parents' homosexuality harms the child, but also tells us that parents' homosexuality does affect the child, even though the effect may be due to social stereotypes rather than the parenting itself.

In sharp contrast to those positions is the harsh stance taken by the American College of Pediatricians, socially conservative former members of the American Academy of Pediatrics who disagree with positions held by the larger Academy on samesex parenting. The American College of Pediatricians discourages adoption by same-sex couples or single parents, arguing that "the fundamental mother-father family unit, within the context of marriage" is the "optimal setting for the development and nurturing of children." The group goes further by condemning gay parenting, maintaining that "rooted in the best available science" is support for their position that "there is significant risk of harm inherent in exposing a child to the homosexual lifestyle" and that it is "potentially hazardous to children and dangerously irresponsible to change the age-old prohibition on homosexual parenting, whether by adoption, foster care, or reproductive manipulation" (Hausman 9).

In addition, Mark Regnerus' report, which is the subject of much criticism from mainstream researchers, is cited by some scholars and detractors of same-sex families like Jennifer Marshall, Director of Domestic Policy Studies for the conservative Heritage Foundation, as an indication that "there is not enough evidence that [children of same-sex households] are going to be the same [as those having heterosexual parents]. There's every reason to believe that different family structures will have different outcomes" (Somashekhar 2). Similar views were voiced by Supreme Court Justices Antonin Scalia and Anthony M. Kennedy during recent arguments on same-sex marriage. Justice Scalia asserted that "There's considerable disagreement" among experts over whether "raising a child in a single-sex family is harmful or not." Kennedy remarked, "We have five years of information to weigh against 2,000 years of history" (Savage and Dolan).

All this disagreement begs the question: how good are we at forecasting social outcomes? It is not difficult to understand why there are conflicting views on the part of those currently attempting to predict the effect of same-sex parenting on the next generation. Years from now, however, when social scientists look back on these predictions and evaluate them against actual outcomes, they may find themselves in the same position as those who now, with several decades of history and data to analyze, disagree on the answer to the question: "Was Moynihan right?"

Ron Haskins, senior fellow at the Brookings Institution, contends that Moynihan was right and that "it was inevitable that the facts would overcome the political correctness of ignoring the family's role in the growth of the black underclass" (282). Acknowledging that "family dissolution has greatly increased among blacks and has spread to all demographic groups in the nation," Haskins, while attempting not to malign the single Black mother, insists that the continuing demise of married-couple families has had the greatest negative effect on Black children:

> Of all the consequences of family dissolution that are harmful to blacks, none is more important than the effect of lone parenting on the development of black children … It is not necessary to demean the efforts of single mothers to observe that their children would be better off on average if the mother and father were married and provided a low-conflict environment for their children. (Haskins 285)

Social science educators and researchers Kathryn Edlin, Laura Tach, and Ronald Mincy, focusing their research on contemporary unwed fathers' involvement in their children's lives and using data from the Fragile Families and Child Wellbeing Study, conclude that from the standpoint of the children affected, Moynihan was right to be concerned about the increasing instances of non-traditional families on future generations. These researchers find that "among U.S. couples, cohabiting unions among parents with children are extraordinarily fragile"; that these unions have led to "repartnering" which may cause children to experience fatherhood as "a series of temporary commitments rather than a lifelong obligation"; and that the impact of these unions now extends beyond Black families to a significant minority

of all American children (Edlin, Tach, Mincy 170,172). Finally, these researchers conclude that "it is unlikely that many children in this situation will receive the same level of emotional or financial investment enjoyed by those who live stably with both their biological mothers and fathers" (Edlin, Tach, and Mincy 172).

When researcher Damaur Quander evaluates "The Moynihan Report," she disputes Moynihan's contention that Blacks' inability to attain the "American Dream" is directly related to matriarchy within Black culture, "a social system Western culture claims is detrimental to the successful development of children" (iv). What Moynihan deemed as "destructive and oppositional to the preferred nuclear family model—where the father figure stabilizes the ascribed imbalance caused my matriarchy," Quander finds to be "the oldest social construct for family … that is reclaiming itself by natural selection in modernity" (v). She concludes that matriarchy, this non-traditional family form by Western standards, is not detrimental to children's well-being and is actually forwardthinking and beneficial in the long term:

> Theirs [Blacks'] was not the small and vulnerable nuclear family of white America, but the extended kinship system of rural folk and of the poor who cooperate that each child may live and survive, no matter what befalls its own father and mother. (Quander 486)

This historical period during which "The Moynihan Report" was written predates the feminist movement and a number of economic, demographic and cultural changes. The effects of these changes on the Western family are yet evolving. While there is no consensus, but in fact sharp disagreement, among scholars over the effects of same-sex parenting on children and on society as a whole, several things seem clear from the research reviewed here. First, the effects of parenting cannot be evaluated by a uniform standard or evaluated on the basis of a single issue, as reinforced by several researchers' concluding that the quality of the parenting is at least as important as the biology and gender identity of the parents. Secondly, as several of the researchers suggest, many of the issues that arise from this non-traditional family form are not due to the family form itself, but rather to how the rest of us perceive and react to it. Even Moynihan, in 1965, and Regnerus, in 2012, agree on this point. Moynihan writes that it is the nonconventionality of matriarchy in an era of male dominance that is the problem:

> There is, presumably, no special reason why a society in which males are dominant in family relationships is to be preferred to a matriarchal

arrangement. However, it is clearly a disadvantage for a minority group to be operating on one principle, while the great majority of the population, and the one with the most advantages ... is operating on another ... A subculture, such as that of the Negro American, in which this [male leadership in public and private affairs] is not the pattern, is placed at a distinct advantage. (Moynihan)

Similarly, Regnerus admits that children do not need a married mother and father joined in a heterosexual union to turn out well as adults and that external forces can contribute to negative outcomes cited by his research as being associated with same-sex parenting:

> The tenor of the last 10 years of academic discourse about gay and lesbian parents suggests that there is little to nothing about them that might be negatively associated with child development, and a variety of things that might be uniquely positive ... the findings reported herein may be explicable in part by a variety of forces uniquely problematic for child development in gay and lesbian families—including a lack of social support for parents, stress exposure resulting from persistent stigma. (Regnerus 766)

It seems obvious that the issue of same-sex parenting is one that goes to people's core values and convictions. It is one that has created a dividing line, not only among society at large, but also within individuals who find themselves torn between their principled or religious objections and their evolving attitudes away from those objections. A shift in attitudes toward support of same-sex parenting is occurring and will likely continue to do so because "same-sex couples ... will continue to raise children [and] American courts are finding arguments against gay marriage decreasingly persuasive" (Regnerus 766), and because of the impact of a younger generation that seems broadly accepting of this family form.

References

Allen, Katherine R. and Demo, David H. "The Families of Lesbians and Gay Men: A New Frontier in Family Research." *Journal of Marriage and Family*, 57:1 (1995): 111–127. *National Council on Family Relations.* Web. 29 Nov 2013.

Edlin, Kathryn, Laura Tach, and Ronald Mincy. "Claiming Fatherhood: Race and the Dynamics of Paternal Involvement among Unmarried Men." *Annals of the*

American Academy of Political and Social Science. 621 (2009): 149–177. Web. 29 Nov 2013.

Haskins, Ron. "Moynihan Was Right: Now What?" *Annals of the American Academy of Political and Social Science.* 621 (2009): 281–314. Web. 29 Nov 2013.

Hausman, Ken. "Pediatric Group Condemns Same-Sex Parenting." *Psychiatric News*, 45:21 (2010). Web. 29 Nov 2013.

Gottman, Julie Schwartz. "Children of Gay and Lesbian Parents." *Marriage and Family Review*, 14:3–4 (1989): 177–196. Web. 29 Nov 2013.

Moynihan, Daniel P. "The Negro Family: The Case for National Action." Washington, D.C., Office of Policy Planning and Research, U. S. Department of Labor, 1965. Web. 29 Nov 2013.

Quander, Damaur. *A nation within a nation: An organic study of the Black matriarchy as a social construct of Black survival in contrast to the Moynihan Report.* Diss. California Institute of Integral Studies, 2013. Ann Arbor: UMI, 2013. Web. 29 Nov 2013.

Regnerus, Mark. "How Different are the Adult Children of Parents Who Have Same- SexRelationships?" *Social Science Research* 41:4 (2012): 752–777. Web. 29 Nov 2013.

Rimalower, Lucy and Caty, Caren. "The Mamas and the Papas: the Invisible Diversity of Families with Same-Sex Parents in the United States." *Sex Education* 9.1 (2009): 17–32. Web. 29 Nov 2013.

Savage, David G. and Maura Dolan. "Justices' Concern Over Gay Parenting." *The Miami Times.* April 2013. Web. 9 Dec 2013.

Sprigg, Peter. "New Study on Homosexual Parents Tops All Previous Research." Washington, D.C., Family Research Council. Web. June, 2012.

Somashekhar, Sanhya. "Social Science Struggles for Data on Effects of Same-Sex Parenting on Children." *Washington Post.* 26 Mar 2013. Web. 29 Nov 2013.

Weber, Scott. "Impacts of Legal Relationship Recognition of Same-Sex Parenting Couples on Family Health and Well-Being." *Journal of Nursing Law* 14:2 (2011): 39–48. Web. 29 Nov 2013.

BRENDA MCKERSON is a graduate student at the University of Houston.

EXPLORING THE ISSUE

Do Adults Need to Place More Value on Marriage?

Critical Thinking and Reflection

1. Do you believe that cohabitation is a stronger threat to marriage than divorce?
2. What are the benefits of traditional marriage? Are these benefits simply a reflection of social norms or is there something intrinsically valuable in marriage?
3. If alternatives to marriage, such as cohabitation, become the norm, would it still be considered problematic?
4. What are the implications for children of different family structures?
5. Are discussions of different family structures always subject to political, religious, and other biases? If so, how do we prevent these biases from impacting policy decisions?

Is There Common Ground?

The evidence that marriage does, on average, associate with good outcomes for adults, children, and communities has accumulated in recent years to the point of guiding social policy. However, it is important to note, the very institutional value we ascribe to marriage may reinforce its advantages and preclude other viable relationship types. Efforts to exclude same-sex couples from legal marriage are only one example of this process.

Does the concept of "traditional marriage" only apply to heterosexual couples? In the YES selection, W. Bradford Wilcox and his colleagues emphasize that traditional marriages are beneficial to individuals and society. However, the argument presented by Brenda McKerson causes us to reconsider our own biases. Might society's negative views of "nontraditional" families impact how we interpret data on these families? Is marriage only positive when it puts people in a position to earn society's recognition and approval?

Create Central

www.mhhe.com/createcentral

Additional Resources

Bloch, L., Haase, C. M., & Levenson, R. W. (2014). Emotion regulation predicts marital satisfaction: More than a wives' tale. *Emotion*, *14*(1), 130.

Graham, J. M., & Barnow, Z. B. (2013). Stress and social support in gay, lesbian, and heterosexual couples: direct effects and buffering models. *Journal of Family Psychology*, *27*(4), 569.

Kurdek, L. A. (2001). Differences between heterosexual-nonparent couples and gay, lesbian, and heterosexual-parent couples. *Journal of Family Issues*, *22*(6), 727–754.

Regnerus, M. (2012). How different are the adult children of parents who have same-sex relationships? Findings from the New Family Structures Study. *Social Science Research*, *41*(4), 752–770.

Vanassche, S., Swicegood, G., & Matthijs, K. (2013). Marriage and children as a key to happiness? Cross-national differences in the effects of marital status and children on well-being. *Journal of Happiness Studies*, *14*(2), 501–524.

Internet References ...

The Alternatives to Marriage Project

http://www.unmarried.org

Institute for American Values

http://americanvalues.org/

Society for Research on Adult Development

http://www.adultdevelopment.org/

Selected, Edited, and with Issue Framing Material by:
Allison A. Buskirk-Cohen, *Delaware Valley University*

ISSUE

Should Grandparents Have Visitation Rights to Their Grandchildren?

YES: Lixia Qu et al., from "Grandparenting and the 2006 Family Law Reforms," *Family Matters* (2011)

NO: Rachel Dunifon and Ashish Bajracharya, from "The Role of Grandparents in the Lives of Youth," *Journal of Family Issues* (2012)

Learning Outcomes

After reading this issue, you will be able to:

- Understand how changes in family structure necessitate changes in family law, and, moreover, an understanding of these systems.
- Recognize that relationships between grandparents, grandchildren, and the parents of the children are often complex with changing dynamics.
- Discuss whether grandparents play an influential role in their grandchildren's lives may be a result of a number of factors including distance, the parent's relationships, and age of child and parent.
- Understand that the parents of children often play a significant role in determining the quantity and quality of time grandparents spend with their grandchildren.

ISSUE SUMMARY

YES: Lixia Qu and colleagues review Australian data on grandparent-grandchild involvement before and after the 2006 legal reforms. They find that that family law reforms are consistent with parental beliefs about grandparent involvement. However, they caution that the reforms do not address many practicalities, including knowledge about the legal system.

NO: However, the research of Rachel Dunifon and Ashish Bajracharya does not find clear evidence that grandparents influence the well-being of their grandchildren. They find that distance, the parent's relationship with the grandparent and child, and age of child and parent all contribute to the quality of the grandparent-grandchild relationship.

Rudy Giuliani once said, "What children need most are the essentials that grandparents provide in abundance. They give unconditional love, kindness, patience, humor, comfort, lessons in life. And, most importantly, cookies." We often envision grandparents as being able to provide all of the fun without any of the responsibilities of parenting. They can play ball, bake cookies, and do any other number of clichéd activities with their grandchildren. But do these images correspond with reality? Most grandparents will tell you that this is no longer the case. The role of grandparents has changed tremendously in recent years.

Today, grandparents often have an active role in raising their grandchildren. According to the U.S. Census Bureau report in 2002, over two million grandparents were raising their grandchildren alone. The parents of these children were absent due to death, substance abuse, or incarceration. In 2010, that number had increased to almost five million. Among children whose parents are still physically present, grandparents may play a larger role today as child-care providers. At least thirty percent of preschoolers with working mothers receive grandparent care. The economic climate certainly contributed to these increases. The numbers increased quickly after the 2007 recession, and have stabilized since 2009 at the recession's official end.

This shift recognizes that contemporary grandparents often assume many parental responsibilities for their grandchildren. While grandmothers are more likely to provide child care, many grandfathers do so as well. While some grandparents act as temporary babysitters for only a few hours a week, this arrangement does not represent the typical pattern. In many cases, grandparents are providing substantial amounts of time, often at no cost. A 2004 report from Child Trends found that among grandparents providing child care on a regular basis, they provided an average of 23 hours of care a week for children age six and younger. Interestingly, this report demonstrated that much of the child care occurred outside of parents' employment hours, indicating grandparent care was more than a substitute for some other type of child-care arrangement.

The website for the American Association of Retired Persons (AARP) along with a host of other organizations provides resources and information for grandparents, particularly around issues of child care. There are checklists and formal agreements for grandparents to use with the child's parents to avoid conflict. These lists include items that range from identifying appropriate foods for snack time to clarifying discipline strategies and methods. Ideas about child-proofing a household have changed in past years, so it is not uncommon for individuals from different generations to clash on basic parenting issues. Parents and grandparents may have conflicting ideas about the role the adult is supposed to play in the child's life (e.g., babysitter, teacher, friend); these organizations provide resources to initiate these conversations at the start of the child-care arrangement.

Child-care arrangements, though, are subject to change, especially given the flux common in family structures today. According to the American Psychological Association, about 40 to 50 percent of married couples in the United States divorce. When couples with a child divorce, child custody and visitation disputes typically involve only the child's parents. As discussed above, many grandparents today are involved in significant care of their grandchildren. However, state laws do not always recognize grandparent rights, but there may be statutes to govern visitation rights of grandparents, foster parents, caregivers, and stepparents. When courts do contemplate grandparent rights, they consider the best interests of the child including the possibility of parental abuse toward the child.

The issue of grandparent rights is hardly resolved, and varies greatly among states. For example, in 2003, the Alabama Legislature revised their statute so that a court may grant visitation to a grandparent if visitation is both in the child's best interest and meets one of five other criteria. Those five criteria include (1) one or both parents of the child must be deceased, (2) the marriage of the parents has been dissolved, (3) a parent of the child has abandoned the child, (4) the child was born out of wedlock, or (5) the child lives with both biological parents, but one or both of the parents has prevented a grandparent from visiting the child. Furthermore, the statute requires courts to consider the moral character of the parents and the age and sex of the child to determine the best interests of the child. In contrast, in Idaho, a court may award visitation rights if visitation is in the child's best interest. Idaho's statute also cuts off visitation rights of grandparents with adoption.

Looking beyond the United States, the YES selection reviews Australian data on grandparent-grandchild involvement before and after the 2006 legal reforms. Previous to these reforms, increased attention was devoted to the role of fathers in their children's lives, and Australia passed the Family Law Amendment (Shared Parental Responsibility) Act 2006. This act made both parents responsible for decisions about their child. While this act was originally part of the fathers' rights movement, it impacted grandparents as well. The legislation recognizes the role that significant individuals (other than parents) can play in children's lives following the dissolution of marriage.

In their article, Lixia Qu and colleagues argue that our legal system should reflect societal norms, which includes grandparent involvement in the lives of their grandchildren. Qu and her colleagues describe how grandparents provide support—physical, emotional, and financial—to their grandchildren and their families. Post-separation relationships can be complex, they note, and the legal system should take these dynamics into consideration. Their review of the family law reforms suggests that these reforms are consistent with parental beliefs about grandparent involvement. However, they caution that the reforms do not address many practicalities, including knowledge of the legal system.

Rachel Dunifon and Ashish Bajracharya, in the NO selection, do not find clear evidence that grandparents influence the well-being of their grandchildren. Their study includes a nationally representative group of young adolescents, ages 14 through 19. Dunifon and Bajracharya identify factors that predict the quality of the grandparent-grandchild relationships, and examine the implications of this relationship for the grandchild. They find that distance, the parent's relationship with the grandparent and child, and age of child and parent all contribute to the quality of the grandparent-grandchild relationship.

Surprisingly, however, they do not find that grandparents influence their grandchildren's school performance or risky behavior (measured by substance use and sexual behavior). If the relationship is not particularly influential, why should grandparents be afforded any legal rights concerning their grandchildren?

YES ⬅

Lixia Qu et al.

Grandparenting and the 2006 Family Law Reforms

Grandparents are often important figures in children's lives. They may provide their grandchildren with care, love and support, while simultaneously imparting a sense of family history. They may also provide financial support to their children's families, especially in times of crisis. Indeed, Mutchler and Baker (2009) showed that children in single-mother families who lived with grandparents were less likely than other children in single-mother families to experience poverty.

Recent research by Horsfall and Dempsey (2011) suggested that around one-half of grandparents spend time with their grandchildren at least once a week, and just under three-quarters spend time with them at least once a month. This time can take several forms; for example, many grandparents provide child care, especially for children under the age of five years (Australian Bureau of Statistics [ABS], 2006), while some assume full responsibility for raising their grandchildren (ABS, 2008; Ochiltree, 2006).

When parents are separating, grandparents can provide their grandchildren with a sense of stability and continuity. This is especially the case when they have already developed a productive, meaningful relationship with their grandchildren. In such circumstances, grandparents are in a strong position to help their grandchildren understand that parental separation is not their fault, that both parents still love them, and that the disruptions in their lives are likely to dissipate or be significantly reduced with time.

At the same time, it is important to recognise that the dynamics of post-separation relationships between grandparents, grandchildren and the parents of these grandchildren can be complex. It is therefore not axiomatic that maintaining these inter-generational relationships will always be of benefit to the family. By "taking sides", some grandparents add fuel to the conflict between the parents and thereby add to the distress of the grandchildren. In addition, not all grandparents have

good relationships with their own adult children and not all parents welcome the input that grandparents might provide at this time.

Previous research suggests that following the separation of their adult children, some grandparents have little opportunity to maintain or strengthen their bond with their grandchildren, and may even lose contact altogether. In particular, grandchildren whose parents have separated are more likely to have an ongoing relationship with their maternal rather than their paternal grandparents. This in turn reflects the fact that grandchildren usually live mostly with their mother after separation (Weston et al., 2011) and are also likely to have established stronger relationships with their maternal rather than paternal grandparents prior to separation (Cherlin & Furstenberg, 1986; Lussier, Deater-Deckard, Dunn, & Davies, 2002; Weston, 1992). Analysis of data from the General Population of Parents Survey, conducted in 2009 (GPPS 2009), confirmed these findings, revealing that while separated parents typically reported that the relationship between their own parents and their children was not affected by separation, non-residents fathers were more likely than resident fathers and mothers to report that this relationship had become distant (Weston & Qu 2009).[1]

One of the aims of the 2006 family law reforms was to lessen the potential for parental separation to diminish or sever the relationship between children and their grandparents and other people who play a significant and beneficial role in children's lives. The *Family Law Amendment (Shared Parental Responsibility) Act 2006* (Cth) recognises that "children have a right to spend time on a regular basis with, and communicate with, both their parents and other people significant to their care, welfare and development (such as grandparents and other relatives)" (s60B(2)(b)). The legislation recognises the important role that grandparents (and other significant individuals, including relatives) can play in children's lives following the separation of their parents. The Government's stated

Box 1

Datasets

The analysis in this article is based on several datasets:

- The General Population of Parents Survey, conducted in 2009 (GPPS 2009), was a nationally representative survey of 5,000 randomly selected parents with at least one child under the age of 18 years.
- The Longitudinal Study of Separated Families (LSSF 2008) and the Looking Back Survey 2009 (LBS 2009) were national surveys. LSSF 2008 randomly selected 10,000 parents who had separated after the introduction of the 2006 family law reforms came into force in July 2006, and LBS 2009 randomly selected 2,000 parents who had separated between January 2004 and June 2005. Parents in both surveys had at least one child under the age of 18 years at the time of interview and had registered with the Child Support Agency.
- The Grandparents in Separated Families Study 2009 (GSFS 2009) was an online national survey of grandparents with at least one grandchild aged 2–10 years whose parents had separated between 1 January 2004 and 31 December 2008. A total of 526 grandparents participated in the survey but it is important to note that the sample may not be representative of the Australian population of grandparents in this position. The survey was first conducted in Victoria in order to derive the necessary information to

select focus group participants. It was subsequently decided that the survey should be extended nationally (with minor changes made, including omission of the invitation to participate in focus groups that had been extended to participants in Victoria). Recruitment was achieved through the placement of advertisements in the *Herald Sun, The Age, The Australian*, and a number of seniors' publications, including state-based newsletters of the Council on the Ageing (COTA) and *The Senior*, a national newspaper for those aged 50 or more years. A sub-sample of grandparents who had completed the online survey then participated in one of a series of focus groups.

- An online survey of Family Relationship Services Program (FRSP) Staff was conducted in 2008 (Survey of FRSP Staff 2008). The study tapped the views of FRSP staff members of services that commenced operation prior to 1 July 2007 (including 40 Family Relationship Centres that were in operation at the time of the survey) in relation to various aspects of the 2006 family law reforms.
- The Family Lawyers Survey, conducted in 2008 (FLS 2008), was an online survey. It focused on views of family lawyers on the 2006 family law reforms, with 319 family lawyers participating in the survey.

objective behind this change was to "facilitate greater involvement of extended family members in the lives of children."[2]

This article addresses the following questions:

- What are parents' views in general about children maintaining contact with each set of grandparents after their parents separate?
- How common is it for parents to consider grandparenting time when developing their post-separation parenting arrangements?
- To what extent have family lawyers and relationship service practitioners noticed any change in the number of grandparents seeking their advice about issues in relation to the time they spend with their grandchildren?
- What impact do grandparents believe the 2006 reforms have had on their capacity to remain involved with their grandchildren?

Attitudes Concerning Children Maintaining Contact with Their Grandparents After Parental Separation

In the GPPS 2009, parents were asked to indicate their level of agreement or disagreement with the following statement: "It is important for children to maintain the same level of contact with their grandparents on both sides after parental separation". The response options were: "strongly agree", "agree", "mixed feelings", "disagree", and "strongly disagree". Some parents expressed uncertainty, and these responses have been combined with the "mixed feelings" category.

Nine in ten fathers and mothers agreed (either strongly or moderately) with this statement, with slightly more mothers than fathers reporting strong agreement (45% vs 39%). Few fathers and mothers

Figure 1

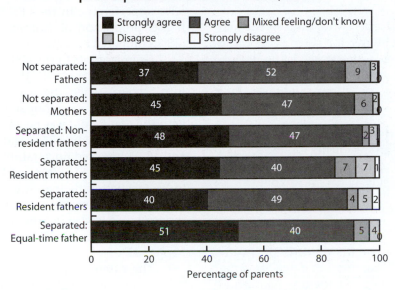

Parents' agreement that grandchildren should maintain the same contact with grandparents on both sides after separation, by whether separated and by post-separation residence status, 2009

Note: The results for non-resident mothers and mothers with equal care-time arrangements are not reported owing to the small number of cases.

Source: GPPS 2009

disagreed (about 3%), and small proportions had mixed feelings (6–7%).

Figure 1 shows the patterns of answers provided by parents (both non-separated and separated with different care-time arrangements) regarding whether they considered that if parents separate it is important that children continue to maintain the same level of contact with their grandparents on both sides.[3]

Strong agreement was expressed by 37–51% of parents across the groups, with the proportions being highest among fathers who had equal care time arrangements (51%) and non-resident fathers (48%), and lowest for fathers who had not separated (37%) and resident fathers (40%). Nevertheless, the overwhelming majority of parents in all groups agreed either strongly or moderately with the statement (between 85% and 94%).

These results suggest that attitudes of Australian parents, including those who have separated, are very consistent with the objective of the reforms: to facilitate the continued involvement of grandparents in the lives of their grandchildren after parental separation.

Consideration of Spending Time with Grandparents When Making Parenting Arrangements

Three surveys—the 2008 Longitudinal Study of Separated Families; the 2009 Looking Back Survey; and the 2009 Grandparents in Separated Families Study—included questions on whether their focus child[4] spending time with grandparents was taken into account when the parents were sorting out their parenting arrangements. It should be noted that parents in LSSF 2008 had separated after 1 July 2006, when the 2006 family law reforms commenced their roll-out, while those in LBS 2009 had separated 1–2.5 years before the reforms came into force. The questions asked are listed in Box 2.

In developing their parenting arangements, it appears that consideration of children's time with their grandparents was by no means uncommon for parents who separated 1–2.5 years prior to the reforms (reported by 40% of parents in the LBS 2009). However, this percentage is somewhat lower than that reported by parents

Box 2

Questions about consideration of time with grandparents

In the LSSF 2008, parents who had sorted out the parenting arrangements for their focus child were asked: "When you were deciding the parenting arrangements for [focus child], was spending time with grandparents, on either side, taken into account?"

In LBS 2009, parents were asked: "When you were deciding the parenting arrangements for [focus child] in [year separation took place], was spending time with grandparents, on either side, taken into account?"

Response options for questions in both LSSF 2008 and LBS 2009 were "yes" or "no".

In the GSFS 2009, grandparents were asked: "At the time your grandchild's parents separated, to what extent did they take the needs of this grandchild to have a continuing relationship with you into account?" Response options were: "fully taken into account", "to a fair extent", "a little", and "not at all taken into account".

who had separated postreform (53% of parents in the LSSF 2008). In the LSSF 2008, a similar proportion of fathers and mothers indicated that time with grandparents had been taken into account during the process of sorting out parenting arrangements for their child (52% and 53% respectively). In the LBS 2009, on the other hand, a higher proportion of mothers reported this than fathers (48% compared to 38%).

Grandparents in the GSFS 2009 also commonly indicated that their time with the focus grandchild was taken into account when the parents of this child separated. Specifically, 53% of grandparents reported that their time with the grandchild was taken into account either fully or to a fair extent, while 34% said that this was not the case, and 13% expressed uncertainty.

Parents in LSSF 2008 and LBS 2009 were also asked to indicate whether their arrangements were mainly reached through: (a) counselling, mediation or dispute resolution services; (b) a lawyer; (c) the courts; or (d) discussions with the other parent; or whether the arrangements (e) "just happened".

The extent to which grandparenting time was considered in the development of postseparation parenting arrangements by these main pathways is shown in Figure 2.[5] Parents who had separated post-reform were more likely than their "pre-reform counterparts" to report that time spent with grandparents had been taken into account, regardless of the main pathway taken. The

Figure 2

Parents indicating that time spent with grandparents was taken into account when deciding parenting arrangements for focus child, by main pathways, parent reports

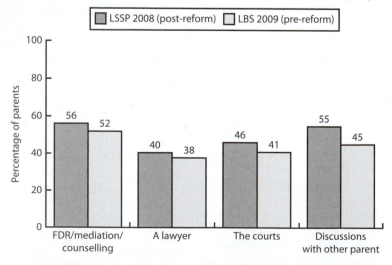

difference was most pronounced with respect to the "discussions with the other parent" pathway and least pronounced with respect to reliance on lawyers.

In short, although some grandparents go to considerable lengths to see their grandchildren, the above-mentioned figures suggest that there may be more willingness among post-reform separated parents to include grandparents in the post-separation parenting equation. The trend is not linked to one resolution or decision-making pathway, though it is least pronounced when lawyers were nominated as the main pathway.

Although a substantial proportion of the separated parents in the pre- and post-reform samples of parents (LSSF 2008 and LBS 2009) and grandparents (GSFS 2009) reported that time spent with grandparents was considered in developing their parenting arrangements, some grandparents who participated in the focus groups in the GSFS indicated that they had to fight through the legal system to have access to their grandchildren. For example:

> I see him [the grandchild] more regular now . . . because I won . . . I see him once a fortnight . . . But I had to go through nine months' court to do it because she said I wasn't going to see him and we tried all the mediation. I went through everything I could. (Paternal grandmother, grandchild lived with mother)

> I was adamant at the outset as [grandchild's] grandmother that I wouldn't lose any contact—I mean, I would have flown to the end of the earth if I had to. But it simply wasn't viable and there was no . . . I wasn't going to lose that contact. As a consequence of that, myself and my husband have a very close relationship with [the grandchild]. (Paternal grandmother, grandchild lived with mother)

It was clear from the discussion in the grandparents focus groups that there were also a number of grandparents who had no choice but to remain involved. At the most extreme end of the spectrum were grandparents who had become de facto parents to their grandchildren due to varied circumstances.

Family Lawyers' and Family Relationship Practitioners' Perceptions of Grandparenting Under the 2006 Family Law Reforms

The Family Lawyers Survey 2008 was designed in part to throw some light on the impact of the insertion into the Family Law Amendment Bill 2006 of the principle that recognised the child's right to spend time and communicate on a regular basis with people, including grandparents, who played a significant role in their care, welfare and development. Two questions in the survey attempted to gauge whether family lawyers had noticed an increase in grandparents seeking advice and the tenor of the advice they may be given. These were: (a) "Since the reforms, more grandparents are seeking advice"; and (b) "Since the reforms, I am more inclined to advise grandparents that they are in a stronger position in relation to spending time with their grandchildren".

The survey suggests that half the family lawyers surveyed thought that there had been an increase in the extent to which grandparents were seeking advice. On the other hand, 37% disagreed with this proposition, and the remainder were unable to say. The majority of family lawyers (57%) agreed that, since the reforms, they were more inclined to advise grandparents that they were in a stronger position in relation to spending time with their grandchildren. But again, 34% disagreed and 10% were unable to say.

In the Survey of FRSP Staff 2008, respondents were asked a series of questions to gauge the extent to which parents and grandparents were seeking to increase the time that children spent with their grandparents since the reforms came into effect. The results are summarised in Figures 3a–3c.

Substantial numbers of FRSP early intervention staff members[6] felt unable to answer the three questions posed in Figures 3a–3c, but of those who did, most of them agreed or strongly agreed that since the 2006 reforms, their service had seen an increase in fathers, mothers and grandparents (taken separately) wanting the children to spend time with the grandparents. Only small percentages disagreed or strongly disagreed.

About three-quarters of Family Relationship Centre staff members agreed (strongly or otherwise) that among their service's clientele, the proportion of mothers and fathers wanting their children to spend time with their grandparents had increased, and 62% agreed that there had been an increase in the proportion of grandparents wanting to spend time with their grandchildren. Only small proportions of Family Relationship Centre staff disagreed (strongly or moderately) that there had been an increase in the proportion of mothers and fathers wanting their children to spend time with their grandparents; but almost a third disagreed that there had been an increase in the proportion of grandparents among their clients wanting to spend time with their grandchildren.

Staff from family dispute resolution services appeared to be less inclined than their counterparts from FRCs to

Figure 3a

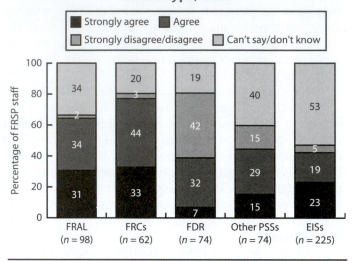

Agreement by FRSP staff that since the reforms an increasing proportion of fathers wanted their children to spend time with their grandparents, by service type, 2008

Notes: FRAL = Family Relationship Advice Line; FRCs = Family Relationship Centres; FDR = family dispute resolution services; Other PSSs = Other post-separation services; and EISs = early intervention services.

Figure 3c

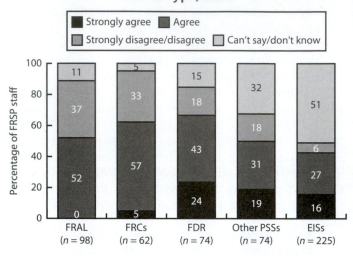

Agreement by FRSP staff that since the reforms an increasing proportion of grandparents wanted to spend time with their grandchildren, by service type, 2008

Figure 3b

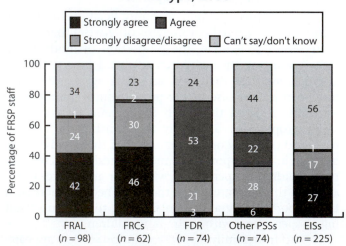

Agreement by FRSP staff that since the reforms an increasing proportion of mothers wanted their children to spend time with their grandparents, by service type, 2008

report having experienced an increase among their clients (fathers and mothers) wanting their children to spend more time with grandparents (24–39%).

The discrepancy in responses from FRC and FDR staff suggests that, at the time of the survey, the services may have had quite different cultures and/or may have been attracting different clienteles. One obvious difference is that after the 2006 reforms, FDR services continued (as they had in the past) to charge a fee, whereas family dispute resolution that occurred in an FRC was free for the first three hours. In addition, it is important to note that Family Relationship Centres offer considerably more than family dispute resolution services, and not all FRC staff members are family dispute resolution practitioners.[7] Responses of Family Relationship Centre staff are much more in line with those of Family Relationship Advice Line staff. This may reflect the fact that, unlike family dispute resolution services, both Family Relationship Centres and the Family Relationship Advice Line grew directly out of the 2006 reforms and may have been culturally more strongly connected with the reforms' aspirations.

Of the other post-separation service staff, 45% agreed or strongly agreed that their service had seen an increasing proportion of fathers wanting their children to spend more time with their grandparents and 33% agreed that this was the case with mothers. Large minorities (40% and 44% respectively) were unable to say, while 15% and 22% respectively disagreed or strongly disagreed with these propositions. Half of this group agreed or strongly agreed that there had been an increase in grandparents wanting to spend time with their grandchildren, but 18% disagreed or strongly disagreed with this proposition and 32% were unable to say.

Grandparents' Perceptions and Knowledge about the 2006 Family Law Reforms

Grandparents who participated in the GSFS 2009 were asked whether they were aware of the 2006 changes in the *Family Law Act* that recognise the right of children to have a relationship with their parents and others important to them, including grandparents. They were asked to indicate whether they were "fully aware", "to a fair extent", "a little" or "not at all aware". They were also asked if, in their opinion, the legislative changes would make any difference in helping children to maintain contact with their grandparents, by indicating if they thought the reforms would be: "a great deal of help", "some help" or "no help at all". In interpreting the patterns of responses, it should be kept in mind that the sample of grandparents is not representative of those who filled the criteria adopted for recruitment (having at least one grandchild aged 2–10 years whose parents separated between 1 January 2004 and 31 December 2008) (see Text Box 1 for details about the sample recruitment).

At least four in ten of these grandparents indicated that they were aware of the explicit reference to grandparents in the legislation, with 17% indicating that they were fully aware of the reference and 27% stating that they had some knowledge of it, while 54% were either a little or not at all aware of the reference and a small number (2%) were not sure about this issue. Grandparents tended to welcome the legislative changes, with 42% reporting that the explicit reference to grandparents would greatly help grandchildren to maintain contact with their grandparents, 38% considering that this would be "some help", and only 13% indicating the change would provide "no help at all". Eight per cent expressed no opinion on this issue.

At the same time, the focus group discussions with grandparents revealed that although they may have heard or read about them, almost all of the grandparents had

only a rudimentary understanding of the 2006 family law reforms or of the services that had been established or expanded. For example:

I thought there were some changes to the financial side of it and, as you said, the amount of time you spend—whether it's 50–50, 60–40—but the contribution from the father, money coming from the father, was actually less now than it was before. (Maternal grandmother, grandchild lived with mother)

The only thing I recently read was they are actually reviewing 50–50 custody. Is that currently happening? (Maternal grandmother, grandchild in shared care time)

I only heard that grandparents now have rights; that's all I heard. I didn't hear *how* you had rights, but I just hear that grandparents now have rights. (Maternal grandmother, grandchild with shared care time)

I don't know a lot about them. I remembered when they were talked about and I read a little bit about [them]. I asked my son what was going to happen. He said that he felt it was going to be a fairer system between him and his ex-wife. (Paternal grandmother, grandchild lived with mother)

A few grandparents had been proactive in their search for service options.

If I find things in *The Age* about family violence or children, separate parents or—and they've usually got a web page or they've got a contact number—I've chopped those out and I fold them into a little thing and I say here's some compulsory reading. We laugh. Other things as well that I think are interesting for child rearing. But at the library, it has the pamphlets on all manner of things. I've seen things there on your role as a parent and grandparent and children and those sorts of things, so I think that's a source. (Maternal grandparent, child living in shared care arrangement)

The extent to which such searches were inspired by the reforms was not clear. Certainly there was very little evidence of direct knowledge of the non-legal services that were available for these grandparents, their adult children or their grandchildren. For example, few grandparents in the focus groups were aware of the existence of more than one of a list of relevant services shown to them at the time[8] and many seemed inclined to continue to see child and relationship issues arising out of separation within the more traditional framework of being essentially legal problems.

Discussion

The data reported in this paper suggest that there is a widely held view among parents that it is important to maintain the same level of contact with grandparents as was occurring before parental separation. This is consistent with the recognition in the 2006 family law reforms that children have a right to maintain their relationship with their grandparents and other people who play a significant and beneficial role in their lives.

A majority of post-reform parents who had sorted out their parenting arrangements felt that time spent with grandparents had been taken into account, and most grandparents confirmed this perception. Pre-reform separated parents, on the other hand, were less likely to have taken grandparents into account. This change is consistent with the aspirations of the reforms. In addition, there is evidence from family lawyers and family relationship practitioners (especially those working in Family Relationship Centres and the Family Relationship Advice Line) that following the 2006 family law reforms, more parents and grandparents had sought advice about the time spent between grandchildren and grandparents as a result of separation.

It is also important to recognise that the data reported here speaks to changes in attitudes and practices that were taking place quite soon after the 2006 reforms had been put in place.

While most grandparents who elected to participate in the survey of grandparents attested to the fact that that their relationship with their grandchildren had been considered, there was also evidence that they had very little knowledge of the services available to assist them in achieving their goals in this respect, and only a rudimentary knowledge (if at all) of the aims of the reforms that refer to grandparents.

In addition, although the data suggest that grandparenting issues are more prominent in the post-reform environment, it also remains the case that the pragmatics of post-separation child care arrangements continue to have a flow-on effect for many grandparents and grandchildren. By this we mean that because mothers continue to be the major postseparation carers of their children in most cases, there is likely to be less time available for paternal grandparents to spend time with their grandchildren. Of course, some mothers with major care obligations will nonetheless encourage continued paternal grandparenting

involvement, but the practical as well as emotional difficulties that pertain in such circumstances can be considerable. It also needs to be acknowledged that, like all relationships, grandparenting covers a wide range of activities and levels of commitment.

Finally, it seems likely that if the legislation continues to act in the direction detected in the research to date, new generations of grandparents will become increasingly knowledgeable about family law systems and services and will increasingly be willing to pursue their grandchildren's rights, under normal circumstances, to maintain and continue to develop relationship with their grandparents.

Notes

1. The GPPS was a 2006 study of 5,000 parents, conducted by the Australian Institute of Family Studies (AIFS) and funded by the Australian Government Attorney-General's Department (AGD) and the Department of Families, Housing, Community Services and Indigenous Affairs (FaHCSIA).

2. Explanatory Memorandum ¶ 39, Family Law Amendment (Shared Parental Responsibility) Bill 2006 (Cth)).

3. The groups represented in Figure 1 were selected because they each comprised at least 40 respondents. The numbers of respondents in each group were: non-separated fathers: $n = 1,802$; non-separated mothers: $n = 2,040$; non-resident fathers: $n = 174$; resident fathers: $n = 82$; resident mothers: $n = 560$; and fathers with an equal care-time arrangements: $n = 57$.

4. Where there was more than one child under 18 years old born of the former couple, questions in each of the three surveys were asked in relation to one child only (the "focus child"). In the LSSF 2008 and LBS 2009, this child was the first listed in the Child Support Agency's database. In the GSFS 2009, this child was the youngest of those grandchildren aged 2–10 years whose parents had separated. Unless otherwise specified, the concepts "child" and "children" refer to the "focus child" of a respondent and "focus children" of all respondents respectively.

5. Some parents who indicated that their parenting arrangements just happened also reported that the time that the focus child spent with grandparents was considered (41–48% in the LBS and LSSF).

6. FRSP services surveyed were divided into early intervention (EIS) and post-separation (PSS) services. EISs consisted of: family relationship

counselling services; men and family relationship services; specialised family violence services; and family relationship education and skills training. PSSs consisted of: the Family Relationships Advice Line; Family Relationship Centres; family dispute resolution; and "others", such as the Parenting Orders Program and Children's Contact Services. While post-separation service practitioners almost always work with families in which a separation has already occurred, pre-separation service practitioners may find themselves working from time to time with families in which a separation has occurred, is about to occur, or occurs during the delivery of the service. It should be noted that the qualitative data suggest that Family Relationship Centres are also seeing estranged grandparents whose grandchildren have not experienced parental separation.

7. The 2008 Survey of FRSP Staff included staff from the 40 Family Relationship Centres that were in operation at the time. While all Family Relationship Centres were included in the 2008 FRSP staff surveys, the questions on grandparenting issues were not asked of all participating staff members.

8. The services listed include: Family Relationships Centres; Family Relationship Advice Line (telephone service); telephone dispute resolution service; Family Relationships Online (web-based service); family dispute resolution services; family relationship counselling services; Children's Contact Services; Parenting Orders Program; Post Separation Cooperative Parenting; Supporting Children after Separation Program; Mensline Australia; Men and Family Relationships Services; Specialised Family Violence Services; Family Relationship Education and Skills Training.

References

Australian Bureau of Statistics. (2006). *Child care, Australia 2005*. (Cat. No. 4402.0). Canberra: ABS.

Australian Bureau of Statistics. (2008). *Familycharacteristics and transitions, Australia, 2006–07*. (Cat. No. 4442.0). Canberra: ABS.

Cherlin, A. J., & Furstenberg, F. F., Jr. (1986). *The new American grandparent: A place in the family, a life apart*. New York: Basic Books.

Lussier, G., Deater-Deckard, K., Dunn, J., & Davies, L. (2002). Support across two generations: Children's closeness to grandparents following parental divorce and remarriage. *Journal of Family Psychology, 16*(3), 363–376.

Mutchler, J. E., & Baker, L. A. (2009). The implications of grandparent coresidence for economic hardship among children in mother-only families. *Journal of Family Issues, 30*, 1576–1597.

Horsfall, B. & Dempsey, D. (2011). Grandfathers and grandmothers looking after grandchildren: Recent Australian research. *Family Relationship Quarterly, 18*, 10–12.

Ochiltree, G. (2006). *Grandparents, grandchildren and the generation in between*. Camberwell, Vic.: ACER Press.

Weston, R. (1992). Families after marriage breakdown. *Family Matters, 3*(2), 41–45.

Weston, R. & Qu, L. (2009). Relationships between grandparents and grandchildren. *Family Matters, 81*, 58–60.

Weston, R., Qu, L., Gray, M., Kaspiew, R., Moloney, L., Hand, K. & the Family Law Evaluation Team (2011). Care-time arrangements after the 2006 reforms: Implications for children and their parents. *Family Matters, 86*, 19–32.

Lixia Qu is a senior research fellow at the Australian Institute of Family Studies. Her research work includes couple formation and re-formation, relationship stability, factors contributing to fertility decision making, the impacts of divorce on financial living standards and personal well-being, parenting arrangements after separation, changes in and determinants of labor force participation of lone and couple mothers, living arrangements and personal well-being.

Lawrie Moloney is a senior research fellow at the Australian Institute of Family Studies and also holds an adjunct professorial position with the School of Public Health in the Faculty of Health Sciences at La Trobe University. He is interested in the theory and practice of dispute resolution, especially within a family context, and in the practice questions and social issues arising out of what is broadly termed "family law."

Ruth Weston is an assistant director at the Australian Institute of Family Studies. Her research focuses on family transitions and well-being at both macro- and micro-levels.

Kelly Hand is a senior research fellow at the Australian Institute of Family Studies. Her work focuses on the area of service provision to families—particularly those in vulnerable and disadvantaged communities.

JULIE DEBLAQUIERE is a senior research officer at the Australian Institute of Family Studies. She has worked in the family law and family transitions area including on the Evaluation of the 2006 Family Law Reforms and a number of national evaluations examining service provision to separating families.

JOHN DE MAIO is a research fellow at the Australian Institute of Family Studies. His research has focused on family law and family transitions. He has also been involved in evaluating family law programs aiming to improve collaboration between family law service organizations and assist parents resolve their post-separation parenting arrangements where there has been an alleged experience of family violence.

Rachel Dunifon and Ashish Bajracharya  **NO**

The Role of Grandparents in the Lives of Youth

Recent trends have increased the potential salience of the role of grandparents in the lives of their grandchildren. Life expectancy has increased from less than 50 years in 1900 to almost 80 years in 2005 (National Center for Health Statistics, 2010), meaning that more grandparents are able to enjoy sustained relationships with their grandchildren as they move into adolescence and adulthood. Increased financial security among older Americans, due to the availability of Social Security and pensions, means older people spend more time in retirement, with potentially greater time available to spend with grandchildren (Szinovacz, 1998). Family sizes have decreased as well—in 1955 the average household with children had 2.18 children; now that number is 1.86—meaning that grandparents may be able to invest more in their grandchildren than before (U.S. Census Bureau, 2009a). While increased migration means that fewer children than before live close to their grandparents, newer avenues for communication, such as email, may facilitate contact between grandparents and grandchildren independent of distance. Thus, grandparents have the potential to play an influential role in the lives of their grandchildren. Despite this, the role of grandparents in the lives of youth remains an under-studied topic.

Using data from a nationally-representative group of youth aged 14–19 from the 1992 Wave Two National Survey of Families and Households (NSFH), this study seeks to better understand the role of grandparents in the lives of grandchildren by addressing the following questions: 1) What factors predict the quality of the grandparent-grandchild relationship? and 2) What are the implications of this relationship for youth?

Theoretical Perspectives

Several theoretical perspectives illuminate the factors that may influence grandparent-grandchild relationship quality, as well as the ways in which this relationship may ultimately influence grandchildren themselves. The life course perspective emphasizes the linked lives of family members, in which intergenerational relationships evolve over time and within social contexts, and family members influence each other reciprocally (see Crosnoe and Elder, 2002). This perspective suggests that the grandparent-grandchild relationship may change over time, and that age (of both the grandparent and grandchild) may play an important role in this relationship. Additionally, this perspective highlights the importance of looking at the roles that other family members (for example, parents) may play in the grandparent-grandchild relationship.

The grandparent-grandchild relationship may also be differentiated by gender—of the grandchild, grandparent, or both. For a variety of reasons, due to evolutionary theory (maternal grandmothers are more certain of their biological connection to their grandchildren), social theory (in which females are conceptualized to be more family oriented), exchange theory (because women are more involved in child-rearing, their own children are more likely to involve them in the lives of their children), or the simple fact that grandmothers tend to live longer than grandfathers (Szinovacz, 1998), it is possible that grandmothers may have a higher relationship quality with their grandchildren than grandfathers, and that this may be particularly so for maternal grandmothers (Spitze and Ward, 1998).

Another perspective suggests that, given limited resources, grandparents adopt a model of "selective investment" (Cherlin and Furstenberg, 1992; p. 96), devoting more resources to grandchildren who are experiencing a crisis such as parental death, divorce, unemployment, illness, or incapacitation. This has been referred to as the latent function hypothesis, and suggests that in general, grandparents may play a minor role in their grandchildren's lives, except during times of crisis (Clingempeel, Colyar, Brand, and Hetherington, 1992). Indeed, children living with a single mother are more likely to experience a very high level of grandparent involvement—living with a grandparent—than are

Dunifon, Rachel; Bajracharya, Ashish. "The Role of Grandparents in the Lives of Youth," *Journal of Family Issues*, vol. 33, no. 9, September 1, 2012. Copyright © 2012 National Institutes of Health.

children living with married parents (in 2009, 9% of all U.S. children were living with a grandparent; 17% of children living with a single mother were doing so; U.S. Census Bureau, 2009b).

Given higher rates of poverty and single-parenthood among African-American families, the latent function hypothesis may manifest itself in race differences in grandparent involvement. However, racial variation in the grandparent-grandchild relationship may reflect cultural differences as well, such as a traditional emphasis on extended family in African-American kinship networks (Hunter and Taylor, 1998). Each of these perspectives would suggest greater grandparental involvement, and perhaps a different type of grandparent-grandchild relationship, in African-American families, compared to white families.

Ecological and family systems theories emphasize the ways in which family members reciprocally influence each other, as well as how they ultimately influence children's development (King, Russell, and Elder, 1998; Lussier, Deater-Deckard, Dunn and Davies, 2002). This concept is further refined by Silverstein, Giarruso and Bengston (1998) as "intergenerational solidarity", or "the sentiments and behaviors that link family members across generations" (p. 144). This suggests that the grandparent-grandchild relationship must be looked at in the context of other family relationships—those between parents and grandparents, as well as between grandparents and their own parents and grandparents.

Factors Influencing the Grandparent-Grandchild Relationship

The perspectives reviewed above suggest several factors that may influence the grandparent-grandchild relationship.

Demographic Factors

One factor associated with grandparent-grandchild relationship quality is age. The type of relationships that grandparents have with their grandchildren changes as grandchildren age. For young children, grandparents often provide direct care (Cherlin and Furstenberg, 1992), while among older children the grandparent may serve as a confidant and emotionally supportive mentoring figure (Tomlin, 1998; Silverstein and Marenco, 2001). Research suggests that grandparents are less satisfied with the grandparent-grandchild relationship as the grandchild enters the teenage years (Cherlin and Furstenberg, 1992); grandchildren may feel the same way, reporting a decrease in reported support from grandparents and an increase in

conflict from 4th to 10th grades (Furman and Burhmester, 1992). The grandparent-grandchild relationship may change again as grandchildren age further. Crosnoe and Elder (2002) report an improvement in the grandparent-grandchild relationship quality when grandchildren enter college.

Grandparent age may be important as well, as older grandparents may have more time to invest in children, but may be limited in their ability to do so due to potential health problems. As noted by Silverstein, Giarrusso, and Bengston (1998), grandparent age and grandchild age may interact with each other in predicting relationship quality. Additionally, age is confounded with the passage of time and cohort effects, meaning that, to truly understand how the grandparent-grandchild relationship evolves over time, longitudinal data is needed.

Race too may play a role in the grandparent-grandchild relationship. Some studies find that black grandparents take on a more parental role in their interactions with their grandchildren, providing discipline (Cherlin and Furstenberg, 1992), teaching life skills (Tomlin 1998), and generally playing a more salient role in their grandchildren's lives (Hunter and Taylor, 1998) than do white grandparents. In a study of 122 highschoolers, Hirsch, Mickus and Boerger (2002) found that black teens were more likely to talk to their grandparents about issues they were having with their parents than were white teens.

Several studies also point to a role for gender in the grandparent-grandchild relationship. Matrilineal grandparents tend to be more involved with their grandchildren than those on the paternal side (Uhlenberg and Hammill, 1998), and grandmothers tend to be more involved than grandfathers (Silverstein and Marenco, 2001). Reports by teenaged and young adult grandchildren indicate that they report a closer relationship with their maternal grandmothers than any other grandparent (Creasey, 1993; Hirsch, Mickus and Boerger, 2002; Elder and Conger, 2000). There is also some evidence that child gender plays a role in the grandparent-grandchild relationship, with one study suggesting that grandfathers tend to be more involved with grandsons than granddaughters (Cherlin and Furstenberg, 1992), granddaughters having a closer relationship with their grandparents than grandsons (Creasey and Koblewswi, 1991), and girls reporting a particularly close relationship to their maternal grandmothers (Lussier et al., 2002).

Grandchildren's relationships with their grandparents may also be contingent upon family structure. Grandchildren's relationships with their paternal grandparents may decline after divorce, especially in cases in which mothers have custody of the grandchildren (Creasey, 1993). On the other hand, grandparents may increase their involvement after a divorce, in order to provide support for a newly divorced parent (Cherlin and Furstenberg, 1992; Johnson, 1998). Indeed, research shows that grandparental involvement is highest in singlemother families, compared to step- and biological parent families (Clingempeel et al, 1992).

Physical Distance

One key factor influencing the grandparent-grandchild relationship is the geographic distance between grandparents and their grandchildren. Studies indicate that grandparent-grandchild relationship quality hinges on frequent contact; living geographically close to a grandparent influences contact, which in turn leads to improved relationship quality (Harwood, 2000; Mueller and Elder, 2003). As noted by Cherlin and Furstenberg (1992), "[i]f you want to predict how often a grandparent will see a particular grandchild, you need to know little more than how far they live from each other" (p. 108). What, then, predicts distance between grandparents and grandchildren? In a study of adult children and their own parents, Compton and Pollak (2011) find that the most consistent predictor of distance is education, with adults who are the most educated living farthest away from their own parents. Other factors associated with living farther from one's own parents include age, and being white (as opposed to black).

Family Interactions

Several scholars have postulated that the interrelationships between family members can influence the grandparent-grandchild relationship in numerous ways. In particular, the parent-grandparent relationship can play a key role in the grandchild-grandparent relationship, with parents serving as "gatekeepers" between the grandchild and grandparent (Mueller and Elder, 2003). Grandchildren are more likely to see their grandparents when their own parents report a better relationship with the grandparents either in adulthood (Cherlin and Furstenberg, 1992; Whitbeck, Hoyt and Huck, 1993) or when they were children (Whitbeck et al., 1993).

Measuring the Grandparent/Grandchild Relationship

The research above describes several factors influencing the grandparent-grandchild relationship. This relationship itself has been measured in a variety of ways. Cherlin and Furstenberg (1992) used grandparent reports to develop three profiles: companionate (focused on pleasurable interactions, but without the grandparent taking direct

responsibility for the grandchild); remote; and involved (with the grandparent taking on a parenting role). Mueller and Elder (2003), also using grandparent reports develop six categories: influential (high on all dimensions); supportive (a close relationship but with no disciplinary role); authority-oriented (high on discipline); passive (in the middle on most measures and no discipline provided); and detached (low on all measures).

Other work (Creasey and Koblewski, 1991; Creasey, 1993; Furman and Buhrmester, 1992; Elder and Conger, 2000) utilizes a multi-dimensional grandparent-grandchild relationship quality measure, reported by the grandchild, assessing concepts such as support, companionship, admiration, nurturance, and intimacy. Creasey's work focused on college students, while Furman and Burhmester examined a sample of relatively affluent mostly Caucasian children and Elder and Conger consider rural Iowa families. Others have used uni-dimensional measures, such as asking grandchildren to rate the quality of their relationship with their grandparent(s) (Whitbeck, Hoyt and Huck, 1993), or more focused measures, such as Crosnoe and Elder (2002), who assessed grandparent mentoring. Some studies have utilized relationship quality measures that combine physical and emotional closeness, assuming that these two are connected (Climgempeel et al., 1992).

The current study utilizes a multi-dimensional measure of the grandparent-grandchild relationship, reported by the grandchild, and drawn from a nationally-representative sample of youth.

The Grandparent/Grandchild Relationship and Child Well-Being

Relatively few studies have directly related the grandparent-grandchild relationship to measures of child well-being. Grandparents may have a direct influence on grandchildren through their interactions with them. For example, if grandchildren have contact with their grandparents, confide in them, or are close to them, grandparents could provide benefits by serving as role models and discussing appropriate behavior, encouraging academic or other success, helping with homework, or providing advice and emotional support. It is expected that, in general, grandparent involvement would have a positive influence on children, although the possibility exists that in some instances grandparents could serve as negative influences through their behavior or advice.

There are also several pathways through which grandparent involvement could influence youth. Grandparents may influence youth through their influence on parental behaviors. If grandparents provide advice and emotional support to parents, this could translate into decreased parental stress or improvements in parental emotional health, which ultimately may lead to positive youth outcomes. Additionally, Coleman's (1988) model of intergenerational closure suggests that involved grandparents may work with the parent to enforce consistent norms and monitor children's activities. On the other hand, it is possible that grandparents could increase stress within families if, by their involvement, they interfere with or subvert parents' parenting behaviors. Finally, grandchildren themselves could have reciprocal influences on grandparents, by providing emotional or other types of assistance.

Some studies have directly linked grandparent involvement to child well-being. Cherlin and Furstenberg (1992) find that grandparent-reported contact and involvement with grandchildren was not associated with children's behavior problems. Ruiz and Silverstein (2007) used data from the second wave of the NSFH (the same dataset used here) and find that, among youth aged 18–23, grandchild-reported closeness with grandparents is associated with lower levels of depression. This was particularly true for those raised by a single parent, and for those with a better reported relationship with their own parent(s). Elder and Conger (2000), in a multi-generational study of Iowa families, found that youth reports of closeness with grandparents was associated with perceptions of academic competence, with personal and social competence, and with self-confidence and maturity. Grandparent closeness was not associated with youth's grades.

Other studies relate specific grandparent behaviors or characteristics to child well-being. Stein, Newcomb and Bentler (1993) find that grandparental drug use influences grandchildren's behavior problems, while Loury (2006) finds that boys with more highly-educated male relatives (including grandfathers) achieved more education themselves, controlling for a host of family-level factors related to education.

Other studies examine how grandparent involvement interacts with parenting behaviors and other characteristics to influence children. Barnett, Scaramella, Neppl, Ontai and Conger (2010) find that, in a sample of 3- and 4-year olds, grandparent involvement (based on maternal reports) reduces the detrimental influence on children of negative reactivity and mothers' harsh parenting. Silverstein and Ruiz (2006) with data from the second and third waves of the NSFH, show that when grandparent-grandchild cohesion was high, mothers' depression was not associated with the depression of young adults, suggesting that grandparents may, in the authors' words "buffer the intergenerational transmission of depression" (p. 609).

Summary

Taken together, the literature reviewed above suggests that grandparents' relationships with their grandchildren can take several forms, and that a variety of factors influence this relationship. While previous research points to specific factors that influence the grandparent-grandchild relationship, few studies have considered the role of multiple factors, and few use national data to do so. Thus, in order to put into greater context our later analyses which focus on the consequences of this relationship for youth, a first step of our analysis is to examine the various factors that influence the grandparent-grandchild relationship.

The core of our analysis is to examine the implications for youth of the grandparent-grandchild relationship. As noted above, adolescence is a time in which the grandparent-grandchild relationship undergoes some important transitions, and a greater understanding of the consequences of this relationship for youth is needed. We examine the ways in which grandparent-grandchild relationship quality may influence youth outcomes that are predictors of young adult success, including grades, risky behaviors, and sexual behavior, using national data. Given grandparents' role during adolescence as potential mentors and role models, these dimensions of youth behavior may be particularly influenced by the grandparent-grandchild relationships.

The goal of this study is to ask: 1) What factors predict the quality of the grandparent-grandchild relationship? and 2) What are the implications of this relationship for youth?

It is important to note that youth who report a closer relationship with their grandparents may be a select group; for example, grandparents may be more emotionally close to children who are already doing well in school, or who are successful in other domains. Alternatively, grandparents may step in when children are faring poorly. Each of these scenarios could lead to biased estimates of the association between grandparent involvement and youth outcomes. Analyses examining the factors that predict the grandparent-grandchild relationship can help to inform this issue.

We also conduct a series of robustness checks attempting to limit the biasing role of selection and reverse-causality in our analyses. To do this, we substitute proxy measures of grandparental involvement for our measure of the grandparent-grandchild relationship quality, using four measures that are likely associated with the grandparent-grandchild relationship quality, but less likely to be associated with unmeasured factors that may differentiate children with various levels of grandparent relationship quality. First, a measure of the number of the child's living grandparents is used as a proxy for potential grandparent involvement, as the more grandparents a grandchild has to choose from, the more likely he or she is to have a good relationship with at least one. Additionally, because other research has shown that matrilineal grandparents tend to be more involved with their grandchildren (Uhlenberg and Hammill, 1998), and that grandmothers tend to be more involved than grandfathers (Silverstein and Marenco, 2001), we also use indicators of whether a child has at least one living grandparent on the maternal side, whether the maternal grandmother is alive, and whether the child has a living grandmother. While these measures are likely somewhat correlated with family characteristics, such as parental education or family income, the death of a grandparent is also an exogenous event, outside of the direct control of the child or his or her parents. As such, we view these analyses as one attempt to isolate, albeit imperfectly, a measure of grandparent involvement that is less likely to be influenced by unmeasured and potentially biasing characteristics of children and their families.

Building off of the research described above, we test the following hypotheses:

H1 Younger children, girls, African-American youth, those living closer to their grandparents, and those with a higher quality parent-grandparent relationship will report a higher quality relationship with their grandparent.

H2 Both a higher quality grandparent-grandchild relationship, and less physical distance between grandparents and grandchildren, will be associated with improved youth well-being.

H3 The relationship between the grandparent-grandchild relationship and youth well-being will be attenuated once issues of selection are addressed.

H4 The grandparent-grandchild relationship will be particularly beneficial for certain youth—those living with a single parent, African-American youth, and girls.

Data

The analyses presented here use data from second wave of the National Survey of Families and Households (NSFH). The NSFH began in 1987–1988 with a nationally representative sample of 13,007 households and consisted of interviews with a randomly selected main adult respondent from each household. In Wave 1, one focal child aged 5 to 18 years old was also randomly selected from among children living in each of the households and the main respondent was interviewed about the characteristics of this focal child. The second wave was collected in 1992–1994 and included telephone interviews with these originally chosen focal children who were aged 10 to 23 years old. A third wave was collected in 2001–2002 and included interviews with these focal children now aged 18–34 (Sweet and Bumpass, 1996).

All together, data was collected on 2,505 focal children through telephone interviews in Wave 2. A majority, (92.74% of our final sample), of focal children were biological children of the main NSFH respondent. The NSFH has the richest data on grandparent involvement of any national dataset. In the second wave, focal children were asked questions about which of their grandparents were living, how often they have contact with each grandparent, whether they ask each grandparent for advice, and how close they feel to each grandparent.

The analyses presented here utilize data from focal children who were aged 14 to 19 years old in Wave 2 and were still residing in the household of the main respondent. We also restrict our sample to focal children who did not have a grandparent living in the household, but who had at least one living grandparent, giving us a final sample of 551 children. We limited our data to the 14 to 19 age range in order to obtain a uniform set of age-appropriate outcome variables for the focal children, particularly in risky behaviors and sexual activity, since questions regarding these outcomes were either not asked for very young children aged 13 or under (e.g. about sexual activity) or could be inapplicable (e.g. for activities such as smoking marijuana). These children were on average 15.58 years old in Wave 2 (S.D. =1.29).

Measures

Dependent Variables

The dependent variables used in this study capture three key domains of youth well-being. First, **school performance** is measured using the focal child's self-reported grades in school. This variable measures grades in categories that range from 1 ("F's") to 8 ("Mostly A's"), with intermediate categories such as "A's and B's" (7), "B's" (6) and so on. A higher score on this scale represents a higher grade. For analyses looking at grades as an outcome, our sample is limited to youth who are still in high school (N = 532).

Second, we utilize an **index of children's risky behavior** that captures the focal child's self-reported substance use. Three dummy variables indicating whether the focal child has, in the last 30 days, a) smoked a cigarette, b) drank alcohol or c) used marijuana are summed together to create a risky behavior index that ranges from 0 to 3. This variable has a Cronbach's alpha of 0.52

Finally, we use a variable indicating whether the child has **ever had sex**. This variable is coded as 1 if the child reported ever having had sex and 0 if they did not. Due to sensitive nature of the question, children were given the option of not answering this question if they felt uncomfortable; thus there is more missing data on this measure than on other variables (N = 522). Children whose responses were missing on this variable differed significantly from other children in the sample on key characteristics. Children who did not answer the question on sexual activity were older, more likely to be male, and more likely to be from minority families. They were also more likely to be from single parent households with less educated parents and lower household income. These children also showed lower grades and higher risky behaviors but were more likely to report that they had good relationships with their grandparents, all compared to children who did answer the questions on sexual activity.

Independent Variables

Relationship of Grandchildren with Grandparents— In order to measure the quality of the relationship of the focal child with their grandparents, we create a composite measure of **grandparent-grandchild relationship quality** using three youth-reported variables taken from the second wave of the NSFH. First is the focal child's rating of how close he or she felt with each living grandparent, measured using a variable that ranges from 0 "not at all close" to 10 "extremely close". While this variable is measured for all living grandparents (up to four), only the closeness of the child's relationship with the highest rated grandparent is used in the scale (following Ruiz and Silverstein, 2007). This eliminates the possibility of an influential and meaningful relationship with one grandparent being cancelled out by mediocre or absent relationships with other grandparents.

Second, we use a variable indicating how frequently a child is in contact with their grandparents through activities such as talking on the telephone or receiving letters. This variable is measured on a scale of 1 ("not at all") to 5 ("more than once a week") with intermediate categories such as "once a year"(2) or "1–3 times a month" (4). Again, we use information from the highest-rated set of grandparents. For this measure, children were not asked

to rate each of four possible grandparents, but rather both the set of maternal grandparents and the set of paternal grandparents. This measure of frequency of contact differs from that used by Ruiz and Silverstein, which measured how often children saw their grandparents in person in the past year.

Finally, the third component of this scale is a single measure of how likely the child is to consult or confide in any grandparent if he or she had a major decision to make. This variable ranged from 1 ("definitely wouldn't") to 5 ("definitely would") and is not asked about a specific grandparent, but rather any grandparent in general.

Following Ruiz and Silverstein (2007), we then construct a composite measure of the quality of the grandparent-grandchild relationship with a factor score using principal components analysis of the three measured described above. The components of this composite variable are fairly internally reliable with a Cronbach's alpha of 0.61.

It is important to note that this composite measure of the grandparent-grandchild relationship quality does not capture children's relationship with a specific grandparent, but rather their overall relationship with their grandparents. This is due to the way that the various questions were asked. The measure of closeness to grandparents was asked separately for 4 different grandparents (maternal/paternal, grandmother/grandfather). In contrast, frequency of contact was asked only about maternal and paternal grandparents as a set. Finally, the measure of whether the child would confide in grandparents was asked about all grandparents as a group. This means that we are not able to create separate composite relationship quality measures for each grandparent. Additionally, our composite may reflect children's reports about different grandparents. For example, the closeness measure may be taken from the child's report of closeness to the maternal grandmother (if this was the highest ranked grandparent), while the measure of frequency of contact may reflect contact with the paternal grandparents as a set (if this is the highest ranked set of grandparents in terms of contact). Supplementary analyses (not shown here) reveal that in 93% of the cases, the grandparent to whom the focal child reports being closest is from the same set (maternal or paternal) with whom the grandchild reports having the greatest contact.

We utilize a composite measure in our main analyses in order to examine the influence on grandchildren of their relationship with their grandparents in the broadest possible sense, not limiting ourselves to certain aspects of the relationship in particular. We also, however, perform analyses in which the individual components of the relationship quality composite measure are examined separately.

Distance to nearest grandparent(s)—We also use in our analysis a measure of physical distance of the youth from his/her closest grandparent(s). We measure **grandparent-grandchild distance** based on the main parent respondent's report of how far, in miles, a) his/her parents (i.e., the child's grandparents) live from the household, and b) how far his/her spouse's parents live from their household. We then use the distance to the child's closest biological grandparent. In our analyses, we use a dummy variable that indicates whether the closest grandparent(s) lives 100 miles or farther from the grandchild. The distance of 100 miles or farther represents the top quartile of the distribution of the distance measure across all focal children in the sample and therefore indicates a grandparent who lives relatively far from the grandchild, compared to most other youth in the sample.

The physically closest grandparent may not necessarily be the one to which the grandchild reports the highest level of emotional closeness or contact (see above). Cross tabulation between these measures, however, suggest that reports of emotional closeness and physical proximity were consistent, with approximately 80% of children reporting that the grandparent to whom they are closest is the same grandparent who lives closest to them in terms of physical distance (results not shown).

Parent-child relationship—Because the grandparent-grandchild relationship may be influenced by the quality of the parent-child relationship, we add a control for child-parent relationship quality. This is based on the child's characterization of his or her relationship to the parent and is measured on a scale of 0 "really bad" to 10 "absolutely perfect". For children living with both biological parents, this is captured through the mean of childreported relationship quality measures for the two parents. For children living with single parents, stepparents or living with unmarried cohabiting parents, the measure reflects the relationship quality with their biological parent.

Number of living grandparents—In our main analyses, we control for the number of grandparents who are alive at the time of the survey in order to account for the fact that some children have more grandparents to draw on than do others. This measure is simply the sum of the number of both maternal and paternal biological grandparents who were alive and ranges from 1 to 4. Another variable used as a proxy for grandparent involvement measures the total number of maternal grandparents alive, ranging from 0 to 2. A third proxy measure is a dummy variable indicating whether the child's maternal grandmother is alive, and a fourth is a dummy variable indicating whether any grandmother was alive.

Control Variables

All analyses control for individual, family and demographic characteristics of children, their parents and their grandparents. Analyses control for focal child age, gender (coded 1 if boy) and for race using a set of mutually exclusive dummy variables indicating whether the child is non-Hispanic White (the omitted category), non-Hispanic Black, Hispanic, or of another race/ethnicity. Parents' educational attainment is measured with dummy variables indicating whether the main respondent parent had: no high school degree (omitted category), only a high school degree, some college, or a college degree. Analyses also control for family structure using a set of mutually exclusive indicators of whether the child is living with married biological parents (the omitted category), a single parent, stepparents, or unmarried cohabiting parents. Other demographic controls include the parent respondent's age, whether the respondent was female and the number of child's siblings in the household.

A series of controls for grandparent characteristics are also included. The parent respondent's closeness with the child's grandparents is based on a scale of 0 "really bad" to 10 "absolutely perfect", and reflects the biological grandparent the parent reports feeling the closest to. We also control for the age and health of the parent respondent's biological parents. If both grandparents are still alive, we calculate the mean of each grandparent characteristic across both. Grandparent age is measured in years. The variable indicating grandparent health is based on the parent respondent's report of the physical health status of the child's grandparents measured on a scale of 0 "very poor" to 5 "excellent".

A variable for total family income is also included in the analysis. This measure includes the income of the main respondent and up to two other household members (if available) from wages and salaries or any self-employment activity in the last year and is measured in thousands of dollars (1992 dollars). We use the natural logarithm of this figure in our analysis. Finally, we control for whether focal child's mother was employed. Due to an unusually large number of missing data points in the maternal employment indicator, we coded the missing data points as 0 in the original variable and created a separate missing data indicator for this variable.

Table 1 presents the descriptive statistics for all variables used here. In terms of distance, youth lived, on average, 274 miles away from their geographically closest grandparent. Approximately half of the youth lived less than 9 miles from their closest grandparent, with approximately a fifth of focal children living less than 1 mile away.

Looking at the three components of the grandparent-grandchild relationship quality scale, we see an average score of 8 out of a total of 10 possible points for the youth's report of the closeness of the highest-rated grandparent-grandchild relationship; the average level of contact with the highest-rated grandparent is 3.94 out of a 5 point scale, representing a frequency of contact of close to 1 to 3 times a month; and the average response for whether the youth would confide in a grandparent is 2.89 points out of a 5 point scale, representing a youth reporting that there is approximately a 50-50 chance that he or she would confide in a grandparent.

Looking at our three measures of youth well-being, the average reported grades were 5.58, which represent a grade of "B's and C's". The mean score on the risky behavior scale is low, only 0.77 out of a total possible of score of 3. Finally, 35.1% of the youth aged 14 to 19 years old who responded to the question regarding sexual activity reported that they had ever had sex.

Among the demographic variables, the average age for children in the sample was 15.6 years and the average adult respondent (child's parent) in the sample was 41.3 years old. In terms of living arrangements, 50.5% of the children lived with their married biological parents whereas about 24% of the children were living with an unmarried parent. The majority of the sample, 73%, was White (non-Hispanic) whereas 17% of the children were non-Hispanic Black and 8% were Hispanic. The average family had a total household income of approximately $46,800 at the time of the survey.

As Table 1 shows, missing data occurs on some of the individual measures used in our analysis. We use listwise deletion to deal with missing data.

Method

As noted above, the goal of this paper is to examine predictors of grandparent-grandchild relationship quality, and then examine the association between the grandparent-grandchild relationship quality and outcomes for youth. First, we examine whether and how characteristics of grandchildren and their families influence the grandparent-grandchild relationship quality. We first utilize OLS regressions to examine the factors that influence youth's reports of their relationship with the grandparents, controlling for the full set of covariates listed above.

Our next analyses relate the grandparent-grandchild relationship quality measure to three aspects of youth

well-being: grades in school, risky behaviors in the last 30 days, and whether the child has had sex. For the dependent variable of youth grades, which is a continuous measure ranging from 1 to 8, we utilize OLS regressions (as noted below, we also perform some analyses using an ordered logistic regression for the grades outcome). To analyze the outcome of youth risky behavior, which ranges from 0–3, we utilize an ordered logit regression, which is appropriate for discrete outcomes with ordinal rankings. In contrast, other options, such as multinomial regressions, do not take account of the fact that the response options are ranked with some being "better" than others (Greene, 1997). Ordered logit analyses are based on the assumption that the relationship between independent and dependent variables is constant across all levels of the dependent variable. We performed a series of Brant test (results available upon request) and found that this assumption held (Stata Annotated Output, 2010). For our ordered logit analyses, we present proportional odds ratios, which show the odds of being in a given category on the risky behavior index, compared to all other categories (i.e., the odds of being in the highest category, 3, vs. being in 0, 1 or 2). Finally, we utilize a logistic regression to examine having sex, and present odds ratios.

Results

Table 2 presents the results of OLS multivariate analyses examining predictors of the composite measure of grandparent-grandchild relationship quality. Results show that that distance is a strong predictor of relationship quality; children who live 100 miles or farther from their grandparent have a relationship quality that is 36% of a standard deviation lower than those who live closer. We also see that children who have a better relationship with their parents and whose parents have better relationships with their own parents, as well as those who have a larger number of living grandparents, report stronger relationships with their grandparents, while children whose parents are older report significantly weaker relationships with them.

We next present results from series of regression models examining the association between grandparent-grandchild relationship quality and youth outcomes. Results in Table 3 show that the grandparent-grandchild relationship quality is not associated with any of the youth outcomes. However, youth who have a better quality relationship with their parent have higher grades and exhibit less risky behavior. The other covariates in the model operate in the expected directions, with older children reporting more risky behavior and increased likelihood of having sex, and youth with more educated parents reporting higher grades, for example.

Table 1

Descriptive Statistics

Variable	Obs	Mean or %	Std. Dev.	Min	Max
Grandparent Measures					
Distance to the Nearest Grandparents in 100's of Miles	537	2.741	9.885	0	90
Nearest GP lives over 100 Miles from Child	493	0.245		0	1
Grandparent-Grandchild Relationship Quality Composite (Standardized)	547	−0.189	1.058	−3.888	1.456
Components of Relationship Quality Composite					
Relationship Quality Score with Grandparents (Maximum)	551	7.998	2.030	0	10
Contact with Grandparents via letters, phone calls (Maximum)	548	3.942	1.261	1	5
Whether Child would Confide in Grandparents	550	2.885	1.243	1	5
Youth Wellbeing					
Grades of Child	532	5.575	1.677	1	8
Risky Behavior Index	551	0.773	0.909	0	3
Child has had sex	522	0.351		0	1
Child's Characteristics					
Age of Child	551	15.584	1.290	14	19
Child is Boy	551	0.485		0	1
Child is White Non Hispanic	550	0.729		0	1
Child is Black Non Hispanic	550	0.169		0	1
Child is Hispanic	550	0.080		0	1
Child is of Other Race	550	0.022		0	1
Child lives with Married Bio. Parents	549	0.505		0	1
Child lives with Single Parents	549	0.239		0	1
Child lives with Step Parents	549	0.230		0	1
Child lives with Cohabiting Parents	549	0.027		0	1
Number of Siblings of Child in the Household	547	2.356	1.967	0	12
Parent Characteristics					
Parent (Respondent) is Female	549	0.687		0	1
Age of (Respondent) Parent	549	41.266	5.521	29	61
Parent has less than a High School Degree	549	0.144		0	1
Parent has a High School Degree	549	0.663		0	1
Parent has a College Degree	549	0.111		0	1
Parent has Some College	549	0.086		0	1
Mother is Employed (Missing=0)	551	0.728		0	1
Mother Employed Variable is Missing	551	0.172		0	1
Parent (Respondent) Relationship Quality with Grandparent	549	8.461	1.692	0	10
Parent Relationship Quality with Child (Respondent)	508	7.824	1.824	0	10
Grandparent Characteristics					
Grandparents' Age (Mean)	517	68.495	8.106	47.5	94
Grandparents' Health (Mean)	508	3.379	0.911	1	5
Parent's Relationship Quality with Child's GP	510	7.616	2.227	0	10

(Continued)

Variable	Obs	Mean or %	Std. Dev.	Min	Max
Proxy Variables for Grandparent Involvement					
Number of Grandparents who are Alive	551	2.650	0.981	1	4
Number of Maternal Grandparents who are Alive	551	1.428	0.642	0	2
Maternal Grandmother is Living	550	0.827		0	1
Any Grandmother is Alive	551	0.966		0	1
Household Economic Status					
Log of Total Household Income	541	10.464	0.889	5.298	13.459

Table 2

Demographic Characteristics and Physical Distance predicting Grandparent Grandchild Relationship Quality

	Grandparent-Grandchild Relationship Quality Principal Components Factor Score
Variable	**OLS Coefficient**
Nearest GP lives over 100 Miles from Child	−0.356*** (0.102)
Parent's Relationship Quality with Child's GP	0.134*** (0.026)
Parent's Relationship Quality with Child (R)	0.131*** (0.024)
Child is Boy	0.034 (0.086)
Age of Child	−0.060* (0.035)
Child is Black Non Hispanic	0.103 (0.127)
Child is Hispanic	−0.196 (0.163)
Child is of Other Race	0.068 (0.319)
Parent (R) is Female	0.076 (0.108)
Parent's (R) Age	−0.030*** (0.011)
Grandparents' Age (Mean)	−0.005 (0.007)
Grandparents' Health (Mean)	−0.006 (0.048)
Number of Siblings of Child in Household	0.031 (0.025)
Number of Grandparents Alive	0.099** (0.048)
Parent has a High School Degree	−0.074 (0.137)
Parent has a College Degree	0.140 (0.184)
Parent has Some College	−0.024 (0.199)
Child lives with Single Parents	0.009 (0.123)
Child lives with Step Parents	−0.126 (0.128)
Child lives with Cohabiting Parents	0.074 (0.270)
Log Total Household Income	0.067 (0.062)
Mother was Employed	−0.089 (0.144)
Mother Employed Missing	0.245 (0.175)
Constant	−0.722 (0.950)
Observations	439
R-squared	0.264

Standard errors in parentheses;
*** $p < 0.01$,
** $p < 0.05$,
* $p < 0.1$

Table 3

Grandparent-Grandchild Relationship Quality Composite Measure and Distance predicting Child Outcomes

Variable	Grades OLS Coefficient	Risky Behavior Index Ordered Logit Prop. Odds	Had Sex Odds Ratio
GP-GC Relationship Quality PC Factor Score	−0.073 (0.091)	0.935 (0.113)	1.094 (0.150)
Parent's Relationship Quality with Child's GP	0.042 (0.049)	0.993 (0.066)	1.103 (0.085)
Parent's Relationship Quality with Child (R)	0.138*** (0.045)	0.829*** (0.049)	0.919 (0.064)
Nearest GP lives over 100 Miles from Child	0.245 (0.191)	0.786 (0.211)	0.720 (0.220)
Child is Boy	−0.491*** (0.159)	1.333 (0.292)	1.583* (0.392)
Age of Child	−0.009 (0.066)	1.693*** (0.151)	2.160*** (0.237)
Child is Black Non Hispanic	−0.411* (0.236)	0.425** (0.145)	2.790*** (1.046)
Child is Hispanic	0.133 (0.303)	0.470* (0.208)	0.642 (0.307)
Child is of Other Race	1.075* (0.585)	1.144 (0.814)	1.185 (1.060)
Parent (R) is Female	−0.090 (0.201)	1.366 (0.396)	0.948 (0.305)
Parent's (R) Age	0.021 (0.021)	0.971 (0.028)	0.939* (0.031)
Grandparents' Age (Mean)	0.009 (0.013)	0.993 (0.017)	1.023 (0.020)
Grandparents' Health (Mean)	0.120 (0.089)	1.050 (0.129)	0.719** (0.098)
Number of Siblings of Child in Household	−0.053 (0.046)	1.055 (0.062)	1.083 (0.081)
Number of Grandparents Alive	0.106 (0.090)	0.804* (0.096)	0.874 (0.121)
Parent has a High School Degree	0.695*** (0.252)	0.551* (0.188)	0.292*** (0.114)
Parent has a College Degree	0.764** (0.340)	0.507 (0.241)	0.475 (0.256)
Parent has Some College	0.749** (0.366)	0.578 (0.290)	0.527 (0.298)
Child lives with Single Parents	−0.012 (0.229)	2.028** (0.633)	1.749 (0.625)
Child lives with Step Parents	−0.473** (0.236)	1.821* (0.567)	1.766 (0.648)
Child lives with Cohabiting Parents	−0.641 (0.516)	3.170* (1.952)	3.607 (2.865)
Log Total Household Income	0.151 (0.114)	1.266 (0.203)	1.024 (0.185)
Mother was Employed	0.179 (0.267)	0.941 (0.352)	3.343** (1.758)
Mother Employed Missing	−0.094 (0.325)	0.797 (0.361)	3.088* (1.843)
Constant	0.240 (1.757)		
Observations	428	439	417
R-squared	0.175		
Log-Likelihood		−365.6	−210.5
Chi-Squared		90.87	127.2
DF		24	24

As noted above, it is possible that children's reports of the quality of their relationship with their grandparents may be associated with unmeasured factors that are also correlated with their outcomes (although this concern is lessened due to the null results in Table 3). We perform a series of analyses to address this issue of selection by using four proxies for grandparent involvement described above. Results (not shown) confirm the results shown in Table 3, suggesting no association between the grandparent-grandchild relationship and the outcomes examined here.

Finally, as noted above, it is possible that grandparent involvement may matter most for certain sub-groups of children. We examined whether the association between the grandparent-grandchild relationship quality index and the outcomes we examined differ by child gender, family structure (single vs. not single parent), and by race/ethnicity (African-American non-Hispanic vs. White non-Hispanic) by interacting these indicators with our measure grandparent-grandchild relationship quality when predicting the three youth outcomes. Results from these analyses (not shown here) suggest that a pattern of different results by groups does not exist.

Additional Analyses

Our main analyses relate a composite measure of the grandparent-grandchild relationship quality to youth well-being, and results from Table 3 suggest that this measure is not associated with the youth outcomes examined here. In additional analyses, we test the associations between the three individual components of this composite measure and youth outcomes. Results (not shown) indicate only one association with youth outcomes—specifically, youth who report a higher overall relationship quality with a grandparent also report having lower grades.

We also performed some analyses including a measure of how often the youth sees his or her grandparents, in order to determine whether in-person contact with a grandparent plays a key role in predicting youth outcomes. Specifically, we used a measure indicating how often the youth had seen each grandparent in the past year, which ranged from 1 (not at all) to 6 (several times each week), using the measure from the highest-ranked grandparent. Results from these analyses (not shown) do not differ from our main analyses, in which this measure is not included. Further, the measure of how often the youth saw the grandparent was not a significant predictor of any of the outcomes examined here.

Discussion

This paper sheds light on the role of grandparents in the lives of youth by examining both the factors that are associated with the grandparent-grandchild relationship, as well as the influence of this relationship on three important dimensions of youth well-being.

Our first hypothesis was that younger children, girls and African-American youth would report a higher-quality relationship with their grandparents. Results show only that younger children have a higher grandparent-grandchild relationship quality than other youth, confirming previous research described above. It is possible that the lack of race differences in grandparent involvement is due to the fact that we controlled for several factors that may be correlated with such involvement and that may differ by race. As the latent function hypothesis (Clingempeel, Colyar, Brand, and Hetherington, 1992) suggests, higher levels of disadvantage among African-American families may precipitate greater grandparental involvement. Indeed, other analyses, which did not control for factors such as family structure, maternal education, and household income that are related to potential disadvantage, did find evidence that African-American youth have stronger relationships with their grandparents.

Our hypothesis that physical distance would be a significant predictor of the grandparent-grandchild relationship was confirmed. Results show that that living more than 100 miles from the nearest grandparent is associated with reduction in grandparent-grandchild relationship quality of 35% of a standard deviation. This is consistent with other studies (Harwood, 2000; Mueller and Elder, 2003; Cherlin and Furstenburg, 1992), and is confirmed and illuminated here in the context of a national sample of youth, and holding constant a wide range of other factors.

Also confirming our hypothesis, results show that another key predictor of the grandparent-grandchild relationship is the parent-grandparent relationship quality. Indeed, we found that a one point increase in the parent-grandparent relationship is associated with a 13% of a standard deviation increase in the grandparent-grandchild relationship quality, controlling for a host of other factors. As suggested by life course theory, interrelationships between family members can influence the grandparent-grandchild relationship in numerous ways. In particular, parents can serve as gatekeepers between grandparents and grandchildren. This gatekeeper role could be a literal one in which parents only permit or facilitate interactions between grandchildren and grandparents when they themselves are close to the child's grandparents. It could also be a more figurative role, in which youth observe their own parents' interactions with the grandparents and model their own relationship accordingly. Regardless, our findings suggest that parents' own strong relationships with the child's grandparents can overcome the barrier of physical distance and help establish a strong grandparent-grandchild relationship. This confirms the gatekeeper role of parents in the grandparent-grandchild relationship (Mueller and Elder, 2003), and extends this finding by considering a national study of teens and by comparing the role of relationship quality with that of a wide range of other factors.

Less examined in the previous literature is the influence of the parent-child relationship on the grandparent-grandchild relationship. We find that a one point increase in the child-parent relationship is associated with an increase in the grandparent-grandchild relationship quality of 13% of a standard deviation, the same effect size as found for the parent-grandparent relationship quality. This could be due to a variety of factors, one of which may be selection—families or circumstances in which children feel close to their parents also the same in which they feel close to their grandparents for reasons that we do not observe. It is also possible that strong parent-child ties, combined with strong parent-grandparent relationships, lay the groundwork for a scenario in which children are encouraged to develop close bonds with their grandparent. Future work could more carefully consider the role of the parentchild relationship in the context of the grandparent-grandchild dynamic.

We also hypothesized that the grandparent-grandchild relationship quality would be associated with youth well-being. We did not find support for this hypothesis. When looking at the three individual components that make up our measure of the grandparent-grandchild relationship we found evidence that one component—a measure of how close the youth is with a specific grandparent—was associated with lower grades. This finding is surprising, but we are hesitant to make too much of it. Out of 12 possible relationships between the grandparent-grandchild relationship and youth outcomes that were tested, only one, or 8% was significant, roughly what one would expect due to simple chance.

There are a variety of factors that could account for these null findings. First, it is possible that, as suggested by Cherlin and Furstenburg (1992), grandparents play only peripheral roles in the lives of their grandchildren, making findings on child well-being difficult to detect. Other studies looking specifically at grades have also failed to find a link between the grandparent-grandchild relationship quality and youth grades (Elder and Conger, 2000). It is also possible that our lack of findings is driven by data limitations. Although the NSFH contains the most detailed information on grandparent-grandchild relationship quality of any national study, it may not capture well the actual ways that grandparents and grandchildren interact with each other. Additionally, it is possible that the outcomes examined here—risky behavior, sex and grades—are not those that are influenced by grandparent involvement. Finally, it is possible that grandparent involvement only matters for youth who are facing difficulties. We tested this by examining whether grandparents played a stronger role for certain youth, such as those living with a single parent; however sample size limitations made it difficult to discern patterns among subgroups.

This study contains several limitations, which should be noted. First, while this study utilized the only nationally-representative dataset containing youth-reported measures of the grandparent-grandchild relationship, the data is somewhat old (from 1992–1994). It therefore does not reflect current ways that youth may interact with their grandparents, such as through email or social networking, and also does not reflect current economic, policy or demographic trends and climate. Including measures of children's relationships with their grandparents in more current, ongoing, studies would allow for a wider set of data on which researchers could draw to address these issues.

Additionally, we utilized only one wave of data from the NSFH, making longitudinal analyses impossible. We did so because of the long lag between assessments of the NSFH, and the resulting change between waves in assessments of youth outcomes and the grandparent-grandchild relationship. The lack of longitudinal data means that we were not able to employ more sophisticated longitudinal analytical methods.

Additionally, we utilized a composite measure of the grandparent-grandchild relationship quality that, while having several strengths, also has some limitations. In particular, the composite contains youth reports on their closeness to, contact with, and willingness to confide in potentially different grandparents—youth closeness to their maternal grandmother, and contact with their paternal grandparents, are combined in the same composite measure. This means that we are measuring the grandchild's relationship with grandparents in general, rather than with one specific grandparent. However, as noted above, in the majority of cases the youth were reporting on the same grandparent or sets of grandparents for the individual measures in the composite.

Finally, the age range of our sample could be a limitation. As noted above, the relatively limited age range could make it difficult to discern patterns of relationship quality by age. On the other hand, the fact that our age ranges from 14–19 means that various ages of youth have had different lengths of time in which to engage in risky behaviors. We addressed this by using data reporting on risky behaviors that reflect the past 30 days' use. However, our measure of whether the youth had had sex is a lifetime measure and therefore is somewhat problematic in this regard. It should also be noted that, because we use a lifetime measure of sexual behavior, this measure could reflect behaviors that took place before the current grandparent-grandchild relationship.

Despite these limitations, this study provides some new knowledge on the ways in which grandparents are involved in the lives of youth. We show that while physical distance between grandparents and grandchildren plays a key role in the grandparent-grandchild relationship, a variety of other factors are important as well—in particular the child-parent and parent-grandparent relationships. Like other studies (Cherlin and Furstenberg, 1992), ours does not provide strong evidence that the grandparent-grandchild relationship is associated with aspects of youth well-being. It remains to be seen whether a fuller set of youth outcomes might be influenced by grandparental involvement, or whether involvement plays a more key role at other stages of the life course. Because the role of grandparents in the lives of youth is such an understudied topic, more work is needed to reinforce these findings and further illuminate the relationships examined here.

References

Barnett M, Scaramella L, Neppl T, Ontai L, Conger R. Grandmother involvement as a protective factor for early childhood social adjustment. Journal of Family Psychology. 2010; 24(5):635–645. [PubMed: 20954774]

Cherlin, A.; Furstenberg, F. The new American grandparent: A place in the family, life apart. New York: Basic Books; 1992.

Clingempeel WG, Colyar JJ, Brand E, Hetherington EM. Children's relationships with maternal grandparents: A longitudinal study of family structure and pubertal status effects. Child Development. 1992; 63(6):1404–22. [PubMed: 1446559]

Coleman J. Social capital and the creation of human capital. American Journal of Sociology. 1988; 94 (Issue Supplement):S95–S120.

Compton, J.; Pollak, R. Working paper. 2011. Family proximity, childcare and women's labor force attachment.

Creasey GL, Koblewski PJ. Adolescent grandchildren's relationships with maternal and paternal grandmothers and grandfathers. Journal of Adolescence. 1991; 14(4):373–87. [PubMed: 1797883]

Creasey GL. The association between divorce and late adolescent grandchildren's relations with grandparents. Journal of Youth and Adolescence. 1993; 22(5):513.

Crosnoe R, Elder GH. Life course transitions, the generational stake, and grandparent-grandchild relationships. Journal of Marriage and the Family. 2002; 64(4):1089–1096.

Elder, G.; Conger, R. Wisdom of the ages. In: Elder, G.; Conger, R., editors. Children of the Land. Chicago: University of Chicago Press; 2000. p. 127–151.

Furman W, Buhrmester D. Age and sex differences in perceptions of networks of personal relationships. Child Development. 1992; 63(1):103–15. [PubMed: 1551320]

Greene, W. Econometric analysis. 3. Upper Saddle River, New Jersey: Prentice Hall; 1997.

Harwood J. Communication media use in the grandparent-grandchild relationship. Journal of Communication. 2000; 50(4):56–78.

Hirsch BJ, Mickus M, Boerger R. Ties to influential adults among black and white adolescents: Culture, social class, and family networks. American Journal of Community Psychology. 2002; 30(2):289–303. [PubMed: 12002247]

Hunter, A.; Taylor, R. Grandparenthood in African American families. In: Szinovacz, ME., editor. Handbook on grandparenthood. Greenwood Press; Westport, CT: 1998. p. 70–86.

Johnson, C. Effects of adult children's divorce on grandparenthood. In: Szinovacz, ME., editor. Handbook on Grandparenthood. Greenwood Press; Westport, CT: 1998. p. 184–199.

King, V.; Russell, S.; Elder, G. Grandparenting in family systems: An ecological perspective. In: Szinovacz, ME., editor. Handbook on Grandparenthood. Greenwood Press; Westport, CT: 1998. p. 53–69.

Loury LD. All in the extended family: Effects of grandparents, aunts, and uncles on educational attainment. The American Economic Review. 2006; 96(2):275–278.

Lussier G, Deater-Deckard K, Dunn J, Davies L. Support across two generations: Children's closeness to grandparents following parental divorce and remarriage. Journal of Family Psychology: JFP: Journal of the Division of Family Psychology of the American Psychological Association (Division 43). 2002; 16(3):363–76. [PubMed: 12238417]

Mueller MM, Elder GH Jr. Family contingencies across the generations: Grandparent-grandchild relationship in holistic perspective. Journal of Marriage and Family. 2003; 65(2):404–17.

National Center for Health Statistics. National Vital Statistics Reports: United States Life Tables, 2006. 2010. Retrieved January 2010 from: http://www.cdc.gov/nchs/data/nvsr/nvsr58/ nvsr58_21.pdf

Ruiz SA, Silverstein M. Relationships with grandparents and the emotional well-being of late adolescent and young adult grandchildren. Journal of Social Issues. 2007; 63(4):793–808.

Silverstein, M.; Giarrusso, R.; Bengston, V. Intergenerational Solidarity and the Grandparenting Role. In: Szinovacz, ME., editor. Handbook on Grandparenthood. Greenwood Press; Westport, CT: 1998. p. 144–158.

Silverstein M, Marenco A. How Americans enact the grandparent role across the family life course. Journal of Family Issues. 2001; 22(4):493–522.

Silverstein M, Ruiz S. Breaking the chain: How grandparents moderate the transmission of maternal depression to their grandchildren. Family Relations. 2006; 55(5):601–612.

Spitze, G.; Ward, R. Gender Variations. In: Szinovacz, ME., editor. Handbook on Grandparenthood. Greenwood Press; Westport, CT: 1998. p. 113–130.

Stata Annotated Output: Ordered Logistic Regression. UCLA Academic Technology Services Statistical Consulting Group; 2010. Retrieved January 2010 from: http://www.ats.ucla.edu/stat/ stata/output /stata_ologit_output.htm

Stein JA, Newcomb MD, Bentler PM. Differential effects of parent and grandparent drug use on behavior problems of male and female children. Developmental Psychology. 1993; 29(1):31–43.

Sweet, J.; Bumpass, L. The National Survey of Families and Households - Waves 1 and 2: Data description and documentation. Center for Demography and Ecology, University of Wisconsin- Madison; 1996. retrieved January 2009 from: http://www.ssc .wisc.edu/nsfh/home.htm

Szinovacz ME. Grandparents today: A demographic profile. Gerontologist. 1998; 38(1):37–52. [PubMed: 9499652]

Tomlin, A. Grandparents' influences on grandchildren. In: Szinovacz, ME., editor. Handbook on Grandparenthood. Greenwood Press; Westport, CT: 1998. p. 159–170.

Uhlenberg P, Hammill B. Frequency of grandparent contact with grandchild sets: Six factors that make a difference. The Gerontologist. 1998; 38(3): 276–285. [PubMed: 9640847]

U.S. Census Bureau. Average Number of Own Children Under 18 Pear Family, By Type of Family: 1955 to Present. 2009a. Retrieved May 2011 from: http://www.census.gov/population/www/socdemo /hh-fam.html#ht

U.S. Census Bureau. Children with Grandparents by Presence of Parents, Sex, Race and Hispanic Origin/2 for Selected Characteristics: 2009. 2009b. Retrieved May 2011 from: http://www .census.gov/population/www/socdemo/hh-fam /cps2009.html

Whitbeck LB, Hoyt DR, Huck SM. Family relationship history, contemporary parent-grandparent relationship quality, and the grandparent-grandchild relationship. Journal of Marriage and the Family. 1993; 55(4):1025–35.

Rachel Dunifon is a professor in the Department of Policy Analysis and Management at Cornell University. She is also an associate director for the Bronfenbrenner Center for Translational Research, and PAM Department Extension Leader. Her research focuses on child and family policy.

Ashish Bajracharya is an associate in the Population Council's Reproductive Health program based in Dhaka, Bangladesh. Bajracharya is a social demographer and policy analyst who evaluates health interventions designed to improve access, use, quality, and equity of maternal and reproductive health care services for poor women in South and Southeast Asia.

EXPLORING THE ISSUE

Should Grandparents Have Visitation Rights to Their Grandchildren?

Critical Thinking and Reflection

1. If parents are undergoing a divorce, should grandparents play a role in custody decisions?
2. What factors do you believe are most important in determining the quality of the grandparent-grandchild relationship?
3. How should parents and grandparents be educated on law reforms? If a grandparent education course were created, what might it look like?
4. At what age should a child have decision-making power regarding custody arrangements? What might the benefits and challenges be in involving children in the legal process?

Is There Common Ground?

The concept of the nuclear family seems rather outdated when looking at current demographic information. Many children today have regular, if not full-time, contact with their grandparents. When individuals divorce, grandparents cannot be assured contact with their grandchildren. In the YES article, Lixia Qu and her colleagues discuss changes in Australia's family law system that recognizes grandparent involvement. However, this shift in policy may be premature as the research by Rachel Dunifon and Ashish Bajracharya in the NO selection does not find that grandparents overwhelmingly influence the well-being of their grandchildren. How do we reconcile these discrepancies?

Scholars have long considered the role of parenting in children's development; now, we are just beginning to explore the role of grandparenting. Both the YES and NO selections describe the complexity of the grandparent-grandchild relationship. It seems that parents, ultimately, may be the deciding factor. When parents support their children's interactions with grandparents by living in close proximity, for example, the grandparent-grandchild relationship is linked with positive outcomes. Attention

to how parents, grandparents, and children interact may help guide policy more effectively.

Create Central

www.mhhe.com/createcentral

Additional Resources

Beiner, S. F., Lowenstein, L., Worenklein, A., & Sauber, S. R. (2014). Grandparents' rights: Psychological and legal perspectives. *The American Journal of Family Therapy*, 42(2), 114–126.

EVALUATIONS, C. (2011). Special feature: A focus on mental health consultants in child custody disputes. *Family Court Review*, 49(4), 723–736.

Strom, P. S., & Strom, R. D. (2011). Grandparent education: Raising grandchildren. *Educational Gerontology*, 37(10), 910–923.

Williams, M. N. (2011). The changing roles of grandparents raising grandchildren. *Journal of Human Behavior in the Social Environment*, 21(8), 948–962.

Internet References . . .

AARP

http://www.aarp.org/research/

Gerontological Society of America

http://www.geron.org/

Trinity University

http://www.trinity.edu/~mkearl/geron.html

Unit 8

UNIT

Later Adulthood

*T*he central question for thinking about later adulthood, generally defined as the period of life after retirement age, is whether it is an inevitable period of decline or merely a period of adaptation. Although we often think of old age as a time of deterioration, research suggests that most people in this stage adjust to the challenges of aging reasonably well. They develop skills and abilities that compensate for lost capacities. Yet, there are unquestionable challenges, including the eventual decline of cognitive functioning and the inevitability of death.

The issues in this section consider each of these challenges, while broadly addressing the nature of old age as a time of continuing development. The first issue considers the role of diagnosis in how we conceptualize old age. The second issue questions whether death is truly inevitable, or whether scientific advances will allow humans to evade it. With both issues, there is attention to the role of science in society, and how we approach philosophical and ethical questions about later adulthood.

Selected, Edited, and with Issue Framing Material by:
Allison A. Buskirk-Cohen, *Delaware Valley University*

ISSUE

Is "Mild Cognitive Impairment" Too Similar to Normal Aging to be a Relevant Concept?

YES: Janice E. Graham and Karen Ritchie, from "Mild Cognitive Impairment: Ethical Considerations for Nosological Flexibility in Human Kinds," in *Philosophy, Psychiatry, & Psychology* (March 2006)

NO: Ronald C. Petersen, from "Mild Cognitive Impairment Is Relevant," in *Philosophy, Psychiatry, & Psychology* (March 2006)

Learning Outcomes

After reading this issue, you will be able to:

- Understand that there is no definitive biomedical test for Alzheimer's disease, dementia, or mild cognitive impairment (MCI)—leading to a blurry line between the disorders and normal aging.
- Discuss the fact that, like many maladies of old age, the diagnosis of MCI may be helpful to health care professionals but it also risks being driven by marketing and pharmaceutical concerns.
- Understand that diagnosing MCI is complicated and while it should not be confused with a "purely biological" disorder, it does offer some hope of early intervention for the types of cognitive decline that can become full dementia.

ISSUE SUMMARY

YES: Philosophers Janice E. Graham and Karen Ritchie raise concerns that rigidly defining Mild Cognitive Impairment (MCI) as a disorder associated with aging artificially creates the harmful impression that the conditions of old age are merely biomedical problems.

NO: Medical doctor and researcher Ronald C. Petersen has been a prominent proponent of defining MCI as an intermediate stage between normal aging and Alzheimer's disease. In this selection he counters Graham and Ritchie by emphasizing the usefulness of MCI as a diagnosis.

Among the sometimes scary aspects of growing old is the prospect of cognitive decline—the gradual loss of intellectual functioning. For many individuals, the decline of the mind is more frightening than the decline of the body. There are numerous nutritional supplements and exercises aimed at improving (or at least maintaining) one's cognitive abilities. Studying cognitive and intellectual changes over the lifespan has thus been an important area for researchers learning about old age. Over decades of study, a general picture has emerged with some consistency. We know, for example, that dramatic cognitive decline is not an inevitable fact of aging, although in some ways our intellectual functioning does inevitably change with time. We also know that not all cognitive and intellectual functioning reacts to aging in the same way. Age-related cognitive decline comes in many diverse forms.

Current research suggests that while certain cognitive abilities decline with age, other skills actually improve. For example, one study at the University of Michigan found that older adults are better at conflict resolution than younger ones. Participants in their 60s were better at considering different perspectives, thinking of multiple resolutions, and suggesting compromises compared to younger adults. A study from Stony Brook University found that people over 50 were happier, reporting less anger and stress, than their younger counterparts. What these studies and others suggest is that general negative stereotypes about old age are typically incorrect. We must be reminded that the ages considered "elderly" have changed as well with life expectancy increasing.

In relatively recent years, health experts have used the term "mild cognitive impairment" to describe the declining abilities associated with advanced aging. The construct of mild cognitive impairment (MCI) is flexible enough to account for a variety of experiences with aging, but does that flexibility prevent it from being a clear disorder? Some experts argue that the symptoms characterizing MCI are those associated with typical aging. For example, the Mayo Clinic's website lists forgetfulness, trouble making decisions, and poor judgment as symptoms of MCI. It also mentions that individuals with MCI also might experience depression, irritability, anxiety, and apathy. Many of these characteristics have social factors that play a role in their development, not just biological ones. For example, elderly people with few social connections are more likely to experience depression than individuals with many friends. The line designating "disorder" is a rather fuzzy one, at best. Furthermore, the age of the individual must be considered, with the relevance of MCI in someone at age 60 is quite different from that of an individual at age 90.

There is increasing concern about the medicalization of our society. Medicalization refers to the process by which human conditions become defined and treated as medical conditions. Sociologists and others use the term to explain how medical knowledge is applied to behaviors which may not be medical or biological in nature. Once behaviors are classified as medical conditions, a medical model of disability is applied and social context is disregarded. Social contributions to a condition, such as the unequal distribution of resources, are no longer considered. Many critics suggest that the pharmaceutical industry has pushed for the medicalization of our society, since it stands to benefit financially.

Another area of criticism concerns the impact of labeling. There are significant costs associated with negatively labeling people with a disorder when they simply may be experiencing normal aging. In other words, is the diagnostic criteria of MCI really reflecting society's negative view of aging rather than a distinct disorder? In 1971, Robert Neil Butler coined the term "ageism" to describe stereotyping and discrimination against individuals or groups on the basis of their age. Most often, ageism has been applied to the experience of the elderly in American society. Societal norms tend to marginalize the elderly, treating them with disrespect, and excluding them from many activities. For example, there are many jokes about the poor driving habits of the elderly even though research actually finds adolescents have the worst driving records.

But we also know that many older adults do experience some degree of cognitive impairment, and that extreme forms such as Alzheimer's disease are a very real problem for our aging population. Alzheimer's disease is the most common type of dementia, which is a general category of enduring cognitive problems that most often occurs during older adulthood. Most forms of dementia, including Alzheimer's disease, are impossible to cure and difficult to diagnose. Despite much attention from researchers and practitioners, there is no single diagnostic test that conclusively defines types of dementia. As such, some scholars worry that focusing on the biomedical aspects of dementia creates a misleading sense that there is a clear distinction between it and normal aging.

Janice E. Graham and Karen Ritchie are among the concerned scholars. When they promote "nosological flexibility," they are referring specifically to nosology as the medical science responsible for classifying diseases. Though such classification may seem to be a simple matter of putting physical symptoms together with labels and definitions, in fact it can be a complex process of interpreting biological and social realities. Graham and Ritchie point out that the relatively new diagnosis of Mild Cognitive Impairment (MCI) offers a challenging example of these complexities. From their perspective, MCI is too similar to normal aging and too poorly understood to merit a distinct diagnosis. In fact, by presenting MCI as an established disorder, Graham and Ritchie are concerned that older adults may be misled by pharmaceutical concerns and doctors toward the conclusion that slight degrees of memory loss or minor deficits in information processing indicate the start of a devastating illness.

Ronald C. Petersen, a medical doctor and researcher at the Mayo Clinic in Minnesota, is more focused on using the diagnosis of MCI to help make progress against more intractable problems such as Alzheimer's. Petersen is often credited with defining MCI as a disorder, and thus has a vested stake in this controversy. But he also makes the quite reasonable claim that simply because a disorder is complex does not mean it is not a disorder. Throughout the lifespan, from childhood behavioral problems to adult struggles with mental health, developmental characteristics regularly tread a fine line between "normal" and "abnormal." As such, thinking about MCI as either a part of or deviation from "normal aging" also provides a valuable opportunity to think through what exactly is "normal" in older adulthood.

YES

**Janice E. Graham and
Karen Ritchie**

Mild Cognitive Impairment: Ethical Considerations for Nosological Flexibility in Human Kinds

. . . This paper examines mild cognitive impairment (MCI), an emerging classification that does not meet all the criteria for dementia, and explores the advantage of allowing nosological flexibility between normal and pathologic definitions associated with aging-related modifications in cognitive performance. We frame the origins of the concept of MCI, and the problems with the premature application of criteria, within a nosological phenomenon: the drive to define a heterogeneous condition as a reified disease entity works against both scientific discovery and human compassion. Who "calls" MCI, and for what reasons? What reliability and validity does this designation have?

The social and ethical implications of identifying and treating those speculated to have an early form of inevitable dementia, a kind of disorder more remarkable for its variability than its predictability . . . , demands attention. Any diagnostic decision is based on anecdotal evidence of improvement or decline, and/or measurements calculated from scientifically standardized instruments. No matter what the source, these everyday and scientific explanatory models serve particular purposes and interests. When potential treatments become available, we must be sure that the market does not determine nosology. We need to examine the possibility that MCI is principally an entity defined to create a market for a product of unknown value.

The micromoral social worlds where decision making takes place contain vulnerable individuals and groups . . . , but the worlds of leading researchers driven by their colleagues' results, and busy clinicians dependent on pharmaceutical representatives, are also laden with opinion and belief. Diagnostic evidence may come from scientific research, a clinician's anticipation of treatment success, or a sufferer's hopes and fears. Research-clinicians, though trying to relieve suffering, may be contributing to premature and speculative hype.

Origins of the Mild Cognitive Impairment Concept

Chronic cognitive deficits, in the absence of neurodegenerative disorder, have been documented since Aristotle as an inevitable feature of the aging process. Such deficits are commonly associated with difficulties in the performance of daily activities. Clinical interest in such conditions has mainly centered on differentiating them from potentially treatable disorders such as depression, metabolic disorders, and toxic reactions and also from early stage neurodegeneration. These subclinical cognitive symptoms are principally distinguished from neurodegenerative disorders such as Alzheimer's disease (AD) by their far slower progression, and by their milder impact on daily performance, and linguistic and visuospatial functions. Nevertheless, recent research into the nature and long-term prognosis of aging-related modifications in cognitive performance has begun to question the extent to which these changes may be considered normal. This questioning is reflected in the evolution of a nosology for these subclinical alterations.

In keeping with the notion that mild cognitive deficits are a common feature of aging, early definitions were based on the comparative performance of young and elderly cohorts on a limited number of cognitive tests. Recognizing particular clinical populations using these concepts began with Kral's . . . concept of benign senescent forgetfulness. Later, Crook et al. . . . defined *age-associated memory impairment* (AAMI) as changes in subjective complaints of memory loss in elderly persons measured by a decrement of at least one standard deviation on a formal memory test in comparison with means established for young adults. Blackford and La Rue . . . refined the excessive inclusiveness of Crook's criteria. They defined their concept of "late-life forgetfulness" as performance between one and two standard deviations below the mean

From *Philosophy, Psychiatry & Psychology*, March 2006, pp. 31–41. Copyright © 2006 by Johns Hopkins University Press. Reprinted by permission.

on at least fifty percent of a battery of at least four tests. Flicker, Ferris, and Reisberg . . . grappled with the normal–dementia divide. Levy et al. . . . introduced *aging-associated cognitive decline,* a concept that stipulated that the deficit should be defined in reference to norms for the elderly and not for young adults. This point signaled a subtle conceptual shift: MCI patients are still judged as normal, but they are now to be compared to an "optimum" level of functioning.

Subclinical cognitive deficit in the elderly had become a clinical entity even in the absence of any specific therapeutic management. Recognition by the major international classifications of disease—of subclinical cognitive deterioration linked to the normal aging process—began with the appearance in DSM-IV (American Psychiatric Association [APA] . . .) of *age-related cognitive decline* (ARCD). It refers to an objective decline in cognitive functioning caused by the physiologic process of aging for which no clinical criteria or cognitive testing procedures are specified. Subsequent attempts to operationalize ARCD using data from two general population studies in France and the United States have concluded that the concept has little value either in predicting clinical outcomes or in identifying comparable populations for research purposes.

As research into the causes of dementia and cerebrovascular disease began to shed new light on the etiology of aging-related neuronal decline, it became evident that many of the physiologic abnormalities seen in these pathologies were also present to a lesser extent in subjects identified as having a normal aging-related cognitive disorder. Consequently, elderly persons with subclinical cognitive deficits have become the subject of neurologic and geriatric research that seeks to discover whether cognitive deficits of this type may be caused by treatable pathologic processes. Alternative concepts have subsequently appeared in the literature linking cognitive disorder to various forms of underlying pathology. As an example of this research, the tenth revision of the *International Classification of Diseases* . . . lists *mild cognitive disorder* (MCD). MCD refers to disorders of memory, learning, and concentration, often accompanied by mental fatigue, which must be demonstrated by formal neuropsychological testing and attributable to cerebral disease or damage, or systemic physical disease known to cause dysfunction. MCD is secondary to physical illness or impairment, excluding dementia, amnesic syndrome, concussion, or postencephalitic syndrome. The concept of MCD, which was principally developed to describe the cognitive consequences of autoimmune deficiency syndrome, but was then expanded to include other disorders in which cognitive change is secondary to another disease process, and is applicable to all ages, not just the elderly. In practice, attempts to apply MCD criteria to population studies of elderly persons suggest it to be of limited value in this context; it has doubtful validity as a nosological entity for this age group. . . . The DSM IV . . . has proposed a similar entity, namely, *mild neurocognitive disorder* (MNCD), which encompasses not only memory and learning difficulties, but also perceptual–motor, linguistic, and central executive functions. Although the concepts proposed by the two international classifications—MCD and MNCD—do not provide sufficient working guidelines for application in a research context, they do give formal recognition to subclinical cognitive disorder as a pathologic state requiring treatment and as a source of handicap, and are thus likely to be important within a legal context.

A provisional classification, in this case meant specifically for elderly populations, is *cognitive impairment—no dementia* (CIND). CIND was developed within the context of the Canadian Study of Health and Aging (CSHA) with an epidemiologic view to research rather than clinical treatment. It is defined by reference to neuropsychological testing and clinical examination. . . . As with MCD and MNCD, persons with CIND are considered to have cognitive impairment attributable to an underlying physical disorder, but they may also have "circumscribed memory impairment," a modifed form of AAMI that accords with Blackford and LaRue's revisions. . . . CIND encompasses a wider range of underlying etiologies such as delirium, substance abuse, and psychiatric illness. MCD, MNCD, and CIND are constructs that have been developed principally for research. They consider cognitive disorder in the elderly as heterogeneous and not necessarily progressive. Their treatment should be determined by the nature of the underlying primary systemic disease. Operational concepts intended for research afford them an heuristic utility unconstrained by the clinical need to relieve symptoms. The first long-term prospective studies of subclinical cognitive disorders suggested that they are not benign, with many neurologists arguing that they are principally, if not exclusively, early stage dementia. These studies mark a complete turn around in the conceptualization of mild aging-related cognitive deficits: whereas in the 1990s, dementia was generally considered to constitute an upward extension of a "normal" process of progressive aging-related cognitive deterioration, subclinical cognitive deficit was now conceptualized as a downward extension of dementia.

In 1997, Petersen et al. proposed diagnostic criteria for a new category, MCI, defined as complaints of defective memory and demonstration of abnormal memory functioning for age, with normal general cognitive functioning and conserved ability to perform activities of daily living. Importantly, MCI was considered to be a prodrome of AD. Neurologists accepted MCI in theory; a period of early cognitive disability in which intellectual difficulties did not yet reach formal diagnostic levels for dementia was self-evident. But MCI criteria were difficult to apply in practice; too much depended on individual clinical judgment and ability to differentiate MCI at one point in time from cohort effects and low intelligence. A later study refined the initial definition by referring to memory impairment beyond that expected for both age and education level. . . . An alternative approach has been to simply define MCI in terms of early stage dementia.

Problems with the Application of Mild Cognitive Impairment Criteria

The identification of subjects for research and treatment for MCI has been problematic owing to the lack of a working definition based on designated cognitive tests and other clinical measures. The result has been that population prevalence, the clinical features of subjects identified with MCI, and their clinical outcomes, vary widely between studies and even within studies where there has been longitudinal follow-up. . . . It is also unclear whether MCI should include any form of cognitive change or whether it should be confined exclusively to isolated memory impairment as initially defined. Although there is some evidence that a purely amnesic syndrome may exist . . . , it appears in only a very small proportion (six percent) of elderly persons with cognitive deficit when the full range of cognitive functions are examined.

An MCI consensus group meeting in Chicago . . . concluded that subjects with MCI should be considered to have a condition that is different from normal aging and is likely to progress to AD at an accelerated rate; however, they may also progress to another form of dementia or improve. This group thus proposed subtypes of MCI according to type of cognitive deficit and clinical outcome distinguishing MCI amnestic (MCI with pronounced memory impairment progressing to AD), MCI multiple domain (slight impairment across several cognitive domains leading to AD, vascular dementia, or stabilizing in the case of normal brain aging changes), and MCI single non-memory domain (significant impairment in a cognitive domain other than memory leading to AD or another form of dementia). It has subsequently been suggested that MCI be further subdivided according to the suspected etiology of the cognitive impairment in keeping with international classifications of dementing disorders: for example, MCI-AD, MCI-LBD, MCI-FTD,

and so on. However, this proposal is complicated by more recent neuroradiologic and post-mortem research that suggests the borderline between the principal forms of dementia (AD, vascular, Lewy body, and frontotemporal) is problematical and calls for a revision of dementia nosology. . . .

Although early identification of memory and language disorders might well mark individuals likely to manifest AD . . . , other forms of dysfunction are also likely to signal early pathologies worthy of clinical observation. To date, evidence supports the prognostic irrelevance of MCI subcategories in identifying specific entities predictive of dementia. . . . Some individuals diagnosed with early cognitive impairment in CSHA did not progress to dementia, and others were diagnosed five years later as having no cognitive impairment. A longitudinal study of a general population sample with subclinical cognitive deficits has demonstrated multiple patterns of cognitive change with variable clinical outcomes including depression, and cardiovascular and respiratory disorders, as well as dementia. . . . Current criteria for MCI pick up all these causes. Should researchers only be focusing on cases at risk of evolving toward AD? Even if we could do these studies based on the identification of MCI in general practice (and it is here that subjects will be principally presenting if a treatment is ever available), results suggest that current criteria have poor predictive validity for dementia in this setting and, applying theoretical criteria for the establishment of a formal diagnostic category, that MCI cannot be considered to be a separate clinical entity. . . .

Mapping Nosologies to Flexible Concepts

Although the recognition of MCI as a pathology marks an early step toward the recognition of nondementia cognitive disorder as an important clinical problem with a potential for treatment, it does not yet meet the criteria for a formal nosological entity. . . . Useful conceptual taxonomies should be able to accommodate more flexible kinds. Clinical research on MCI focuses narrowly on forms that lead to AD, the specter of which drives researchers, policymakers, and the public . . . to identify research subjects earlier. The expansion of the potentially affected population coincidentally provides a potential pharmaceutical market of from one quarter to one half of the population over sixty-five.

Ian Hacking's writing on natural and human kinds and his concept of "dynamic nominalism" can inform this discussion. The concept shows how new objects can be introduced into the world; these facts and categories are both socially created and real. Hacking describes the effects of this phenomenon,

> People classified in a certain way tend to conform to or grow into the ways that they are described; but they also evolve in their own ways, so that the classifications and descriptions have to be constantly revised. . . .

How might Hacking's looping of cause and effect, the way observation and identification changes the subject under study, affect those subjects who are identified early? Furthermore, how might those who escape this surveillance fare? How can the diagnosis of MCI be sustained when it has such poor predictive validity? Case identification remains a key issue in MCI as it did in dementia. . . . Accommodating the effects of education continues to require special screening and diagnostic criteria. Cognitive decline in both the normal and CIND groups is associated with older age, lower MMSE, and education, and increased functional impairment at baseline. . . . Concern about missed cases in MCI research outweighs concern about including individuals who are not cognitively impaired (false positives).

Dynamic nominalism stresses how much the act of classifying people changes both the classifier and the subject of classification. . . . Abnormal must predicate normal as a deviation from it, yet some absolute state of normal is itself simply constructed from an averaging of the cases selected. This paradox prompted Schneider to differentiate disease from abnormal variations in the early half of the last century, and both Canguilhem . . . and Foucault . . . to challenge the presumed stability of normal health. Recently, Davis has creatively employed the paradox to address the dynamic flexibility of health as a "plurality of possibilities and potential transitions to new norms." . . . New norms represent flexible adaptation to a new environment. Flexibility as a marker for health can be usefully compared to frailty, a benign accumulation of comorbidities and progressing severity. . . . But the progression from healthy flexibility to frailty is neither linear nor inevitable; it is less a paradigmatic dualism of incommensurable biological and social factors than a balancing board with often undetectable weights dropped on and off and interacting synergistically and antagonistically with one another. . . .

Although individuals do age, and they do become subject to pathologic processes marked by inadaptability and disease, evidence suggests that there is considerable deviation in cognitive impairment within and among individuals. In contrast to Davis's view . . . that dementia "tolerates no deviation" different processes may well play varying roles; cognitive degeneration is neither inevitable nor "natural" and it remains subject to interpretation, for

example, by ascertainment bias. An individual identified as having MCI might embody behavioral symptoms that are a response to the diagnosis itself. These characteristics, in turn, are associated with progressive decline (i.e., agitation, irritation, depression, apathy). Moreover, the worried well may turn to self-monitoring, evaluating, discussing, and further data gathering. The act of identifying provides a comfortable prompt category and repository for information. What would be normal in the unhailed . . . , serves to reinforce pathology. Researchers, clinicians, patient advocates, or pharmaceutical companies can then mobilize these new human kinds to exert influence on policy decisions. . . .

MCI, like the dementias that it is presumed to precede, is a heterogeneous condition with no certain biomarker or known etiology. At this stage, MCI still incorporates multiple patterns of pathologic, cognitive, behavioral, and functional criteria. Useful conceptual nosologies should be able to accommodate a plurality of causal explanations as they consolidate research operational definitions with empirical evidence to build new models to explore etiologies. Although suggesting causal subtypes of MCI, Petersen's . . . focus on Alzheimer's disease constrains his "MCI" to a specific ontological passage, and should perhaps more accurately be identified as "mild AD." As noted, clinical research is focused on forms of MCI that lead to AD. Practical kinds offer a way out of this etiologically constrained box. They accommodate dimensional approaches and combine theoretical and empirical evidence to help us understand cognitive impairment and cognitive decline within a complex matrix of social and biological determinants of health. . . .

Technical, Social, and Corporate Relationships

The pathologic process of neurodegeneration is situated in sociodegeneration, or what Davis . . . refers to as *socioneurologic degeneration*. The quality of disintegrating relationships defies a simple normative–pathologic dualism. These relationships only have meaning, can only be defined in historically contextualized complex exchanges of shared memories and experiences, social interactions that are situated, embodied expressions of agency. . . . The persistence in viewing cognitive impairment as a purely biological process, as a natural kind that sits in contrast to some ideal normal healthy state, lacks internal validity—the complex heterogeneities of a variable sociodegenerative process incorporate redundancies, synergies, and antagonisms of intricately woven biocultures. . . . For Canguilhem . . . , pathology was a product of the clinical encounter, the therapeutic intervention between a doctor and patient. If only recognized upon the clinician's diagnosis, then pathology or disease have no relevance or meaning beyond that clinical encounter. Over half a century ago, Kurt Schneider suggested that suffering be a criterion for pathology. . . . Is the diagnosis of MCI cause for more suffering?

Treatments for cognitive impairment show only modest benefits in individuals with dementia . . . and, therefore, have given rise to a need to show efficacy through new clinically meaningful treatment outcomes. Clinicians are using qualitative methods to ground their judgments in refined operational definitions and criteria that evoke patient and caregiver perceptions, meaningfulness, and hope for symptomatic relief in anticipation of a progressive decline in memory, thought, and action. Tests such as the MMSE and ADAS-Cog are cognitive scales with an emphasis on logical and linguistic dimensions. These standardized packages categorically reify some evoked pathology . . . in a person who then too easily becomes a Clinical Dementia Rating Scale 2, MMSE 15, ADAS-Cog 47; these categories contribute little insight into personhood or identity. The real, clinically meaningful markers are localized in actions and relationships . . .—working, doing housework, canning fruit with a daughter, washing oneself in front of a mirror, walking the dog along a worn mnemonic path. Such everyday activities received scant attention before their affectual qualities were realized to mark a potential "treatment success" whose documentation as "clinically meaningful" might further the treatment's sales. This clinical turn places patient desires and expectations at the top of clinical management and treatment goals and it is an important and worthy movement; nevertheless, we need to reflect on the reasons for it and who profits from it.

We are now in the midst of a quiet revolution, as the desires and responses of the patient as subject, if not quite participant, are brought into focus. At the heart of the issue remains measurement. Formerly, the hold of quantitative psychometric and biometric gatekeepers, there is a growing body of research that measures qualitative everyday events and the values that individuals attach in the context of their socioneurodegeneration. Efforts to assess these measures are continuing. . . . But with earlier ascertainment of subtle cognitive impairments and the availability of questionable techniques to link individual responder subtypes to therapies . . . comes a responsibility.

The 1990s saw a turn away from a command and control regulatory apparatus. The U.S. Food and Drug Administration, concerned that pharmaceutical companies might not be rigorous enough in their testing procedures when it set out standardized criteria for measuring efficacy . . ., adopted partnerships with sponsor companies and now relies almost exclusively on company data

to show efficacy and safety. There is a pressure to get products to the market faster. Rather than relying on objective psychometric measures of efficacy, as was outlined by the committee in 1990, there are increasing calls to adopt more clinically meaningful outcomes . . . that necessarily require a different approach to measurement. Research-clinicians and industry now ask what the quantitative data actually mean in everyday life. They look to patient expectations to measure success. Whether the rush to market has an effect on the methods and findings of these studies and whether data are subject to equally rigorous critical appraisals requires further analysis. New operational definitions require evidence that stand up to standards of accountability, reliability, and validity; consensus decisions to adopt these methods must be subject to scrutiny.

But what happens when new operational criteria and methods are proposed that equate treatment improvement to maintenance or "staying the same"? A common sense argument is constructed that accepts no further decline as a positive finding for an elderly person. Clinicians elicit narrative meaning from their patients; the existing assessment tools that cannot establish efficacy for a treatment get replaced by patient testimonials; panels of scientists agree that no decline is improvement. They form consensus committees, publish practice guidelines, set international standards, and authorize this paradox. Moreover, the emotionally resonant influence of personal testimonies from sufferers is used as evidence. A constellation of signs, symptoms, and social and technical relations are being mapped based on patient and caregiver hopes and fears, not the least of which is the concern about affordable access to their only hope. The noise from these heterogeneous sociotechnical relations creates accounts that cannot make sense. . . . Pharmaceutical grammar (in the form of hopes and fears and treatment success) feeds clinician desires to assist the sufferer who wants access to anything that might possibly work. If treatment effect is to be used to identify the category boundaries for practical kinds, but operational definitions for response continue to be diluted to maintenance, they may well mimic the variable states found in untreated Alzheimer's patients. . . . A vulnerable incipient disease population can be created by excessively loose inclusion criteria. . . .

Although the pharmaceutical industry may be pushing the treatment of MCI at a pace that is detrimental to clinical validity, it must be acknowledged that it is fulfilling its role as a market provider. It has played an important role, responding rapidly to changing social attitudes toward aging and a demand for increasing intervention to improve quality of life in the elderly, in the face of a lagging public health policy that has, for too long, neglected psychogeriatrics. Although it has promoted these causes to their shareholders gain, it is clearly the role of the clinicians implicated in industrial research, and not the industry itself, to ensure that the clinical limits of trial outcomes are adequately discussed.

Despite poor clinical predictive validity, MCI has market appeal to an anxious public. Personal testimonies of modest results risks exaggerating the efficacy of treatments, but it also overlooks the fact that many people do not respond to treatment. In identifying subgroups who may be more prone to treatment effects than others, researchers could underestimate the true potential of a therapy by averaging results across heterogeneous patient subgroups. Although MCI cannot be considered a formal nosological entity (it is rather a heterogeneous syndrome in which dementia is "nested"), it is being treated as though it were and may thus risk being used as a diagnosis in a legal sense—as such it could be evoked in damages, to exclude persons from responsibilities and services (notably elderly care admission) or employment. On the other hand, we have to be careful—MCI is important

socially: we are no longer saying that cognitive decline is just normal aging, which the elderly have to tolerate (thus also underlying common attitudes to the elderly as incompetent), but that they should be investigated as practical kinds. Various treatments that might be detected using more flexible nosologies, which allow researchers and clinicians to understand more practical kinds better, might be actively sought. The cholinesterase inhibitors may be only one approach among many provided we are clearer about who we are giving them to and why. . . .

Janice E. Graham is a medical anthropologist and Canada Research Chair in Bioethics at Dalhousie University in Halifax, Nova Scotia. Her work takes an interdisciplinary approach to cultural, technical, and moral issues related to health.

Karen Ritchie is a neuropsychologist and epidemiologist. She is currently a research director with the French National Institute of Medical Health and Medical Research

Ronald C. Petersen

Mild Cognitive Impairment
Is Relevant

Graham and Ritchie . . . have contributed a scholarly document that implores us to reexamine nosological categories and certain diagnostic outcomes. They have chosen mild cognitive impairment (MCI) as the target of their scrutiny and have raised several interesting issues. I would like to comment on their approach and suggest that MCI is a useful clinical entity that does serve a practical function and hopefully will lead to a better quality of life for aging persons.

There are several clarifications concerning the construct of MCI that need to be emphasized. Graham and Ritchie have asserted that all persons with MCI eventually evolve to Alzheimer's disease (AD) and have claimed that this is the inevitable outcome of the disorder. Although it is true that many of the early studies on MCI focused on the amnestic subtype as a precursor to AD . . . , subsequent work has expanded the construct to include prodromal forms of other disorders. . . . As such, the construct of MCI has become flexible in recent years to account for alternative types of intermediate cognitive impairment.

The authors state that MCI addresses those individuals speculated to have an inevitable dementia. Certainly, we do not presume that dementia is inevitable in the aging process; rather, we posit that if certain criteria are fulfilled in persons who are aging, the likelihood of a person progressing to a certain type of dementia is quite high. As such, this is an important precondition about which to learn, because interventional strategies may be available.

Graham and Ritchie argue that some cognitive changes with aging are "normal" and trying to classify these individuals as "abnormal" is performing a disservice to much of the aging population. We draw an important distinction between the cognitive changes of normal aging, as they are recognized to exist, and what we feel constitutes the pathologic changes of MCI. We believe that the abnormal cognitive function found in MCI has a high probability of progressing to a greater degree of cognitive dysfunction in a relatively short period of time and these behavioral changes are accompanied by pathologic brain changes that are manifested on magnetic resonance imaging scans, positron emission tomography scans, cerebrospinal fuid biomarkers, and autopsy studies. . . . This type of progression is in contradistinction to other individuals who are experiencing cognitive changes of normal aging. These individuals do not progress rapidly to greater degrees of impairment and autopsy studies reveal that their brains do not harbor the pathologic changes found in the MCI population. . . .

The cognitive and behavioral changes accompanying persons with MCI are devastating and cannot be ascribed to "senility" or "He is just getting old." It is a mistake to imply that by labeling people with a condition such as MCI we are doing them a disservice. Most of these individuals are seeking medical attention for their perceived difficulties. Consequently, addressing these concerns and educating the individuals on the implications of their symptoms are important services. Although we may not have adequate therapies at present, this does not imply that we should ignore the symptoms.

We cannot treat many conditions at present, yet we do not avoid the opportunity to characterize the condition and make a diagnosis. Even if this were part of the aging process, this does not mean that we should ignore the disability and refuse to treat it. Most individuals develop an inflexibility of their optical lenses as they age, yet corrective lenses of one type or another are believed to be extremely beneficial at alleviating this disability associated with the aging phenomenon. No one would argue that it is inappropriate to treat this condition because it is "just a part of aging."

It should be noted that I have stressed the situation in which individuals are seeking medical attention for their cognitive concerns. It is quite a different situation if an investigator were proactively to enroll a subject in, for example, an epidemiologic study and then label subjects as having some type of disorder such as MCI. In this instance, the individual subject is not seeking attention for any medical concerns and consequently it is inappropriate to intrude proactively on their daily activities and put a research label on them. This is particularly important while MCI is still evolving with regard to its refinement, and as such has not been completely delineated. However, in the clinical situation whereby an individual is seeking medical attention, the responsibility of the evaluating clinician is quite different.

Graham and Ritchie strongly imply that the entire research and clinical enterprise in MCI is driven by the pharmaceutical industry. Statements such as ". . . the possibility that MCI is principally an entity defined to create a market for a product of unknown value . . ." . . . are false and an inappropriate indictment of the research community. Virtually all of the MCI research that has emanated from the Mayo Clinic has been supported by the National Institute on Aging (NIA). Similarly, most of the major longitudinal studies on which these data are based—the Religious Order Study, the Cache County Study, the Cardiovascular Health Study, and the Monongahela Valley Epidemiologic Study—are all federally funded. These investigators do not have ties to the pharmaceutical industry. Furthermore, the MCI criteria currently in place have been adopted by federally funded agencies to promote research such as the NIA-sponsored Alzheimer's Disease Centers research program and the NIA-supported Alzheimer's Disease Neuroimaging Initiative. . . . To imply that this work is driven by pharmaceutical interests to create a market for marginally effective products is a distortion of the intents of the academic community.

Our work in Rochester, Minnesota, grew out of a longitudinal study on aging and dementia in which we observed individuals who exhibited cognitive concerns and impaired performance through a longitudinal follow-up study. We appreciated that these individuals progressed more rapidly to dementia and particularly AD than would be expected solely on the basis of aging. This observation led us to codify the criteria for these subjects and perform a longitudinal observational study. After many years of scrutiny, it became apparent that these individuals were progressing more rapidly than would be expected on the basis of age, and that this condition likely was the clinical precursor of dementia. There was no influence from the pharmaceutical industry in the design, execution, analysis, or reporting of these data. Yet, Graham and Ritchie would assert that the entire MCI research enterprise was spawned by the pharmaceutical industry.

This is not to say that the pharmaceutical industry has not appreciated this line of research as a marketing opportunity, and partnerships have developed between federally funded grants and industry, for example, the Alzheimer's Disease Cooperative Study, in an attempt to develop treatments for this condition. As such, with appropriate oversight and scrutiny, the public is likely to benefit from a combination of resources of these two partners. Having said that, when the Alzheimer's Disease Cooperative Study reported its MCI treatment trial involving donepezil and vitamin E, the final analysis, interpretation, and reporting of the data were under the auspices of the Alzheimer's Disease Cooperative Study without pharmaceutical company authorship. . . . Strict guidelines were in place in the Alzheimer's Disease Cooperative Study restricting the key investigators from having collaborative relationships with sponsoring pharmaceutical companies. Consequently, these assertions are false and distracting from the essential discussion.

Claiming that MCI research is the product of the pharmaceutical industry would be tantamount to saying that the diagnosis, cognitive impairment—no dementia (CIND) from the Canadian Study of Health and Aging was motivated by the development of a market for the pharmaceutical industry. CIND has not been the study of clinical trials because the overall concept lacks the specificity required to test certain pharmaceutical interventions. However, some Canadian researchers have defined subcategories of CIND that are virtually identical to the subtypes of MCI, and hence have demonstrated the utility and similarity of these two constructs. . . .

Graham and Ritchie claim that the identification of MCI subtypes for research and treatment has been problematic. That is, in part, true. However, with increasing attention and education of clinicians, these subjects are being recognized at an increasing rate. The threshold for detection of a meaningful cognitive impairment is shifting toward lesser degrees of impairment, and subjects are being recognized at earlier stages. A significant number of people with full-blown dementia still go unrecognized in general practice, and this problem would be magnified as one considers milder degrees of impairment. Yet, the threshold is moving and many individuals in general clinical practice are now becoming aware of more subtle forms of impairment and national organizations such as the American Academy of Neurology have recommended that clinicians identify these individuals because they are at increased risk of progressing to dementia. . . . With increased refinement of the criteria including subtypes and etiologies, a great deal of the variability among the studies in the literature can be avoided.

An issue raised by Graham and Ritchie concerns the worry that the act of classifying might alter the classifier and the subject of the classification. This is a relevant and valid; since both the classifier and the classified are probably changed by the process. However, one can look at this issue from a positive as well as a negative perspective. That is, as noted, as clinicians become more aware of the subtleties involved in identifying early impairment, they may refine their own techniques for classification. In a similar fashion, the process of classifying may well have an impact on the subjects of that classification system. Investigators have a moral responsibility for monitoring the labels they place on individuals and this needs to be respected. On the one hand, some individuals appreciate the classification of concerns about their own symptoms, although we must be concerned that labeling people with a condition that is still under refinement may be problematic. We need to caution people about the uncertainties involved in the classification system and indicate the research that is underway. Nevertheless, if this is done in a responsible fashion, this should not dissuade the clinician from exploring new constructs that may be of potential benefit to their patients.

Finally, Graham and Ritchie claim that conceptual nosologies should accommodate a plurality of causal explanations. The authors criticize MCI as a heterogeneous condition as if that were a detrimental quality. They claim that the depiction of MCI is driven only by a treatment focus. Once again, this appears to be an oversimplification of the issues. MCI is by definition heterogeneous because in its broadest sense, it is a precursor to a variety of dementing illnesses. If dementia is characterized by a loss of cognitive capacity of a sufficient degree to impair daily function, then by definition, there must be multiple causes. As we know, from many of the diagnostic manuals, dementia is the first step in a multilayered process of arriving at an ultimate diagnosis. Once the diagnosis of dementia is made, then the clinician must decide the etiology of that dementing syndrome, for example, degenerative, vascular, metabolic, or traumatic. After that determination is made, then a specific diagnosis can be entertained, such as AD, frontotemporal dementia, dementia with Lewy bodies, or vascular dementia.

In a similar vein, if many of these conditions have a prodromal state (e.g., MCI), then MCI should have multiple causations as well. Therefore, the most recent iteration of the MCI diagnostic process includes a specification of a particular subtype based on clinical features such as amnestic or nonamnestic and single or multiple domains. This type of clinical classification leads the process in the direction of diagnostic specificity. However, stopping at this stage produces variability in the longitudinal outcomes of the various clinical subtypes. That is, if a study only classifies the subjects syndromically, then one would expect variable outcomes owing to the multitude of etiologies that could produce the clinical syndrome. Therefore, when an epidemiologic study claims that the syndrome of MCI is "unstable" because some subjects get better and some get worse, this is what one would expect. This is not a problem with the MCI entity itself. Some persons with a memory impairment caused by an evolving degenerative condition will likely get worse; others with the same clinical syndrome caused by depression or medication would be expected to improve once the offending cause has been eliminated. This is not an indictment of the construct of MCI; rather, this variable outcome is to be expected if the consideration of an etiology of the syndrome is not considered. This would be analogous to someone making the diagnosis of dementia and then claiming that dementia is unstable because all of the cases do not ultimately turn out to be AD. Dementia can have multiple etiologies in a similar fashion to the broad syndromic definition of MCI. Therefore, after the designation of the clinical syndrome is made, the clinician must assess the likely etiology. If an amnestic MCI subtype is determined and the likely cause is believed to be cerebral degeneration, then and only then can the specificity of amnestic MCI leading to AD be determined.

All this is to say that MCI does accommodate a plurality of causal explanations and the result and heterogeneity of the construct is a positive attribute. When MCI diagnostic algorithms are utilized to their fullest extent, they do exhibit the appropriate sensitivity and specificity to make the construct a useful clinical tool.

In closing, it is probably quite obvious that I am not a philosopher. The arguments of Graham and Ritchie are forceful and well expressed. Ultimately, I must classify myself as a pragmatist. I believe we can contest these issues interminably, probably to little avail. It is my contention that data will ultimately settle the issues. Prospectively designed longitudinal studies employing the most recent iteration of the diagnostic schemes and tools for MCI will determine the ultimate utility of the construct. Finally, I would contend that although academic exchanges are useful to clarify the issues, the final determination regarding the viability of the construct will be made by the clinicians and patients themselves. If clinicians find the construct of MCI useful, predictive, and helpful with patients, and if patients similarly find the construct explanatory and useful in communicating with each other and with their physicians, then the construct will prevail. At the very least, the construct of MCI has spawned a great deal of interest, debate, and research and that in and of itself is likely useful. . . .

RONALD C. PETERSEN is a medical doctor, researcher, and director of the Mayo Clinic's Alzheimer's Disease Research Center. His scholarly work focuses on aging, mild cognitive impairment, dementia, Alzheimer's Disease, and neuroimaging.

EXPLORING THE ISSUE

Is "Mild Cognitive Impairment" Too Similar to Normal Aging to Be a Relevant Concept?

Critical Thinking and Reflection

1. What are the relative advantages and disadvantages to "creating" disorders associated with the declines of aging before fully understanding their cause and treatment?
2. At present there are few treatments for cognitive decline, and no "cures" for Alzheimer's disease. How might this create a contentious situation for pharmaceutical companies and doctors working with older adults?
3. Graham and Ritchie identify MCI as part of a broader problem where complex changes with age are defined as exclusively bio-medical concerns. What other changes and characteristics might also fit as part of this problem?
4. Petersen claims that he is more of a pragmatist than a philosopher, and argues that MCI is a pragmatic diagnosis. What are the relative advantages and disadvantages to approaching the study of older adulthood as a pragmatist?
5. These selections are primarily concerned with the way professionals define and think about MCI. How might those considerations relate to the actual experience of older adults confronting cognitive impairment?

Is There Common Ground?

Aging has long been characterized by declines in physical, cognitive, and emotional health. The selections in this issue focus on cognitive decline. The question they pose is at what point does cognitive impairment become a disorder. All aspects of the human experience exist on a continuum, but establishing a cut-point becomes both necessary and useful, particularly when thinking about dysfunction. For example, while everyone experiences feelings of anxiety, but at what degree do those feelings constitute an anxiety disorder? This question has been at the center of every medical classification system; the creation of the debate surrounding MCI is not new.

The concerns expressed by authors of both selections also have historical significance. Both selections commented on the long-standing distress and distrust regarding the involvement of the pharmaceutical industry in classification systems. For example, the Diagnostic and Statistical Manual (DSM) used by mental health experts and produced by the American Psychiatric Association has experienced its share of criticisms related to panel members having financial ties with pharmaceutical companies. To a certain extent, it makes sense to have cooperation among physicians, patients, and the companies producing treatments. While the authors of each selection may differ

on whether the pharmaceutical industry was involved in the creation of MCI, neither doubts the difficulty in balancing that role.

Another concern presented by both selections was the trouble identifying MCI subtypes for research and treatment. The subtypes were intended to help differentiate among patients and assess risk. However, results have been mixed. It is important to note that scholarly definitions do not always have clinical utility. In this regard, additional data clearly is needed. As Petersen noted, "the final determination regarding the viability of the construct will be made by the clinicians and patients themselves."

Create Central

www.mhhe.com/createcentral

Additional Resources

Albert, M. S., DeKosky, S. T., Dickson, D., Dubois, B., Feldman, H. H., Fox, N. C., … & Phelps, C. H. (2013). The diagnosis of mild cognitive impairment due to Alzheimer's disease: Recommendations from the National Institute on Aging-Alzheimer's Association Workgroups on diagnostic guidelines for Alzheimer's disease. *FOCUS: The Journal of Lifelong Learning in Psychiatry, 11*(1), 96–106.

Koen, J. D., & Yonelinas, A. P. (2014). The effects of healthy aging, amnestic mild cognitive impairment, and Alzheimer's disease on recollection and familiarity: A meta-analytic review. *Neuropsychology Review, 24*(3), 332–354.

Petersen, R. C. (2011). Mild cognitive impairment. *New England Journal of Medicine, 364*(23), 2227–2234.

Petersen, R. C., Caracciolo, B., Brayne, C., Gauthier, S., Jelic, V., & Fratiglioni, L. (2014). Mild cognitive impairment: A concept in evolution. *Journal of Internal Medicine, 275*(3), 214–228.

Internet References . . .

Alzheimer's Association

www.alz.org

The American Geriatric Society Foundation for Health in Aging

www.healthinaging.org

Mayo Clinic

www.mayoclinic.org

National Institute on Aging

www.nia.nih.gov

Selected, Edited, and with Issue Framing Material by:
Allison A. Buskirk-Cohen, *Delaware Valley University*

ISSUE

Should We Try to "Cure" Old Age?

YES: **Michael J. Rae et al.**, from "The Demographic and Biomedical Case for Late-Life Interventions in Aging," in *Science Translational Medicine* (2010)

NO: **Ezekiel J. Emanuel**, from "Why I Hope to Die at 75," *The Atlantic* (2014)

Learning Outcomes

After reading this issue, you will be able to:

- Discuss how many Western societies have had great success extending the lifespan, but that success has coincided with an aging population that often requires costly care.
- Understand that today's longer lifespans are largely a result of improvements in standard health care, particularly in combating illness and disease, but little science has addressed the aging process directly.
- Explain how extending the lifespan without attention to the physical, cognitive, and emotional health of the individual may be detrimental to both the individual and to society.
- Discuss how immortality brings with it a host of ethical and practical questions for both the individual and society.

ISSUE SUMMARY

YES: Michael J. Rae was lead author on an article presenting the position a group of prominent antiaging scholars. They promote more funding and support for what they consider promising research directions towards slowing or even curing aging.

NO: Ezekiel Emanuel, an oncologist and bioethicist, presents a contrasting view. He argues against an ever-expanding lifespan. Instead, he believes this article suggest our focus should be on maximizing our quality of life and accepting the inevitability of death.

Why do we have to get old? Though often asked as a rhetorical question by those frustrated with the realities of aging, this question is surprisingly difficult to answer. There is no obvious or necessary reason that the human body and mind has to deteriorate, nor is there a perfect logic to the current limit of the human lifespan. In fact, we all know that the lifespan of different animals varies considerably such that we regularly refer to abstract things such as "dog years." There are examples of living things that do not indicate signs of dying. For example,

an Aldabra giant tortoise was estimated to have lived 250 years. There is a bristlecone pine tree in California's White Mountains, called the Methuselah, thought to be almost 5,000 years old. Researchers believe some species of sponges living in the ocean near Antarctica are 10 millennia old.

The logic and appeal of antiaging and life-extension certainly has an enduring appeal. Tales of a "fountain of youth" have appeared since ancient Greece. This fountain is thought to be a spring that restores the youth of anyone who drinks from or bathes in it. It has held different names throughout history, including Water of Life and Bimini. Mention of this type of fountain appeared in writings as early as those by Herodotus in fifth century BCE. The legend became most well-known during the sixteenth century, with the explorations of the Spaniard Juan Ponce de Leon. In more contemporary culture, the Fountain of Youth is associated with longevity and immortality.

The modern media is full of schemes for longer life from cryogenic chambers to ozone therapy that offer hope despite little scientific support. Science has, however, offered some legitimate promise and life expectancy has increased dramatically through recent centuries. In the United States, for example, life expectancy went from 49.2 years in 1900 to 77.5 years in 2003, according to data from the National Center for Health Statistics. In other words, improvements in health care and decreases in environmental risks have added almost 30 years to the average lifespan in the past 100 years. At that rate of change, by the turn of the next century, the average life span for Americans will well exceed 100 years. But is it reasonable to expect such rapid change to continue? And, is it a good thing if it does?

The fact that people are living longer already poses significant social challenges to many nations who have to support longer years of retirement at a time when decreasing fertility rates in the West make for fewer workers. An aging population stresses health care systems, financial systems, and the environment. There is also the impact on heterosexual relationships, since women typically outlive men. There are ethnic and cultural differences in longevity as well. For example, African Americans have a much lower life expectancy than European Americans. But since asking people to live shorter lives is obviously not an option, countering the debilitating effects of aging may be a more pragmatic alternative. People do not die of old age; rather, they die of a physiological failure that is more likely to occur as they get older.

There are several well-established biological theories that account for aging. The aging by program theory argues that aging is programmed into us, and it may be related to capacities of the brain. The aging by program theory is supported by evolutionary processes and theories. The homeostatic imbalance theory, on the other hand, suggests that aging occurs because of a failure in the systems that regulate the proper interaction of the organs. An older body is not as effective in reacting to stress as a younger body, which is why stress can be so detrimental for the elderly. The cross-linkage theory posits that when cross-links are formed between peptides, the proteins are altered in negative ways. For example, when collagen's proteins are altered, we see sagging and wrinkles in the skin. Researchers also point to the role of autoimmunity

in aging. With increasing age, the body's immune system rejects its own tissue. Diabetes and hypertension exemplify this process. Finally, there are genetic theories of aging, such as the telomere shortening theory that suggests changes in tiny pieces of DNA create problems in cell division leading to cells' aging and dying.

Another way to examine the impact of aging is to look at centenarians. Centenarians are people who live to be one hundred years or older. Research suggests that these individuals may be more resistant to cancer and other diseases, but they also may be responding to other factors as well. For example, some of the age modifiers studied by researchers include nutritional status, stress level, educational level, occupation, personality type, and socioeconomic status. Relationships and social networks also have been related to longevity, though not directly. Intimacy and friendship are linked with positive mental, physical, and emotional outcomes. For example, individuals with strong social support tend to deal with stressful events in healthier and more positive ways. Participating in leisure, cultural, and social activities are associated with good health and well-being throughout life.

In the YES selection, Michael J. Rae and his colleagues argue that countering the effects of aging would be good policy. They point out that most of what science has contributed to the increase in life expectancy to this point is based on "conventional, disease-centered medical innovation." That is to say that the field of medicine has effectively managed to decrease the toll of communicable diseases such as small pox and to manage chronic illness such as heart disease. Rae and his colleagues propose large-scale investment in a newer "antiaging" science that would use a variety of techniques to "directly target age-related changes themselves." In this vision, scientists would not just respond to illness as a threat, but also proactively deter the cellular and metabolic changes of aging.

In the NO selection, Ezekiel Emanuel argues against an ever-expanding lifespan. In fact, somewhat sarcastically, he asserts that 75 is the correct age to end one's life. In essence, Emanuel's article is about the more than increasing life expectancy; it is about the active lifespan. The active lifespan refers to the number of years an individual lives in an independent state, free from significant disability. While Americans are living longer than they have in the past, they are also living longer with more diseases. The larger point of this article is to discuss our inability to accept decline and death. He discusses the functional limitations on the elderly, pointing to elderly declines in creativity, originality, and productivity. Of course, Emanuel is only 57, so his wish to end life at seventy-five might change.

YES

Michael J. Rae et al.

The Demographic and Biomedical Case for Late-Life Interventions in Aging

Introduction

Age is the greatest risk factor for most major chronic diseases in the industrialized world and to an increasing degree in the developing world. After adolescent development, functionality declines progressively with age, and mortality rates increase exponentially, doubling roughly every 7 to 8 years after puberty. This exponentiality manifests as a progressive, roughly synchronous rise in the incidence of disease, disability, and death from chronic diseases beginning after midlife and suggests a causal—rather than a casual—relationship.

The physiological basis of these phenomena lies in the progressive lifelong accumulation of deleterious changes in the structure of the body at the molecular, cellular, and tissue levels. These changes (aging damage) arise primarily as damaging side effects of normal metabolism, aggravated by environmental toxins and unhealthy lifestyle. Aging damage contributes to pathology either directly (by impairing the function of specific biomolecules) or indirectly [by eliciting cellular or systemic responses that generally serve near-term protective functions but ultimately are deleterious]. As damage accumulates, organisms suffer progressively diminished functionality, homeostasis, and plasticity, reducing the capacity to survive and recover from environmental challenge. These changes both contribute etiopathologically to specific age-related diseases and increase the organism's vulnerability to other insults that contribute to them, leading to increasing morbidity and mortality.

The surprising conclusion from the past two decades of research on biological aging is that aging is plastic: Within a species, maximum life span is not fixed but can be increased by dietary manipulation [particularly calorie restriction (CR)] or genetic manipulation [particularly dampened insulin/insulin-like growth factor–1 signaling (IIS)]. These interventions generally reduce the generation, enhance the repair, and/or increase the tolerance of the molecular and cellular damage of aging. Although our ability to assess "health span" in model organisms remains incomplete, these interventions generally preserve "youthful" functionality in regard to tested parameters and reduce the incidence of age-related disease.

There have long been calls for greater efforts to translate this research into clinical interventions to expand the healthy, productive period of human life. By targeting the aging damage that is responsible for the age-related rise in disease vulnerability, such interventions would reduce the incidence of most, if not all, age-related diseases in unison, by modulating the underlying biology that drives them all, rather than treating each in isolation, as in conventional medicine. To date, however, investments in such research by the National Institutes of Health (NIH) and its international equivalents have been disproportionately low relative to their potential return; for example, the NIH $28 billion budget allocates <0.1%—perhaps as little as $10 million—to research on biological aging. Contrast this allocation with the costs of medical care for today's aged, such as the current Medicare budget of $430 billion, and with projected outlays many times that number to treat future increases in the diseases of aging.

Calls for an intensive agenda of research on the biology of aging have particular salience today because of two converging trends: one demographic and one scientific. Demographically, we are entering a period of unprecedented global aging, as the ratio of retired elderly to younger workers increases dramatically within the next decades in both developing and industrialized nations. Age-related disease and disability greatly increase medical costs, even when adjusted for survivorship, and are major determinants of the decline in productivity and labor force participation after midlife. Thus, the results of biological aging are both a rise in social costs and a decrease in a national workforce's ability to produce the goods and services necessary to meet those costs. The costs of global aging to individuals and societies are therefore high and are projected to inflate into an unprecedented economic and social challenge in coming decades.

Scientifically, this phenomenon coincides with the first robust reports of effective interventions into the biological aging of mammals that are already in late middle age when treatment begins. In 2004, CR was first shown to extend life span in mice as old as 19 months, which is broadly equivalent to the current average age of postwar "baby boomers." And 2009 saw the first demonstration of pharmacological intervention into the biological aging of similar-aged mice, with preliminary evidence of delays in cancer incidence and other changes in gross pathology.

Intervention in the degenerative aging process need only lead to a simple delay in the appearance of age-related disability and rising medical costs in order to alleviate the projected social costs and challenge of global demographic aging. This alone would increase the ratio between productive workers of all ages and the dependent frail elderly, simultaneously expanding the resources available to bear the costs of supporting a subpopulation of frail elderly and reducing the relative size of that subpopulation during the critical period of demographic transition. The benefit to be gained from intervention in biological aging would be even greater, however, if it were able to not only delay the onset but reduce the absolute ultimate burden of age-related disease. Preliminary evidence from animal models of retarded age-related degeneration [for example,] and the identification of human subpopulations characterized by extreme survivorship with surprisingly little morbidity (possibly indicative of a phenotype of slow biological aging) suggest that such intervention might have this even more beneficial effect. Whether it would actually do so, however, is uncertain.

Preliminary glimpses of the benefit to be anticipated from therapeutics targeting the underlying degenerative aging process can be gleaned from two studies performed a quarter-century apart. Recently, Manton et al. demonstrated that, by improving the health of older adults, investment in conventional medical technology in the late 20th century buffered projected declines in labor force productivity and thereby contributed significantly to economic growth. Such investment thereby constrained the growth of health care costs as a share of gross domestic product, effectively paying for itself; the authors provide analysis to suggest that ongoing investments can be projected to continue to do so. Economic modeling performed independently in the 1980s indicated that even greater economic benefits can be

expected from interventions that successfully slow the rate of biological aging. But this analysis is probably an underestimate, because it preceded and does not factor in the rapid rise in dependency ratios that lies ahead today, the alleviation of which represents a significant part of the benefits now projected to be realized by expanding investment in even conventional medical technology. Incorporating this new demographic challenge into the analysis of the economic impact of interventions targeting the underlying degenerative aging process would clearly substantially amplify the benefits to be expected.

In light of these convergent scientific and demographic phenomena, we advocate an intensive, dedicated, and focused R&D agenda by developed and rapidly developing nations globally, to devise interventions to restore and maintain the health and functionality of humans in late middle age and older.

Research Roadmap

Our consensus is that a realistic path toward this goal exists, by targeting age-associated changes that, based on existing research, are known or thought to be important primary components of human age-related degeneration and thus drivers of vulnerability to age-related disease. Here we outline such an agenda, focusing on targets that are likely to be biomedically tractable, even later in life, and would make efficient use of intellectual, capital, and temporal resources.

We propose a global biological aging research agenda focused on the detailed understanding of the following overlapping core age changes and developing therapies for decelerating, arresting, and reversing them: (i) the loss of proliferative homeostasis, (ii) neurodegeneration, (iii) somatic mutations in both nuclear and mitochondrial DNA, (iv) nonadaptive alterations in gene expression, (v) immunosenescence, (vi) nonadaptive inflammation, and (vii) alterations of the extracellular milieu. See the supporting online material (SOM) for brief elucidation.

To ameliorate age-related changes, we identify three broad modes of intervention that should be exploited in addition to ongoing conventional, disease-centered medical innovation: (i) reduction in exposure to environmental toxins and amelioration of other risk factors through improved public health; (ii) modulation of metabolic pathways contributing to age-related changes; and (iii) a more broadly conceived regenerative medicine, to embrace the repair, removal, or replacement of existing aging damage or its decoupling from its pathological sequelae.

Public Health and Medical Advancements

There remains substantial room to improve healthy life expectancy through improvements in public health and lifestyles, medical control of disease risk factors, and traditional disease-oriented medicine. However, we note their limitations in the late-middle-aged cohorts in whom intervention is most urgent. These improvements are most effective when applied relatively early in life, especially during development; in later life, the effect of environmental influences declines. In fact, age-related changes lead to paradoxical relationships between disease risk factors and outcomes in the elderly: The relationship between well-established risk factors—such as overweight, hypertension, and hyperinsulinemia—and adverse outcomes often declines in magnitude or even reverses relative to their relationship in younger people. The causes and implications of these changes are often unclear. Some may be the result of "reverse causation," in which the causal relationship between two closely associated phenomena is mistakenly taken to be the reverse of what it actually is; for example, mild overweight in older adults is associated with longer life expectancy, which may not indicate a protective effect of excess weight but rather that thinness in older adults is often the result of medical conditions that themselves cause weight loss (such as cancer, chronic obstructive pulmonary disease, or depression) or of the cachexia (wasting syndrome) and sarcopenia (the loss of muscle mass, strength, and function) of aging. But others may represent genuine age-related changes in the causal relationship between a risk factor, its underlying metabolic basis, and clinical disease. This uncertainty creates potential for unintentional worsening of patient health through mismanagement of the risk factor. Improvements in public health and conventional medicine will therefore contribute primarily to the future health of currently young people rather than people already in late middle age and beyond.

Modulation of the Metabolic Determinants of the Aging Damage

Interventions that mimic the modulation of metabolic pathways influencing the rate at which aging damage accumulates in model organisms—such as pharmacological mimetics of CR and down-regulation of IIS—have thus far received more attention than alternative routes to postponing human age-related degeneration. This avenue is undoubtedly promising, but we note possible limitations. Many of these promising interventions have been demonstrated in model organisms with simpler signaling

systems than those of humans; the inbred laboratory strains of model species that have dominated research to date may create experimental artifacts; and whereas life-span extension is readily quantitated, effects on age-related functional decline (reduced health span) are difficult to assess and characterization is limited. Accordingly, the benefits of even faithfully translated interventions in the health and functionality of aging humans remain uncertain.

Additionally, the modulation of metabolic pathways typically imposes substantial side effects in model organisms, such as impaired immunity, low bone mass, vulnerability to cold, and lower fertility. Rapamycin, a likely CR mimetic because its inhibitory effects on a nutrient-sensing pathway parallel those of CR and several longevity mutations, was recently shown to extend life span in mice when first administered late in life. This drug is an immunosuppressant, induces hyperlipidemia in humans (which would only modestly affect mouse life span, because wild-type mice are not susceptible to atherosclerosis), and might interfere with normal brain function—none of which were assessed in the recent report.

Finally, even if interventions that favorably modulate the metabolic origins of aging damage can be fully translated to humans and any deleterious side effects mitigated, there remains the progressively reduced efficacy of such interventions the later in life they are initiated. These interventions decelerate age-related decline but cannot arrest or reverse its course. Thus, even assuming full human translatability, a rough extrapolation from results to date suggests that a CR mimetic might extend human life expectancy by 25 years beyond the 85-year life expectancy that would otherwise result from "aging as usual" if begun at weaning but only 9.3 years if begun at age 54.

Regenerative Therapies

A third mode of intervention in the degenerative aging process is to directly target age-related changes themselves, rather than their environmental and metabolic determinants. This is the goal of regenerative medicine, a term often limited to cell therapy and tissue engineering: replacing lost cells and tissues with versions that are new and structurally youthful to restore function. We propose to broaden its scope to include conceptually similar interventions targeting other age-related changes.

Where they are possible, regenerative therapies would have the advantage of being effective even after youthful functionality has been lost. This feature also implies simpler and more rapid clinical testing, because any effects will necessarily be more immediate and direct. Regenerative therapies are thus especially attractive because they have effects even when initiated late in life, when the body has already accumulated extensive age-related changes.

Regenerative therapies, too, would have limitations. Their effects would necessarily be segmental, specifically affecting changes linked to the particular damage that a given therapy repairs. Further, it is unclear whether such therapies could be developed to address all age-related changes, although proofs of concept exist and other potential interventions can be foreseen from existing developments.

It is possible that therapies of different types might be used complementarily. Whereas regenerative therapies are segmental, metabolic interventions (especially CR) are highly pleiotropic, decelerating many, if not all, degenerative aging processes. The two approaches could thus be synergistic, with metabolic interventions decelerating age-related degeneration systemically and regenerative therapies used to restore functionality in particular tissues more fully. If regenerative therapies strengthen the weakest links in the chain of age-related changes decelerated by metabolic modulation, a disproportionate increase in healthy life span might result.

Policy Priorities

Funding

Recognizing the potential of this research agenda to avert enormous economic, social, and human costs, we advocate that substantial new investments be made by governments, while engaging and facilitating the participation of the biomedical industry. A previous proposal that included one of us (R.N.B.) as an author suggested that the United States invest $3 billion annually (<1% of the current Medicare budget) in a broadly similar agenda; we suggest that this funding level is inadequate to deliver interventions in time to avert demographic crisis. We therefore urge a larger investment, targeted specifically to late-life interventions, matched by other developed and developing nations in proportion to the means and demographic urgency of each.

Regulatory Changes

Because they would reverse existing age-related changes, the effects of regenerative therapies may be so rapid as to be amenable to direct testing for their effects on specific diseases in time frames similar to those of conventional medicines, allowing their evaluation in clinical trials within existing regulatory frameworks. However, new regulatory structures will also need to be developed for the unique

features of this class of medicines, especially for interventions targeting modulation of the metabolic determinants of the rate of accumulation of aging damage, whose effects will be more global and will emerge more gradually.

Regulatory agencies such as the U.S. Food and Drug Administration (FDA) should be charged with developing new guidelines for testing interventions that do not necessarily target a single specific disease but that retard, arrest, or reverse the structural degeneration and loss of functionality associated with aging. Preliminary meetings exploring a subset of such issues have occurred between geriatricians and FDA officials; they will need to be expanded into interdisciplinary working bodies drawing in experts in the basic biology of aging (particularly experimentalists with extensive experience in lifelong interventional studies in mammals) and translational medicine. The ability of an agent to extend life span and health span in mammalian models, based on evidence of a broad spectrum of health effects in rodent models with robust historical controls, should be evaluated as sufficient preclinical evidence of efficacy for clinical trials.

For human testing, new surrogate outcomes will need to be designed that would offer evidence for parallel effects without necessitating a measurement of life span, such as the panels of nonspecific deficits used in cohort frailty studies, reducing the acceleration of total mortality rate over the course of 8 years, and the cautious use of metabolic changes observed in animal models that are thought to be mechanistically important to the observed deceleration of the rate of biological aging.

We also advocate that regulatory agencies charge interdisciplinary panels with identifying age-related dysfunctions that are sufficiently well characterized to merit consideration as new licensable therapeutic indications (that is, medical conditions for which regulatory bodies will approve effective therapies for marketing). A pressing example is sarcopenia, which occurs even in master athletes and in which loss of mass is only one relatively reversible element. Sarcopenia is a major contributor to age-related frailty and adverse outcomes, ranging from loss of activities of daily living to institutionalization, fracture risk, and increased mortality. It is estimated to cost the United States $18.5 billion ($11.8 billion to $26.2 billion) per year (~$1.5% of total health care expenditures) in direct medical costs alone. Exercise and supplemental energy and protein consumption can increase muscle mass to a limited extent but do not address the degradation of myocyte and neuromuscular unit structure. Beyond this, clinicians can at best resort to non–evidence-based off-label use of medications, risky and minimally effective hormone therapies, or unregulated, putatively ergogenic dietary supplements. Yet because sarcopenia is not a licensable indication, no incentive exists to develop therapies specifically targeting it. New treatments targeting determinants of sarcopenia other than loss of muscle mass could greatly benefit the health and functionality of older adults, and expert panels should explore this and other causes of age-related disability as possible new licensable indications.

We also advocate efforts to include more people over the age of 65 in clinical trials. Older adults are the largest consumers of prescription medications and have the highest prevalence of the diseases for which many drugs are indicated. Yet they are sorely underrepresented in clinical trials and are often perversely excluded from trials precisely because of their burden of other age-related disease. For example, an analysis of 3470 community-living older adults with possible or probable Alzheimer's disease (AD) found that >90% would be precluded from participation in either of two trials for cholinesterase inhibitors, the main drug class approved to treat AD symptoms. Extrapolation of the results of trials performed in younger adults into older patients is fraught with potential artifacts because there are substantial differences in drug pharmacokinetics and in the range and severity of adverse reactions, because of primary and secondary age-related changes.

This exclusion of older people is a major problem in conventional medicine testing and will almost preclude the testing of agents whose purpose is to retard, delay, or reverse age-related changes in late life. In addition to implementing comprehensive reforms to address weaknesses in the existing system (proposals from the American Geriatrics Society and the American Association for Geriatric Psychiatry merit consideration), we advocate that trials of therapeutics specifically targeting biological aging or new indications for age-related diseases should be required to undergo testing in persons 50 years old and above, with significant representation of people over 65, beginning no later than in phase II trials.

Conclusions and Beginnings

We therefore advocate the development and implementation of all three forms of intervention in age-related degeneration discussed above, but with emphasis on metabolic and regenerative interventions, and on the most aggressive schedule possible, bearing in mind the urgency of the demographic challenge before us. We cannot be certain of success. Nor can the full range of social impacts, positive and negative, of a dramatic increase in healthy human life span be known with certainty in advance.

One obvious and quantifiable challenge that would result from a rapid decline in late-life mortality would be upward pressure on global population. Contrary to what is widely assumed, however, the net effect should be relatively minor. Because the effect on global population of adding each additional entire human life span (and one future parent) to the world is greater than the effect of adding some fraction of a life span onto each extant life, the effect of birth rates on population growth is much greater than the effect of late-life death rates. Without intervention in biological aging, the emerging global shift into subreplacement fertility is likely to lead to the stabilization and later ongoing shrinkage of world population at ~9 billion in the 2050–2070 range. Demographic modeling in the contemporary Swedish population of the effect of a reduction in the rate of acceleration of mortality of the same magnitude (50%) as is required to achieve our proposal finds that population would continue to decline over the next century. In fact, even a much more radical intervention into age-related mortality than we envision, in which the rate of age-related mortality is arrested at the equivalent level of today's 50-year-olds, would result in a surprisingly low increase of 35% in global population over the critical 50-year period of concern for global demographic aging. And of course, fertility rates themselves can be the subject of policy decisions, both directly and indirectly.

But it should also be emphasized that the social challenge posed by overpopulation is not determined by sheer numbers but by a variety of factors within the sphere of public policy, such as the efficiency of resource use and the equity of resource distribution, as well as the rate of economic growth. Moreover, the predictable early expansion of productive capacity resulting from intervention in biological aging will increase the resource pool available to meet the population and other challenges to which such intervention may contribute and with which it will interact.

This and other potential impacts of intervention in the degenerative aging process must be the subject of open, early, and serious public dialogue; in our view, such challenges should be met under the broad approach called the "vigilance principle:" that action should be taken for the greater social good based on current knowledge, acknowledging uncertainty surrounding its possible future ramifications (positive and negative), and monitoring such consequences actively. The resilience and adaptability exhibited by human cultures throughout history should be recognized and engaged, with more specific policy-based remedies applied judiciously in cases in which organic social response proves insufficient to mitigate specific deleterious effects that actually (rather than hypothetically) emerge.

In the case of late-life intervention in human age-related degeneration, what we can be certain of today is that a policy of aging as usual will lead to enormous humanitarian, social, and financial costs. Efforts to avert that scenario are unequivocally merited, even if those efforts are costly and their success and full consequences uncertain. To realize any chance of success, the drive to tackle biological aging head-on must begin now.

MICHAEL J. RAE is a researcher and science writer at the SENS (Strategies for Engineered Negligible Senescence") Foundation, where he serves as a research assistant to prominent antiaging scientist Dr. Auvbey de Grey.

Ezekiel J. Emanuel    **NO**

Why I Hope to Die At 75

An argument that society and families—and you—will be better off if nature takes its course swiftly and promptly

Seventy-five.

That's how long I want to live: 75 years.

This preference drives my daughters crazy. It drives my brothers crazy. My loving friends think I am crazy. They think that I can't mean what I say; that I haven't thought clearly about this, because there is so much in the world to see and do. To convince me of my errors, they enumerate the myriad people I know who are over 75 and doing quite well. They are certain that as I get closer to 75, I will push the desired age back to 80, then 85, maybe even 90.

I am sure of my position. Doubtless, death is a loss. It deprives us of experiences and milestones, of time spent with our spouse and children. In short, it deprives us of all the things we value.

But here is a simple truth that many of us seem to resist: living too long is also a loss. It renders many of us, if not disabled, then faltering and declining, a state that may not be worse than death but is nonetheless deprived. It robs us of our creativity and ability to contribute to work, society, and the world. It transforms how people experience us, relate to us, and, most important, remember us. We are no longer remembered as vibrant and engaged but as feeble, ineffectual, even pathetic.

By the time I reach 75, I will have lived a complete life. I will have loved and been loved. My children will be grown and in the midst of their own rich lives. I will have seen my grandchildren born and beginning their lives. I will have pursued my life's projects and made whatever contributions, important or not, I am going to make. And hopefully, I will not have too many mental and physical limitations. Dying at 75 will not be a tragedy. Indeed, I plan to have my memorial service before I die. And I don't want any crying or wailing, but a warm gathering filled with fun reminiscences, stories of my awkwardness, and celebrations of a good life. After I die, my survivors can have their own memorial service if they want—that is not my business.

Let me be clear about my wish. I'm neither asking for more time than is likely nor foreshortening my life. Today I am, as far as my physician and I know, very healthy, with no chronic illness. I just climbed Kilimanjaro with two of my nephews. So I am not talking about bargaining with God to live to 75 because I have a terminal illness. Nor am I talking about waking up one morning 18 years from now and ending my life through euthanasia or suicide. Since the 1990s, I have actively opposed legalizing euthanasia and physician-assisted suicide. People who want to die in one of these ways tend to suffer not from unremitting pain but from depression, hopelessness, and fear of losing their dignity and control. The people they leave behind inevitably feel they have somehow failed. The answer to these symptoms is not ending a life but getting help. I have long argued that we should focus on giving all terminally ill people a good, compassionate death—not euthanasia or assisted suicide for a tiny minority.

I am talking about how long I *want* to live and the kind and amount of health care I will consent to after 75. Americans seem to be obsessed with exercising, doing mental puzzles, consuming various juice and protein concoctions, sticking to strict diets, and popping vitamins and supplements, all in a valiant effort to cheat death and prolong life as long as possible. This has become so pervasive that it now defines a cultural type: what I call the American immortal.

I reject this aspiration. I think this manic desperation to endlessly extend life is misguided and potentially destructive. For many reasons, 75 is a pretty good age to aim to stop.

What are those reasons? Let's begin with demography. We are growing old, and our older years are not of high quality. Since the mid-19th century, Americans have been living longer. In 1900, the life expectancy of an average American at birth was approximately 47 years. By 1930, it was 59.7; by 1960, 69.7; by 1990, 75.4. Today,

Emanuel, E. (2014). "Why I Hope to Die at 75." *The Atlantic.* http://www.theatlantic.com/features/archive/2014/09/why-i-hope-to-die-at-75/379329/. Reprinted by permission of The Atlantic Monthly Group.

a newborn can expect to live about 79 years. (On average, women live longer than men. In the United States, the gap is about five years. According to the National Vital Statistics Report, life expectancy for American males born in 2011 is 76.3, and for females it is 81.1.)

In the early part of the 20th century, life expectancy increased as vaccines, antibiotics, and better medical care saved more children from premature death and effectively treated infections. Once cured, people who had been sick largely returned to their normal, healthy lives without residual disabilities. Since 1960, however, increases in longevity have been achieved mainly by extending the lives of people over 60. Rather than saving more young people, we are stretching out old age.

The American immortal desperately wants to believe in the "compression of morbidity." Developed in 1980 by James F. Fries, now a professor emeritus of medicine at Stanford, this theory postulates that as we extend our life spans into the 80s and 90s, we will be living healthier lives—more time before we have disabilities, and fewer disabilities overall. The claim is that with longer life, an ever smaller proportion of our lives will be spent in a state of decline.

Compression of morbidity is a quintessentially American idea. It tells us exactly what we want to believe: that we will live longer lives and then abruptly die with hardly any aches, pains, or physical deterioration—the morbidity traditionally associated with growing old. It promises a kind of fountain of youth until the ever-receding time of death. It is this dream—or fantasy—that drives the American immortal and has fueled interest and investment in regenerative medicine and replacement organs.

But as life has gotten longer, has it gotten healthier? Is 70 the new 50?

Not quite. It is true that compared with their counter parts 50 years ago, seniors today are less disabled and more mobile. But over recent decades, increases in longevity seem to have been accompanied by increases in disability—not decreases. For instance, using data from the National Health Interview Survey, Eileen Crimmins, a researcher at the University of Southern California, and a colleague assessed physical functioning in adults, analyzing whether people could walk a quarter of a mile; climb 10 stairs; stand or sit for two hours; and stand up, bend, or kneel without using special equipment. The results show that as people age, there is a progressive erosion of physical functioning. More important, Crimmins found that between 1998 and 2006, the loss of functional mobility in the elderly increased. In 1998, about 28 percent of American men 80 and older had a functional limitation; by 2006, that figure was nearly 42 percent. And for women

the result was even worse: more than half of women 80 and older had a functional limitation. Crimmins's conclusion: There was an "increase in the life expectancy with disease and a decrease in the years without disease. The same is true for functioning loss, an increase in expected years unable to function."

This was confirmed by a recent worldwide assessment of "healthy life expectancy" conducted by the Harvard School of Public Health and the Institute for Health Metrics and Evaluation at the University of Washington. The researchers included not just physical but also mental disabilities such as depression and dementia. They found not a compression of morbidity but in fact an expansion—an "increase in the absolute number of years lost to disability as life expectancy rises."

How can this be? My father illustrates the situation well. About a decade ago, just shy of his 77th birthday, he began having pain in his abdomen. Like every good doctor, he kept denying that it was anything important. But after three weeks with no improvement, he was persuaded to see his physician. He had in fact had a heart attack, which led to a cardiac catheterization and ultimately a bypass. Since then, he has not been the same. Once the prototype of a hyperactive Emanuel, suddenly his walking, his talking, his humor got slower. Today he can swim, read the newspaper, needle his kids on the phone, and still live with my mother in their own house. But everything seems sluggish. Although he didn't die from the heart attack, no one would say he is living a vibrant life. When he discussed it with me, my father said, "I have slowed down tremendously. That is a fact. I no longer make rounds at the hospital or teach." Despite this, he also said he was happy.

As Crimmins puts it, over the past 50 years, health care hasn't slowed the aging process so much as it has slowed the dying process. And, as my father demonstrates, the contemporary dying process has been elongated. Death usually results from the complications of chronic illness—heart disease, cancer, emphysema, stroke, Alzheimer's, diabetes.

Take the example of stroke. The good news is that we have made major strides in reducing mortality from strokes. Between 2000 and 2010, the number of deaths from stroke declined by more than 20 percent. The bad news is that many of the roughly 6.8 million Americans who have survived a stroke suffer from paralysis or an inability to speak. And many of the estimated 13 million more Americans who have survived a "silent" stroke suffer from more-subtle brain dysfunction such as aberrations in thought processes, mood regulation, and cognitive functioning. Worse, it is projected that over the next 15 years there will be a 50 percent increase in the number of Americans suffering from stroke-induced disabilities. Unfortunately, the same phenomenon is repeated with many other diseases.

So American immortals may live longer than their parents, but they are likely to be more incapacitated. Does that sound very desirable? Not to me.

The situation becomes of even greater concern when we confront the most dreadful of all possibilities: living with dementia and other acquired mental disabilities. Right now approximately 5 million Americans over 65 have Alzheimer's; one in three Americans 85 and older has Alzheimer's. And the prospect of that changing in the next few decades is not good. Numerous recent trials of drugs that were supposed to stall Alzheimer's—much less reverse or prevent it—have failed so miserably that researchers are rethinking the whole disease paradigm that informed much of the research over the past few decades. Instead of predicting a cure in the foreseeable future, many are warning of a tsunami of dementia—a nearly 300 percent increase in the number of older Americans with dementia by 2050.

Half of people 80 and older with functional limitations. A third of people 85 and older with Alzheimer's. That still leaves many, many elderly people who have escaped physical and mental disability. If we are among the lucky ones, then why stop at 75? Why not live as long as possible?

Even if we aren't demented, our mental functioning deteriorates as we grow older. Age-associated declines in mental-processing speed, working and long-term memory, and problem- solving are well established. Conversely, distractibility increases. We cannot focus and stay with a project as well as we could when we were young. As we move slower with age, we also think slower.

It is not just mental slowing. We literally lose our creativity. About a decade ago, I began working with a prominent health economist who was about to turn 80. Our collaboration was incredibly productive. We published numerous papers that influenced the evolving debates around health-care reform. My colleague is brilliant and continues to be a major contributor, and he celebrated his 90th birthday this year. But he is an outlier—a very rare individual.

American immortals operate on the assumption that they will be precisely such outliers. But the fact is that by 75, creativity, originality, and productivity are pretty much gone for the vast, vast majority of us. Einstein famously said, "A person who has not made his great contribution to science before the age of 30 will never do so." He was extreme in his assessment. And wrong. Dean Keith Simonton, at the University of California at Davis, a luminary among researchers on age and creativity, synthesized numerous studies to demonstrate a typical age-creativity

curve: creativity rises rapidly as a career commences, peaks about 20 years into the career, at about age 40 or 45, and then enters a slow, age-related decline. There are some, but not huge, variations among disciplines. Currently, the average age at which Nobel Prize-winning physicists make their discovery—not get the prize—is 48. Theoretical chemists and physicists make their major contribution slightly earlier than empirical researchers do. Similarly, poets tend to peak earlier than novelists do. Simonton's own study of classical composers shows that the typical composer writes his first major work at age 26, peaks at about age 40 with both his best work and maximum output, and then declines, writing his last significant musical composition at 52. (All the composers studied were male.)

This age-creativity relationship is a statistical association, the product of averages; individuals vary from this trajectory. Indeed, everyone in a creative profession thinks they will be, like my collaborator, in the long tail of the curve. There are late bloomers. As my friends who enumerate them do, we hold on to them for hope. It is true, people can continue to be productive past 75—to write and publish, to draw, carve, and sculpt, to compose. But there is no getting around the data. By definition, few of us can be exceptions. Moreover, we need to ask how much of what "Old Thinkers," as Harvey C. Lehman called them in his 1953 *Age and Achievement*, produce is novel rather than reiterative and repetitive of previous ideas. The age-creativity curve—especially the decline—endures across cultures and throughout history, suggesting some deep underlying biological determinism probably related to brain plasticity.

We can only speculate about the biology. The connections between neurons are subject to an intense process of natural selection. The neural connections that are most heavily used are reinforced and retained, while those that are rarely, if ever, used atrophy and disappear over time. Although brain plasticity persists throughout life, we do not get totally rewired. As we age, we forge a very extensive network of connections established through a lifetime of experiences, thoughts, feelings, actions, and memories. We are subject to who we have been. It is difficult, if not impossible, to generate new, creative thoughts, because we don't develop a new set of neural connections that can supersede the existing network. It is much more difficult for older people to learn new languages. All of those mental puzzles are an effort to slow the erosion of the neural connections we have. Once you squeeze the creativity out of the neural networks established over your initial career, they are not likely to develop strong new brain connections to generate innovative ideas—except maybe in those

Old Thinkers like my outlier colleague, who happen to be in the minority endowed with superior plasticity.

May be mental functions—processing, memory, problem-solving—slow at 75. Maybe creating something novel is very rare after that age. But isn't this a peculiar obsession? Isn't there more to life than being totally physically fit and continuing to add to one's creative legacy?

One university professor told me that as he has aged (he is 70) he has published less frequently, but he now contributes in other ways. He mentors students, helping them translate their passions into research projects and advising them on the balance of career and family. And people in other fields can do the same: mentor the next generation.

Mentorship is hugely important. It lets us transmit our collective memory and draw on the wisdom of elders. It is too often undervalued, dismissed as a way to occupy seniors who refuse to retire and who keep repeating the same stories. But it also illuminates a key issue with aging: the constricting of our ambitions and expectations.

We accommodate our physical and mental limitations. Our expectations shrink. Aware of our diminishing capacities, we choose ever more restricted activities and projects, to ensure we can fulfill them. Indeed, this constriction happens almost imperceptibly. Over time, and without our conscious choice, we transform our lives. We don't notice that we are aspiring to and doing less and less. And so we remain content, but the canvas is now tiny. The American immortal, once a vital figure in his or her profession and community, is happy to cultivate avocational interests, to take up bird watching, bicycle riding, pottery, and the like. And then, as walking becomes harder and the pain of arthritis limits the fingers' mobility, life comes to center around sitting in the den reading or listening to books on tape and doing crossword puzzles. And then …

Maybe this is too dismissive. There is more to life than youthful passions focused on career and creating. There is posterity: children and grandchildren and great-grandchildren.

But here, too, living as long as possible has drawbacks we often won't admit to ourselves. I will leave aside the very real and oppressive financial and caregiving burdens that many, if not most, adults in the so-called sandwich generation are now experiencing, caught between the care of children and parents. Our living too long places real emotional weights on our progeny.

Unless there has been terrible abuse, no child wants his or her parents to die. It is a huge loss at any age. It creates a tremendous, unfillable hole. But parents also cast a big shadow for most children. Whether estranged,

disengaged, or deeply loving, they set expectations, render judgments, impose their opinions, interfere, and are generally a looming presence for even adult children. This can be wonderful. It can be annoying. It can be destructive. But it is inescapable as long as the parent is alive. Examples abound in life and literature: Lear, the quintessential Jewish mother, the Tiger Mom. And while children can never fully escape this weight even after a parent dies, there is much less pressure to conform to parental expectations and demands after they are gone.

Living parents also occupy the role of head of the family. They make it hard for grown children to become the patriarch or matriarch. When parents routinely live to 95, children must caretake into their own retirement. That doesn't leave them much time on their own—and it is all old age. When parents live to 75, children have had the joys of a rich relationship with their parents, but also have enough time for their own lives, out of their parents' shadows.

But there is something even more important than parental shadowing: memories. How do we want to be remembered by our children and grandchildren? We wish our children to remember us in our prime. Active, vigorous, engaged, animated, astute, enthusiastic, funny, warm, loving. Not stooped and sluggish, forgetful and repetitive, constantly asking "What did she say?" We want to be remembered as independent, not experienced as burdens.

At age 75 we reach that unique, albeit somewhat arbitrarily chosen, moment when we have lived a rich and complete life, and have hopefully imparted the right memories to our children. Living the American immortal's dream dramatically increases the chances that we will not get our wish—that memories of vitality will be crowded out by the agonies of decline. Yes, with effort our children will be able to recall that great family vacation, that funny scene at Thanksgiving, that embarrassing faux pas at a wedding. But the most-recent years—the years with progressing disabilities and the need to make caregiving arrangements—will inevitably become the predominant and salient memories. The old joys have to be actively conjured up.

Of course, our children won't admit it. They love us and fear the loss that will be created by our death. And a loss it will be. A huge loss. They don't want to confront our mortality, and they certainly don't want to wish for our death. But even if we manage not to become burdens to them, our shadowing them until their old age is also a loss. And leaving them—and our grandchildren—with memories framed not by our vivacity but by our frailty is the ultimate tragedy.

Seventy-five. That is all I want to live. But if I am not going to engage in euthanasia or suicide, and I won't, is this all just idle chatter? Don't I lack the courage of my convictions?

No. My view does have important practical implications. One is personal and two involve policy.

Once I have lived to 75, my approach to my health care will completely change. I won't actively end my life. But I won't try to prolong it, either. Today, when the doctor recommends a test or treatment, especially one that will extend our lives, it becomes incumbent upon us to give a good reason why we don't want it. The momentum of medicine and family means we will almost invariably get it.

My attitude flips this default on its head. I take guidance from what Sir William Osler wrote in his classic turn-of-the-century medical textbook, *The Principles and Practice of Medicine:* "Pneumonia may well be called the friend of the aged. Taken off by it in an acute, short, not often painful illness, the old man escapes those 'cold gradations of decay' so distressing to himself and to his friends."

My Osler-inspired philosophy is this: At 75 and beyond, I will need a good reason to even visit the doctor and take any medical test or treatment, no matter how routine and painless. And that good reason is not "It will prolong your life." I will stop getting any regular preventive tests, screenings, or interventions. I will accept only palliative—not curative—treatments if I am suffering pain or other disability.

This means colonoscopies and other cancer-screening tests are out—and before 75. If I were diagnosed with cancer now, at 57, I would probably be treated, unless the prognosis was very poor. But 65 will be my last colonoscopy. No screening for prostate cancer at any age. (When a urologist gave me a PSA test even after I said I wasn't interested and called me with the results, I hung up before he could tell me. He ordered the test for himself, I told him, not for me.) After 75, if I develop cancer, I will refuse treatment. Similarly, no cardiac stress test. No pacemaker and certainly no implantable defibrillator. No heart-valve replacement or bypass surgery. If I develop emphysema or some similar disease that involves frequent exacerbations that would, normally, land me in the hospital, I will accept treatment to ameliorate the discomfort caused by the feeling of suffocation, but will refuse to be hauled off.

What about simple stuff? Flu shots are out. Certainly if there were to be a flu pandemic, a younger person who has yet to live a complete life ought to get the vaccine or any antiviral drugs. A big challenge is antibiotics for pneumonia or skin and urinary infections. Antibiotics are cheap and largely effective in curing infections. It is really hard for us to say no. Indeed, even people who are sure they don't want life-extending treatments find it hard to refuse antibiotics. But, as Osler reminds us, unlike the decays associated with chronic conditions, death from these infections is quick and relatively painless. So, no to antibiotics.

Obviously, a do-not-resuscitate order and a complete advance directive indicating no ventilators, dialysis, surgery, antibiotics, or any other medication—nothing except palliative care even if I am conscious but not mentally competent—have been written and recorded. In short, no life-sustaining interventions. I will die when whatever comes first takes me.

As for the two policy implications, one relates to using life expectancy as a measure of the quality of health care. Japan has the third-highest life expectancy, at 84.4 years (behind Monaco and Macau), while the United States is a disappointing No. 42, at 79.5 years. But we should not care about catching up with—or measure ourselves against—Japan. Once a country has a life expectancy past 75 for both men and women, this measure should be ignored. (The one exception is increasing the life expectancy of some subgroups, such as black males, who have a life expectancy of just 72.1 years. That is dreadful, and should be a major focus of attention.) Instead, we should look much more carefully at children's health measures, where the U.S. lags, and shamefully: in preterm deliveries before 37 weeks (currently one in eight U.S. births), which are correlated with poor outcomes in vision, with cerebral palsy, and with various problems related to brain development; in infant mortality (the U.S. is at 6.17 infant deaths per 1,000 live births, while Japan is at 2.13 and Norway is at 2.48); and in adolescent mortality (where the U.S. has an appalling record—at the bottom among high-income countries).

I am not advocating for 75 in order to ration health care. What I am trying to do is delineate my views for a good life.

A second policy implication relates to biomedical research. We need more research on Alzheimer's, the growing disabilities of old age, and chronic conditions—not on prolonging the dying process.

Many people, especially those sympathetic to the American immortal, will recoil and reject my view. They will think of every exception, as if these prove that the central theory is wrong. Like my friends, they will think me crazy, posturing—or worse. They might condemn me as being against the elderly.

Again, let me be clear: I am not saying that those who want to live as long as possible are unethical or wrong. I am certainly not scorning or dismissing people who want to live on despite their physical and mental limitations. I'm not even trying to convince anyone I'm right. Indeed, I often advise people in this age group on how to get the best medical care available in the United States for their ailments. That is their choice, and I want to support them.

And I am not advocating 75 as the official statistic of a complete, good life in order to save resources, ration health care, or address public-policy issues arising from the increases in life expectancy. What I am trying to do is delineate my views for a good life and make my friends and others think about how they want to live as they grow older. I want them to think of an alternative to succumbing to that slow constriction of activities and aspirations imperceptibly imposed by aging. Are we to embrace the "American immortal" or my "75 and no more" view?

I think the rejection of my view is literally natural. After all, evolution has inculcated in us a drive to live as long as possible. We are programmed to struggle to survive. Consequently, most people feel there is something vaguely wrong with saying 75 and no more. We are eternally optimistic Americans who chafe at limits, especially limits imposed on our own lives. We are sure we are exceptional.

I also think my view conjures up spiritual and existential reasons for people to scorn and reject it. Many of us have suppressed, actively or passively, thinking about God, heaven and hell, and whether we return to the worms. We are agnostics or atheists, or just don't think about whether there is a God and why she should care at all about mere mortals. We also avoid constantly thinking about the purpose of our lives and the mark we will leave. Is making money, chasing the dream, all worth it? Indeed, most of us have found a way to live our lives comfortably without acknowledging, much less answering, these big questions on a regular basis. We have gotten into a productive routine that helps us ignore them. And I don't purport to have the answers.

But 75 defines a clear point in time: for me, 2032. It removes the fuzziness of trying to live as long as possible. Its specificity forces us to think about the end of our lives and engage with the deepest existential questions and ponder what we want to leave our children and grandchildren, our community, our fellow Americans, the world. The deadline also forces each of us to ask whether our consumption is worth our contribution. As most of us learned in college during late-night bull sessions, these questions foster deep anxiety and discomfort. The specificity of 75 means we can no longer just continue to ignore them and maintain our easy, socially acceptable agnosticism. For me, 18 more years with which to wade through these questions is preferable to years of trying to hang on to every additional day and forget the psychic pain they bring up, while enduring the physical pain of an elongated dying process.

Seventy-five years is all I want to live. I want to celebrate my life while I am still in my prime. My daughters and dear friends will continue to try to convince me that I am wrong and can live a valuable life much longer. And I retain the right to change my mind and offer a vigorous and reasoned defense of living as long as possible. That, after all, would mean still being creative after 75.

Ezekiel J. Emanuel is Vice Provost for Global Initiatives and chair of the Department of Medical Ethics and Health Policy at the University of Pennsylvania. He is an oncologist and bioethicist, who also serves as a columnist for the *New York Times*.

EXPLORING THE ISSUE

Should We Try to "Cure" Old Age?

Critical Thinking and Reflection

1. Why is an aging population considered a social problem for many Western countries?
2. Do you believe government funding for research should be allocated for antiaging research and technology? Why or why not?
3. What are the implications of extending the lifespan for both the individual and for society?
4. Why are some people so eager to live longer? Why might others embrace death?

Is There Common Ground?

The debate around antiaging science really involves two distinct questions: Is it possible to "cure" aging? And, is it a good idea? These particular selections touch on both questions, with an emphasis on a better understanding of the aging process. While Michael J. Rae and colleagues in the YES selection promote further research toward curing aging, Ezekiel Emanuel in the NO selection instead encourages accepting the inevitability of death.

For experts in both articles, the issue is not just about extending the lifespan, but also about maximizing quality of life. The topic of mortality (and immortality) raises all sorts of questions—practical, legal, psychological, and ethical. As individuals and as a society, we will have to address these questions and consider their implications.

Additional Resources

Gilinsky, A. S., Ehrlich, M. F., & Craik, F. I. (2014, January). Aging and cognitive function: Cross-cultural studies. In *Cognitive Psychology Applied: A Symposium at the 22nd International Congress of Applied Psychology* (p. 225). Psychology Press.

Huang, C. Q., Wang, Z. R., Li, Y. H., Xie, Y. Z., & Liu, Q. X. (2011). Cognitive function and risk for depression in old age: A meta-analysis of published literature. *International Psychogeriatrics*, *23*(04), 516–525.

Jacoby, S. (2012). *Never say die: The myth and marketing of the new old age*. Random House LLC.

Schaie, K. W., & Willis, S. L. (Eds.). (2010). *Handbook of the Psychology of Aging*. Academic Press.

Create Central

www.mhhe.com/createcentral

Internet References . . .

American Geriatric Society Foundation for Health in Aging

http://www.healthinaging.org/

Gerontological Society of America

http://www.geron.org/

National Institute on Aging

http://www.nia.nih.gov/

Snescence Information

http://www.senescence.info/

SENS (Strategies for Engineered Negligible Senescence) Foundation

http://sens.org/